MW01629909

BOB BILYEU CAMBLIN

AN ICONOCLAST IN HOUSTON'S EMERGING ART SCENE

SANDRA JENSEN ROWLAND

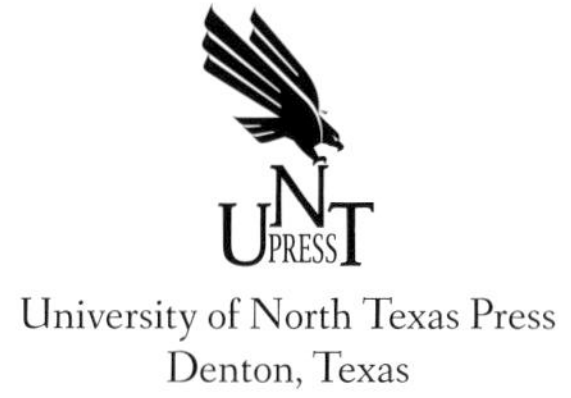

University of North Texas Press
Denton, Texas

10 9 8 7 6 5 4 3 2 1

Permissions:
University of North Texas Press
1155 Union Circle #311336
Denton, TX 76203-5017

The paper used in this book meets the minimum requirements of the American National Standard for Permanence of Paper for Printed Library Materials, z39.48.1984. Binding materials have been chosen for durability.

Library of Congress Cataloging-in-Publication Data

Names: Rowland, Sandra Jensen, 1942- author.
Title: Bob Bilyeu Camblin : an iconoclast in Houston's emerging art scene / Sandra Jensen Rowland.
Description: Denton : University of North Texas Press, [2020] | Includes bibliographical references and index.
Identifiers: LCCN 2020001905 | ISBN 9781574417890 (cloth) | ISBN 9781574418019 (ebook)
Subjects: LCSH: Camblin, Bob Bilyeu, 1928-2010. | Artists--Texas--Houston--Biography. | Art teachers--Texas--Houston--Biography. | Painting, American--20th century.
Classification: LCC N6537.C3435 R69 2020 | DDC 709.2 [B]--dc23
LC record available at https://lccn.loc.gov/2020001905

Cover and text design by Rose Design

The electronic edition of this book was made possible by the support of the Vick Family Foundation.

This book is dedicated to F. Cruser Rowland Jr.,

my beloved husband who always makes things better.

His motto is "I can fix anything from a broken heart to the crack of dawn";

thus he has his hands full.

CONTENTS

ACKNOWLEDGMENTS

In the early 1970s I was a student of art history at Rice University in Houston. My second semester of study, I enrolled in a life drawing class. My professor was Bob Bilyeu Camblin. He performed for us, and he taught, entertained, and challenged our hands, eyes, beliefs, and minds. So began our long friendship, which allowed me to be a witness for Camblin during his twenty-one years in Houston. Nearly six months after our meeting, he asked me to be his historian. I promised that I would honor his request. This long overdue manuscript is the fulfillment of that promise.

Cruser Rowland, my beloved husband, never wavered in his stalwart support for this project. He buoyed me along on this journey. His faith was absolute. I dedicate this book to him.

I want to thank Mike DeGeurin for his insights into Camblin which attest to their long and deep friendship.

My appreciation knows no bounds for the clarity and vision of Karen DeVinney, Assistant Director & Managing Editor for the University of North Texas Press. Her editorial suggestions, unflagging patience, and expertise made this book happen. I am ever grateful for her talent and her time.

Ronald Chrisman, the Director of the University of North Texas Press, gave me encouragement when I needed it most. What better letter for a writer to receive than one written by the Director of a major press that ends with "I look forward to seeing this book published."

Great designers are at the top of an artbook's major needs. Carol and Eric Sawyer of Rose Design undertook the task with great success. Indexers Peter Brigaitis and Marie Nuchols were the final team working with the book.

Elizabeth (Bess) Whitby, UNT Press Marketing Manager, not only worked on marketing, she also graciously gave assistance whenever asked.

Without help from Camblin's family, this enterprise would have been less complete. I am especially thankful to his widow, Nancy Giordano-Echegoyen, and to his children, Brian Camblin and Robyn Camblin Rodriguez, who provided me with documentation, information, photographs, scrapbooks, their own books on Camblin, and their continuous positive energy.

Essential support for the book came from the following collectors and friends who allowed their Camblin works to be photographed. They also added to the personal history of Camblin through their stories about him. Camblin's support group included:

Carolyn Farb, a force majeure, instantly agreed to have her Camblin art included in the book. She had her artwork photographed and encouraged other collectors to do the same. Her continuous encouragement was a positive influence.

Penny Cerling, artist and etcher, was always willing to help with research and to provide information on Camblin's printmaking. The clarity of her thinking and her prose was inspiring. I am especially grateful for her history of printing in Houston.

Pete Gershon is the expert on this particular time in Houston's history, as evidenced by his book, *Collision: The Contemporary Art Scene in Houston 1972–1985*. Gershon was enthusiastic about this project the minute he heard about it. His unfailing encouragement and expertise gave me the confidence to carry on.

Earl Staley, artist and Camblin collaborator, formed part of B & E Productions, B E & J Productions and The Holding Firm. Earl answered every email and telephone inquiry I made. He also provided a summary of his thoughts on Camblin as well as the Super 8 footage of the Galveston Beach happening.

Richard Newlin, of Houston Fine Art Press, offered comments and editorial suggestions that helped move me along.

The DeGeurin/DeGuerin families: Michael and Gayle DeGeurin, Dick and Janie DeGuerin, and Annie DeGuerin, all supported Camblin by collecting his work, offering their friendship, and allowing their Camblin collections to be photographed. Every family member has been helpful and gracious whenever called upon.

Laura H. Fain and Elizabeth Oliver, caretakers of the Lollie Jackson Collection & Archives, allowed me to see their mother's Camblin collection.

Sarah Balinskas, professional framer, cared enough about Camblin to hold a fundraiser for him after his stroke. She also graciously permitted her Camblins to be reproduced in the book.

Robert Fowler III, architect and son of Camblin's contemporary and friend Robert Fowler, Jr. (1931–2010), graciously allowed his family's Camblins to be photographed; however, he first had to get his mother's permission since Camblin's works still hang in her home. Kay Sheffield of ProseWorks, Flo and Douglas Hannah, Ray and Lourdes Balinskas, and Bob and Su Su Ross opened their homes to photographer David Gray, who documented their Camblins.

Thanks to those who offered unfailing moral support and encouragement: George O. Jackson, Joseph Martin, Larissa Madrid, Forrest Prince, Jack Massing, Marjorie Synder, David Null, Allan Otho Smith and Margo Jensen.

Institutions & Individuals who helped with Research Related Inquiries and Photography

Alex Gregory, Curator of Art at the Smithsonian Institution Archives of American Art.

Margaret C. McKee, Imaging Services Specialists at the Amarillo Museum of Art.

Geraldine Aramanda, Archivist at the The Menil Collection in Houston, Texas.

Lynn Wexler, Reference Librarian at the Hirsch Library, Museum of Fine Art, Houston, Texas. Also Jamie Teich, Lorraine Stuart, Sunyoung Park, Library Assistants & Acquisitions at the Hirsch Library,

Julie Schilder, Rights Specialist VAGA, New York, New York

Janet Landay, Project Director, Museum Curator, Administrator, Author who organized, curated, and wrote the catalog for *Collaborators: Artists Working Together in Houston 1969–1986*, exhibited at the Glassell School of Art, MFAH. Landay now is the Director of the CAA-Getty International Program and Fair Use Initiative College Art Association, New York, N.Y

Renee Hawkins, Director (now retired) of Longview Museum of Fine Arts.

Christopher Manly, Administrative Assistant at the Longview Museum of Fine Arts.

Lillian Stephen, Institutional Archives Intern at the Art Institute of Chicago.

Youngmin Chung, Chief Registrar and Exhibition Manager of the Blaffer Art Museum at the University of Houston.

Nancy Warren, Archives Clerk at the Blaffer Art Museum at the University of Houston.

Julia Hendrickson, Assistant Curator of The Contemporary Museum in Austin.

Clint Wilhour, Curator (retired) at the Galveston Arts Center.

Wendy Griffiths, Assistant Registrar at the Modern Art Museum of Fort Worth.

Allie Heath, Assistant Registrar & Database Administrator at the Modern Art Museum of Fort Worth.

Jason Francis, Production Manager of Signature Books.

Becca Maksym, Curator of Utah Museum of Contemporary Art.

Photography

Camblin's children, Brian Camblin and Robyn Camblin Rodriguez, made photographs from their father's scrapbooks and sketchbooks available for publication.

James Mahood took photographs of Camblin's art in Salt Lake City.

Thomas Dubrock took photographs of Carolyn Farb's Camblins.

Frank Martin captured Camblin with Bert Long and James Surls in his photo.

Marc St. Gill took photos of Camblin shortly after the artist's arrival in Houston.

Tammy C. Campbell provided the Longview Museum of Fine Arts' *Two Versions of the Galveston Deadfall.*

David P. Gray photographed Camblin's work in Houston.

Scott Peterson photographed Camblin's work in Utah.

Sandra Jensen Rowland added photographs of Camblin.

George O. Jackson documented Houston's Allen Parkway Kite Festival.

Why should anyone read or care about artists? Are we fascinated with artists because their convictions and their need to create set them apart from others? For most, even to the ardent, creativity is a mystery just as the reasons behind our passion for art often remain mysterious. What is clear: an effective work of creativity engages the viewer's eyes; their intellect, their emotions, their spirit. Art has the power to charge and change thought processes via an aesthetic experience. In our fascination with art creation, we become mindful of the artist's power to enrich society as well as our own humanity.

Bob Bilyeu Camblin was an artist who, as a child, fell in love with the creative act. Creating was just what he did. Art chose him. A career in art was not the easiest way to make a living, but for Camblin, the option was not his. His existence was an artist's existence: he was a questioner, a stimulator, an awakener. His art was meant to jar preconceptions held by his audience through the combination of images, words, visual puzzles, and surprising contrasts. The category-defying artist believed that thinking itself was an art form that needed to be continuously developed and honed. So he never stopped drawing. He thought with his pencil and filled his art with beautiful interlacing lines and symbols meant to capture our attention, to make us think and reflect. His non-traditional vision led him to study, observe, question, and create. Camblin's inventiveness and constant experimentation invite us to access our own inner depths through contemplation and recognition of the unique interpretations our lives bring to his work.

Those who appreciate beauty and talent, who are stimulated by great art, who like a challenge and a good puzzle, will revel in the art and life of Bob Camblin. He lived his beliefs and hoped his particular way of seeing things might suggest to us that while there is no absolute truth in art, being absolutely true to oneself is essential. This book celebrates Bob Camblin's originality and authenticity in his life and in his art.

SJR

It takes fifty to one hundred years for an artist to find his true audience.[1]

—Marcel Duchamp

INTRODUCTION

This book should never forget the process of making art, but it will, since, as in everything, one's attention wanders: the painter, the writer, the watcher, the talker, the waiter are all part of the process . . . doing and making. I am aware that art is style now. I'm not just being eclectic. Fashion is somewhere else. I want to make the paint please me as it has all my life—something, sometimes, someways to get past art and be sunsets, fish, streets, Time.

—Bob Camblin. Written in a sketchbook, November 1976, Venice, Italy.

This book is the story of Bob Bilyeu Camblin, an elusive, polymorphic artist who was consumed by his ability to create. A gifted watercolorist and a powerful draftsman, he wanted his art to be more than something that hung on a wall. He wanted to manifest Time itself. Paint pleased him all his life, and from that pleasure came work that was dense, replete with puzzles, language, cosmic allusions, contradictions, sexuality, and scientific references. He was fascinated with the hidden, the masked, the mysterious, the secret. Not afraid to add additional egos to his endeavors, he experimented with mind games that he and his close friends first played, then collaboratively shaped into art projects during the two decades he worked in Houston.

As a teacher, artist, collaborator, and friend, Camblin asked difficult questions intended to perplex. As a professor he challenged his students' beliefs. As an artist he filled his art with overt and covert messages. As a collaborator he instigated group projects and queried design decisions. His conversations with friends were not always easy, but he absolutely believed in the Socratic method as a tool for self-awareness. He could alienate the insecure, but conversationalists who held their ground and who "gave as good as they got" delighted him. He was not part of a generation intent on instant gratification and afflicted with shrinking attention spans. A vapid 140-character tweet in response to a complex issue would have appalled him. When bested in a conversation, he was always willing to re-think his ideas. He lived his beliefs.

Major cultural events occurred during his lifetime and influenced his thinking: the Depression, World War II, the Atomic Age, the Cold War, the Korean War, the Vietnam War, the Hippie Era, the excesses of the 1970s, and the inevitable burnout of the 1980s. Existentialism played a large role in the development of his personal philosophy as did Italian, French, German, and Russian films. If Camblin wasn't drawing or writing, he was reading everything from novels to philosophy. Western Music, Motown, the Moody Blues, the Rock and Roll of the Rolling Stones, and the Folk Rock of Cat Stevens all provided him with a musical soundtrack for his creation. His inquisitive mind added a contrariness to his personality and allowed him to consider and to believe both sides of an issue. He joked that the Jesuits had taught him how to win any argument but not how to change the debater's mind.

In the mid 1970s, Camblin began separating the components of his identity through the creation, control, and performance of a cast of characters, each one personifying a facet of his personality. (It was almost as if one individual were too limited a space to contain many interests and ideas.) He gave each created persona a name, then inhabited one of his creations. Donning psychological masks he would entertain, frighten, provoke, amuse, and educate his audience. Indeed, all the world became his stage,[1] and he was the star. Being omnicredulous (a favorite description for himself), he expanded the largess of his beliefs to art. His motto became "It's all art!" Bob entwined his work and his convictions with his existence throughout his life.

CHAPTER ONE

Setting the Stage for Bob Bilyeu Camblin: Ponca City, Oklahoma

For those unfamiliar with the artist's beginnings, here are some distinguishing facts about Camblin and the town that provided the environment for his upbringing. Twenty-one years after Oklahoma achieved statehood, Bob Camblin was born on August 1, 1928, in Ponca City.[1] His childhood evolved against a setting of Spanish Revival architecture, large brick office buildings, and oil refineries. Camblin was an only child for twelve years. His brother Michael was born in 1940 and Dennis in 1942. Two major historical events served as the backdrop for his first seventeen years: the Great Depression (1929–1939) and World War II (1939–1945).

At the beginning of the Depression, Ponca's largest employer, Marland Oil, merged with Continental Oil and Transportation Company and formed a new company: Conoco. With headquarters in Ponca City, Conoco's pervasiveness influenced Camblin's childhood. His father, Donald, went to work for the company shortly after he and his new wife Viva moved from Tulsa to Ponca. The couple's first child Bob Bilyeu Camblin was born in the Ponca City Hospital. To support his family, Donald worked steadily at

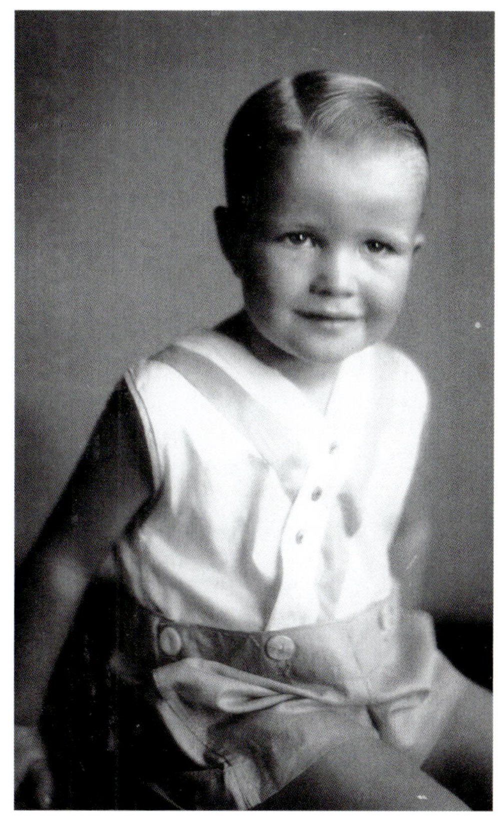

Birthday photograph of Camblin at age three, August 1931.

1

Conoco for thirty-five years before retiring. His paycheck assured that the Camblin household need not worry about necessities even during the Great Depression and World War II.

The Ponca City of Camblin's youth was largely a product of the largesse of oil-rich entrepreneurs, one of whom was named E. W. (Ernest Whitworth) Marland[2] who arrived in the dusty town in 1908, twenty-one years before the Depression and twenty years before Camblin's birth. Marland came looking for oil. After drilling seven dry holes, the wildcatter discovered his first Oklahoma gusher in 1910 on the Willie Cries-for-War Ponca allotment. In keeping with its name, Willie Cries-for-War spewed a plume of oil, quickly transforming Ponca City into a boom town. Marland and the well's investors became wealthy men.[3] Rather than take his riches to a glamorous metropolis, Marland opted to live in Ponca City where he remained until his death in 1941.

During the time it took for a newborn Camblin to grow into adolescence, Marland called the city "home" (except for his four-year term as the state's governor).[4]

Camblin heard the local gossip that swirled around the businessman,[5] who not only fueled the world with oil, but also supplied Ponca City residents with the sort of intrigue that one might otherwise only find inside a romance novel.

Marland completed his Ponca City mansion, his "Palace on the Prairie," in 1928 (the same year Camblin was born). He commissioned a work of art for the people of Ponca in gratitude for his bountiful wealth: a Regionalist, seventeen-foot-tall bronze statue known as the *Pioneer Woman*.[6] The monumental mother holds a Bible in her right hand. With her other hand she leads and guides her boy child in the same fashion that his own mother led him to view the statue during his childhood. A young Camblin was impressed by the giant, bronze woman and child. Perhaps the Regionalist mother-son image even imprinted itself

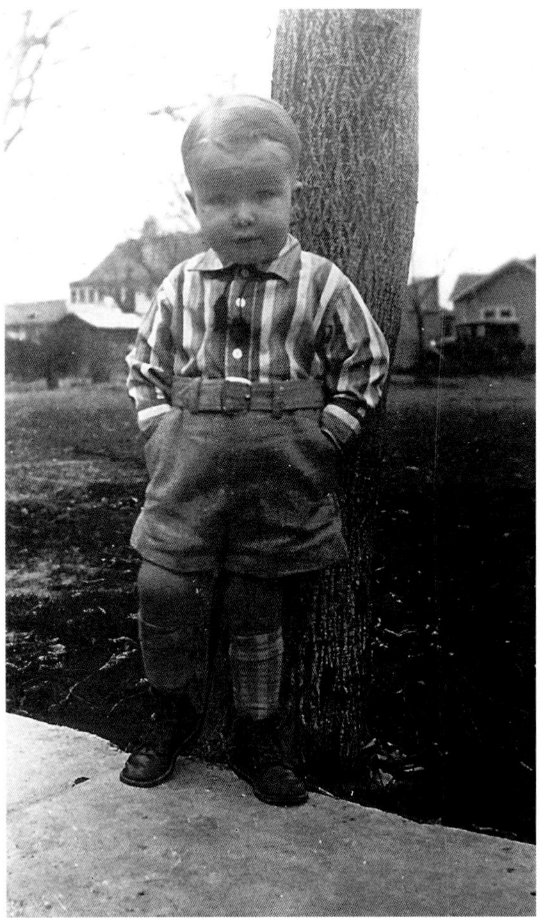

Family photograph of Bob Camblin at age two from the scrapbook kept by his mother, Viva.

on his young mind, because he forever connected that statue with his own mother and with his hometown. He would later include *The Pioneer Woman* in his art as a tribute to his mother, Viva.[7]

Even though Camblin was born after Ponca City's glory days, he was aware of his home town's history and of the buildings constructed as testament to the town's oil wealth. The Arcade Hotel[8] was such a place (built in the late 1800s to accommodate speculators who came to the boomtown and needed a place to stay). *The Ponca City News* reported, "At its peak, the Arcade [Hotel] . . . had 22 out of the nearly 100-room hotel rented to 22 millionaires." Presidents Taft and Teddy Roosevelt stayed in the hotel as did E.W. Marland and his wife when they first arrived in the city. Will Rogers, Ty Cobb, and Williams Jennings Bryan were among the celebrities who graced the Arcade. During Camblin's boyhood, the Arcade functioned as a hotel, but more importantly, the building served the collective imagination of local Poncans by providing tales of ghosts, power, and money. If prodded, Camblin could regale friends with tales that originated in the Arcade Hotel.

Tales of men going from rags to riches titillated Ponca's residents. Besides Marland, one such man was Lew Wentz who had come to Ponca City penniless in 1911. It didn't take him long to develop an interest in the oil business. By 1927, he had amassed enough oil properties to add a million dollars a month to his bottom line. When Camblin was born, Wentz was one of the seven richest men in America, Though he was a modest man and shied away from opulence. Instead, he preferred the role of philanthropist. Ponca City was one of the biggest beneficiaries of his generosity. He gave the town a golf course, camps for boys and girls, and a wildlife sanctuary, all of which remain open to this day. Of all his gifts, the kids of the town preferred the Olympic-sized, public swimming pool Wentz built for the city. At the time the

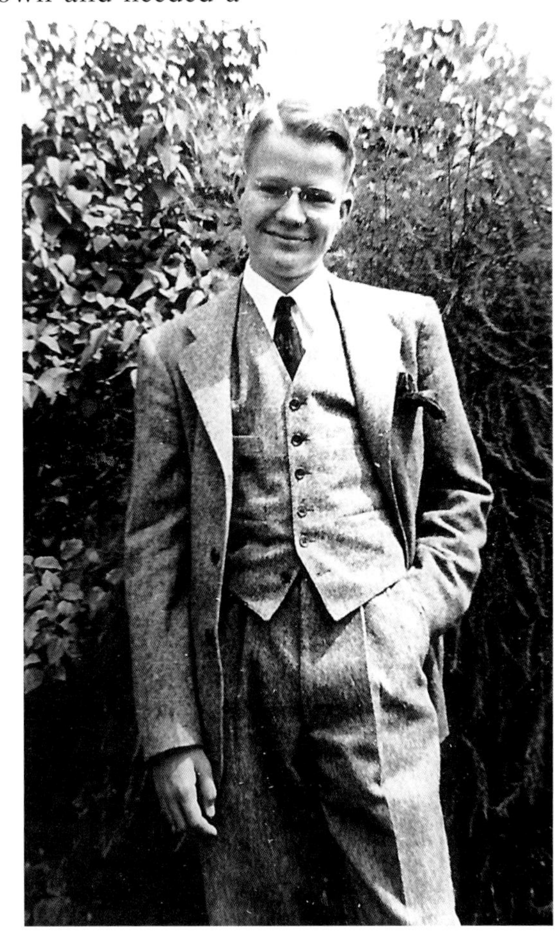

Bob Camblin, May 16, 1942.

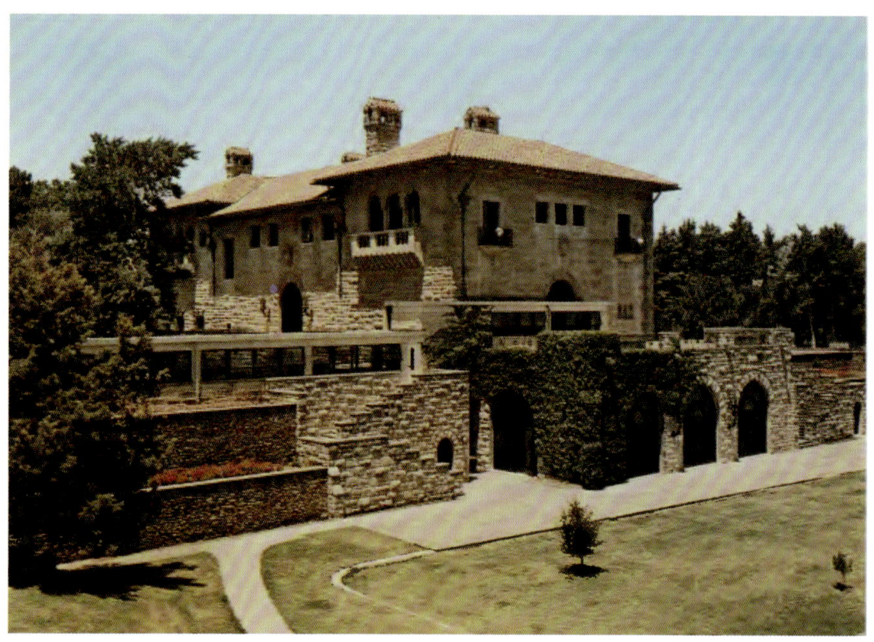

Side view of the Marland Mansion in Ponca City. Marland referred to his home as the Palace on the Prairie.

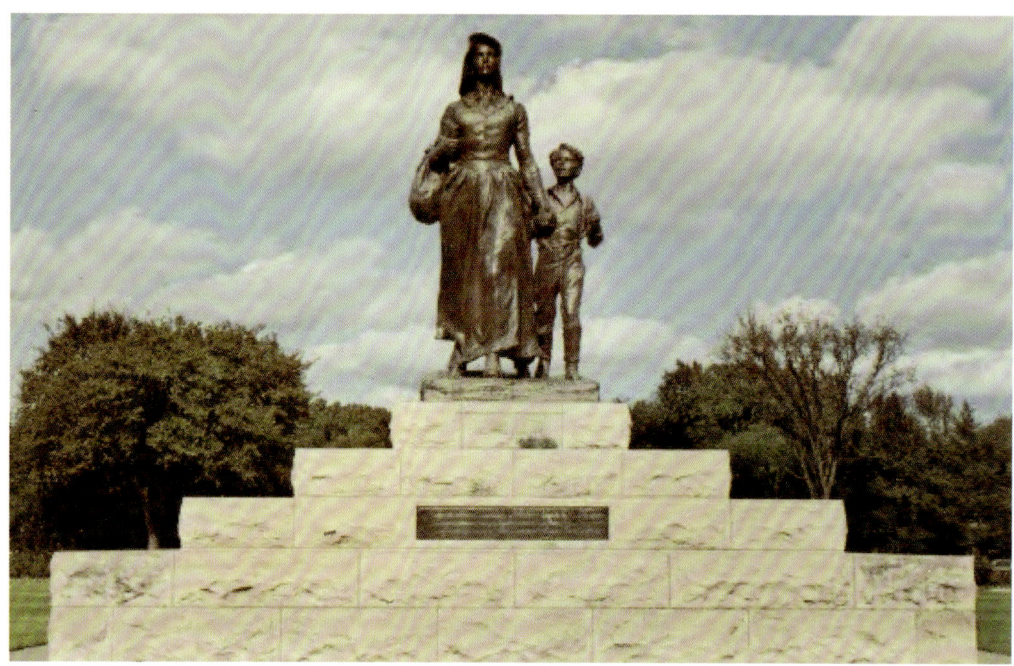

The Pioneer Woman. The seventeen-foot-tall bronze was the singular piece of sculpture that Camblin saw repeatedly during his upbringing in Ponca City.

pool was considered the most beautiful public pool in America. Camblin spent many hot summer days in the pool's cool waters. The crenellated sandstone towers and cascading terraces leading to the water fueled his over-active imagination, and he enjoyed hearing the stories that swirled around the town's larger-than-life benefactor.[9]

Swimming helped amuse Camblin during summers, but movies provided year-round entertainment. Two years before the Great Depression and one year before Camblin's birth, the city of 16,000, built the Poncan Theatre. National celebrities came to entertain on its stage, but with the popularity of "the talkies," the space was converted into an atmospheric[10] movie theatre in 1929. Camblin's romance with the movies began in the Poncan's plush seats. On Saturdays, the theatre provided special movies and live entertainment for the town's youth. Sitting in the darkened theatre in 1939, a wide-eyed, eleven-year-old Camblin fell under the spell of *The Wizard of Oz*, an enchantment he carried with him for most of his life. Outlasting Camblin and Ponca's philanthropists, the Spanish Colonial style Poncan Theatre celebrated its ninetieth birthday in 2017.

Inexpensive family excursions were part of a small-town upbringing. Camblin's father took his son camping and fishing to the nearby lakes and streams. He taught him survival skills including how to build rabbit traps. During their outings, Camblin watched his father sketch, so he followed suit. He also learned to draw and to watercolor by observing his mother. Besides emulating his parents, Camblin found the models for his art in the linear representation used by the popular media. He undoubtedly gathered his affection for linear drawing at the breakfast table while he studied the illustrations on cereal boxes. It is easy to imagine his eyes tracing the cartoonish designs drawn in blue lines on Straight Arrow In-jun-uity cards inside Nabisco Shredded Wheat cartons, or the mask cut-outs on Wheaties boxes. He read Hearst newspaper comic strips and saw the "Draw Me" promotions in magazines. He went to movies and read comic books. Camblin's assimilation of the 1930s and '40s media culture would serve as the foundation for his art.

Camblin was not seriously impacted by the Great Depression. He was busy with art, family, camping trips, and school (even though the global calamity carried on into World War II). On September 1, 1939, Germany invaded Poland. That same year Ponca City was selected to establish a training school for war pilots. According to the Oklahoma Historical Society, "The next six years [1939–1944] of worldwide conflict freed the Sooner State[11] from the grip of the Great Depression and produced change on a scale seldom equaled in American history . . . Even before the United States entered the war, federal dollars poured into the state for training pilots, establishing military installations, and constructing wartime production facilities. The Selective Service Act of 1940 reduced unemployment and eventually placed so many men in uniform that women entered the work force in unprecedented numbers. Before the attack on Pearl Harbor, programs for training British Royal Air Force (RAF) pilots operated in Oklahoma, and the Darr Flight School in Ponca City trained more than eleven hundred pilots."[12]

War was very much on the minds of Oklahomans, and Sooner State citizens knew their training schools were helping the war effort. Even so, when the conflict ended, 5,500 of Oklahoma's young men had given their lives in combat.

Camblin attended Ponca City High School during the three years, eight months, and twenty-two days of America's involvement in World War II.[13] Built a year before Camblin's birth, the high school cost a third of a million dollars and offered "every modern convenience" as well as a "progressive curriculum." While attending Ponca City High, Camblin participated in extra-curricular activities that included playing on the football and wrestling teams and serving as art director for the school yearbook. He also made a lifelong friend in Forrest Harrisberger, who too loved to draw.

In high school, Camblin read everything he could find on art, and he shared his ideas and his books with Harrisberger, the only other student in Ponca High who seemed to care about art as much as Bob did. Camblin came from a creative household, and he understood his need to develop his own style. He was completely uninterested in Regionalism (rural) and Social Realism (urban) but didn't dismiss their influence. Instead of working in the predominant styles of the time, he was experimenting with line, color, and perspective.

When the USA detonated atomic bombs over Hiroshima and Nagasaki in 1945, Camblin, like almost all Americans, was stunned. Japan's horrific surprise military strike on the Naval Station in Pearl Harbor on December 7, 1941, killed

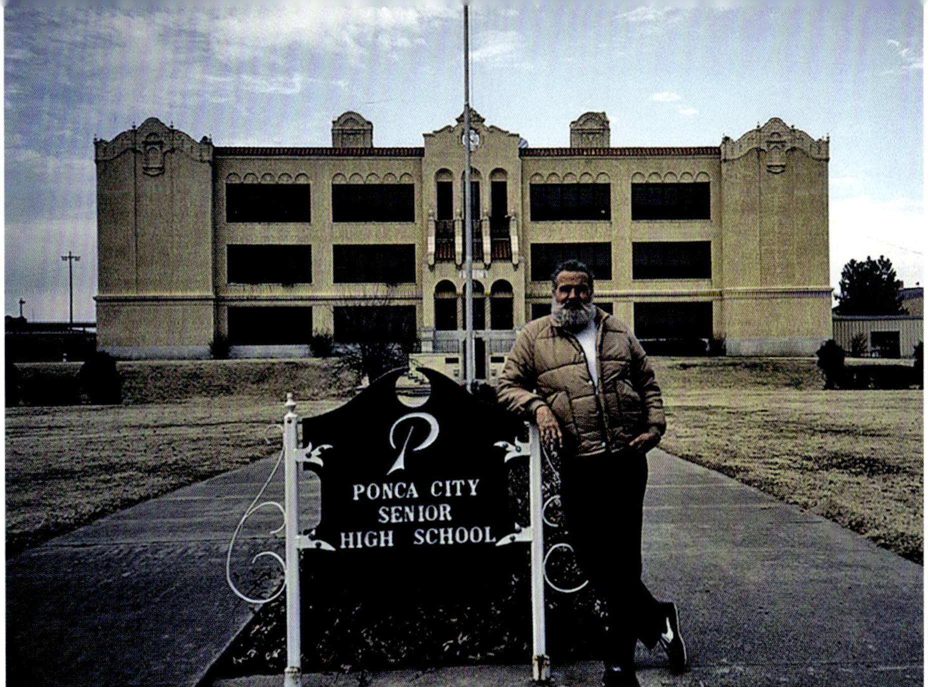

Ponca City Senior High. An older Camblin stands in front of school.

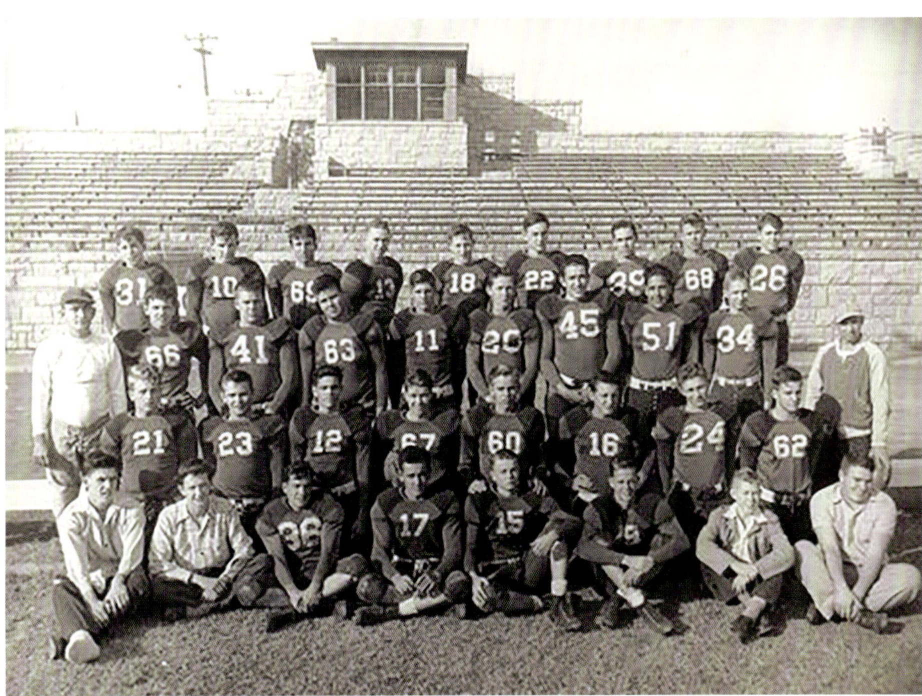

Ponca City Wildcats football team, 1945. Camblin is number 67 in the middle of the second row.

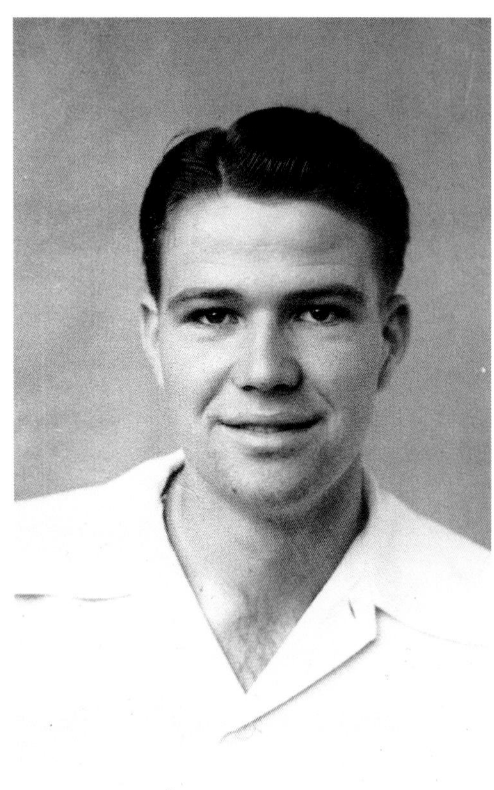

Camblin's High School Graduation photo, May 1946.

2,403 people, 68 of whom were civilians. Camblin was thirteen then, and in his still-teenaged mind, the almost-four years that followed seemed like too long a wait for payback. He knew that Nagasaki and Hiroshima were large cities filled with a quarter of a million civilians who were killed (the true total will never be known) only days after his seventeenth birthday. The bombings, credited with ending WWII, catapulted Camblin into adulthood. He believed Japan had proven its stealth and inhumanity with the Pearl Harbor attack and America had proven its military prowess and its own inhumanity with the deployment of atomic bombs. Instantly Regionalism and Social Realism seemed archaic. The world changed, and Camblin fixated upon the news concerning the aftermath and long-term effects of radiation. For him, high school became insignificant, though he still graduated.

Upon receipt of his diploma in May 1946, Camblin was in limbo. For the first time ever, the thought of nuclear annihilation entered mainstream thinking. The possible end of the world and the devastation of nuclear fallout were all Camblin could think about. He felt he had to do his part to stop possible bombings, but he felt helpless. His father got him a job at Conoco, hoping that his son would stop obsessing about nuclear war, and would instead follow in his own footsteps and see the value of a company job. Camblin did not. His employment with the company was short-lived. Instead of staying with Conoco, Camblin wanted to participate in the bigger world. He enlisted in the U.S. Army five months before he turned nineteen, on March 11, 1947.

Besides wanting to be a patriotic American, Camblin had practical reasons for joining the military. The aftermath of the war produced a mass migration of servicemen into art on the back of the GI Bill,[14] and Camblin needed to secure the bill's educational benefits if he wanted to get out of Ponca City. He didn't want to end up an hourly worker without a college education: the idea terrified him. He knew he did not want to be a lifetime employee of Conoco. He was ready to meet life head-on, though Camblin's idealism did not preclude his common sense.

The year 1947 was also an important year for the larger world of art. The same year, Pollock began his "drip" paintings, though news of Pollock's new and radical painting technique barely made a ripple in Ponca City or US military bases. At eighteen and nineteen, Camblin wasn't interested in abstraction that focused on flatness or the personal act of creation, but he was intrigued with his own personal, evolutionary art. With no studio to call his own, he was not concentrating on the elimination of depth perception on canvas like the abstract expressionists. Instead, he chose to focus on the development of his own inner depth through new experiences, new environments, and new work.

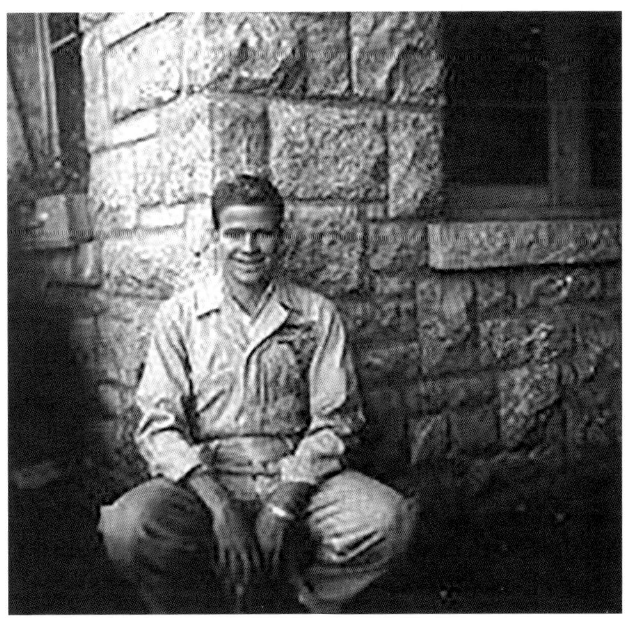

During his summer employment by Conoco Oil Company, Camblin wore the company uniform, 1946.

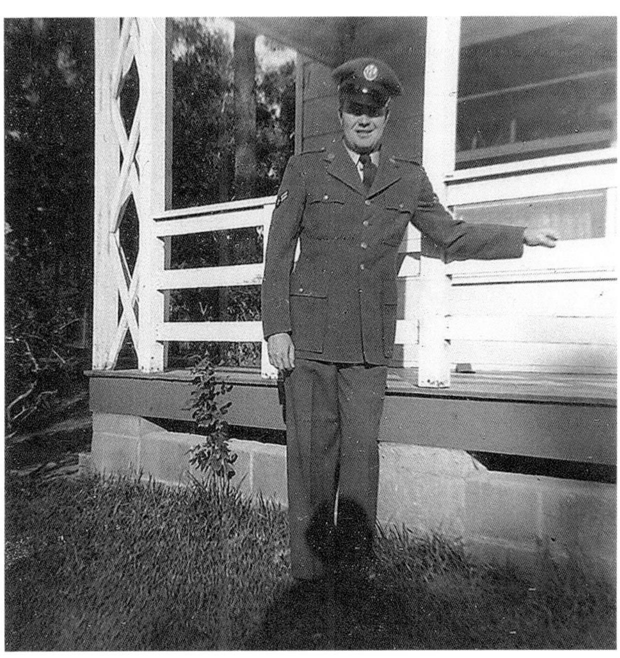

Camblin in the military wearing a uniform with the insignia of a chevron which most enlisted men wore in every branch of the service.

Gaining a Larger Artistic Context through the Military and Kansas City Art Institute

Being in the Army did not eliminate Camblin's thoughts of nuclear annihilation, but his fears did grow quieter. Recognizing the young GI's quick and curious mind, an Army chaplain gave him books on the religious traditions of Taoism and Zen Buddhism. Raised Catholic, he was intrigued by the new philosophies, and the fact that both philosophies originated centuries before Christ fascinated him. Following the messages found in the teachings of the two closely bound schools of Eastern thought, Camblin began trusting his own intuition. Rather than give up Catholicism, he viewed his birth church's dogma as a foundation for his new self-understanding in his nascent quest for his own true Buddhist nature, a nature he found inseparable from his art.

The Army sent Camblin to Fort Ord, California, for basic training before transferring him to Fort Sill, Oklahoma, where he worked as an artillery mechanic: book in one hand, a wrench in the other.

After an honorable discharge from the Army in 1948, Camblin decided to apply to the Kansas City Art Institute in Kansas City, Missouri (KCAI).[1] He knew that his resume was impressive: High school honor student, football player, wrestler, writer for the school paper, art director for the yearbook followed by an honorable discharge from the U.S. Army after his enlistment. No longer worrying about the destruction of the world, Camblin was ready to get serious about art. He knew that Thomas Hart Benton had taught at KCAI from 1935 to 1941 and that his Regionalist influence still lingered at the institute, even though he had departed seven years earlier. Two of Benton's colleagues, who had also been his students, were still perpetuating Regionalism at KCAI: Glen Gant and Frederic James. KCAI was a small institution, and Camblin likely took classes from the two landscape artists. Landscape would play a large role in his own work over his lifetime.

Examples of Camblin's artwork during his early years at KCAI exhibit no Regionalist influence. Instead, the works demonstrate the artist's experimentation with abstracted realism and mergers of three and two dimensionality. The media culture of his youth re-emerged. There was an example image of a figure with some foreshortening, which was meant to imply depth and volume. Camblin drew a boy child who appears to be playing with an elaborate "tinker toy" of cubist angles and flatness, a sort of cubist grid. In other artwork he combines unusual perspective with totally flat planes.

Camblin's art did not follow any movement, and even though he was interested in Freud, he did not consider his paintings Freudian. He preferred the ideas of Joseph Campbell, whose book, *The Hero with a Thousand Faces*, Camblin read and reread. He added Campbell's archetypal hero to his own personal journey and mythology. Critically astute about his unique and complex makeup, he opened himself to the mysterious process of creation and allowed his art to flow from his unconscious. Consequently, the meaning behind his art was often masked, even to himself.

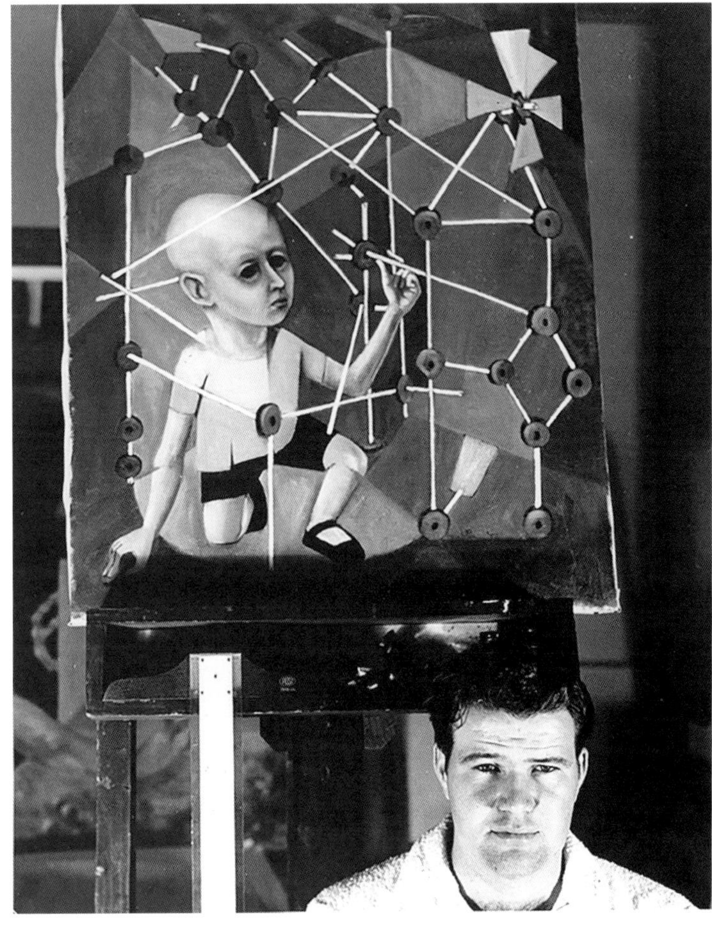

Camblin posing in front of one of the artworks he created while attending Kansas City Art Institute in the '50s.

Like Campbell, Camblin studied Carl Jung's archetypes and personae, focusing on the everyday masks (public faces) we all wear when we interact with others. Jung's profound connections between dreams, culture, and art impressed Camblin who felt the existence of universal, mythical characters within his own psyche. The idea that he was a part of a universal, genetically inherited, collective consciousness greatly appealed to him. He especially enjoyed learning the Swiss psychiatrist believed art, myth, religion, and dreams were the only methods through which archetypes could be deduced, making all presentations of art—abstract, realist, religious, symbolic, primitive, ritualistic—about the artist. Bob Bilyeu Camblin became the center of his own art, even as he unconsciously shared universal memories common to every man. He spent much time going over Jung's writings.

The study of Jung did not increase Camblin's finances. He did not want to become the struggling artist archetype. Instead, he turned into the warrior archetype.

While living in Kansas City, he had reconnected with Forrest Harrisberger, and the two shared a room in a boarding house. Another renter happened to be a pilot who encouraged the two men to join the Air Force Reserve. The pilot told them he doubted their unit would be called to active duty. He added that the Reserve's monthly stipend was pretty good and the weekend flying was exciting. The job market hadn't presented them any interesting offers so in early 1950, Camblin and Harrisberger enlisted for one year in the Air Force Reserve. They especially looked forward to flying. Both felt confident that there would be no new threats of war, though Chinese and Korean communists had other ideas.

Four months after Camblin joined the Air Force Reserve, North Korea invaded South Korea. President Truman committed the United States to the conflict in Korea without a congressional declaration of war. Shortly thereafter, the American intervention in the Korean war began. The U.S. Air Force called Camblin's reserve unit to active duty and extended his one-year enlistment another year and a half. Both men must have considered the possibility of having to fight on Korean soil, but they got lucky. He and Harrisberger were not deployed to Korea but were instead stationed at Selfridge Air Force Base in Detroit, Michigan. Camblin was transferred to Hamilton Air Force Base in Novato, California, and Harrisberger reported to duty somewhere near Sacramento. During their service, the two friends managed to find time to get together and sketch the California coastline.

While stationed at Hamilton Air Force Base, Camblin found an old *Life* magazine from 1943. The magazine introduced him to the work of Buckminster Fuller, whose views Camblin would champion for decades. The magazine's article on Fuller explained the inventor-philosopher's alternative vision for the world: the Dymaxion Map.[2] The only flat map of the entire surface of the Earth provides humans a way to visualize the whole planet as one island, one ocean. Fuller thought understanding the map would help make mankind "better equipped to address challenges as we face our common future aboard Spaceship Earth."[3]

Fuller's Dymaxion Map was arguably the quintessential example of the cubist grid. As Camblin would say, it was a "bigger idea." He respected Fuller and his creative thinking and lectured on Fuller's "One-world island. One-world ocean" for the entirety of his teaching career.

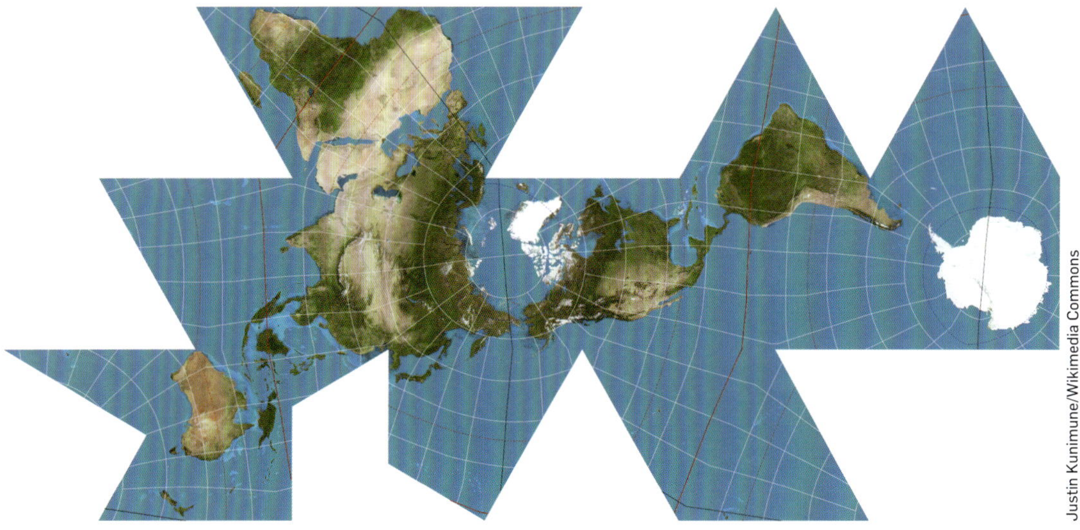

Buckminster Fuller's Spaceship Earth: The March 1, 1943 edition of *Life Magazine* included a photographic essay titled "Life Presents R. Buckminster Fuller's Dymaxion World."

Writing about Camblin's and Harrisberger's friendship, Camblin's son Brian noted: "After their respective hitches were over, Harrisberger, who already had his BFA, landed his first job as an illustrator, and Camblin (with his second GI bill in hand) returned to KCAI to finish his education . . . They kept in touch for over 66 years until Camblin's death in 2010."

While Camblin was serving Uncle Sam as an active Air Force Reservist in 1950, New York was reeling from Jackson Pollock's fourth solo show at Betty Parsons' gallery where he exhibited thirty-two "drip paintings." Created through the motion of dripping or flinging paint on a canvas, Pollock's paintings[4] catapulted American art into international prominence and made Pollack the first American superstar artist. The year of 1950 also introduced Willem de Kooning's *Woman I*, the figurative component of early Abstract Expressionism. Fame and fortune rewarded both Pollock and de Kooning despite their positions at opposite ends of the art spectrum. The US Air Force did not offer such rewards to Camblin or Harrisberger.

During the New York artists' ascent, Camblin was twenty-three years old and counting off the days until his military service was completed so that he could resume his art education. In the military, he was isolated and far removed from art movements and events. Abstract Expressionism did not interest him any more than Regionalism had. He ignored the pieties and posturing of the action painters and embraced comics and advertising. The work he created during his service employed his knowledge of the graphic arts, relying on line and tone. He created flat, cartoon-like imagery set in unusual perspectives. In an example titled *The Artist*, the viewer looks

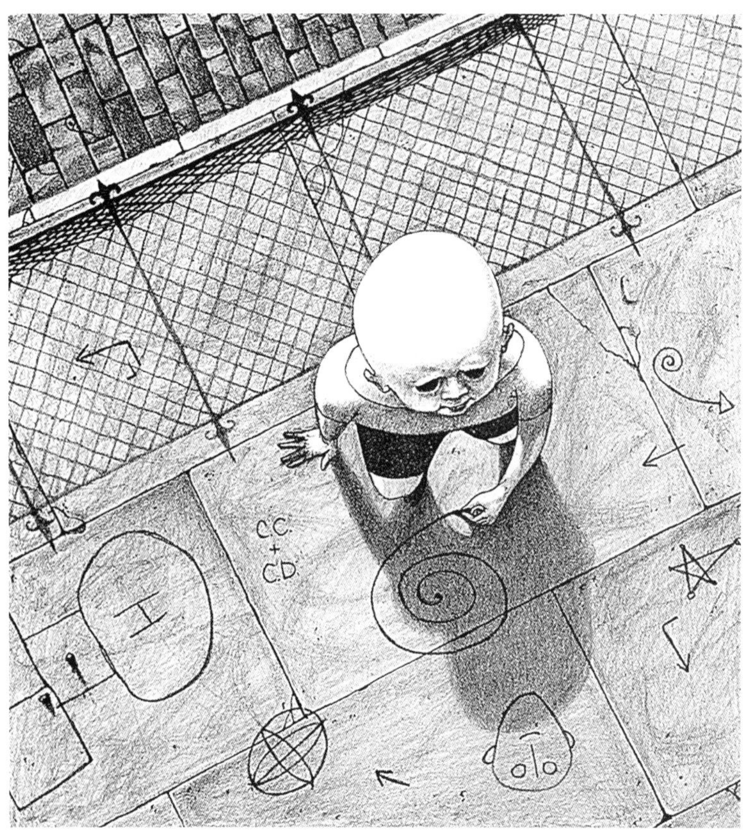

The Artist 1956

down upon the bald head of a child who is drawing spirals and other linear configurations on a sidewalk. The central cartoon figure in another work is a Catholic nun standing between a bald boy child and a girl hiding behind the flat planes that create the nun's habit. The nun looks down and vaguely smiles at the boy child. The cartoon drawing perhaps belies the artist's desire for the simplicity of childhood as well as the benevolent protection and concern of Catholicism as practiced by the nun.

The subject of a third early piece is a pair of hands emerging from the blue heavens. Three fingers have strings that attach to an earthbound marionette with elbows up and head down. The heavenly hands suggest a higher force controlling the movements of the earthbound. *The Marionette*, masked, is dated 1950. In the work, twenty-two-year-old Camblin referenced his Catholic belief in "higher forces" animating mere mortals. His world view, as well as his artistic capabilities, expanded exponentially over the years, but he never completely abandoned influences from his Catholic upbringing.

Realizing that he needed to complete his education, he applied for readmission to KCAI and was accepted. At the institute, Camblin met a young woman, Bonnie Bertram, a Kansas City native. After a whirlwind courtship, they married on September 5, 1953.

Before receiving his Bachelor of Arts degree, Camblin saw a notice posted on a KCAI bulletin board: a "Call for Artists" to submit their work for consideration in the *8th National Missouri Valley Exhibition*. Feeling confident, he sent his art to the exhibition judges. He was exhilarated when his work was selected for the show, his first formal exhibition. He felt even more positive when he won a purchase prize for his entry.

After receipt of his B.A, he remained at KCAI to work toward a graduate degree. He believed a Master of Fine Arts would help

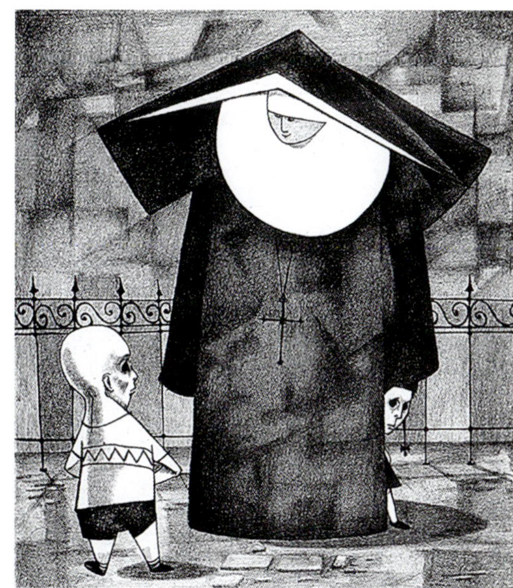

The Boy and a Nun, 1956

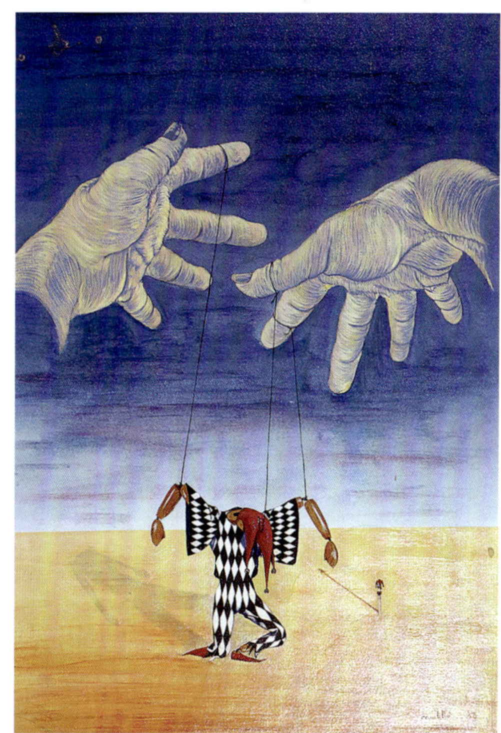

The Marionette, 1950

him find a better job. To assist him financially during his studies, the art department made him a graduate teaching assistant. Camblin recognized that abstraction was the dominant discourse in art during the mid-1950s. But Camblin was a reactionary, and he preferred representation over total abstraction even though he simplified, fractured, outlined, and abstracted his representative work.

In a photograph taken during his solo exhibition, Camblin, in a suit and tie, stands in front of a triptych that demonstrates his painting techniques. The figures in the painting are taken from a Greek or Roman myth, but which myth remains a mystery. Camblin continued working with myths for the next decade. When he received his M.F.A., Camblin was awarded the Margaret Allen Barnett Memorial Award as the outstanding student of the class of 1955. Recognizing his award as well as the quality and originality of his work, the art department faculty asked him to mount a one-man exhibition, *Bob Camblin, Paintings and Drawings.*[5]

The school year 1954–55 had been good to Camblin despite what was happening in the world. He was proud of his art, his experience, and his credentials, but finding a job in his chosen field was still difficult. After applying for numerous positions, Camblin went to work defining parcels of land for Kansas U.S. Map Compilation. Bored with mapping, he continued to apply for a teaching position in art. On a whim, he filled out an application for a Fulbright grant. He was ready to experience life outside the Midwest, but Europe had not seriously factored into his expectations. Six months after submitting his application, Camblin was awarded a Fulbright for one year's study abroad. He and his wife Bonnie both rejoiced.

Camblin's new wife, Bonnie, became his favorite model.

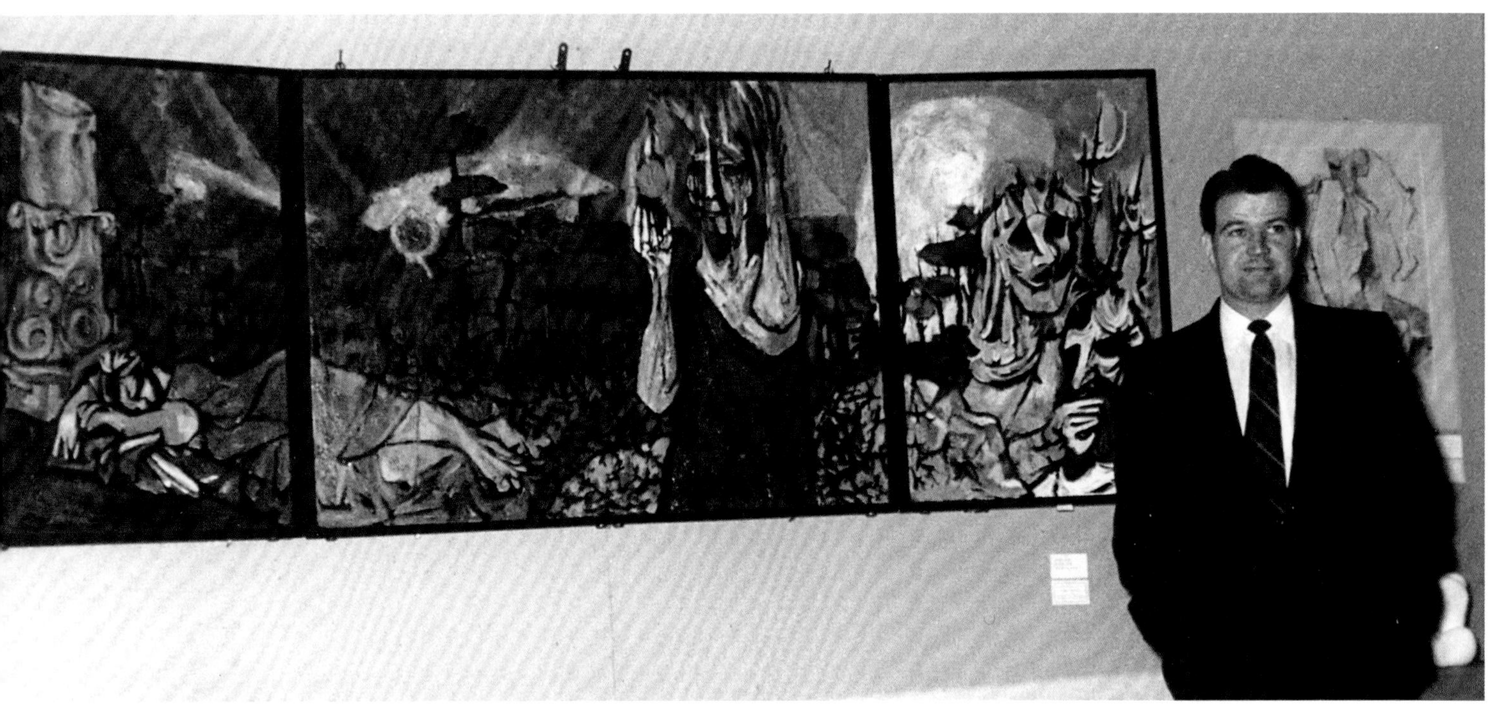

Bob Camblin standing in front of a triptych he painted as a student at Kansas City Art Institute. The painting was exhibited in a oneman show that KCAI gave for the artist upon his completion of his Master's Degree in 1955.

Fulbright in Italy

Before their departure for Europe, Camblin and Bonnie were required to select the city in which they wished to live during their Fulbright. Paris had been the center of the art world since the beginning of the twentieth century, but New York City became art's epicenter after WWII. When Camblin received news of his Fulbright, eleven years had passed since the war's end. Not having participated in the New York art scene but having received a traditional "French focused" art education, for Camblin, like most American art students, Paris would seem a logical place to spend his Fulbright immersed in art. Camblin went to Rome.

So why did Camblin choose Rome? The answer is relatively obvious: Roman Catholicism. Bob Bilyeu Camblin had been an altar boy with a great imagination fired by the liturgies of his parish church. He wanted to absorb Michelangelo's Rome (where the Vatican is sovereign): within St. Peter's Basilica, Bernini's twisting, spiraling Baldacchino covers St. Peter's tomb. The heart of Catholicism! But the most celestial station in the Vatican is the Sistine Chapel. Photographs could never do justice to the Sistine's frescoes. Camblin wanted to walk among Michelangelo's gigantic figures, to surround himself with their beauty and power, to imagine the artist in his act of creation. That is why Camblin opted for Italy: he made his pilgrimage to the country with 3000 years' accumulation of the Western world's greatest art and architecture, much of which was commissioned by the Catholic church.

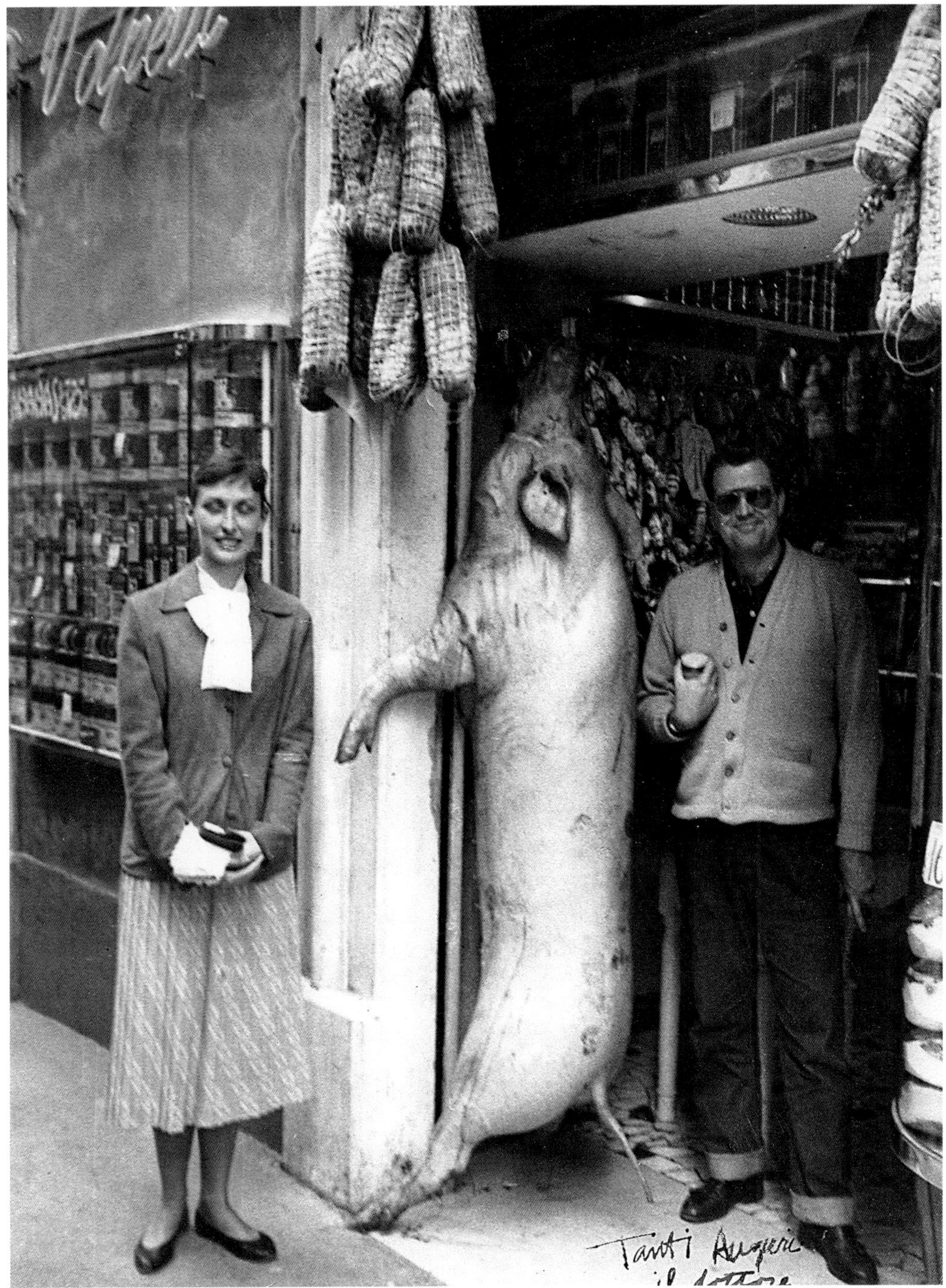

Bonnie and Camblin in a Roman Market, 1957.

In Rome, Camblin was in his element. He had dreamed of European travel, of living in the city where Roman mythology, a longtime theme in his work, evolved. He wanted to see the art and architecture he first discovered in books, to experience the exhilaration of life in another culture, to learn a new language, to indulge in a new cuisine.[1] His grant freed him from financial worries, and his wife was by his side. He knew he was living *la dolce vita* (the sweet life).

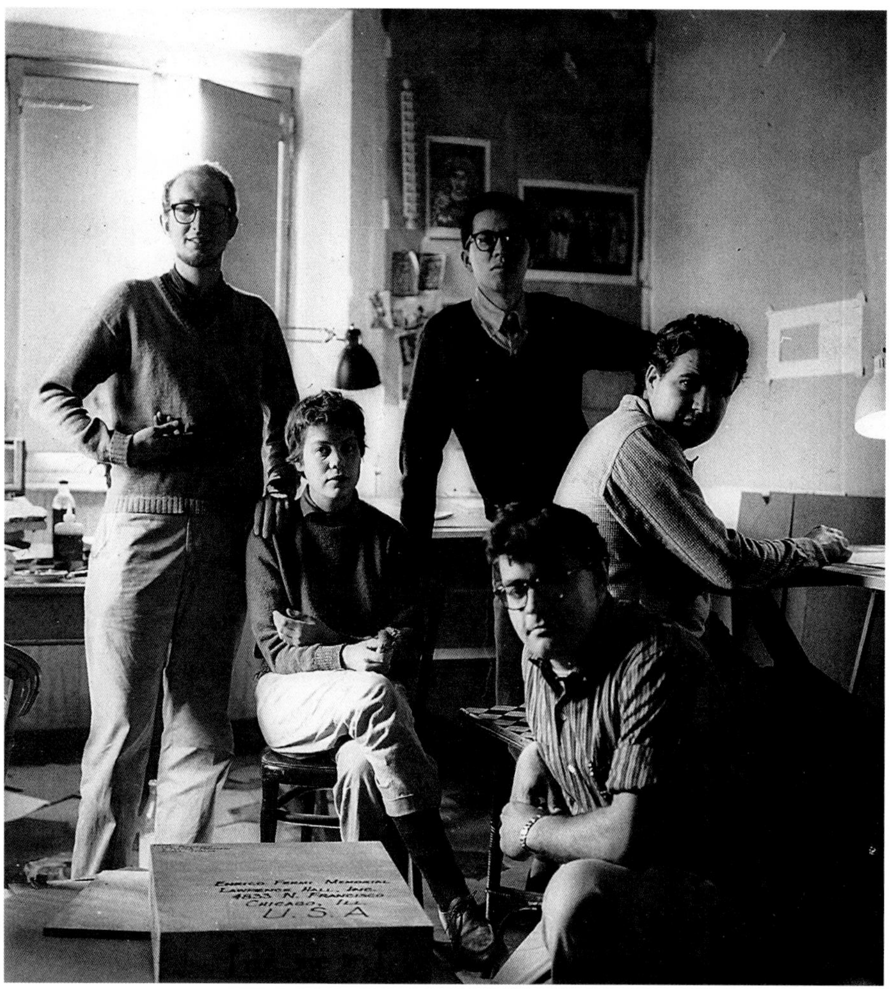

Camblin seated at drawing table in his Roman studio, surrounded by artist friends including Lee Bontecou, center, 1957/58.

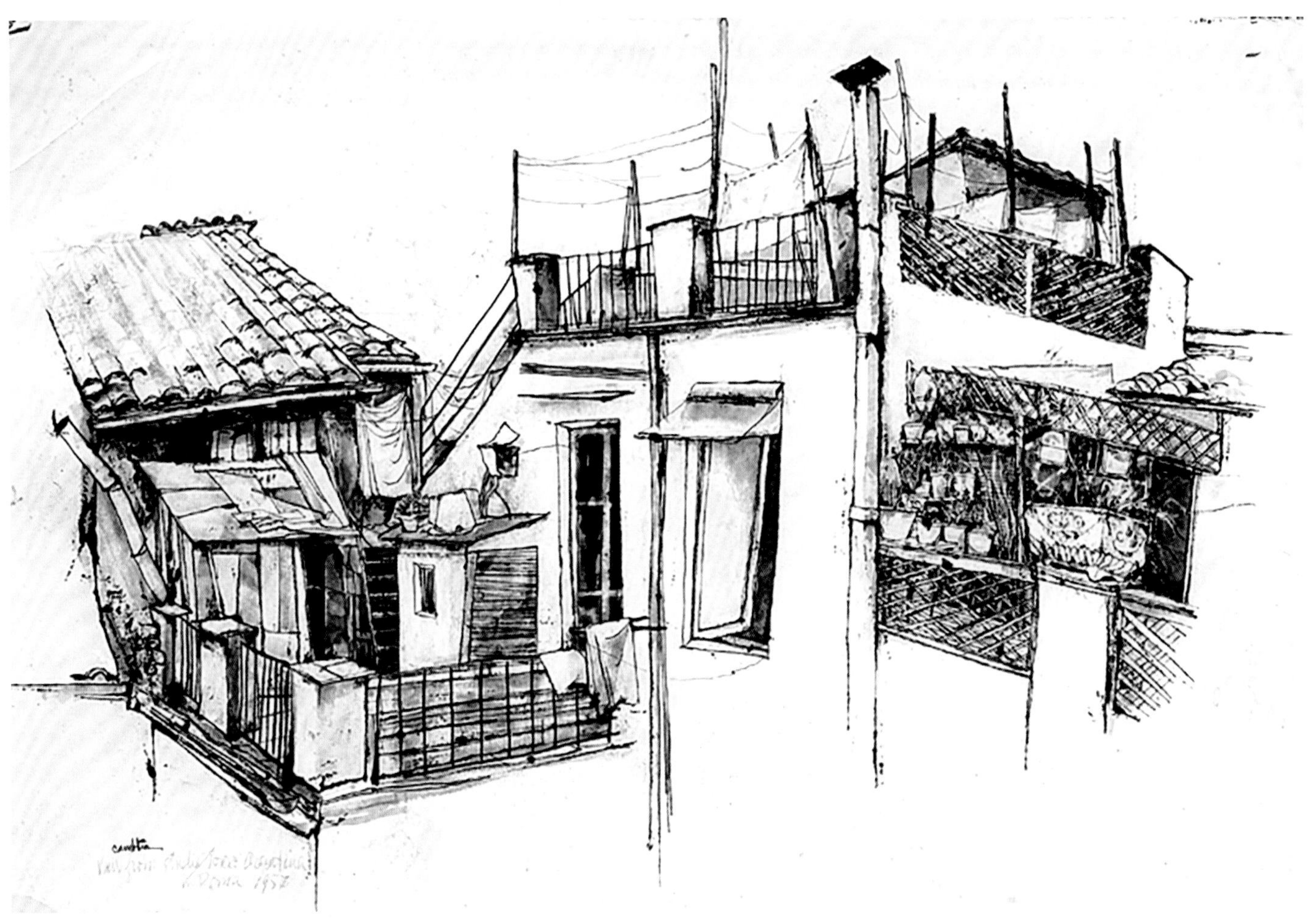

Bob Camblin: *The View from my studio window*, 1957/58.

He wasn't without American contacts. His studio in Rome became a gathering place for expats living in the city, including Lee Bontecou. Camblin appreciated his studio's location in the city square of *Largo di Torre Argentina*. He lived among ruined and reconstructed Roman temples, as well as the remnants of Pompey's Theatre where Julius Caesar was assassinated. Wandering through Rome, his imagination worked overtime to the point he felt as if he had entered a time warp. The history and muscularity of the city inspired him.

Camblin described his Italian influences in a 1958 exhibition catalogue from a Fulbright artists' show sponsored by the Smithsonian Institution and the Institute for Education: "Now take a boy from the Midwest, from Ponca City, Oklahoma, for instance, teach him to speak Italian, then put him in an apartment that is twenty years older than his own country's government; put this apartment in the center of Rome about a block from where Julius Caesar was killed; where from his studio window he can see the church in which the first act of 'Tosca' takes place; where each morning he can feed the cats in the *scavi* in front of his apartment and where a short walk will take him to the *Colosseo* and *Foro Romano*. Let him become acquainted with many of the people in this area and close friends with several Italian families. Let him visit the major museums and cities of Europe and live the last three months in Venice. Then bring him back and put him again in the Midwest . . . the results are these paintings."[2]

Morning walks led him past some of Rome's greatest treasures. Because of the central location of his studio-home, he was also near local galleries that represented the art of his Italian peers. One such gallery was the Galleria dell'Obelisco,[3] where he discovered the work of Leonardo Cremonini and Renzo Vespignani. Camblin noted his admiration of the art of both men in sketchbooks and may have met the artists during a visit to the gallery. Cremonini drew and painted stylized animals and figures, often children, against a background of geometric shapes. Artists and writers including Francis Bacon and W. H. Auden appreciated his work. Camblin studied and experimented with the spatial construction of Cremonini's paintings and the simplified forms of his figures. Vespignani used a blotted ink method, similar to a Rorschach test, to inspire a drawing. First he would splatter an

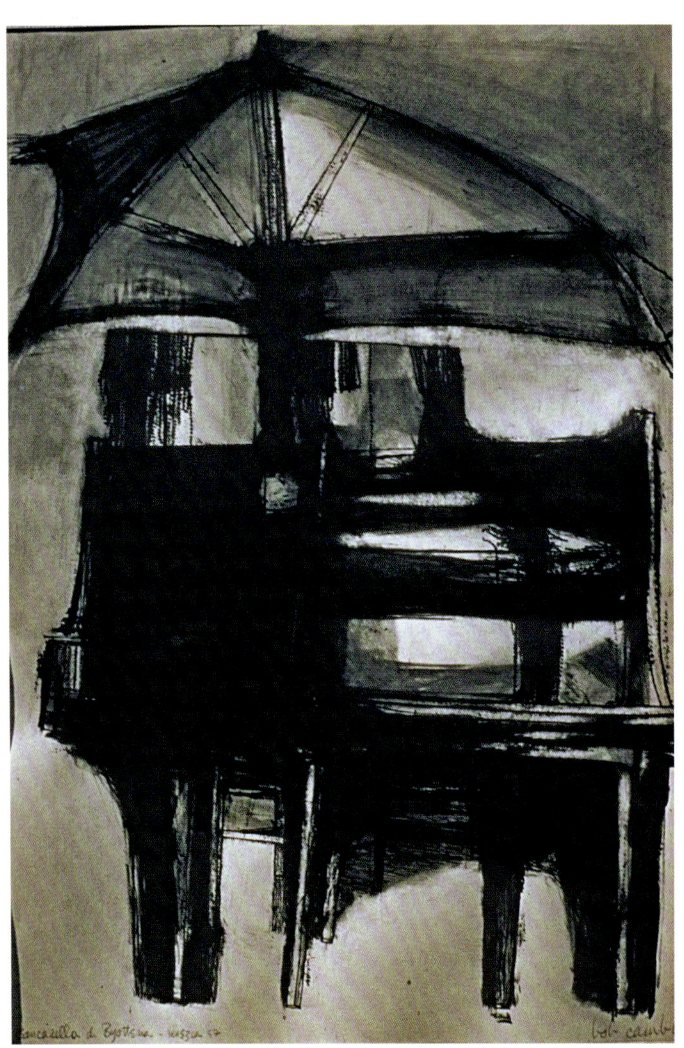

Sancalella di Bijotteria, 1957

inkblot on paper. Then he would search for an image in the blot,[4] elaborating the image into a drawing. Camblin applied the inkblot method to his own work and would later expand the technique to find images suggested by color gradations and drips in watercolor and oil washes. He wrote, years later, on a sketchbook page with a blotted ink drawing: "Yes, Vespignani. Now that he is dead for me, In memory—BLOT!"

In Camblin's personal library there is a book titled *Franz Kafka*.[5] Written in Italian and illustrated with Vespignani's blot technique drawings, the book seems to have served as both philosophical and artistic inspiration for Camblin whose personal library also includes an English volume of Kafka's "The Metamorphosis," (first published in 1915) a tale describing the transfiguration of Gregor Samsa[6] into a giant insect. Kafka's short story and Vespignani's double page illustration of the creature undoubtedly reinforced Camblin's interest in alienation, transformation, absurdism, and existentialism.

Camblin and Bonnie made numerous day trips to Rome's surrounding areas. They also made a side trip to Palermo, a drive to Sicily, Italy, which took twelve or thirteen hours. The Catacombe dei Cappuccino (Capuchin catacombs) intriqued Camblin with its 1,252 mummies and 8000 corpses, which line the walls and fill the burial chambers. The description from the catacombs' website is apt: "A macabre spectacle that brings out the uses, customs and traditions of the Palermo society from the seventeenth to the nineteenth century."[7]

Rather than maintain the religious sanctity of burial tombs, the Italians still exhibit their indelicate humor toward their beloved religion by placing skeletons, skulls, and bones in arranged lifelike settings. Like many Italians, Camblin was drawn to the bizarre and the macabre. He described his visit to the catacombs in a sketchbook:

Palermo—1956–57 . . . Paper crowns, wooden hearts—the macabre jingling of lire in a leather pouch held by a monk—a sound to remind you that your morbid interest should help pay the expenses of the monastery—That silent sandaled, bearded, rebel saint following discreetly and bouncing his leather bag—A wall of the men, a wall of the women and a wall of the priests—perfectly and properly segregated for eternity The children were the only ones that created any empathy—so may gaping sockets a [*sic*] slack jaws reminded you of an enormous silent choir practice, but the gray gloved and dusty remnants of the children.

There was one recent waxy improvement of the embalming art so commercial in its perfection that it made death lose its dignity and gave the others a sort of glory. Needless to add: She was so life-like, they didn't make photographs of her.

Mold, decay and all the figures in burlap sack along the wall. I wonder if the family must keep up the repair?

At Ferrocavallo we swam in crystal water and trapped conches and sea urchins. We also watched a funeral in which the hearse was pulled by four enormous black horses and the wheels were higher than the roof of the VW Sedan.

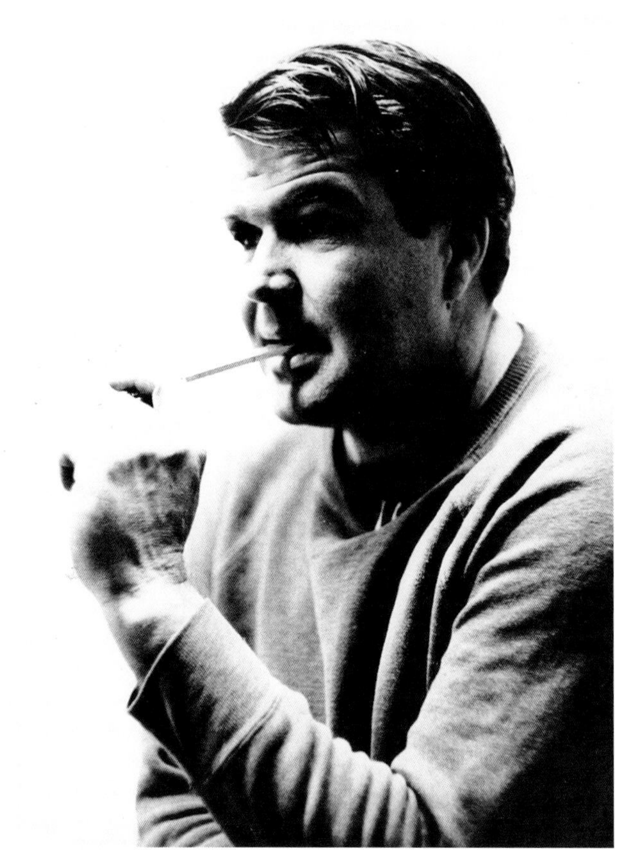

Camblin in Rome, 1958

To this day Romans elaborate or satirize morbid vitrines to venerate mummified saints whose decay has slowed to a crawl: an existential absurdity in its own right. In the late 1960s, Camblin would use a similar sarcastic cleverness by starting a group of works about a fictitious St. Bambola, about as far from Modernist geometric abstraction as a Catholic boy could stray.

Italian influences permeated Camblin's work for decades. In 1957, he looked to Italian contemporaries for inspiration, though as a draftsman, Camblin found his greatest influence in Leonardo da Vinci's observations, sketches, and drawings of unusual faces. Camblin's shapes and lines seem like enlargements of Leonardo details, suggesting that he stayed with his Italian experiences more than with modern art. For the most part, Camblin worked with abstracted, yet still recognizable, subject matter during his time in Italy. He added geometric forms and patterns to his subjects via his preferred media: ink, wash, and casein.

Before the Camblins' year in Italy concluded, they traveled to Venice and fell in love with the "City of

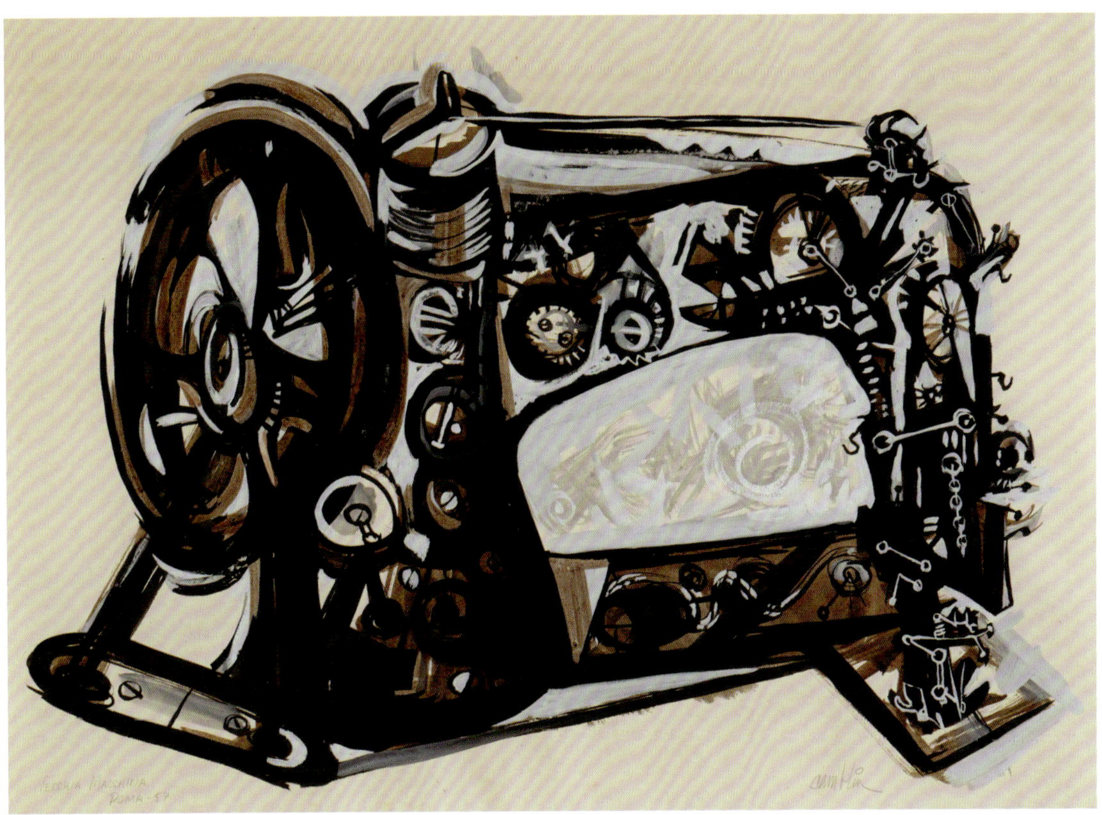

Camblin elaborated the form of an old sewing machine in *Vecchia Macchina*, Roma, 1957. *Photograph by Scott Peterson.*

Lions." Leo was his birth sign, and Camblin felt he had come home. While there, he and Bonnie visited Peggy Guggenheim's museum the Palazzo Venier dei Leoni, so called, it is thought, because of the lion heads on the museum's facade. The city's wealth of architectural gems, the troves of great paintings together with the romance of the canals, gondolas, and lagoons captivated them. Camblin vowed to return. Venice generated an ineffable artistic power, and he wanted to absorb more of its influence.

Camblin felt surrounded by a culture that stimulated all his senses, and he drew inspiration from the Italian tradition, the architecture and art in Rome, Florence, and Venice, the food and wine, the rhythmic lilt of spoken Italian, the vibrant scenes on every cobbled street, and the great art that hung in museums (his favorite being the Uffizi in Florence).

Turning into an Existentialist in Rome

Though Camblin was overjoyed to be in Italy in 1956, the scars of World War II still lingered. Camblin's exuberance became muted whenever he turned a corner and came upon bombed-out buildings yet to be rebuilt. He felt the Italians were generally optimistic because the war was eleven years behind them. However, remnant evidence of Mussolini's fascist regime, the German occupation that followed, and a collective memory of trauma seemed to temper Italian enthusiasm. So too did the continued post-war reconstruction that was still part of daily life in Italy.

Curiously, Italy did not produce any known writers who explored existentialism, despite having weathered the absurd governance of a despotic autocrat for twenty-two years. Being in a country that lived through the horrors of a world war spurred Camblin to continue his study of existentialism. The Lion Bookshop in Rome provided him with Soren Kierkegaard's writings. The Danish philosopher, considered the first existentialist philosopher, examined personal choice, existence, individualism, and authenticity: concepts central to existentialism and to Camblin. Kierkegaard's philosophy led the artist to other writers and philosophers like Franz Kafka, Albert Camus, and Jean-Paul Sartre.

Camblin was making himself into an artist. He came to accept that existence precedes essence, that everyone has the responsibility and freedom to define themselves, and that with total freedom comes total responsibility. He forged a path influenced by Jean-Paul Sartre's "Man is nothing else but that which he makes of himself," despite the cliché of it.

Whether in Europe or anywhere else, he enjoyed quoting French authors Sartre and Camus, who both wrote of the difficulty of being authentic in an absurd and meaningless universe. Existentialism posits that people are completely on their own and must therefore accept responsibility for their choices. For the existentialist, free will both defines and gives the self meaning in the face of an indifferent, arbitrary, and irrational world. Sartre wrote: "Man first of all exists, encounters himself, surges up in the world—and defines himself afterwards."[8] The human need for a "defined" and meaningful life coupled with the inability to find a reason for being can result in existential angst. If an individual acts in "bad faith"[9] to quell the anxiety, the result is an act of self-deception. Sartre defined bad faith as "hiding the truth from oneself,"[10] an act that results in inauthenticity, or in masking inner realities. Camblin determined to be personally authentic and to create authentic art.

Before his trip to Rome, Camblin read many books on the ancient city. He knew that during the Renaissance, Rome worked to regain its ancient prestige, but at the time Florence was the city state that embodied the cultural transition from the dark ages to the cultural and humanist revival, which placed man, not God, at the center of everything. One such example was Brunelleschi's rediscovery[11] of one point perspective (c. 1420), which turned the viewer into a participating point of reference. Camblin wanted to participate.

The *Portinari Altarpiece*

While living in the Eternal City, Camblin also spent time visiting Florence where he frequented the Uffizi Gallery and became fascinated with a triptych painted by the Netherlandish artist Hugo van der Goes:[12] the *Portinari Altarpiece*. Van der Goes began the altarpiece in 1475, the same year Michelangelo was born. The triptych was painted with oil on wood and is huge—eight by twenty feet when open. And rather than a single, flat perspective, the central panel utilizes several axes, which give a sense of depth to the painting's geometry.

The complexity of these compositions intrigued Camblin as much as he appreciated van der Goes's personalized portraiture (perhaps best exemplified in the *Portinari* by the shepherds' faces). Even though humanism was an intellectual movement of the Renaissance, van der Goes's realistic portrayal of unrefined but emotional shepherds was unconventional. The inclusion of common men (abetted by the central panel's title *The Adoration of the Shepherds*) is one of the first examples of mere mortals being admitted into a holy birth scene. The triptych impacted the development of realism in Renaissance art and greatly influenced the artwork of Bob Camblin nearly five centuries after its creation.

The Uffizi houses masterpieces by Botticelli, Raphael, Titian, and Caravaggio: why did Camblin fixate on Hugo van der Goe's triptych that hangs on the wall

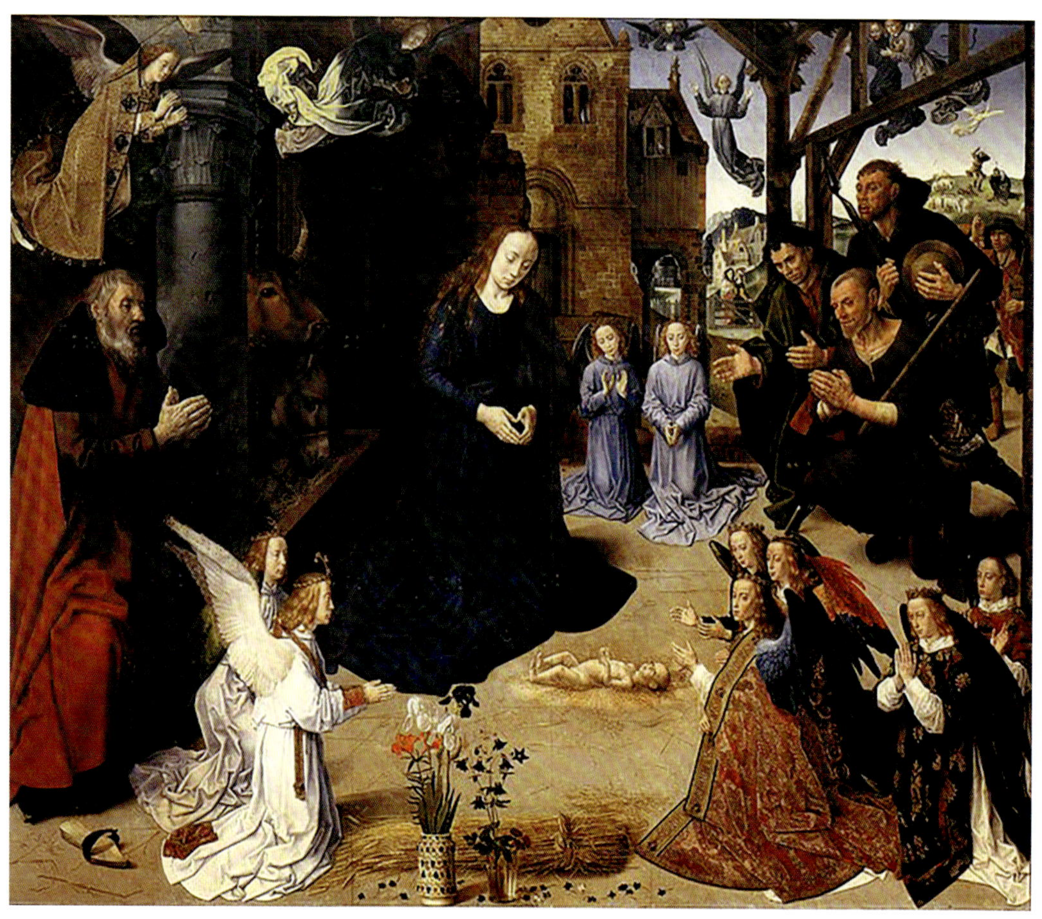

Central Panel of the Portinari Altarpiece by Hugo van der Goes, c. 1475.

opposite Sandro Botticelli's *Birth of Venus*? Perhaps Camblin saw humanity reflected in the eyes of the shepherds. Maybe the nativity scene triggered his mental imprint of the *Pioneer Woman*, mother-and-boy-child. Or perhaps Camblin had read Erwin Panofsky's book *Early Netherlandish Painting, Its Origins and Character*, published in black and white three years before Camblin left for Italy on his Fulbright. Panofsky considered the *Portinari* one of the greatest Late Netherlandish paintings and theorized about its unusual diagonal compositional format. Part of Panofsky's compositional analysis concerns van der Goes's

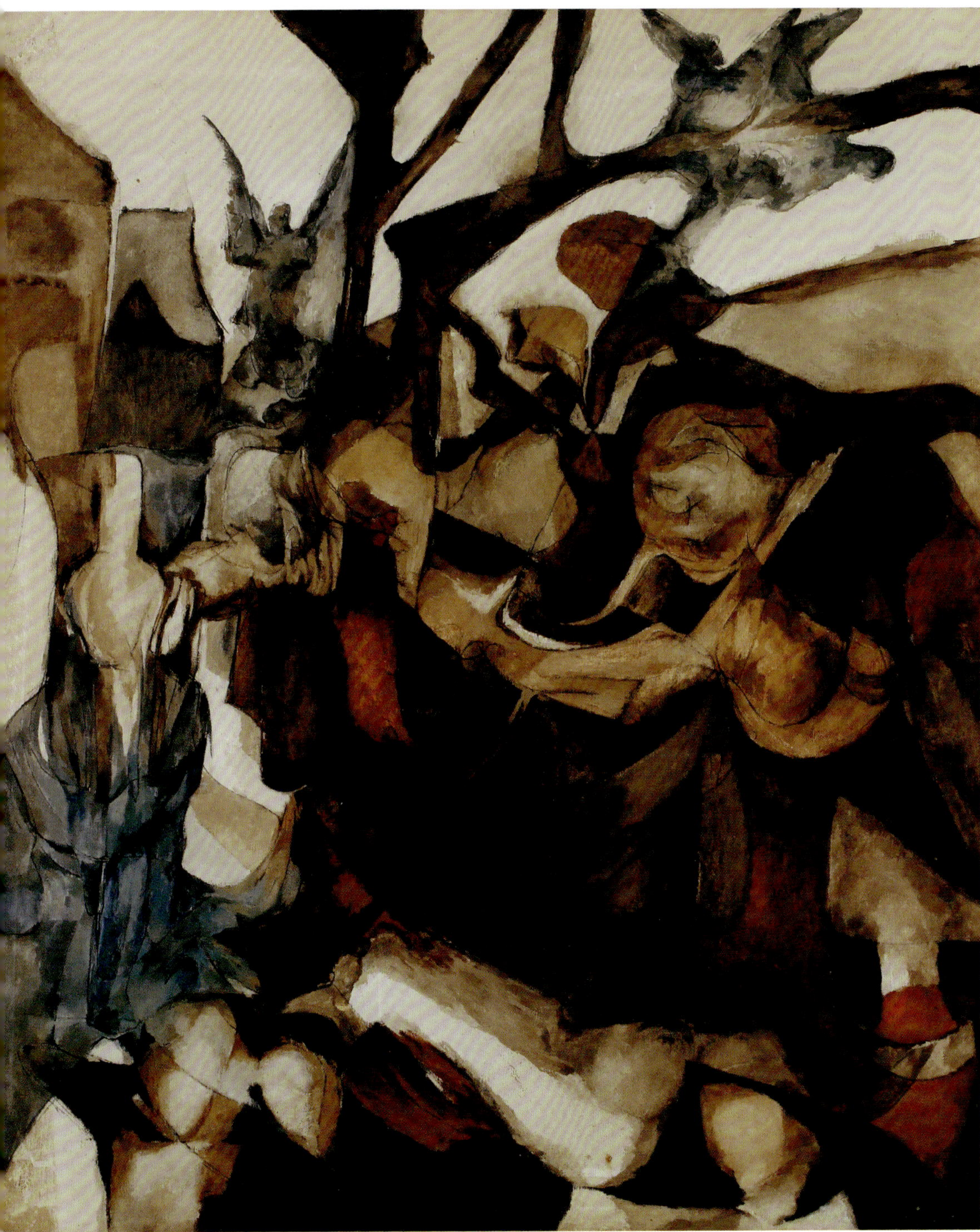

Camblin interpreted van der Goes' *Adoration of the Shepherds* in his *Homage to Hugo, 1959–60*. Oil on canvas, 6' X 5'. *Collection of Sandra and Cruser Rowland. Photograph by David P. Gray.*

organization of dark and light areas. Camblin studied the composition of the central panel and experienced an epiphany during a visit: he realized that structure preceded narrative. All structural lines lead to the Virgin's face.

Van der Goes's work influenced numerous artists including Vincent Van Gogh who wrote to his brother Theo in 1883:

> You remember the painting *The Madness of Hugo van der Goes* by Wauters? In some things B. [Dutch artist, George Hendrik Breitner] faintly reminds me of a state of mind like Van der Goes's.
>
> I had recently become wild-eyed, a bit like Hugo van der Goes in the painting by Emile Wauters.
>
> I'm once again nearly reduced to the state of madness of Hugo van der Goes in Emile Wauters's painting.

In an interview for *The Kansas City Star*, Camblin stated, "I looked at van der Goes's masterwork for a long time . . . before I suddenly became aware of the incredible exactness in its composition. I realized I could lay a grid over that painting and find every component of the work in perfect balance of order. [Organization] is like practicing on the piano. Regardless of how much talent you think you have, you must work and work until the basic skills are part of you."[13]

The visual compositional elements intrigued Camblin more than the realistic subject matter. He saw the interaction of compositional abstractions: shapes, colors, textures, forms, and the light elements played with dark elements. His discoveries gave his work a new foundation.

Another Camblin painting, albeit far removed from the *Portinari Altarpiece* homage, demonstrates the artist's interest in composition and abstraction. In *Mare Tirreno* the background consists of an abstracted sea and a flat, planar but stormy sky. The middleground shows a turbulent, whitecapped sea, while the foreground is filled with skeletal forms reminiscent of a whale rib cage. The white curves play off the vertical and horizontal greens and blues. The motion of the sea contrasts with the staid, boney structures on the beach, their white abstracted forms echoing the whitecaps.

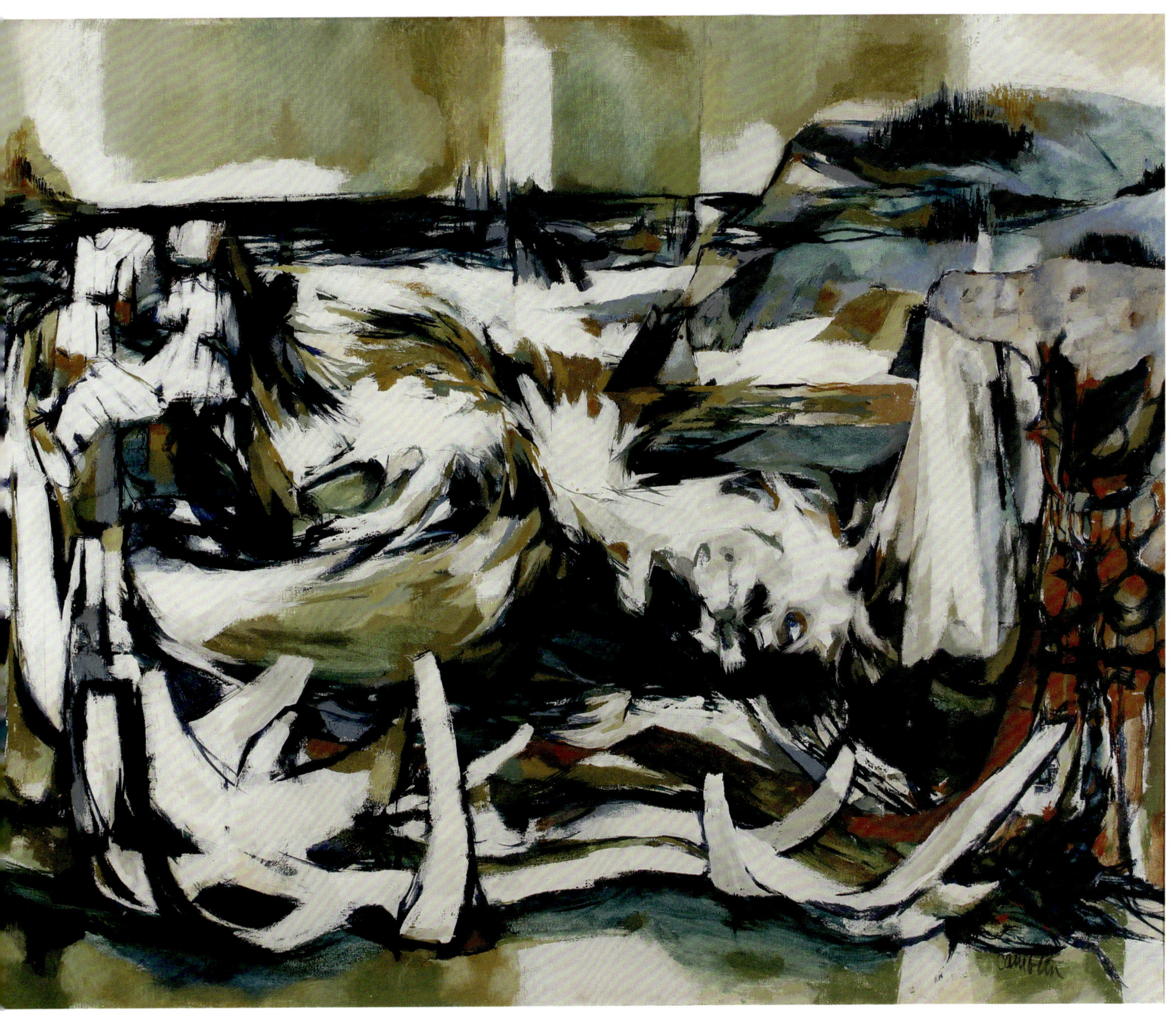

Mare Tirreno (*Tyrrhenian Sea*), late 1950s. Polymer tempera on canvas, 29.5" X 39". *Collection of Kay Shefield.* A part of the Mediterranean Sea off Italy's west coast where Camblin loved to paint and sketch. *Photograph by David P. Gray.*

Professing in Sarasota, Florida; Urbana, Illinois; Detroit, Michigan; and Salt Lake City, Utah

Florida 1958–60 Red Tide and Birth of Venus series following the Homage to Hugo paintings and the large carousel drawings. The space in the drawings & ptgs was conscious a tension to edges as if they were stretched hides on a frame. Positive and negative emphasis.

—notes from a Camblin sketchbook

After the completion of his Fulbright, Camblin returned to the U.S.A. armed with firsthand experience of great art, a new language, a renewed interest in abstraction, and stronger existentialist beliefs. He faced a world devoid of meaning and sought to give significance to his art and his life. He was ready to teach and sent job applications to several universities and museums. Before he found a teaching position, he worked as a cartographer for Trans World Airlines for nearly a year. He found drawing maps pleasurable but was more than ready to move on to the creation of art, when he received an offer of a teaching position at the John and Mable Ringling Museum of Art School in Sarasota, Florida. He accepted immediately. He had seen photographs of the Ringling estate's buildings, which were constructed in the "Venetian manner." Camblin did not believe it was coinci dence that his first teaching job after falling in love with Venice was in a recreated Venetian environment. He felt the universe was buffering his readjustment to life in America. This new echo of the city of canals blended American culture with a vision of Venice. Built on Florida's Gulf Coast, the new museum and mansion even offered water with better beaches.

John Ringling and Mable Burton married in their thirties. Mable had left Ohio to find a rich husband, and find him she did. When she met John, he was one of seven Ringling brothers, five of whom had joined together to start the Ringling Brothers Circus in 1884. They went on to acquire the Barnum and Bailey Show in 1907, which became a world-class circus that dominated the field of traveling circuses. The profits from the enterprise enabled John to invest wisely, and he made a fortune, some of which he invested in art, and more of which he used to build his and Mable's Sarasota mansion and museum. Their 36,000-square-foot home, named Ca' d'Zan (house of John) was designed in the style of Venetian Gothic pala-zzos. After moving in, the Ringlings discovered the palace wall space was too lim-ited for their art (at the time one of the world's major collections). In order to house their Baroque masterpieces, they built a museum modeled on the Uffizi Gallery.

Mable died first, then upon John's death in 1936, creditors discovered he had bequeathed his estate to the people of Florida; however, his creditors tied the estate up for ten years. In 1946, the estate was restored and opened to the public. When Camblin arrived in 1958, little had been done to maintain the estate since John Ringling's passing. Camblin joked that the state of Florida was allowing Ringling's Venice to become more authentic through decay. Between classes, Camblin often sat on the marble terrace of Ca'd' Zan where he could sketch the bay front or the buildings and grounds of the property.[1]

Curiously, none of Camblin's paintings of Floridian Venice survived. Perhaps he resisted painting the Ringling buildings because he gained a sense for their art-ficiality at some point during his two years in Sarasota. He may have felt that painting those imitations would not be in accordance with his contemplation of existentialist virtue, particularly the importance of living an authentic life. Perhaps in painting the Ringling buildings, he would not have been true to himself, to his work, or to Venice, the city he loved. It is also possible he may have been too busy, or the work was lost.

Rather than focus on Sarasota's Venetian influences, Camblin decided to return to his studies of the *Portinari Altarpiece* that hung in Florence's Uffizi. During his two years in Sarasota, he employed his "basic skills" for the creation of his first totally abstract paintings, based on the *Portinari's* central panel: *The Adoration of the Shepherds*. Camblin incorporated the central panel's diagonal structure, the balance of light and dark areas, as well as the work's color palette. He eliminated the subject and narrative through the total abstraction of forms, knowing that the removal of realism and religious allusions would not compromise structure. He discussed his work with a local reporter: "The paintings are a transformation of the figures in 'Adoration' into abstract color relations, with an attempt to retain the poetic suggestions . . . I have found a direction and it's nice to be going somewhere . . . Remember, however, that when I say I have found something that is right for me, I don't mean it's wrong for someone else . . . The greater the painting, the less the viewer will be aware, at casual glance, of the secrets of its greatness."[2]

Camblin also created a totally abstract work based on the colors and forms he had used in his earlier homage to Hugo. In this work he completely ignored narrative. He based the colors and forms on his earlier *Homage to Hugo*.

Camblin may have been drawn to the van der Goes in the Uffizi, but he did not ignore Botticelli's *The Birth of Venus*. Nudes were rare in medieval art but began making a comeback in the early Renaissance. Botticelli began painting full-figure, life-size nudes for the Medici family in the early 1480s. He was the first Renaissance artist to create large-scale backgrounds based on mythology into which he placed his nudes. For his model in *The Birth of Venus*, Botticelli referred to an ancient statue of Aphrodite. He painted a subtle dark line around the figure of Venus, a technique that Camblin used in many of his works. In Italy, Camblin completed several sketches of *The Birth of Venus*, but it wasn't until he taught at the University of Detroit Mercy's School of Architecture that he began painting his version of the work. He again found structure more important than figural representation. He told a reporter: "*The Birth of Venus* is an exercise in organization. [For me] painting gradually became secondary to drawing, even superfluous.

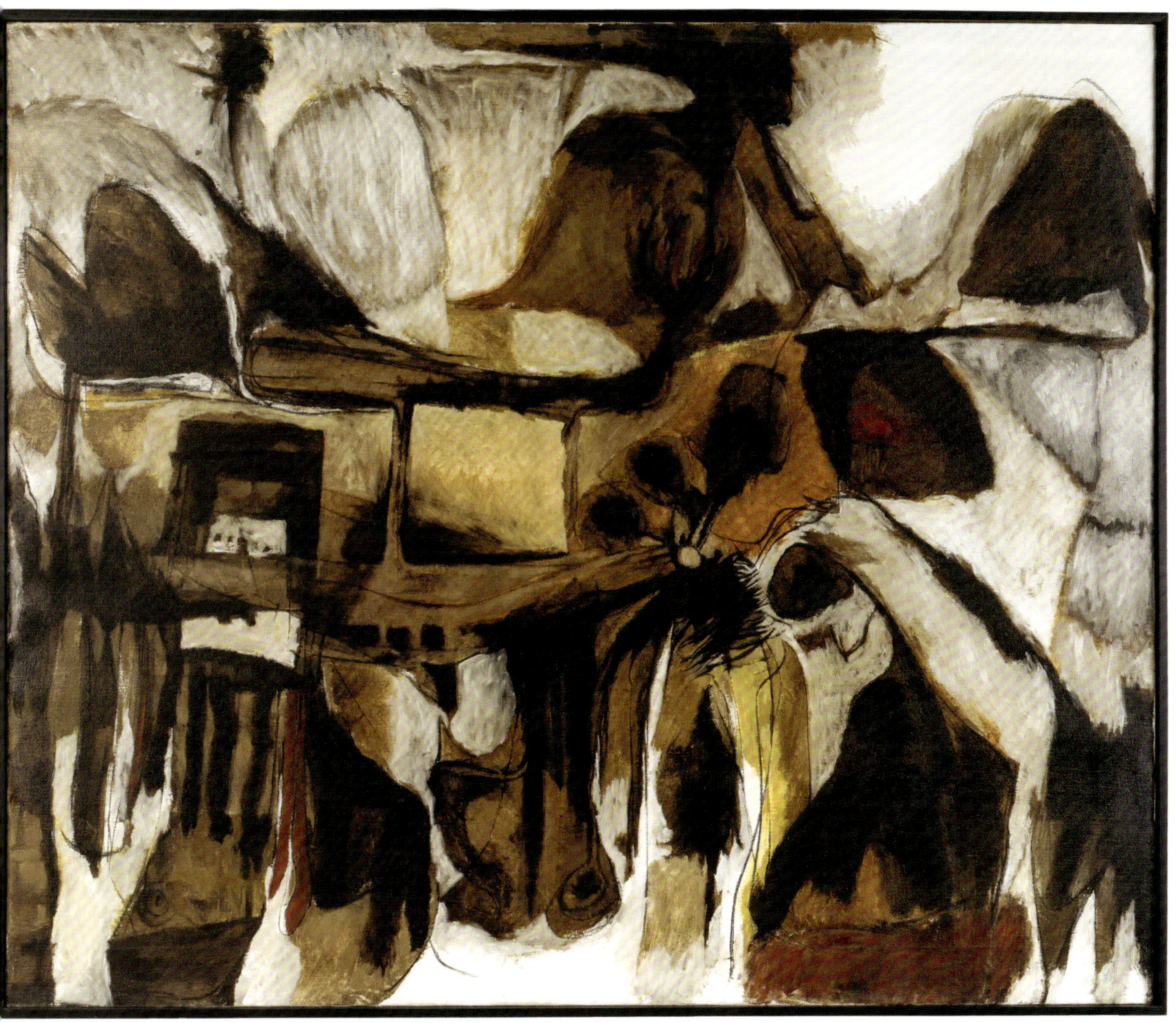

Homage to Hugo, abstraction, 1960–61. Camblin experimented with the geometry of the van der Goes altarpiece for years. He completely abstracted this example. *Photograph by Scott Peterson.*

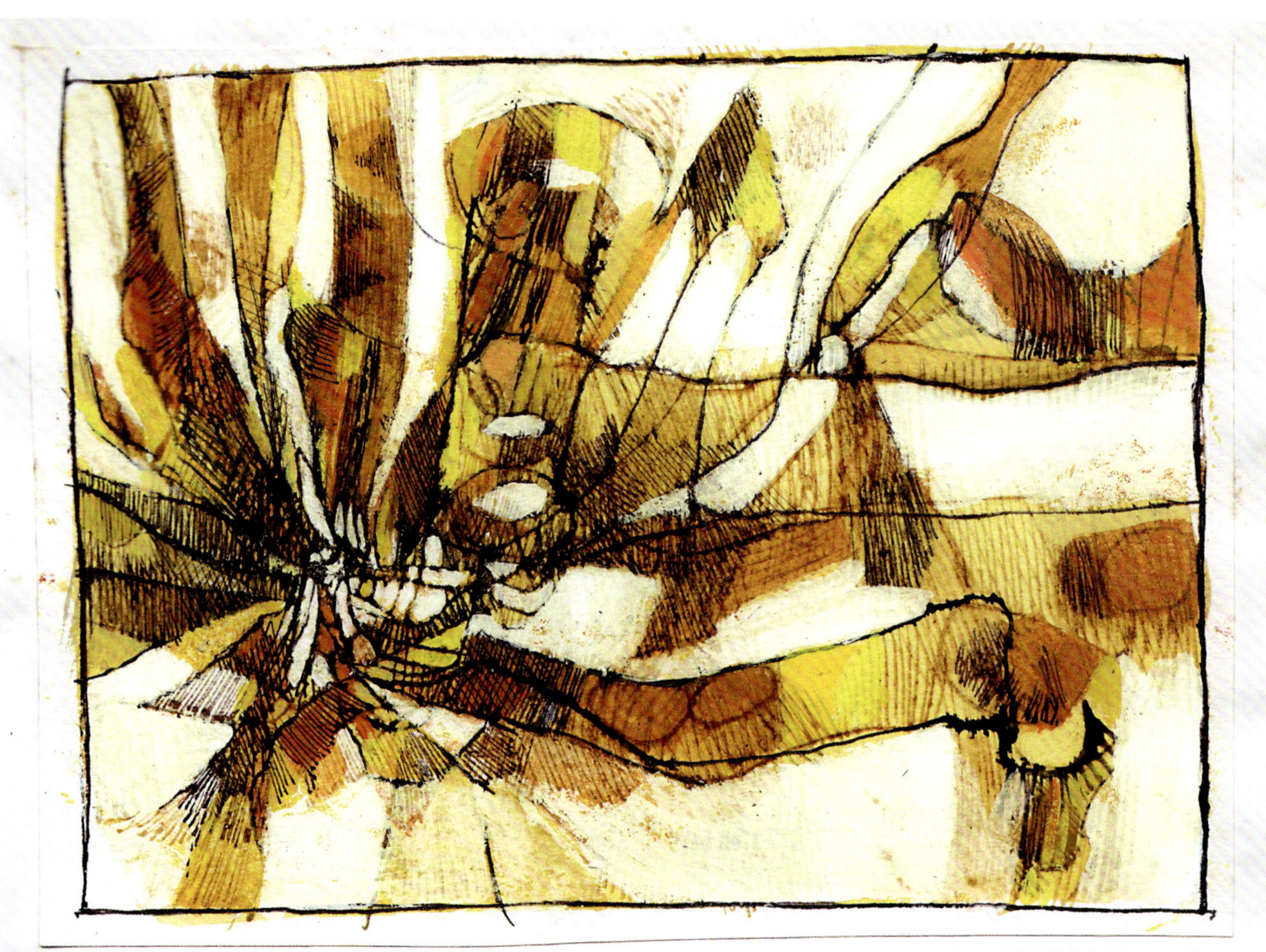

Icarus Descending, 1959. The influence of myths in Camblin's work is apparent in his titles. *Photograph by Scott Peterson.*

I sluffed off color as I went along. Drawings provide a real insight into an artist. I've been looking at old master drawings, and I have discovered there is a contemporary feeling in them all. The paintings are period pieces."[3]

Urbana, Illinois

After Sarasota, Camblin relocated his family to the public research University of Illinois, Urbana, for the 1960–61 school year. During his stay in Urbana, he contacted some old faculty member friends at the Kansas City Art Institute who asked him if he would like to exhibit his new work at the Institute. He was flattered and responded positively. A week before his exhibition was scheduled to open, Camblin made the six-hour drive to Kansas City, Missouri, pulling a rental trailer full of his art. He helped hang his one-man show *Bob Camblin—Recent Drawings and Paintings* at his alma mater. *The Kansas City Star* reviewed the exhibition:

> Bob Camblin is an artist who believes that paintings are a 50–50 proposition— they should bring something to the viewer and the viewer should bring something to them. That is why, for himself, he likes neither abstract art (which demands too much) nor social realism (which screams too loud). He has tried both, and found the results a little forced. Now he is working somewhere between in a manner that might be called allegorical. 'I have found a direction, and it's nice to be going somewhere, Camblin said genially last week when he visited the Kansas City Art Institute.[4]

Later in a sketchbook he noted: "Illinois 1960–61 Elaboration of the Birth of Venus into a metamorphosis series—change of scale due to a pastiche of Picasso's Minotauromachy—The meta-morphosis begins to be about a conscious (?) evolutionary effect. This links all the preoccupation since 1947 with TAO-ZEN et al.— with a myth—a new myth. (The drawings are super rational compositions.)"

Camblin was busy. Besides teaching, creating a new series of paintings, and exhibiting his art, he continued his studies of the *Tao* and Zen Buddhism, his favorite subjects since high school. He nurtured the evolution of his art and his ideas. Gerald Purdy, who had just recently received both his BFA and MFA from the University of Illinois, made regular visits to his alma mater during Bob's time there. Purdy and Camblin became fast friends after they encountered one another. They would share a glass of beer, discuss art and ideas, and relish the relaxation they felt in each other's company. Their bond lasted a lifetime.

Detroit, Michigan

Michigan 1961–65 Continued elaboration of the myth making and major change was the metamorphosis existential comic strips (joke!) This writing and drawing combination starts with the Great Scavenger of the Birth of Venus-Frog-Fish-Sunflower story. (Drawings become more intuitive over a classical composition.)

—notes from a Camblin sketchbook

After his year in Urbana, Illinois, Camblin accepted a teaching position at the University of Detroit Mercy. Given his Catholic upbringing, he felt comfortable at the private Roman Catholic university. He was in the first group of artists to be hired by the university's architecture department headed by Bruno Leon, who provided the Camblins with a home of Leon's own design in Grosse Isle Township. The Township residence was twenty-five miles south of Detroit and situated on the largest island in the Detroit River: it provided a four-year haven for the Camblins.

Aside from supplying an architect-designed house for a faculty member, Mercy's forward-thinking architecture department was a champion for Detroit homes like Frank Lloyd Wright's Dorothy H. Turkel House. The city itself offered numerous examples of exemplary architecture. Architect Minoru Yamasaki, best known for designing the World Trade Center's Twin Towers in New York, designed the McGregor Memorial Conference Center at Wayne State University in the heart of Detroit. His design inspired a new style of architecture: New Formalism.

The largest collection of residences by Mies van der Rohe can be found in Lafayette Park, a historic district just east of downtown Detroit.

Camblin likely saw the twenty-seven 1933 fresco murals by Diego Rivera glorifying workers at the Ford Motor Company. The Rivera frescoes were commissioned for the Detroit Institute of Art, and surround the institute's Rivera Court.

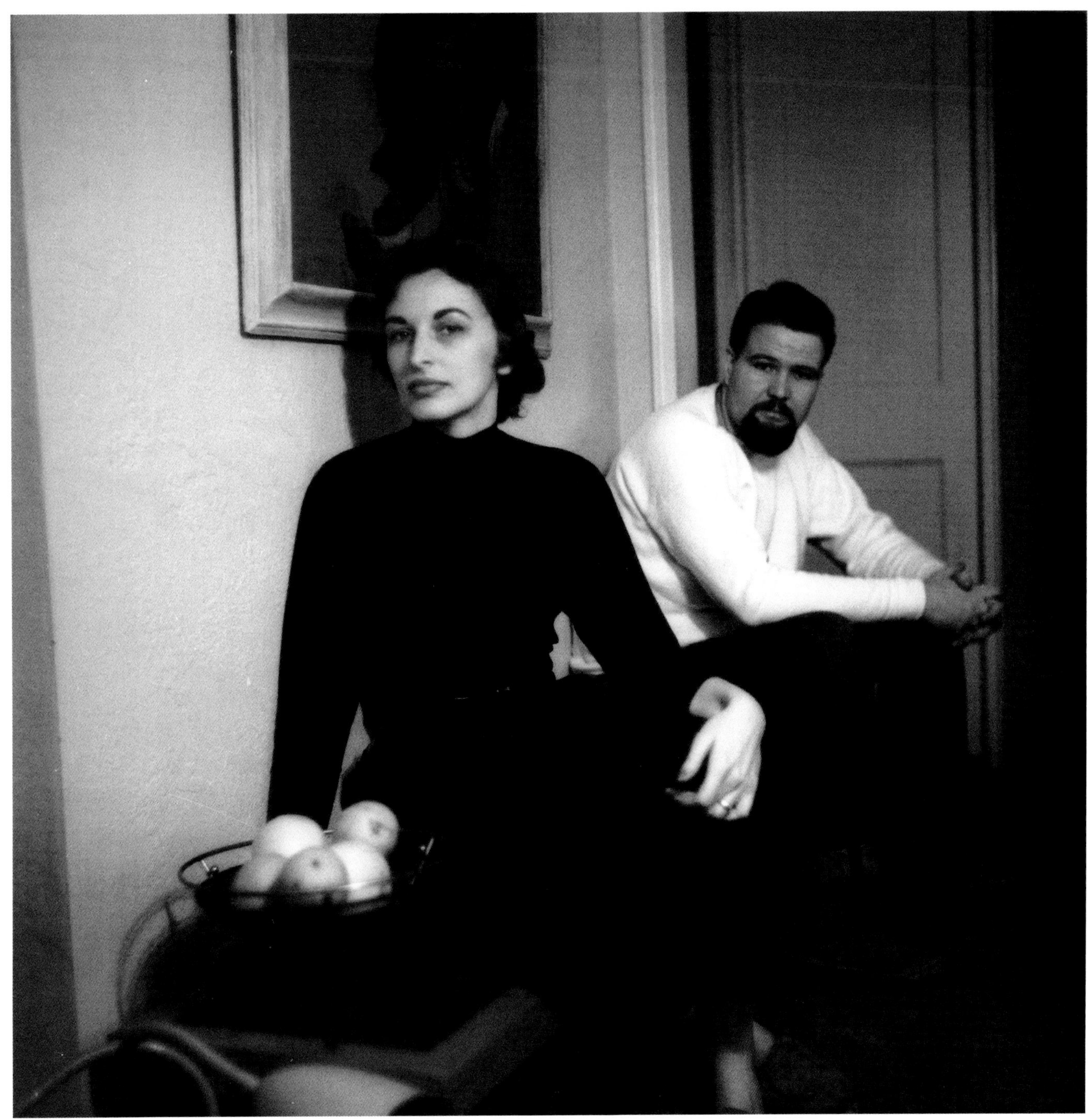

A photograph of Bonnie and Bob in the 1960s.

Detroit's Guardian Building, Briggs Stadium, the Hudson Department Store, the Masonic Temple, and the Palms Theatre are but a few buildings exemplifying the development that resulted from the auto industry's exponential growth. Camblin experienced the power of America's burgeoning automotive heritage.

Often in the company of Leon, Camblin visited notable architecture built in nearby cities including Marcel Breuer's 1964 St. Francis de Sales Church in Muskegon, constructed shortly before Camblin left Michigan. Eliel Saarinen's Cranbrook Academy of Art in Bloomfield Hills, and his son Eero Saarinen's General Motors Technical Center in Warren along with Alden Dow's visionary 1936 home in Midland (designated as a National Historic Landmark in 1989). Dow's Midland Center for the Arts and a library named after his mother, Grace A. Dow Memorial Library, were among Leon's favorite architectural designs.[5] Leon relished sharing his love of architecture with Camblin, and their friendship blossomed. Aside from taking architectural road trips to Michigan, Camblin and Leon travelled to Europe together. No records remain from their journey, but judging from their lifelong friendship, the trip was a complete success. Bob's experiences with likeminded friends, his experiences in Detroit, its energy and its environs, all helped imbue his creativity with kinetic momentum.

Camblin lived through the art movements associated with Modernism including Regionalism, Abstract Expressionism, Pop Art, and Minimalism but did not feel motivated to follow any of them. Instead, while in Detroit, he created his own form of Modernism, "existential comic strips." The format for the strips consists of single, small drawings in rows, with individual cells of three or four per row, similar to storyboards for film and to cartoon lay-outs. He did not include text on his first comic strip format compositions, but the individual drawings within a single work shared a common theme. He drew images in the cells: masks, babies in specimen bottles, fish heads, tubing, skulls, toads, and discarded dolls. He titled a multi-celled work, *Series of Masks*. Other than his signature and the title, there is no explanatory writing. He was drawn to the mysteries of hiding behind a false face, and the viewer is never sure if the faces in the individual cells are faces as masks, or masks covering faces. Under the subsequent celled works he wrote his own fables. He titled one series *Time Machine*,[6]

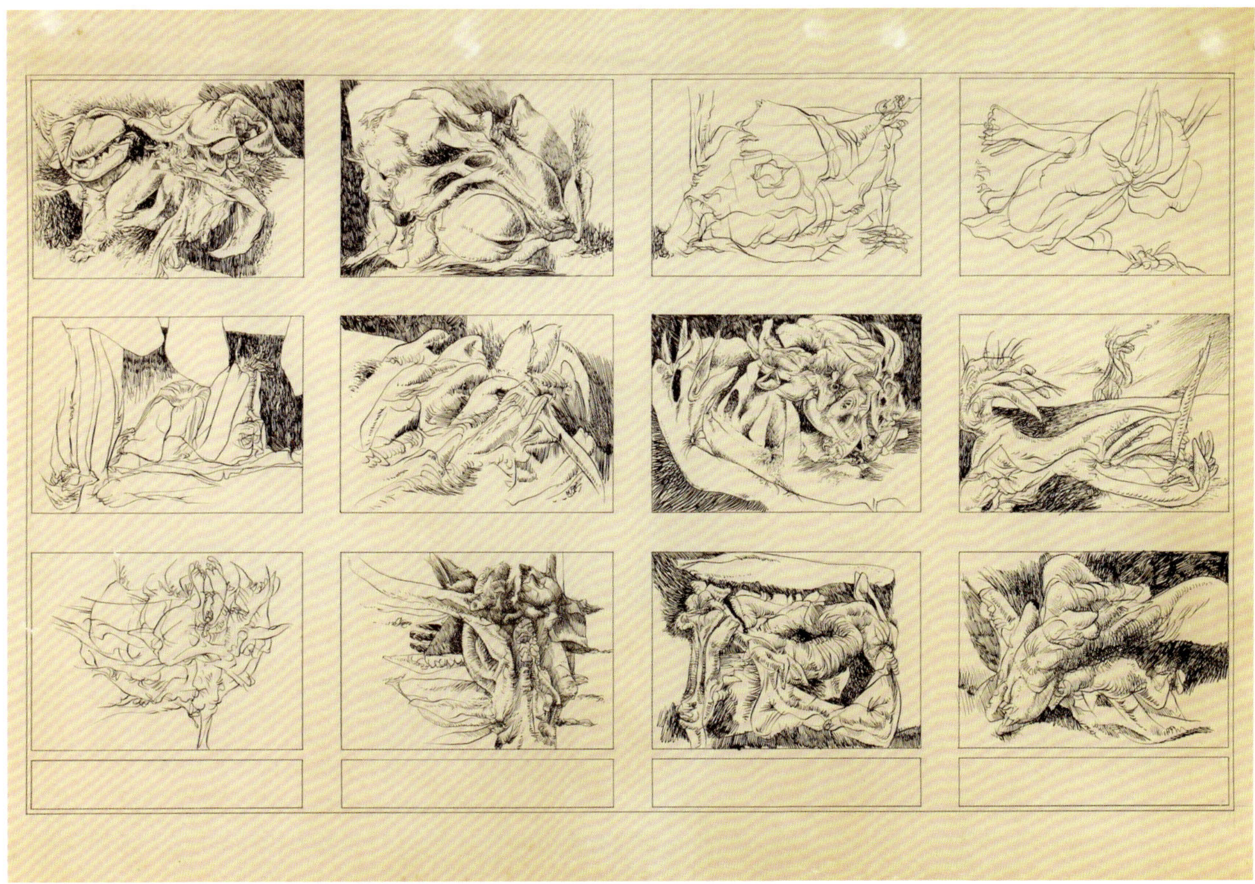

Time Machine cells c. 1967. Ink on paper, 22.5" X 32.5". *Collection of Robert Fowler. Photograph by David P. Gray.*

in which he christened a cast-off doll, St. Bambola. Beneath the cells of *Time Machine* he wrote:

(Beginning cell) Here begins the dream in which barnacle lips sing the song of St. Bambola, her martyrdom and internment in the glass reliquary. And the sea-sounds from the sea-stained green glass bottle sing of fortune, fate and toads that must appear—the empty vial waits . . . (Cell Two) We follow the mysteries of the many layered Bambola into the husk of a Sicilian catacomb where red wooden hearts beat slowly in the olive-oil of memory; their faint message pumped into a decanter of pink, plastic fingers that tell us by tapping that Braun Z. Cox has been cured by faith and they wish also to be free and phallic . . . (Cell Three) A large

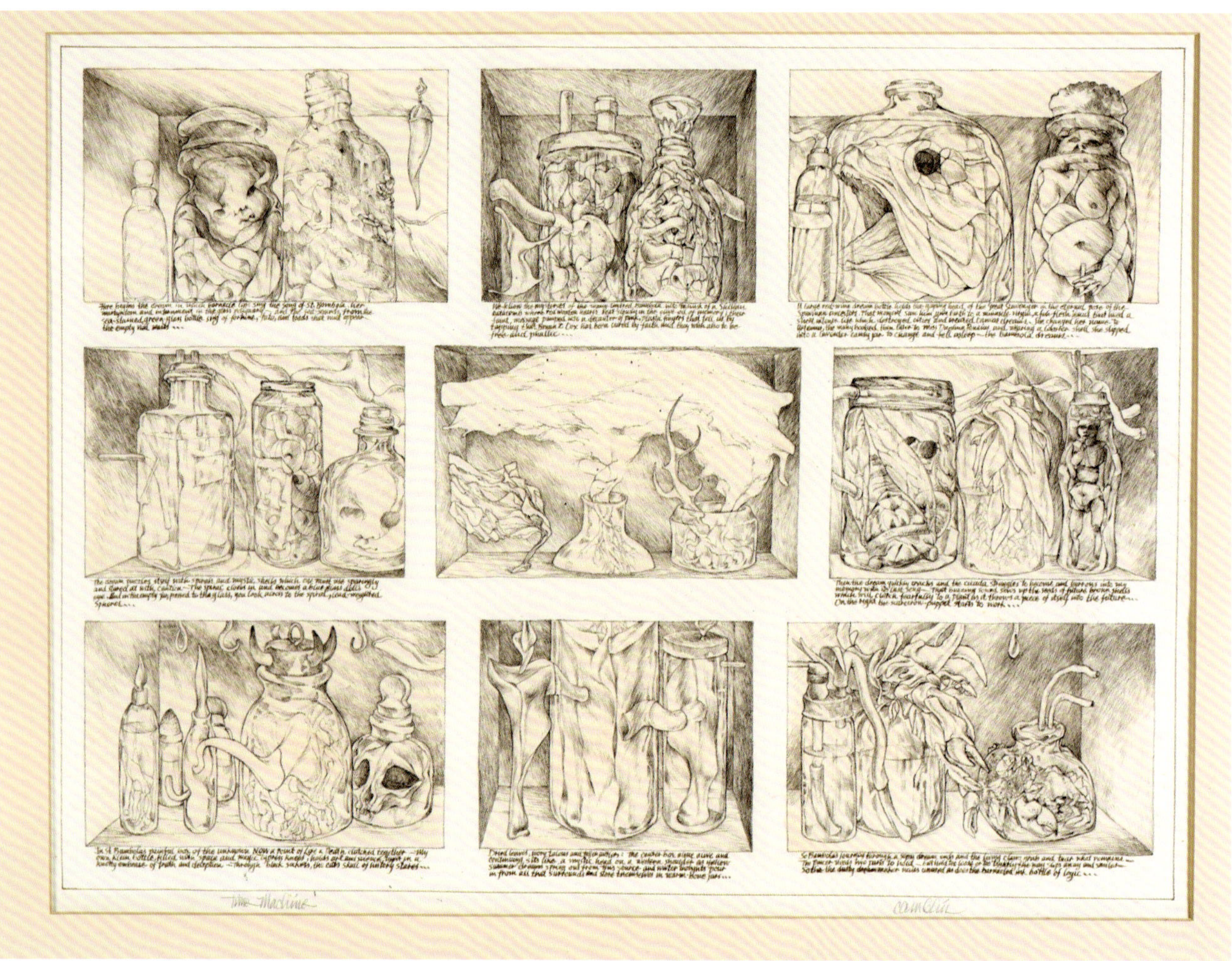

Time Machine, Robert Fowler Collection. Photograph by Scott Peterson.

red wine dream bottle holds the gaping head of the Great Scavenger in the eternal pose of the Spavinaw ancestors. That moment saw him give birth to a minuscule virgin, a fish flesh Venus that lived a short, intense life which destroyed cities and created canvas dreams. She changed her name to Artemus, the many boobed, and later to Miss Daphne Peneius and wearing a lobster shell slipped into a lavender candy jar to change and fell asleep—the bambola dreams . . . (Cell Five) Then the dream quickly cracks and the cicada struggles to become and burrows into my memory with its last song—That buzzing sound sews up the seeds of future

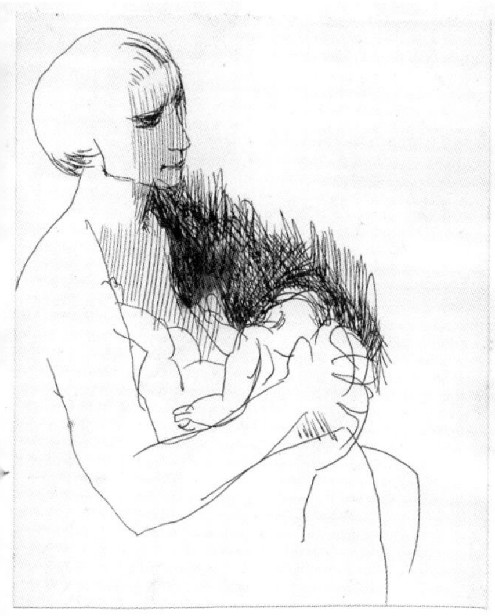

Haiga: *First Child*, 1961. Camblin adopted the 17th century Japanese drawing style called a haiga, which incorporates text into a drawing, to celebrate the birth of his son, Brian. *Photograph by Scott Peterson.*

brown shells which will clutch fearfully to a plant as it throws a piece of itself into the future . . . on the right the scarecrow puppet starts to work . . . (Cell Six) In St. Bambola's painful box of the unknown NOW a point of life and death clutched together—My own Klein bottle, filled with space and magic cypress knees, holds art and science tight in a knotty embrace of truth and deception—Through black sockets, the cats skull of history stares.

The comic strips pleased him. They required both drawing and text. He lamented now and then that because of his love of words, he probably should have been a writer.

Not only did he create a new art form for himself, he also became a father while teaching at the University of Detroit Mercy. In 1961 Bonnie gave birth to a son Brian. He knew and was appreciative of the fullness of his life. He had also made a lifetime friend in Leon. There never seemed to be a shortage of conversation or inspiration. When his daughter Robyn was born in 1963, Camblin knew that his family was complete.

The old masters had always intrigued Camblin, and he had copied works of various artists during his school years. After the creation of his existential comic strips he began experimenting with his *Variation on Turner's The Parting of Hero and Leander.* His depiction of Joseph Mallord William Turner's painting mirrored the composition and referenced the allegory's narrative: the work's title names the lovers but Camblin's drawing does not depict the figures' deaths. Rather than imitate

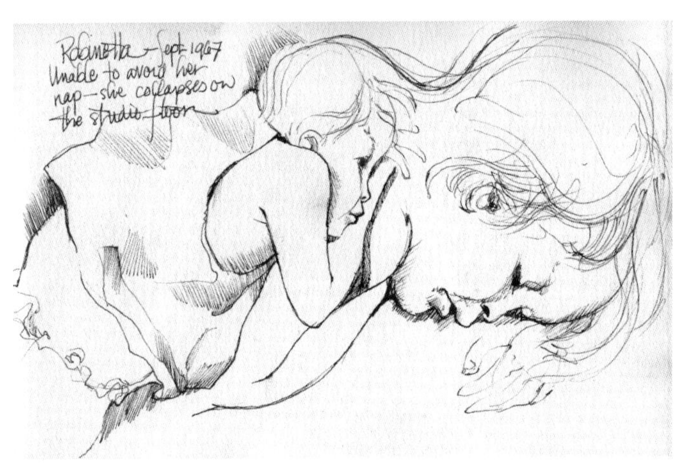

Robinetta, 1967. The birth of his second child, Robyn, prompted more visual poetry. *Photograph by Scott Peterson.*

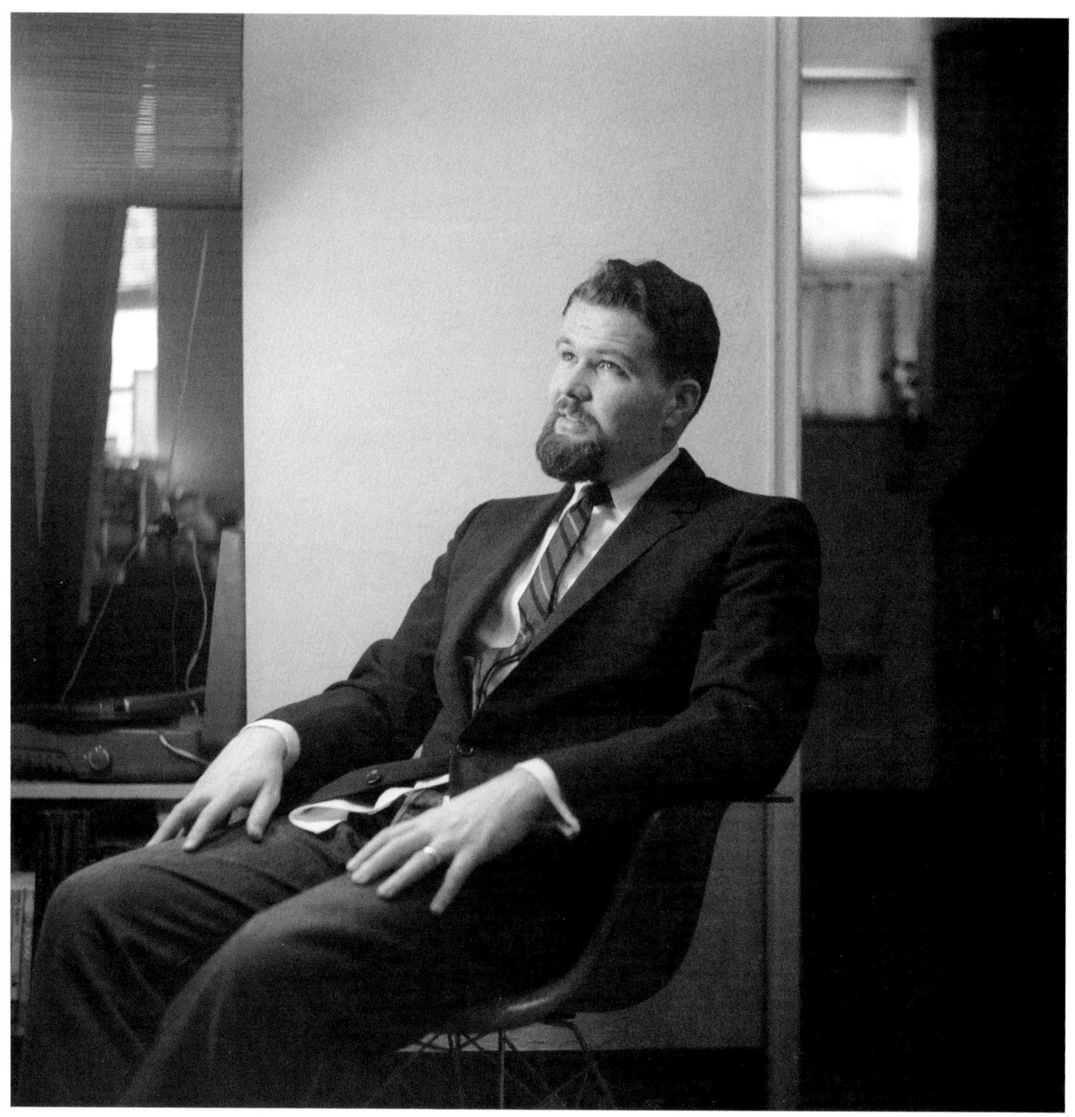

Bob Camblin at the beginning of his career as a university professor.

Turner's brush strokes, Camblin utilized dense ink lines to draw the viewer's eye to the surface of the work instead of to the vanishing point. His clouds have specified outlines instead of evanescent Turner clouds, allowing his drawing technique to dominate the work's structure.

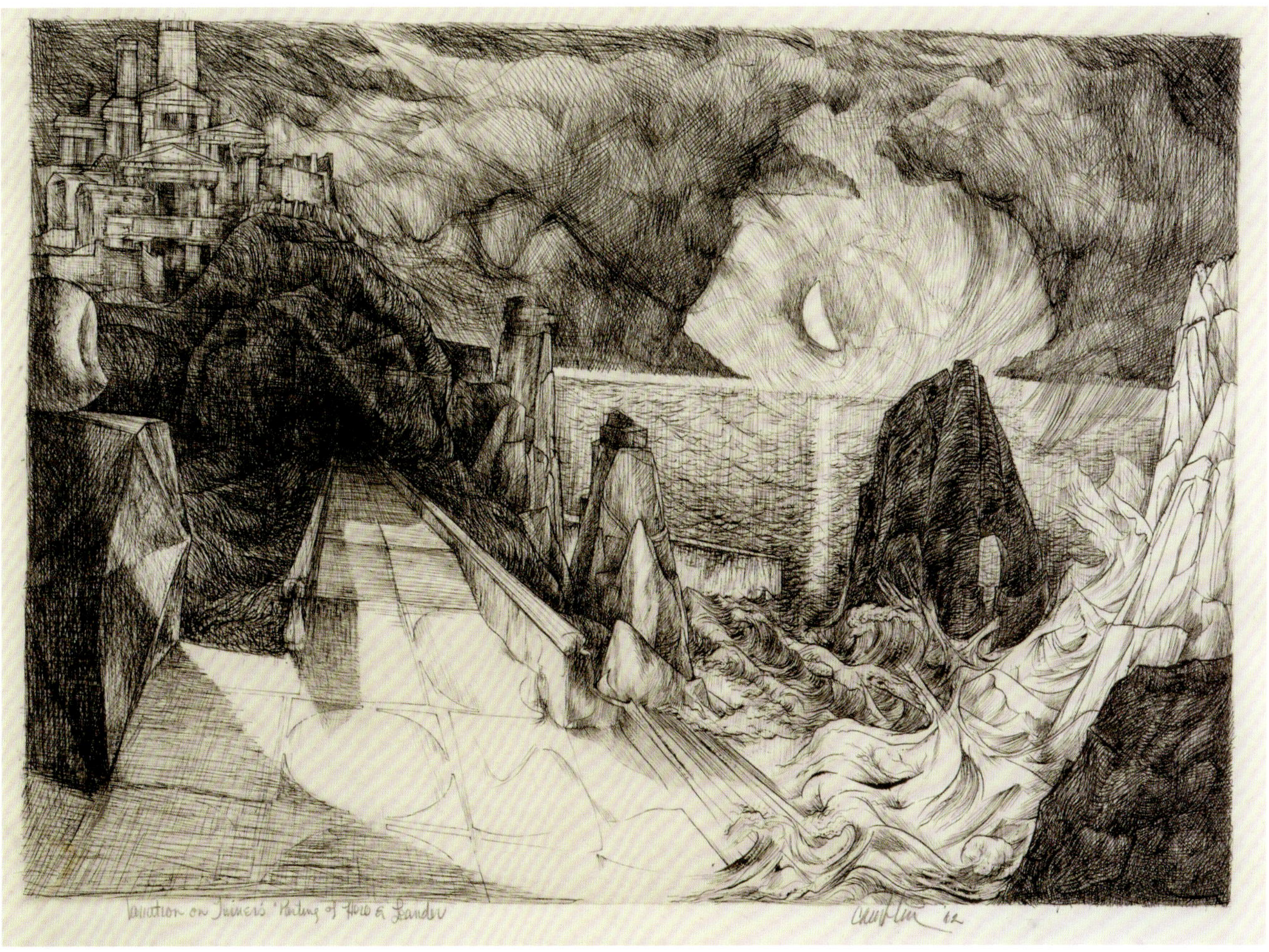

Hero and Leander, 1964. Ink and wash on J. Perrigot Arches Special MBM (France) paper, 21" X 28". Camblin's homage to Turner's artwork of the same subject. *Collection of Sandra and Cruser Rowland. Photograph by Scott Peterson.*

Camblin created *Hero and Leander* in 1964, the same year he drew *The Return of the Archer*, the inspiration for which is not known. The work's narrative emphasizes the death of innocents. The largest figure in the drawing is a seated male reminiscent of Francisco Goya's *The Colossus*, 1808–12. The warrior sits in a chair with one leg over a nude woman and a skull near his foot. The woman smiles slightly while the male figure shows no emotion. A larger, similarly-hatted male, possibly a type of satyr, rises above a decomposing head. Four female corpses hang in the background. The women appear to have been defenseless against brutality.

The predominance of death charges the work with the power of misfortune as well as with the indifference of those who perpetrated the horrors. He did not explain the shift from structure to narrative. The drawing demonstrates Camblin's exquisite lines and his interest in existential helplessness against the supremacy of death. Existential thoughts were never far from his mind or his art. His anxieties could be seen in his work.

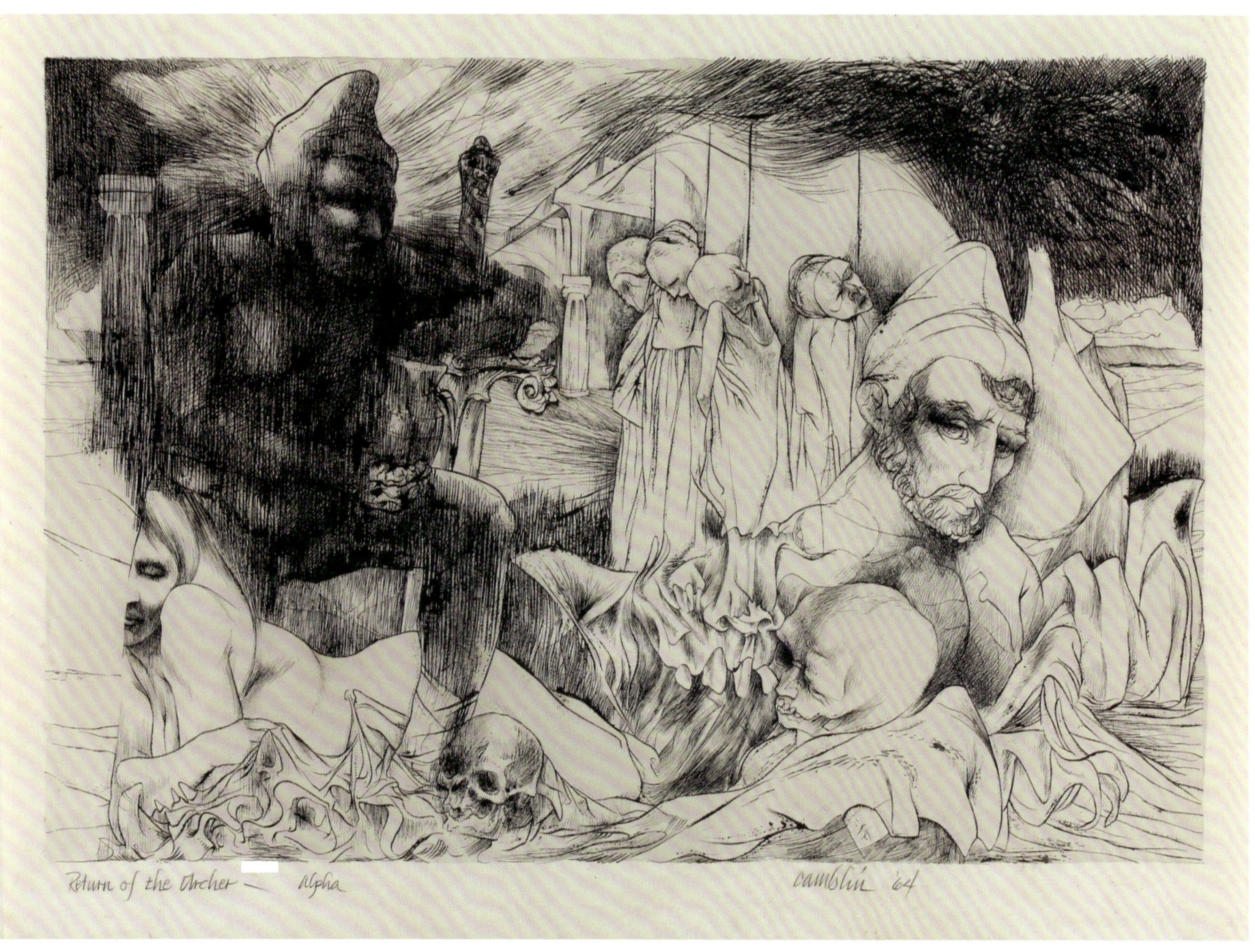

The Return of the Archer, 1964. Ink on paper, 30" X 42". *Collection of Robert Fowler*. This work exemplifies the absurdities of life and death and the inconsistencies of scale and perspective. *Photograph by David P. Gray.*

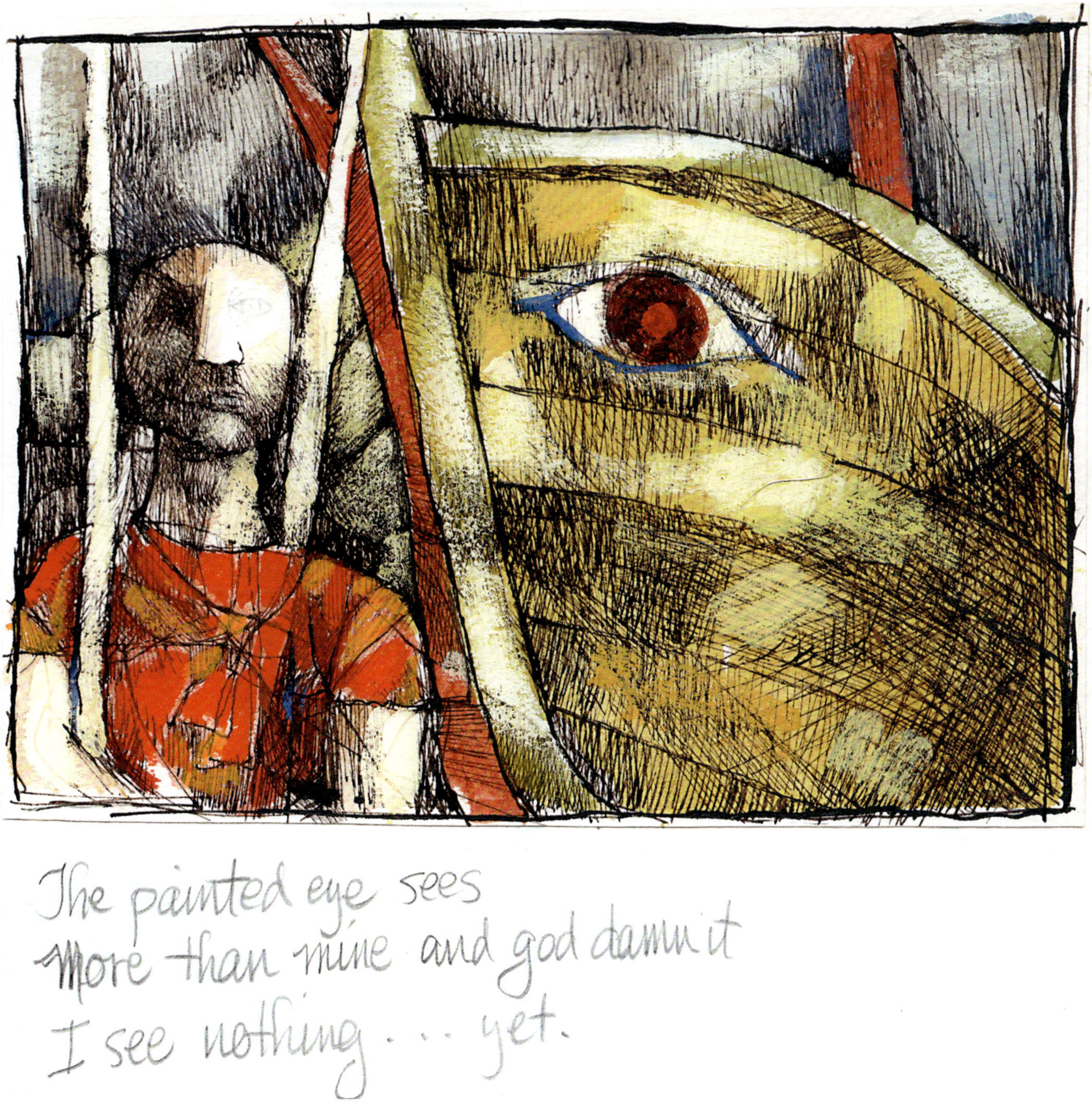

The Painted Eye Sees, 1964. Camblin used the haiga when he was poetic and when he was frustrated. *Photograph by Scott Peterson.*

Salt Lake City, Utah

After four years in Michigan, Camblin received and accepted an offer to teach at the University of Utah in 1965. He knew his friend Gerald Purdy, who had preceded him to the University of Utah in 1963, was behind the invitation. Camblin looked forward to working with Purdy. During phone calls, they had discussed the issues involved in the University of Utah's purchase of a Charles Brand intaglio press for $2,000, a hefty sum in 1965. Purdy had been successful in his perseverance to get the press, the only one of its kind between Denver and the West Coast. Purdy believed he could make prints an important part of the university's art department and a major art form. He kept in touch with Camblin and told him Utah would be a safe environment for his growing family. The two friends often discussed the rising racial tensions in Detroit. Beside the promise of safety for Camblin's young family, Purdy knew the opportunity for Camblin to work with a new press would hook him.

Purdy played his hand well. Camblin moved his family of four from Michigan to Salt Lake City, Utah, where the only significant buildings in the city were the Mormon Temple, a spired Bavarian castle, and the Cathedral of the Madeleine, a Roman Catholic church with a Romanesque Revival-style exterior and a Neo-Gothic interior. After the vitality of Detroit, the culture shock must have been great, but the Camblin family was pleased to see Catholicism thrive in the largely Mormon environment. The University of Utah rewarded Camblin with peace of mind, artistic freedom, and a new medium to explore. He welcomed the change and the challenges.

A decade after his Fulbright, Camblin continued to profess his existential belief in the inevitability of change. While teaching at the University of Utah in 1966, he told a newspaper reporter: "An artist is [anyone] who can live in an open-ended society, can adapt to constant change. The prevailing philosophy in our society is now existential. Politicians don't agree. Religions don't agree. Parents don't agree—so each person has to construct his own values . . . Artists are always a threat to the status quo, to the existing values and attitudes of society. They are iconoclasts, establishing the next steps that society will take. Not that all creativity

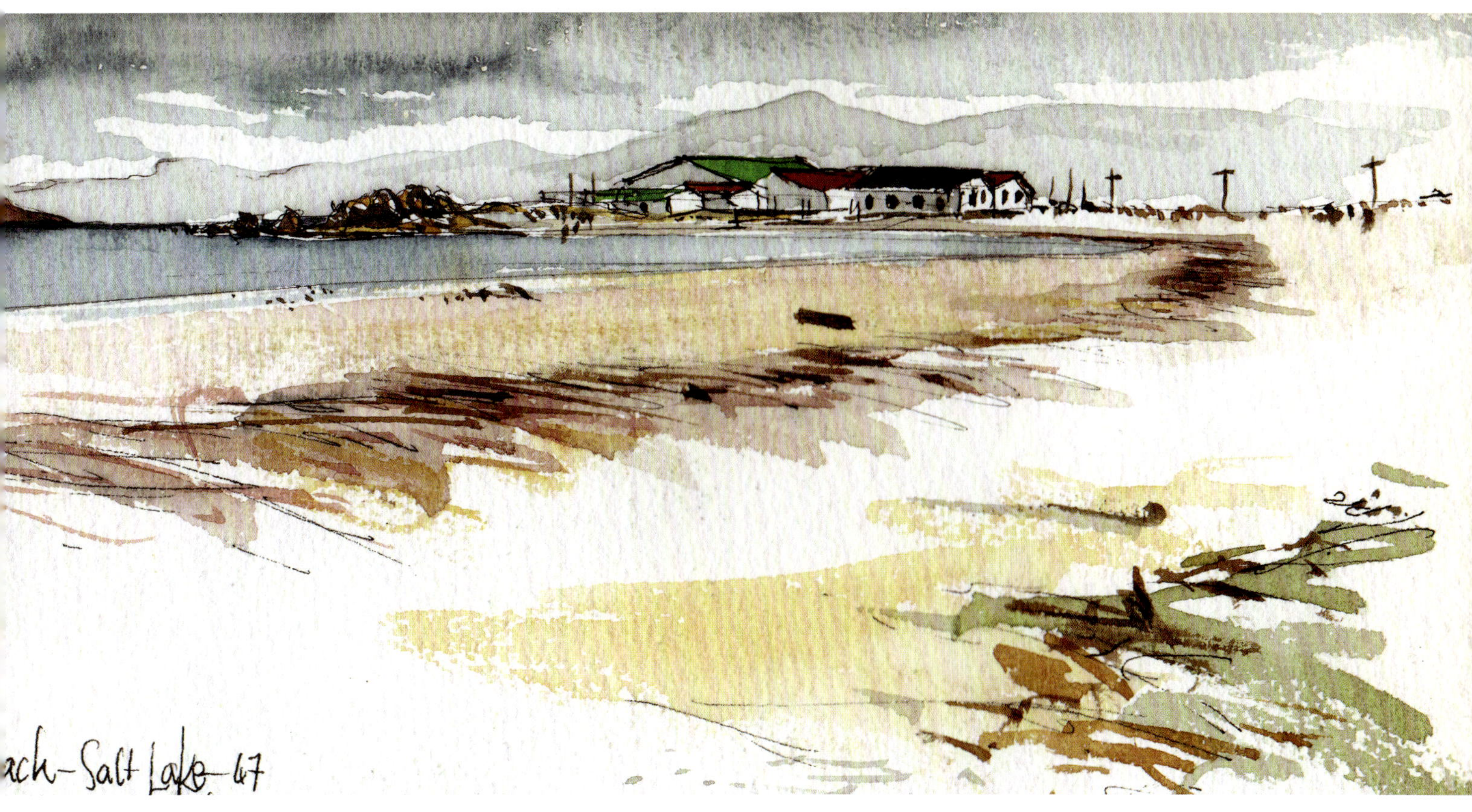

Great Salt Lake Beach, 1967. *Photograph by Scott Peterson.*

is necessarily good, in the sense of being beneficial to society, but change is inevitable and it is the natural role of the artist to point out new ways."[7]

Existentialism was Camblin's way, and it was a philosophy he continued to follow. In a personal letter, he wrote: "tell your friend: that I was surprised (!) when he said he was going to 'become' an artist because I had assumed since he was an author he was an 'artist' (that wrote). Tell him that breaking away from the university and having published 'Ideas' puts him in the same existential place that all of us operate out of—A Halfway House of belief and doubt and that we all record the NOW! That is all we can do and do the best we can. We know too much to pretend we are only watching and that what we are doing is not what we are doing—We are in History! There is no way not to be an artist now if we are to survive! Get rid of any doubt you can."

During most of his teaching career, Camblin counseled his students to examine their ulterior motives and to take responsibility for their actions.[8] He created art with existential themes, some titled *mauvaise foi*, bad faith. (The ranks of American and European writers and artists who were interested in existential ideas in the late 1950s and 1960s are too large to consider in relation to influences on Camblin.) The existentialism found in the Theatre of the Absurd,[9] especially in the plays by Samuel Beckett, did impact Camblin,who had begun to see and to refer to his own life as theater.

He noted his own responsibility for his existential life choice in a sketchbook: "I am living as I have chosen—and old Camus knew that writing is easier than pushing a rock."[10] He quoted Albert Camus: "Man stands face to face with the irrational. He feels within him his longing for happiness and for reason. The absurd is born of this confrontation between the human need and the unreasonable silence of the world."[11]

Did Camblin believe in the unreasonable silence of the world? Doubtful. He spent his iconoclastic life in free-willed rebellion against most everything, even his Catholicism, though he never gave up his faith.

CHAPTER FIVE

Birthing a Saint While Studying Zen Buddhism in the Land of the Mormons

Life in Salt Lake City may have prompted Camblin to create his sainted doll series, a theme he would pursue for most of the next decade. Images of saintly martyrdom fired Camblin's youthful imagination and he remained intrigued by sainthood throughout his life. In Utah he learned that Mormons officially call themselves "Latter-day Saints."[1] Residing among the Salt Lake City saints renewed his interest in his fallen-by-the-wayside, sanctified doll *St. Bambola*.[2] Camblin noted in one of his sketchbooks: "Utah 1965–67: St. Bambola was almost my downfall since the theme was so humorous and it related to Italy and tied down all my previous use of symbols, and turned me on like a faucet. There was no end of variations but could and did become a bit stereotyped while still provocative. (Derived from assemblage but built from [imagination??]"

The iconography of *St. Bambola* is mystifying: was the *Pioneer Woman*'s mother-and-boy-child creative fuel for

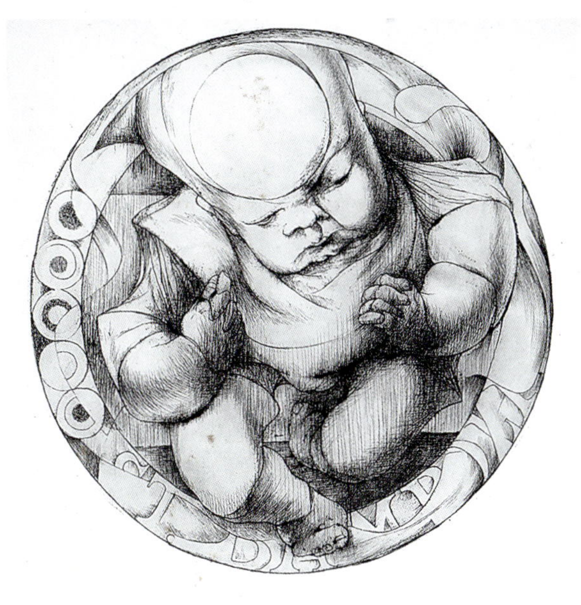

The Medallion of St. Bambola began the evolution of the sainted doll. *Photograph by Scott Peterson.*

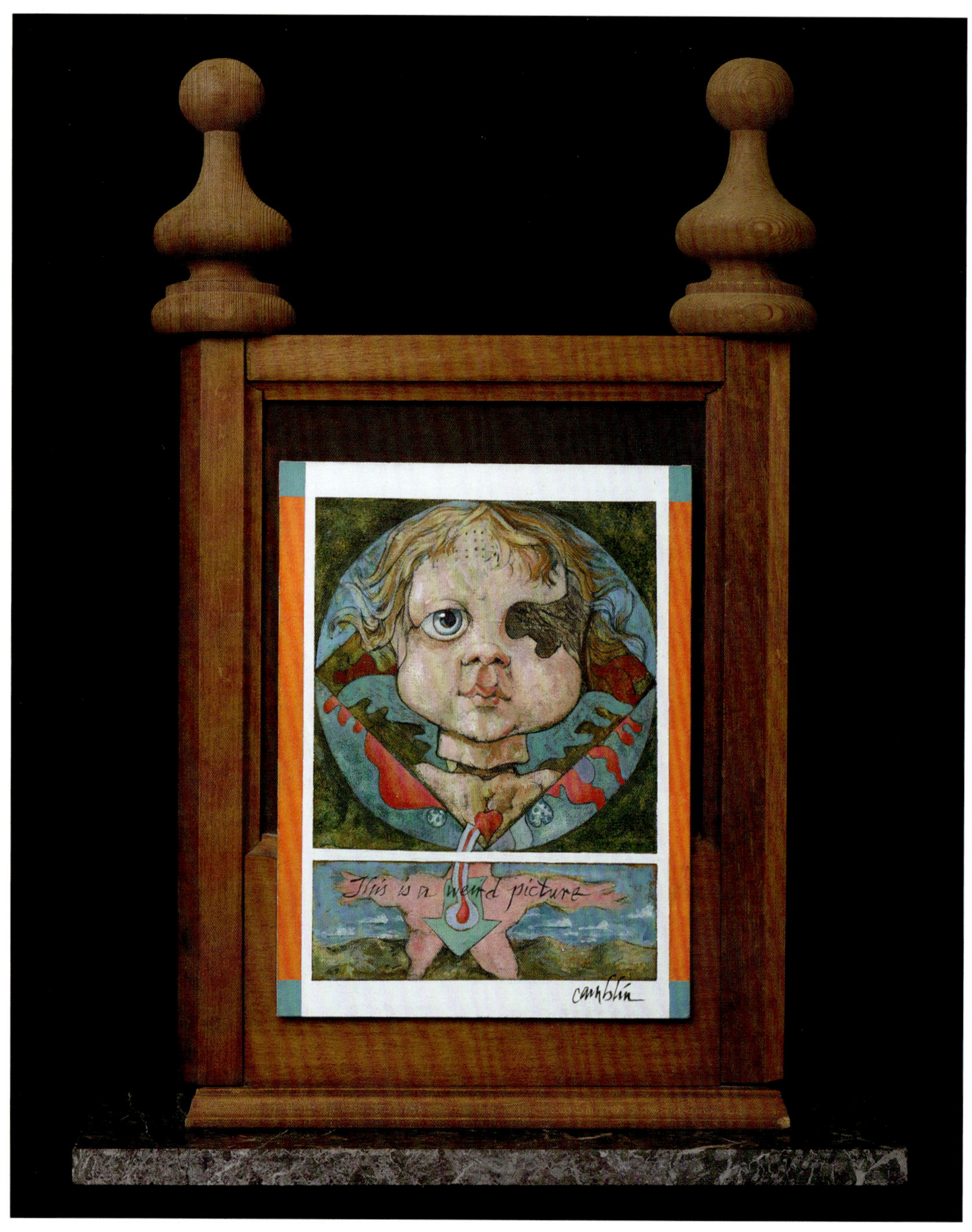

St. Bartholomew, c. Mid 1960s. Mixed media, 24" X 18" X 7" deep. Camblin wrote on the painting, "This is a weird picture." *Carolyn Farb Collection. Photo Credit: Thomas DuBrock.*

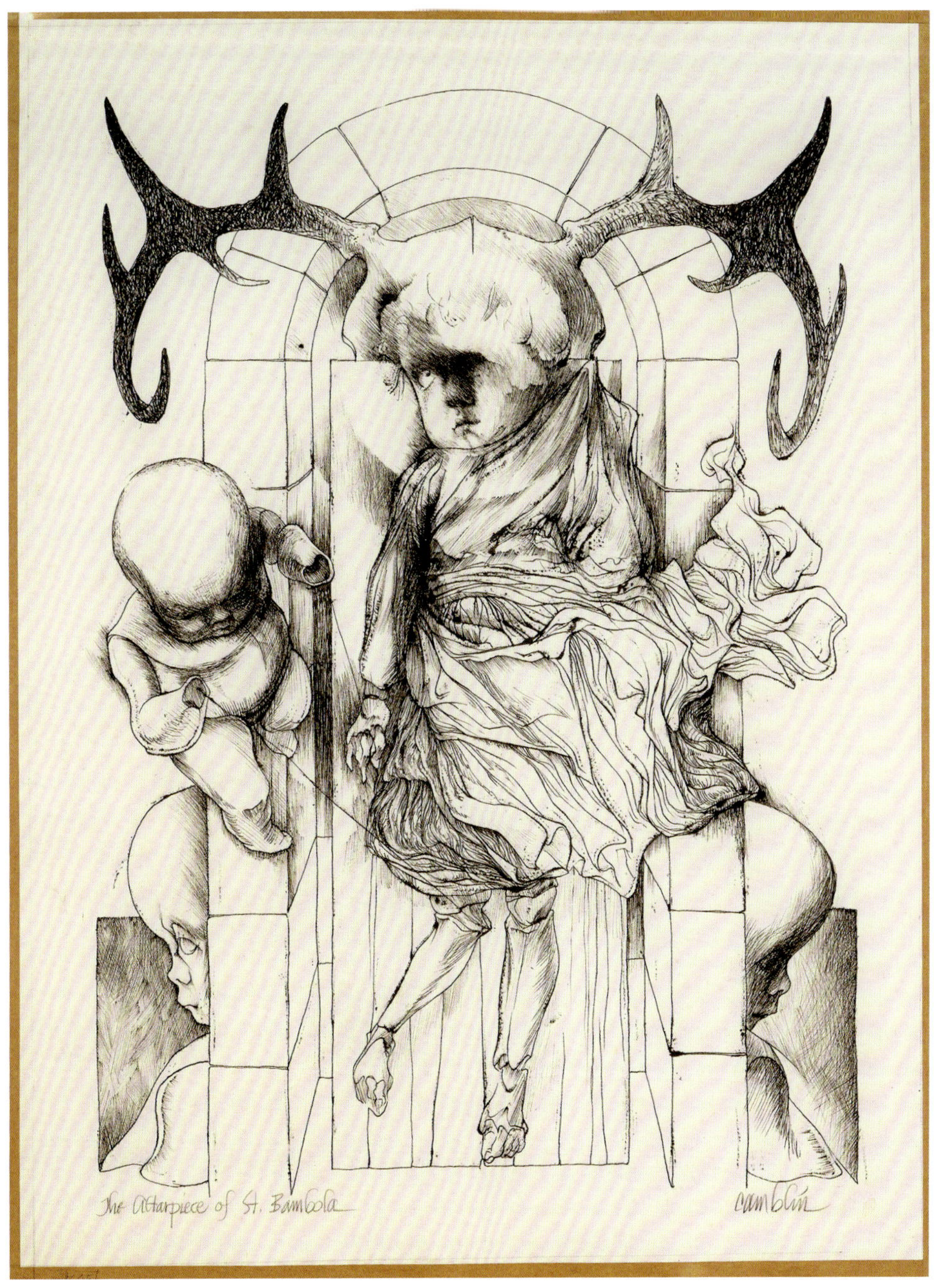

The Altarpiece of St. Bambola, c. 1968. Pen and ink on paper, 28.25" X 20.75". *Collection of Sandra and Cruser Rowland.* Camblin often joined his sainted dolls to pagan horns. He also gave them masks to hide behind. *Photograph by Scott Peterson.*

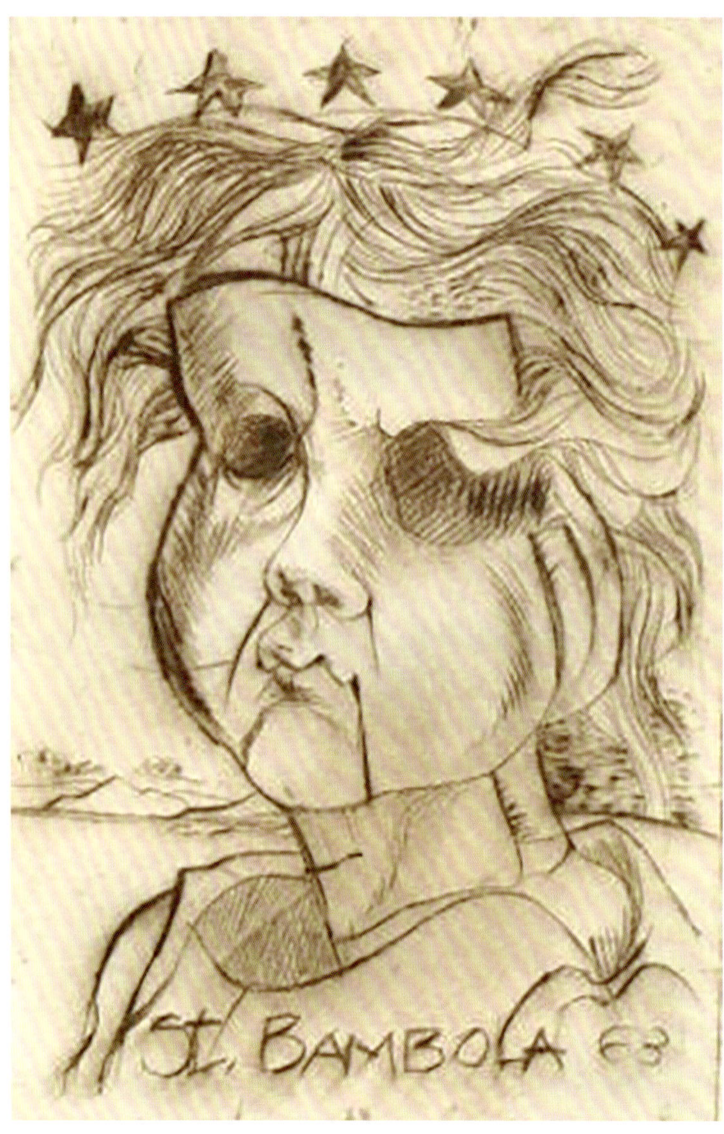
St. Bambola, 1968. *Photograph by Scott Peterson.*

Camblin's sanctified child? If so, does the sanctified child suggest anything about Camblin's own sense of self? He wrote that dolls relate to a time in Italy when he came in contact with doll vendors. Were the numerous doll-like *putti*[3] that appear in Italian art the source of his inspiration? What was the attraction? Did he see a doll as a symbol of innocence and the loss of childhood? Why would an adult be drawn to the image of an abandoned doll? Why transform a doll into a saint? Why preserve the saint in a bottle or shrine? (In a sketchbook he wrote that he always liked to see faces in bottles.) Why partially mask the saint's face with the face of another broken doll? Could Camblin have considered St. Bambola a spirit guide[4] or his anima?[5] Did he see childhood as a sort of mask for the adult burgeoning within the child? He answered none of these questions. His saint did not seem troubled, nor did it generate humor. St. Bambola was just cast-off; battered by use and no longer needed. Camblin's doll saint seemed transformed by the ravages of love, and time, and by the loss of childhood.

Camblin was not the first artist to give dolls a prominent place in his art. For centuries, artists had used models and life-sized mannequins to study proportion, the drapery of clothing, the effects of light and shade and the arrangements of composition. In the nineteenth century, the mannequin became the artist's subject. A few twentieth-century artists fetishized mannequins sometimes adding misogyny, pornography, and sexploitation.

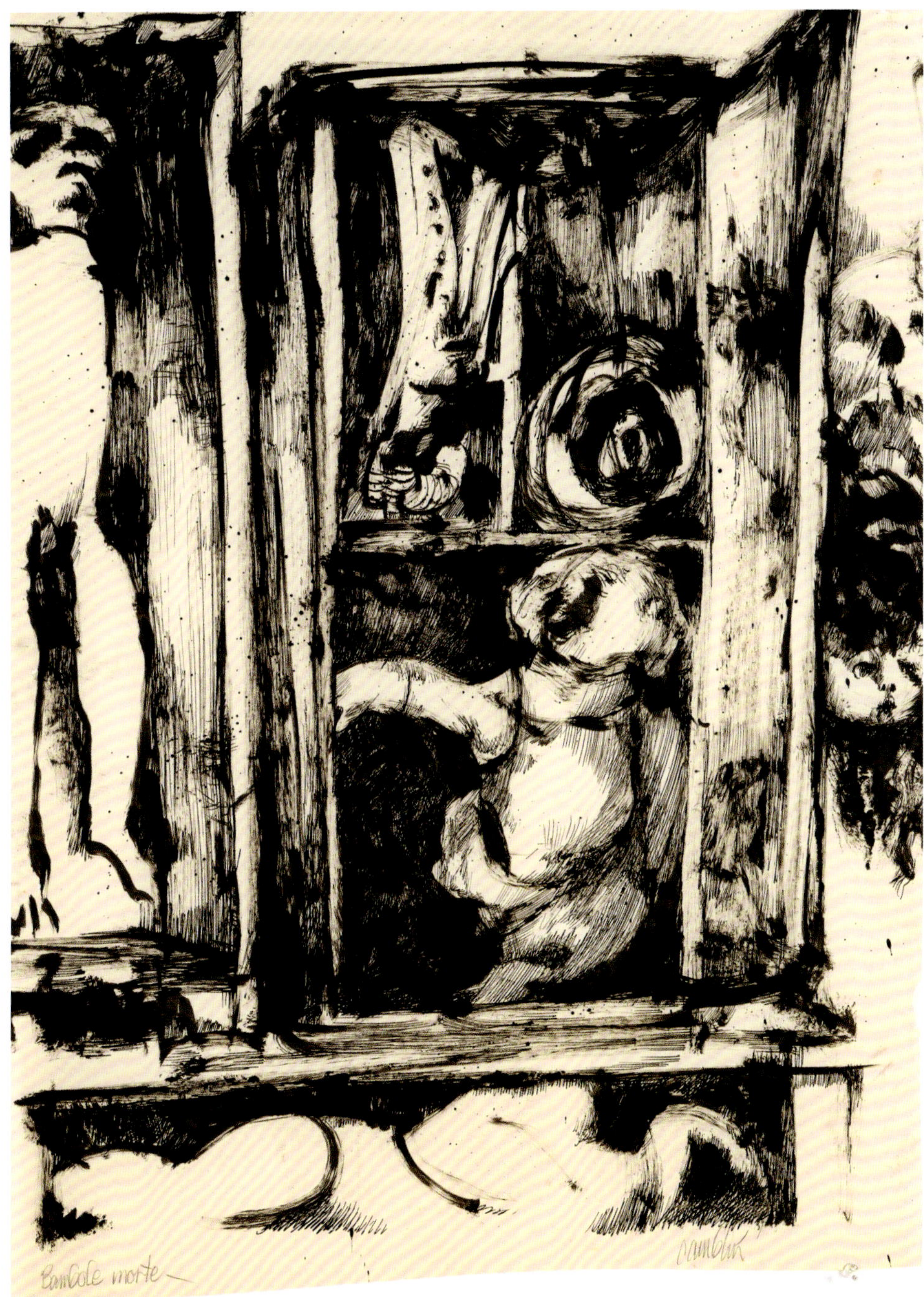

Bambole Morte. One of numerous examples of Camblin's compartmentalized doll series. *Photograph by Scott Peterson.*

Twentieth-century Austrian expressionist Oscar Kokoschka demonstrated one of the most troubling examples of a doll obsession. When his lover, Alma Mahler (widow of Gustav Mahler), grew tired of him and left, the artist was inconsolable. He wanted her to return, but she refused. To replace her, Kokoschka commissioned a replica doll with Alma's physical attributes. The doll took six months to complete. After the delivery of the Alma doll, Kokoschka feverishly sketched and painted her in the same poses his ex-lover had assumed. He asked his maid to spread rumors about his obsession with his doll, which he dubbed the "Silent Woman." After some time Kokoschka was finally free of his sexual obsession with Alma, so he threw a party to introduce the Alma "substitute" to his friends where, after a night of drinking, he beheaded the doll. Some of Camblin's St. Bambolas are headless, but the missing heads were not removed by violent decapitation. They remain dolls, not sexual obsessions.

Kokoschka's contemporary Hans Bellmer was a German artist who likewise became obsessed with a doll. (Like the Surrealists, he was a fan of the Marquis de Sade.) Two years before he created his first doll, he became enamored with his beautiful teenage cousin. When he made his first doll in 1934, he sexualized the doll as a pubescent girl and titled his life-sized mannequin *The Doll (Die Puppe)*. With the aid of moveable ball joints, Bellmer positioned his doll in poses indicative of sexual violence. After placing *Die Puppe* in *tableaux vivant* (living pictures), he took photographs. Looking at his work, the spectator may find it difficult to discern the line between erotic, sadistic, and pornographic; adjectives that do not apply to Camblin's saint.

His interest in St. Bambola is intriguing but not troubling. The dolls in his work lack the blatant eroticism of Bellmer or Kokoschka. St. Bambola did not exhibit the misogyny, explicit sexuality, or life-size scale found in the Kokoschka and Bellmer dolls. Camblin did not make his dolls; he used those that had been manufactured, played with, and then discarded. He also canonized his doll after the Catholic tradition, not the Marquis de Sade.

A 2014 exhibition at the Fitzwilliam Museum in Cambridge, England, *Silent Partners: Artist and Mannequin from Function to Fetish* included "180 paintings and drawings by [artists including] Fra Bartolommeo, Cézanne, Poussin,

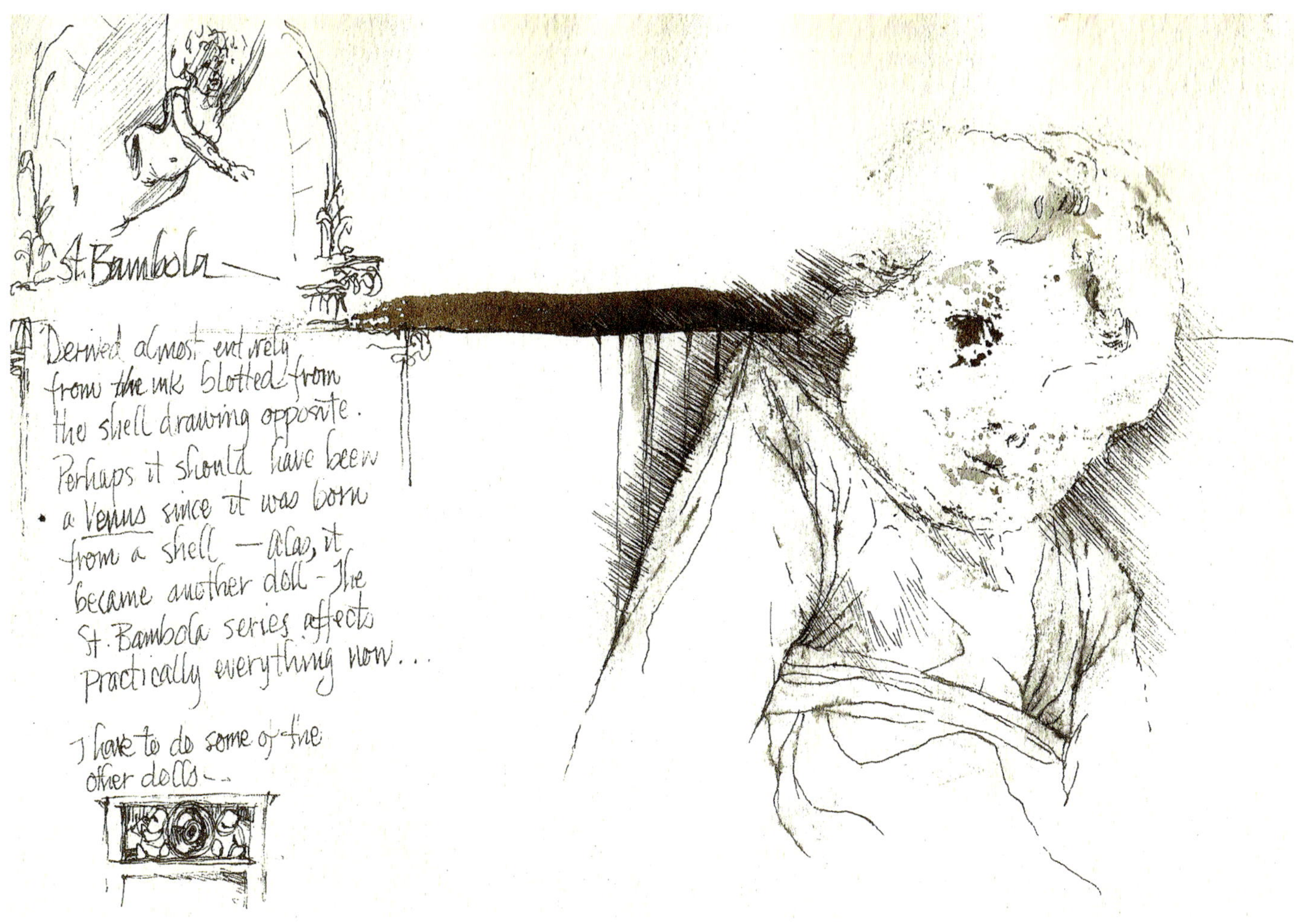

An inkblot inspired this one-eyed St. Bambola.

Gainsborough, Millais, Ford Madox Brown, Courbet, Wilhelm Trübner, Kokoschka and Degas as well as photographs by and of Surrealist artists such as Bellmer, Raoul Ubac, Dalì and Man Ray; two works by Jake and Dinos Chapman will form a twenty-first-century coda."[6] Apparently numerous artists beside Camblin, Bellmer, and Kokoschka have been and still are intrigued by dolls.

With the evolution of the psychological sciences in the twentieth century, new understandings of the complex relationship artists had with mannequins and dolls can be analyzed ad infinitum. The subject of analysis is too large even to consider in this context. Camblin's intentions and fascination with *St. Bambola* remain a mystery, possibly even to him.

A page from an undated Camblin sketchbook may give clues: Camblin drew a putto[7] emerging from an architectural niche. On the right half of the page he also drew a larger patchy image of a babydoll, defining only one eye. To the left of the doll he wrote:

> *St. Bambola.* Derived almost entirely from the ink blotted from the shell drawing opposite. [The referenced drawing has not been found.] Perhaps it should have been a Venus since it was born from a shell—Alas, it became another doll. The *St. Bambola* series affects practically everything now . . . I have to do some of the other dolls.

The explanation suggests Camblin's first *St. Bambola* was created using Vespignani's blot technique. Camblin saw a doll in the inkblots. His line, "I have to do some of the other dolls," alludes to a prior and continuing interest in drawing dolls.

Camblin's *St. Bambola* does not conform to traditional fifteenth-century cherubs. She is a doll, not a putto, and is a girl rather than a boy. Though Camblin canonized her, she inspires no religiosity. Her unkempt condition may suggest the saint is also a sinner. His interest in the subject seemed to mystify even him. In a sketchbook he wrote, "I want to turn off my myth-making machine and escape the seductive powers of *St. Bambola* and extend the evolution that stopped with the *Cicada* series."

An undated photograph of a large St. Bambola Shrine, inhabited by a living nude female and an authentic skeleton plus dozens of dolls, shows the degree to which Camblin was entranced by his saint. Perhaps the large assemblage was the culmination of the artist's obsession with sainted and antlered dolls.

Camblin found *Bambola* difficult to escape, however. She reasserted herself whenever he was in Italy. During a stay in Venice in 1976, he wrote of her mask, "My own mythology is going along on its own. I think I'm waiting for *St. Bambola* to reappear in her new mask and tell me new stories—TRAGI-COMEDY that still end . . . and they lived happily ever after."[8]

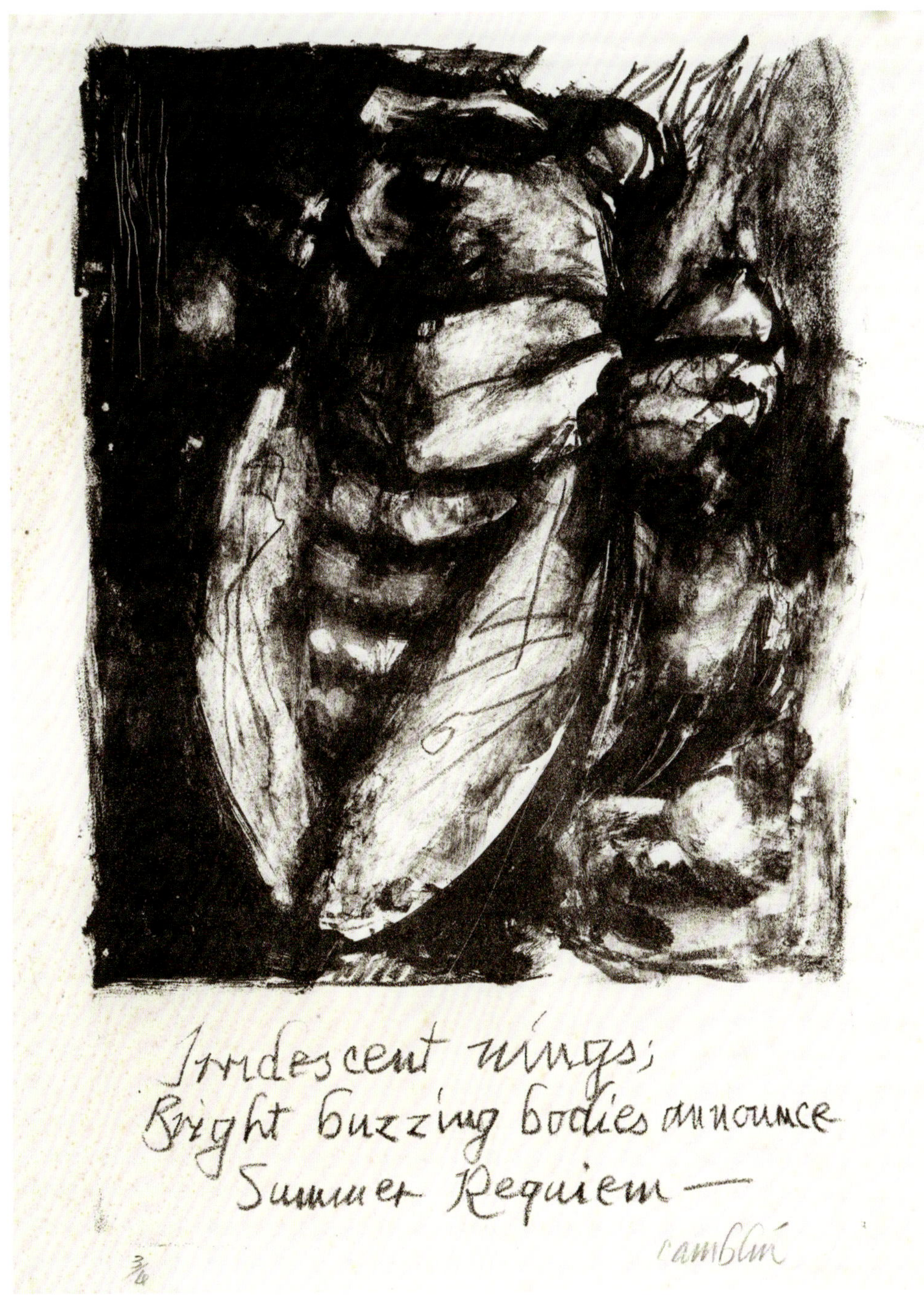

Summer Requiem Cicada. The inevitability of change often dominated Camblin's art as seen in his continuing use of the cicada as subject matter.

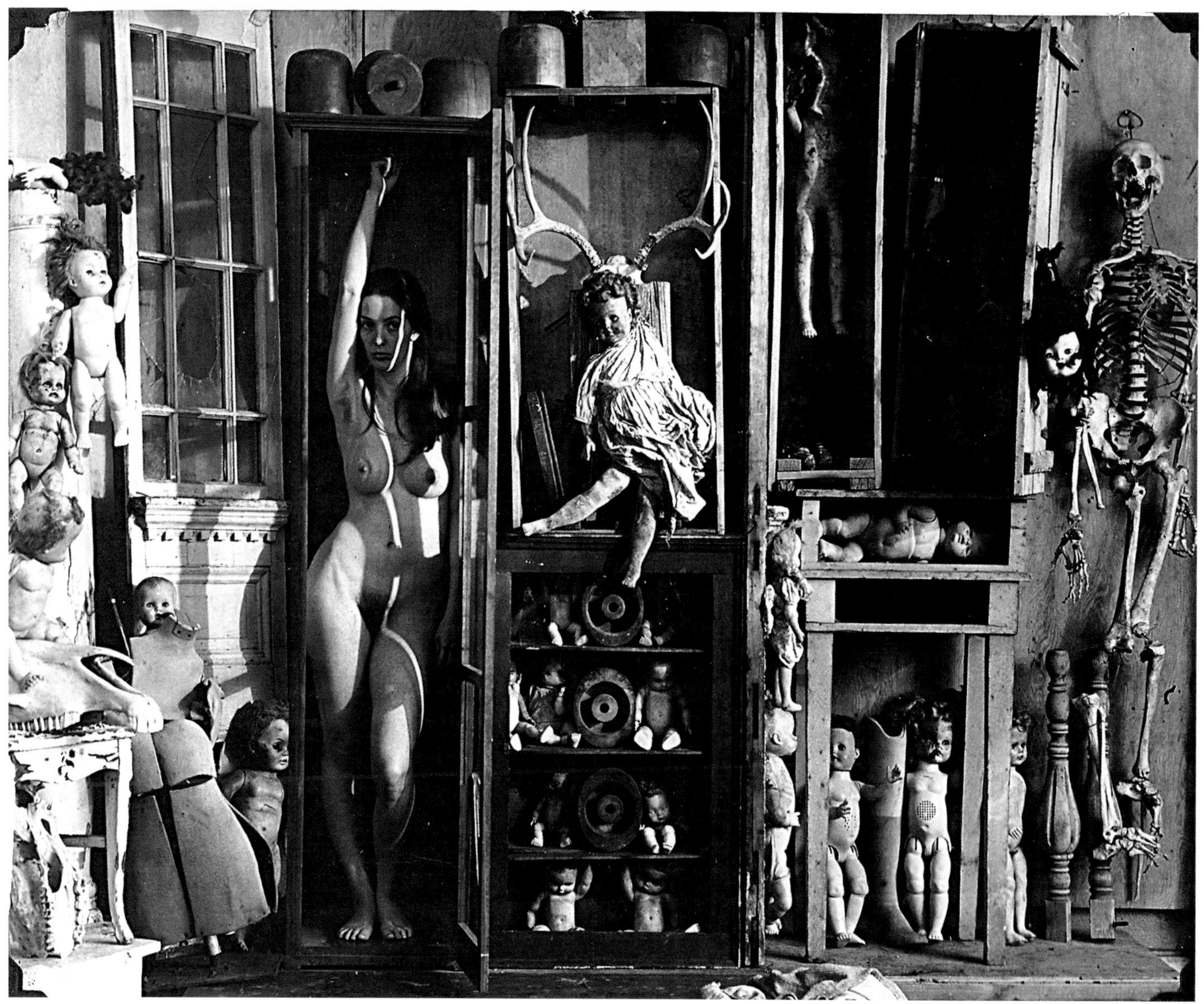

Shrine of St. Bambola constructed for a Camblin exhibition in the David Gallery.

Of course, Tragedy and Comedy are often portrayed as smiling and frowning masks and are symbols of the ancient Greek muses: Thalia (muse of comedy), and Melpomene (muse of tragedy).

In the late 1960s Camblin's art was not about happy endings. His work focused on dark images from his imagination. He started a series of scarecrow drawings

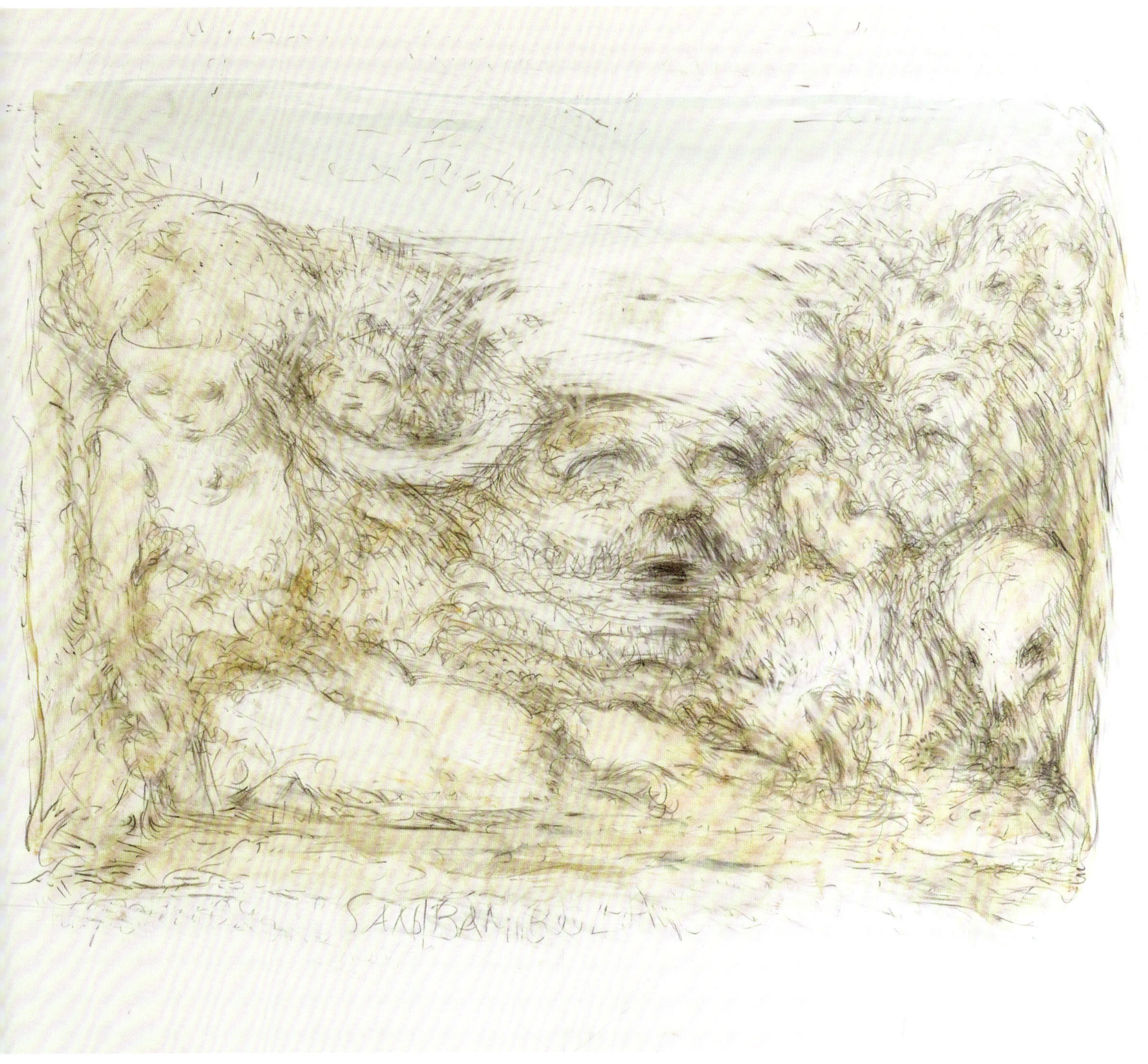

Untitled: Masked St. Bambola with Camblin self-portrait and masks. *Photograph by Scott Peterson.*

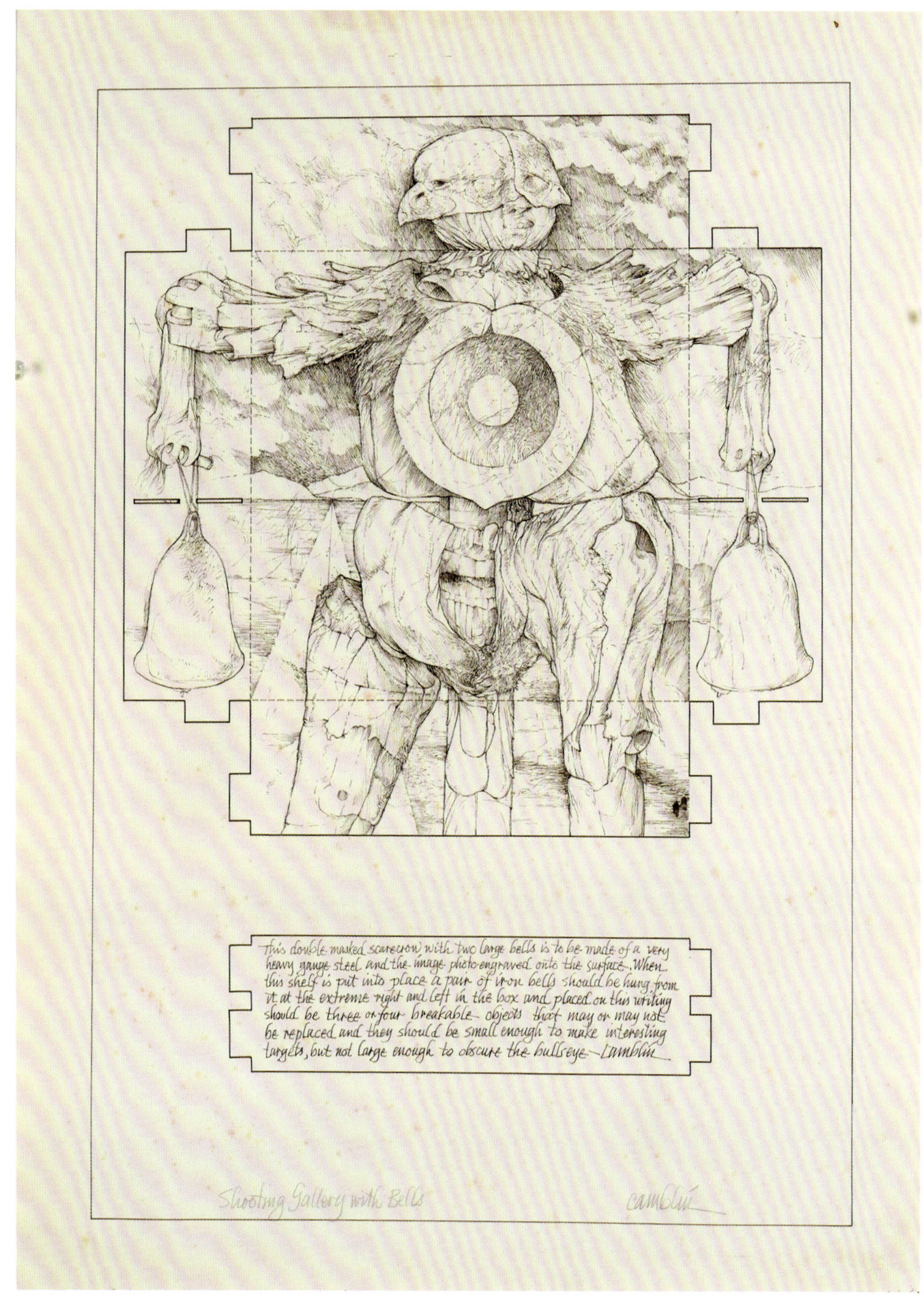

Sketch of double-masked scarecrow. *Photograph by Scott Peterson.*

while he continued work on *St. Bambola*. On the back of a pen and ink draw-ing, Camblin wrote, "Rich man, poor man, beggar man, etc. Giving credit: Gunter Grass's verbal images of the scarecrows in Dog Years . . . December 16, 1966 was the beginning of this series—It's great because it links the Chrysalis (Cicada Husk), *St. Bambola* and *Metamorphosis*."[9]

Camblin's scarecrows are not menacing effigies. They appear to be shells of men, visual boogey men, not Grass's symbols of a barbaric past and a Nazi pres-ent. Like the Roman god Janus, the scarecrows often have two faces, each wearing a mask. Sometimes two masks cover the sides of the head. Camblin's figures cause "free-floating anxiety," not terror. The stuffed men can be seen as a metaphor for empty men who hide behind masks because they lack substance or integrity; they can be understood as manifestations of the everyman, or they may simply be an artist's fascination with a writer's verbal description of an object.

Camblin knew existentialism rejects the notion of God, yet he chose to draw and write about a saint. The doll appears to have been cast out, perhaps supply-ing Camblin with a surrogate for his broken attempts at casting out his religion. As he noted, he "holds art and science tight in a knotty embrace of truth and deception."

Aside from the multi-celled *Time Machine* drawings he began in Detroit and continued in Salt Lake, Camblin also created single, titled works with no accom-panying text that focused on subjects from the *Time Machine* series. In *Glass Reliquary* (1962), he simplified the composition but not the iconography. The sub-ject matter includes a horned mask (the image of his wife Bonnie), sitting on the top of a glass specimen bottle. Arms and legs attach to the bottle that rests on toy-like wheels. Inside the body of the container is a one-eyed doll on which a heart rests while a cicada nymph rests on the bottom exterior of the bottle. The horned mask, bodily attachments, and contents of the bottle add secular dimensions to the usual religiosity of a reliquary. Camblin transformed the traditional representation of a shrine for relics into an inexplicable pagan artifact.

Reacting to the conservative culture of Salt Lake City, Camblin dove back into his studies of Zen Buddhism. He read D. (Daisetsu) T. (Teitaro) Suzuki[10] who wrote:

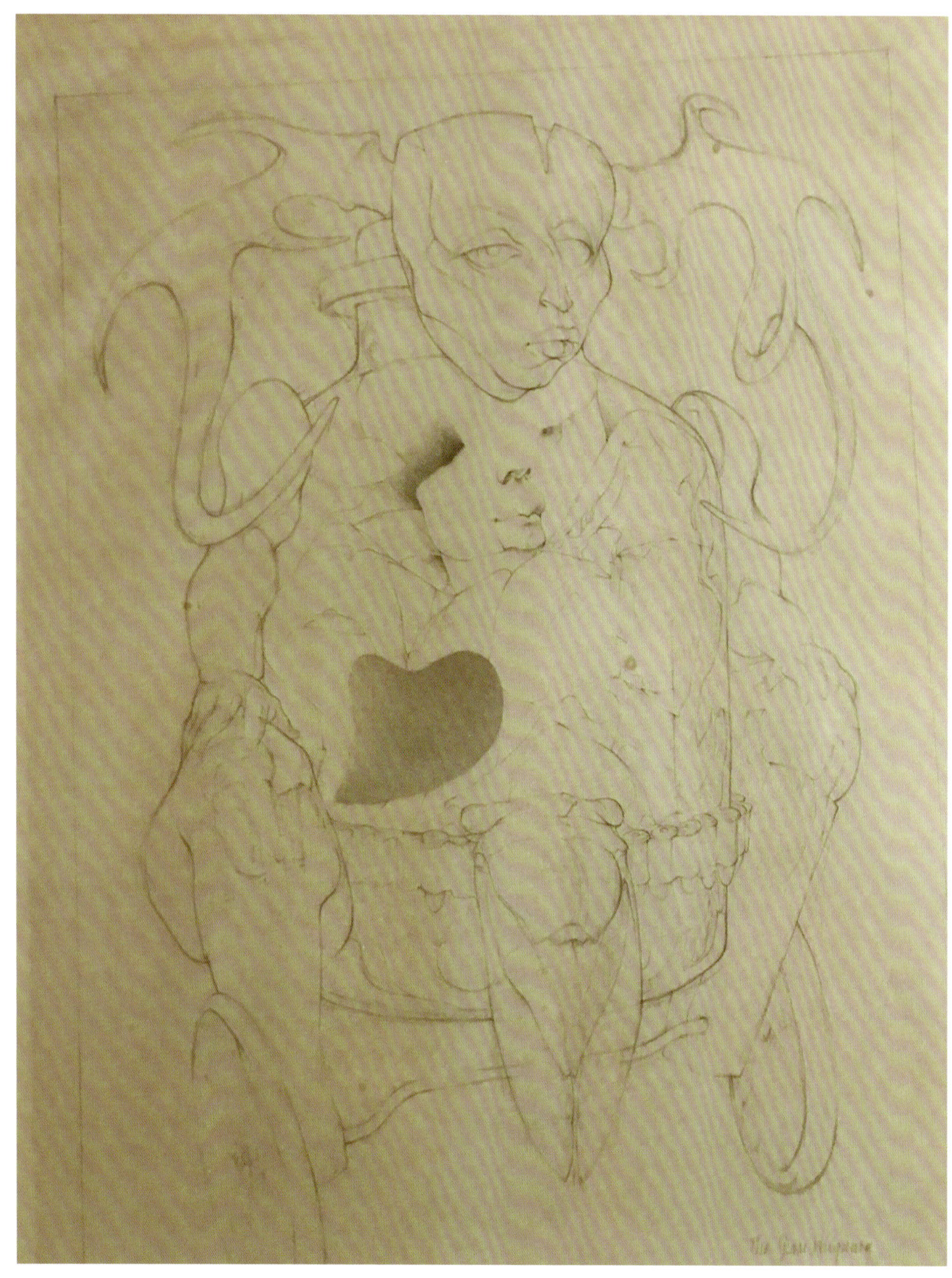

Glass Reliquary sketch. *Photograph by Scott Peterson.*

Zen is not a religion for Zen has no God to worship, no ceremonial rites to observe, no future abode to which the dead are destined, and, last of all, Zen has no soul whose welfare is to be looked after by somebody else and whose immortality is a matter of intense concern with some people. Zen is free from all these dogmatic and "religious" encumbrances. . . . In Zen God is neither denied nor insisted upon . . . Zen, therefore, is emphatically against all religious conventionalism. . . .[11]

Camblin's continuing study of Zen Buddhism led him to the discovery of Sengai Gibon, a nineteenth-century Japanese Buddhist monk. Remarkably, at some unknown date, Gibon had created a standalone work of art in *The Universe: Circle, Triangle, Square.*[12]

European and American art in the nineteenth century was antithetical to the simplicity found in Gibon, who also made a painting entirely of a brushed circle, an enso, perhaps the purest sign of abstraction ever devised. Gibon's drawings entranced Camblin. From his time in Salt Lake City until he died, he would draw the enso. Like the Zen philosopher, Camblin used the circle to empty his mind and to allow the universal to enter his thinking. Before he began writing or drawing in his sketchbooks, he often drew the circle at the top of a page.

The Zen practiced by Gibon and later by Suzuki echoed the beliefs Camblin found in existentialism. Suzuki even added daily Zen exercises to his texts, including *zazen* (seated meditation). In an effort to gain non-conceptual insight and to settle into the moment, Camblin worked to empty his mind through meditation; this was not an easy task for the typically loquacious professor.

Camblin also integrated Zen drawing into his work to help him understand the "inner workings of being."[13] He continued to create the enso in his art in an effort to open his psyche to an "intangible space where there is an interconnectedness to everything."[14] He wrote haikus and combined the poetry with Japanese-style paintings to form haigas.[15] In some of his haigas, Camblin returned to a favorite subject: the transformation of the cicadas, or the shedding of one's original mask to reveal the true self. In a sketchbook he wrote,

After seventeen years the cicada sings not knowing how long the day lasts for it is not as anything he ever knew before. The light he sings. The wind he sings. Joyous he drills with his voice the universe.[16]

Dust from a bird's wing

Etching outlines on the glass—

End of summer's song . . . 1965

—From a Camblin haiga

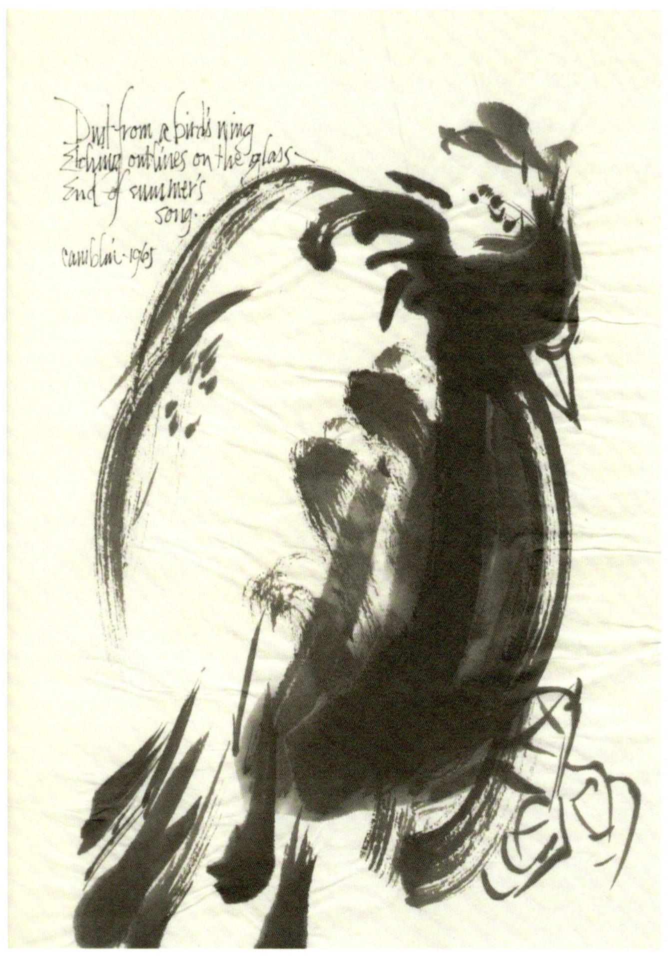

Camblin practiced the Japanese ink painting technique called Sumi-e.

In an effort to internalize his meditative transformation, Camblin spent time contemplating the Taoist-based Chinese idea of *Wu-Shih*,[17] which notes the interconnectedness of nature. *Wu-Shih* speaks to a reality so omnipresent it is taken for granted, thereby becoming "nothing much special" (a loose translation of the term). Camblin described himself as "perfectly average," aligning his beliefs with *Wu-Shih*. He asked his University of Utah students to experience "nothing much special" for a week. He outlined the task:

"Nothing much special: Some Chinese and Japanese landscape paintings are magnificent panoramas of mountains, forests, temples, gardens and lakes. But the taste of Zen prefers something like this—the simplest landscape imaginable, something we might ordinarily pass without notice. A creek is winding through the sand hills of a beach—just such a creek as one may see anywhere on a thousand beaches. There is nothing in the least spectacular. But it has the virtue of wu-shih—'nothing special.'" According to *Mustard Seed Garden*, "Extraordinary events and breathtaking scenery may have their own particular religious appeal, but common mud strikes him who sees it at all as even more holy. The Lotus flowers of the Taj Mahal may be uplifting for the Life of the spirit, but what slams right on the nose with the bare fact of existence is the indomitable mediocrity of trampled little weeds on the side streets of Hong Kong . . .”

Camblin incorporated these ideas into his teaching. He wrote the following “Assignment: Finish a texture problem of objects of ‘not much importance’ but have the drawing be meticulous say, more than junk . . . have your own observation and efforts reduce your world to a microcosm of rust, rot and beautiful nothings . . . The drapery is nothing much special either since it is the way cloth has folded and fallen since the first piece was woven. Technically we have studied texture and value. Esthetically we have explored the zen world of wu-shih. Starting today and the weekend you must try to find some more wu-shih in nature and your drawing will reflect 3 aspects of reality . . .”[18]

He wrote about wanting his art to rise above commerce, yet remain nothing much special, at least in the Zen sense: “‘Ahh—there’s the rub . . .’ To do it [art] so that it will be visible always as part of humanity and not commerce. Always more than just the money but now what comedy to convince; what tragedy to prove—Nothing Much Special. Just the things I love to do. No more, no less and the hope they won’t be lost, but not to care—they are my snake skins at any given moment. The one I’m growing is the most important—especially if it grows on one someone, in the future.”[19]

CHAPTER SIX

A Point That Moves

Throughout his life, Camblin created lines. Drawing was his artistic foundation. His pens, points (nibs), and pencils became extensions of his left hand. He said he could not remember when he did not draw. The Getty Museum defines line: "A line is an identifiable path created by a point moving in space. It is one-dimensional and can vary in width direction, and length. Lines often define the edges of a form. Lines can be horizontal, vertical, or diagonal, straight of curved, thick or thin." But line is so much more. Line is a tool that can recreate images stored in one's memory and can transform a blank piece of paper into a work of art. Lines can be drawn with less preparation than other media and can delight the eye almost instantaneously. Line gives a viewer insight into its creator. Drawings inspire us to see. Creating "a point that moves" allowed Camblin to craft his own unique worlds, often full of visual conundrums and challenges. His lines dissolve from one thing into another. Some camouflage, others shock; some are bold but most are fine. Camblin's lines work together to create a unified whole.

Trained to see and to visualize, artists depict volume by light and contrast. A line flattens. When artists draw with lines, they are graphic signifiers of edges. Camblin liked edges. He lived on the edge culturally, philosophically, and artistically. When Camblin drew, he traveled down his lines into universes he recreated with his pen or pencil. Paul Klee said drawing was taking a line for a walk. Camblin took lines for extended excursions.

Aside from giving him access to his inner worlds, why did Camblin prefer lines? Illustrators universally rendered with pen and India ink. Camblin assimilated art from illustrators, from the newspaper comics, from Vespigiano and Ben Shahn, from his parents' drawings, from Botticelli, from Leonardo, and from Michelangelo. Camblin drew and sketched compulsively. He filled the last half of his life with his drawritings.[1] He created so many sketches that his son Brian reported his dad often rolled up drawritings and used them to start a fire in the fireplace.

Participation in one of mankind's oldest modes of communication appealed to Camblin. Drawing preceded written alphabets. Historians believe stylization and simplification of drawn images, otherwise known as pictograms, led to written language. By putting pen or pencil to paper, Camblin resolved problems, created studies, investigated ideas, demonstrated concepts, created art, and doodled. Intaglio and lithography enamored him, largely because he could draw or etch directly into the plate or the thin coating applied to the plate. He liked edges, outlines, the rhythm of one becoming another. He liked the feel of the pen or pencil tip on paper. He liked recording his creativity, his environment, his poetry, his thoughts. Drawing helped empty his mind and set it free.

He was a master draftsman, and he spent hours looking at the drawings of other artists, especially those of Rembrandt—probably the greatest draftsman who ever lived—and of course, Leonardo da Vinci. In Italy, Camblin studied the pen and ink drawings of Guercino and Tiepolo. Albrecht Durer, Peter Paul Rubens, Van Gogh all drew—and Camblin would study reproductions of their work for hours. The endless possibilities for creation through the simple act of drawing lines captivated him. When the 39,000-year-old cave drawings were found on the island of Sulawesi, Indonesia, in the 1950s, Camblin sought out articles on other ancient drawings. He examined the photographs of Lascaux Cave in France, Altamira Cave in Spain, and Aboriginal rock art in Australia.[2] Drawing appears to be mankind's common denominator for recording spiritual, historical, and creative acts.

Camblin combined line with sculpture for an exhibition of his *Chrysalis Series* at a local Salt Lake City gallery: first he cast plaster forms on which he drew his images. Then he enclosed the forms in a plastic bubbles and created his own chrysalises: work that promised change. Robert Fowler, the son of Camblin's friend Bob

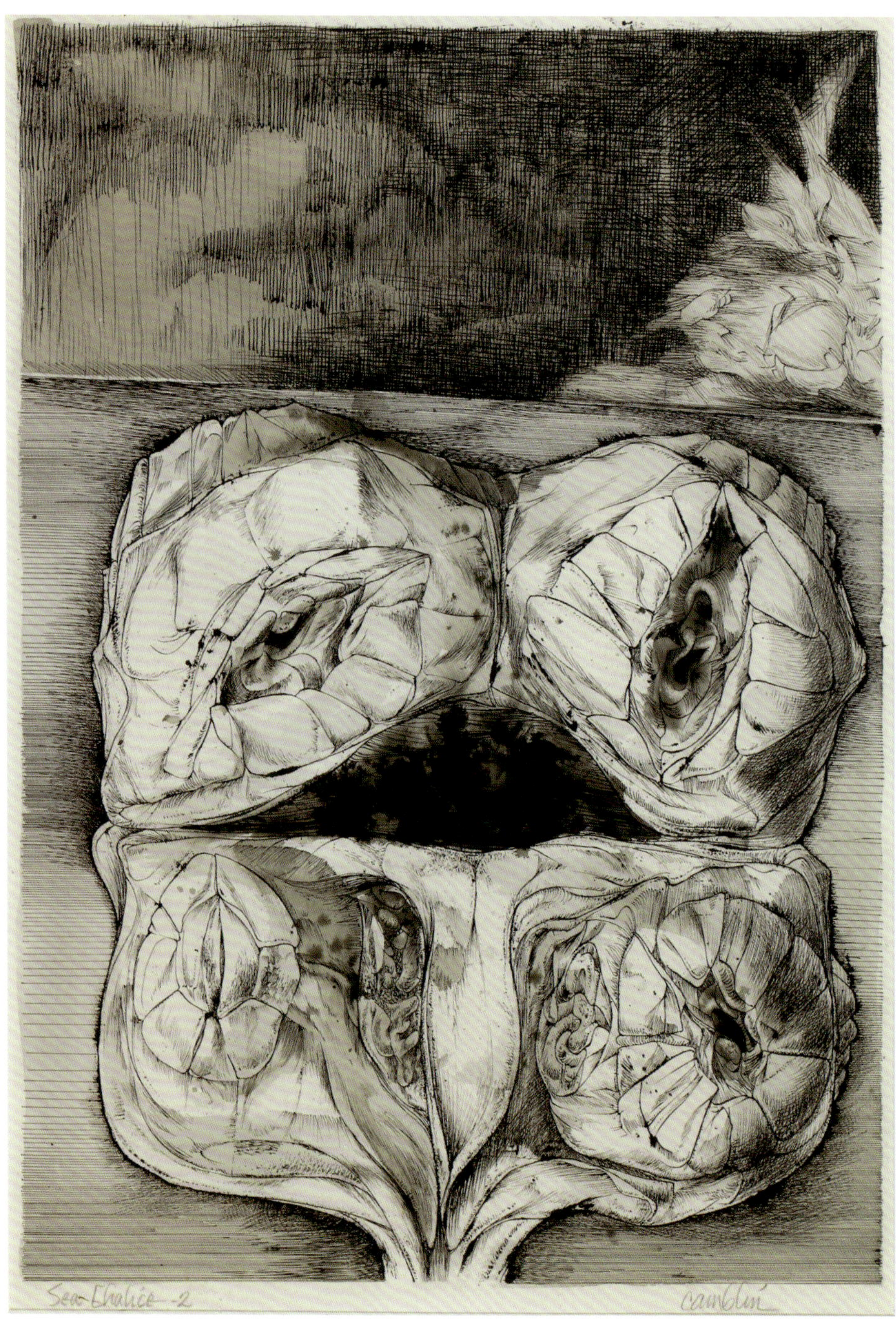

Sea Chalice, 1967. Ink on paper, 33" X 24" framed. *Collection of Mike and Gayle DeGeurin*. The drawing shows Camblin's love of the drawn line. *Photograph by David P. Gray.*

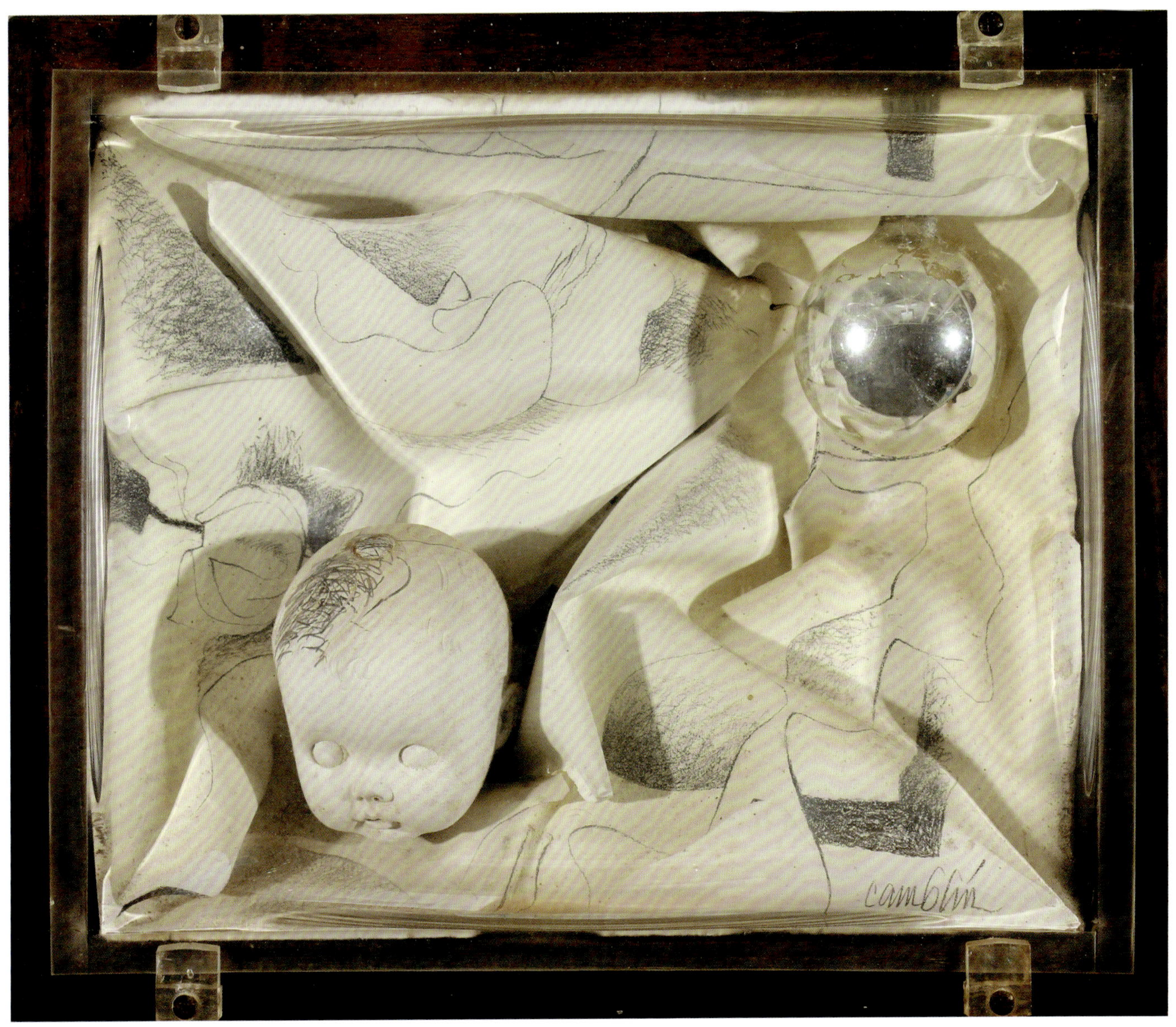

Bob Camblin, *Untitled Assemblage*, 1966. Mixed media: Plaster of Paris, pencil, doll head, silver ball in wooden box covered with acrylic bubble, 11" X 14" X 8.75". *Robert Fowler Collection. Photograph by David P. Gray.*

Fowler Jr., and owner of a Camblin piece from the series, wrote: "Camblin and his bunch were very tight-lipped when it came to expository discourse where their work was concerned. The only piece in the group that received any explanation

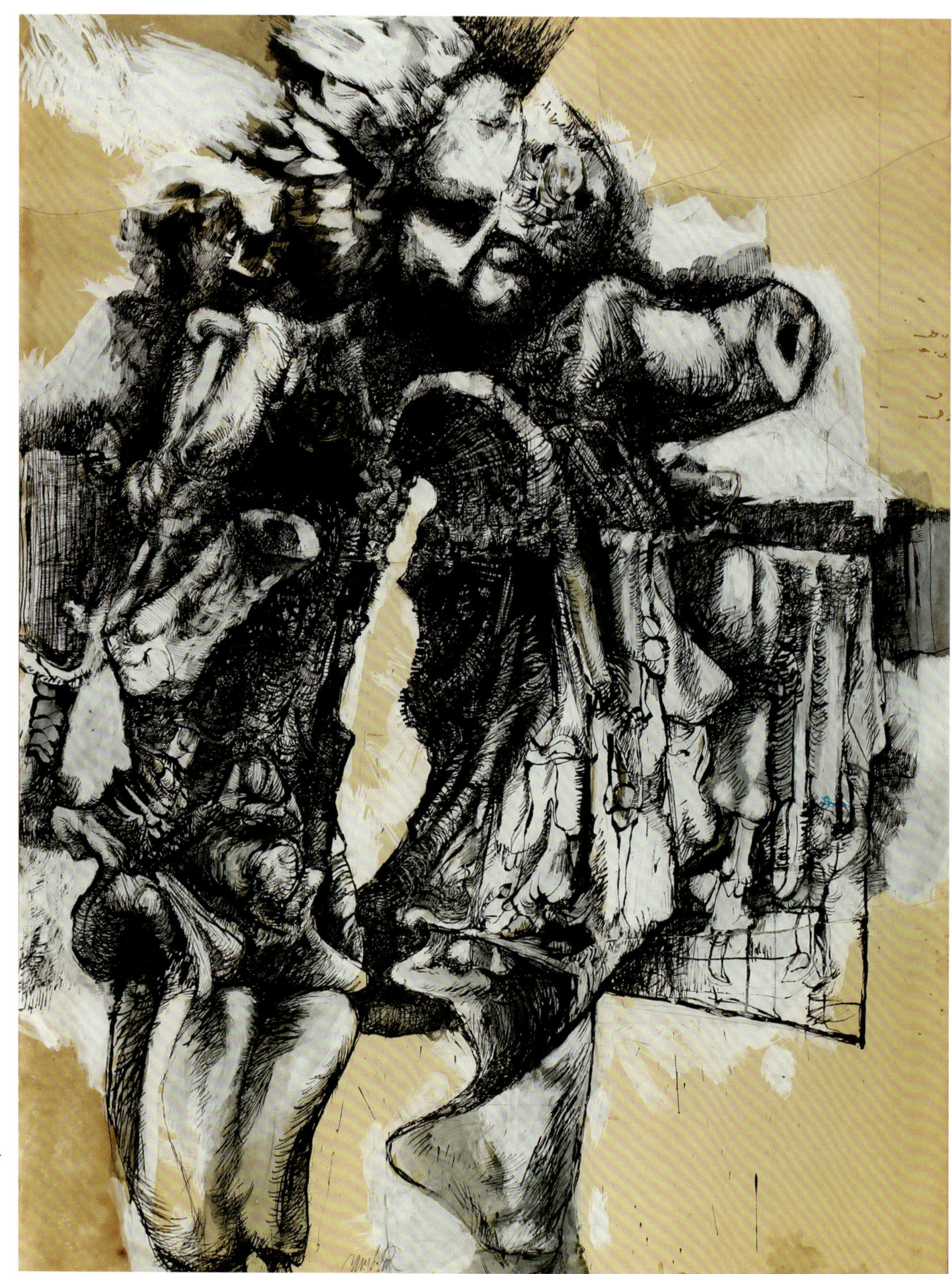

Angel, c. 1966. Ink, gouache, & wash on paper, 54" X 36". *Robert Fowler Collection. Photograph by David P. Gray.*

from Bob was the untitled 'baby head' casting. He simply claimed the work depicted an unborn child in the womb and that the mirrored orb represented the divine spirit itself or that it represented the instant when the new life was endowed with an immortal soul."[3]

Belief in an immortal soul is not part of Zen Buddhism. By combining vestiges of his Catholic beliefs with his acceptance of the Zen experience, Camblin may have demonstrated his omni-credulousness, a word he used to explain his openness to ideas. The professor professed that he "believed in it all." He liked trying on new skins and transforming old concepts.

While he had been interested in Zen Buddism for decades, it was Catholicism that manifested itself in his work. Chirstianity's angels captivated him much more than Buddhist Devas. Using line, wash, and casein, Camblin created an unusual angel. The angel's right hand and most of the left arm are missing. The sharp endings of the bones suggest they were cut off. Wings are only partially realized. A black eye may indicate a seeing eye in the darkness but the other other eye has a shaded, white covering. The head rests above a vaulted center under which is an opening that ends in the pelvic area. Two strange legs descend to the bottom of the work. The ink and wash are applied directly to paper that has gradually turned into a light caramel color. The complexity of ink lines unifies the whole. Camblin created a disfigured angel, not a protective angel. This is an angel that needs assistance, which poses the question: Is mankind in need of angels or do angels need the support of believers? This angel offers no solutions. Instead it inspires pity, unless of course, the viewer just contemplates the beauty of the lines. Perhaps Camblin was presenting an angel that a normal church-goer could imagine metamorphizing into rather than creating an angel who seems too lofty to be within reach. After all, who knows how to transform into an angel?

Camblin thought the cicada was a perfect example and symbol for metamorphosis. As a young boy in Ponca City, he heard the cicada's song and through it, he came to appreciate the insect's life-cycle. Cicadas spend the majority of their lives underground (between two and seventeen years) after which the nymphs emerge and climb the nearest tree. The male sings loudly to attract a female, who deposits

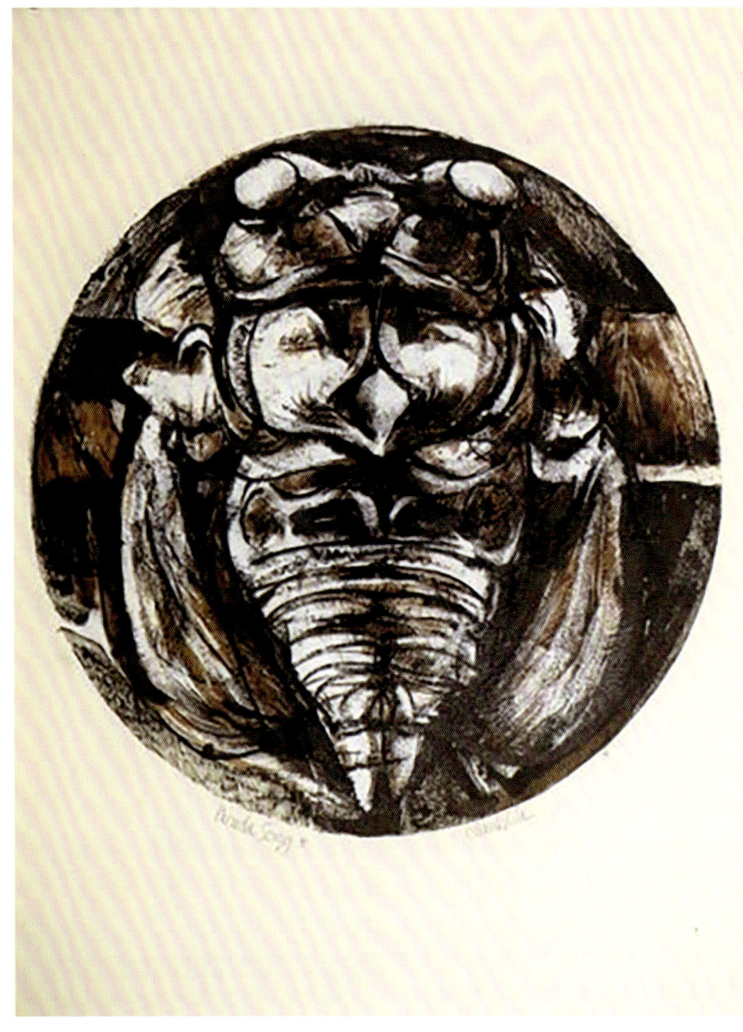

In *Cicada Song*, Camblin saw transformation within the perfection of a circle. *Photograph by Scott Peterson.*

her eggs in the bark. In order to grow, they shed their hard exoskeletons and leave their husks behind.

Camblin painted and drew cicadas to represent change, metamorphosis, transformation. Perhaps in his explanation to the Fowlers for his *Chrysalis* work, Camblin used "divine spirit" and "immortal soul" to reference his Catholic upbringing, showing that he never totally relinquished his religion. Perhaps he found it difficult to adopt Zen completely. Then again, he believed in the creative process. He believed in Catholicism. He believed in Zen. He believed in his art. He had the capacity to believe everything. All aspects of his beliefs were ineffable, but that didn't stop him from trying to explain them. To clarify, he labeled his way of thinking as "omni-credulous."

The process of creation was paramount for Camblin. In an interview for *The Salt Lake Tribune*, he noted: "There are two sides to people. There's the intuitive and the rational. And they're both important. We use rationality for the next giant step into intuition. Art is a success if the student can get back to being a child again. It's all a process—becoming something. And it's important for the artist to recognize the process."[4]

Camblin recognized that "the process of becoming something" began in childhood. He had been fascinated with Biblical stories when he was an altar boy. Later, he found subjects for his art in the apocalyptic Book of Revelations. Wanting his drawings to compete favorably with paintings, he increased their scale. *The*

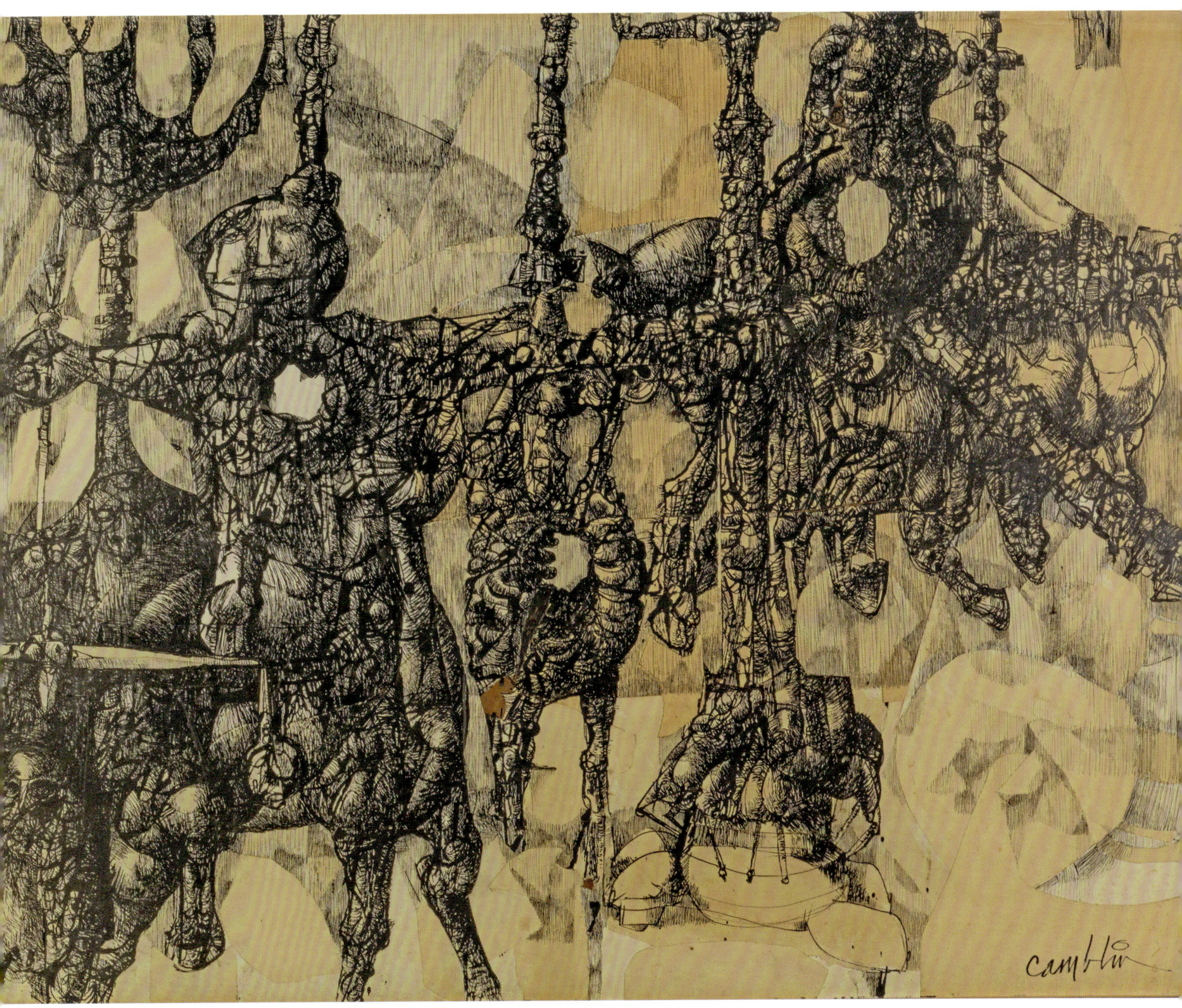

Four Carousel Riders or Riders of the Apocalypse? 1965–1966. Ink on collage background on Masonite, 37" X 49" framed. *Anonymous Collection. Photograph by Scott Peterson.*

Carousel of Four is one of his large pen and ink collages. For the ground, he tore various types of blank paper into random shapes and glued them on a surface of masonite. Over the collage, he drew four mounted figures that appear to be skeletal, armored knights. The density of the black ink gives the abstracted figures and their steeds a heftiness that defies the layered effect of the background on which the riders paradoxically appear to float. With no horizon or perspective, the knights seem to be apparitions from a dream or vision, harbingers of famine, war, conquest, and death—a manifestation of the prophecy of the arrival of the Four Horsemen of the Apocalypse.[5] They are not riders of a merry-go-round or carousel but are masked forerunners of the Last Judgment.

As Camblin wrote in a sketchbook: "*Carousel of Four* was the first—a large pen &ink collage but it started the drawings that have preoccupied me for the last 10 years. It was related to the Four Horsemen of the Apocalypse, the wheel of Life, a minor disagreement with Kerouac's' Dharma Bums and an enchantment with Laotse & Zen. . . . I felt at the time I was right—I still do, but now there is room for more than one opinion . . ."

In 1966, Camblin's opinion was not one shared by Utah's faithful Mormons. They believed, and still believe, that they are God's chosen people. Mormons' guiding principle is obedience to their prophet, whose directives are not to be questioned. Camblin declared blind faith anathema. For him, the inexplicable, including the existence of God, provided reasons for reflection: questioning was the process that led to knowledge. He missed curious minds.

CHAPTER SEVEN

Returning to the Land of His Youth

When Camblin received an offer to teach at Rice University in Houston, Texas, he had been in Salt Lake City for two years; and even though Salt Lake was a safe place to raise children, Camblin believed that a more diverse culture would better instill curiosity in his children. Situated 490 miles south of Ponca City, Houston is considered southwestern while Ponca City's northern position makes it more of a midwestern city. Even with different geographic designations, the two cities share many similarities, topographical and cultural. Both were shaped by the petroleum industry; both have humid and hot summers; both are flat, both are politically conservative; both are proud of their cowboy heritage, and cicadas sing in both environments.

Camblin was returning to the land of the cicadas. Before leaving Utah, he drew several versions of cicadas. He felt he had spent nine years, like a cicada, developing "underground." He was ready to emerge, to shed the mask of his chrysalis and to sing until he died. He left Salt Lake City and didn't look back.

From a sketchbook: "The dew has not yet washed the mud from that cicada shell."[1]

An ebullient Bob Bilyeau Camblin, with his wife and two young children, moved out of their home in Salt Lake City, loaded up their Volkswagen van, and headed south toward the siren call of Rice University. Three cold winters in Utah had been enough. They were all ready for the more temperate climate of Texas. They didn't even worry about the humidity. The Camblins arrived in Houston two and a half years before the tumultuous '70s. Shortly after moving into a house located north of the Rice campus, near Houston's Museum District, Camblin began teaching art at Rice University. He was thirty-nine years old and in his prime. Acknowledging his penchant for existentialism, he welcomed the new responsibilities that awaited him.

Just before Camblin departed Salt Lake City, he and Bonnie watched the deadly race riots in Detroit on their TV. They held tender memories of the city, and the killings, injuries, and burning of buildings made them worry about their Michigan friends. The couple was grateful to have their family safely out of Detroit. Even so, the news of the deadly events depressed them greatly. Camblin noted the two branches of the military that had been called in to quell the disorder were the two branches in which he had served: the US Army and the National Guard. In 1948, Camblin received an honorable discharge from the US Army, the same year that President Harry S. Truman abolished racial discrimination in the US Armed Forces. Truman's executive order was largely implemented by Eisenhower, but the desegregation of all military units was not fully accomplished until 1954. At some point during this process Camblin realized just how much work stood in front of true and genuine equality.

The homogeneity in Utah bothered him throughout his time there. Nearly everyone in the state was white, so the issue of segregation never felt truly relevant for the residents of the state. He wondered if blacks stayed away because they simply didn't want to live in a predominantly blond-haired, blue-eyed environment. He knew something had to be done about discrimination, but he didn't know what he could do to help eliminate prejudice.

When Camblin was a child, very few African Americans lived in his hometown. When Camblin enrolled at KCAI in 1948, the first black student, Leonard Pryor, had also just been admitted to the institute. With such a small student body, Camblin must have met Pryor, but no record of the meeting exists. When he taught in Sarasota, Florida, Camblin noted few, if any, blacks at the Ringling School of Art.[2]

Camblin expected Houston to be different. Blacks had been a part of Houston since its beginning. In fact, an African-American community came into being there in 1836 when Houston was founded. Yet by the time Camblin moved to the city almost 150 years later, 90 percent of the African-American demographic still lived in informally segregated neighborhoods. A mere thirteen years later the city had one of the largest black populations in America, 440,257 African-American residents. When Camblin left Houston, very little had changed. "As of 1987[3] most African Americans in Houston continued to live in inner-city black neighborhoods, even though they gained the legal right to move to any neighborhood."[4] The demographics of Houston's population and Utah's population were polar opposites. Camblin appreciated the diversity found in Texas, but he knew the state still had a long way to go before equality could be achieved.

Houston wasn't a cowtown in the late 1960s. The Museum of Fine Arts, Houston, [MFAH] was founded in 1900. Twenty-four years later, William Ward Watkin designed a Neoclassical building to house the museum's small art collection. The Blaffer Memorial wing by architect Kenneth Franzheim opened in 1953, and five years later the MFAH hired Ludwig Mies van der Rohe to design a signature wing to front the original building.[5] Aside from their visionary directors, the museum had forward-thinking patrons. Jean (anglicized to John in 1962) and Dominique (nee Schlumberger) de Menil arrived in Houston in 1944 from their native France, where the couple had begun collecting contemporary art. Once in Houston, they became active at the MFAH as well as the Contemporary Arts Museum (CAMH). Their influence brought Jermayne MacAgy to the city in 1955. Six years later the MFAH, where John was a board member, hired James Johnson Sweeney as director. (John de Menil made the call to ask Sweeney to come to Houston.) From 1935 to 1946, Sweeney had been a curator at the Museum of Modern Art, New York, and was the second director of the Solomon R. Guggenheim Museum. Together with the Menils and Jermayne MacAgy,[6] Sweeney greatly expanded Houston's cultural footprint.

Four years after MacAgy's death in 1964, Mrs. de Menil organized and hung a memorial exhibition of MacAgy's private collection entitled *Jermayne MacAgy: A Life Illustrated by an Exhibition* at St. Thomas, November 1968 to January 1969. Camblin visited the show and delighted in the unusual objects MacAgy had collected. Rumors about MacAgy swirled among her fans. A favorite was that MacAgy had never paid more than modest amounts for anything she collected, including partitioned boxes of glass eyes, exquisitely cut rock crystals, old signs (one with a single eye in an oval frame that hung outside a shop), sixth-century Greek animal sculptures, numerous boxes created by Joseph Cornell, art by Mark Rothko, small paintings by Texas eccentric Forrest Bess, and early works by Houston artist Jim Love, who credited MacAgy for turning him into a sculptor. The quirkiness of her collection held great appeal for Camblin who too collected the bizarre and the unusual. He realized how completely the cultural environment of the city had been influenced by John and Dominique de Menil and by Jermayne MacAgy.

Postmodernism arrived on the art scene about the time Camblin arrived in Houston. The city itself interested Camblin much more than any particular art movement. Houston was primed for new ventures, and Bob Camblin fit right in. Free from constraint, he reinvented himself as a wild-man artist who happened to be a Rice professor. He described Houston upon his arrival: "In 1967–68, Houston was a place with no past history, lots of money and open doors."[7] NASA's Manned Spacecraft Center was five years old when he moved to the city. Thirteen months after his arrival, on July 20, 1969, Neil Armstrong addressed NASA with, "Houston," the first spoken word from the moon. The "Eighth Wonder of the World," the Astrodome, had been open for three years. Houston Intercontinental Airport had broken ground for construction. The fifty-mile-long Houston Ship Channel connected the city to Galveston Bay and was adding hundreds of millions of revenue dollars per year to Harris County.[8] Houston was on its way to becoming the third biggest port in the USA, and oil and energy-related firms were turning Houston into the "Energy Capital of the World."

With the flood of new money, the city was developing an "only-in-Texas" identity: a retired upholsterer John Milkovisch was covering his house with flattened beer cans of the beer he had drunk. When completed, the city designated the house a Houston landmark. Another eccentric folk artist, Jeff McKissack, transformed his home and yard into a sculptural homage to the orange, his favorite fruit. Using recycled junk he created an architectural maze populated with iron figures. Through the help of a wealthy patron, the place evolved into the Orange Show Center for Visionary Art. Mickey Gilley opened his honky tonk in 1971, and crowds flocked to the bar to ride a mechanical bull. Houston's refusal to have city zoning embodied the free-for-all spirit of the scrappy and stubborn city with a population of over a million. Houston in the 1970s seemed a place where anything was possible. The city generated an optimistic energy, which lured and then welcomed immigrants, refugees, and anyone interested in its promise of a bright future.

Houston did have a major flaw, however. In 1967 the city did not have a museum dedicated to collecting its own artists nor an art journal committed to representing Texas artists to the rest of the world. Sadly, the existing museums seldom held exhibitions of local artists, except for the CAMH. Even so, Texas artist shows were usually hung in the basement. The city was growing quickly, and local artists were hopeful that a museum for their work would be forthcoming. Camblin counted himself among that group and welcomed all the changes. He wrote in a sketchbook, "Texas 1967—Bambola died here, but her ghost still is haunting the premises. The Time Machine and Spavinaw Ancestors are not removed enough yet to exist completely {on their own?}"

Camblin easily adapted to the Texan identity. The comparative leap from Ponca City to Houston was significant. Ponca shared much of the same western identity as Texas, but Ponca was a small town. Camblin felt more connected to the larger artistic venue of Houston. He was a gifted talker, a talent who was much appreciated by the locals. He had long heard of Texas bravado, and he didn't mind indulging in Texas braggadocio from time to time. Hearing that "if you ask a Texan a question, he will tell you a story," he felt his natural Irish gift of gab would serve him well.

The fact that Texas was the only state in the union that had operated as an independent, sovereign country for nine years before becoming part of the USA gave Camblin, the new Texan, something to brag about. Texas independence and pride were real, and as a proud and independent man, Camblin was primed to assume the Texan mantle. He never passed up BBQ or Tex-Mex and was naturally friendly, so he was practically home free already. He added a cowboy hat to his Oklahoma cowboy boots, listened to Texan music, and felt only a little uncomfortable dancing the Texas two-step. He was quick on his feet and didn't suffer fools.

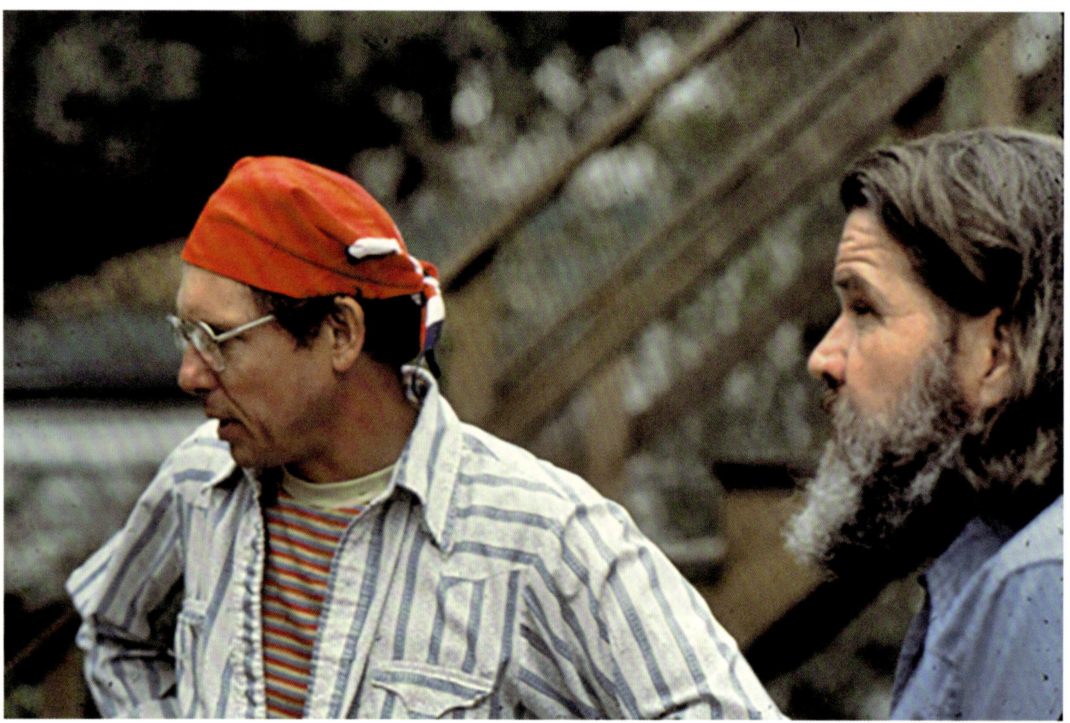

Earl Staley and Bob Camblin in Earl's backyard, Houston. *Photograph by author.*

Camblin felt drawn to the characteristic individualism his new neighbors seemed to possess in spades, and he expected his own personal and artistic eccentricities to be readily accepted in Houston. He reported for his teaching job at Rice University's Department of Fine Arts in the fall of 1968 with a readiness to push the edges of Houston's cultural envelope and a personal aesthetic that was augmented by a certain Texan pastiche. Camblin did exactly what he set out to do: he challenged people to think with his liberal outlook and tolerant disposition. Though, sometimes that sort of provocation did not fare well outside of his classroom.

When Camblin first arrived at Rice, the art department was only two years old. Three teaching artists were in place: John O'Neil, David G. Parsons, and Earl Staley. The university was known to be conservative, but the Rice studio atmosphere exuded the thrill of possibility. Camblin was ready to spark outrage. His new colleague Earl Staley was like-minded—the two quickly became friends. They both taught at Rice for one year before the university fired Staley, who was then immediately hired by the University of St. Thomas, a Catholic college only a few miles from the Rice campus.

Pat Colville and Jack Boynton were already teaching at St. Thomas when Staley began work at the university. Together with Staley, the two artists offered a summer art workshop in which Camblin participated. The class concluded with a two-week visit from William Wiley (who introduced the group to California Funk).[9] The Texas artists were attracted to this new art movement's references to pop culture, art history, humor, as well as the absurdist imagery Wiley used in his watercolors. Camblin's previous work with visual media-plus-incorporated text enabled the artists to immediately recognize their mutual love for the haiga approach. Both continued to develop the use of language and lines in their work.

CHAPTER EIGHT

Collaborative Endeavors

Camblin was energetic and enthusiastic; and after teaching in Houston for a year, he decided to make art more enticing and fun for his classes. Camblin wanted to introduce his students to the excitement and exuberance of the New York art scene in an effort to expand their understanding of the larger art world. Accomplishing the task was difficult from Texas, but he felt compelled to try. Eight years earlier, while teaching at the University of Illinois, Urbana, Camblin had been impressed with the collaborative performances that were occurring in New York City. Two leading pioneers of the events were Allan Kaprow[1] and Claes Oldenburg.[2] Both artists chaffed at the prevailing definition of art as a precious object, and each created and performed in happenings of their own creation. In fact, Kaprow was the first to call the events "happenings."[3] "Happenings are events that, put simply, happen. Though the best of them have a decided impact . . . they appear to go nowhere and do not make any particular literary point. In contrast to the arts of the past, they have no structure beginning, middle, or end. Their form is open-ended and fluid."[4]

Improvisation, chance, and group involvement played large parts in this new collaborative art form. Kaprow's first event entitled *18 Happenings in 6 Parts* occurred in 1959.[5] The audience was able to become part of the production by following the instructions printed in their programs.

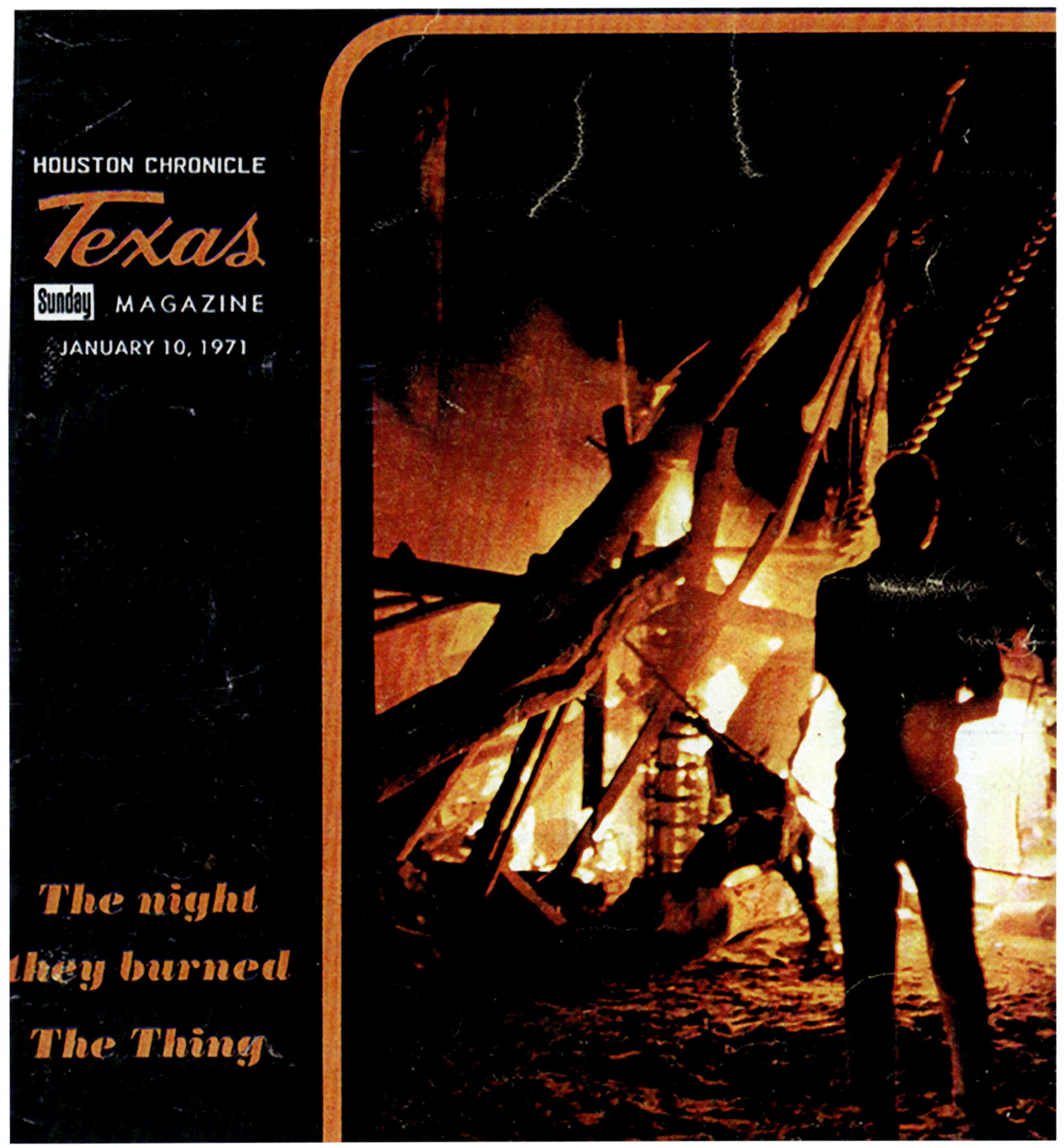

"The night they burned The Thing," documents the beach happening for the students of Camblin and Staley.

Three years later, Oldenburg also performed in front of an audience when he put on his own personal productions he called *Ray Gun Theater*. He improvised presentations with help from his friends. He wrote *I AM for ART*, thereby outlining his irreverence for traditional art. The first sentence sets the tone: "I am for an art that is political-erotical-mystical, that does something other than sit on its ass in a museum." So too Camblin decided he wanted his students to "do something other than sit on their asses in a classroom."

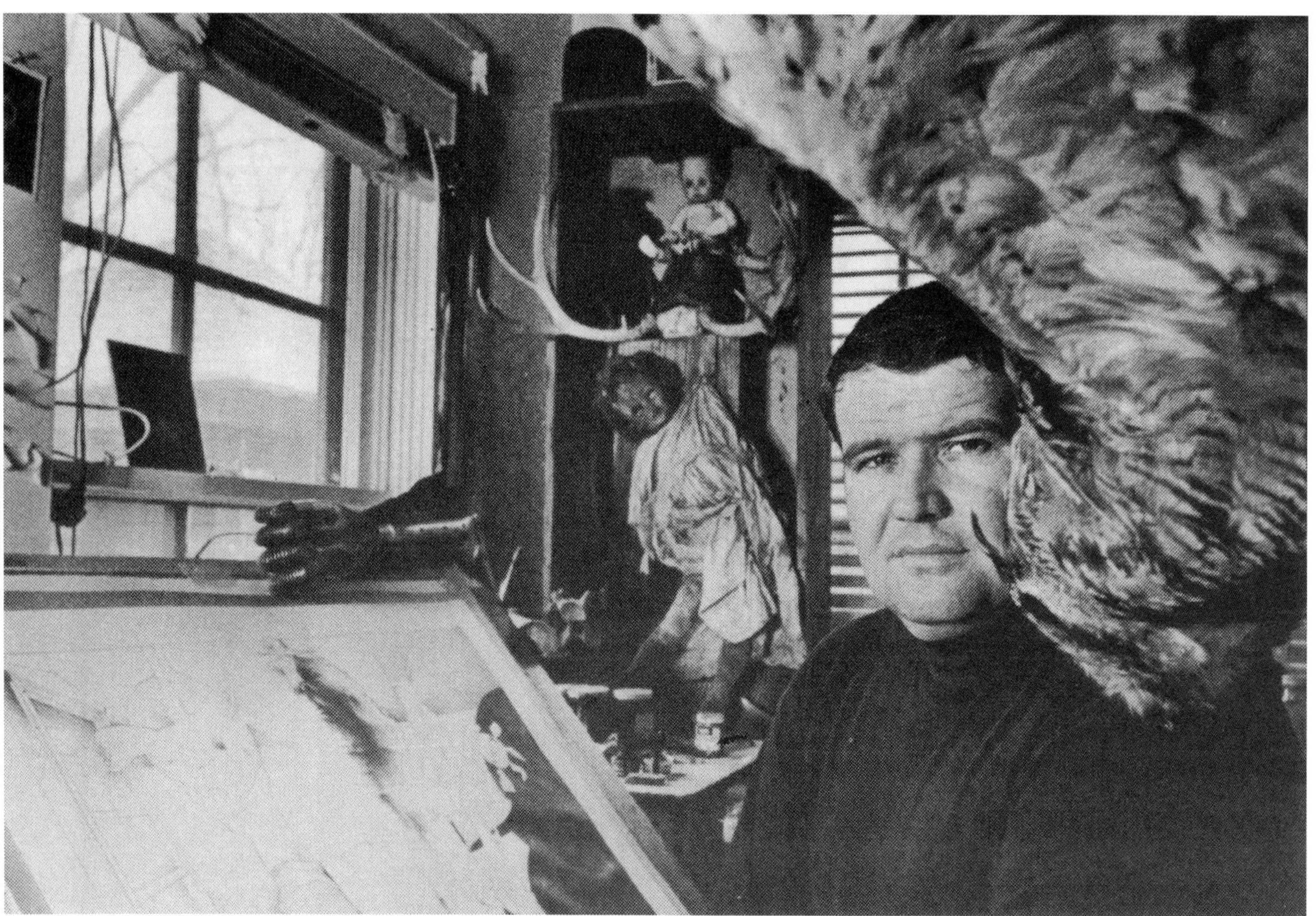

Camblin in his first Houston studio. Photo by Marc St. Gil. Note St. Bambola on side wall.

In 1968,[6] the year before Staley was fired, he and Camblin escorted a group of students to Galveston's West Beach on an excursion for a Construction/ Destruction happening.[7] Staley made a film of the event titled *Side Show.*[8] The professors and their group built freeform structures from beach debris, then set their artistic creations on fire. The camaraderie and excitement of the students turned their excursion into an extended, all-night adventure. A year later the Camblin-Staley duo (who now called themselves B & E Productions [Bob and Earl]), led another Galveston Construction/Destruction event. A third collaborative happening in Galveston followed in January of 1971 when Camblin and Staley were joined by Joe Tate, who had recently joined the art department faculty at Rice. The trio added a "J" to their moniker, becoming B E & J Productions. Bob galvanized his classes with the theatricality of happenings and the romance of the beach at sunset. Everyone in attendance participated. For his part, Camblin saw the beach events as a manifestation of his belief in artistic cooperation—he was in his element.[9]

After each happening, the University of St. Thomas, where Staley[10] was now art department chairman, held exhibitions of both the surviving creations and the charred remains from the outings.[11]

The David Gallery

In 1969, Camblin began exhibiting his work at the David Gallery in Houston, owned and run by Dianne David. The gallery dealer had a lightning-quick mind and a razor-sharp wit, which she demonstrated via her uninhibited tongue. Camblin found his verbal match. So the pair both agreed to a rule for their verbal combat to eliminate the possibility of collateral damage to their shared sense of camaraderie lest they step over the line of friendship into the abyss of psychological warfare. If either sparring partner observed tension or heard an edge in the other's voice, they would simply redirect the conversation entirely without explanation. Mostly, their exchanges played out in a teasing fashion.

Camblin and Staley, as B & E Productions, collaborated with David on shows for the David Gallery including: *Painting and Drawings by Bob Camblin, Stable*

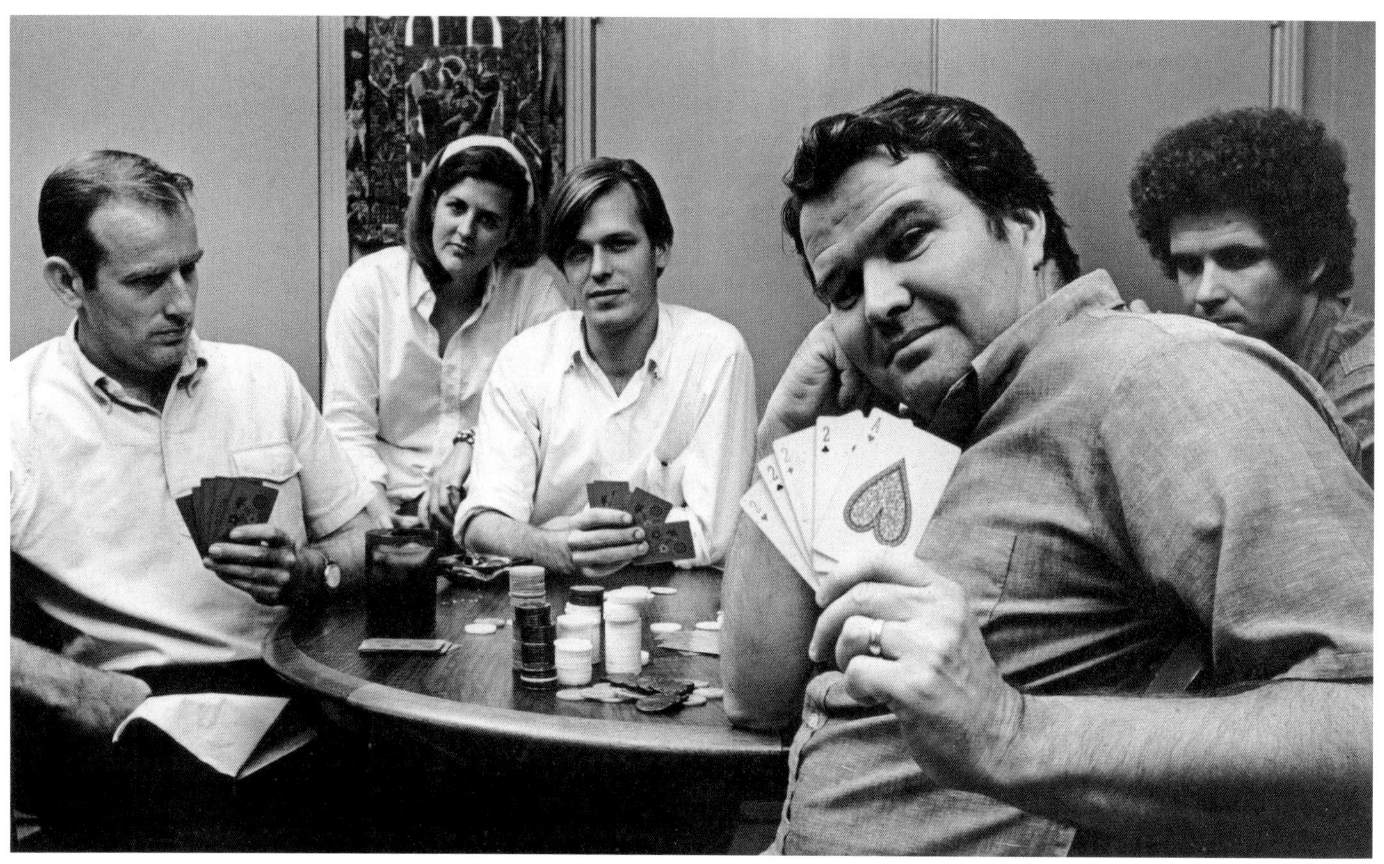

Counter clockwise: Bob Camblin, Dennis Camblin, Lucas Johnson, Dianne David, and Bob Fowler.

Works by Stable Artists in 1969, *Boxscapes* in 1970, *The Tattoo Show* in 1970, and a *Document Show* in 1971.

In an interview, Dianne David said: "I started showing the artists I thought were really good: Jim Love, Roy Fridge, Bob Camblin, Don Shaw, Lucas Johnson. When I closed the gallery, I think in 1970, Bob Camblin, who was one of my artists, told me that the thought that art had died and that the galleries were going to stay open—I think that was the main reason I closed the gallery—he said that the galleries that were going to stay open were going to be like tombs and that if I would watch, that the art was going to start becoming more minimal, more non-perceptive—no realism. He was really right, because

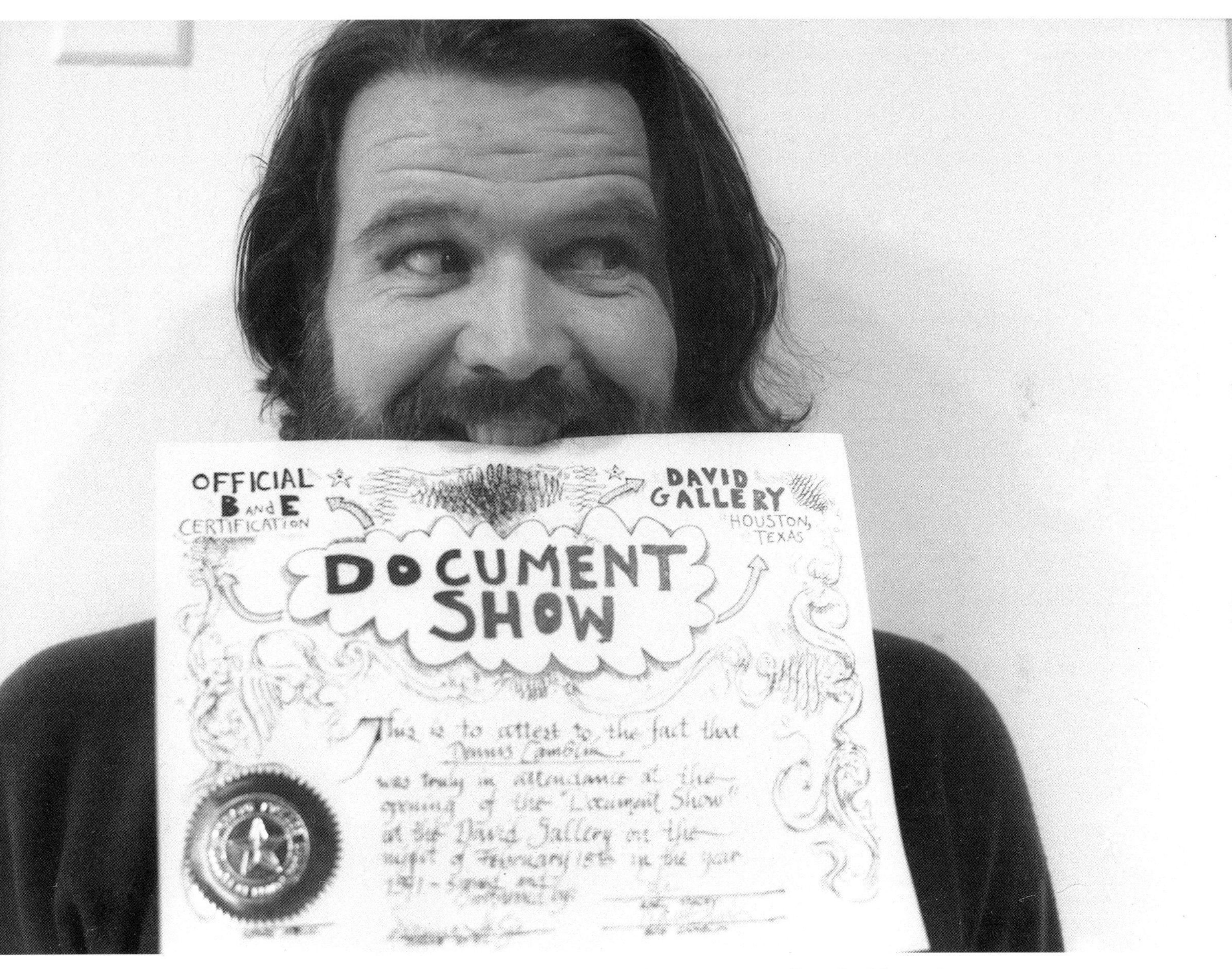

Camblin and Staley, as the Holding Firm, helped organize and run the David Gallery's Document Show. Camblin posed with a document in his teeth, 1971.

the galleries that are staying open are showing very, very minimal art that I could do myself, lines, showing art by people who cannot draw. Like Salvador Dali said, he thinks we ought to get back to realism so we can find out who's got some skill."[12]

In the watercolors for the *Boxscapes* show, Camblin elaborated the themes he had begun in Detroit: catfish heads (Spavinaw Ancestor Masks), rubber gloves, St. Bambola and tubing, traps, body parts—all placed in drawn boxes. His only three-dimensional work in the show was a wooden cabinet filled with compartmentalized boxes, the beginning of his *Wunderkammer*[13] (cabinet of wonder). He filled each small box within the larger cabinet with his personal collection of objects, memorabilia, and tubing. The cabinet provided a cypher for the watercolors. On the subject of the *Boxscapes* show, Camblin said, "For me, it is all part of the birth-death cycle. You have to get your mind past what it is you are seeing. We get conditioned to think certain things are ugly. I see, instead, transformation—Venus born of the red tide of dead fish."[14]

When a reporter asked Camblin to interpret one of his works, he answered: "[It] took him forty-two years to begin to understand his work and [he] doesn't see why it should be made any easier for the viewer."[15] Despite his naturally talkative nature, Camblin seldom explained his work for anyone from this point in his career onward. He was wary of interpretation, but he did offer clues to help give insight into his art. Camblin's "Notes on Drawings" follow:

These drawings link up all the previous styles and are tied directly to Time Machine #1, the organic drawings of the Birth of Venus and Metamorphosis have altered themselves and become "mechanized." Built, but aging

Built, not with technology, but by hand

Existing, but superfluous

Functioning, yet functionless

Introspective, but impossible to comprehend

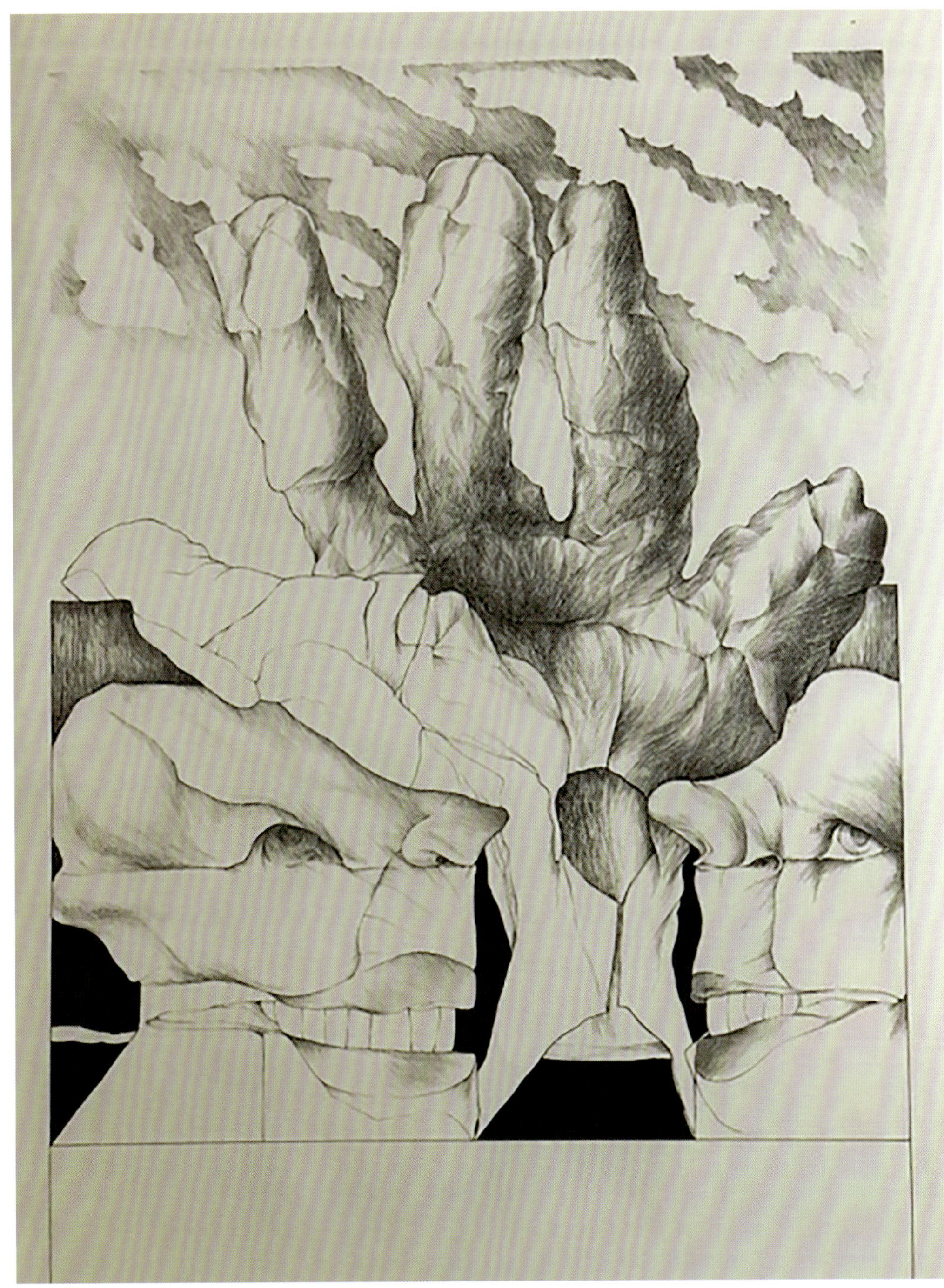

Camblin explained that gloves are functionless without a human hand. *Photograph by Scott Peterson.*

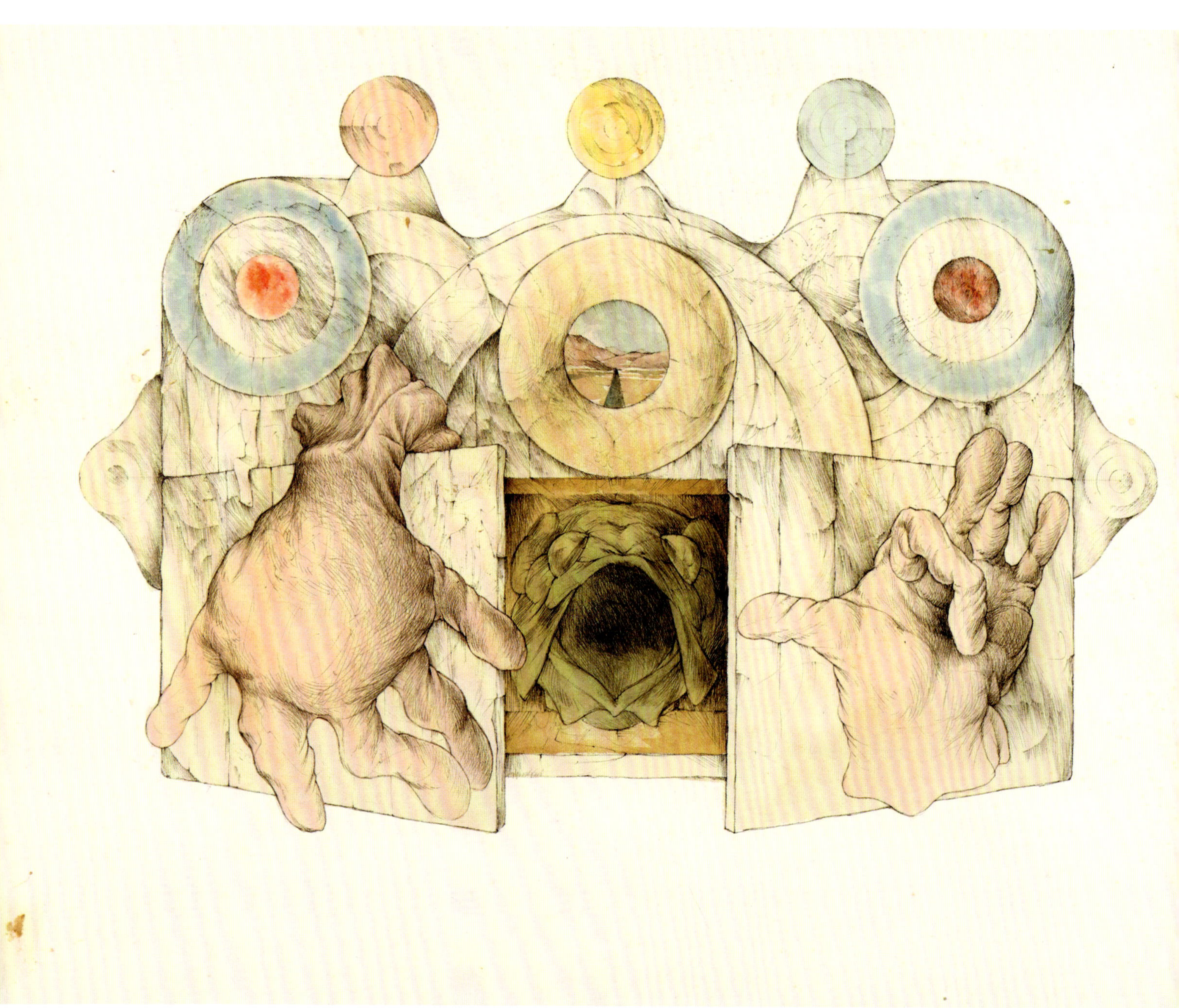

Untitled Fish Head and Gloves. A box with gloved hands guards the mounted fish head. *Photograph by Scott Peterson.*

Glove Drawings fit in here as first generation change—part organic—The glove is skin—reflects the human organism—without which it is functionless. In the drawings it is always immobilized further by being covered with a synthetic resin.

There occurred the word ISLOMANIA which was described as a rare but by no means unknown affliction of the spirit. There are people . . . who find islands somehow irresistible. The mere knowledge that they are on an island, a little world surrounded by the sea, fills them with an indescribable intoxication. These born "islomanes," Durrell used to add, are the direct descendants of the Atlanteans, and it is toward the last Atlantis that their subconscious yearns . . .

   L.

     —Durrell's *Reflections on a Marine Venus.*

A year after Camblin's *Boxscapes* for David Gallery, B & E Productions decided to collaborate with Dianne David on an edgier side of Houston living: local tattooed bikers. Camblin and Staley undertook the task of finding great tattoos for a *Tattoo Show*. In 1970s Houston, tattoos challenged middle-class values and were considered the domain of biker-fringe culture. The "skin art" played into the ideas of "suffering for one's art," lifetime commitments to creativity, and the recognition of the growing value of marginalized lifestyles. The David Gallery exhibited drawings of tattoos or works inspired by tattoos. Camblin created his *Family Portrait*. He outlined the right arm of each member of his family and filled the arms with tattoos. "Family Portrait can take each member of the family and do a montage of events depicted by symbolic tattoos. The traditional tattoos seem to be hearts, arrows, ribbons, roses, birds (predatory and song) knives and panthers—plus skulls and flags."[16]

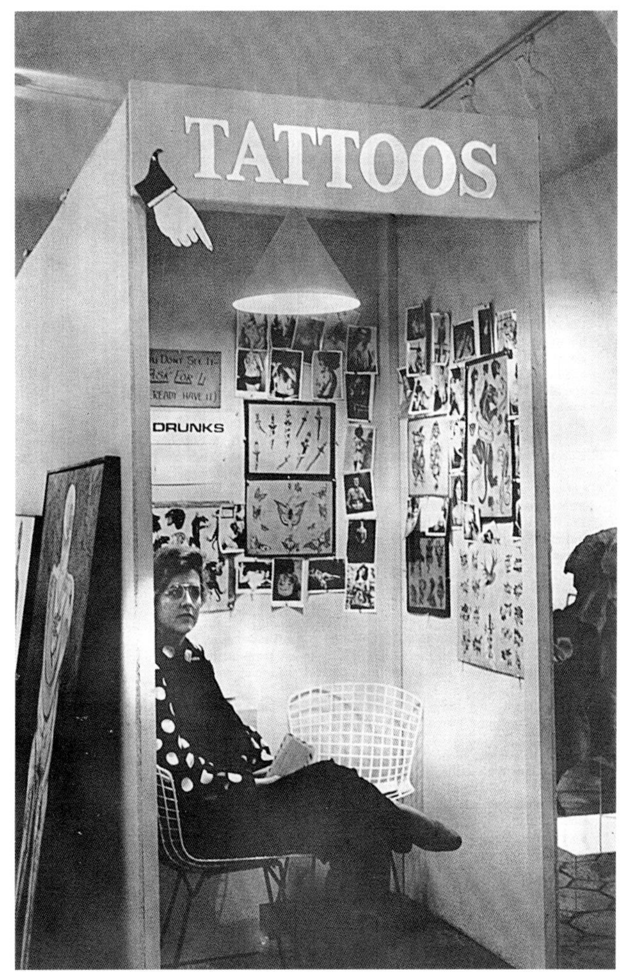

Dianne David in a tattoo booth built for her gallery's *Tattoo Show*.

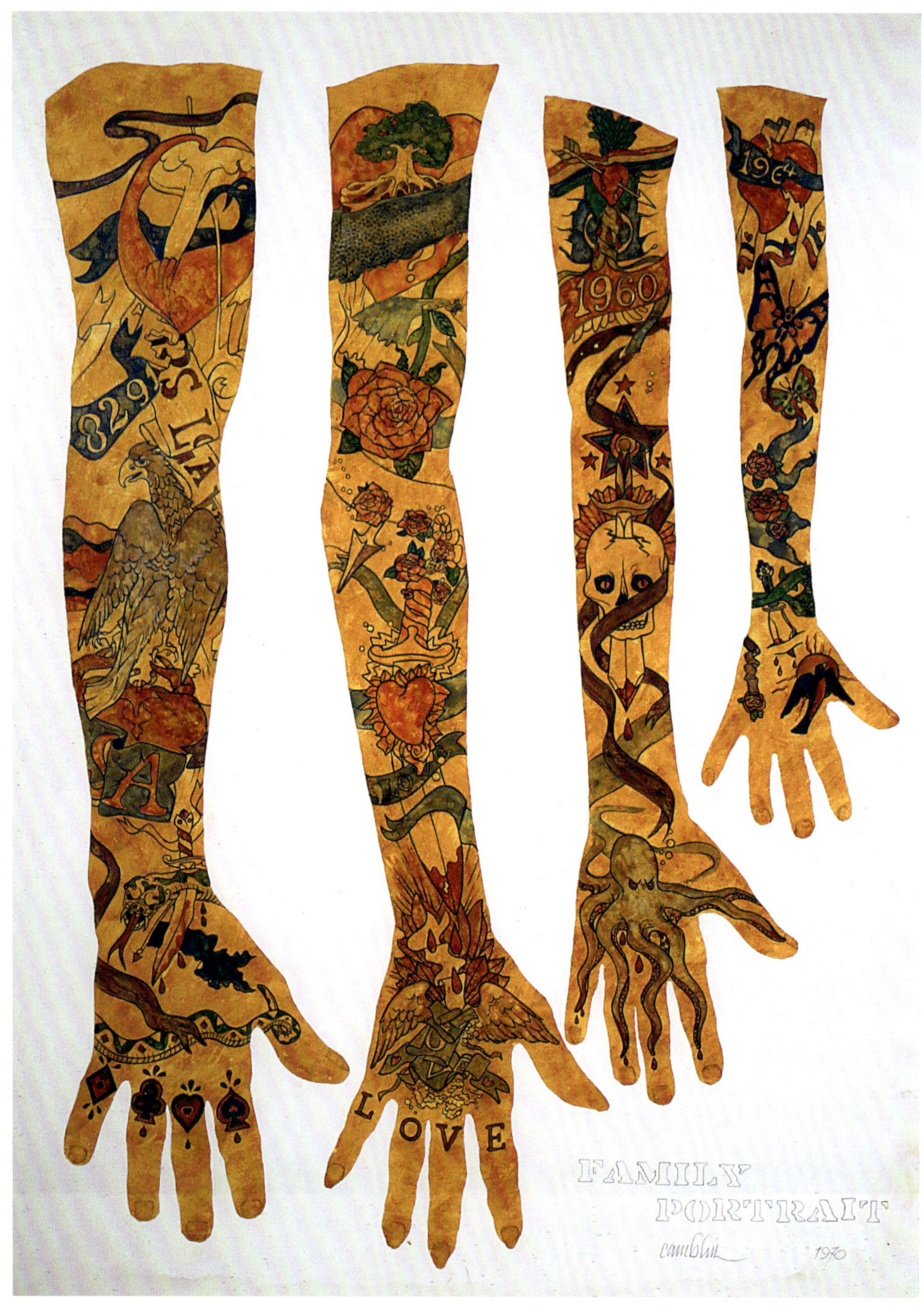

For *Family Portrait*, 1970, Camblin drew the right arm of each of his family members, and filled the arms with tattoos. *Photograph by Scott Peterson.*

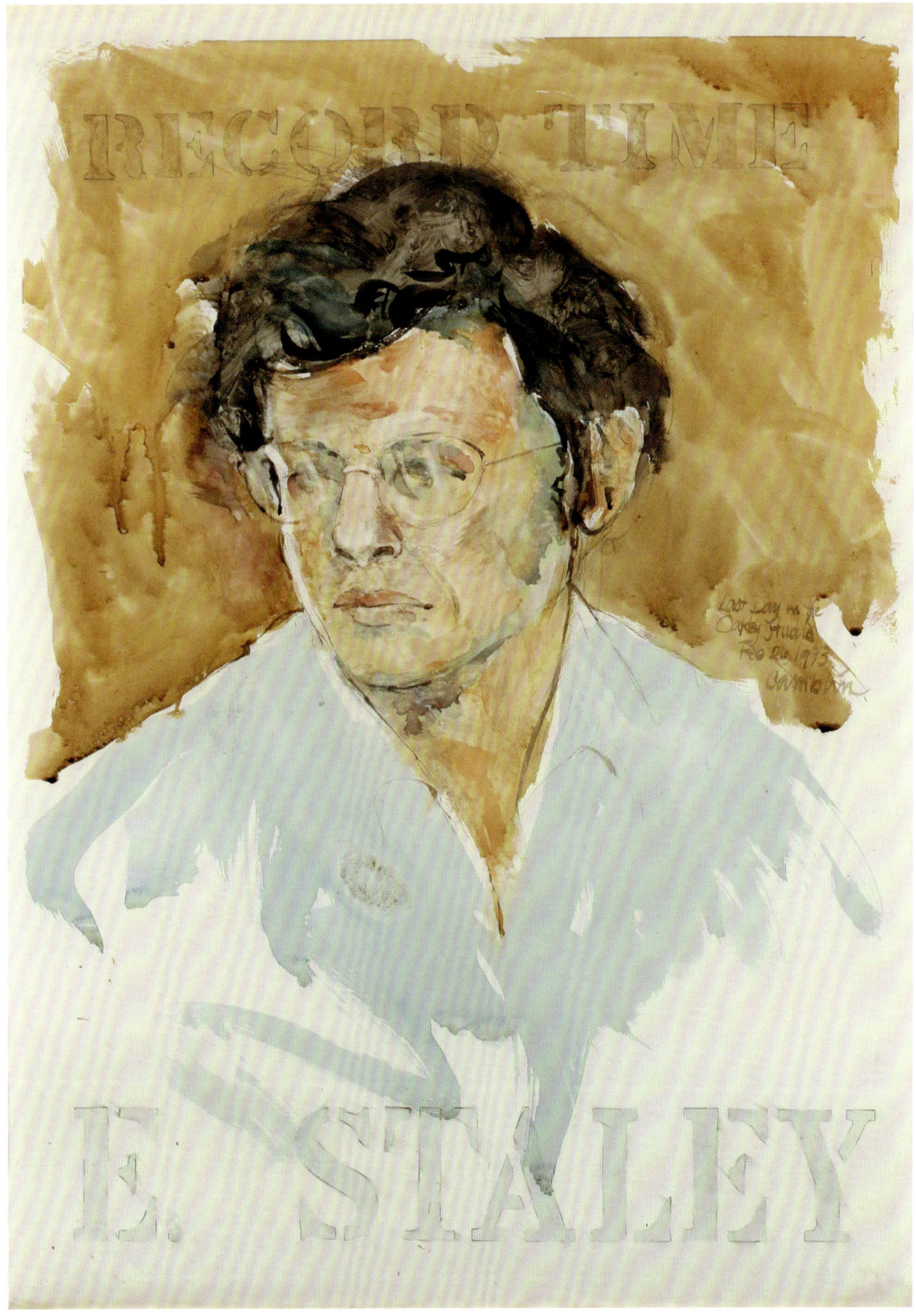

Bob Camblin portrait of Earl Staley, 1973. Watercolor on paper. *Collection of Earl Staley.* Staley said Camblin painted the portrait in minutes; thus the title, *Record Time. Photograph by David P. Gray.*

The most eye-catching and controversial attraction in the *Tattoo Show* involved the tattoos sported by the nude or seminude attendees. During the show's opening, the nudity of the tattooed participants flustered some gallery attendees; others welcomed a more liberal milieu not usually found in "respectable" Houston. Three years later, tattoos were given a seal of approval: the first world tattoo convention took place in Houston.

To some, tattoos are considered "skin documents." To Camblin it seemed logical that the *Tattoo Show* would be followed by a *Document Show*, exhibited in February 1971. The exhibition paid homage to its German predecessor *documenta*, which originated in 1955 in Kassel, Germany. *Documenta*'s purpose was to exhibit the work of artists who influenced modern art and to banish all traces of Nazi influence in the new art of the time. Camblin and Staley wanted to omit politics and to have only an exhibition of documents since they had no evil empire to banish. They invited participation of artists "across the board . . . of repute, of no repute and even of ill repute."[17] Potential exhibiting artists received the following letter, on B & E Production letterhead:

> A document show is being planned by the David Gallery in Houston, Texas. B & E Productions has been asked to coordinate this endeavor. We are inviting a number of significant artists to submit work. The interpretation of the word DOCUMENT may be left to the individual artist. Our only limitation is that the article submitted be sent to us by parcel post. Should you decide not to participate, a letter of refusal (handwritten) would be appreciated.[18]

In the original Statement of Purpose: "Knowledge demands documentation. Art is documented knowledge."

The year California artist Joe Tate replaced Staley at Rice, Camblin's life intersected with my life. He had already joined forces with Staley. Being socially, politically, and artistically compatible, the trio became B E & J Productions in 1971. They changed their collaborative identity to The Holding Firm[19] the following year. A Camblin entry from a sketchbook cautioned, "We are object makers. We do the best we can. You get more than you bargained for when you do business with the Holding Firm."

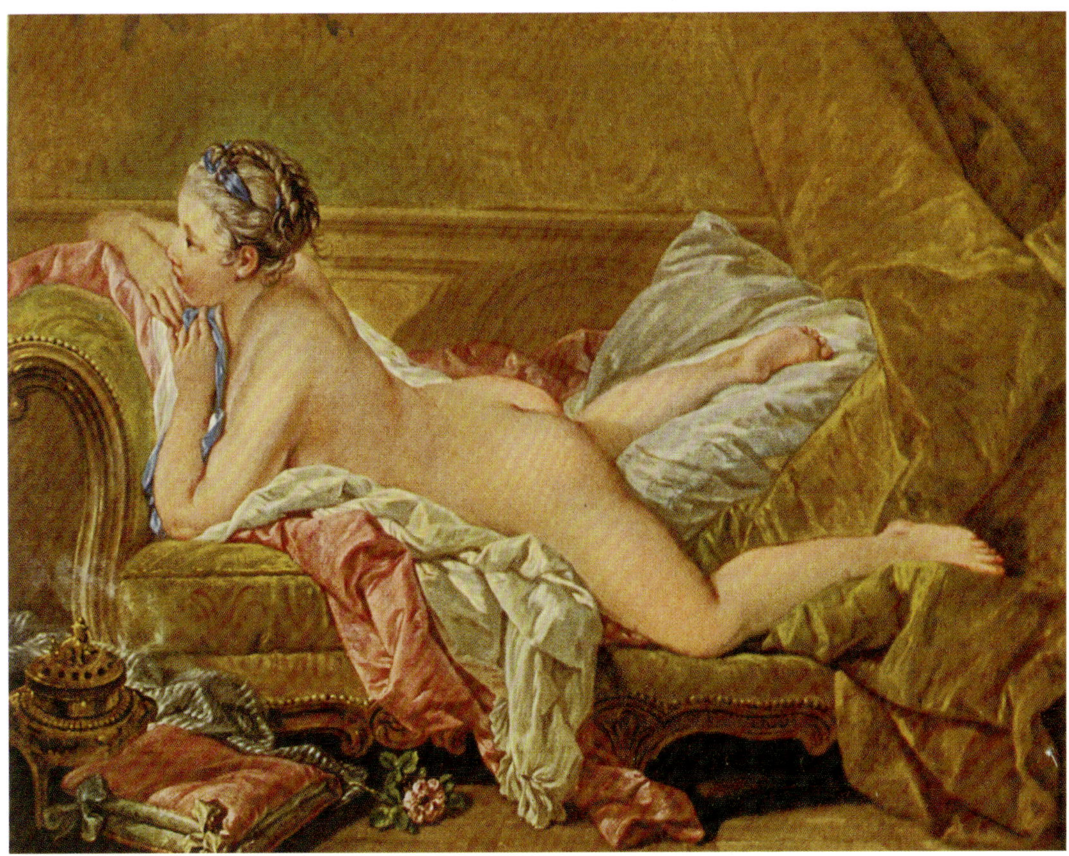

Boucher's eighteenth century portrait of the mistress of French King Louis XV. *Louise O'Murphy.*

A Private Collaboration

During Tate's year at Rice, I was one of the students who enrolled in Camblin's life drawing class. As a professor, he made his students believe they could learn to draw. He spent individual time with everyone and fired up our enthusiasm for the creation of art. His eloquence made the subject become an important part of each individual's life. He also helped soften the blows that arrived with classmates' brutal critiques by quickly pointing out something positive about the student's work, without offending the critic. Most of his class fell in love with him, with art, and with the possibility of becoming an artist. The semester flew by, almost like magic.

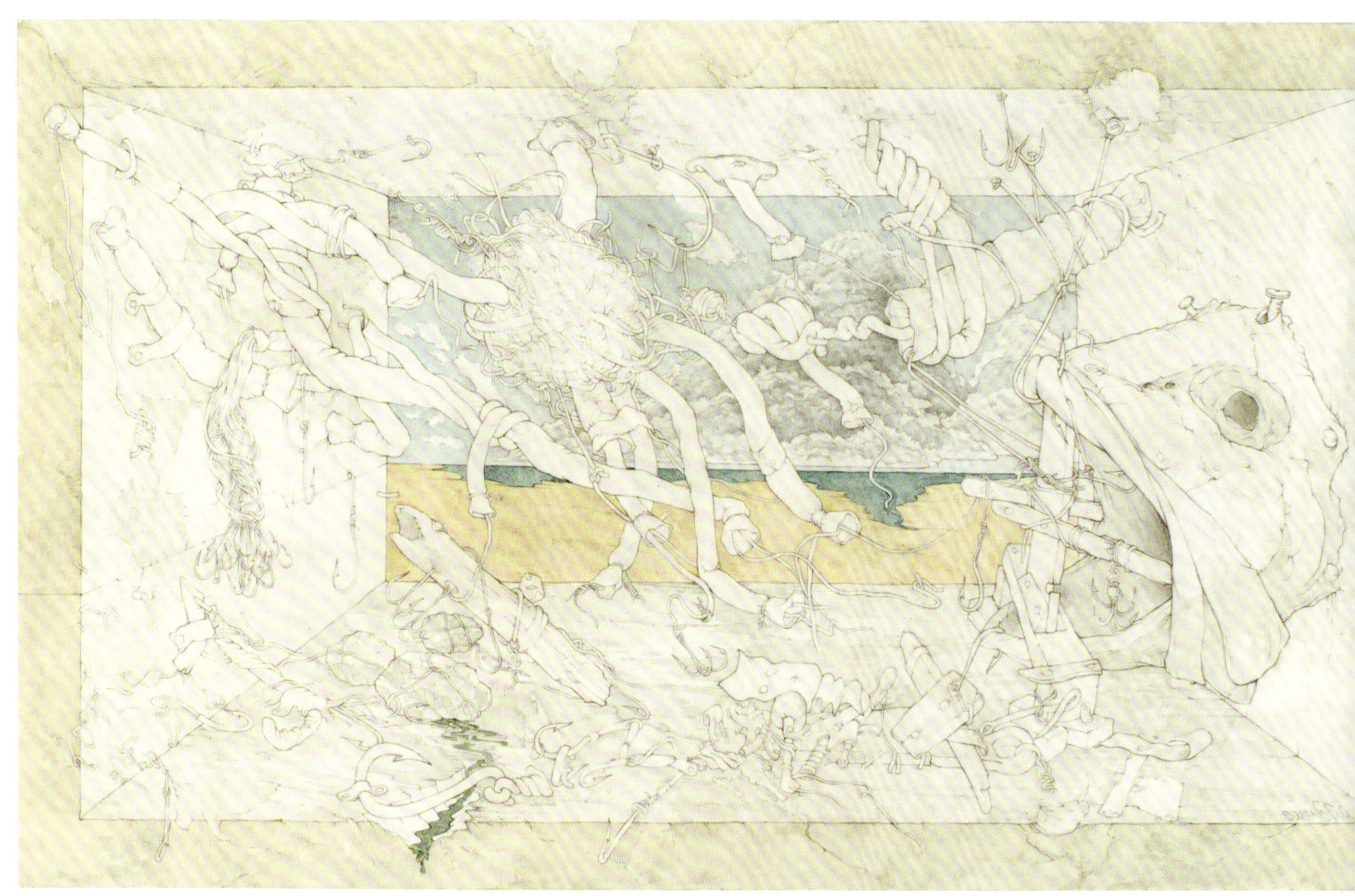

Trotline Memorial, 1971, watercolor and pencil on paper, 22" X 30½", *Menil Collection*. The delicacy and beauty of *Trotline Memorial* exemplify Camblin's exquisite line and complex subject matter. The surreality of the pale rectangular container backed with a colored landscape and filled with disparate objects challenges and disorients the mind.

During one watercolor outing, Camblin spent extra time with me, perhaps with reason, since I was hopeless with watercolor. The next week he hardly acknowledged me. He would later confess that he knew indifference would get my attention more easily than attention. For his end-of-semester assignment, he asked the class to draw a nude self-portrait. The results were surprising. Being intensely shy,

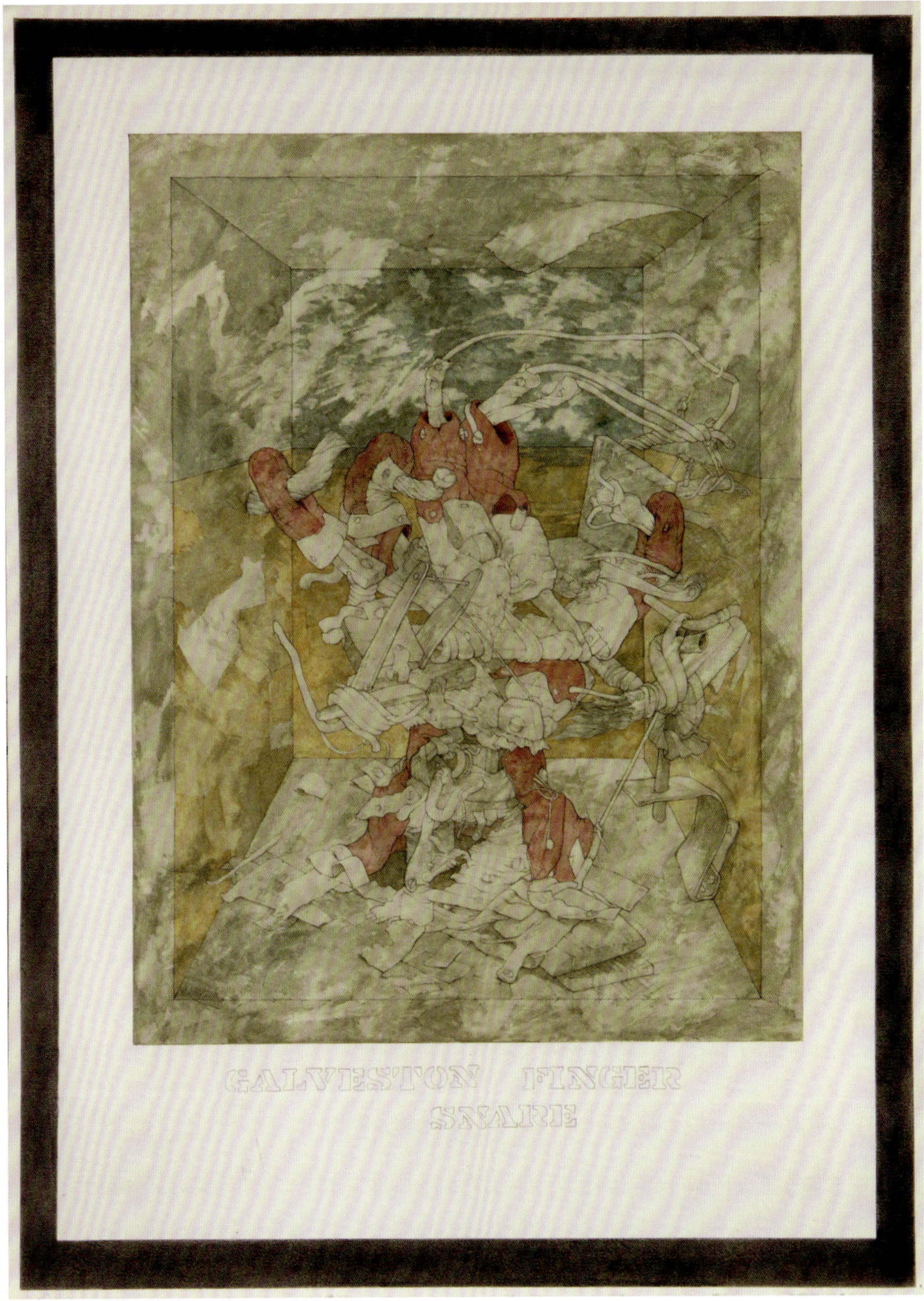

Galveston Finger Snare, 1971, watercolor and pencil, 30" X 22", went to The Modern Art Museum of Fort Worth. Harkening back to Cambln's use of gloves, boxes, and traps, the viewer decides if the gloved fingers are the snare or are being snared.

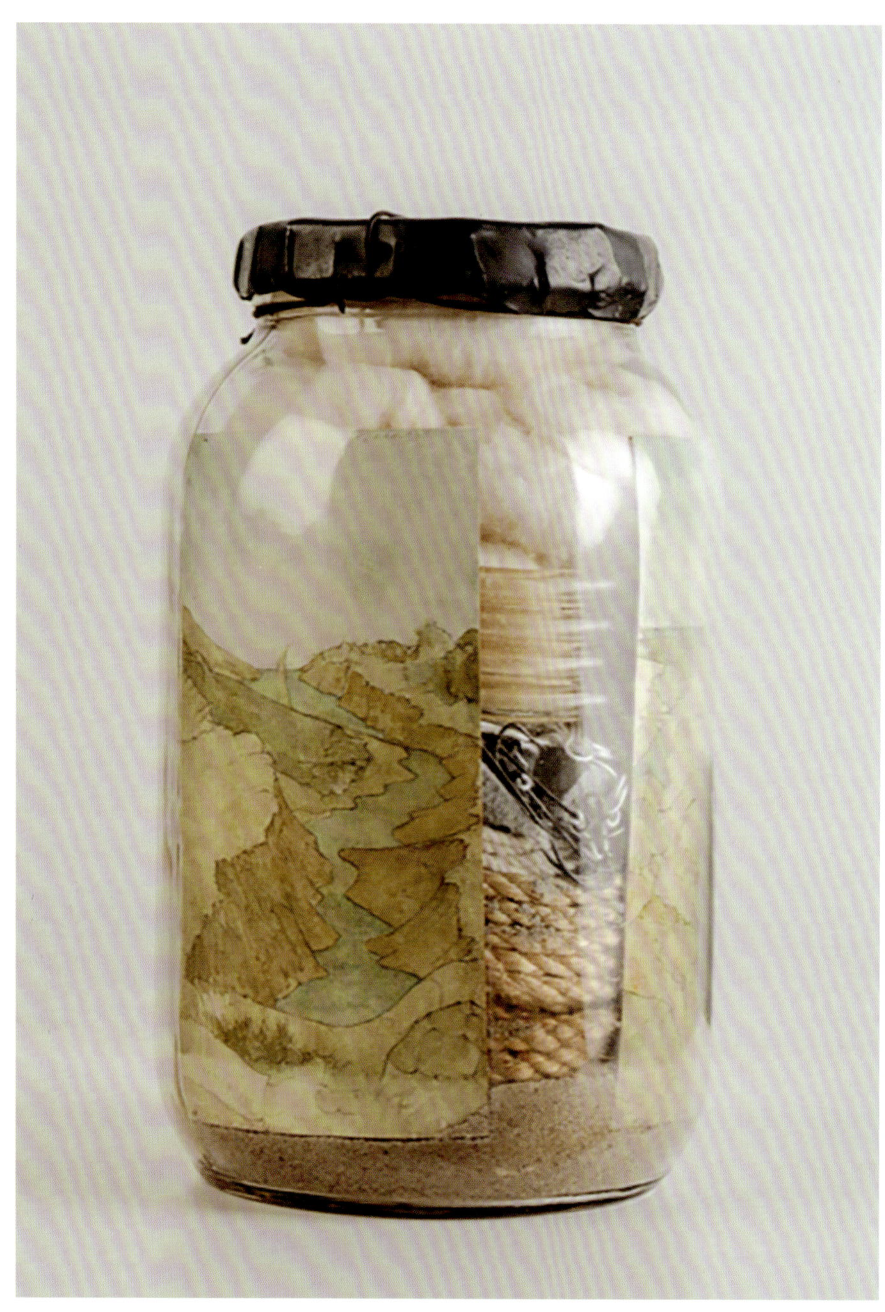

Lining a large bottle with a watercolor landscape, Camblin left a gap through which his layers of tubes, hooks, sinkers, and sand, which comprised his interior landscape, are visible.

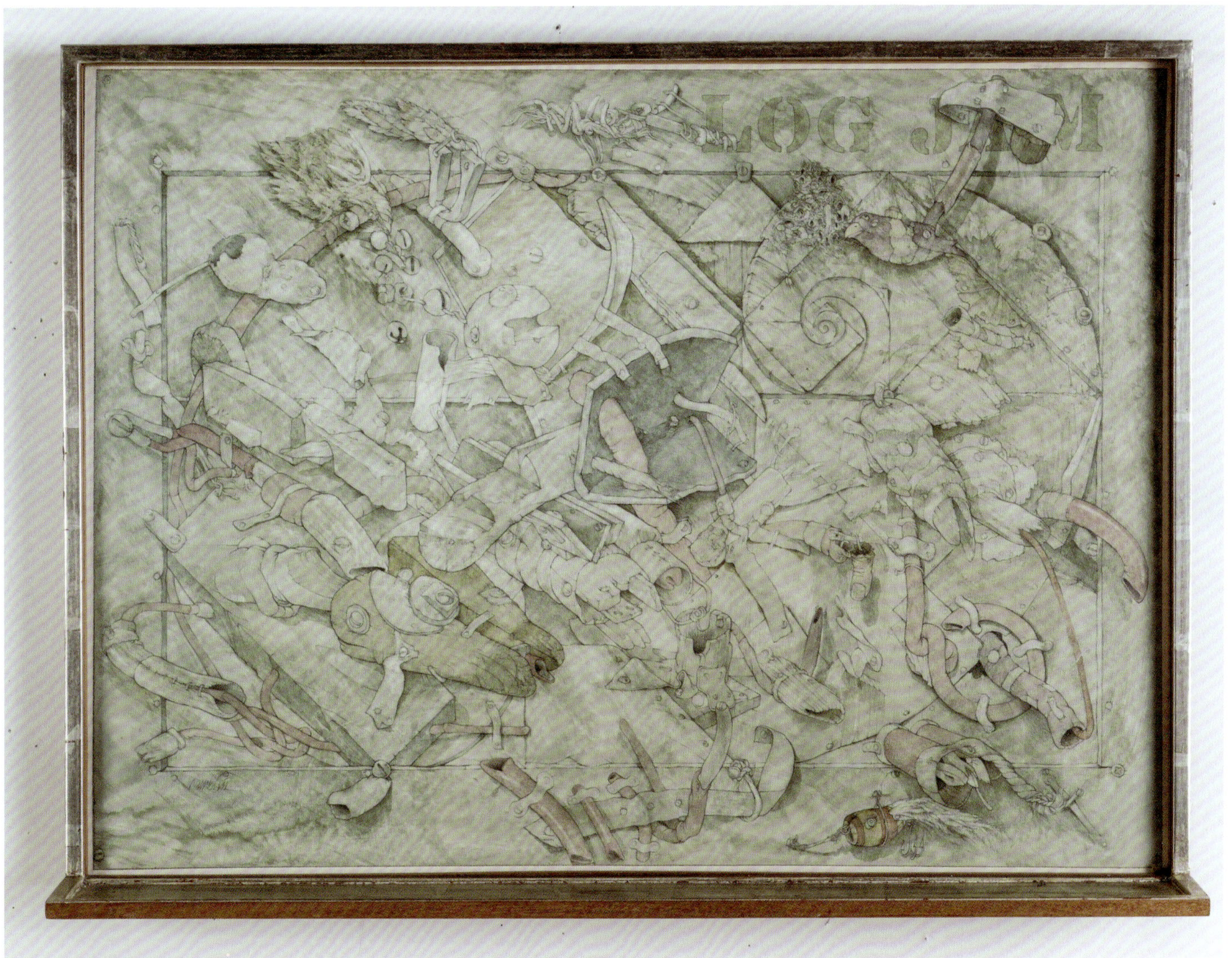

Logjam. The light green totality of *Logjam* gives the artwork a unity that initially defies the visual complexity of the composition. *Photograph by Scott Peterson.*

I looked through art books in an effort to find the least revealing pose possible. Not having much of an eye at the time, I opted to copy the nude back of François Boucher's *Louise O'Murphy* or *Mademoiselle de Morphy*, an Irish mistress of French King Louis XV, c. 1752. I would later find out that the painting is considered to be one of western art's most erotic paintings.

In my pitiful attempt to draw *O' Murphy*, I left the pose and surroundings intact and simply replaced her head with my own. Believing (or at least trying to make myself believe) that Camblin would appreciate the Irish connection as well as my desire to hide my own nudity behind that of *O'Murphy*, I handed in my assignment. All Camblin saw was "mistress." When Camblin returned my drawing, it was ungraded. A nonchalant invitation to visit his studio to discuss my drawing soon followed. I had recently separated from my husband so I did not immediately take him up on the offer. Plus, I had heard many rumors

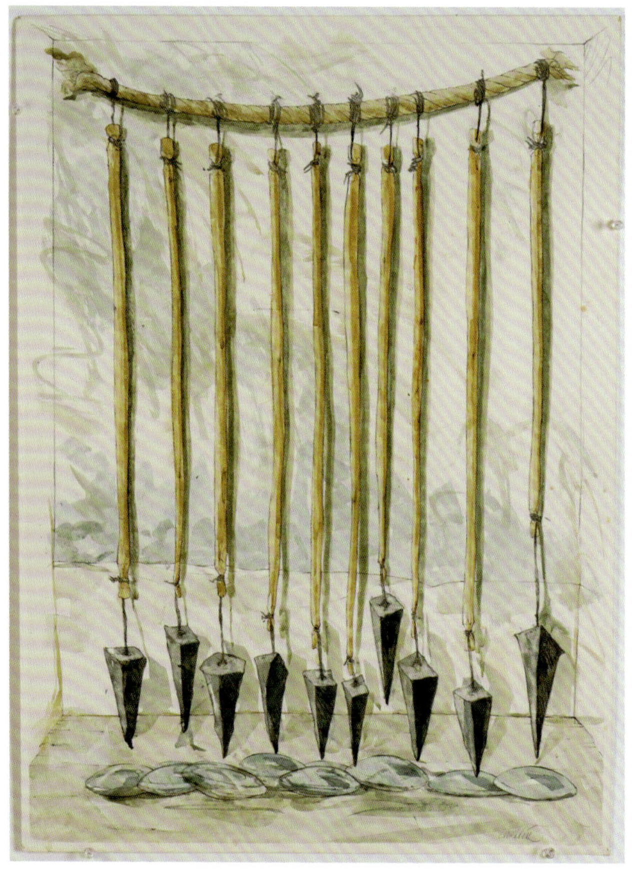

Untitled, (suspended weights). Pointed lead weights hang perilously over a line of convex/concave glass circles. Perhaps the artist's metaphor for potential perils that threaten the fragility of an untroubled existence. *Photograph by Scott Peterson.*

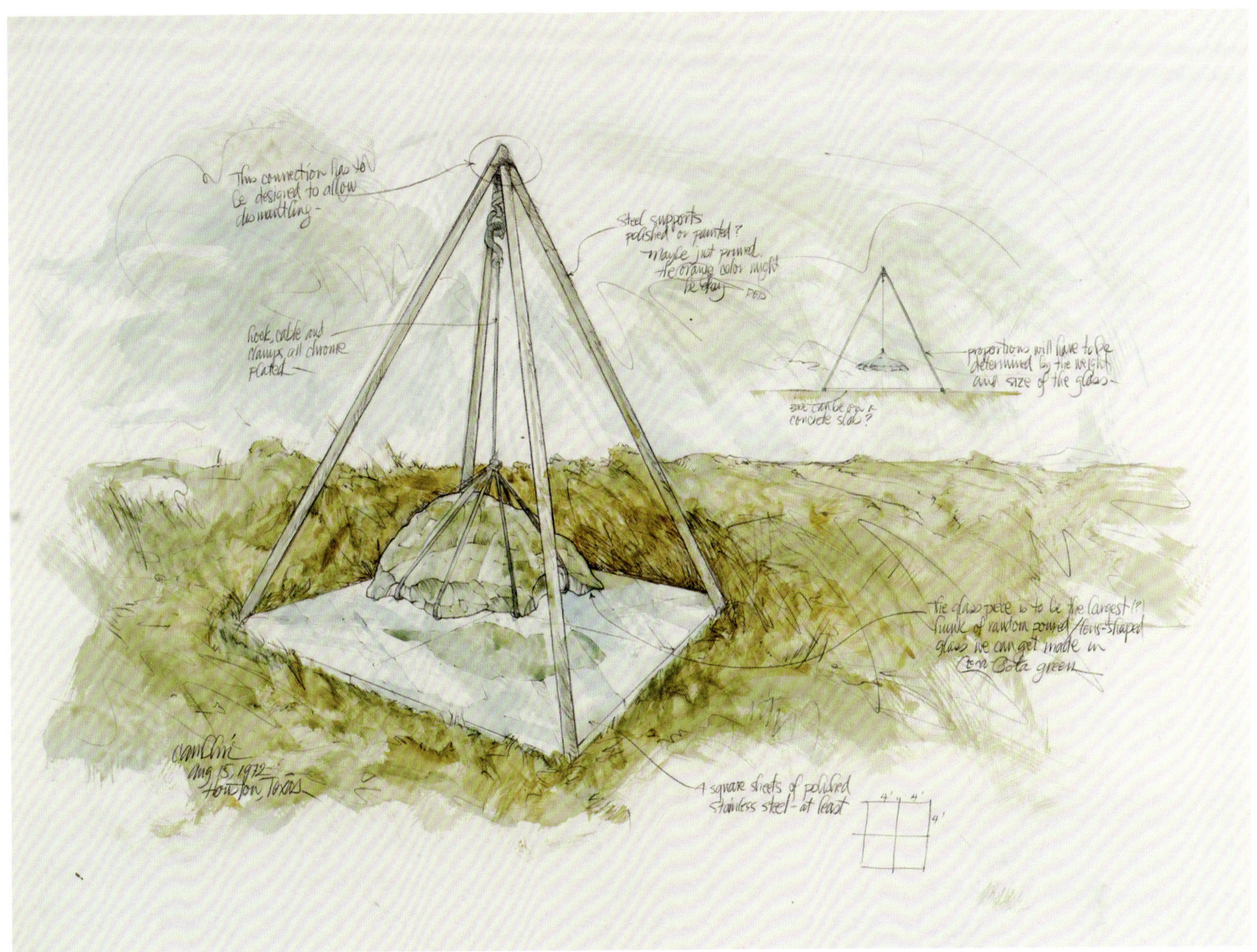

Suspended Glass. A fractured glass weight is suspended over a shiny, stainless steel base, showing Camblin's intrigue with the triangle and the square. *Photograph by Scott Peterson.*

about his one-night stands, and I knew he was married. During class breaks, Camblin's students gossiped about their professor. Many speculated about his love life. Some noted that he always drove his nude female models home after class ended. Most were convinced that he was not faithful to his wife, but none offered proof.

Camblin was happy and busy. His art was selling well. The Menil Collection purchased *Trotline Memorial, 1971.* Rainbow Pie, also created in 1971 sold to

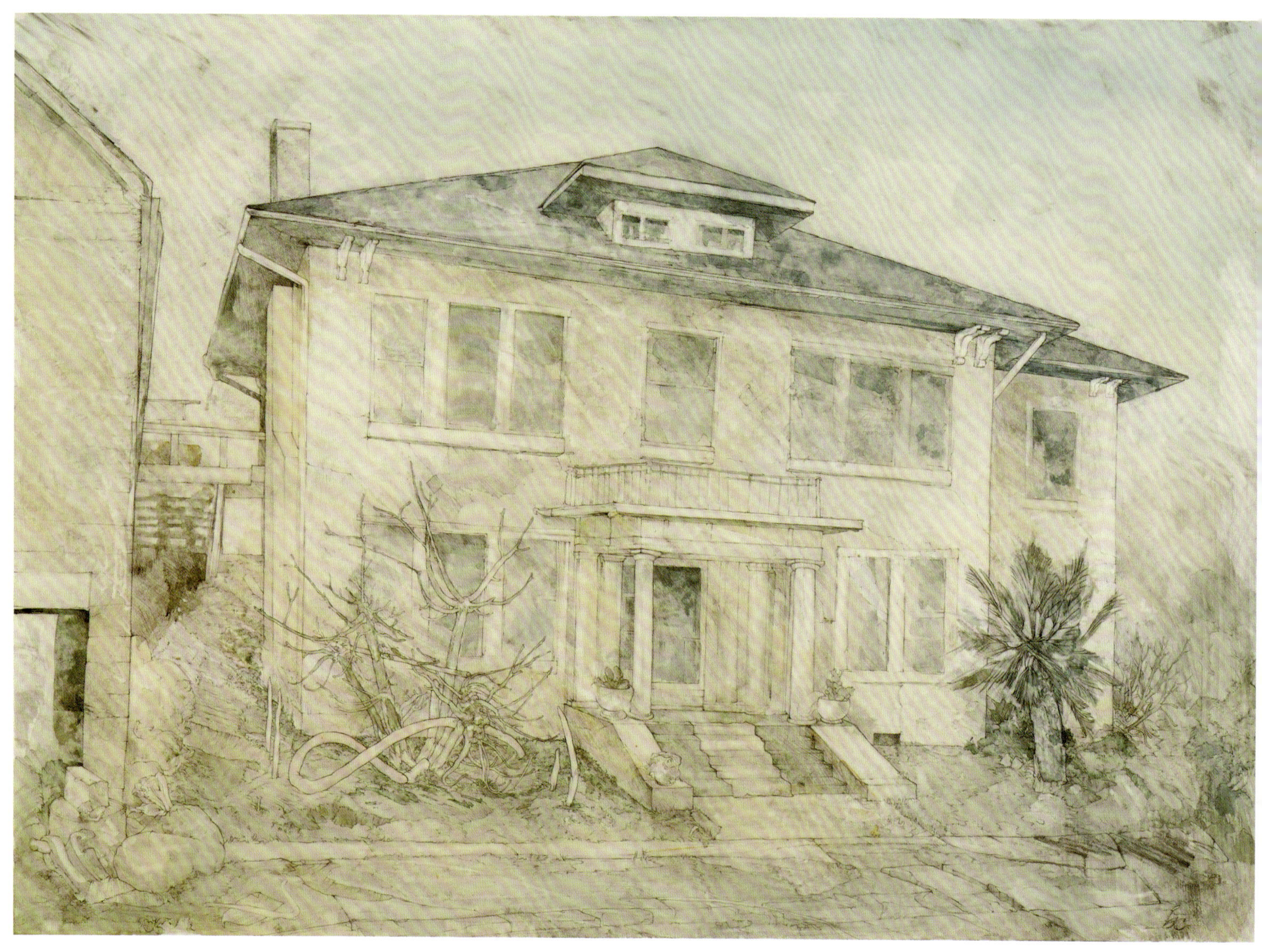

To document his first studio in Houston, Camblin drew *Oakley Street Studio, 1973. Photograph by Scott Peterson.*

a private collector (as did numerous other works), The Modern Art Museum of Fort Worth added the *Galveston Finger Snare, 1971,* to their collection and *Two Versions of the Galveston Deadfall* was purchased by the Longview Museum of Art. Several years later, the Amarillo Art Museum would purchase *It's All Natural,* a William Wiley collaboration, and two pieces by Camblin and Jack Boynton.

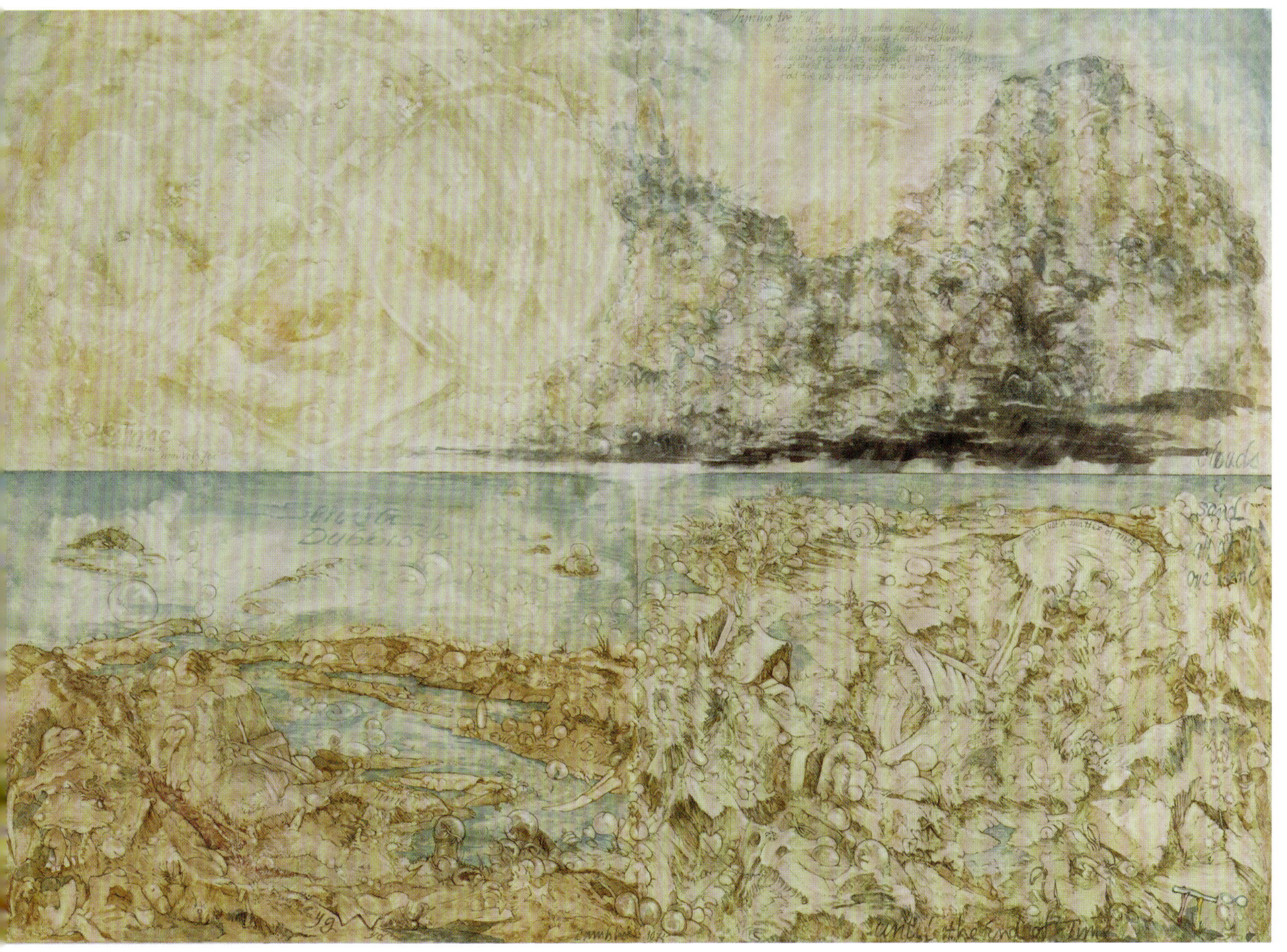

Camblin wrote on the artwork, "Clouds and sand, all at one time until the end of time," 1974. *Photograph by Scott Peterson.*

Hoping his art would offer insight into the maker, I sought out his work in Houston galleries, and I purchased my first work by the artist. In *Logjam*, the viewer's eye discovers a picture plane filled with visual impasses, suggesting a hidden depth. The plethora of fragmentary objects from everyday reality implies a logjam in every man's personal context. The art becomes an expression of the complexity of all our lives. The juxtaposition of unrelated objects in the composition gives the whole a coherent narrative. Camblin enjoyed creating visual puzzles in works that, at first, appear to be traditional landscapes.

During the time the David Gallery represented him, the staff had provided examples of his art, and the gallery owner Dianne David happily shared her views on the artist whom she adored. The dealer reinforced my belief in the complexity of Bob Camblin as well as those who surrounded him. I definitely felt out of my league. Feeling a victim of suspended animation myself, I was drawn to two Camblin works involving suspended objects:

My marital separation turned into a divorce, and I didn't want to complicate my life any further. I was a mother of two, had a job working for Dominique de Menil at The Institute for the Arts, Rice Museum, and was a full-time art history student at Rice. I had enough happening in my life without adding situations that could, and probably would, present serious problems for me. Still, I was smitten. I had never heard anyone talk like Camblin, seen anyone draw like Camblin, or experience anyone flirt like Camblin. He was confident and seemed to enjoy performing for his class. He made everyone feel welcome. He gave me something new to look forward to, and I began to practically count the hours between classes.

At the time, Camblin felt himself in transition. He was in his last year as a university professor, a change that would interrupt the reliable income to which he had grown accustomed. He shared a studio on Oakley Street with Earl, but the small rooms needed upgrading. The space limited his privacy but not his determination. Romantic beginnings are usually enchanting, and ours continually delighted us. We spent hours entertaining each other with our stories. We picnicked, drew in each other's company, visited museums, and drank endless cups of coffee together. We recounted our past histories and talked about our families. He told me of his wife's love for his best friend, Bruno Leon. I had no idea if the story were true or if it were meant to excuse his infidelity. We both opened ourselves to the hormonal and chemical changes caused by the insanity induced by Cupid's arrow. We brought each other enormous joy. Camblin thought about little else and created artwork that reflected his obsession. To his closest friends he admitted that he had fallen in love "hook, line and sinker." As he wrote in a sketchbook, "The world, USA, Texas, Houston and Sand and I are alone and in LOVE. appearing, vanishing, Hide and Seek in our tiny oasis, Playing out the game of balancing ourselves in this fragile moment, out of all times, making it the Best of All the Worlds, both Body and Soul together at last (slowly) and yet . . . 'senza dubbio' I pray."

But Camblin was still a (non-practicing) Catholic and he loved Bonnie, so he remained in his marriage, though he spent less and less time at home, even when I was out of town. Unable to control his preoccupation with our affair, Camblin increasingly focused on the concealed parts of his life. He decided to transform some of his sketchbooks into hidden treasure. He accomplished this by placing his bound drawings, notes, and observations into fairly large wooden boxes that he labeled "sculpture" and constructed, sometimes with the help of others. A watercolor, with pen and ink, records one such box. Titled *Making the Best of It*, Camblin wrote "hand-made or ready-made." Above a watercolored red heart he added, "Sculpture container for Hook, Line & Sinker." On the heart he wrote "?maybe walnut stain and finish as furniture or maybe leave it alone. Que scais-je?" Aside from placing a sculpture inside the box, he planned to add, "A. Letter certifying that sculpture was crated by Don Prince (a local craftsman who specialized in the crating and shipping of fine art) B. Photograph of sculpture C. Bonnie Camblin signed Notary Public statement by Bob Camblin that the crate has been unopened since packing." He added "Pandora's Box sealed by a Prince." He signed "Camblin & Prince or Prince/Camblin." The "sculpture container" was for "Hook, Line & Sinker." Whether or not the box became a reality is not known. The drawing serves to illustrate A. Camblin's interest in leaving behind clues and boxed sculpture; B. his having fallen in love hook, line, and sinker; C. his love of collaboration, this time including his wife, Bonnie and his friend, Don Prince; D. his beginning use of the French *Que Scais-je?*, Middle French for "What do I know?" The phrase was sixteenth-century French philosopher and writer Michel de Montaigne's skeptical questioning of his own knowledge. From this time on, Camblin used the remark freely. He also continued to make and to seal boxes filled with his sketchbooks and sometimes with his art.

CHAPTER NINE

A New Studio and a Collaborative Scaffolding Backyard Project

When space became cramped in the Holding Firm's Oakley Street studio, B E & J found a two-story house on the corner of Sul Ross and Jack Streets in Houston. After moving into the new space in 1974, they fenced the backyard before beginning to build a "three story tower" they titled *An Imaginary Scaffolding for the Renovation of the Statue of Liberty, to be Completed by the Bicentennial in 1976.* Allan Otho Smith,[1] a young artist who helped B E & J with projects, and Mark Batista, a student of architecture at Rice University, also assisted with the creation of the tower. Once completed, the view itself provided the artists, literally, with a new perspective. From a 1974 sketchbook: "Every evening we sit on the tower. Everything is green—the catalpa is higher than we are. The sunsets are again forever incredible. Nothing is ever finished—but summer plans are near."

The tower proved to be very romantic.

Dianne David was pleased with the Sul Ross and Jack Street studio. She decided that bringing potential art buyers to the space would help create business for Camblin and the Holding Firm. Being an affluent and outgoing art dealer, she had access to wealthy friends and collectors, and she introduced her artists to as many as she could. Her best friend at the time was the heiress and shy eccentric, Lollie (Laura) Reed Dyke Jackson. Jackson didn't often attend public openings. Instead

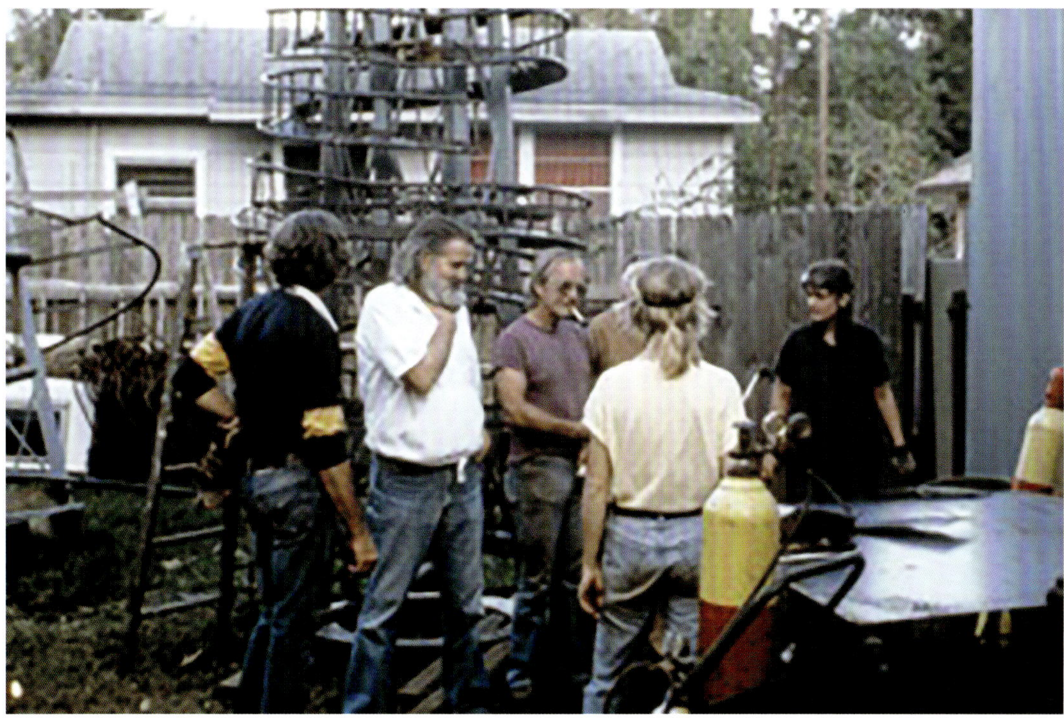

Bob Camblin and David Folkman (in purple shirt) building the backyard tower with assistants.

she invited the local up-and-coming attorneys, artists, patrons, and the occasional famous person to parties at her home. She and Camblin became instant friends and confidantes. Through Lollie's gatherings, Camblin met John Huston, the movie director and actor. He also became friends with some of Houston's brightest legal minds, including the DeGeurin/DeGuerin brothers. Lollie's photographer husband George O. Jackson was an excellent chef and could grill anything to perfection. Together they provided an ideal environment filled with all sorts of entertainment: music, food, drink, and almost anything anyone desired.

Lollie's gatherings were eventful and fun, but private moments with the heiress held the most allure for Camblin. He maintained that Lollie provided the perfect shoulder for his lamentations when I was gone. She commissioned a portrait and spent considerable time sitting for the artist. During the hours that ensued, Camblin and Lollie began their custom of sharing personal beliefs and thoughts.

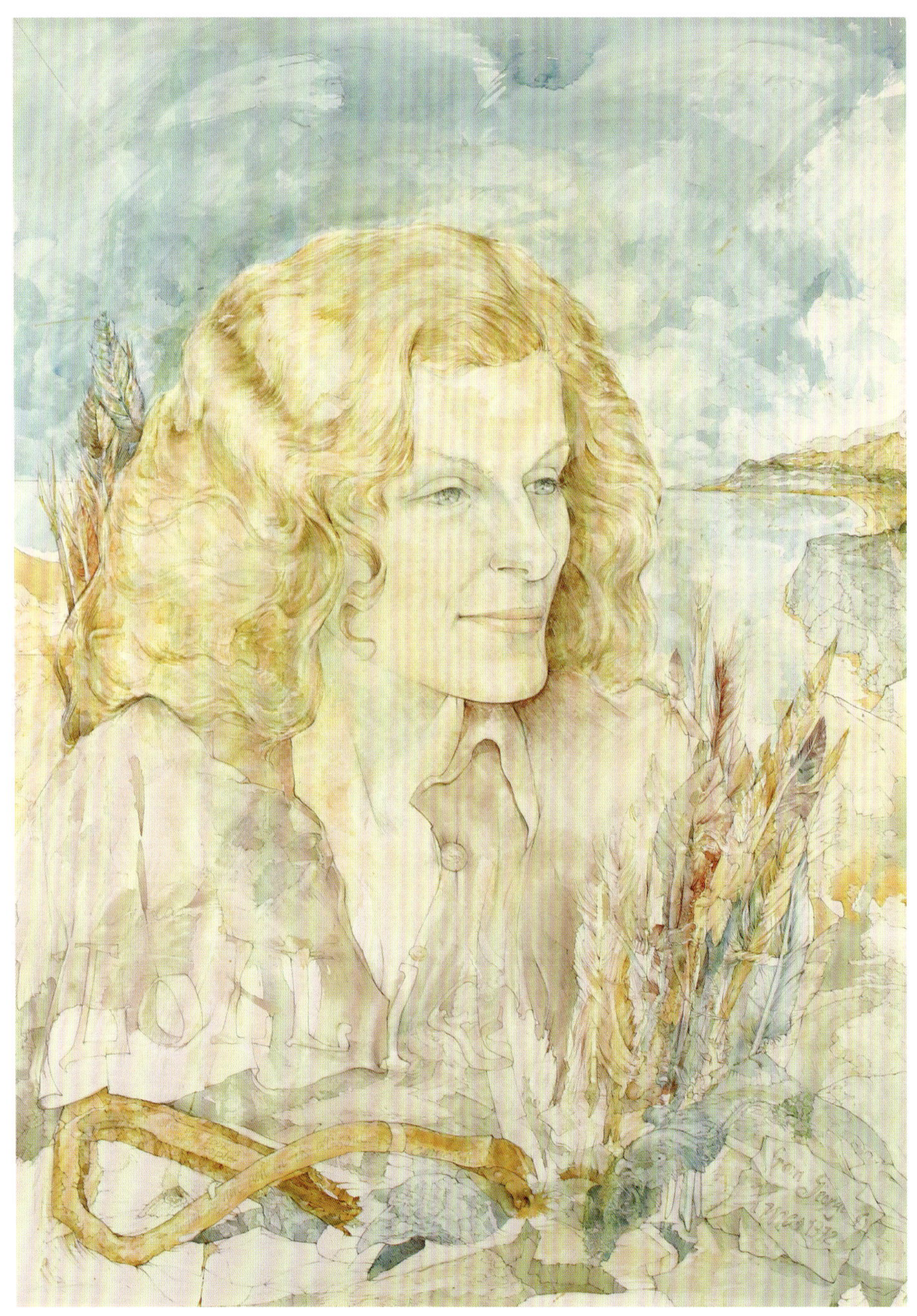

Camblin's *Portrait of Lollie*, on which he wrote: for George O., December 1972. Watercolor and pencil. *Collection of Laura (Lollie) Dyke Reed Jackson Estate. Photograph by David P. Gray.*

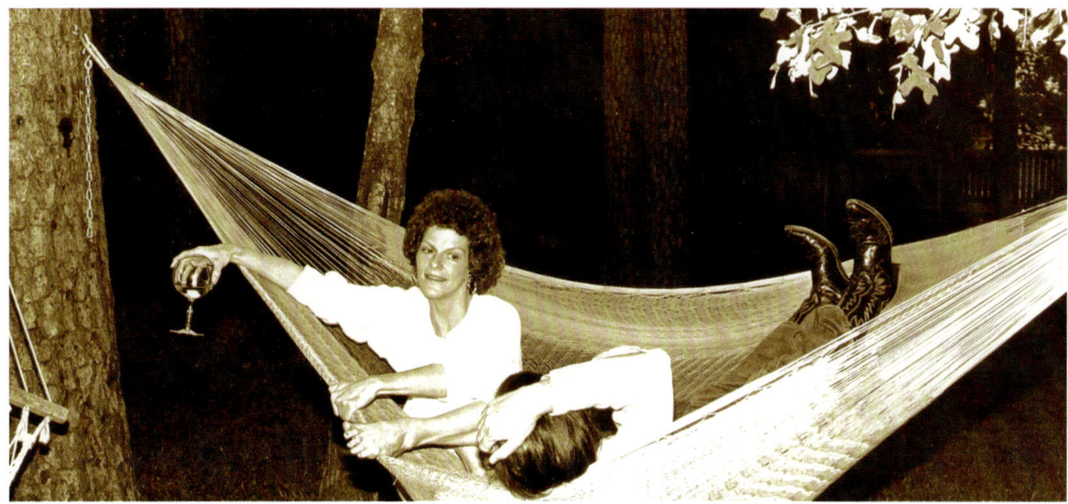

Camblin and Lollie Jackson enjoying the hammocks and a glass of wine in Lollie's backyard. *Photograph by author.*

Their friendship blossomed, often in the company of Lollie's two daughters, Elizabeth and Laura.

Lollie was a bird woman. Her home was filled with cages of colorful parrots, many of which spoke Spanish phrases, but it was the Jackson backyard that was most intriguing. Filled with huge and beautiful bird cages, exotic and rare plants, a free roaming emu, a swimming pool, and numerous hammocks strung between towering trees, the multi-acred outdoor space added exotica to Houston's naturally green environment. Rather than be confined by a house, Lollie and Camblin preferred to communicate outside where Lollie's Scarlet and Blue Macaws flew in and out of the trees while the friends swung in hammocks and sipped good wine or cold Margaritas. The yard provided a perfect respite from stress. The chilled Margaritas helped.

I often accompanied Camblin when he visited the Jackson home. He encouraged friendships between the women in his life, although Lollie and I spent most of our time together in the presence of Camblin. We all were acutely aware of the position we held in the triad: patron, artist, girlfriend. Camblin was the connection; and while Lollie and I both liked each other, a close female friendship was not to be. To observers, but possibly not to Camblin, Lollie seemed smitten with the artist. She listened attentively and responded in a manner that pleased him. Camblin was living his dream, and part of that dream was being and working with friends. Lollie's unique and exotic setting offered a perfect backdrop. She and Camblin remained lifelong friends.

Producing Art and Energy through Collaboration with Friends

Camblin's enthusiasm for working on projects with people he enjoyed resulted in a series of collaborative endeavors. As Janet Landay noted in the catalogue she produced for the exhibition she curated, *Collaborators, Artist Working Together in Houston 1969–1986*, "Over a three year period, and amidst a great deal of discussion, the Holding Firm produced a remarkable amount of art." In 1971–72, the trio began a *Bestiary* series of six highly detailed drawings: a bat, a seal, a composite beast, an anteater, a vulture, and an alligator. Collaboration invigorated Camblin. He drew the outlines of the beasts after which he, Staley, and Tate energetically filled the creatures with doodled sketches of anything and everything that came to mind. All three signed the works. Tate's signature is a heart that overlays Staley's and Camblin's signatures. (Little Egypt Enterprises created lithographs from the drawings in 1975.) The three artists also completed an ink on board drawing of a rhinoceros.

The Holding Firm years were rich with collaboration. Tongue-in-cheek, Camblin and Earl Staley created a *History Test*. First they drew a cubist, Picassoesque image on a blank page torn from a spiral-bound sketchpad. Then they wadded up the drawing, un-wadded it, and pasted it to the left side of a large paper board. To the right of the collaged sketch, they drew a replica image that included the crumpled wrinkles and the torn binding holes, matching the collaged sketchpad page. Not only did the finished artwork challenge the perception of the viewer, the piece also tested the viewer's sense of humor.

In 1971, he and Dallas artist David McManaway worked on a *Jomo Collaboration*—Jomo[2] being the term used by McManaway for his assemblages, which resembled fetishes. The following year, he and Joe Tate created a *Portable Beach Vacation*. Camblin painted the top of a box with a rock, driftwood, and

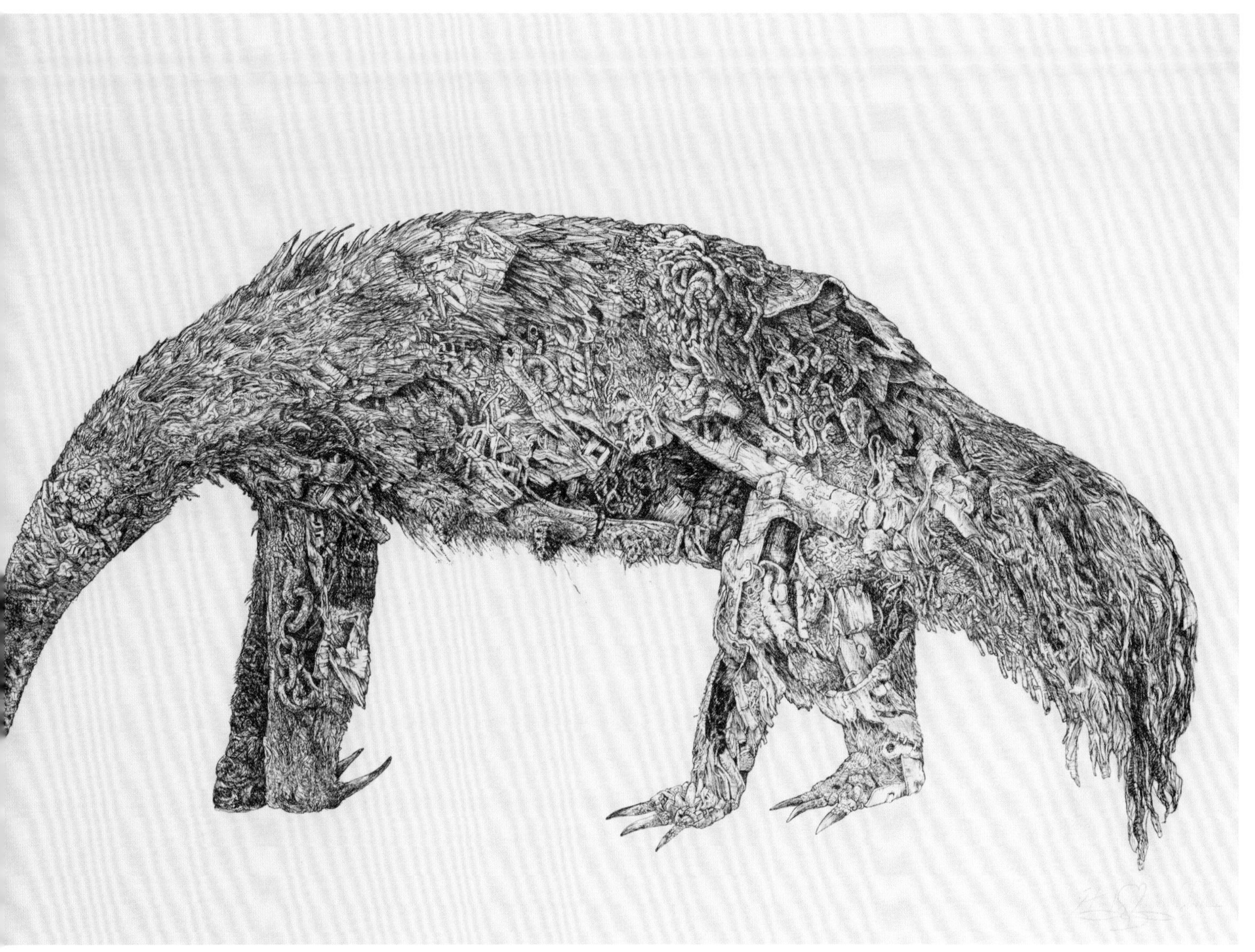

Anteater from the *Bestiary Series* which was created in 1971–72 and printed by Little Egypt Enterprises in 1975. Created by Camblin, Staley, and Tate. *Photograph by Scott Peterson.*

sand. He stenciled ART SIGN under the painting. Inside they place a leather pouch containing the objects depicted on the top of the box, including sand. The Holding Firm, together with "friends," created a large mixed-media piece *Flatonia*, with objects they collected on an outing to the small Texas town. Together with Robert

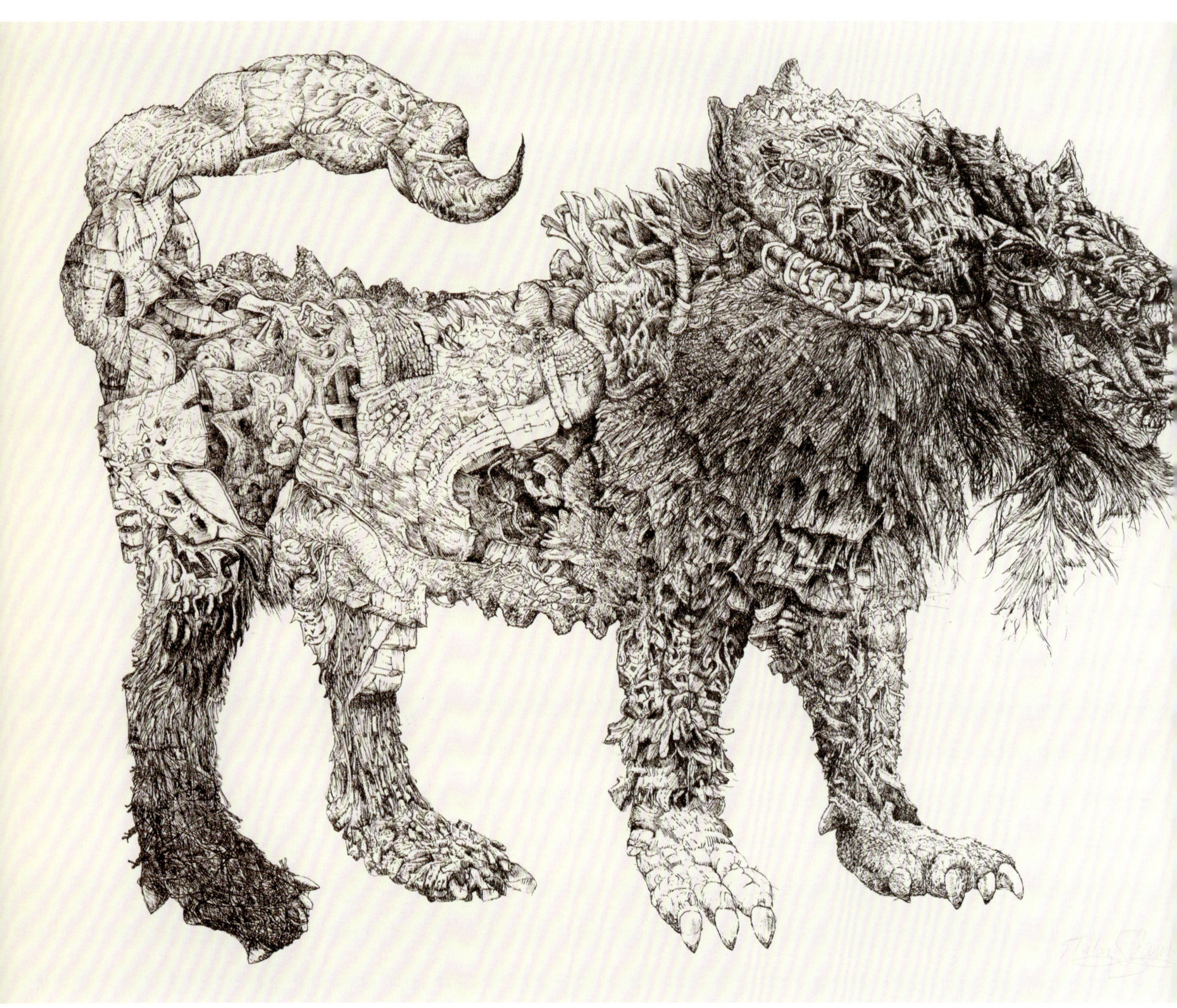

Camblin, Staley, Tate collaborative lithograph, Beast from the *Bestiary Series. Photograph by Scott Peterson.*

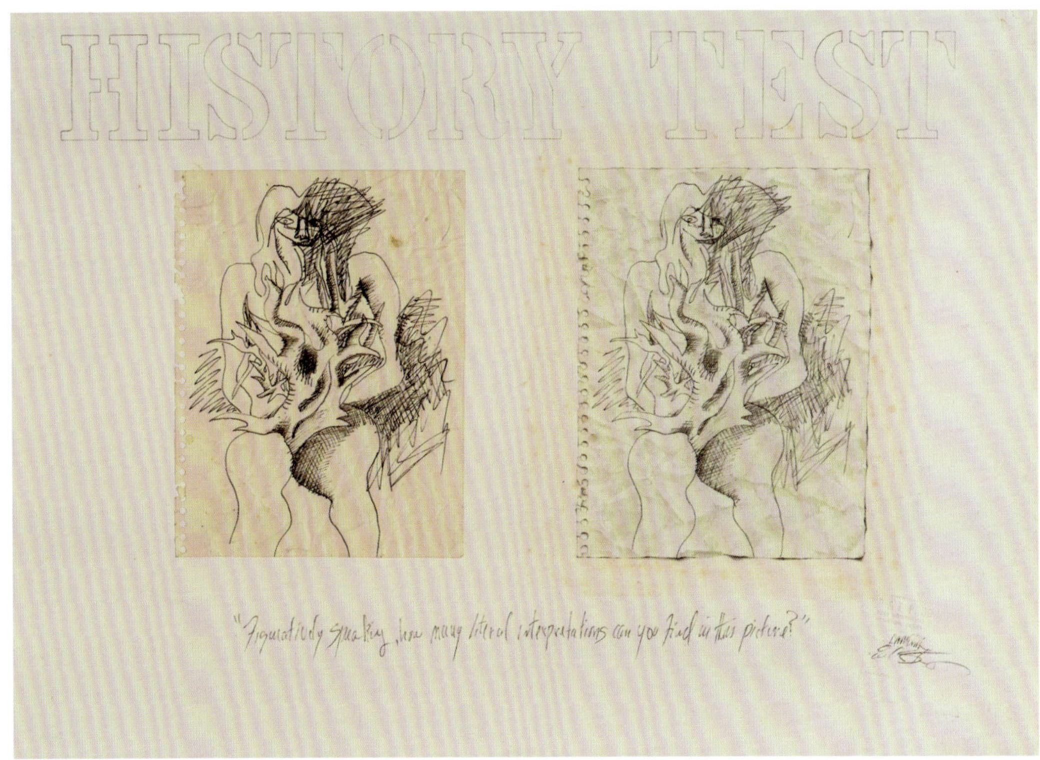

A collaborative drawing/collage by the Holding Firm (Camblin and Staley), *History Test. Photograph by Scott Peterson.*

Heintges, a young student of architecture who worked with photo collage and assemblage, Camblin made his *Figure Four Trap*, using a two-foot by three-foot suitcase, which he covered with rabbit pelts. Inside he embedded a figure four trap with a small rabbit head.

The green backdrop of Houston inspired The Holding Firm to begin painting *en plein air.* Taking advantage of the immediacy of watercolor, they started a series of backyard paintings. Using oil, their artistic endeavors changed to a larger scale and together they painted *Joe Tate's Backyard* on a six-foot by twelve-foot canvas. The Holding Firm's next project involved Ralph Waldo Emerson. They copied the words from Emerson's essay "Self Reliance," etched them into a plate, and hand-colored the prints.

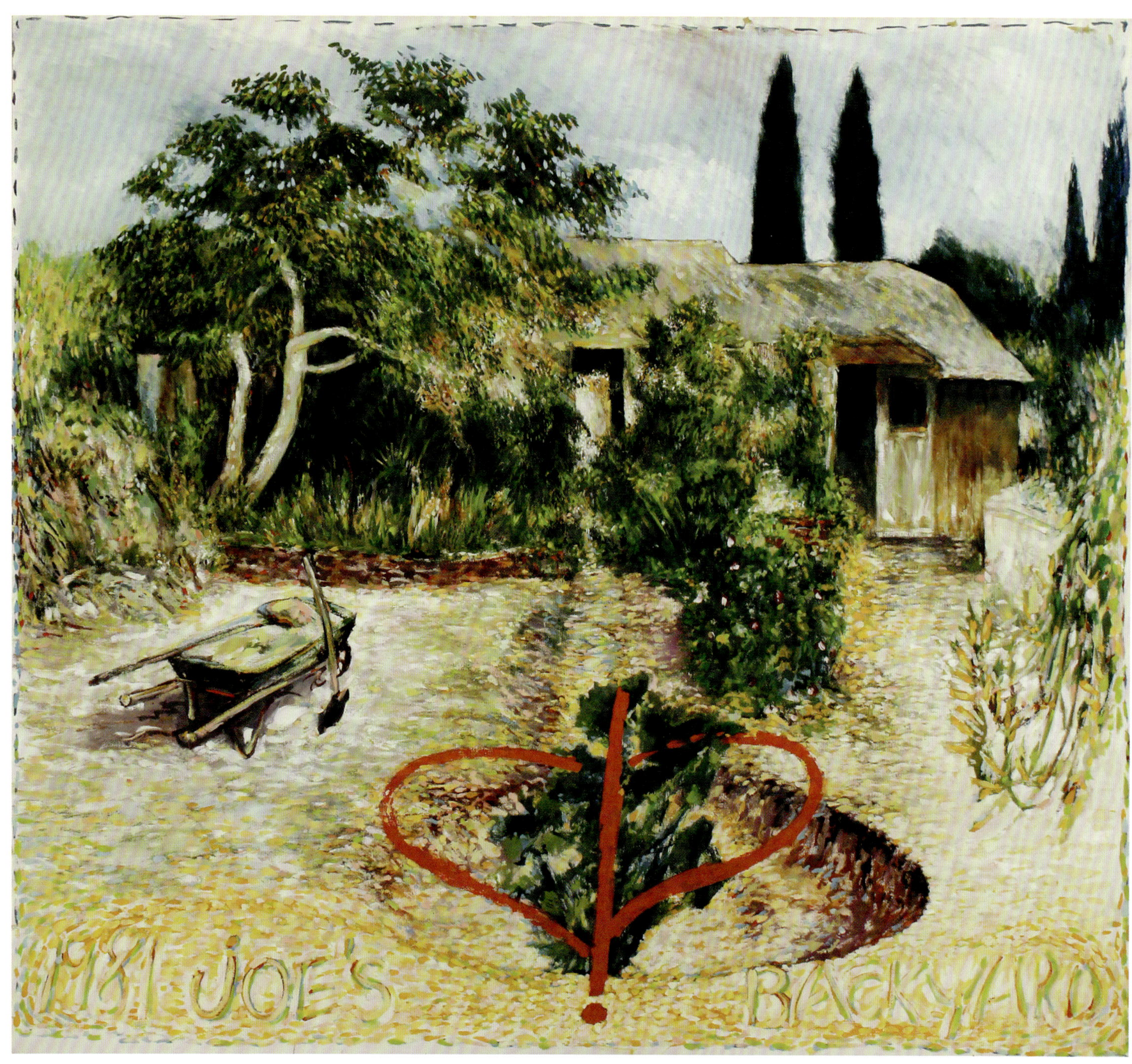

The Holding Firm, which now included Joe Tate, painted several canvases of *Joe Tate's Back Yard*, this example being from 1980. Oil on canvas, 48" X 60". *In the Hannah Collection. Photograph by David P. Gray.*

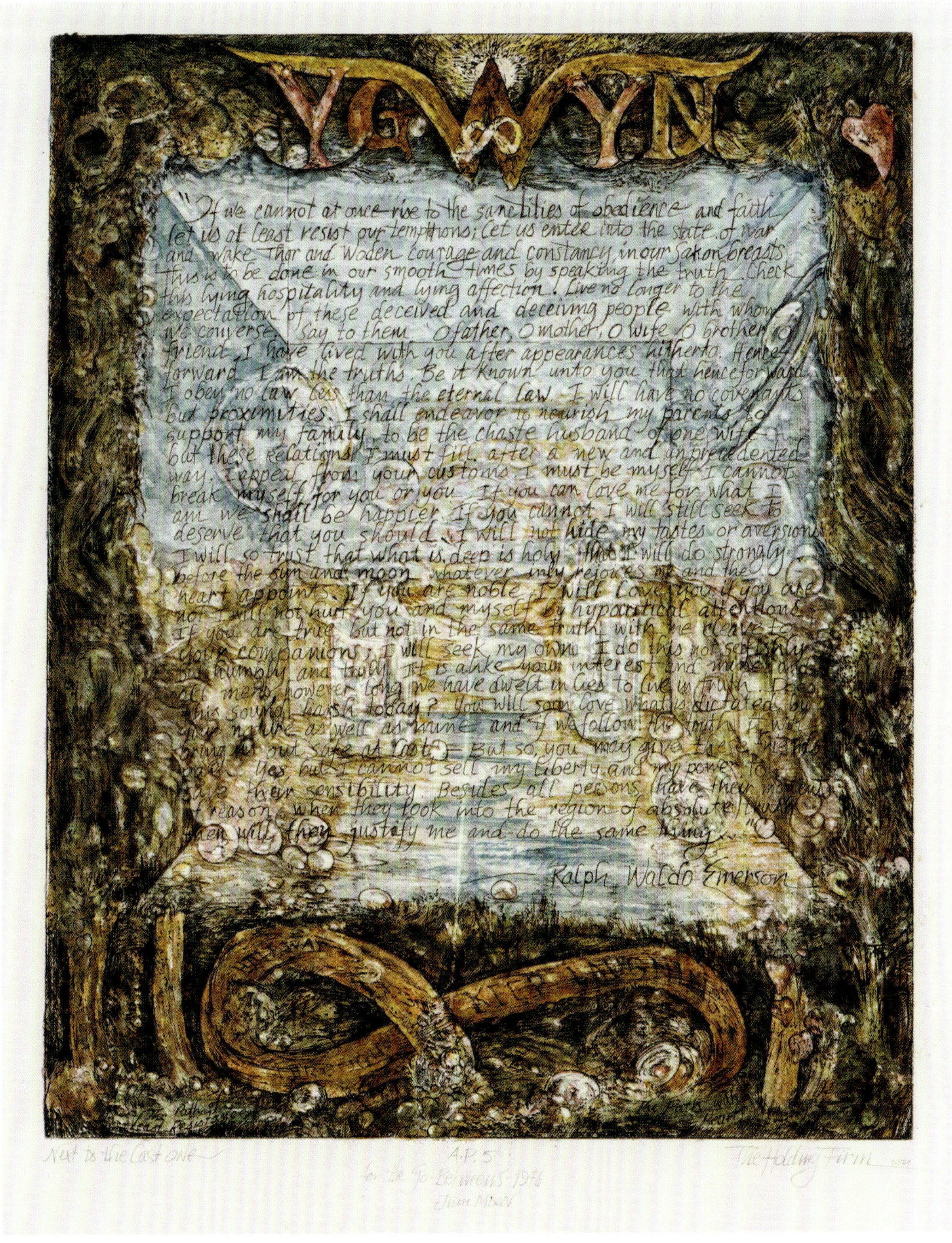

Whenever Camblin felt he needed a dose of common sense, he read Ralph Waldo Emerson. He gave all his friends Emerson's *Complete Works*. He copied the essay "Self Reliance" for this work. *Photograph by Scott Peterson.*

Even though B E & J held firm, Rice dismissed Tate the year following his arrival. Camblin was outraged. He sent a letter to the university president, the dean of students, and to the art department faculty outlining his grievances: "On closing I would like to state that if the University, Faculty and Students permit themselves to be used in this manner knowingly, then as an artist I would have to find this environment unsuitable for my approach to art and teaching which always will be to create 'humanity.' Since art is not only pencils and pigments, but is seeing one's life as an In-Process art form, then I must live it as honestly as I paint."[3]

Four months after his written protest, Camblin received a termination letter from the university president, Norman Hackerman. On the back of the envelope containing the letter, Camblin wrote, but never sent: "Dear Pres. Hackerman, I am in receipt of your letter of April 6th notifying me of the termination of my contract next June 30, 1973. I wanted to thank you for the offer of assistance in finding a suitable position elsewhere, but in a discussion with Prof. Camfield I find that since the department feels that I am valuable to them, I will be offered the post of Artist-in-Residence. Thank you again for your concern."[4]

Shortly after Camblin received Rice's "thank-you-for-your-service" letter, Brooke Alexander traveled to Houston to ask Camblin if he could represent his work at Alexander's eponymous gallery in Manhattan. Camblin accepted. Later in the year, Camblin visited the University of Manitoba, Winnipeg, Canada. The university's architecture department invited him to conduct design labs, freehand drawing classes, and a seminar in the theory of environmental design. Because of the increased interest in his work, Camblin felt vindicated in his defense of Tate.

CHAPTER TEN

Barter Show to Wunderkammer

Dianne David closed her gallery in September 1972. Camblin persuaded her to reopen the exhibition space for a December *Barter Show* of his devising. The invitation announcing the event noted, "Money is no object." David added, "We'll trade his [Camblin's] strange and unusual art for your stranger and unusual objects." Camblin included the art he was willing to barter, and he and Staley conducted the exchanges. Because Camblin lived his belief, "it's all art," he was willing to include the marvelously artless and the artfully commonplace. No differentiation was made between the worthless and the worthy object. He added bartered items to his personal collection of objects, from an Apache wife beater to a nineteenth century medical school training doll of a fetus and placenta. In reference to bartered art Camblin said, "We all have our magic snake skins. We slough them off. That is what I have done."[1]

With an artist's touch, Camblin turned his studios into his personal treasure chests, his cabinets of wonder. Each was a mini-museum much in the way that *Wunderkammers* had been precursors to sixteenth century museums of Europe.

In his blog, Earl Staley wrote about Camblin: "His place was a treasure tableau of the curious and outrageous that he had collected or traded . . . it was as entering a wizard's den."[2]

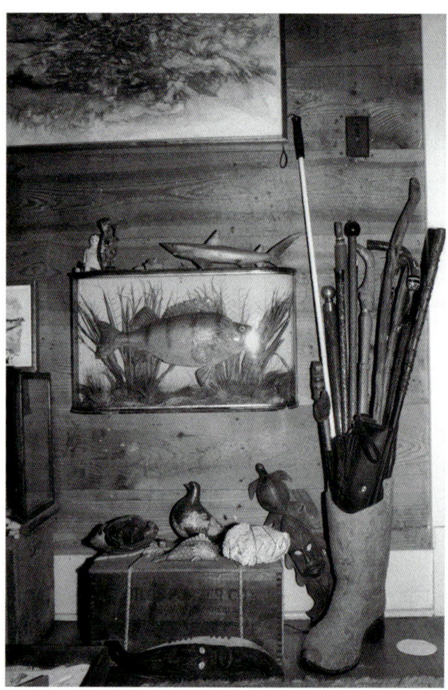
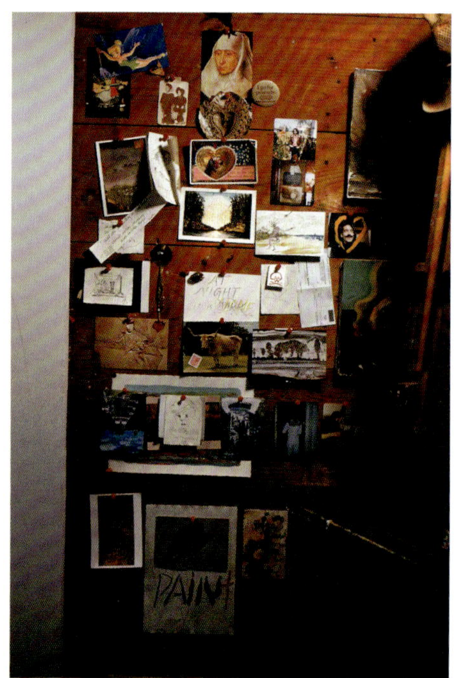
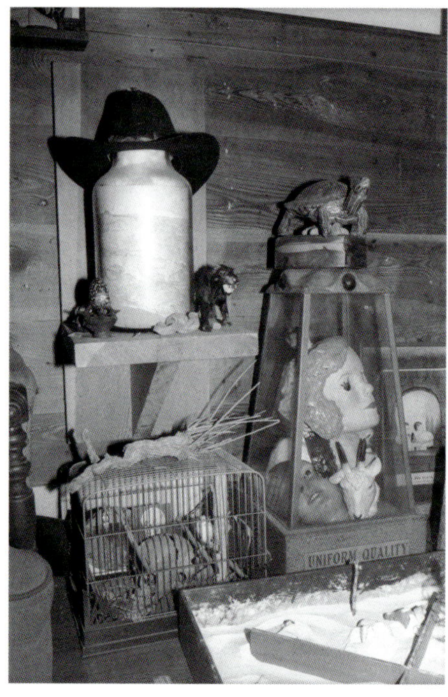
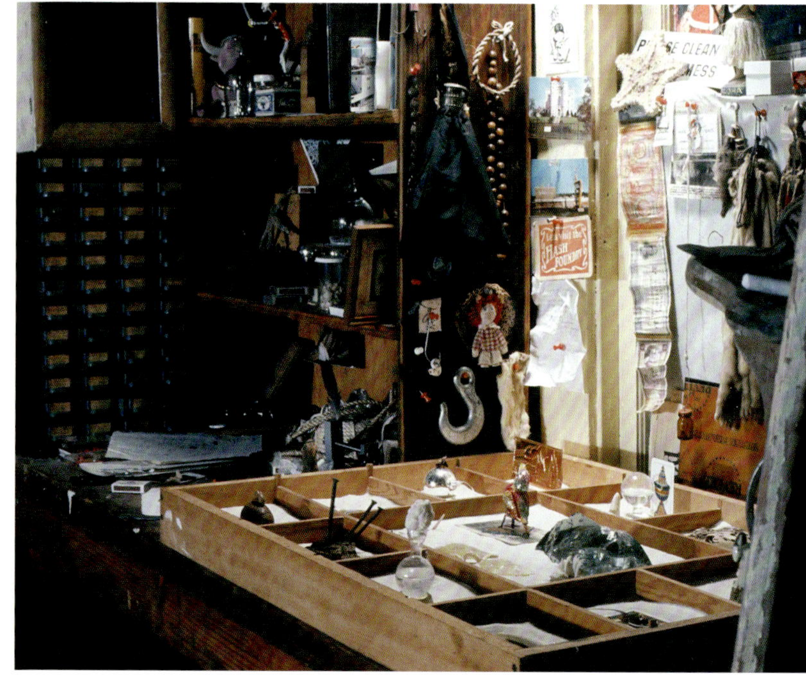

A series of photographs of Camblin's W. Bell Street studio, *all taken by author.*

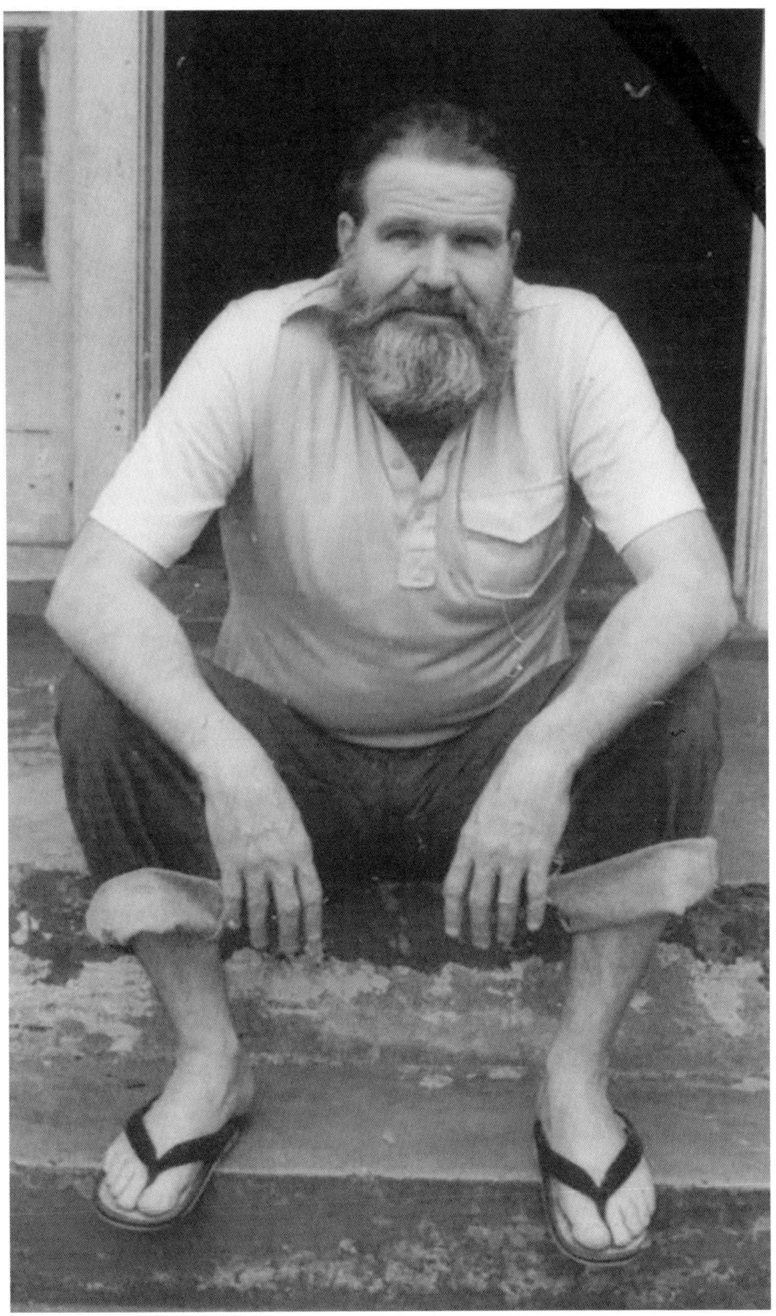

Camblin sitting on the step of the entrance to his West Bell studio. *Photograph by author.*

Reporter Eleanor Freed wrote, "On the mantel piece in Camblin's studio stands an array of strange, strange objects . . . a stuffed armadillo, a head from a wax museum, a penitent rattle, an ivory elephant train, a polished bone, rattlesnake rattle and entire skin, a rather askew set of antlers, bells, fur, feathers, trade beads, an apache wife beater, a walrus tusk, dinosaur fragment, books with escutcheons and other insignia . . . a leather medical school training doll from the nineteenth century complete with fetus and placenta . . . a trunk full of childhood tricks. Much of Camblin's work contains the aura of magic."[3]

Open to the unusual, the bizarre, and the exotic, Camblin amassed collections of disparate objects, most of which he later gave away. He was especially fond of masks and felt he belonged to the world's ancient masking culture. He filled a large glass container from the '30s with antique masks. Eye milagros, nearly big enough to be half-masks, decorated his studio wall along with two large, feathered masks and a Bauta mask from Venice.

In a sketchbook, Camblin noted: "Slowly as a mollusk builds a shell, I find my hideaways and keep in [like a] 'Hermit crab' . . . adding bits and pieces, loving the world and yet never a part of it. There doesn't seem to be any way to change . . . at some levels no one cares and there I float—watching the caring that does go on in the world. The poor can do nothing except care verbally and watch—and so I join them in our helplessness and watch . . . but the children, always the children, may be escaping, perhaps not, to the future—whatever it is . . ."

Selective about whom he let visit his hideaways, the "Hermit Crab" enjoyed friends but was unwelcoming to the uninvited. He found pleasure in his private, treasure-strewn refuges. The "bits and pieces" he collected reflected his love of the natural world even though he felt secluded in his shell. In the mid-1970s, he included some of his favorite small objects in sandboxes. He built compartmentalized wooden boxes or used old cigar boxes or Japanese jewelry boxes and filled them with a fine, white sand into which he would bury his "bits and pieces." Most boxes included a fine bristled paint brush with which to brush away the grains of sand, revealing the hidden riches. He gifted me with three of his mysterious sandboxes.

CHAPTER ELEVEN

Figure Fours, Fish, and Friends

Besides collaborating on the *Figure Four Trap* with Robert Heintges, Camblin created a series of paintings based on the trap. He and his father had gone on camping trips and had built their own rabbit traps. Camblin excelled at the task, thus beginning his fascination with deadfalls. As an artist, he was interested in the figure four trap's simplicity, visual clarity, and symbolism: since traps mean death for the trapped and conversely mean life for the trapper, Camblin added a cartoonish "hare trigger" to his trap drawings, diluting its menace. By adding a decapitated rabbit head to the object of death, he reversed the usual symbolism of a hare's fecundity.

Camblin found the figure "4" very versatile. For him, four was a number, a subject, a glyph, a stand-in for the word *for* and a reference to works of other artists. He was intrigued by the *trompe l'oeil* (fool-the-eye) paintings of American painters John Frederick Peto and William Michael Harnett, whose forgotten works had been rediscovered the same time Camblin had enrolled at KCAI. Harnett and Peto created and "trapped" (with illusionistic pinned strips of cloth tape) envelopes and postcards to the vertical plane of the background walls in their paintings. A particular work by Peto may have captured Camblin's imagination: *The Cup We All Race 4*, ca. 1900.[1] Rather than paint a number as the subject[2] of a work of art, the possibility exists that he preferred and adopted Peto's number-for-word substitution in the written text of his own watercolors.

Perhaps inspired by all the postcards Camblin received from me during my travels, as well as by Peto and Harnett's use of painted postcards and envelopes for their paintings, he began painting compositions filled with many postcards of his own creation. Camblin took the postcards a step further: he pinned real postcards to many of his works. For numerous years part of his *modus operandi* involved attaching postcards to artworks, often painting over the postcards.

While making figure four traps, he worked on another series of watercolors with fish as the subject, and many of his fish are out of water. He drew them in surreal boxed landscapes[3] and created dioramas for single fish. He also made sculptural wall hangings from lead or leather strips that were formed into mounted, open-mouthed bass heads. The materials he used resulted in an object that appeared closer to a fish mask than a fish portrait. Camblin's interest in fish began in childhood during fishing excursions with his father. He described a trip to Oklahoma's Lake Spavinaw:

What is the thing that makes your heart jump, your stomach knot, the hair on your neck bristle at the knowledge that without speaking you know that, *senza dubbio* [without doubt], for some RNA/DNA reasons, you are "triggered" by a set of experiences: A lake in the early morning sunrise, fishing with my father. The orange sky/water with black shadows and only silhouette edges and void. The silence, trying to move making no noise or even a ripple to disturb the glass—small ripples of fish feeding, bird sounds, silence and small discreet fishermen sounds, etched deep. Fog burning off—sunrise.[4]

The writings of Richard Brautigan also spurred Camblin's interest in fish. He was especially taken with the writer's *Trout Fishing in America.*[5] Camblin and Brautigan were fellow travelers who were both part of the countercultural path of the times. Brautigan did with words what Camblin did with drawing. The two artists drew from their personal visions using unconventional images and metaphors. Both employed unexpected connections. Their works invite yet resist analysis or standard categories except in the broadest sense. Camblin liked the writer's disconnect between anecdotes, an example being when the character named Trout Fishing in America mistakes an old woman for a trout stream:

"Excuse me," I said. "I thought you were a trout stream."

"I'm not," she said."[6]

Brautigan and Camblin both understood the attraction of the absurd and the significance of masking identities.

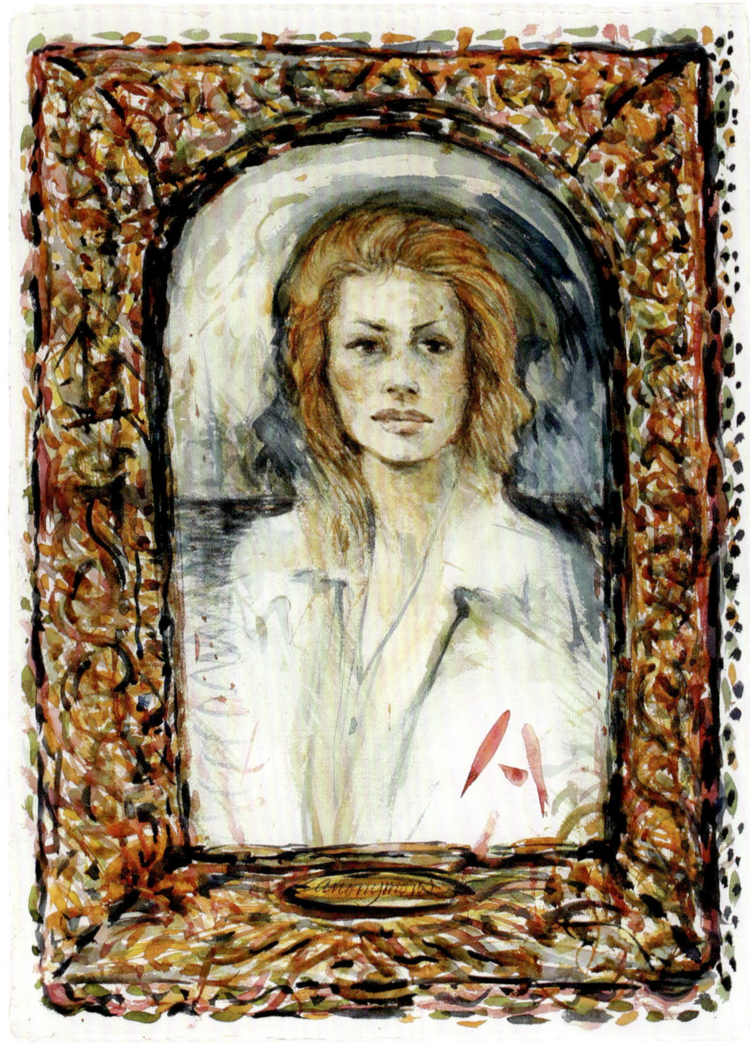

Portrait of Annie DeGuerin, c. 1970s. Watercolor on paper, 29.5" X 21.5". Annie's beauty was captured by Anonymous in both her obvious portrait but also in the profile near her hair on the right. *Collection of Annie DeGuerin. David P. Gray photograph.*

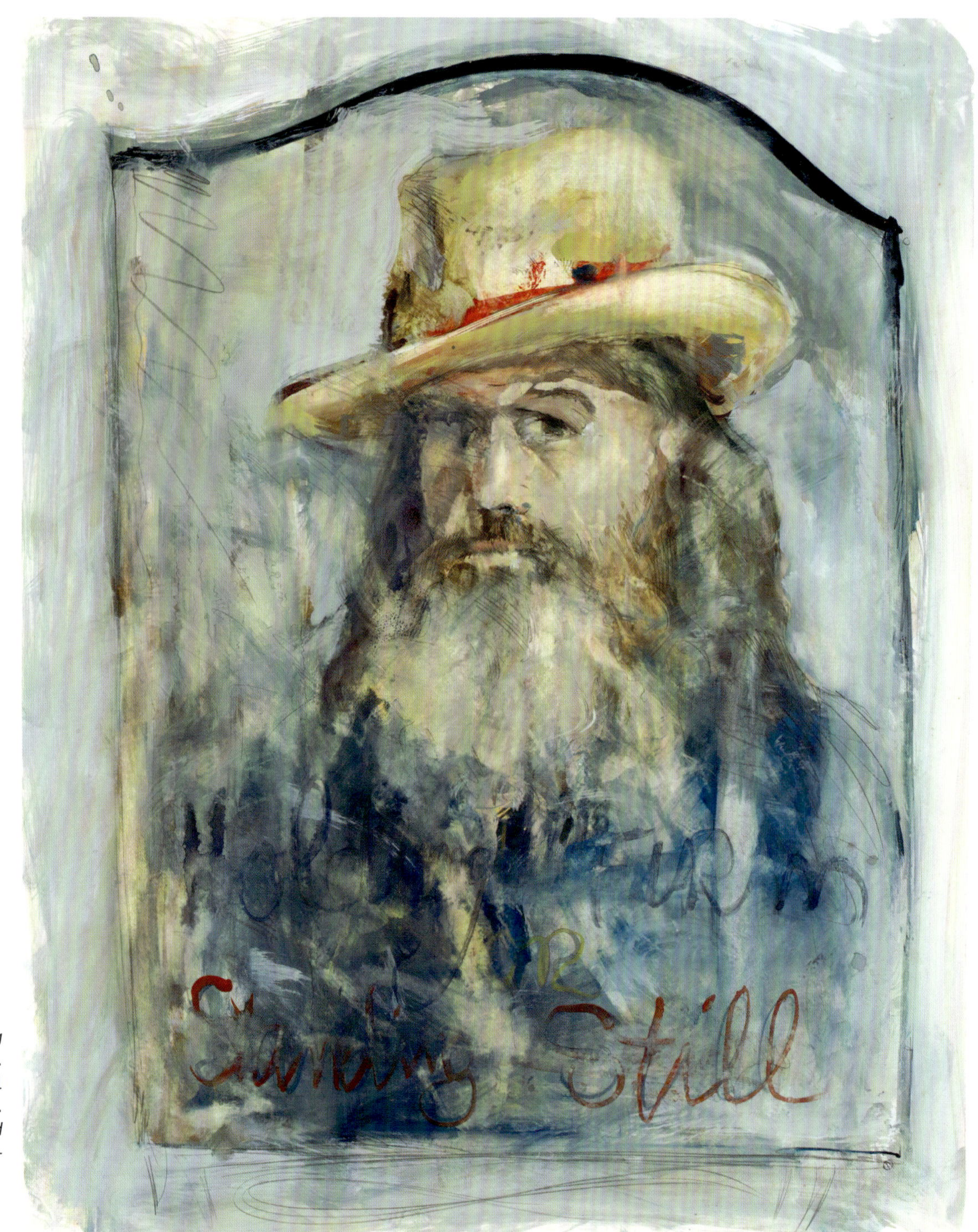

Holding Firm or Standing Still (Self Portrait), 1977. Watercolor and pencil on paper, 29" X 23". Collection of Sandra and Cruser Rowland. Photograph by Scott Peterson.

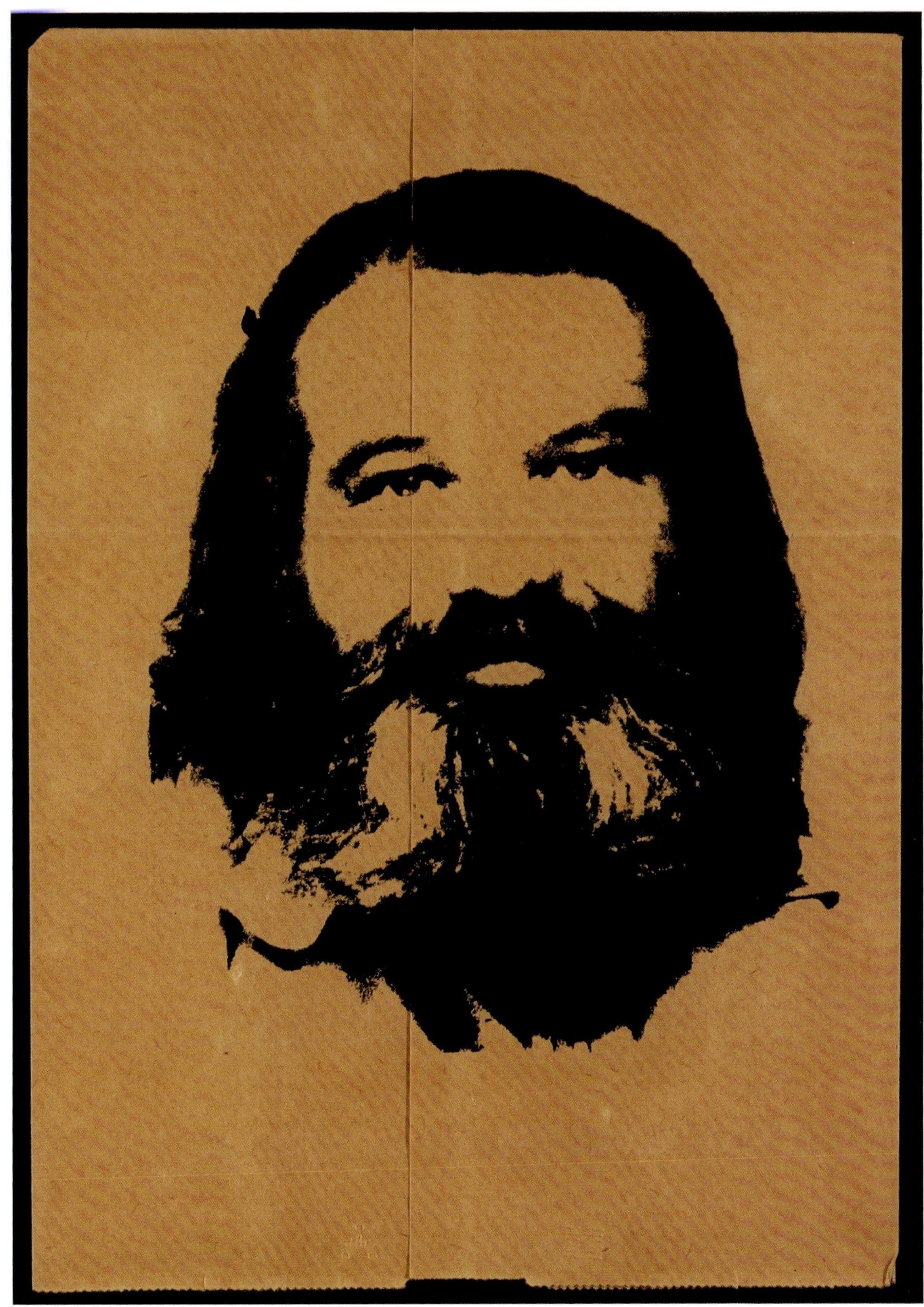

Bob on a Paper Bag, early 1980s. Allan Otho Smith printed the seriograph, 17" X 12". *Penny Cerling and Jeff Skarda Collection.*

A remnant from a Camblin watercolor evidences a link with another artist, Robert Rauschenberg (1925–2008). The saved fragment shows a fish with its head in a ring, reminiscent of the car tire around the midsection of the angora goat in Rauschenberg's *Monogram*, 1955–59. The incongruity of a round object encircling the body of a living creature, fish or goat, would seem to suggest Rauschenberg's influence even though no other evidence exists.

During the late sixties and through the eighties, Camblin continued creating portraiture, mostly of friends. Occasionally he would contemplate the confrontation of his own image and paint a self-portrait. Sometimes artist friends would create a portrait of Camblin.

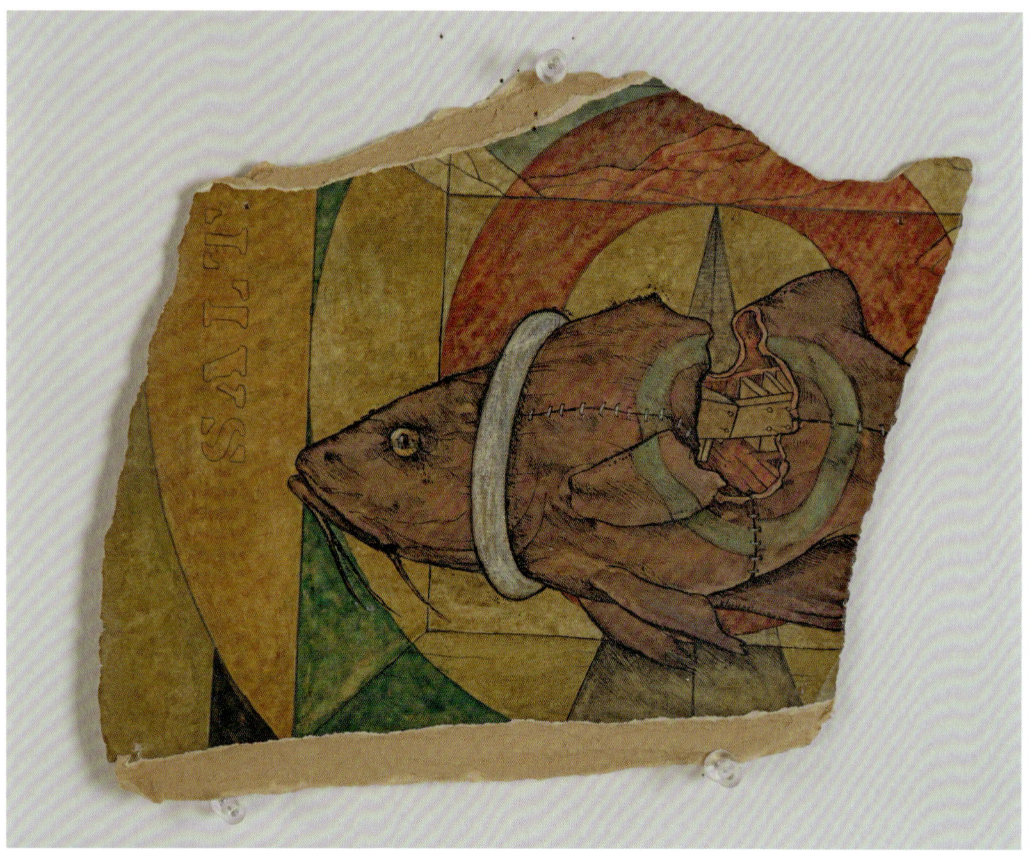

Rauschenberg fragment

CHAPTER TWELVE

The Aesthetic Appeal of Unemphatic Landscape

The Holding Firm's collaborative landscapes and the background landscapes for Camblin's trap and fish series evolved into his main preoccupation from the mid-seventies through the 1980s: landscape. The Texas landscape is unemphatic except for the vistas of Big Bend National Park, the state's largest park, located in a remote part of the Chihuahuan Desert in Far West Texas. Camblin visited Big Bend with Jack Boynton and Earl Staley. Except for a few small paintings of West Texas, mountains did not factor into Camblin's work, even though he reminisced about the Wasatch Range in Utah and the Chisos Mountains[1] of Big Bend. As an avid camper since his childhood, Camblin explored and camped out in Oklahoma, Kansas, Florida, Illinois, and Michigan. His time in each state's hill country gave him confidence in his survival skills. Living in the Rockies made him doubt his ability to overcome high altitude hardships. Perhaps the Rockies were too muscular to consider as stand-alone subject matter or as a background for his art. Camblin said the Rockies sucked the air out of his work because the presence of the Wasatch Range dominates everything around it. Whatever the reason, the grand mountains did not inspire his paintings. Ponca City has some rolling hills, but the tallest point in the state is Black Mesa in the extreme northwest corner of the Panhandle. With an elevation of 4368 feet, the mesa rises a mere 142 feet above the altitude of Salt Lake City. Camblin did not want mountains to overpower his more intimate creations.

Growing up as a flat-lander may have made the looming presence of the Rockies somewhat troubling when he lived in Salt Lake City. Not wanting to document real geographical places, Camblin's landscapes were his own creations. Because Ponca City shares a similar topography with Houston, Camblin understood the issues of

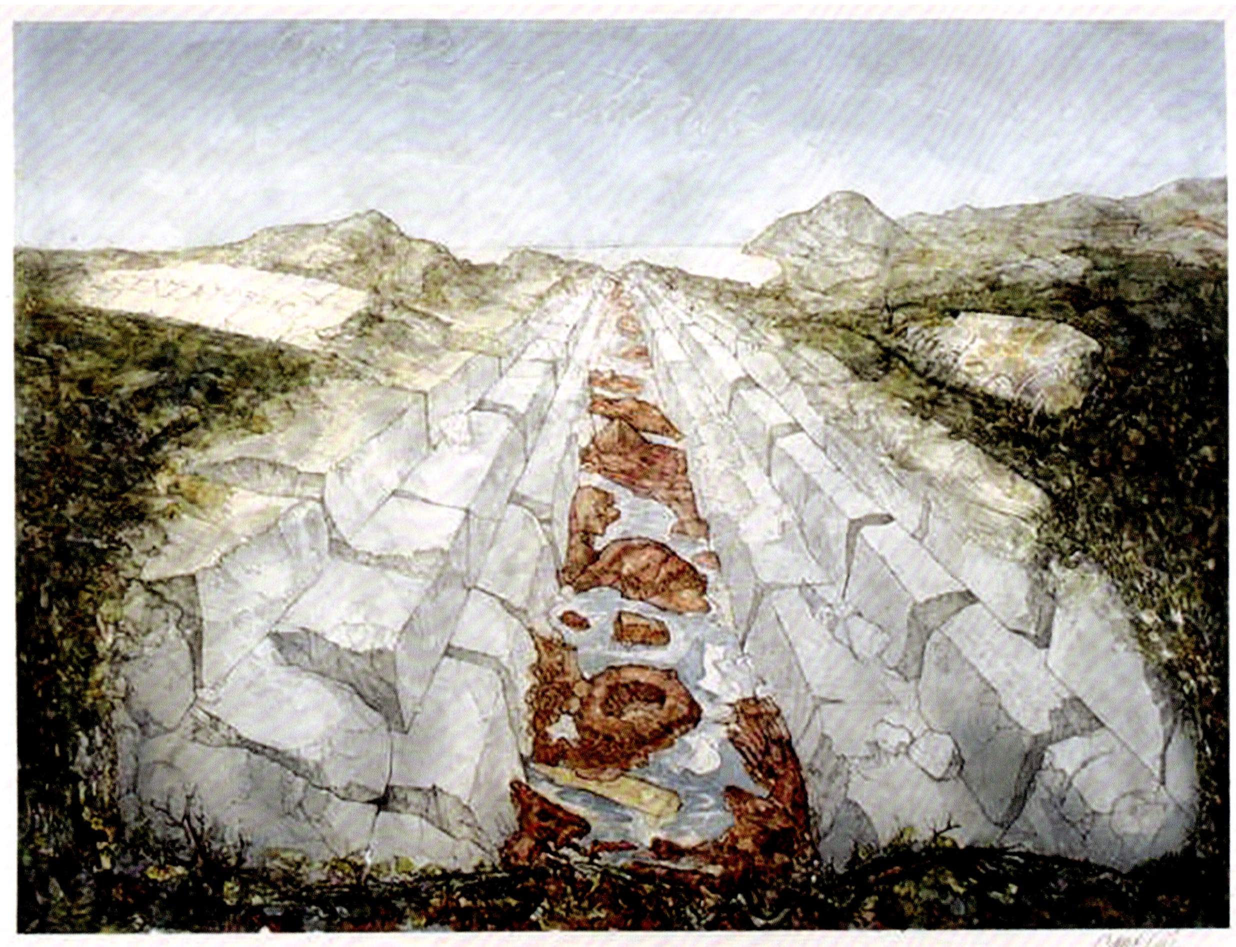

It's All Natural, 1979. Watercolor on paper, 22¼" X 30¼". *Amarillo Art Museum Collection.* A quizzical, incomplete, man-made, sharp edged stone aqueduct in the middle of nowhere, strewn with unidentifiable red objects could be considered "all natural" in a world filled with conscientious, if neurotic, humans.

flat land: drama comes from the sky, and the placement of the horizon determines perspective as well as what can be depicted in a landscape.

Camblin created self-referential landscapes with gully washers, man-made canals, and valleys[2] largely using traditional perspective. None of his landscapes contain complete figures. He revived a Manifest Destiny trope by painting landscapes devoid of humans, creating a record of an idealized nature without corruption and sin. Prelapsarian longings had been a theme in Western thought since the Enlightenment, but Camblin's Arcadian depiction of innocence is skewed. He did not try to depict paradise before original sin. His landscapes may be empty of figures, but they are filled with manmade detritus and body parts, including mask-like faces. Zeroing in on the details of the nature created by Camblin reveals that his landscapes need to recover from man's neglect and manipulation before they can be considered Arcadian.

In the catalog for *Contemporary Landscapes*,[3] Jim Edwards captured Camblin's open approach to collaboration: "I doubt he [Camblin] would consider himself a landscape painter in the traditional sense. Of the three paintings included in this exhibition, two were done in San Jose, California, at the home of his friend, the painter Joe Tate. In both 'Joe's Backyard' and '507 Bascom—The Studio' Camblin depicts the home's front and backyard with lush color and paint application. The yard has a domesticated wildness about it, seemingly not so much for lack of care as for a preference for the untamed. A narrative quality creeps in as titles are written across the base of the paintings. At nearly dead center of '507 Bascom—The Studio' Camblin has collaged a post card to the surface of the painting only to paint over it. Energy and a robust nature breathe through these works. They are in a true sense collaborative in that Camblin asked Joe Tate to also contribute to them. Without knowing Bob Camblin we can still imagine him handing a loaded brush to his friend and saying something like 'Here, Joe, you do something to it.'"

Camblin also experimented with the landscape genre's format and created works that were complex in their structure and dense in their imagery. He drew visual and intellectual puzzles. Defying visual logic in some of his rectangular compositions, Camblin often incorporated a curved wall over which he drew a landscape background with traditional one-point perspective. Other watercolors depict

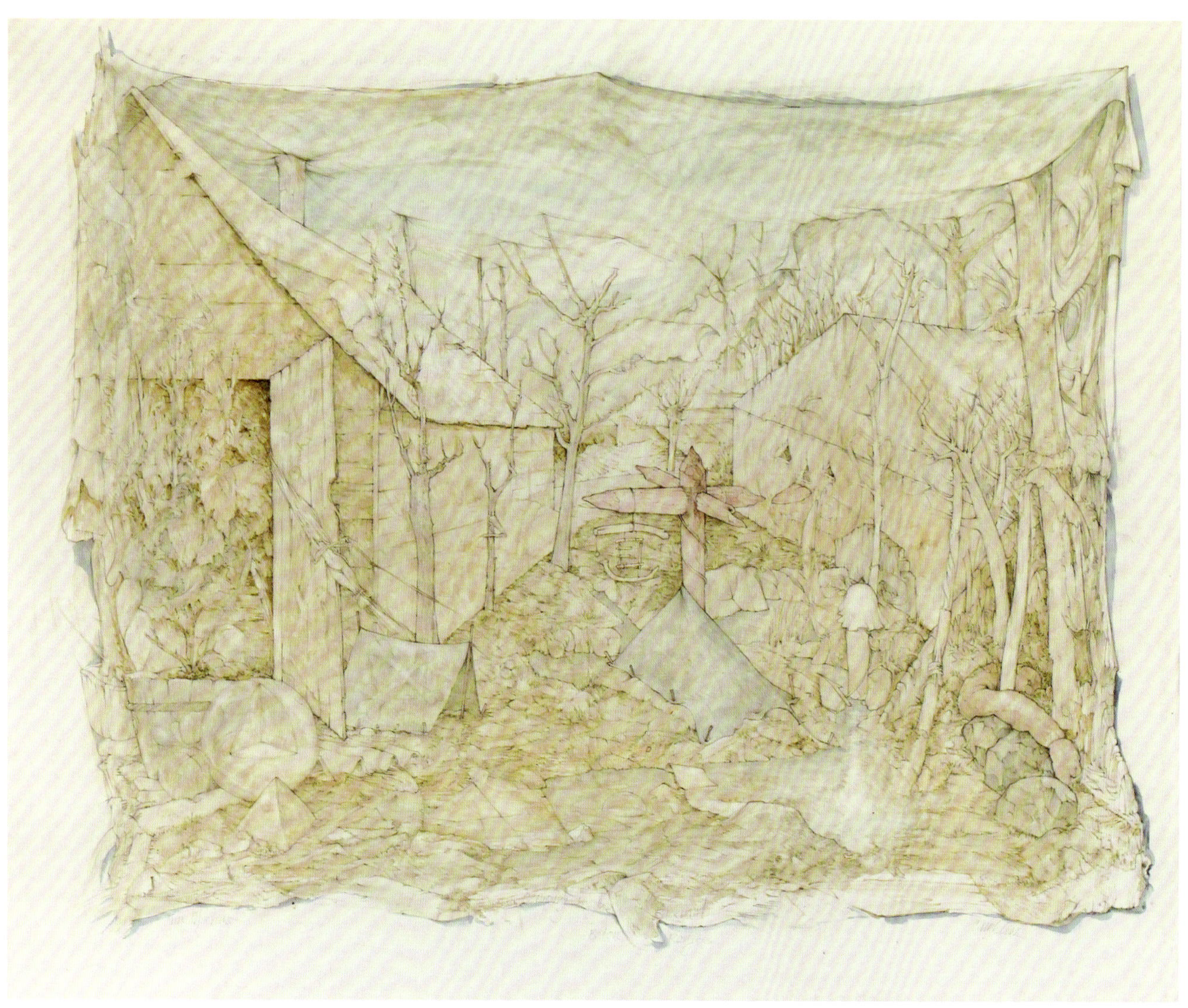

Time Machine, Camping in the Backyard, c. 1970s. Watercolor and pencil on paper, 33" X 30". *Dick and Janie DeGuerin Collection.* Camblin incorporates a draped curtain format that casts shadows under the edges. Leafless trees appear to be piercing the sky curtain, a pumpkin face with tongue out, and a sign post create a delightful if perplexing back-yard. *Photograph by David P. Gray.*

an incongruous, corner-pinned drapery background on to which he drew land-scapes with defined perspectives that do not conform to the folds of the drapery. He sometimes drew the horizon just below the top of his watercolor paper. Other times he painted his landscape in a box, often with multiple vanishing points;

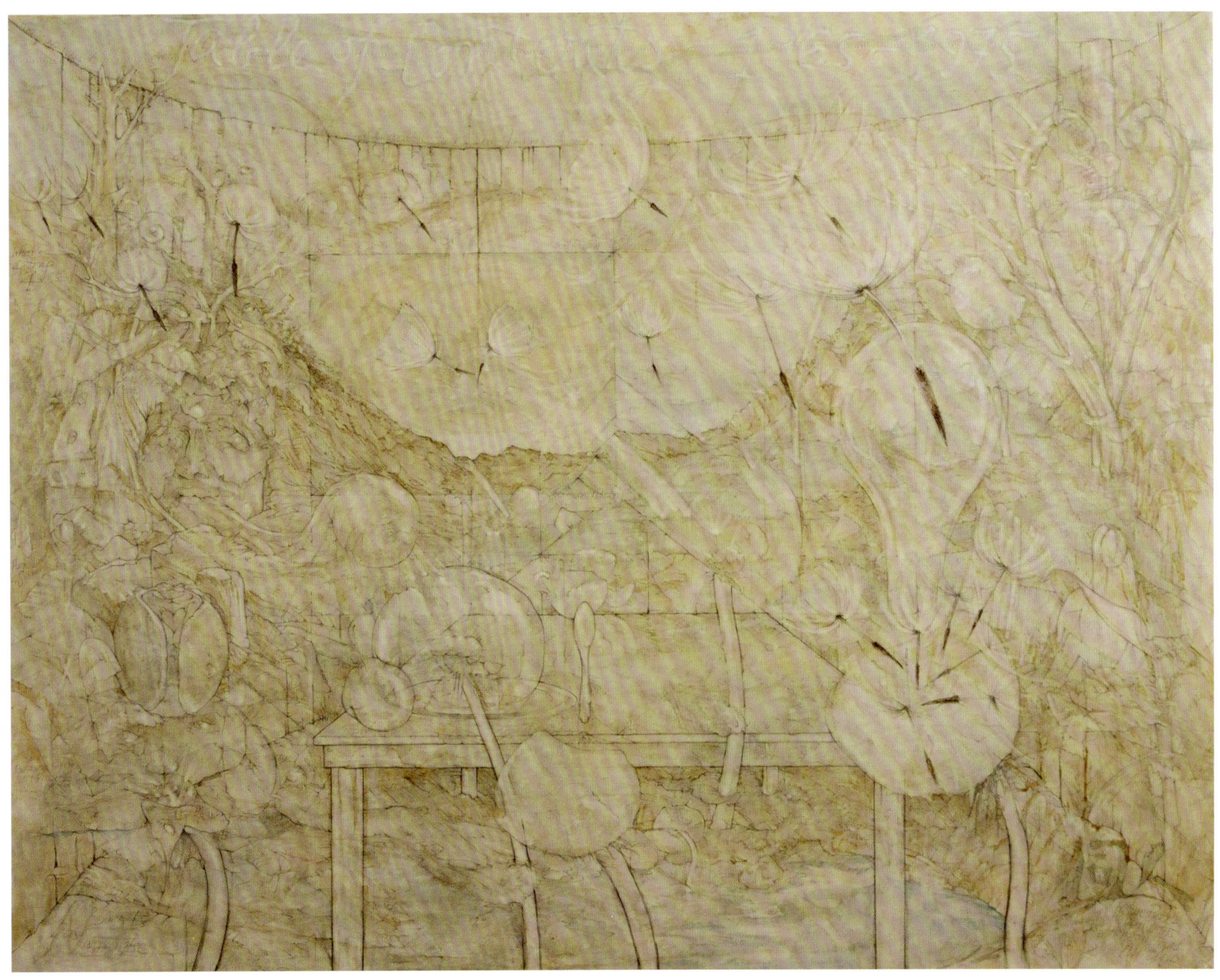

Table of Contents, 1975. Watercolor and pencil on paper, 21" X 27" A mysterious face on the left appears to be blowing bubbles. A table, painted with one point perspective, recedes until it disappears in the background turning the table top into a triangle. *Photograph by Scott Peterson.*

occasionally he used no horizon or vanishing point. Instead, he filled the entire surface with bits and pieces of individual drawings, creating a surface that roils with flotsam and jetsam. He did also paint conventional landscapes, especially those from his *Backyard* series.

At the close of 1972 and continuing through the beginning of 1973, the Houston Chamber of Commerce Cultural Affairs Committee organized *Main Street II: Fort Worth, Dallas, Houston Invitational: 11 Artists*. The show was exhibited at the Fort Worth Art Center, the Contemporary Arts Museum, Houston, and the Dallas Museum of Fine Arts. For the exhibit Camblin painted three watercolors from his trapped fish series and also included a fish trap sculpture.

CHAPTER THIRTEEN

Life After Life After Academia

In 1973–74 Camblin assumed his visiting artist position at Rice University and participated in fifteen exhibitions including three in New York. (Staley filmed a Super 8 movie that documents Jasper Johns attending an unspecified art opening in Houston.) Camblin continued to focus on watercolor landscapes that became more Arcadian but no less enigmatic. Text grew in importance. He included words to shift the viewer's focus and to emphasize themes of time and change, and he continued to develop subjects involving transformation and metamorphosis.

The artists' summer plans included classes in the new tower. B E & J posted notices at local art galleries and art supply stores: "THREE HOUSTON ARTISTS are opening their private studio at 519 Sul Ross for the study of Fine Art."

The trio taught their classes, an experience they believed would be stimulating and in demand, but lack of local support forced the tower-teaching venture to close in less than a year. Seldom home, Camblin decided it was time to move into his studio.

Surrounded by and working with friends, Camblin was happy and productive. He realized that his demands in his letter had been too angry and forceful for the university deans and department heads. He hated university bureaucracy and decided against trying to find another faculty position, even though money was becoming an issue. His ability to support himself and his family with his art worried him; but he felt positive about himself, his art, and his power to create work that would generate income. Brooke Alexander Inc. in New York and Covo de Iongh Gallery in Houston, owned and operated by Patricia Johnson, represented his work, giving him confidence to remain in Texas as an "unemployed" artist.

Fortuitously, Brooke Alexander returned to Houston to commission Camblin to create a set of twenty-six hand-colored etchings for a traveling exhibition Alexander was organizing, *Hand Colored Prints*. Camblin found the inspiration for his print in the *10 Bulls of Zen* series[1] found in D. T. Suzuki's *Manual of Zen Buddhism*. He used the Texas Longhorn rather than traditional images of bulls to represent "the stages of awareness" that lead to enlightenment. But more than that, Camblin felt at home in Texas and chose to title the piece *Round-Up: See King The Longhorn*[2] as a tip of his hat to the King Ranch, which was known for its longhorns. The Texas Longhorn has a 500-year legacy in Texas. Natural adaptation, rather than help from man, is the key to the longhorns' endurance. Camblin viewed the longhorn print as a document that illustrated his philosophy of survival.

For the bull's horns, he used his "Flying Double-You," designating the work as "Texas Brand Art." The artist's earlier use of the "Flying W" was incorporated into five letters, YGWYD for "You Get What You Deserve." For the longhorn, he wrote the saying in the composition. He was drawn to the letter W because it began so many questioning words: what, who, where, why, when. He also noted that the query "how" ended in a W. His *See King the Longhorn* is a tribute to questing and to questioning. To provide guideposts for understanding, Camblin added sentences and words to *Round-Up: See King the Longhorn*, all of which he intended the viewer to ponder here "Patience is a virtue" and "Follow the path of least resistance." He had used text in his art prior to the etching for Alexander, but in 1973 he increased his incorporation of words.

Camblin wrote, "a last thought for 1973—We talked of changing the world, he listened then took 21 cents from his coin purse to pay for his coffee and left . . ."

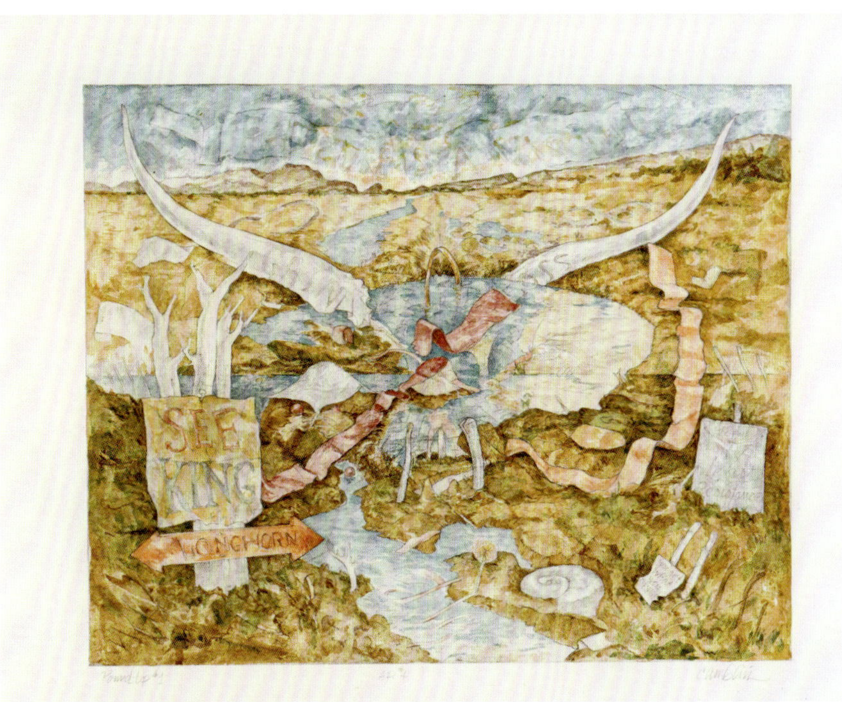

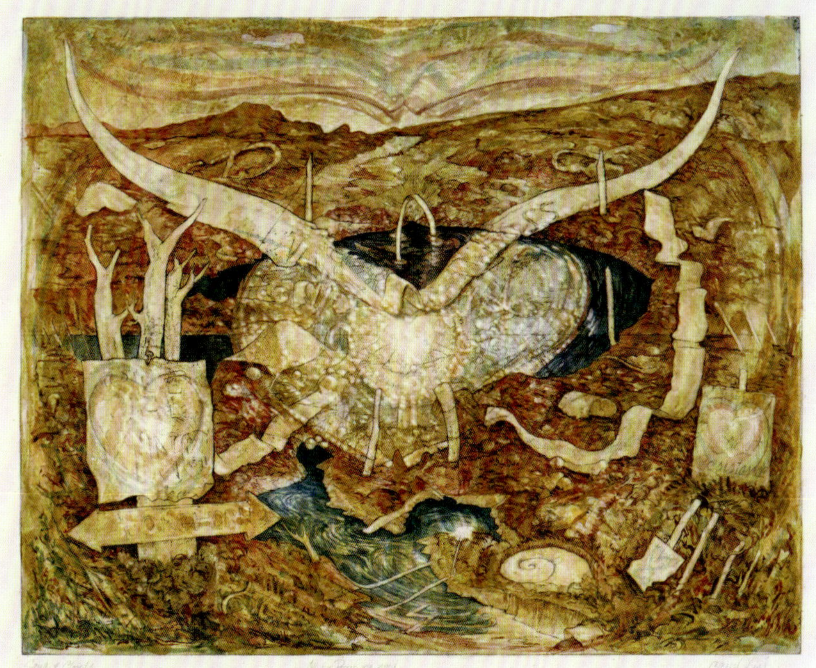

Above: Brooke Alexander commissioned 26 hand-colored etchings of Round-Up: See *King the Longhorn. Scott Peterson photograph.*

Left: Another version of Camblin's *See King the Longhorn*, 1975. He wrote his favorite sayings in the print. *Scott Peterson photograph.*

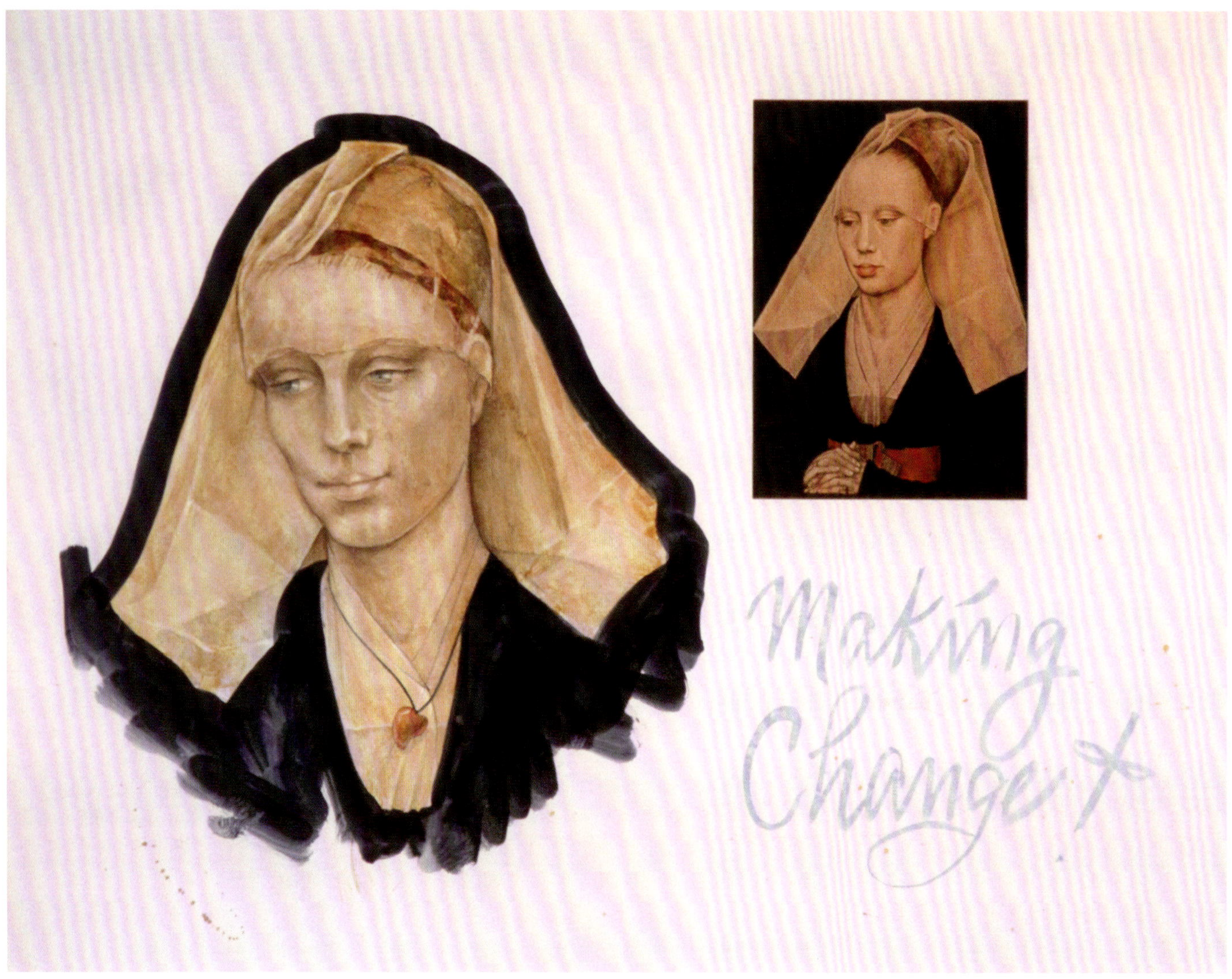

Making Change. Camblin was at a point in his life when he wanted to make changes. *Photograph by Scott Peterson.*

The Wonder of Words

Painters and sculptors often reject words as dangerous to the perception of their art. Although being human, artists and critics like to talk their two cents worth and much of it is meaningless garbage. And yet, communication continues to grow, as well as the sophistry in explaining art. The end result would be that to see an image of the

Sistine ceiling and discuss the aesthetic, social, and philosophical content of it would be deemed adequate enough to experience it in its own terms. This kind of experience creates a verbal awareness overlapping a century of wariness. Eventually it no longer becomes important to do more than recognize a potential for something to be art. The object disappears and the idea remains.

—notes from a Camblin sketchbook

Even though Camblin felt ambivalent about the importance of words as concepts in art, in the early 1970s he began giving the titles of his art more significance. He used two-inch stencils to make titles on the top and bottom borders of his watercolors. Next, he incorporated titles into the structure of the work, followed by the merger of hand-lettered words and drawn images. He wanted a literal visual vocabulary to infuse itself into his imagery. The flexibility of words and the complexity of the mental images they evoke became components of his art. For Camblin, the interface of art and language added clues, ciphers, and a density of information to the puzzles he hid in his watercolors.

At the time universities across the US and in Europe were awash with talk of linguistics and semiotics.[3] The degree to which Camblin inserted himself into the discussion is a matter of conjecture. The text in his art indicates a familiarity with the early writings of Ferdinand de Saussure, cofounder of semiotics, who examined the arbitrariness of linguistic signs in culture, especially language. He argued that languages do not produce different versions of reality; they produce different realities,[4] something that Camblin excelled in. In the 1970s Camblin's multiple vanishing points, word overlays, and linguistic signs helped create his alternate realities. He was enthusiastic about language and signs. He read Michel Foucault, who wrote:

> modern man no longer communicates with the madman . . . There is no common language: or rather, it no longer exists; the constitution of madness as mental illness, at the end of the eighteenth century, bears witness to a rupture in a dialogue, gives the separation as already enacted, and expels from the memory all those imperfect words, of no fixed syntax, spoken falteringly, in which the exchange between madness and reason was carried out.[5]

Foucault believed that some artists tap into their unique madnesses from which they distill wisdom, reason, and subject matter. Camblin speculated with friends as to which artists' visions came from personal madness. He wrote,

"Notes for the Historian of the Holding Firm," January 1, 1975:

"This year ends with the feeling that I am free and accept the fact that I am truly mad but not dangerous."

Besides a history of madness, Foucault wrote a history of cultural semiotics.[6] In the first chapter of the book, he discusses the complexity of Diego Velazquez's painting *Las Meninas* to illustrate the linguistic assumptions that underlie a period of history. Camblin was drawn to Foucault's interest in artists. He was especially intrigued by Foucault's interest in Velazquez to whom he would later pay homage.

Jacques Derrida, another French philosopher, studied under Foucault. Derrida's system of semiotic analysis became known as deconstruction. He wrote that speech is the original signifier of meaning, and the written word is derived from the spoken word.[7] Both written and spoken words are derivative and refer to other signs.[8] For Camblin, words were signs. His philosophy shared the general principles of Foucault and Derrida who both collapsed visual art to a textual construct, allowing words to enter into visual rhetoric.

In addition to signatures and titles, artists have also appropriated text into their art for centuries. Consider Albrecht Durer's *Melencolia I*, 1514. The title is part of the compositions and is printed on a scroll held aloft by a bat-like creature. In the early twentieth century, text became a component of artwork when Georges Braque and Pablo Picasso added words to Cubist works, but the words were not the central idea of their art. Foreshadowing Conceptualism, Francis Picabia and Rene Magritte gave added importance to the use of text.

With the arrival of Conceptual Art in the mid-1960s, the concept became the most important component of art. Language-based works grew in significance. Ed Ruscha, Joseph Kosuth, Robert Smithson, Sol LeWitt, and Lawrence Weiner, among others, employed text as subject matter to convey the idea, design, and meaning of the work. Camblin felt that Conceptualism was too easy. He appreciated the words that Jasper Johns included in *Map* (1961) and he liked the added road signs "Stop" and "One Way" that Robert Rauschenberg included in *Overdrive* (1963). However, numbers did not carry Johns's and Rauschenberg's work. Both artists had an effect on, but were not considered part of Conceptualism.

Unlike some Conceptualists, Camblin did not want text to become his subject, to overpower his images or to eclipse his artistic skills. He remained an intimist in his preferred means of expression: drawing. With text, he added a playfulness to his work even though he was serious about his art. His plays on words seem whimsical, and he added to the whimsy by giving double meanings to words. For example, Camblin was left-handed; he called his left hand his "writehand." Other examples include "Good old daze," "Miss Takes," "Sin King City" (Venice), "mASKed," "X-Isle," "X-ess," "Chair Rubs," "Free Dumb," "Sins of Humour," "Coeur Age," "see level," "SezAnn," "heART," "in-to-it," "render unto Seize Her," "Fool Moon," "St.art." The Spanish *si* could either mean "see" as in "O say can u si?" or "yes." For emphasis he often used "hook, line and sinker" and "s*enza dubbio*" (Italian for "without a doubt"). Occasionally he painted a word such as "world" and then drew a slash through a letter, in this case the "l," making use of world and word. Cosmic with the "s" slashed out was one of his favorites.

Camblin also incorporated run-on words, numbers in place of words, alternate spellings, or combined words, often drawing them on top of other words, necessitating the viewer's need to unravel the layers and meanings in his multivalent writings. A few examples are "kuwaiting," "objetdart," "fences," "electricage," "onemortime," "ncompleat," "whatitwants2b," "MYOMYLIFESANOPENBOOK." "God" turns into "good" when the o gets twisted into an infinity symbol pierced by a ray of light. Happenings blurred the line between art and life; text-based works blurred the line between drawing and writing.

Besides single words, Camblin wrote short sentences or maxims in his art. Reflecting his appreciation of the *Tao Te Ching*, he wrote his own version of the truths. Compare the writings in the *Tao* to Camblin's words:

Tao: In action, watch the timing.

Camblin: Timing is everything. It's just a matter of time.

Tao: Be really whole, and all things will come to you.

Camblin: You get what you deserve.

Tao: He who does not trust enough, will not be trusted.

Camblin: First, trust yourself.

Tao: Therefore the sage is guided by what he feels and not by what he sees.

Camblin: Follow the path with heart.

Tao: I will walk on the main road and my only fear will be of straying from it.

Camblin: Follow the path of least resistance.

He created his own calligraphic script, filling sketchbook pages with formal Asian-like shapes, sometimes including a word or two of English.

By summer 1974, Camblin was without a university teaching position for the first time since receiving his MFA. He separated from his family and lived alone. Having long preached the importance of personal freedom, he was shocked to discover the destructive passions that came with being truly free. Change challenged his life as a family man and as an artist, but his art continued to flourish. He outlined his interests in an undated work-in-progress, ca. 1974, titled *Time. What's a Big Idea? 1 through 5—Halfway Through*. Camblin wrote in ink on the acetate overlay of the lithograph: "No Doppler. Isometric View of the Universe. It's About Time. This too shall pass. No matter! Patience is the virtue. Get into [the 'o' being an infinity symbol] it. Omnidirectional Halo. Sun/Fire, Clouds, Lava, Water . . . moving as long as the heat's on! Time wounds all heels or YGWYD [You Get What You Deserve], The path of least resistance. We all evaporate in time."

Near the center of the lithograph is the figure "1." On top of the number he wrote: *Il piu del uno* (Italian for "One of the most"), under which he wrote: "ineffable." The number 1 over a 5 is drawn in the middle of the large figure 1, under which he wrote: "Sex & Love equal One." He drew the numbers 2 through 5 into the landscape. On the left of the composition Camblin drew a triangle containing a circle used to depict "the absolute within the self." Next to it, he drew a circumcircle of a triangle. Another triangle in a circle with a wormhole into the triangle was the last of the series. "Triangulation" is written above a pool with shadows forming a skull, a *memento mori*.

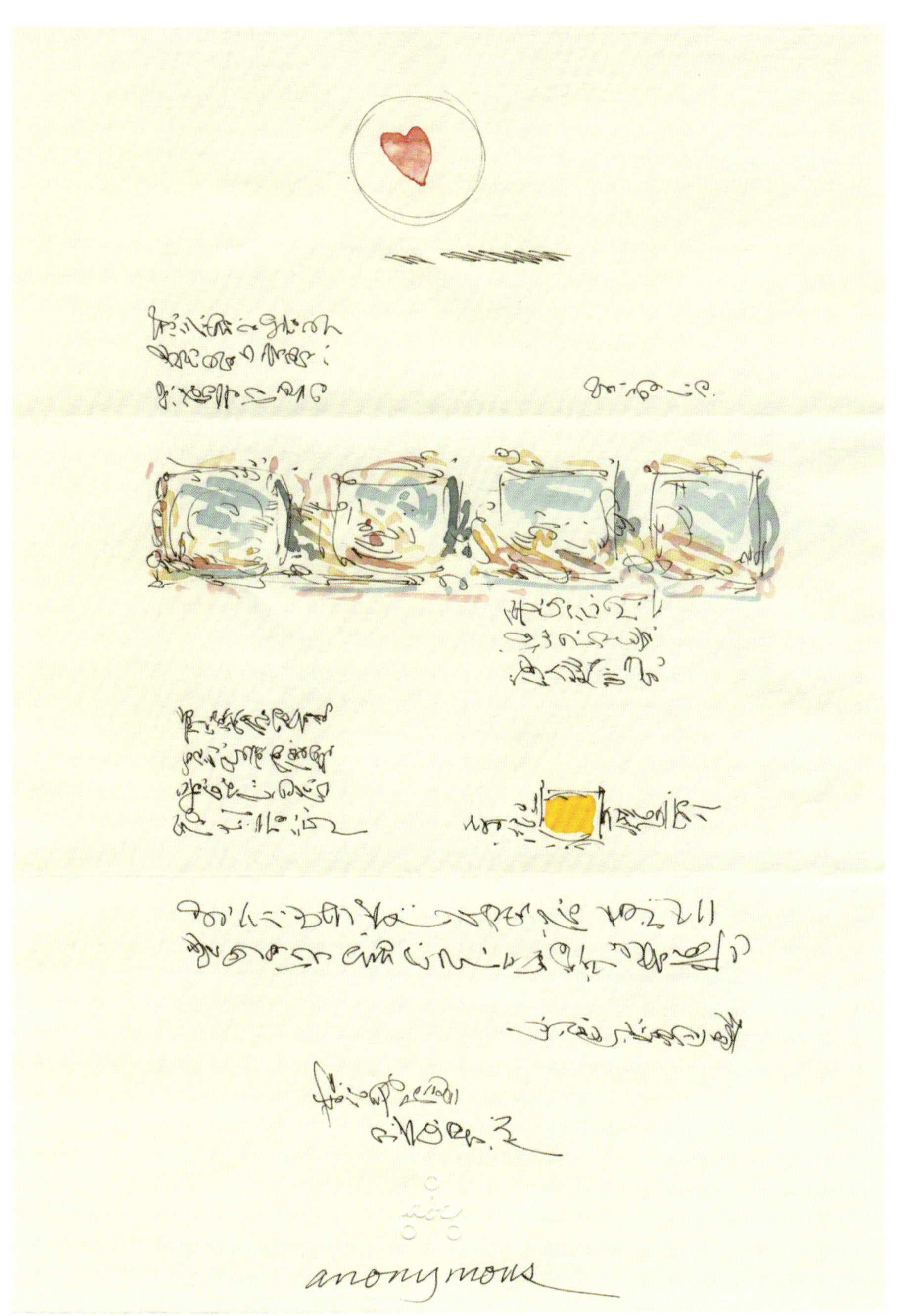

An example of Camblin's own hieroglyphic script.

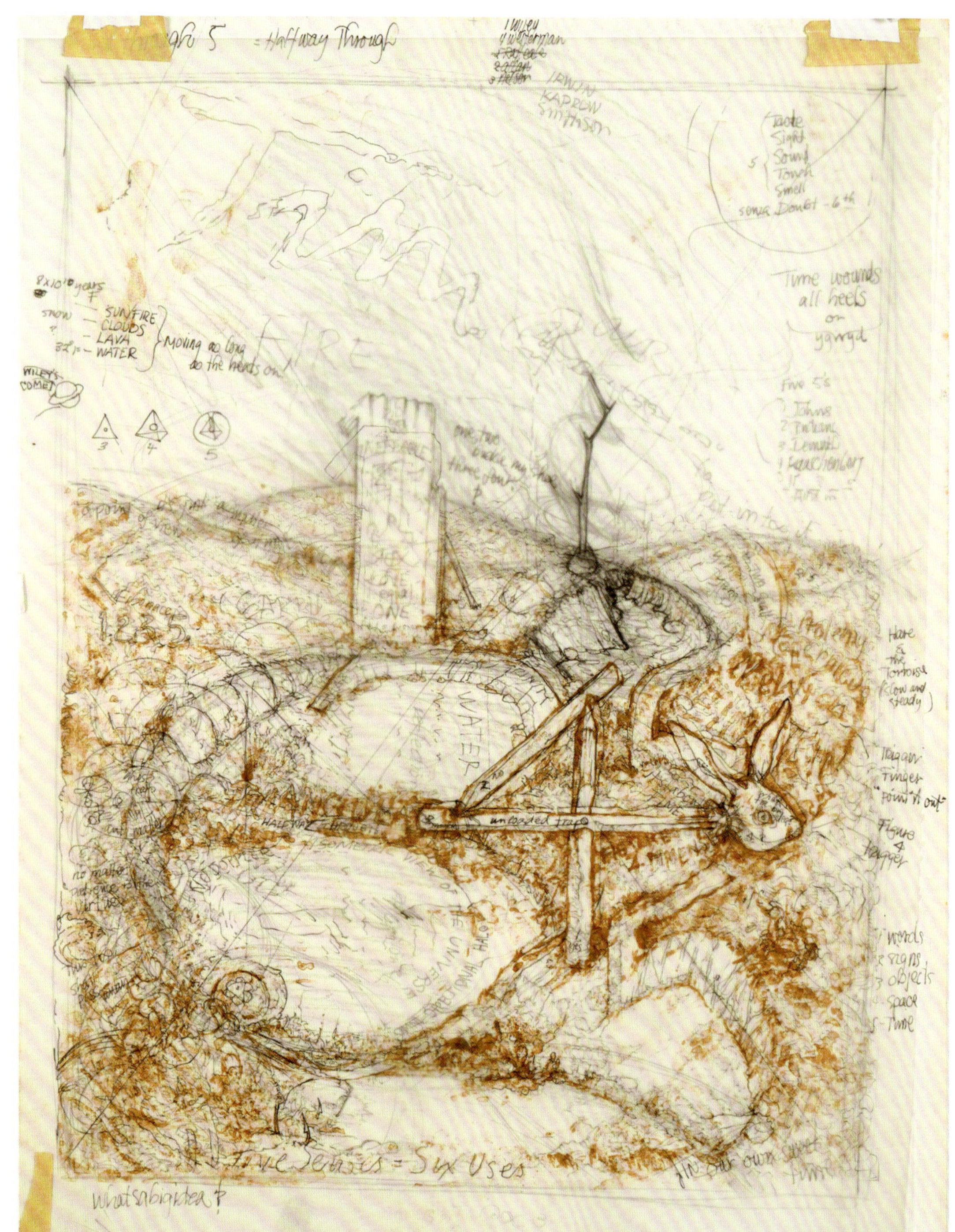

1 Through 5, Halfway Through.
Photograph by Scott Peterson.

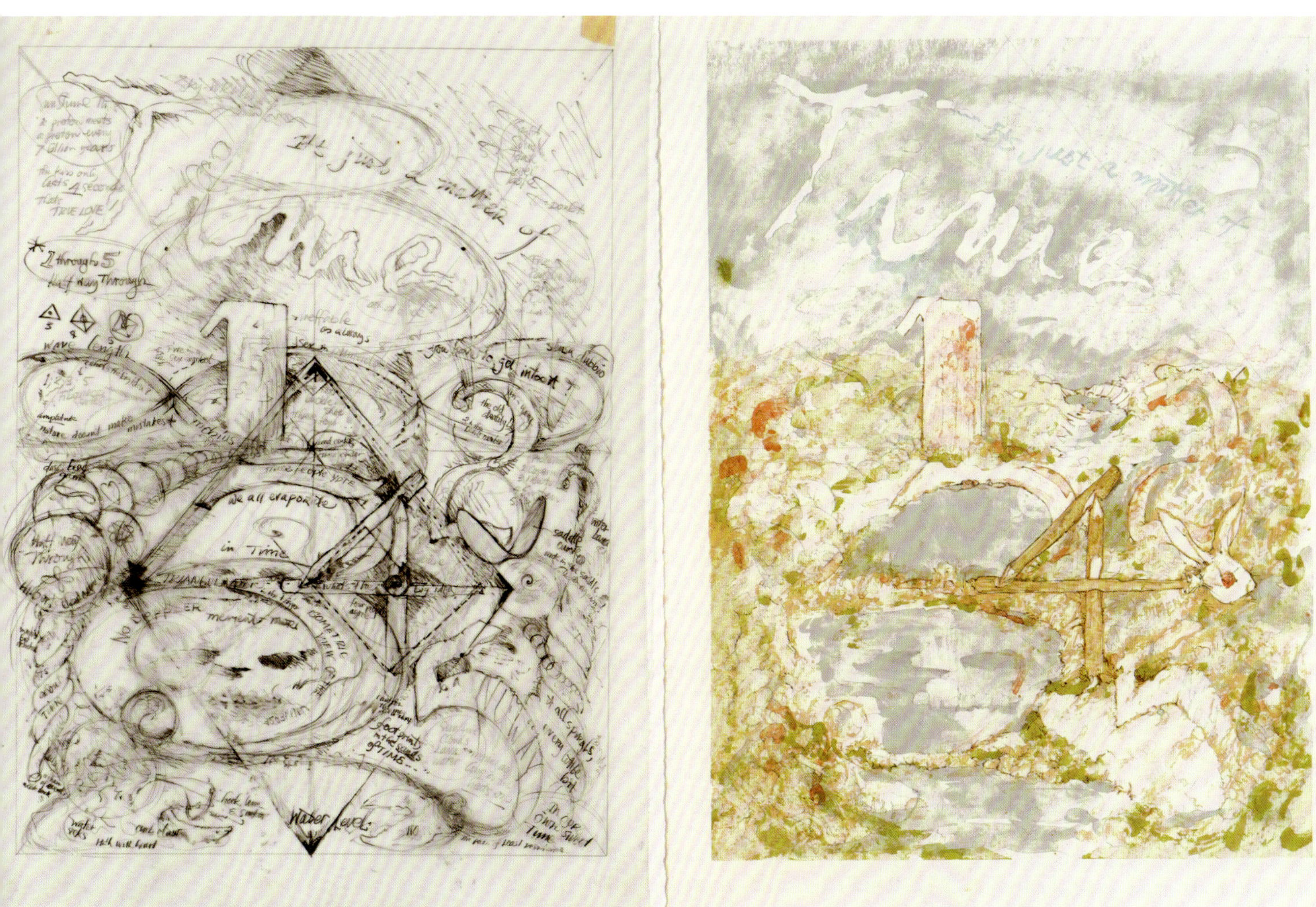

1 through 5, Halfway Through, 1974. A lithograph began this work-in-progress. Camblin placed a piece of acetate over the lithograph and began detailing the underlying images, including a figure 4 trap with a hare trigger. *Photograph by Scott Peterson.*

He listed five artists on the lithograph: (1) Wiley, (2) Allan (crossed-out, replaced with Kaprow), (3) Nelson (crossed-out, replaced with Smithson), (4) Westermann, (5) (Joseph) Raffael (crossed-out, replaced with Irwin). The five senses: (1) Words, (2) Signs, (3) Objects, (4) Space, (5) Time. He listed "Five 5s:" (1) Johns, (2) Indiana, (3) Demuth, (4) Rauschenberg. He left the fifth space blank and wrote, "Fill it in."

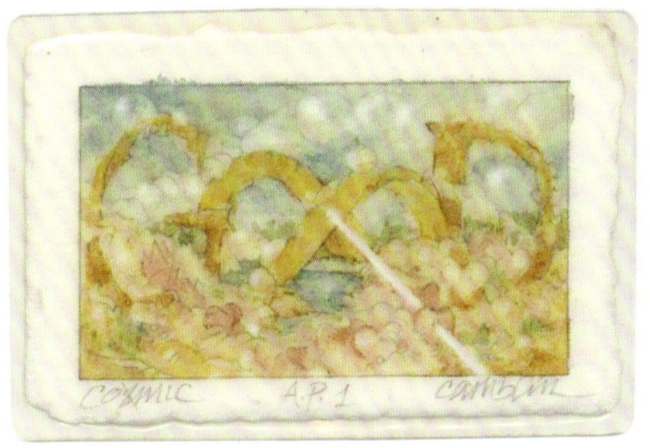

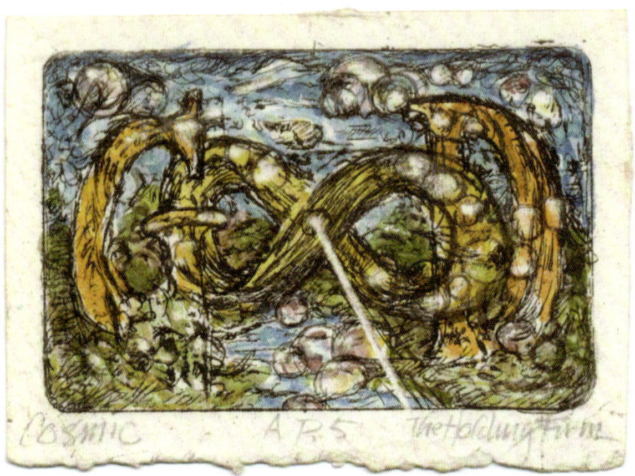

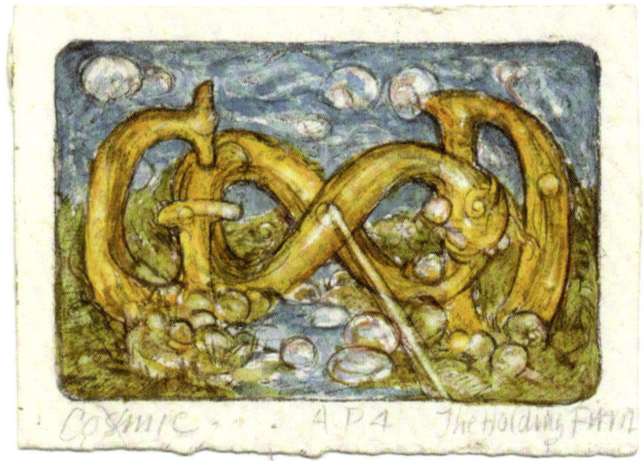

Camblin created his own business cards. *Photograph by Scott Peterson.*

In the work, Camblin's scientific references include a listing of scientists: Ptolemy, Copernicus, Newton, Einstein and "?." He drew mathematic symbols or wrote, "Saddle Curve, Fibonacci sequence and the Golden Spiral." Under and right of the central figure 1, he drew a figure 4 trap with a "hare" trigger.

The work was intended as one of several decoders for his watercolors and attests to the fact that Camblin was, as he professed, omnicredulous; he did believe in IT all. He talked about vector algebra and calculus from Euclidean space and would extrapolate his theories on the quantum mechanics of Hilbert space with an infinite number of dimensions. From there he would ponder a universe of an infinite number of dimensions, considering our universe as only one in an infinite number of universes. Exploiting the quantum model allowed him to say, "It is all art," because the classic Renaissance field of art could be comprehended as an infinity of infinities. By foregrounding the sign for infinity into some of his works, Camblin proclaimed the way to get there. On one side of his hand-drawn and colored calling cards, he drew an infinity symbol with a ray of light piercing its center.

Camblin knew that Hilbert space is only a model, a mental construct. He ventured into the space knowing that it was no more or less real than any other model, that infinity is meaningless, that we simply know nothing at all. Infinity is the end point of what we think we know, the placeholder for the limits of our models.

The print's title, words, signs, and numbers, however, point to encrypted markers in Camblin's work and indicate that a secret narrative flows through his art. There are visual and philosophical treasures to be found, but Camblin did not intend to have the text in his watercolors tell a story. His words are signs to be used to mask, to complicate, or to solve his riddles. He recorded his experiences into phrases or sentences based on facts or science and expected the informed viewer to seek clues in the images and words found in his work. Even with clues, Camblin's work offers so many disparate elements that the viewer knows that the works will remain ever enigmatic, possibly even to their creator.

In 1974, perhaps in an effort to help decipher his art and his words after the year 2000, Camblin placed sketchbooks from 1956 to 1974 in an Atlas Powder Dynamite box. On the top he carved "All Fool's Day 1974 Closed—Open 2000." He sealed the crate with rope and wax before wrapping it with fish nets, hooks, and anchors. He put the mysterious box in storage where it remained for forty years. Camblin's family opened the crate in 2014 and subsequently published pages from the "lost sketchbooks." Besides personal musings, the written entries and sketches contain numerous references to scientific and literary influences, to tattoos, to Zen, and to masks: Spavinaw ancestor masks, scarecrow masks, St. Bambola masks, masks in bottles, and "Masques: Man mask masked, no mask or a collection of one time masks."[9]

He begins a sketchbook with "Jacob Bohme attained enlightenment while staring at a reflection in a pewter pitcher—I attained 'absolute' love of you in a reflection on the corner of a stainless steel sink in the One's a Meal. . . . Beginning the second book I realize I may be letting you know too much about my feelings. . . . Vulnerable, I sit in the cab of my truck with the motor running, hoping she loves me, the poems, the art, et al. . . . I have never done this in my life—this rush of love letters, a feeling of despair, every corny song, every trite cliche, C'est moi!!"

CHAPTER FOURTEEN

Little Egypt Enterprises and Cerling Etching Studio

In 1974 David Folkman brought his lithographic workshop, Little Egypt Enterprises (LEE), from Illinois to Houston. Camblin was the first artist he contacted. Folkman moved his press into Camblin's Sul Ross studio, which he shared with Staley and Tate. There Camblin created a set of lithographs for the publisher Robert S. Lowe. Titled *The Elements*, the suite consisted of "four original hand printed lithographs in editions of fifty plus ten Artist's Proofs, Color Separation Proofs, Bon a Tirer, a Printer's Proof and Archive Impressions." Five months after beginning *The Elements*, he wrote, "Lithography has really set me free. I should say not lithography but the master printer/artist collaboration in your own studio. It allowed me to 'experience' what Picasso 'enjoyed' when he had the printers in his studio for a year doing the Erotic Prints."[1]

In an article by Charlotte Moser for the *Houston Chronicle*, "Master Printmaking in Houston," May 31, 1975, Folkman noted, "I'm not interested in reproducing an artist's drawing into a lithograph . . . I collaborate with the artist." Sharing a love of working with friends, Folkman and Camblin would continue to create numerous lithographs until Folkman left Houston.

Describing the process for the creation of *The Elements*, Moser wrote in the *Houston Chronicle* article "Master Printmaking": "Camblin designed the images

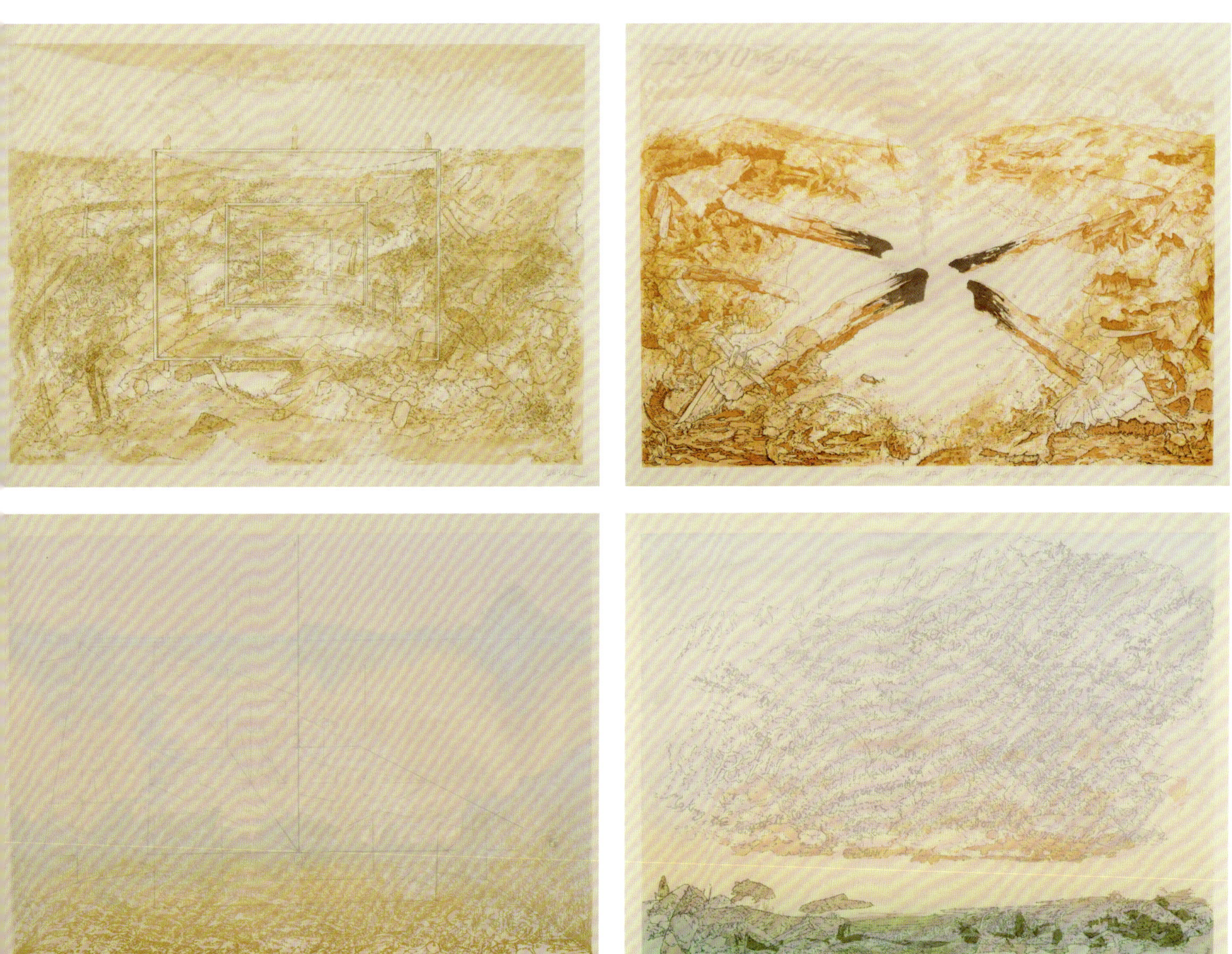

Dave Folkman's press, Little Egypt Enterprises printed Camblin's *The Four Elements: Air, Water, Earth, and Fire*, 1974. *Scott Peterson photographs.*

on aluminum lithography plates, but Dave helped with color and execution of his idea. Paper used was 100 percent rag from Twin Rocker Handmade Papers in Indiana. The results show new ideas from Camblin and perfect printmaking by Folkman. So fine is the series that it has been selected for review in the Print Collectors newsletter."

Ten plates were used for each print. The series took over a year to complete. Folkman carefully stored all the plates, believing they would become great teaching tools for any newcomer to lithography or for any university with a print department.

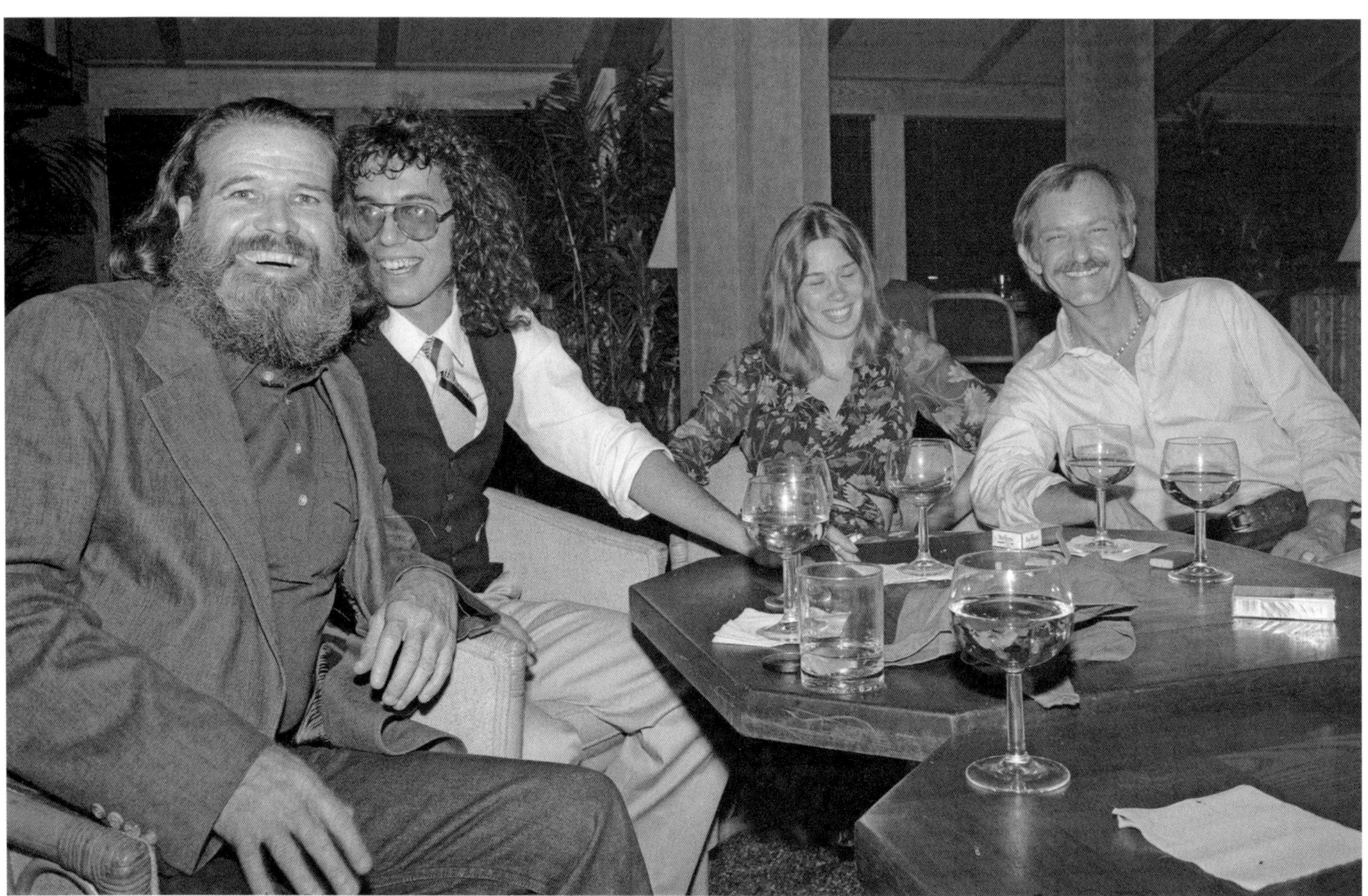

Left to right: Camblin, Enrique Leal, unknown girl, and Dave Folkman, 1974. *Photograph by author.*

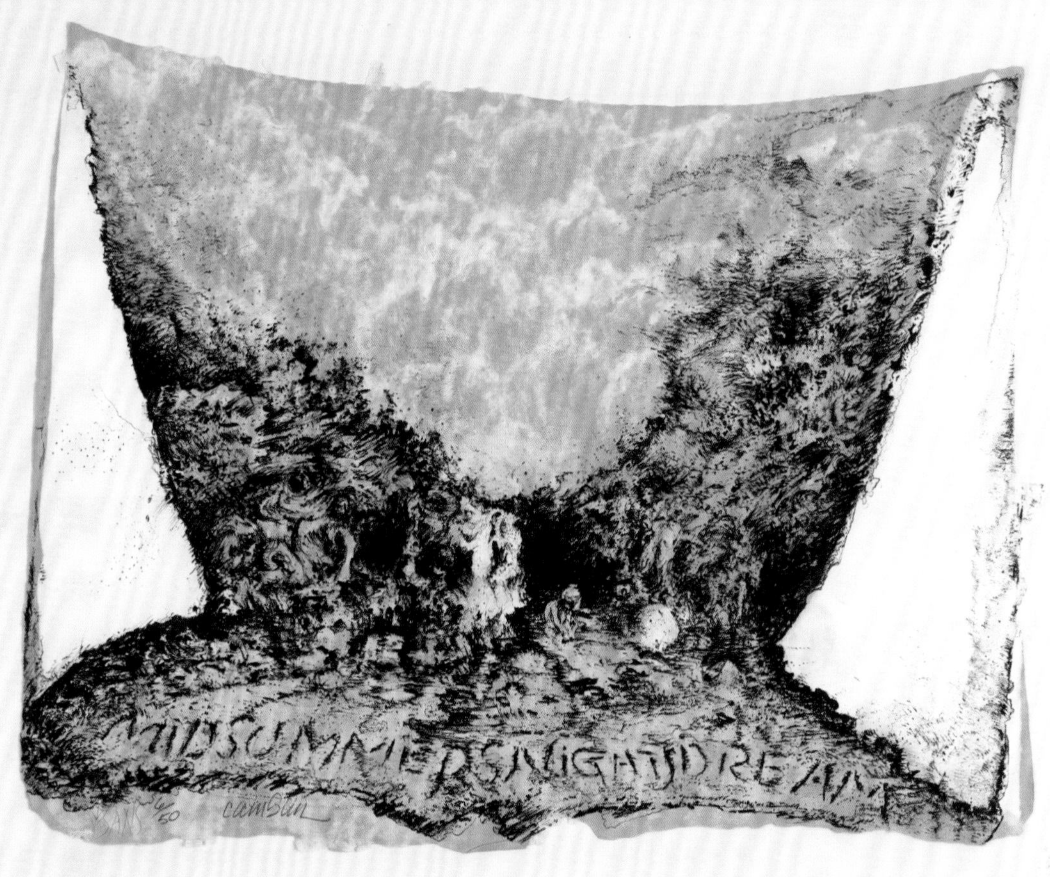

Camblin and Folkman collaborated on *Midsummer Night's Dream. Scott Peterson photograph.*

Camblin and Folkman had a strong friendship and worked well together. They collaborated on many projects over the ensuing years. For *Midsummer Night's Dream*, first they handmade the paper for the Shakespearean homage. The sides of the paper appear to fold in at the bottom, like the fabric of a stage curtain. The folds frame the blue interior with a white cloud-like surface onto which the black inked landscape image is printed. The composition contains a fairy, contemplating a bubble, sitting in the center of the forested landscape. For Camblin, the bubble worked as a metaphor. The perfection and transparency of a sphere that could float, reflect light, and cast a shadow intrigued the artist. Obviously if the bubble were large enough, as it is in Camblin's Shakespearean piece, it could reflect the image of its viewer. A bubble's beauty and fragility, its constantly shifting and spiraling colors, its penchant to evaporate or pop suddenly, combined with the complexities of the Zen enso made it a favorite image of his. Of course, *Midsummer Night's Dream* has to include a sprite.

Allan Otho Smith set up silkscreen printing for Little Egypt from 1979 to 1985. (During that time he created *Bob on a Bag* among other works.) Penny Cerling, a Houston artist, worked as an etching printer for Little Egypt from 1980 to 1990. Her first project with LEE was assisting in the completion of Camblin's *Scrapbook*. Another printer had begun work on the project, but the work had languished until Cerling took the job of providing Camblin etching plates so she could print them. She encouraged Camblin to finish etching the plates for the *Scrapbook* undertaking, and when her work as the etching printer was completed, she helped Camblin assemble his series of *Scrapbooks*.

Camblin continued to collaborate on lithographs and three-dimensional works with Folkman. For one joint effort, Folkman carved a hinged box to enclose a Camblin watercolor. The finished wood feels like satin. Leather straps, to hold the box open, can be inserted into carved depressions in the inside lid, which also holds a magnifying glass with which to examine the treasures found by the landscape.

In 1993, Cerling organized a retrospective of Dave Folkman's work for DiverseWorks Artspace. The exhibition included the lithographs and etchings that Camblin created at LEE. Days after the show's opening, Folkman died.[2] Recalling her time working with Camblin, Cerling wrote:

Camblin was an enigmatic artist, pulling personalities out of his head, creating art and questions to go along with obscure characters such as Mr. Peanut, Red Stick the Pirate, Anonymous and many others. He said "Anonymous" was the most famous painter in the world and signed his work "Anonymous." We watched him create puzzles in his drawings and paintings. The paintings held secret, hidden meanings and we looked closely at each line and brush stroke for clues. Everything was questioned. He questioned life from the visible to the invisible. He questioned

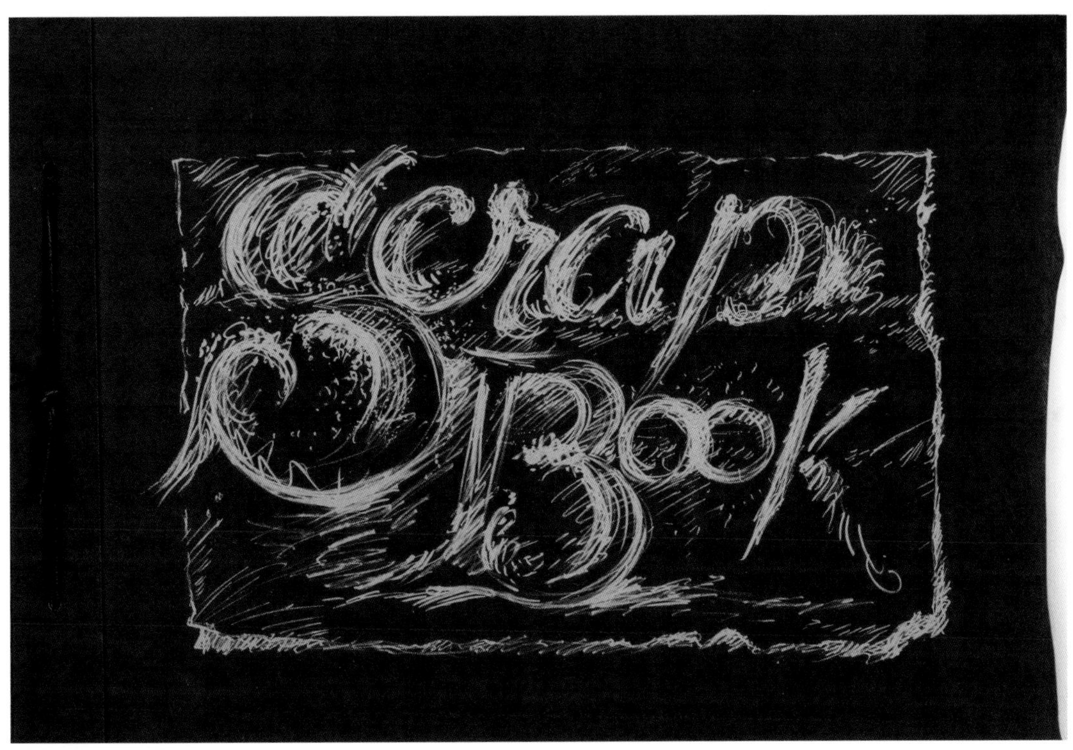

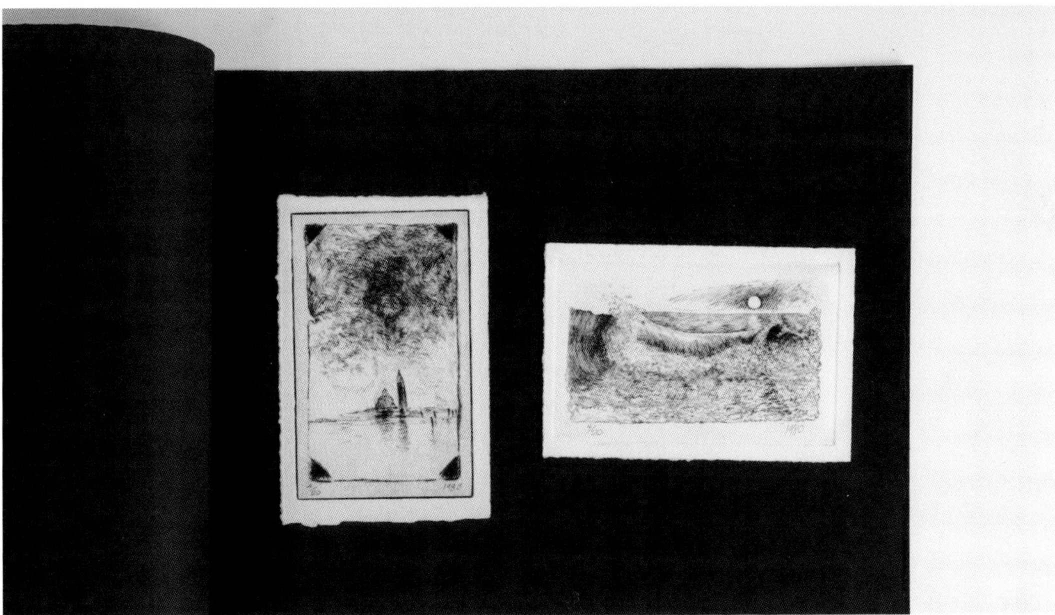

Camblin created a *Scrapbook* filled with his etchings. *Scott Peterson photographs.*

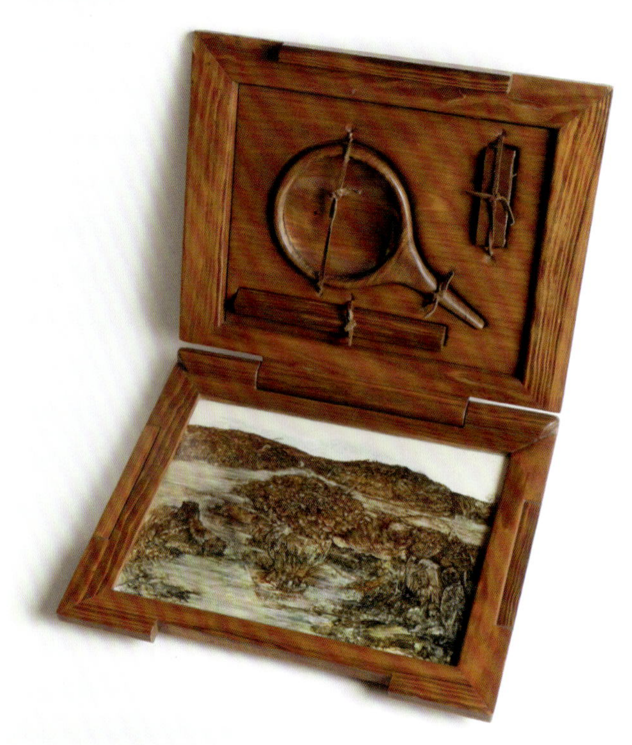

Folkman carved the box and Camblin added the watercolor. *Scott Peterson photograph.*

electrons and what we were made of, arguing that as artists in Houston we could do anything and think anything we wanted because we were isolated and far from the important art scenes on either coast. This gave a sense of freedom: that we didn't need to worry about having fashionable work because we could explore whatever question came to mind as we looked into our physical and mental world, producing drawings, paintings, prints, sculpture. The attitude was to just do it and don't worry about earning money because the impetus of creation through thinking was the most important goal. However, worry about money was an immediate, conflicting pressure that often undermined goals, and Camblin was a conflicted man. He would furiously make paintings when he needed money and give them away when he didn't. Sometimes he would place impossible demands on a dealer or collector and later walk away with nothing but heartburn and unsold work.

Collaboration was a special love of his which created problems because it was difficult enough for a dealer to handle work created by multiple artists, and most especially because of the casual way Camblin handled what should have been sensible negotiations. As he argued absurd points I sometimes wondered if we were watching his blood pressure rise and whether there was pleasure in the elevation.

Collaboration, for Camblin, also meant inclusion. Being around him and the artists who frequented Little Egypt taught me about the Houston Attitude. The world has looked on in surprise as Houston's spirit of inclusion, acceptance and generosity have been brought to national attention with Hurricanes Katrina in 2005 and Harvey in 2017, but those of us who live here learned that happy attitude from Camblin and others who came to Houston before us.

Camblin, Boynton, and Folkman: A Fine-lined Friendship

When Dave Folkman moved his press, Little Egypt Enterprises, to Houston in 1974, Camblin and Jack Boynton had worked together, on and off, for about five years. When Camblin discovered that it was Boynton who inadvertently caused Little Egypt Enterprises [LEE] to relocate from Carbondale, Illinois, to Houston, Texas, he believed LEE's move to Texas was kismet. Fate had stepped in when Boynton traveled from Houston to Carbondale in the early 1970s. He went to Illinois to create plates for a new series of lithographs with LEE. After Boynton completed the plates he returned to Houston, while Folkman printed the plates in Carbondale. To get Boynton's signature on the work, Folkman traveled to Houston, lithographs in hand. He journeyed from chilling snows in Illinois to the warmth of a Texas winter. Folkman found Houston's weather and year-round green environment irresistible and decided to move to the Bayou City. Pleased with Folkman's decision to set up shop in Houston, Boynton took him to meet the city's artists, first introducing him to Camblin.

When Camblin arrived in Texas to teach at Rice University, Jack Boynton was one of Houston's best-known artists. At the time, he was teaching at the University of St. Thomas where he had created the studio art department. He and Camblin became good friends. They often met for coffee or lunch at Shipley's Cafe on West Gray Street. They shared ideas on art and life. Both appreciated the other's ability to create beautiful lines. They would stop by each other's studio with regularity, often staying long enough to draw a few lines on the work at hand. They collaborated on watercolors, drawings, and prints. Both enjoyed Texas iconography. While Camblin preferred the Texas Longhorn, Boynton created drawings and prints of the "Amarillo Boot" that he filled with Texas landmarks, bluebonnets,

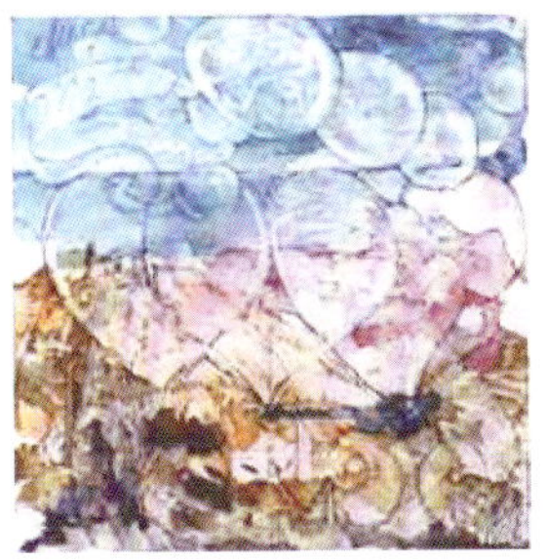
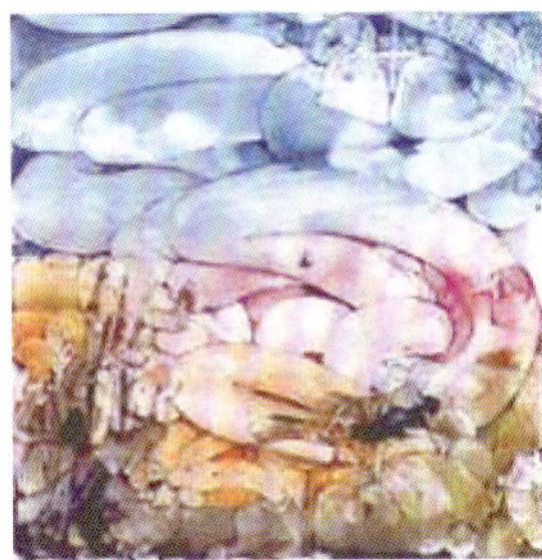

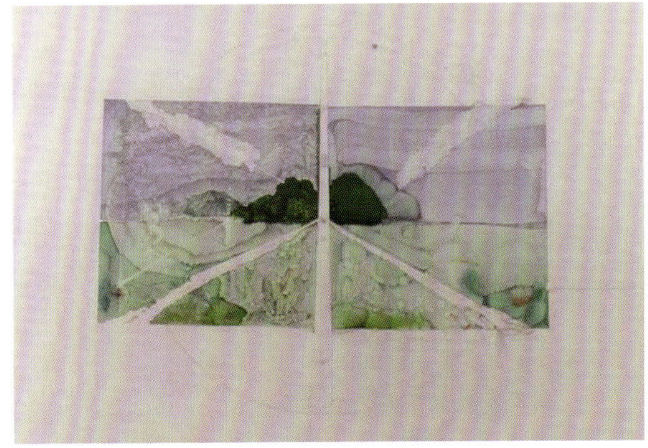

Above: Cosmic Co-Mix, 1975. Watercolor and pencil on paper, 23" X 23". *Collection of the Amarillo Museum of Art.*

Below: Through the Looking Glass—Lightly, 1975. Watercolor on paper, 23" X 29". *Collection of the Amarillo Museum of Art.*

and other symbols of the Lone Star State. Both incorporated words into their art. He and Camblin were known to combine their classes for outings. Even though they had dissimilar temperaments, they had much in common philosophically and artistically. Oddly, they were both born in 1928 and both died in 2010.

Life Changes in 1975

January 1, 1975

Notes for the historian of the Holding Firm

Now watching it happen!

Earl and Betty are getting a violent divorce. Joe and Diane split quietly. Joe and I parted with some rough edges. Bon and I are separate and trying to get halfway between Tate's and Staley's [divorces]. Mark just disappeared—moving in his own strange fashion. Al [Smith] came back and helped me get ready to move, to keep still, to change. Dave and I are finishing the suite of prints. Bob Lowe—Brooke Alexander—Murray Smither still in my business reality. (Que scais-je?) Teaching one class at the museum school. McManaway—Love—Fridge—watching their theater. Wray—Shaw—Dianne (in the wings of whose theater?) George O. & Lollie [Jackson]— flying objects identified. The De Menil Dynasty—local Medici theater. Museums, galleries, Houston in toto—observing the patient.

I am eclectic, excessive, eccentric and trying to keep a perfectly average point of view so as not to miss anything. not even what my own body will do on its own. It is a marvelous world and Love is the answer—

—notes from a Camblin sketchbook

But love was complicated. At the beginning of the year, I left Houston with my daughter for a trip around the world. Foreign countries understood me. Camblin couldn't understand how I could leave him for months on end. He filled sketchbooks and sent long and lonely love letters. My ex-husband had moved to Bahrain by this time, and my sister lived in Kuwait. Before leaving Texas, I explained my situation to Mrs. de Menil. She told me that I should take the trip and that I was not to worry because my job would be waiting for me when I returned. With open tickets and my daughter in hand, we began a journey to circumnavigate the globe. I knew Camblin would be hurt, but I rationalized that I might never again have this opportunity. I assured him that I would write, that I would be faithful, that I would use his eyes to open the world for me. Nothing helped.

While I was gone Camblin spent his time filling sketchbooks with love letters and erotic drawings. Our lives became rollercoasters of opposing emotions. He recorded his feelings and his dreams in his writings and drawings.

From sketchbooks:

"Five or six o'clock and you are starting to wake up on Thursday morning, when I go to car pool tomorrow your day will have been spent a world away from me and as I start my day—you will see the sun setting—Time to come home!!"

"Looking at vanishing images in the drawing, I begin to desire you. Seven in the morning in India—France—Italy—Nepal, somewhere I can't reach you no matter how I try. If I could quit wanting, maybe you'd come home NOW"

"day after day . . . night after night . . . Haven't you seen enough ruins— Look at this one waiting for you!"

"I have your letter! Touching it, a thrill, a delicious shudder of anticipation through my body. Opening the letter was almost as exciting as undressing you in the old studio—The fragile leaves of an airmail containing all that explosive eroticism for a mad Irish anarchist. Love—talking leaves and my window . . . Aeons of Time, Egypt dreamed. The lips of Teye whisper, "remember" and Aida-like I remain in the tomb of silence with my love waiting—I wait—willlingly."

"Love is not Blind when it is the LOVE—"

"It's about 5 o'clock in the evening where?? I wish my eyes could feel what you have seen today—can we fix it so we can look at the slides in bed? My free one, return to my cage . . . A word to describe my physical mood—going slowly, I almost touch you. I . . . eye . . . thou—we us together your skin, smooth surfaces melting into me—molding—through your eye I see everything in Venetian gold—my Byzantine dreamer—silk something embroidered and held in front of you. gold filigree flowers—touching it—touching me glide across marble/terrazzo floors and nearing sunset—a spectrum of lights—getting ready—you are looking tonight. I kiss your "sweet" soul. glasses, reflections—Bohme—in the reflections find me tonight, and in the darkness and now the rain starts in long slow streaks—my raindrop world—a cloud so far away—I'm parched and want you to move this way.

"My dreams are all for you sweet dreams of you glowing in the Orient—I wonder if you know how much I love you and how I begin to wonder if anyone else ever felt this way . . . (another human conceit) No tragedies, please, to reduce this dream to reality—come back safely. don't let my desire rock the cosmos I don't want to tempt fate or move a muscle that isn't our destiny—I want it all to continue—no prayers or wishes except that lovers around the world make constantly to great inexorable NATURE and then submit—willingly to FATE. Senza dubbio—I can do nothing but love you.

"So many words, so much that remains unsaid and yet for me the words focus the crystal and I'm with you knowing you will soon read all of this—bad poetry, but my body sits here—looking into space—rambles, wishing you were here and had to listen as I would try to seduce you verbally with honeyed words and images—cold words—inert—dear without that tiny ear near my shoulder and that porcelain thigh across my stomach . . ."

Camblin knew his friend Bruno Leon had been nursing his dying wife. He had also been watching Bonnie and Bruno struggle with their love for years. Bruno was in Detroit, so for Bonnie, phone calls and letters had had to suffice, with only brief and occasional visits. Camblin loved Bonnie and Bruno, so he wanted the best for both of them. After the death of Bruno's wife, Camblin received the following letter from him on March 4, 1975, explaining the situation and apologizing for taking his wife from him:

Dear Bob—

This is a letter that requires writing because of our long friendship. Yet, it will be difficult to write because it may cause some pain which I certainly hope will not be true.

I have not seen you in a long time so I do not know your feelings and/or attitudes at this time. However, I will write to you as we always did in the past.

I am aware that you left home, a fact you conveyed to me yourself, and that you and Bonnie are in the process of getting a divorce. That news I received from Bonnie several months ago and have talked with her on the phone several times since that time. That reality is the basis for this letter.

You know that I have loved Bonnie for all these years and although that affection was never fulfilled, I also knew of her strong feelings for me. After Louise died my thoughts naturally gravitated to Bonnie, but that is where they stayed. A large part of my reason for not stopping in Houston was to avoid any intrusion on my part that my new status might imply, create or instigate in my own behavior. That is not the only reason but a prime motivator. That has changed now that you two have decided upon divorce because my actions or presence would no longer intrude in the relationship you had at one time. What this all states is that I am coming after Bonnie. In the discussions I have had with her recently we have decided to allow ourselves the chance to get together and see if we could build a new life as partners. At my request she has remained silent about this possibility because I felt I wanted to tell you myself . . . an emotion based upon my friendship and respect for you, both of which I hope will continue in the future. It is upon this latter basis I write you even though, under the circumstances, there is no essential dictum that requires me to do so.

Should all of this come about in reality, I want you to know that not only do I want you to continue to be my friend but that I would in no manner create impediments to your free access to your children and to my encouragement in them of continued affection and respect for you. The only problem would occur because of the change in geographical location since it is very unlikely that I would ever move to Houston.

I am not certain when Bonnie and I would make this move but it seems to me that when school is out for the children would be an ideal time.

Despite what possible difficulty it may present for you, I would encourage you to consider taking as positive a response as possible to your children in terms of moving because for them and Bonnie it would be a much easier transition, and as I can testify after these past two years, the needs of young people require more attention than we men can give or often even understand.

Insofar as all your other issues are concerned in the divorce proceedings, I have told Bonnie that it is none of my affair nor do I want any involvement in them ever. I have told her that I want her to come with the children and we will start from that basis alone.

Well, that is it! To speak of other things hereon seems sort of ludicrous so I will not do so. I hope that those discussions will continue in the future when all of this is resolved in what I hope will be a manner as humane and painless as possible for you, Bonnie and your children.

One last thought. I write you because my affection for you remains as it always was.

Bruno

With Camblin's blessing, Bonnie and the Camblin children moved to Detroit to be with Bruno as soon as the kids' school year ended. Bonnie and Camblin signed official divorce papers the following year. Feeling that he had let his family down by not providing enough income through the sale of his art, Camblin contemplated the possibility of getting a new job. On April 1, Camblin filled out a resume, though he never bothered to send it:

On April 1, 1975, at 12:01 A.M., C.S.T., I passed through the chronological matrix of one billion four hundred fifty five million three hundred seventy six thousand seconds of Real Time . . . This stated, let me begin: For whatever it means and to the "best of my knowledge" and with proper documentation, I, Bob Camblin, was born on August 1, 1928, to Viva Faustena Camblin nee Bilyeu and Donald Barr Camblin in Ponca City, Oklahoma, U.S.A., World, Galaxy, et.al. The rest is perfectly average.

Camblin included his education experience, his working experience, and his family experience. He added, "1973–75: Working full time as an object maker, specifically in graphite and watercolor pigments as applied to 100% rag paper, although I have continued: 1. Small three dimensional objects; lectures, teaching: A. design at the Museum of Fine Arts School, Houston B. guest lecturer, University of Winnipeg, Canada 3. Mosaic murals A. Sacred Heart Byzantine

Rite Church, Detroit, Michigan 4. Prints: A. collaboration with Dave Folkman of Little Egypt Enterprises in a suite of 4 prints. My work is handled by: Myself, Houston; Brooke Alexander Inc. New York, New York; Delahunty Gallery, Dallas, Texas. I am located at: 1426 West Bell, Apt. #5 Houston, Texas, 77006 U.S.A. North America; Latitude 30 degrees Longitude 95 degrees; World; Third Planet-Solar System; Galaxy, et. al. More information available on request. Love, Camblin 1975."

Camblin received and accepted an offer for a one semester position as visiting artist at Louisiana State College in Baton Rouge. He needed the money.

After months of travel with my daughter, Larissa, we returned to the States. Our first re- entry into the USA was in Hawaii. Camblin traveled to Honolulu to meet us. Hawaii also meant time with his brother Dennis who lived on the island.

"All new poems from the new 'me' in a new studio and a trip to Hawaii—to begin this love affair again with an adventurer. How I begin is how I end so how much nicer it will be to try and add to your dream and not mine.

"Beginning in the Far East, a blending of our Far West and we begin again on an island and carry it with us forever. Dreamer—dream us on. You know the way. I will follow you in complete faith—the first I've ever had—and yet I'm free and know you are too. . . .

"While you were in Egypt, I discovered that I couldn't control you or make you come back to me. I discovered selfishness and Love through my obsession."

After our joyous reunion, Larissa and I flew to Salt Lake City, and Camblin returned to Houston. He only had a brief stay in Texas before he moved to Louisiana to fulfill his Visiting Artist position at Louisiana State University in Baton Rouge. In a letter to me dated August 30, 1975, sent from Baton Rouge, he wrote,

Rain, just got drenched walking back after class. Listened to a tape. I say the same things [as my students], but the last [thing I overheard while teaching my class] was a girl talking to another girl. She is into Zen and Ram Dass and her 3 year old affair is changing. She is young but making sense. Tuesday I've got an ex-helicopter pilot, a medical hypnotist and an art student talking to the class. Thursday I think

I'll ask the girl to talk on Zen and Ram Dass. Her friend is into Body Language and Personal Space—maybe I can get them to "draw on all they know . . ."

Tired, lonely—the weekend stretches out into torpor, LA. Fuzzy . . . I don't think I'm into teaching anymore. I feel they have heard it all and I'm just movin' around. So young—how can they be so much more together than my age group? Does age just break most of us as prison does?

I'm ready for a silence. the loneliness here in the apt. is preferable to listening to the "average"—not perfectly, but the ones just spending/wasting TIME. They "mean" well . . .

This started out to be a love letter, but it's too soon after class—I'll de(com)press and finish this evening—I love you (read that Leary article and pretend it is us and see how far they have to go to have a separate reality.)

Time machine this morning. Up and down. Read my Chuangtse book and it restores my balance. The isolation is good. It frees me in spite of my desires. If I pretend it is forever, and not a prison, but I am the outsider without you, then I would, in time, have an Al, Dave, Joe, Jack, Earl et al pass by again and go to "work." And yet to know, to believe without a doubt that what we have is, although rare, not unique. (It was or would have been easier to never have known it.) and now, to know there is no loss or gain and yet in this isolation to know that our precarious & precious treasure an (will?) fade in Time . . .

Oxymoronic—Bitter/Sweet, pain/pleasure, that I do to myself imagining futures without you, they come unbidden! and so do tears. This is passion!

There are so many possibilities of our remaining separated that I can really "scare myself"—must stop wallowing.

Kind of bogged down on working. Nothing is getting started. Did two watercolors (sort of similar to the Waterfall) and the overlay to the Treasure Map. Can't do much with that until I get back. What images next—I know I won't do the big one—although I might when I get back.

RED STICK CAMBLIN ROBIN GOODFELLOW

I'm sort of trapped in too much time in my own game here. Red Stick is in Houston with his mistress and other pirates. Robin Goodfellow doesn't get stoned alone much and has no other practical jokers to talk to. So, Camblin, the old professor, can't go into it with his old friends and the rest of the faculty have not come around at all, so I sit here unable to let in the Magic Theater—Watching Woody Allen in Love and Death alone in the theater, should have warned me that it was a premonition. I was doing this for the money and so that is all I'll get out of it.

Make me a list of things to eat that are good for me and don't take any cooking.

I'll write again tonight. This morning is dribbling away and I can't get in.too. it. All my love . . . bob

I wish I could teach what I feel instead of using words to make it sound like I know—a typical thought by anonymous Bosh.

> —from a letter Camblin wrote from Baton Rouge dated Aug 30, 1975.

Camblin was no less in love, and his jealousies had not diminished. Our relationship was still poetic and powerful. His time in Baton Rouge, preceded by my absence, brought out his insecurities in the relationship and made him anxious and volatile. Eventually jealousy gained the upper hand. Camblin chastised himself for being unable to control his emotions and for relying on me to keep him happy. He needed a way to vent his frustrations. Thus, the character Red Stick the Pirate, with his symbolic skull and crossbones, came into being. Through the alter-ego, he developed his "sins of humor." The ruthless and acerbic outlaw allowed him to be outrageous and to express his anxieties, regardless of decorum. The pirate was beyond censure and he took no prisoners.

In the Baton Rouge letter Camblin also noted his disenchantment with his New York dealer, Brooke Alexander. "Have to go along with Brooke, he made me feel guilty again and that's twice. One more time—I have to not want anything from him since he is not interested in me, but in the object."[3]

Brooke Alexander had made numerous efforts to work with Camblin, undoubtedly believing that requesting more work was a good thing, not that he was trying to cause guilt or to indicate that he was not interested in the creator of the work. But Camblin followed his own set of rules; if someone did not live up to his enigmatic standards, he walked away. Before demanding the return of all his work,

Camblin decided to have me act as his representative. He told Alexander that he would only communicate with him through his partner. Alexander graciously accepted the new "conditions." Numerous letters ensued between Alexander and me, even though I did not feel comfortable with the process. Camblin's romantic vision of the ideal artist/dealer relationship doomed long-term gallery representation. Compromise was not part of his nature. He felt justified by changing the game plan.

CHAPTER FIFTEEN

Cast of Characters: Cindy Claus to Santa Claus

Acknowledging the absurdity he found in his own human nature, Camblin appreciated existential preposterousness, exemplified by the Theater of the Absurd. He filled sketchbooks with notes on existentialism and absurdity. His life was his "magic theater," and he was the main attraction. Rather than perform on stage, he instead transformed into whatever persona he felt filled the requirements of the moment. In doing so, he created and played the roles of an entire cast of characters, hiding himself in numerous guises. Or perhaps he was displaying different aspects of his true nature for all to see? In an effort to understand an absurd world, Camblin accepted the preposterousness of an absurd human nature. When he inhabited one of his characters, he was demonstrating that acceptance. He was revealing the fluidity of his self-image.

In earlier self-portraiture Camblin had drawn mimetic likenesses. In a 1965 drawing, a mask of his face rests on the partial head of a doll puppet with one lidless eye. He titled the work *Plastic Mask for Doll—Vacuum Formed over Death Mask*. The use of his own death mask as a disguise for a doll gives the portrait absurdist and macabre overtones. The death mask ties the image to the *danse macabre* (dance of death) and to funerary masks. Camblin does not conceal his identity behind the mask; rather he uses the mask to reveal himself while obscuring the doll,

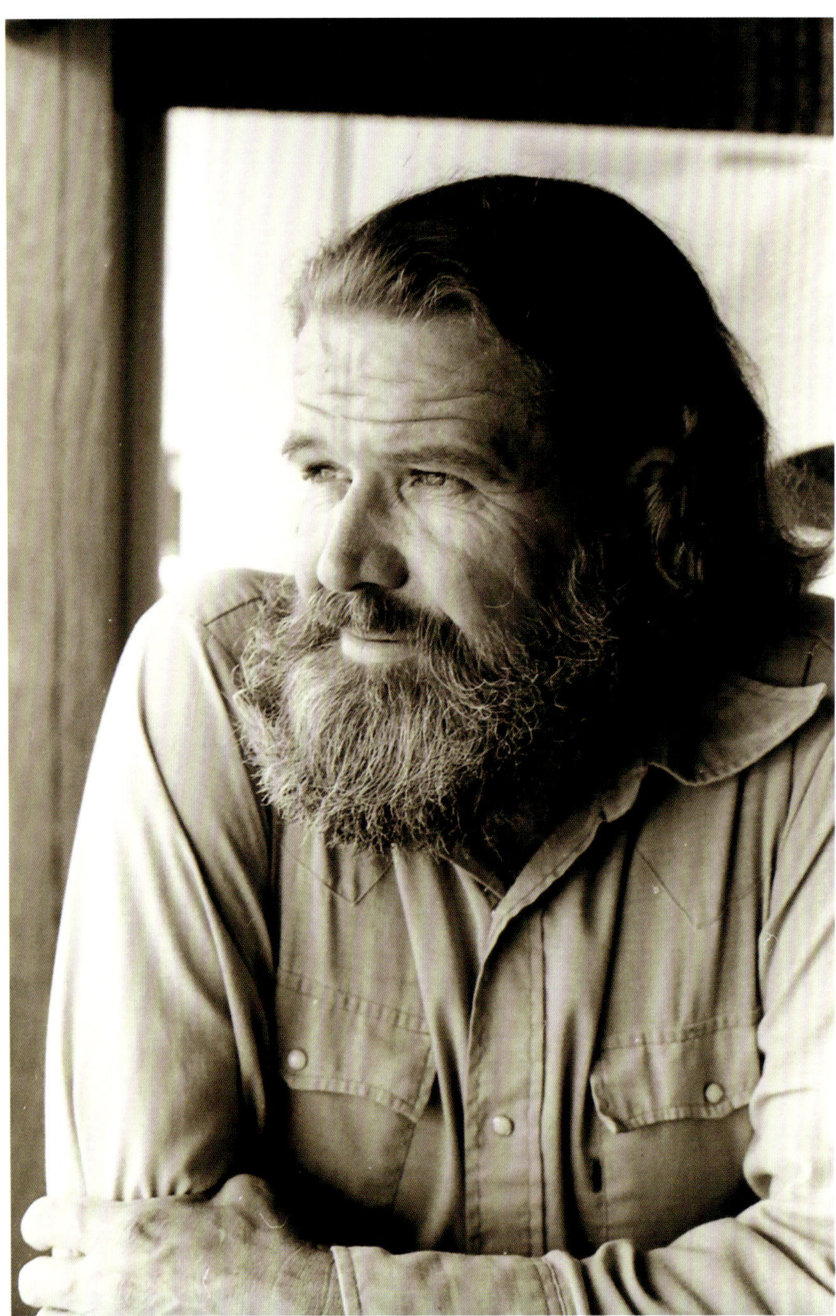

Photo of Camblin by author, 1975

demonstrating his interest in masking and the personification of dolls.

A year later he drew a self-portrait with hatching obscuring half his face. The right eye looks directly at its creator or viewer, making the portrait confrontational. Camblin attached a newspaper image of a mounted, antlered stag over his portrait using masking tape. On the tape he printed "CAUTION."[1] Underneath the deer he wrote, "Portrait of the artist in Salt Lake City, Utah." A mounted deer head suggests the deer no longer needs to be careful, but that perhaps the male hidden under the newspaper clipping should take caution. Masking his own identity with a warning, Camblin suggests that it will take more than a mounted deer head to keep death at bay.

Employing symbols, he created an etching with his portrait drawn on hanging fabric nailed to a neutral background. A self-portrait on a hanging veil, tied or pinned at the corners, is, *prima facie*,[2] lifted from the Spanish artist Francisco de Zurbaran's paintings of the *Volto Santo* or *Holy Face*.[3] Zurbaran's paintings[4] are examples of Spanish mysticism. Camblin's face on a hanging fabric reveals his own view of himself as a mystic.

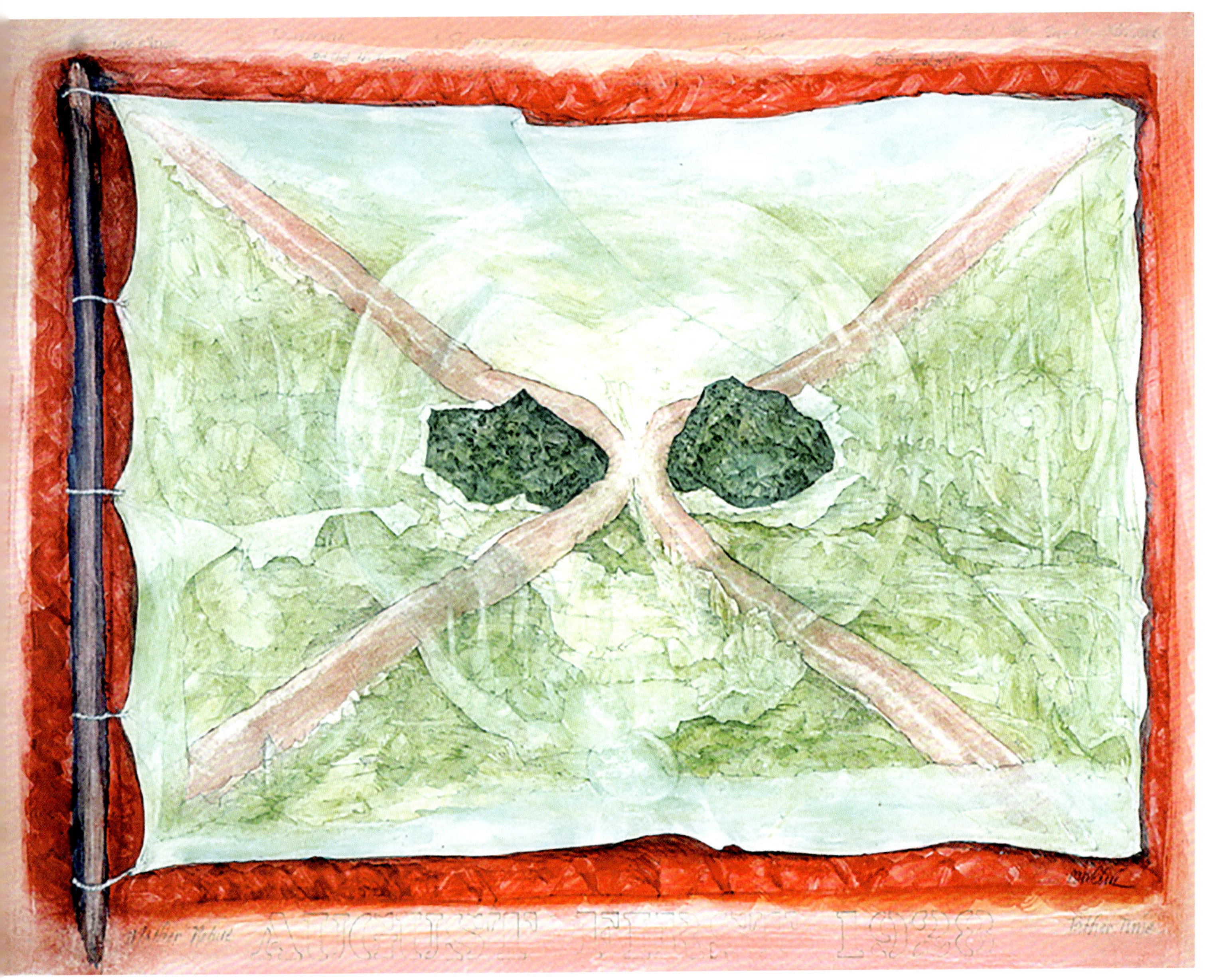

Camblin painted skull in *August First 1928*, his birth date. *Photograph by Scott Peterson.*

Self-portraits with masks (to reveal, conceal, or confuse) as well as an image of himself as a mystic may have piqued Camblin's interest in alternate personalities. He had begun using alter egos prior to his 1975 Baton Rouge semester

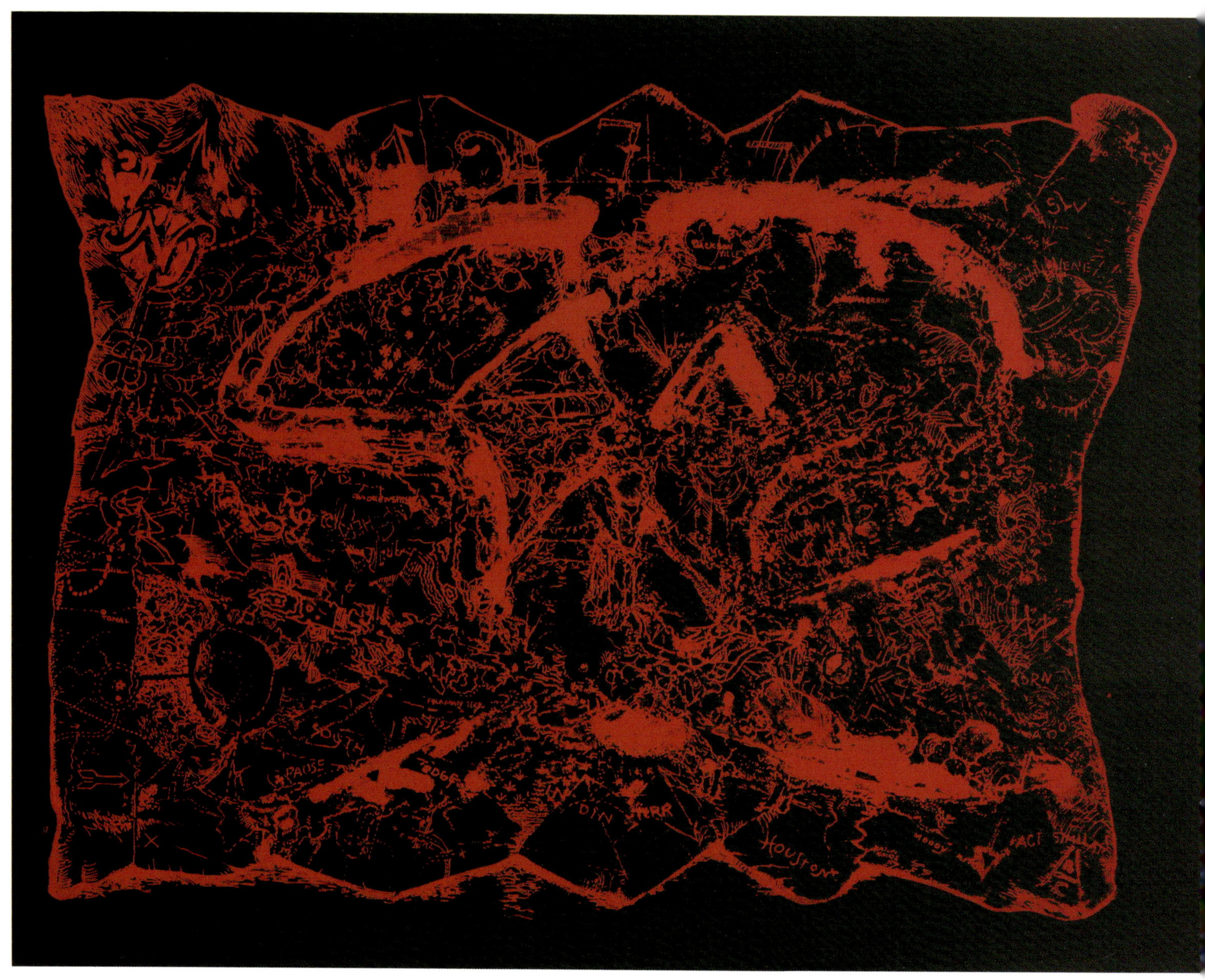

The red abstracted skull drawn on black paper adds an aggressive mood to the flag. *Photograph by Scott Peterson.*

during which time he created Red Stick the Pirate. Several years earlier, his daughter, Robyn, had given him some Santa Claus stickers that turned into a female with a large hairdo if viewed upside down and from the back. He drew a generic female face on the reversed Santa silhouette and christened her Cindy Claws (sometimes Cindy Claus). He went on to use the image of Santa Claus as a jovial elf throughout the rest of his life, even seeing himself as a Santa. Camblin never, however, assumed the Cindy Claus identity. He only employed her name and form in sketchbooks, letters, and drawings. Two characters originating from one sticker appealed to his sense of the absurd.

As a professor, Camblin had long used the trilogy of King, Shaman, and Fool to depict archetypes that individuals and groups use when interacting. The King governs, thinks, and rules. The Shaman is the intuitive teacher, often with religious overtones. The Fool entertains, makes art, and often speaks the truth. (Camblin chose to omit the hunter or military archetype, a presence not wanted in his world.) He would slip from one persona to another, often to demonstrate the self-deceptions or *hintergedankens* used by us all.

Rather than simply lecture about King, Shaman, Fool archetypes, Camblin decided to take role-playing more seriously. During his semester at LSU in Baton Rouge, he taught as Red Stick[5] the Pirate,[6] which was not a benign role. Red Stick painted pirate flags with skulls and crossbones (or large red *X*'s) bordered by red. For him, skulls were the framework for the mask of flesh we call the face. The skull remains long after the face mask disappears. He operated under his flag of Death, giving grim overtones to his character. Camblin likened artists to outlaws: "Artists live on the fringe of society and steal ideas." He seemed comfortable in the role of Red Stick. He believed he could speak the truth no matter how brutal. The character cost him friends and acquaintances.

He tied his skull imagery to his earlier "Flying W" by creating a jawless skull with the sides of the W curved in to form the cranium. He employed triangles for the empty eye sockets. He was drawn to the image and tried various papers and techniques to create the pirate flag.

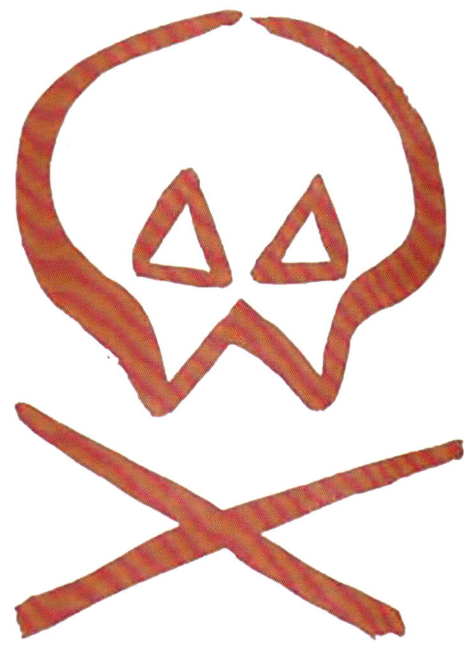

This rendition of a *Skull and Cross Bones* became Camblin's mark.

Back in Houston, Camblin wanted to lessen the dominance of Red Stick and replace the character's influence with something softer, something beautiful.

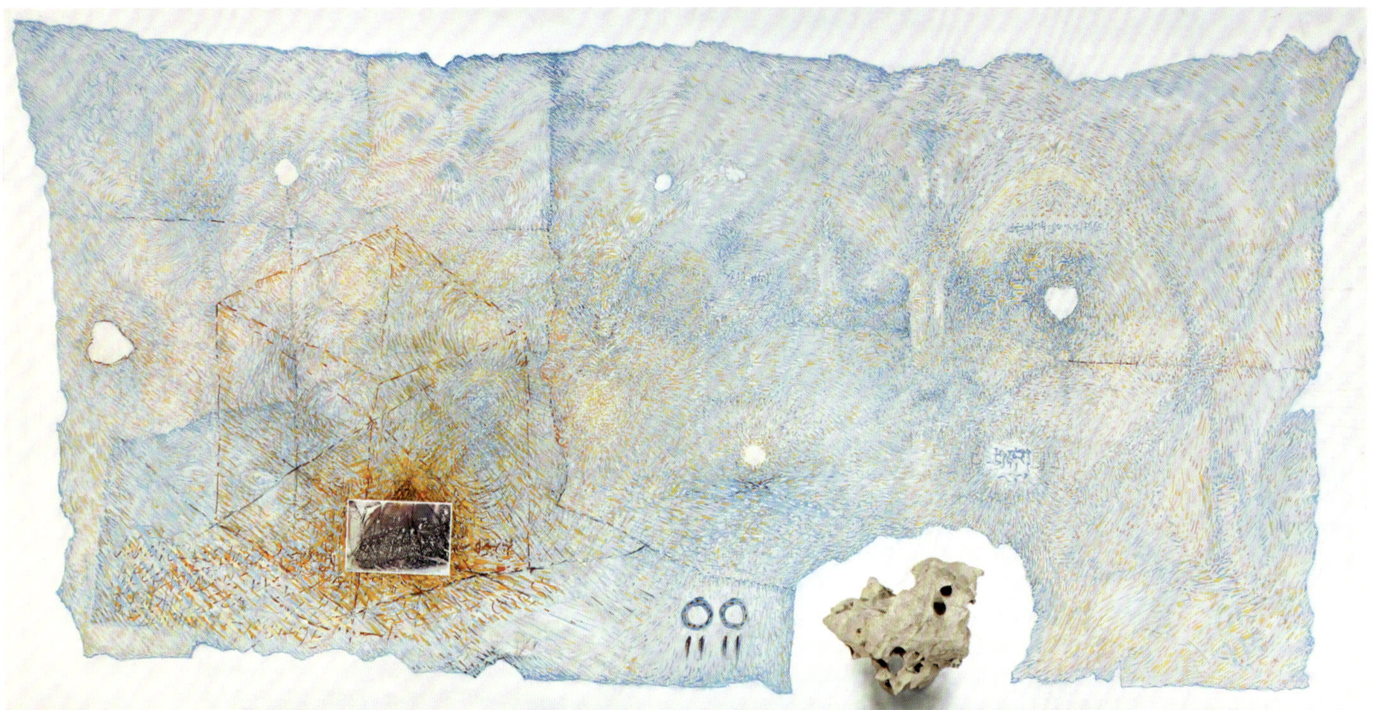

Treasure Map, c. 1980s. Watercolor, 41" X 79". *Collection of Annie DeGuerin. Photo Credit: David P. Gray.*

Inspired by Sandro Botticelli's *Primavera*, he painted a portrait of Flora, whom Zephyrus, from Greek mythology, turned into the goddess of spring. Camblin's *Flora or Kay Sage* wears a half-mask with her enigmatic smile. Like Botticelli's Flora, her hair is full of flowers, and her neck is encircled with a garland. However, Camblin's flowers seem to be closer to electrons and scientific symbols. His Flora is flanked on the right by a large red exclamation point, similar to a red baseball bat, that, together with the mask and scientific symbols, add some of Red Stick's pirate spirit and mystery to Camblin's Flora. He, tried but couldn't quite rid himself of the pirate.

Alongside Red Stick the Pirate, Camblin created The Professor, an entertaining *raconteur*,[7] a role that Camblin had nurtured during his teaching career. He fit the part. To balance the pirate outlaw and staid professor, he created the flirtatious and charming Robin Goodfellow,[8] a practical joker. An article from Louisiana State University's newspaper announced, "Visiting Artist—On display in the Union

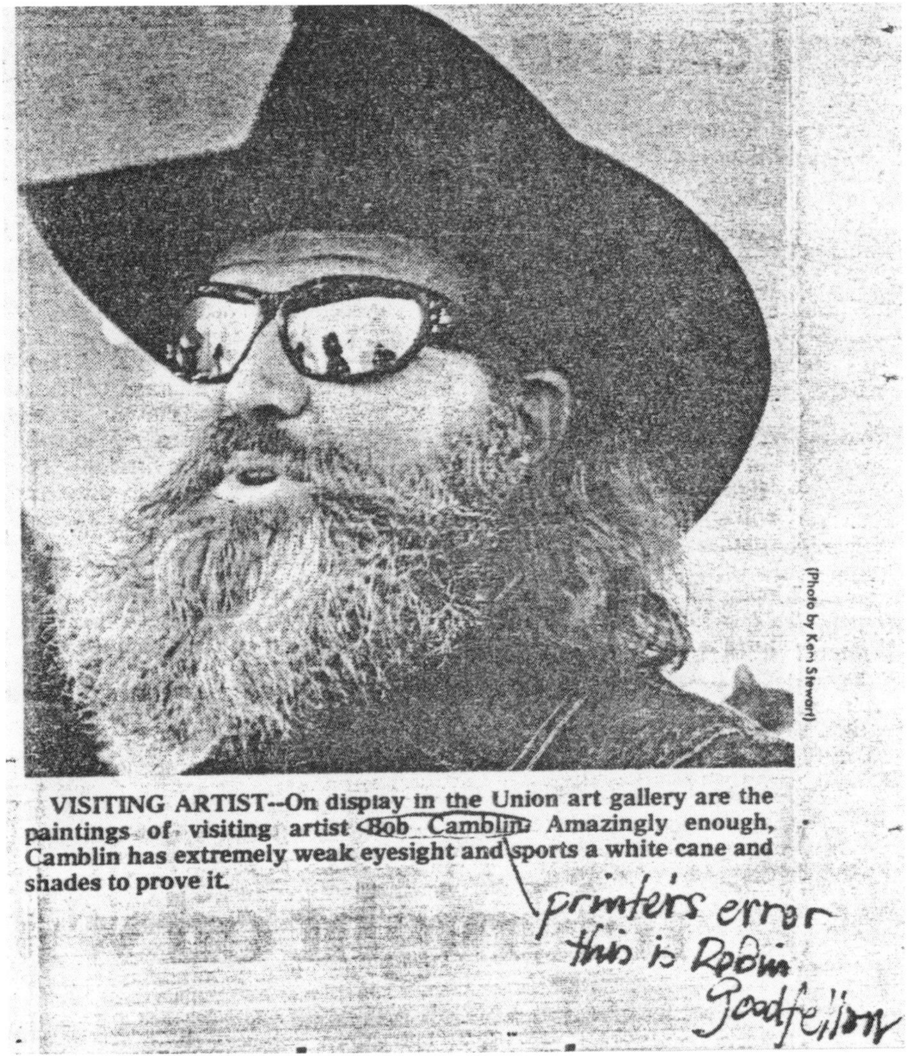

The births of Red Stick the Pirate and Robin Goodfellow occurred at Louisiana State University in Baton Rouge where Camblin taught for a semester in 1975.

art gallery are the paintings of visiting artist Bob Camblin. Amazingly enough, Camblin has extremely weak eyesight and sports a white cane and shades to prove it."[9] The photograph shows a headshot of a bearded Camblin in a black cowboy hat and sunglasses. Underneath the photograph Camblin wrote: "Printer's error. This is Robin Goodfellow."

In a letter from Baton Rouge, dated September 15, 1975, Camblin paid tribute to Duchamp: "I will have to make the best of my being in Red Stick, Louisiana, by letting it flow and watch me. 'C'est la vie, Rrose.'"[10]

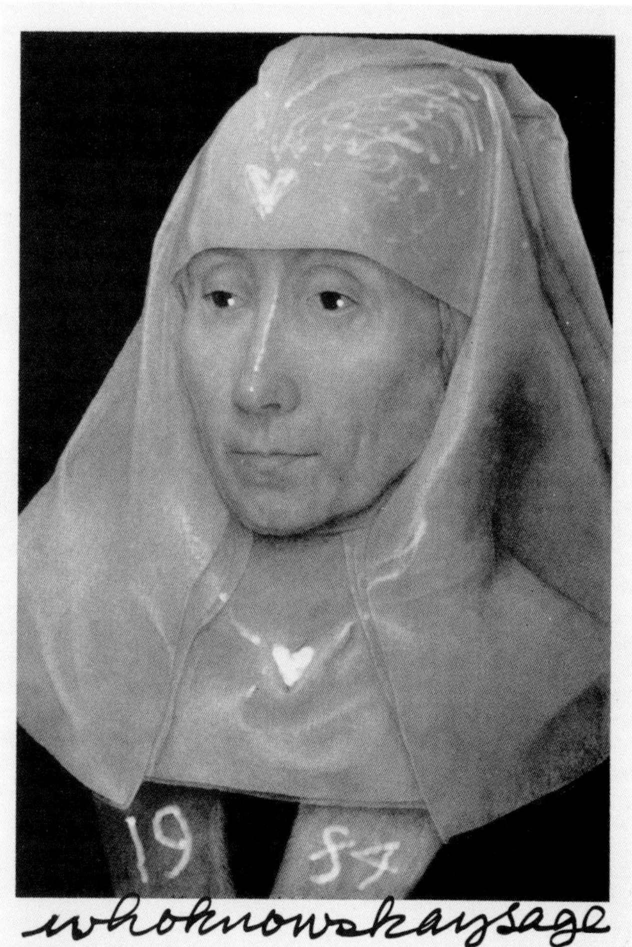

Camblin used the French pronunciation of *Que Scais-je?* to create Kay Sage.

Referencing Duchamp's Rrose Selavy, Camblin created a gender neutral entity, Kay Sage.[11] Camblin had been borrowing Montaigne's[12] skeptical question *Que Scay- je?*[13] for some time (What do I know?). When spoken, Montaigne's French query sounds similar to Kay Sage: Kay and *Que* are close in pronunciation and *sais-je* sounds like Sage. Camblin included Kay Sage's name, signature, and initials in his writings and in his art. Unlike Duchamp, he did not impersonate or dress as the character.

The name Kay Sage offered Camblin a loophole: He could avoid or escape verbal and visual traps by uttering or writing *Que sais-je?* or Kay Sage. He could answer questions he did not like with the same retort. The query gave him a way around any obstruction. He could end any discussion or argument with a shrug and the question. He used Kay Sage. What did she know? She knew she could mask Camblin's entire identity, at least momentarily.

Extending his cast of characters, Camblin added Old Paint, the artist's view of himself as a used, bent tube of paint; a blind Impressionist artist (eyes masked) who painted with the help of an assistant, who described images to him; and Anonymous Bosh, an homage to Hieronymus Bosch (Camblin intentionally omitted the "c" in Bosch, noting that he, Camblin, was the missing "c"). As he aged, *Mort* (French for death) joined his cast. He brought Santa Claus back to life as a sprightly old elf, bearer of Christmas presents (or troubled by the lack of gifts). Camblin chose a magical realm from pre-Christian Irish lore for Santa's setting: *Tir Na Nog*, Land of the Young. Because Santa is a cultural icon for the young as well as for everlasting joy and giving, an aging Camblin confirmed his wish for a suspended mortality.

Santa is a common character, at least every December, but Mr. Peanut is not. Camblin never explained his reasons for personifying the enigmatic nut. In a sketchbook from 1971 Camblin drew Mr. Peanut, beside which he wrote, "I saw Mr. Peanut on the streets of Tulsa, Oklahoma in 1936, in the winter." Obviously, the sighting of the nut remained an indelible memory for most of his life. The eight-year-old's imprinted memory was reinforced through advertising, begun in 1906, by Planters Peanuts, for one of America's first "everyman" snack foods. He would have seen the logo and the accompanying nuts for sale his entire life. Camblin's Mr. Peanut[14] came into existence sometime in the 1970s. He was drawn to the legume's ubiquitous, commercial, American presence, and to the absurdity of anthropomorphizing a nut. The duality between the nut's omnipresence versus the costume's singularity intrigued him, as seen in his numerous drawings of the character. Foucault wrote late in life on the aesthetics of the self: the individual emancipated him- or herself from the isolation and alienation of the modern condition by turning him- or herself into a work of art, such as a self-proclaimed existentialist hiding in public as Mr. Peanut.

Camblin owned a full-scale Mr. Peanut costume (Planters logo) with monocle and cane. He once placed the costume behind him during an art opening, but he never wore it, possibly because it was too small.[15] He did don dark glasses, a hat, gloves, and cane: a masked enigma in his version of a peanut suit. He doubtless chose the disguise to mystify the collectors and to cause a disturbance in the dimension, but his choice of such a popular advertising icon was meant to demonstrate his solidarity with Pop Art's "consumer image into icon."

He was not alone in his use of a peanut for inspiration. Horace Clifford (H. C.) Westermann,[16] an artist Camblin admired, carved a giant, two-foot-long peanut out of pine, (*Untitled First Peanut*) in 1973. The possibility exists that the sculpture reinforced Camblin's connection to Westermann whether Westermann was aware of Camblin or not. It is also possible that Camblin's Mr. Peanut character might have been a personal homage to other peanut eccentrics, including a Canadian who

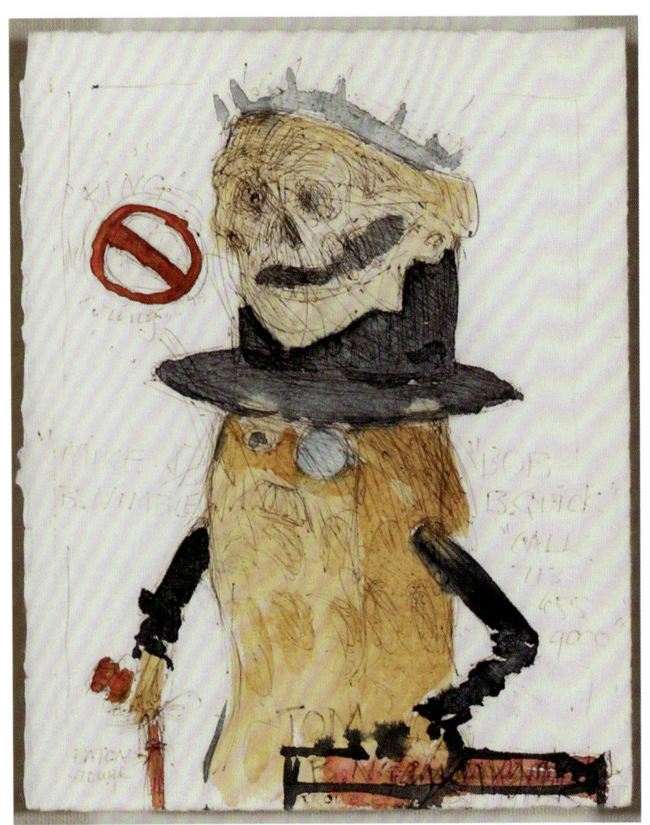

Left: A handmade *Mr. Peanut* postcard from Camblin to Mike and Gayle DeGeurin. *Above:*
Back of postcard. Watercolor and ink on paper, c. 1980s, 7" X 6". *Photographs by David P. Gra[?]*

also created a Mr. Peanut persona. Vincent Trasov, a performance artist, began his
Mr. Peanut act in 1972. Two years later Trasov took his Mr. Peanut persona, in
costume, to numerous cities including New York and San Francisco. For his most
famous Mr. Peanut performance, he dressed in a Mr. Peanut suit and ran for mayor
of Vancouver. His *Mr. Peanut Mayoralty Campaign of 1974* performance ran for
twenty days. Mr. Peanut's "art-centric platform" included the acronym PEANUT:
P for Performance, E for Elegance, A for Art, N for Nonsense, U for Uniqueness,
and T for Talent. Trasov walked around the streets of Vancouver as Mr. Peanut,
pretending to campaign. John Mitchell, his manager, followed him around the
streets proclaiming platitudes like, "People are as ready for one nut as the next."
William S. Burroughs, who happened to be in Vancouver during a performance,
publicly endorsed the candidate. Trasov once commented: "Once I got in my shell,
I assumed the identity of Mr. Peanut. It wasn't Vincent Trasov anymore. People

started calling me Mr. Peanut. The name stuck. That's how I could do my identity change, my research on identity, adopting the identity of Mr. Peanut. Getting out of my own ego. It was an empty shell. People could pour their ideas into the empty shell. I was just a vehicle for other people's imagination."[17]

No record exists that could prove Camblin knew about the Canadian's Mr. Peanut although it seems unlikely, but not impossible, that two contemporary artists would create equivalent characters at basically the same time. The 1974 publicity[18] generated by Trasov would have been hard to miss. Several years after Camblin began drawing Mr. Peanut, he began assuming the persona of the nut. He continued adding Mr. Peanut to art into the late 1980s.

Camblin, Westermann, and Trasov were not the only artists to be drawn to the peanut. 1986, the year before his death, Andy Warhol included Mr. Peanut in his silkscreen of Leonardo da Vinci's *The Last Supper*, collapsing two images—one sacred and one profane. That would epitomize Camblin. A well-known optical illusion challenges the brain to recognize a spotted dog in a scattering of high-contrast camouflage. How much can be removed from the ordinary world of details for a viewer to cohere an image? At the other extreme how much can be piled on? Warhol's *Mr. Peanut Last Supper* challenges both extremes. He exposed a reproduction of *The Last Supper* at such low contrast that the image is mangled. Then he layered it on top of an aggressive hunting gear camouflage pattern, itself an optical illusion. Added to that, Warhol stationed Mr. Peanut ridiculously hovering like the risen Christ above the sacramental table. The Polish Warhol had been a Byzantine Catholic boy. Camp satire and optical illusions notwithstanding, the juxtaposition of Jesus and Mr. Peanut would, to a great many viewers, be sacrilegious. Similarly Camblin's use of Mr. Peanut and *St. Bambola* imagery gave off more than a whiff of sarcasm. Bambola could suggest fetuses in apothecary jars: biological oddities preserved for Victorian *wunderkammer*, the ultimate objectification. Contempt for the preciousness of Camblin's own Catholic upbringing! Good or not, an artist gambling his career on such imagery had better take the temperature of the New York appetite. Or maybe he didn't give a damn.

Camblin masked his identity with Red Stick, Robin Goodfellow, The Professor, Mr. Peanut, and to a degree, Kay Sage. While he could not compartmentalize his creativity, he could personalize aspects of his character by giving them names. Risking a broad generalization, people, especially men, are conditioned to employ public personalities. Our culture expects us to play the roles prescribed by professions, and men especially seem to identify with the mask their "job" role requires. One becomes the artist, the doctor, the merchant. Private identities are reserved for intimates. The possibility exists that inner complexities may reflect unresolved identities.

Camblin knew that Carl Jung used "persona" to describe the social mask that everyone hides behind: "The persona is a kind of mask, designed on the one hand to make a definite impression upon others, and on the other hand to conceal the true nature of the individual."[19] Camblin, however, did not appear to hide behind his masks; he inhabited the character he presented. Audience interaction, pro or con, validated his performances. Each alter-ego, though masked, was an attempt to understand aspects of his own personality, regardless if his characterizations were misunderstood by others. Then again, Camblin may have wanted his role-playing to be misinterpreted, his masks to obfuscate and magnify. He consistently refused to explain himself or his art, and by doing so, he revealed his desire to become unknowable. Did his cast of characters give him freedom to act in whatever manner pleased him without revealing his true self, or did his personae offer glimpses of the man behind the curtain? He even referenced studios with his personae. On a watercolor and ink study of his Bell Street Studio, Camblin wrote, "After Red Stick 4San."

Camblin was indeed investigating himself through the use of his cast of characters. Foucault argued that for an individual to be free, he or she must turn away from all theories that claim to be global or radical, refuse to submit to authority, and direct oneself to an investigation of the self. The reading of Foucault may have helped Camblin turn inward and stay there rather than throw himself into the dynamics of the New York art world. Foucault felt that the individual must critique society, authority, and dogmas as much as critiquing oneself. The Mr. Peanut suit functioned as an aesthetic self-critique of the culture. The suit also connected Camblin to Image Bank[20] and to Trasov's acronym PEANUT. Mr. Peanut defined the terms of its critique. Camblin could simply use the suit as a prop. The critique came with it.

In June of 1976, Camblin cut his ties with Brooke Alexander. He asked for all his unsold work to be sent back to him. In a letter to Alexander, he wrote that he

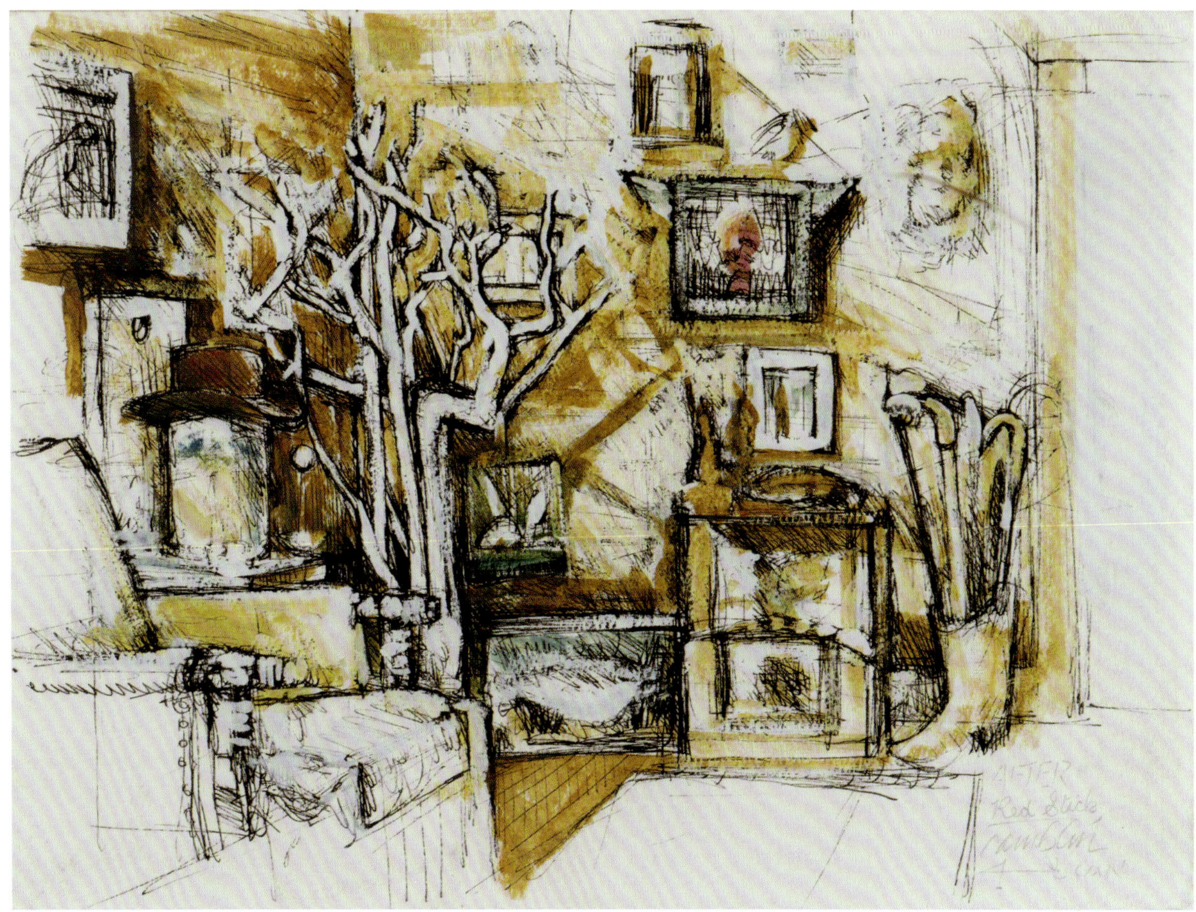

West Bell Studio, c. 1977. Watercolor and ink drawing, 11" X 14". *Photograph by Scott Peterson.*

and the New York dealer "were not on the same page." Alexander expressed his desire to continue the artist-dealer relationship, but Camblin insisted on the return of his work. Alexander graciously complied.

To some, Camblin's exit from the New York art world seemed to be an act of self-sabotage. Alexander had successfully promoted Camblin through exhibitions in his eponymous gallery. He commissioned the prints for *SeeKing the Longhorn* and included them in a traveling show, which toured extensively. Alexander traveled to Houston to spend time with Camblin even though the New York dealer was seldom met with enthusiasm. Besides Alexander, Nancy Hoffman Gallery had included Camblin's work in a 1974 exhibition. The Whitney Museum of American Art

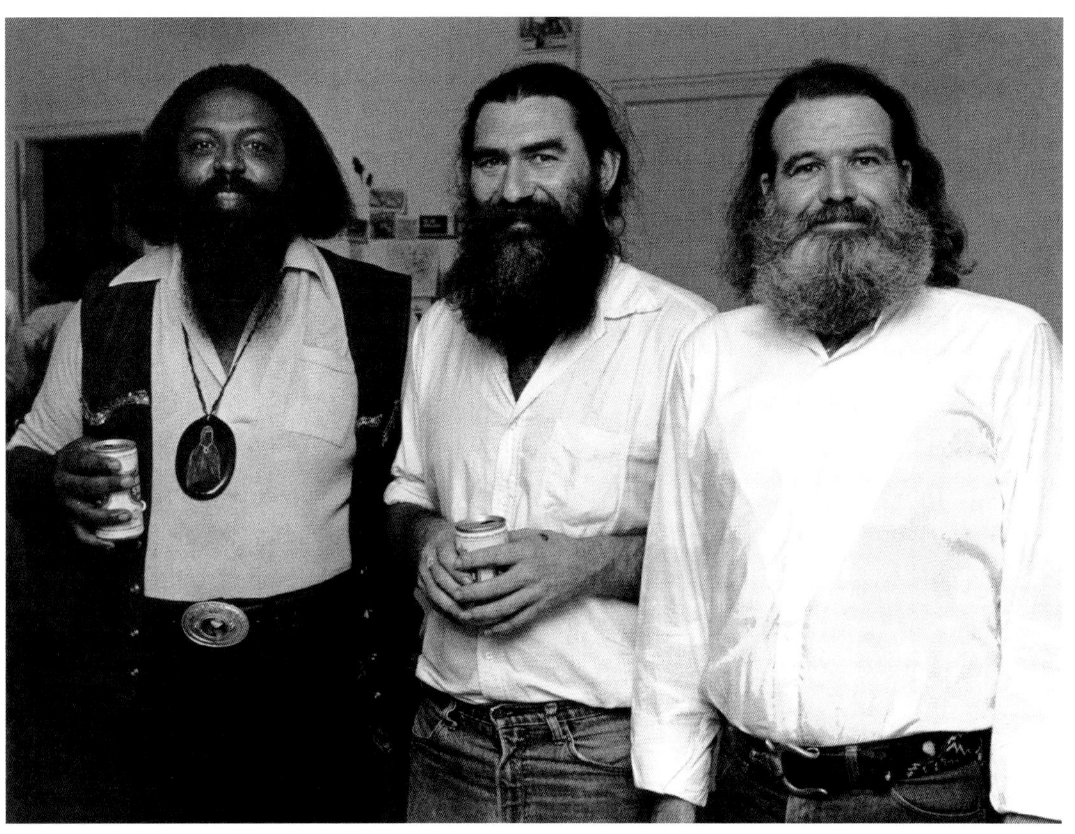

Frank Martin photo of, from left to right: Bert Long, James Surls, and Camblin

showed his art in its *American Drawing 1963–1973* show as well as in the museum's *Extraordinary Realities* exhibition. For whatever reasons, Camblin did not spend any time or energy trying to have his work represented in New York. Perhaps he felt so strongly about his Texas cowboy identity that he felt New York would compromise him. Fearing that he would be perceived as a country bumpkin, he may have been reluctant to participate in the "slick" NY art scene. He enjoyed being an eccentric and dominant player in the Houston art world, preferring his audience, collectors, and dealers to participate in his world. He enjoyed interacting with his admirers and friends. In Houston his cast of characters intrigued and amused his collectors. He may have worried that his role-playing would be less well received outside of Texas, a state where eccentrics are venerated. Then again, he simply may not have cared.

During the year, Camblin not only developed his cast of characters, he also created art for twelve shows, and moved his studio to a different space in 1426 W. Bell, #5. Covo de Iongh represented his work in three shows, including the *Box Show*. He wrote about his new boxes:

The New Boxes:

The boxes are several things—they pull several periods together and perhaps are going to be more open than I first supposed. I must recopy some of the notes on the latest drawing since this morning opened up several observations and levels of understanding to me. Since I never analyze what is happening until there seems to be enough pieces that it begins to make sense, it is good that a number of things fell into place.

A. The distance of the picture plane and its meaning

B. The box and its one-point perspective/its relationship to earlier works. The similarities of subject matter and their similarities to earlier works, especially organic—man-made.

The concept of metamorphosis again revisited, but approached from new directions.

1. The box as inscape/mindscape/body interior

2. The box as chrysalis in new metamorphosis series

3. The box as man-made but functionless and non-technological

Covo de Iongh's April 1976 exhibition, *Origin of the Birds*, combined Camblin's intricate art with Bill Steffy's jewelry. Camblin's piece of art, from which the title of the show originated, is surrounded by a handmade frame with a lower shelf. The frame is finished with gold gilt, adding to its preciousness. The originality of the frame that Camblin designed played into the artist's concept of the numinous.[21] The shelf allowed the owner to add small precious objects, adding mysterious spiritual power to the piece, thus turning the work into an altar. Camblin continued using his shelf/altar frame for some years.

Louisiana Gallery in Houston included Camblin's art in a show. He had work in exhibits at The Museum of Modern Art in Fort Worth, the Indianapolis Institute of Art, the Memorial Art Gallery at the University of Rochester, New York, Louisiana State University, Baker University in Baldwin City, Kansas, and The Akron Art Institute. He and Bonnie officially divorced in the spring of 1976 and in the fall of '76 she married Bruno Leon. Camblin felt completely free to pursue his dreams, which included a return visit to Venice. He traveled to Italy alone, knowing I would join him whenever possible.

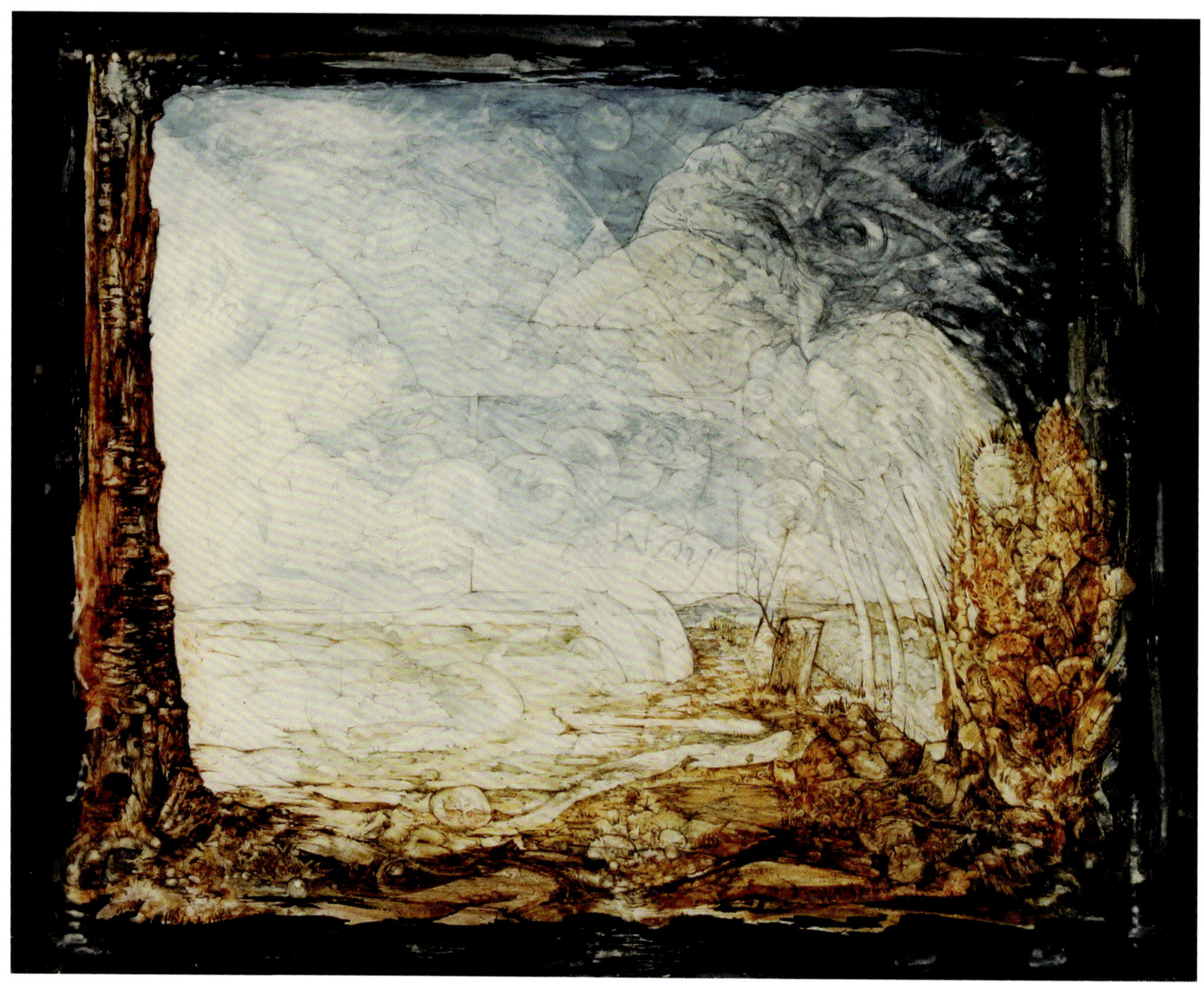

Origin of the Birds, c. 1974. Watercolor and pencil on paper, 12" X 15". *Collection of Lourdes and Ray Balinskas. David P. Gray photograph.*

CHAPTER SIXTEEN

Venice in His Own Words and Through His Unique Vision

"Over the Everglades, cumulus giants and a rainbow around out plane. Flying to Milan on the way to Venice from London. Among the clouds, some of them are hard! the Alps! Lightning and rain in Venezia. Left Houston in a flood; going to bed tonight in a rain."

—From Libro di Ricordare *sketchbook*

Twenty years had passed since Camblin's Fulbright year in Italy, and with Bonnie and his children with Bruno in Michigan, he felt the timing was right to return to Venice. He wanted to be in the city he loved with the woman he loved. To that end, he created Subscriptions for Future Art to finance his venture and, with Betty Moody's help, sold enough subscriptions to pay for his journey. His cast of characters accompanied him. I visited him in the watery city for several month-long sojourns. When I traveled, he sent me letters filled with watercolor illustrations. At every arrival I was greeted with numerous and beautiful sketchbooks filled with longing, drawings, and watercolors.

"Memories jostling to be remembered. None will get in line. My memories act like Romans, except they don't even say, '*Permesso.*' My memories, each part of

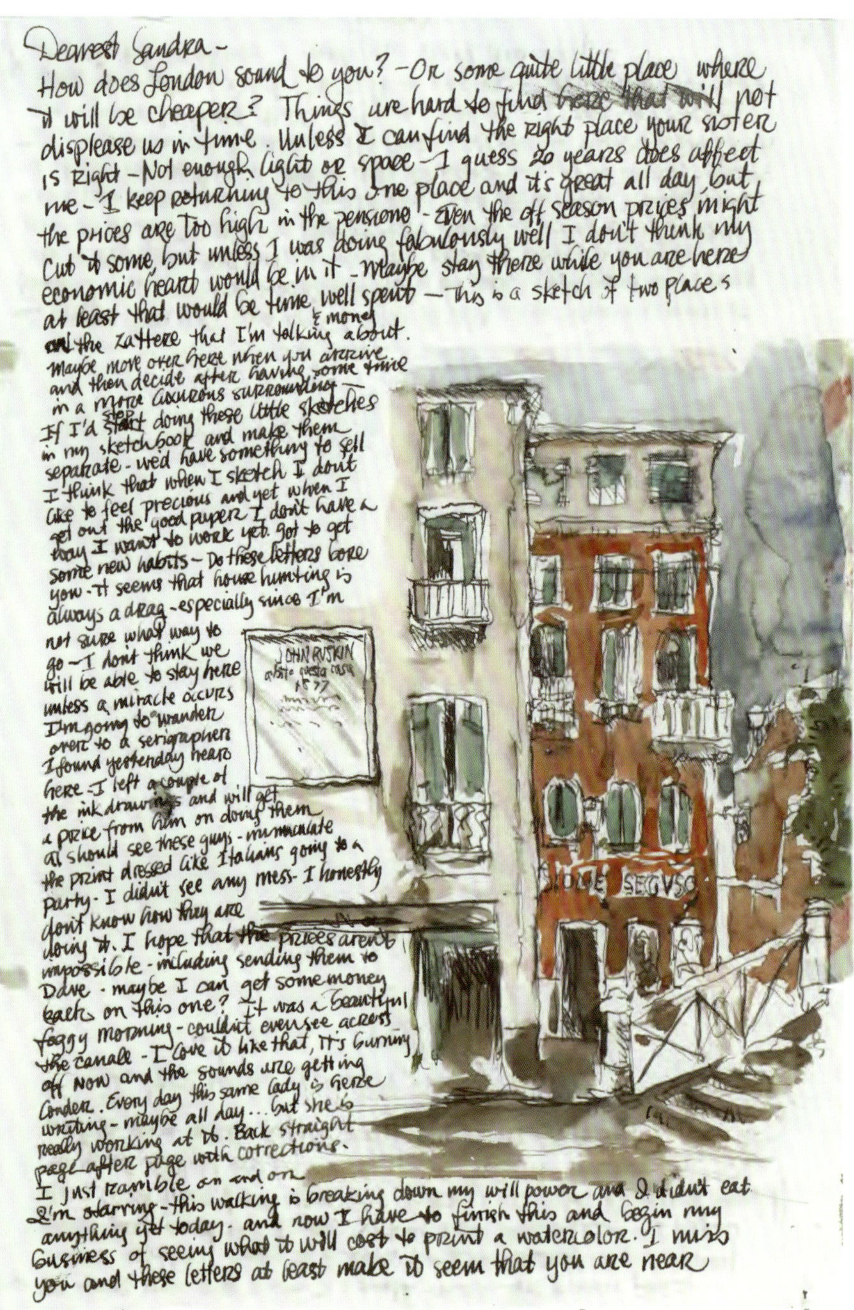

Dearest Sandra—

How does London sound to you? —Or some quite little place where it will be cheaper? Things are hard to find here that will not displease us in time. Unless I can find the right place your sister is right—Not enough light or space—I guess 20 years does affect me—I keep returning to this one place and it's great all day, but the prices are too high in the pensione—Even the off season prices might cut to some, but unless I was doing fabulously well I don't think my economic heart would be in it—Maybe stay there while you are here at least that would be time well spent—This is a sketch of two places on the Zattere that I'm talking about. & money

Maybe move over here when you arrive and then decide after having some time in a more luxurious surrounding.

If I'd start doing these little sketches in my sketchbook and make them separate—we'd have something to sell. I think that when I sketch I don't like to feel precious and yet when I get out the good paper I don't have a way I want to work yet. Got to get some new habits—Do these letters bore you—It seems that house hunting is always a drag—especially since I'm not sure what way to go—I don't think we will be able to stay here unless a miracle occurs. I'm going to wander over to a serigrapher I found yesterday hear here I left a couple of the ink drawings and will get a price from him on doing them. I should see these guys—immaculate the print dressed like Italians going to a party. I didn't see any mess. I honestly don't know how they are doing it. I hope that the prices aren't impossible—including sending them to Dave—maybe I can get some money back on this one? It was a beautiful foggy morning—couldn't even see across the canale—I love it like that, it's burning off now and the sounds are getting louder. Every day this same lady is here writing—maybe all day... but she is really working at it. Back straight page after page with corrections.

I just ramble on and on. I'm starving—this walking is breaking down my will power and I didn't eat anything yet today—and now I have to finish this and begin my business of seeing what it will cost to print a watercolor. I miss you and these letters at least make it seem that you are near

Letter w/watcolor of Jon Ruskin's Venetian home.

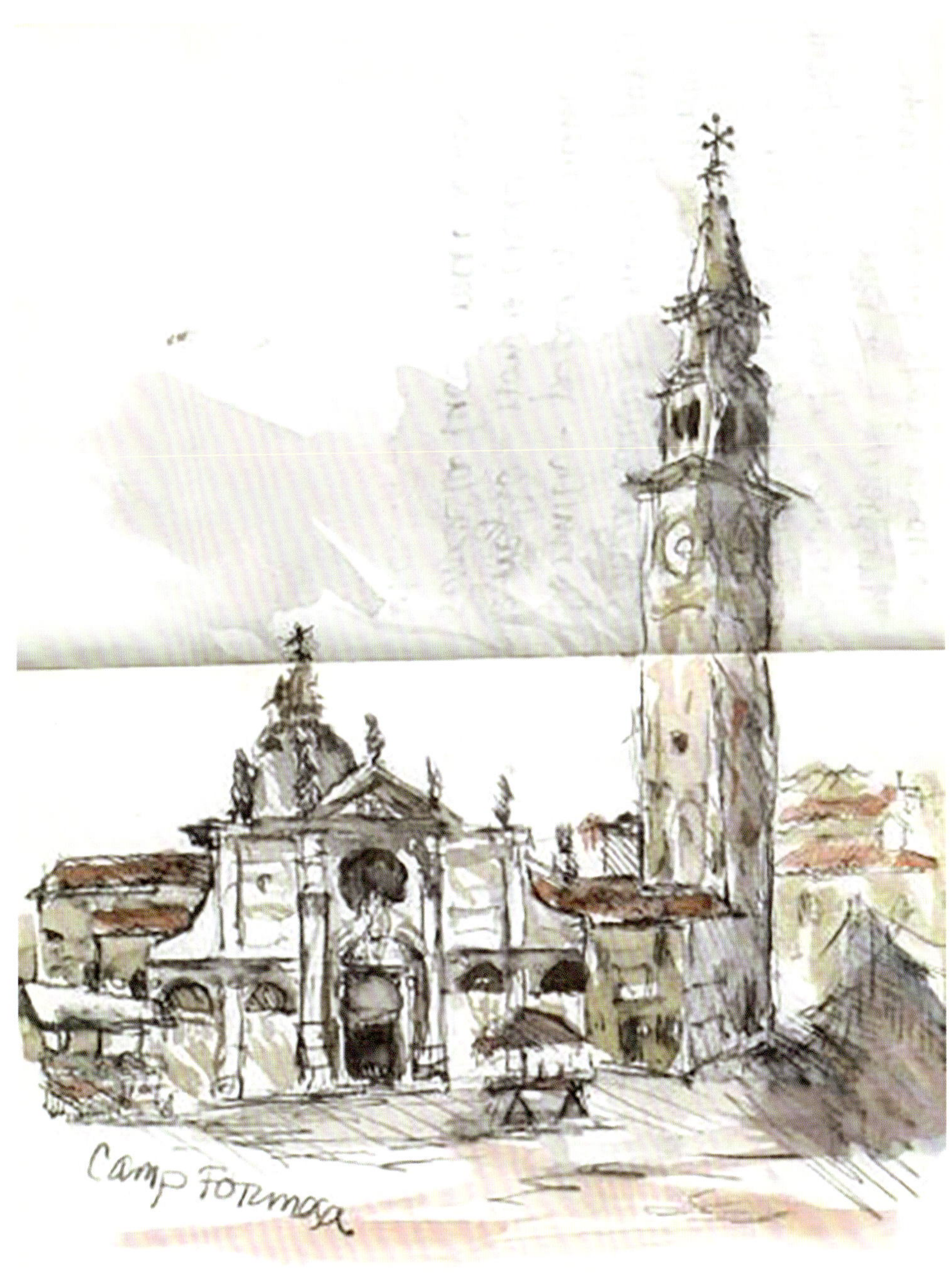

Sketchbook entries made in Venice. Camblin used front and back pages for *Camp Formosa* in Venice.

the rope of my existence, want to be pulled out and say, Look at Me, Look at Me, don't you remember? All mythology—Things I remember are the ones that get in without asking, well or ill. They reflect the parts of me that I know, that no one else can see or even be aware of . . . since we all see only the facets we present or are presented with, accepting the descriptions we hear come back in dialogues with others. Our composite Past/Future is not nearly as accurate as hitting the moon. Our inner computers can only say Yes/No, and let our actions lead to the next action/reaction."—From a 1976 Camblin sketchbook "*Livre de Luxe Scrap Book Venezia 1876–1976*:

> "Mr. Peanut goes to Italy" or "The Blind Impressionist paints in Venice from memory" or The Retired Professor studying the effects of Light 'n Water in classical painting of Venezia 1879–1976 or Mr Peanut and his neuro-electric painting machine that is programmed to paint only the true effects of light 'n water."

A month after Camblin arrived in the City of Masks, I joined him. He welcomed me with the gift of several sketchbooks. In one of his gifts he wrote,

> I am very much in love with a young lady that is coming to Venice—and when I give her these books, I will be very, very happy . . . These are the times that I would love to be a writer, one who could make the words caress and bite and etch their meanings and shapes in your existence, but mine wallow, bleat, whine, and other shabby tricks just to fill page after page of meaningless chatter just to keep you visible while I sit here ALONE to anyone watching.
>
> Now coffee and thoughts of you. I can always see your eyes. I can always remember you in the brown (tan) suite that you wore in class—I can always see you putting on your make-up.

For Camblin, Venice was a living watercolor. The literal fluidity of the city, rising from one hundred small Adriatic islands, makes Venice ethereal. He worked to capture the reflection of the water on the stone bridges and palazzi. The light appeared to erode the surfaces, surfaces already eaten away by time. The Renaissance and Gothic architecture reflects the light from the water, and in turn, is reflected onto the water. With the flickering light on the water and the dancing reflections on the buildings, Venice seems to be in constant motion, and yet, paradoxically, the constancy of the dance exudes a timelessness, an eternal present. Camblin felt he belonged in the city, but he felt intense loneliness when he was by himself: "Sitting here on the columns, I keep thinking how nice it would be to see you . . . in the distance. Now and then, I do see you, your hair or something, but never really. A bit closer and the illusion fades. How much longer must I wait for you? Forever?"

During the fall and winter months, Camblin tried to paint the frequent lavender fog that rose from the canal thoroughfares. The mists often obscured the cityscape, turning the buildings into ghostly apparitions. Only the fog stopped the visual evidence of the corruption that resulted from the ravages of time, creating conflict, or perhaps injecting reality, into the hearts of those who love Venice. In spite of the exquisite light and incomparable beauty of the city, a constant awareness of the destructive nature of time combined with the erosion from the water that filled the city's 400 canals, is impossible to ignore. Drawing the worn edges of Venice, Camblin felt his own worn edges even though he was only forty-eight. "Sun and Shade: My emotions seem to reflect the day. When the sun is out, I feel we can conquer it all. When a cloud passes over, I fall into my gloom of needing you as my light, my heart, my source."

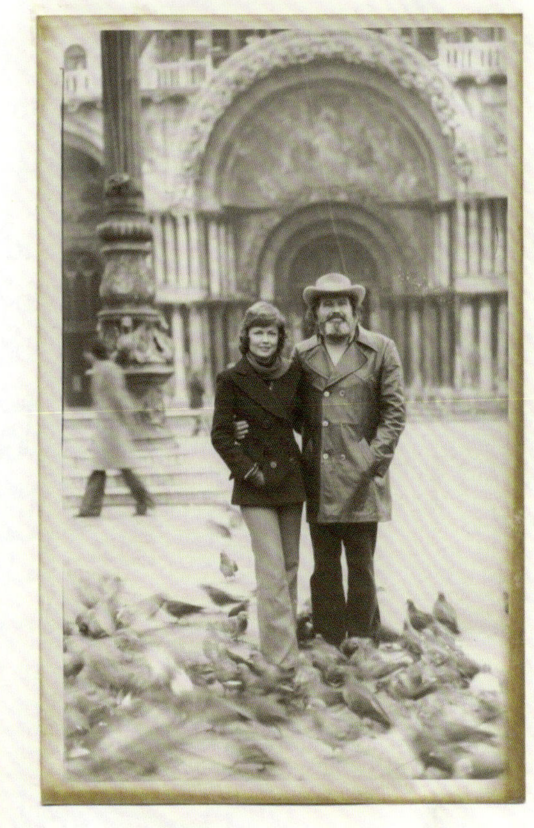

Author and Camblin, Piazza San Marco

Inhabitants of the watery city choose not to dwell on the inevitable. Deciding to be more Venetian, Camblin decided bravely to face an uncertain future with unwavering Italian aplomb. He meticulously recorded his observations in sketchbooks, journals, and letters. Camblin notes from *Libro Di Recordare, Sept. 20th, 1976 to October 14th, l976:*

Domani [tomorrow] is a new day.

Walking all over—feet killing. Rio Garibaldi is a nice wide street that has San Giorgio as a focus and the Giardini at the end of it, unlike the main part of Venice. Less likely to draw, but not bad for living.

Sunday morning sitting at the floating bar behind the Accademia facing Guidecca writing a few letters and waiting for something. Now I sit and ponder this Now/Future. Last night the concert—too much—an experience easy to remember—unique for me: Wings [with Paul McCartney] in Piazza S. Marco. Stampede, no manners, lasers, smoke, sound, *Basta e basta*. [It's enough]

I met a printer but he only works for himself, but he sent me to a place where they train printers. This afternoon I will return to talk to them about the price of Lastri [offset plates] and someone to print them. Also I'm beginning to trust the sketching. I don't want to give them away now, so they must be improving. Also the Pelican ink I got here is not black, but runs when you hit it with water and turns blue with a lot of water and green with a little . . . plus watercolor, I got it made—*Spero*! [I hope]

This afternoon—*verso casa e comincia di lavorare* [towards new forms of work], but on what? An imaginary landscape from some post cards? Campo Formosa and do some more details, some of the canals nearby, maybe some people drawing, although that turns into caricature. Listening they talk about the cost of things, my concerns are also theirs, but in a different way. I'm on vacation—I think. Clear sky then clouds. Ruskin and Turner both loved the Zattere.

Streams of people over streams of water: lunchtime in Venice. In another place, even the canals are asleep. Only the reflections are awake. Quietly it comes—the silence of early afternoon; no children laughing; no men talking. The day is slowly changing, a moment ago *Come piove* [as it rains]. . . . now clear again . . .

The lights at night on the water are a whole new thing. They change the appearance of the city, but it is better when there are even fewer tourists. A slow walk to Margherita . . . find something along the way. I haven't seen anything to collect yet.

Saturday morning—*Primo di Ottobre*: [First of October] Out again only today I buy a small folding umbrella . . . Another painter went by with a folding easel. I think they really mean it. This morning really looks like rain.

It is quite cool, but pleasant. Think today may be one for staying inside and reworking drawings, just like the good old days. Actually doing some things that are more likely in the South than in Venice—going to work. Moving, always in pulses, but time to stop for coffee. most standing up. Me? I always sit down. This morning there is a radio playing Italian songs. How nice for a change! Pigeons are the color of winter in Venice.

Clearing sky seen in a rock. Watching the stones dry in Campo San Formosa and in several low areas, the water reflects the campanile. 9:00 A.M. The sun is casting shadows and Venice is entirely different. Dogs with muzzles—everywhere and seemingly content with their outfits—Italian shoes . . . All of the pigeons will, at one time, fly from one side of the church out over the campo and then fly back to the other side . . .

It seems that asleep my dreams have been strange and unique—people I've never met complete stories of regular events in an unreal ambience that I can't place. When awake, my surroundings here are not as real as my dreams. I am a tourist, and each morning will be like the one before. Waiting for Godot again.

Blue skies, the fog/clouds have burned off early and now the morning is really real . . . Tourist here all winter. Sit here a little longer, and then laundry, *Chiaroscuro* is a nice word and when the sun shines Venice isn't flat. I rather like the lavender gray 2-dimension that winter creates. Now much more aware of contrasts, too many for a painting but good for architecture.

The filling of this cafe is nice, different tongues. A girl with hair that cascades in black/ red/auburn waves. . . . Titian would have loved her.

Columbi pigeoni eating crumbs, brown eyes; red feet. A girl sitting near looks just as Lee Bontecou did 20 years ago. *Stranieri fra stranieri, come strano.* [Foreigners among foreigners. How strange.]

Silhouettes across the canal, Sun setting behind that woman's eyes . . . Haiku time: Sipping beer, a minute ago I believe she was crying. Blue/orange ball— Rainbow roll and the flow of people . . . Home. Child's laugh behind me. Choose—sunset or turning?

Twilight is her time of day, *Crepuscolo* [Dusk]—10:00 a.m. There—I'm watching.

In Venice nothing goes to one vanishing point. This is not Renaissance Italy. It wanders, it breaks, it changes. a straight line, an unbroken line is unseen and unheard of here.

This morning I'm to go to the printers and pick up a larger plate—but some thinking today about ART/me/76—because there seems to be a blocking of sensations—perhaps just as 1956—I felt something changing and it was Pop Art or rather a continuous flow of American contributions for 20 years and now I feel something else is coming and it is not that I can change or get into it. I may already be doing it. I can't help thinking that the Paraphysical side of things is the next idea, but a great place for phonies—as always and I can't let my way turn into that. If it is just going to be business as usual—with the Dada boys going strong and AE [abstract expressionism] the stronghold of the intellectuals—Regionalism is the next one—and that is a laugh unless they understand it. Texas Funk, part of it, thousands of miles away. What do I believe now? That it's Business is as usual and there is very little soul left in the business or the artist—just theater, not art. Just show business and painters are usually lousy actors.

Tempo Passato [Time Past or Past Time]

Working on the plate has been good . . . allows me to drift. The point was too heavy—had to buy one—Then it began to relax. Now I think I have to start a larger one and just doodle on it until something happens. Feels good, but mainly it lets me be out of Time. Houston is a Future/Venice is a Past, and it makes my mind float to work in this old medium. It isn't important what picture my hands make. It is the free Time it gives my mind. I guess I don't have anything to say and this is just what I do. Just as the metronome hammering of the guy knocking rust off his boat. Somehow it isn't irritating. It is constant, even striking. It is what he is doing—as these people are doing . . . The children in the piazza live a separate existence, surround by adults and yet free.

If I look at just the top of that cottonwood against this blue sky, what difference is there from the dreams in my tree house in Ponca City. An old man rowed into my dreams, and a sea gull. The gull is easy—cottonwoods & gulls in Salt Lake City.

Time and time—so difficult to let them bleed into one another. I have to slow it down even more. Houston moved in a slower rhythm than Venice, for me.

A white gull, just barely touching its reflection.

October 14, 1976: Picasso opened a door and Duchamp stood in it—The rest of us have to crawl through the window and wait.

Sketchbook, October 1976 Venezia:

I'm afraid that oil painting is the only way to do Venice. There is so much Turner around here, plus all the usual scenes. I'm going to be forced to move to more abstract effect or they will slide from Impressions to imitations. It is so easy to be eclectic in Venice—Everyone has left tracks here.

(Describing Venice): Worn bricks, wet and dry, small shrines with electric lights, slivers of light canyons of dark—gulleys of architecture—sealed up windows— lock and iron bars insides and outside—trees and leaves "CE" and "A" carved in the paving stones—writing on the walls—GRAFFITTI—the source of writing in a painting—a footnote . . . What I am: wants to talk, requires silence—tries to be nice, but wants to rage—knows that rage wastes energy—convinces no one— confuses some—and friends deserve better . . . my doubts come from another source—any pedant can waste your time like putting sandbags against a flood— you know it will pass, but you have to save something. Scholars are like floods and locusts—they never know when they've eaten too much or gone over their own heads. They hate the living body. I think, maybe most people do. They dwell in the past and complain into the future—even I can hardly wait for the present to become past so I can use it and let my future become now. . . . The radio is play- ing Italian Pop songs—The campo is dark, the Vecchia Romagna warm—and I am writing—No matter how I complain, I am living as I have chosen—and old Camus knew that writing is easier than pushing a rock. [referencing Albert Camus's *The Myth of Sisyphus*] This is pleasure, but you, my dearest reader, don't Ever do this/ that except that you have to! HAVE TO!! Once known, enjoy even the misery, and leave tracks. Searching for the Longhorn, blaze a trail. If it's a dead end, then your mark will, in Time, be CAUTION SIGNS: Nothing is this way, but a "path with heart" always ends up . . . somewhere. Forget the words, nothing. The process is me sitting here, alive, watching, pausing, thinking, loving, dreaming, sad, happy, my children, my life, my love. This is just a micro-second in a life of consciousness . . . going so fast—a mathematical probability that will never be where this was written again. (Even the underlining marked the past.) I'm reaching the "speed of enlightenment" so I must stop and accept the outside, more overwhelming than my inside—just RAIN—Nov 7, 1976, 6:00 PM Venice Italy All my love, Roberto Cambolinni, Signor Arachide [Mr. Peanut] et Al.

Dreaming is a way of Life . . . the dream that you can never tell and will never know until the end . . . R. G. [Robin Goodfellow]

You may guess, but who knows? anonymous

A fool Moon and accompanying star tonight—Clear as a crystal tonight. She is a woman in the moon here, Mama Luna.

Clear day, Monday Nov 8, 1976. First song was Country Western, just like Ponca City on a cold wintery morning, only it never looked like this . . .

The future arrives here just like always; find a spot and sit and wait for it to appear. Perhaps I feel that it can't find me if I'm inside since the life is outside my room in Venice. In Houston, it knew where to find me. Venice is a small town and I'm in it, but the world is in the Solar System, which is in the galaxy which is in the Cosmos, et. Above and below, at this wave length, I'm always here I am. Frying pan or fire, it's just a matter of Time . . . every time.

Suspended animation, that is what kind of cartoons I draw . . . anonymous

Sketchbook, November 1976 Venezia:

Kodachrome color back in my room, bright splashes of sunset on the walls. Memories of sunshine daze and yet, in my memory and in this reality, it is the purple, lavender, blue gray, gray muted, foggy days of Venezia that tug at my "soul," I guess.

Is this Venice where fishermen go? St. Peter was a fisherman. What did St. Mark do for a living? The Lion is everywhere in Venice.[1]

Reflections find me tonight in the darkness and now the rain Starts in long slow streaks, molecule after molecule falling to be in another form for some time to come. 80% of my body feels the sadness/sweetness of rain. For water to be free as vapor—to fly, to be pulled to the sun and not gravity—to float up and not down stream. To be drawn to the light and not into a plant . . . maybe water molecules don't think about happy/sad, knowing ice, plants, deep wells, oceans, evaporation are all the same—a part of the cycle—poor humans, we wonder so much.

My raindrop world—a cloud so far away."

In an undated sketchbook Camblin wrote:

A quote from Nietzsche, Thus Spake Zarathustra:

Voluptuousness: to free hearts, a thing innocent and free, the garden happiness of the earth, all the future's thanks over-flow to the present.

Voluptuousness: only to the withered a sweet poison: to the lion-willed, however, the great cordial and the reverently saved wine of wines.

Voluptuousness: the great symbolic happiness of a higher happiness and highest hope . . .

From another sketchbook:

Cold, clear—yesterday the clouds arranged themselves equally over the sky and each of them lay there looking like new Egyptian mummies sliding to the south.

While in Venice, Camblin wrote down his favorite William Blake quotes in a sketchbook:

To see a World in a Grain of Sand And a Heaven in a Wild Flower,

Hold infinity in the palm of your hand

And Eternity in an hour.

He who binds to himself a joy Does the winged life destroy.

But he who kisses the joy as it flies Lies in eternity's sunrise.

Love to faults is always blind, Always is to joy inclin'd,

Lawless, wing'd and unconfin'd,

And breaks all chains from every mind.

Children of the future Age Reading this indignant page,

Know that in a former time,

Love! sweet Love! was thought a crime.

Camblin continues:

(Unfortunately we are back to my loose tongue and scratchy pen. I avoid Blake for I'm afraid that I'm doing a pastiche of him without knowing it—)

I see that madness and I hope I never step over that edge. I may get involved with myself at times, but I don't go on forever. I can't look for signs until Sand is here!

I keep working at some level even though I have no idea of how it will turn out. The prints will look fine, I'm just not sure how to tint them. Maybe the edition will be smaller by the time I finish.

As long as I'm drawing or writing, then Death or something less surprising, can come along and I can keep doing what I do. Just my talisman—my flimsy paper armor and pen sword. So many pictures, so many words in the world, and they just erode away—N TIME FRAGMENTS—a piece here and there, a name, a memory dug up, dropped out of Time and Space. Not to be used for fame and fortune, but as a protection, lenses—to use the TIME harm/less/ly . . . and perhaps a dried flower or two that will last a bit longer than expected. This magic book is just about used up—They are only magic for me while they have empty pages. As soon as the pages/sand have run out, I have to quickly turn the glass/book over and begin again.

I think I will sign my prints, Venezia—1976 1/25 anonymous b.c. a.b.c.? anonymous b.c.? A (with B & C on the interior the letter). Well maybe the Durer chop is best, more puns A teepee too. Killing Time, Wasting Time, Spending Time, Doing Time, Making Time, Losing Time, Finding Time, About Time and all in Space . . .

There are times that make me more lonesome than others, and so I write you another letter. Arrive SAFELY. I need you! and love you! Soon—I thought it would never happen."

The Magic of the Light

Besides the magic of the light, Venice was Camblin's favorite city for numerous other reasons. He never tired of the magnetic pull he felt in the Piazza St. Marco, the Doges Palace, and Saint Mark's Basilica. Being Catholic and a Leo, he couldn't help but respond to a sacred building that was built to house relics of the Evangelist, St. Mark, whose symbol of the winged lion became the city's symbol. "Venetian tradition states that when St. Mark was traveling through Europe, he arrived at a lagoon in Venice, where an angel appeared to him and said 'Pax tibi Marce, evangelista meus. Hic requiescet corpus tuum.' (May Peace be with you, Mark, my evangelist. Here your body will rest.)"[2] St. Mark's original burial place was in Alexandria, Egypt, where it remained until 828. At that time two Venetian merchants stole the relics and relocated them to Venice. To house the relics, the first basilica was begun in 829 but burned down in 976. Another basilica followed, but it is the eleventh-century Byzantine basilica, consecrated in 1094, that remains today. The city claimed St. Mark as its patron saint. Employing the saint's lion, Venice erected a towering column at the entrance of the Piazza St. Marco and topped it with a bronze, fifteen-feet-long winged lion with his paw on an open book. St. Mark's representative lion proliferates all over Venice, appearing in all sizes and in every medium. Indeed, the city of lions spoke to Camblin's pride in being a Leo. A constant reader, he also appreciated the combination of the book and the lion.

Famous for its lions, Venice is also notable for its elaborate masks, displayed in almost every shop window. The history of Venetian masking goes back centuries, and every resident in the city knows the characters the masks depict, from the plague doctor to the larva. Originally used to hide identities in a dangerous city, masks are now largely restricted to the Carnival of Venice. Of course the etymology of masquerade is self-explanatory. Even though Camblin had been drawn to hidden identities prior to his initial trip to Venice, the city's masking culture stimulated his interest in masks. During his first trip to Venice, he had purchased the red, Bauta half-mask and hung it on his studios' walls.

During Camblin's time in Italy, we spent as much time together as possible, but I still had to travel a good deal. While Camblin was sketching in the Piazza San

Marco, I was in Houston where I organized an exhibition of works on paper by seven Houston artists: Jack Boynton, Bob Camblin, David Folkman, John O'Neil, Allan O. Smith, Gael Stack, and Earl Staley. After collecting the work, I hand-carried the art from Houston to Kuwait where my sister Margo had arranged for an exhibition space. The year 1976 was a little early to take Western abstract or representative art to viewers who were not familiar with Western art. The Muslims believe that the prophet Mohammed cannot be depicted in art for fear his representation might become an object of worship. Any person blasphemous enough to make an image of God could face death. The basic tenet of Islam is that God alone can be worshipped. All art is suspicious. (Now Arabs are some of the biggest collectors of art.) Islamic proscription against representation resulted in the rich Islamic abstraction that adorns Islamic architecture. In 1976 the ex-patriates living in Kuwait City attended the *Texas Artists* show and purchased art created by their countrymen.

Even though we spent months together in Venice, Camblin resented my time away, and he couldn't keep from complaining about my lifestyle. When together, we mostly spent our time wandering around and exploring the maze of the city. He showed me his favorite, non-touristy areas. We ate in out-of-the-way restau-rants he had discovered. We visited museums and marveled at the Gothic-styled palazzi. We bought each other gifts from a local silversmith. We tried on masks. We stood up in the vaporetti (water buses) like the natives. We both painted the scene outside his apartment window. We relaxed in each other's company and pretended this idyllic life would continue forever. We tried to give up and to for-get schedules.

When he relinquished his worries, Camblin became a part of Venice. He even enjoyed the romantic, melancholic loneliness during some of his time there; how-ever, forlornness brought out his insecurities and his need for friends and family. He sketched and did prints with an etcher he had met through an Italian acquain-tance from his Fulbright year, but did not feel motivated to paint, partly because he didn't have an appropriate studio. He completed some watercolors, filled numer-ous sketchbooks, and wrote endless letters. The Leo experienced extremes in Venice from the romance of sharing his city with me, to the solitude that overwhelmed him

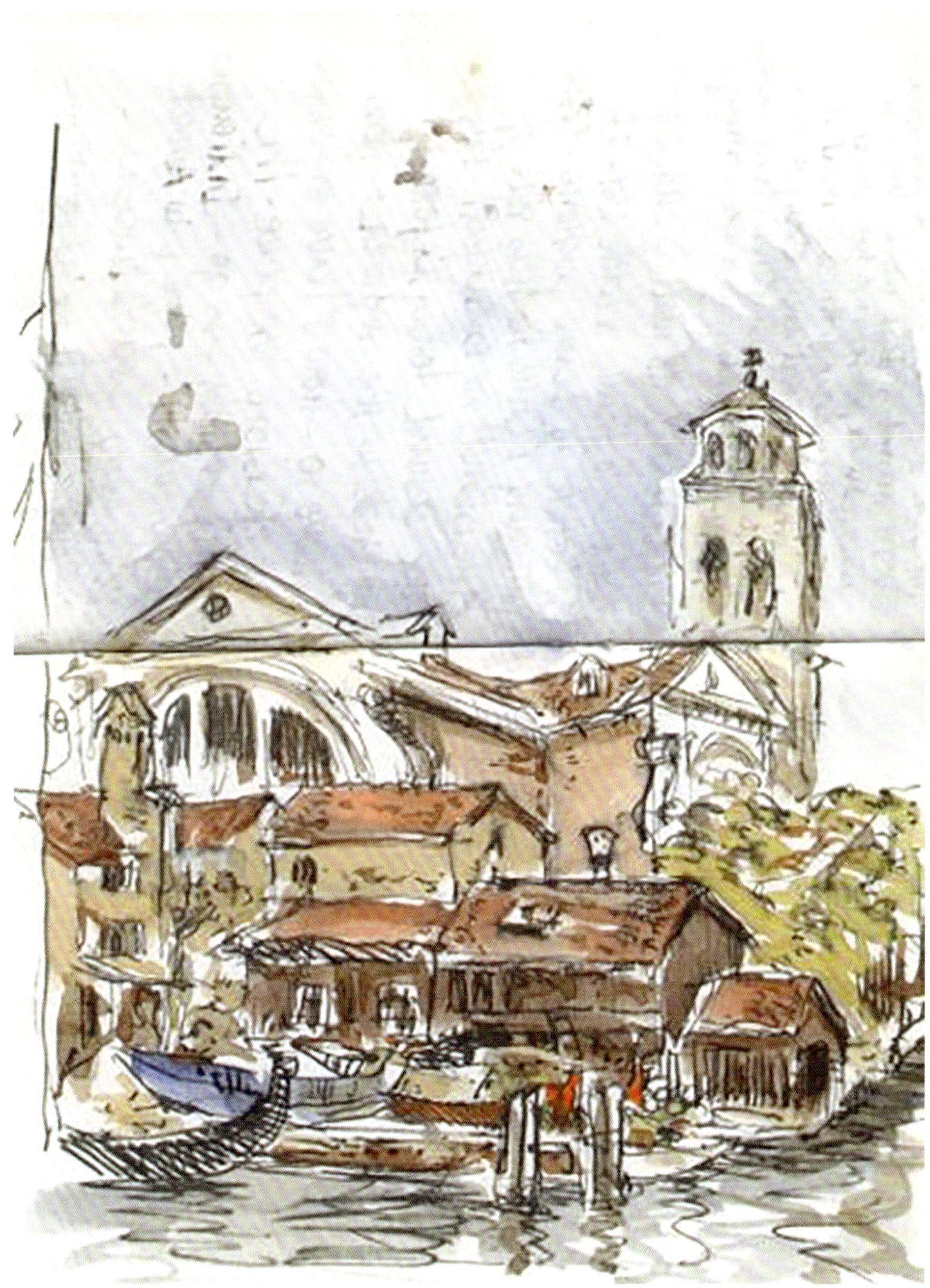

Page from Camblin's Venice sketchbook

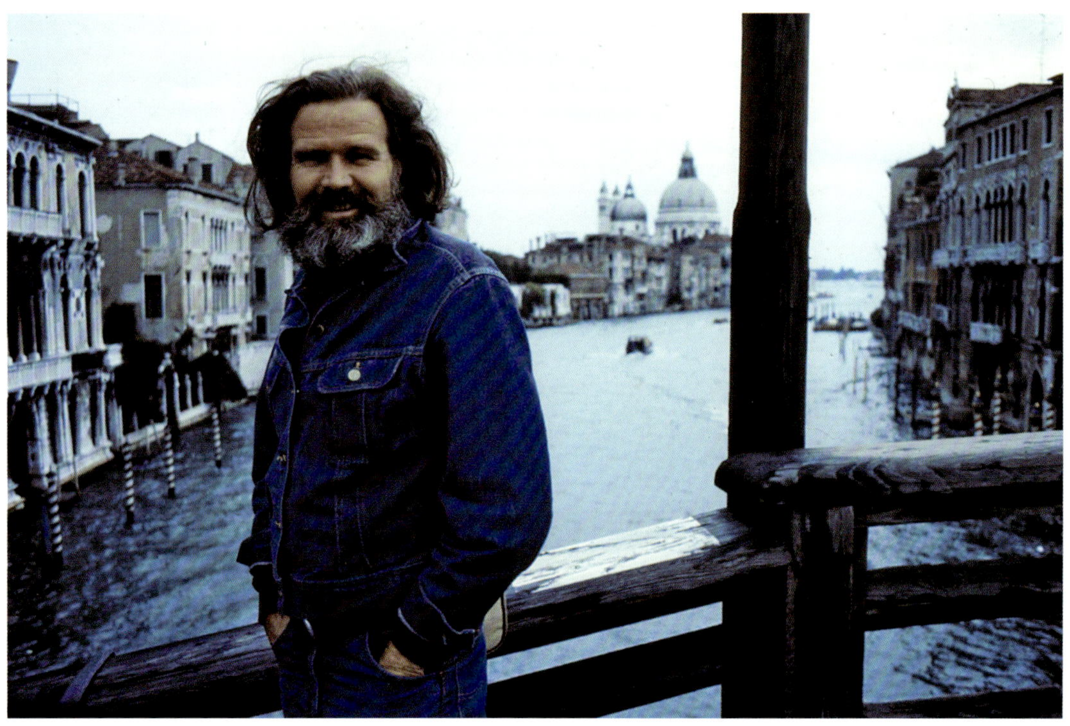

Camblin fell in love with Venice the first time he visited the city of canals during his Fulbright year in Italy. He was overjoyed to be able to return in 1976. *Photograph by author.*

during my absences. The tug of Texas pulled Camblin to an early exit from Europe, but first he made visits to Brittany, France; Glasgow, Scotland; and Dublin, Ireland. Like *Babbo Natale* (Santa Claus), he arrived in Houston on Christmas Eve.

CHAPTER SEVENTEEN

Leaving the Canals
and Returning to the Bayous

Shortly after settling back into his Houston studio, Camblin made a visit to Moody Gallery. He took some of the art he had created in Venice for Betty Moody to distribute to the collectors who had purchased subscriptions for his work prior to his leaving for Italy. Moody was very enthusiastic and asked Camblin if she could represent his work. They had been acquainted for over two years, and Camblin agreed. Moody's attention seemed to ease his worries. She listened to his laments about being alone and assured him that all would be well. During one of his daily afternoon visits, the gallery dealer told him that she would like him to participate in upcoming group shows before she staged a one-man exhibition of his work in November 1977. She also said she wished he would consider having another solo show in 1979. Camblin slowly cast off his negative mood. He welcomed having to create work for Moody shows, especially those that showcased him and his art. He had not completed all the art that was due his Venice subscribers so he worked to deliver on his promises. He appreciated being busy and tried to focus on work rather than on me and my new job in Guatemala.

Enjoying his friendship with his dealer, Camblin began spending more time at the gallery. Moody was always cheery and encouraging. When alone in the city, Camblin took her to dinner, and she occasionally cooked for him. Together

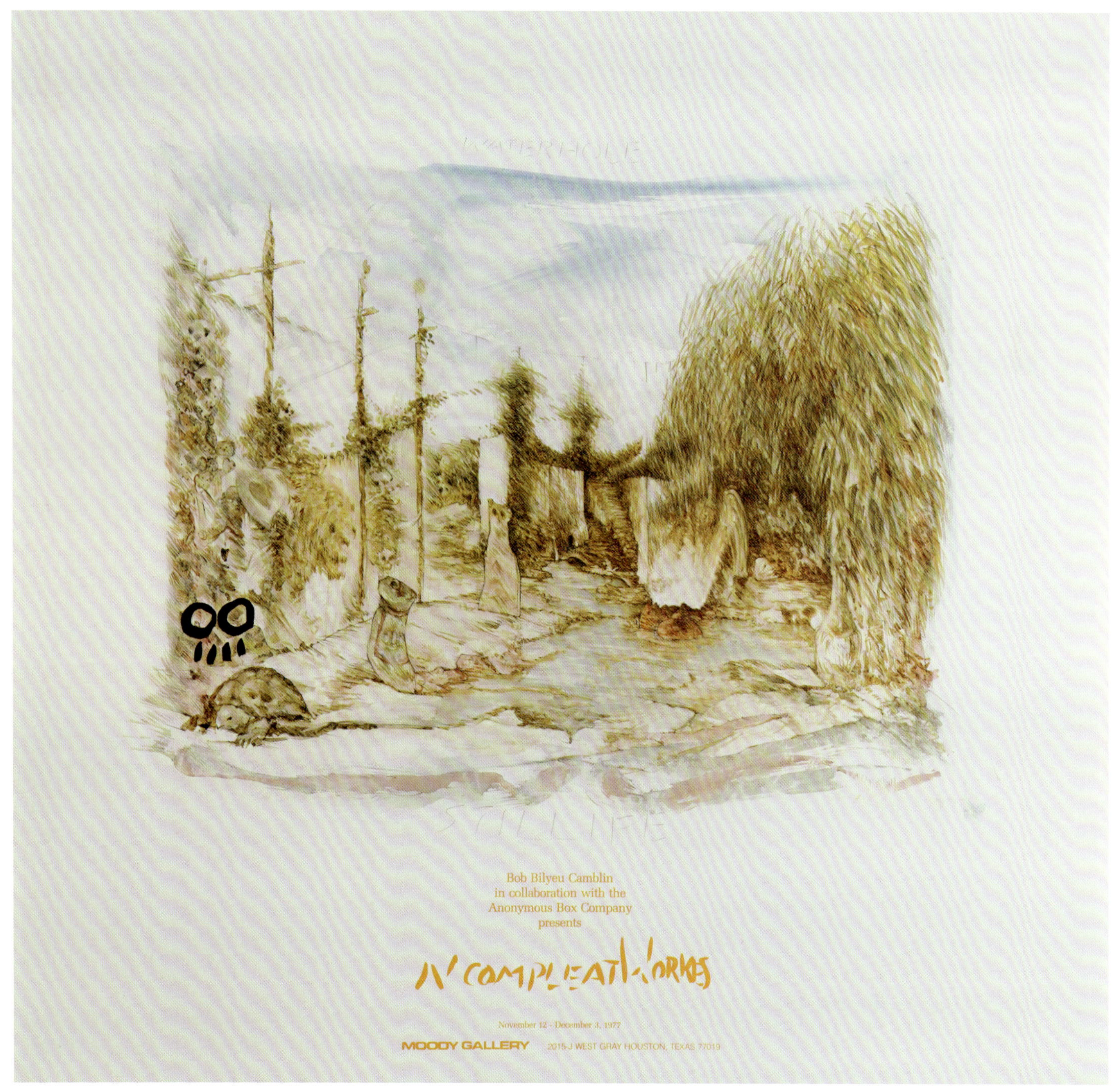

The Moody Gallery poster for Camblin's exhibition 'NCompleatWorkes, 1977.

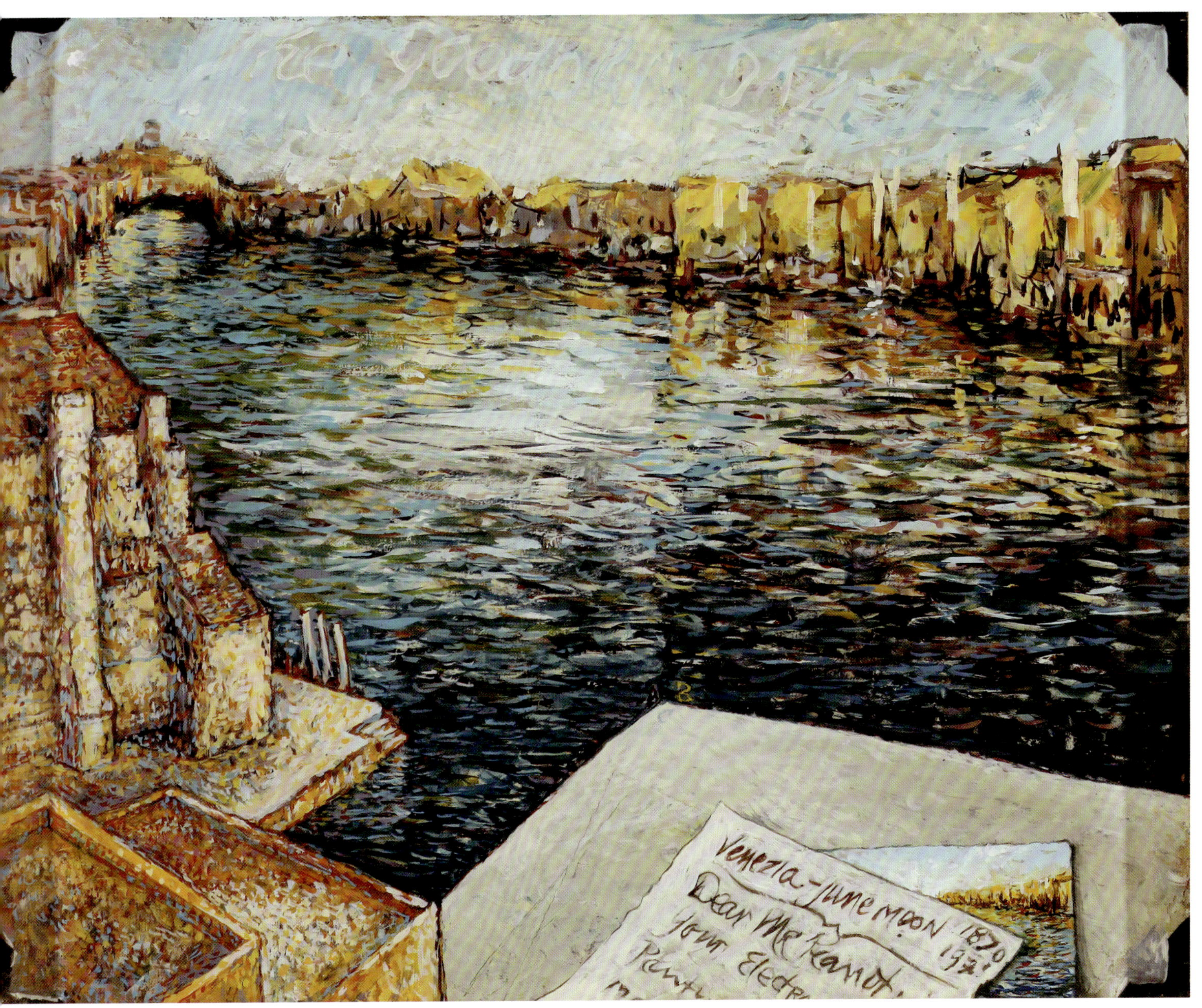

The Good Old Daze, Venezia, c. 1996 (to mark twenty years since Camblin lived in Venice. Exact date of creation unknown) 11" X 14". Camblin's brushstroke grew more impressionistic and textured, giving motion to the canals. *Collection of Gayle and Mike DeGeurin. David P. Gray photograph.*

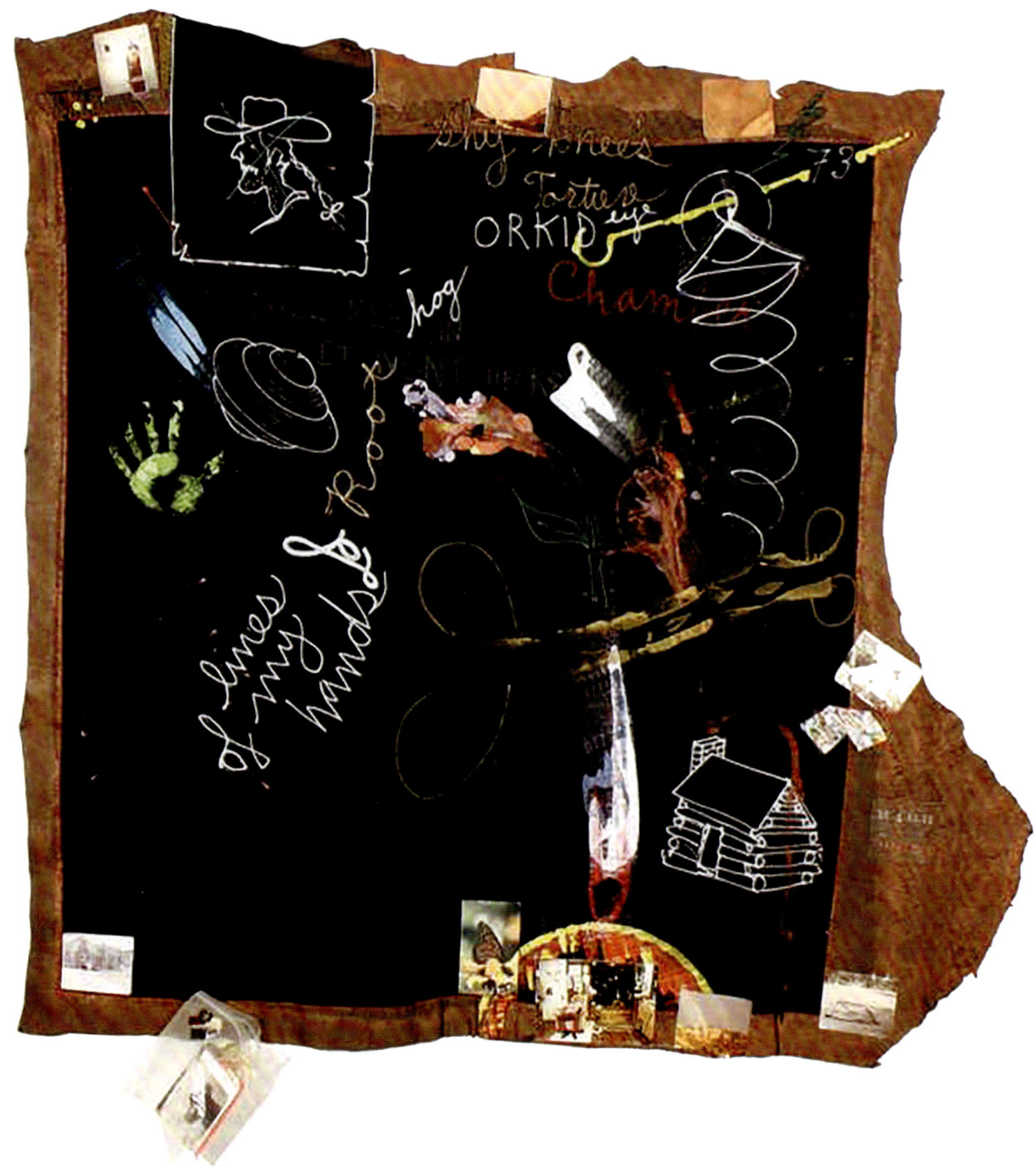

The Amarillo Museum of Art also added an Untitled, 1977 William Wiley, Bob Camblin, Jack Boynton, Al Smith, et al. collaboration to the museum's collection. Mixed media: Paint, photographs, wire, and wood on black felt, 5' X 5'.

they planned his shows and discussed his art. They started to depend on one another. Lives changed. Camblin's first solo show at Moody Gallery was titled *NCompleatWorkes*. The drawing for the invitation is a series of autobiographical postcards that sit atop the pages of his open *Texas Scrapbook*. One of the cards is addressed to The Holding Firm, one has a drawing of Mr. Peanut, and another is a photograph of the Texas Longhorn. Kay Sage or K.S. appears on several cards. The exhibition showcased numerous watercolor landscapes and drawings from Camblin's postcard series. "The watercolors of the last few years allowed me to lay in the 'ground' and 'play my games.' Their existence would be enough 'homework' if someone wants to check."[1]

Camblin continued to fill his art with visual games, hidden codes, personal references, and cyphers. He expected his viewers to play his games and to find the masked messages in his art. His art again became his major interest.

During 1977, William Wiley[2] once more visited Houston. Camblin and Wiley, together with Jack Boynton, Sharon Boynton, Earl Staley, Richard Cabral, Robert Hudson, and Allan O. Smith, created a five-by-five-foot untitled collage of paint, postcards, photographs, wire, and wood on black felt. A handprint and the words "lines of my hands," "shy knees," "ORKID eye," "Root," and "hog" are written on the work and accompany random, whimsical drawings. Collaborating with a group of friends buoyed Camblin's spirits.

Working on the large oil canvases he had contemplated while in Venice, he noted, "Now I want to enlarge that scale, those grounds, those landscapes—and Venice is the beginning backdrop. Big Bend wouldn't have worked because it has no human scale—mountains never work for me."

"Gothic gullies always have the reference of man."[3] Camblin painted several Venice-scapes: oil paintings he created with impressionistic brushstrokes, which reflected the refracted and broken light of Venice. He also painted *The Bottom Line*, a tongue-in-cheek tribute to François Boucher's 1751 painting of *Girl Reclining*, (*Miss O'Murphy*), the painting I had used for my nude portrait. He added my face to his painting. That same year he painted *They Only Mate This Way Once*, an atwork that epitomizes his technical skill as well as his creativity.

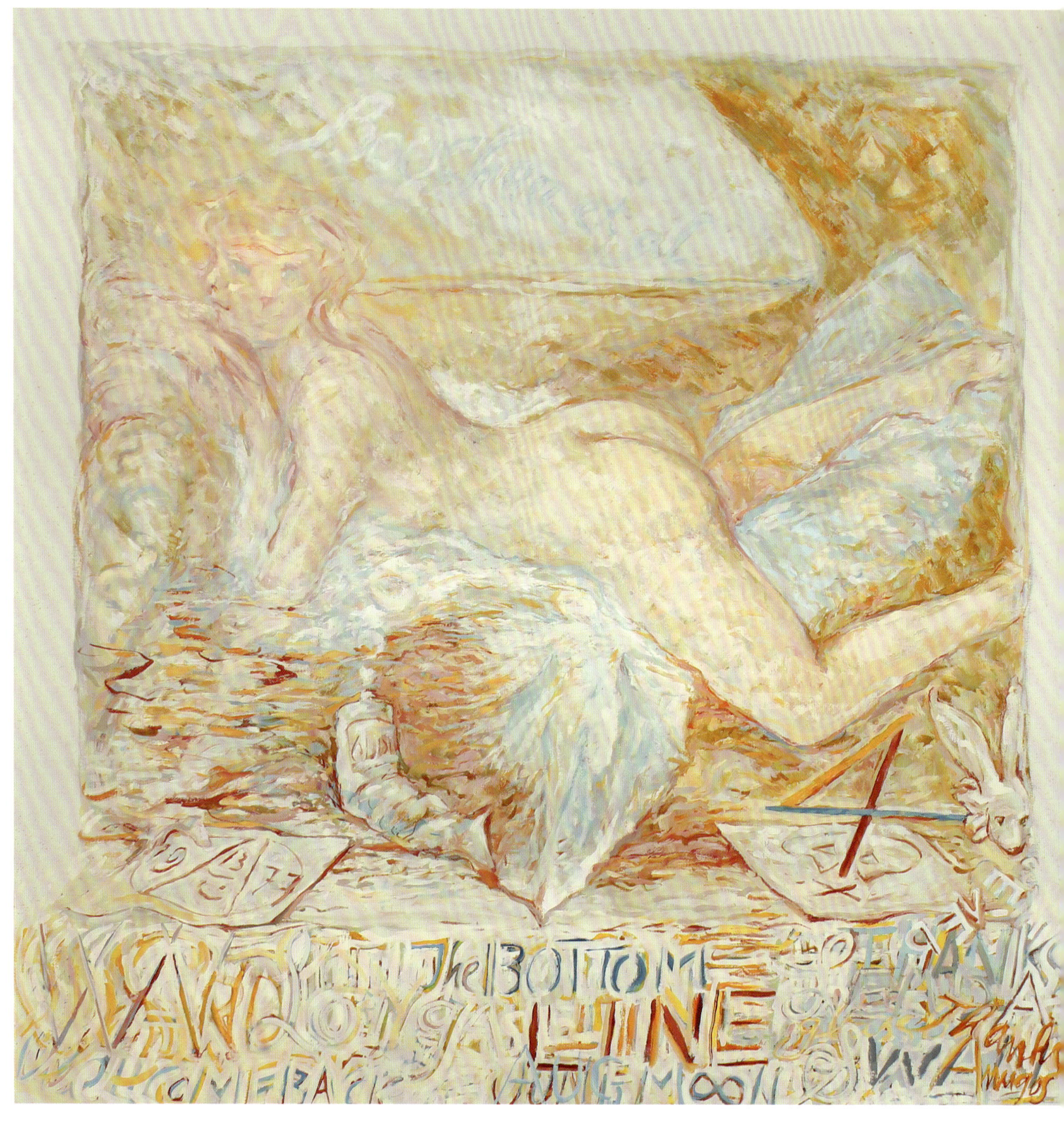

Camblin's *The Bottom Line*, 1974. Oil on canvas. was based on my earlier copy of Boucher's nude. *Collection of the Jackson Estate. David P. Gray photograph.*

When I was in Houston, Camblin was mostly content. However, he couldn't help badgering me from time to time. Knowing of the Moody imbroglio during my absence, I was less than understanding. Eventually Camblin's jealousy gained the upper hand. He chastised himself for his inability to control his emotions and for relying on me to understand and accept his needs. He wanted to be as important to me as I was to him. Somehow he thought his jealous nature proved his love. I did not have a jealous nature. He continued to plead for marriage and security, the very things he had counseled me against when our romance had begun. His efforts to change my schedule and my life seemed attempts to destroy the very things in me that attracted him. He regretted his having championed the importance of freedom and trust. And he hated himself for it. Strife entered Eden.

Camblin's concentration shifted from mistresses to mortality. Time grew longer between our visits; and when I did appear, he harangued me about what little time we spent together. He focused on skulls and paintings of dead flowers. In the watercolor, the dead arranged bouquet is inside the window, which reveals an exterior of vibrant green life. Realizing he had less than a year before he turned fifty, his preoccupation with death grew. His postcard collection included Hans Holbein the Younger's *The Ambassadors* with its anamorphic[4] perspective of a skull. Another card that played into his mindset was Allan Gilbert's *All Is Vanity*: a *memento mori* of a woman applying make-up in front of a mirror that, together with the woman's reflection, forms a skull. He pinned Holbein's and Gilbert's postcards above his drawing table and wrote, "The thoughts of things dying spring from the fear of love's demise."[5]

During Camblin's time in Venice, my sister, Margo, had commissioned him to create a large oil painting for her Kuwaiti home. He started painting "the Middle Eastern project," as he called it, using a painting technique he labeled "dot and dash." Camblin outlined the development of the commission in a sketchbook: "1978 ABC . . . Variation on Las Meninas as\ A *Memento Mori* after Velazquez and Picasso et al\ The Skull behind all things (even our children have one) and yet. . . ."[6]

Camblin sought inspiration in Diego Velazquez's painting, *Las Meninas*, 1656. The masterpiece's visual and psychological puzzles as well as the painting's

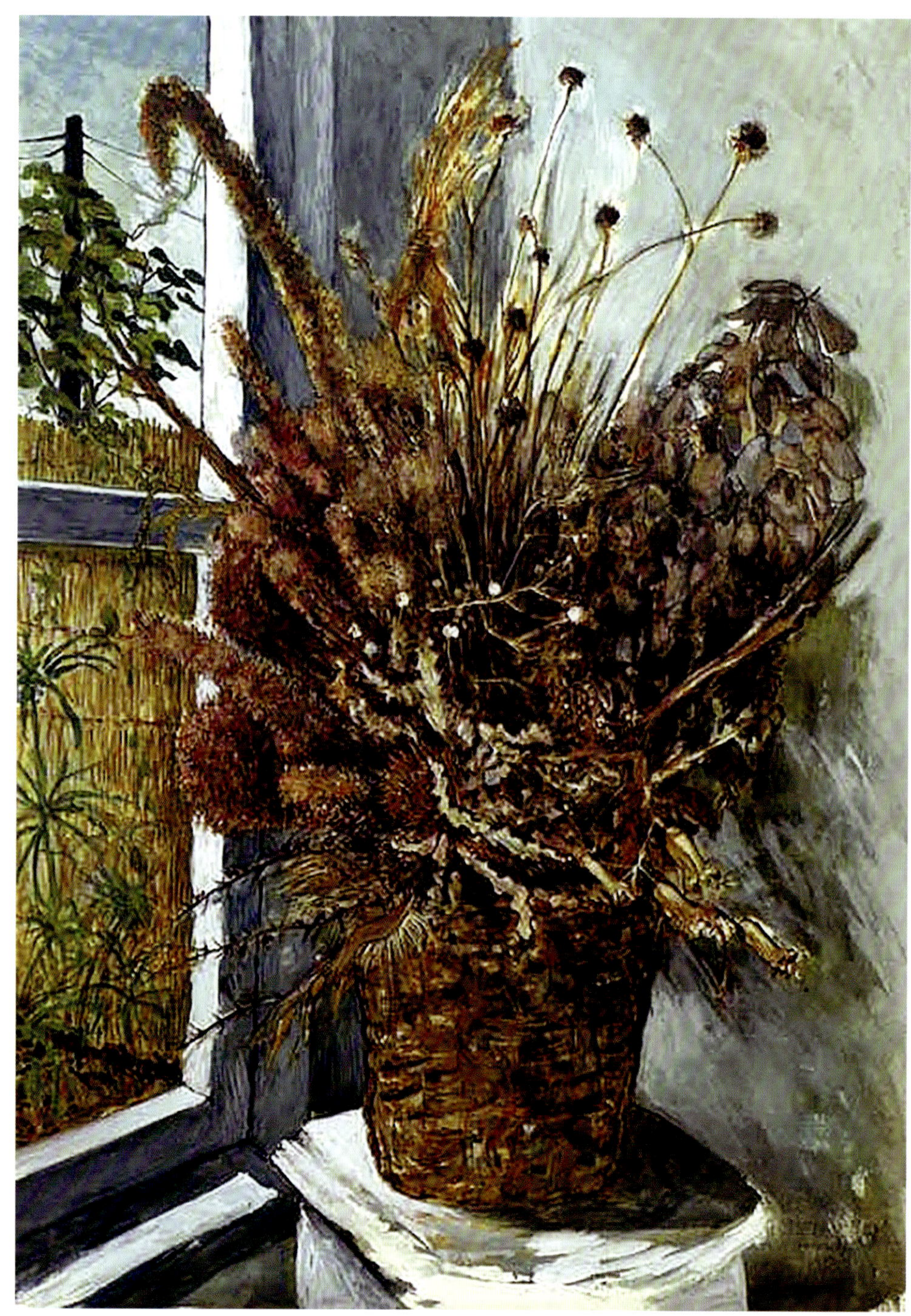

Dried Still Life contrasts life outside with death inside the window.

skull structure had long intrigued him: "Beyond the mirrors of every imaginable KIND the man stands in the DOOR\ with his BACK to the Light and Reflects on it . . . Flickering brush eye and MIND and in Time\ We stand in this/that ROOM and the Difference disappears and we SEE Velazquez, Picasso and ME2\ watching the YEARS ROLL BY."[7]

Spending more and more of his time alone in his studio, Camblin's moods swung from feeling lonesome to anger, from feeling remorseful to hateful. Urged on by his feelings, he tried to get control of his emotions through the creation of art. When he "came up for air," however, his self-imposed situation made him angry. I had declared us both free to see other people, making him less comfortable participating in the Houston art scene. He sent me letters and sketches. Not hearing back from me, he decided it was time to leave Dodge and to travel independently.

> I will always be the same, but for a time, it seems that I cannot control my passions (even though I have some control over my desires). I can't go on hurting myself and then hurting you . . . So I must silence myself and in the future, someday I hope that I can honestly see you again and be as I always wanted to be, a friend *senza* dubbio! As soon as I can think of you without hurting myself . . . with my own time machine, then perhaps a note now and then, a card and sooner or later, I can speak again. I can love no other. It came too late in my life to do anything but honor your wishes. Until the future, I remain—All my love—bob
>
> —From a letter dated August 1978.

To get out of Houston, Camblin drove to Claremont, California, to see his long-time artist friend, Gerald Purdy. He then journeyed to San Jose, California, and spent time with Joe Tate. Next he traveled to Kalamazoo, Michigan, to reconnect with Bruno and Bonnie. Being with friends helped lift him out of his melancholy but did not completely ameliorate Camblin's frame of mind. He reluctantly returned to Texas to complete the Kuwaiti commission and to assemble work for a one-man exhibition at the Art Museum of South Texas in Corpus Christi.

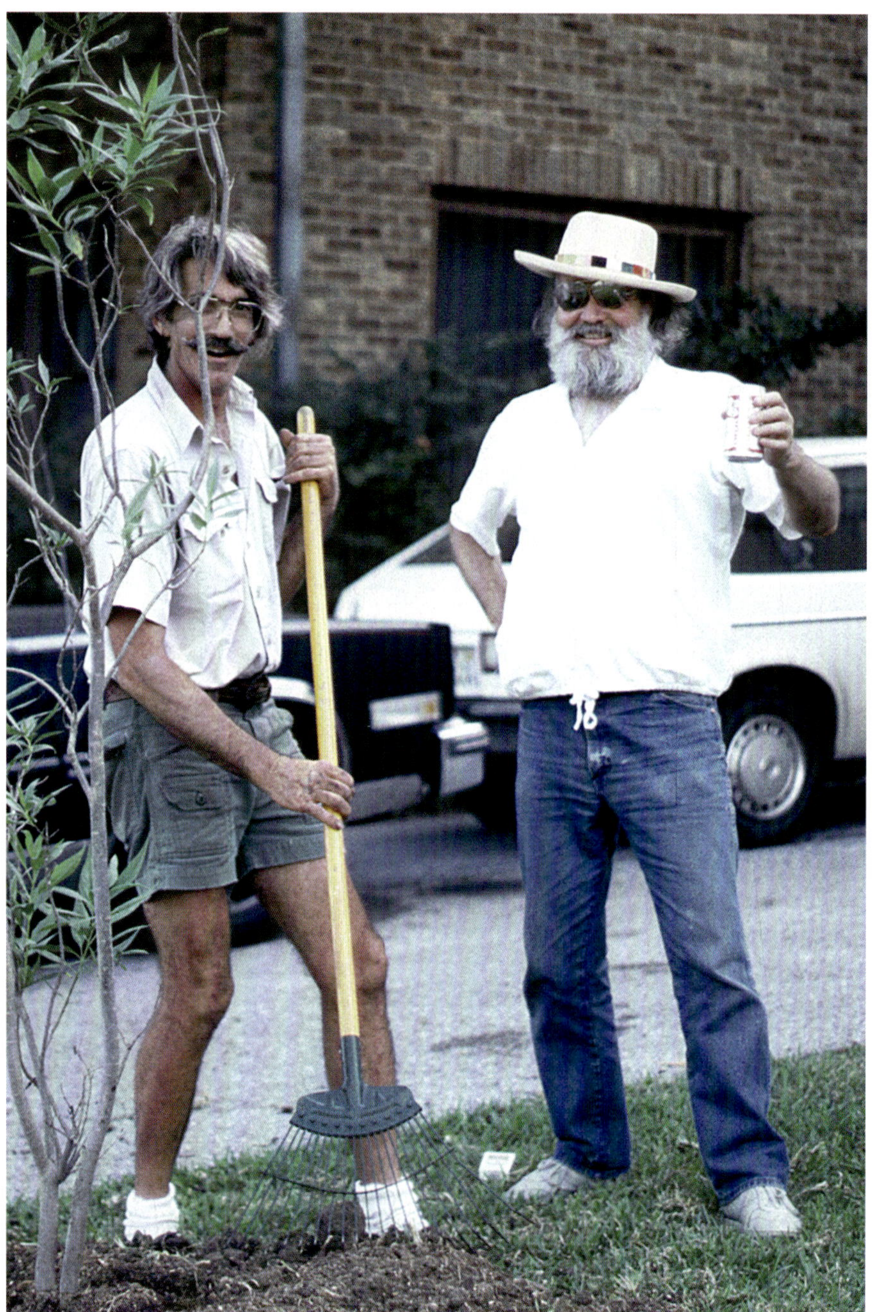

Tate and Camblin Planting a tree.

The Transience of Life: Vanitas

Being in Houston didn't help Camblin's frame of mind. Every turn brought back too many memories of happier days. He decided to move to Oaxaca, Mexico, in August of 1978. He stayed at the Casa Marcum for months of solitude. He called his visit a voluntary "ex-isle." With Halloween approaching, Camblin became obsessed with Mexico's ancient tradition of skull art, he sought examples of skeletons painted on pots, carved into stone and woven into garments.[1] He looked for the necklace of human hearts with a skull pendant worn by the Aztec goddess of death and earth. The reminders of death were relentless. Trying to clear negativity from his mind, he read. He drew. He painted. He walked. He wrote.

> I feel that my plans are to return to Houston sometime in November—a longer stay here without a car is difficult. This voluntary X-isle has worked admirably. I have found it possible to "go on living" with no one around, but it is not my true nature. Rex and Lollie Marcum have been excellent hosts for my recovery—as she is an X-English teacher and taught Hardy and at this moment is looking for the "Mayor of Casterbridge."

A visit by Earl Staley, his wife Susanne, Dave Folkman, and Betty Moody transformed Camblin into the happy host and guide. The exoticness of Mexico, the camaraderie of the group, and the shared past histories elevated everyone's feelings.

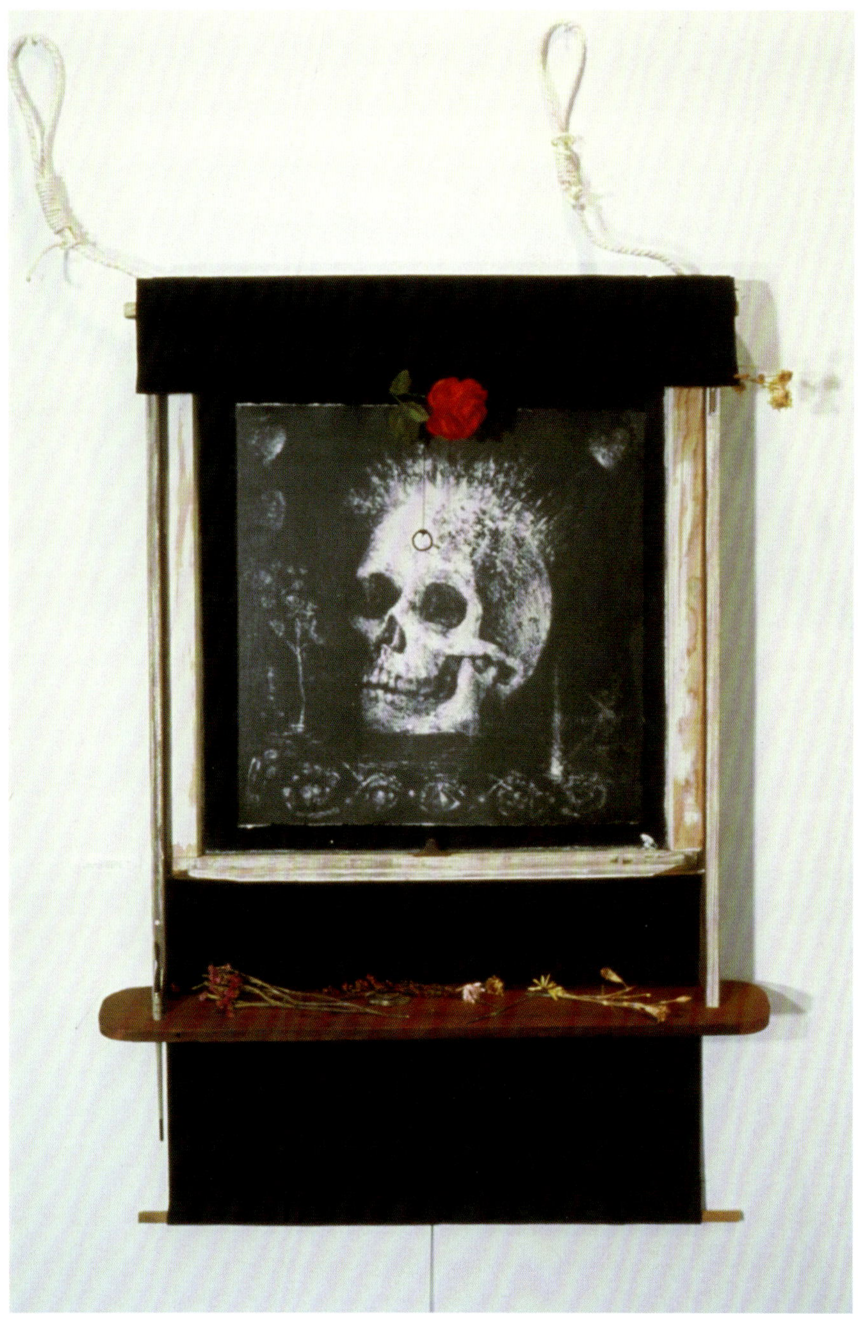

A trio of Reliquaries reflects Camblin's continued interest in death, 1978. Friends helped him build them.

Camblin realized how much he truly loved Oaxaca as well as how much he missed Houston. After his guests departed, he spent time in the local market where he purchased boxes of the sugar skulls to distribute to the friends he thought had forgotten him during his ex-isle.

Camblin did remain in Mexico long enough to celebrate the *Dia de los Muertos*. The first day of the celebration (October 31)[2] honors deceased infants and the second day remembers adults. Relatives and friends of the dead go to the cemeteries with marigolds, sugar skulls, tissue paper decorations, and traditional foods. If the gifts are satisfactory, departed souls are encouraged to make visits to graveyards to hear the prayers of the living.[3] Feeling old, Camblin no longer saw anything celebratory about death. He saw the skull as a final portrait. He left Oaxaca and returned to Houston mid-November.

Back in Houston, Camblin's skull imagery dominated his art and his thoughts. Rather than work alone on a piece of art in his studio, he decided it was time to make another print with Little Egypt Enterprises. He wanted to be surrounded by friends. He created a twenty-four-by-twenty-four-inch lithograph of a smiling skull, which seems animated through the disturbing smile and the suggestion of rays emanating from the top of the head.[4] He printed one skull red, one yellow, and one blue. Together with Allan O. Smith and Ron Arena, he built three large wooden reliquaries and placed a lithograph in each. Camblin hung a black blind behind one reliquary and used hangman nooses on two sides to anchor the piece to the wall. Under the print he made a shelf atop a drawer that was filled with *memento mori*. He certainly dwelled on the fact that he was going to die. Another reliquary was a free-standing, rounded-top, coffin-like sculpture that stood sixty-seven inches tall. A third hanging work incorporated a large shelf for mementos, including candles, *milagros*,[5] and dead flowers. Each piece was powerful and haunting. Sadly, the three works no longer exist.[6]

Camblin had long encouraged me to befriend Betty Moody. He believed he needed us both. The friendship was not to be, however. The ratio of one man and two romantically involved women did not serve as a pattern for longtime relationships.

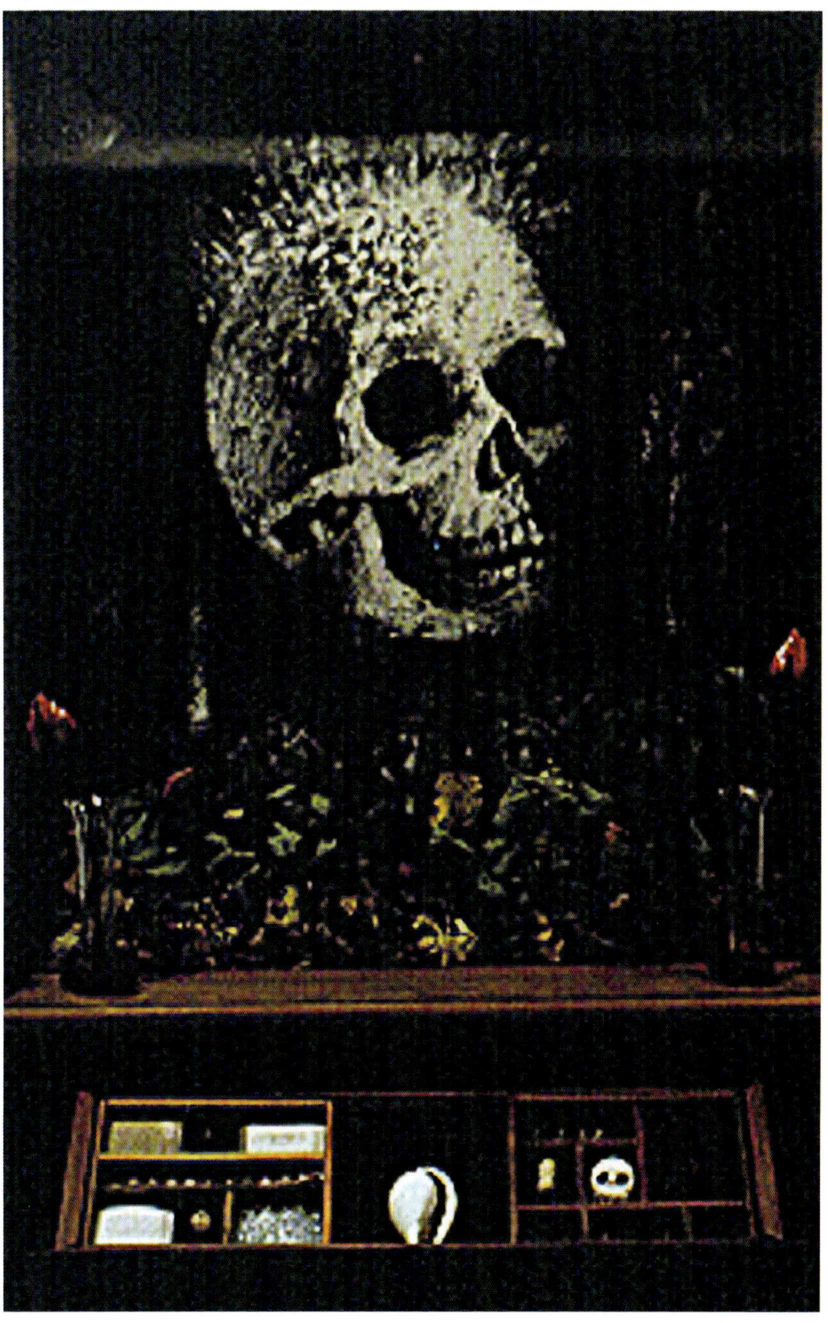

A reliquary with a drawer and a shelf for precious objects.

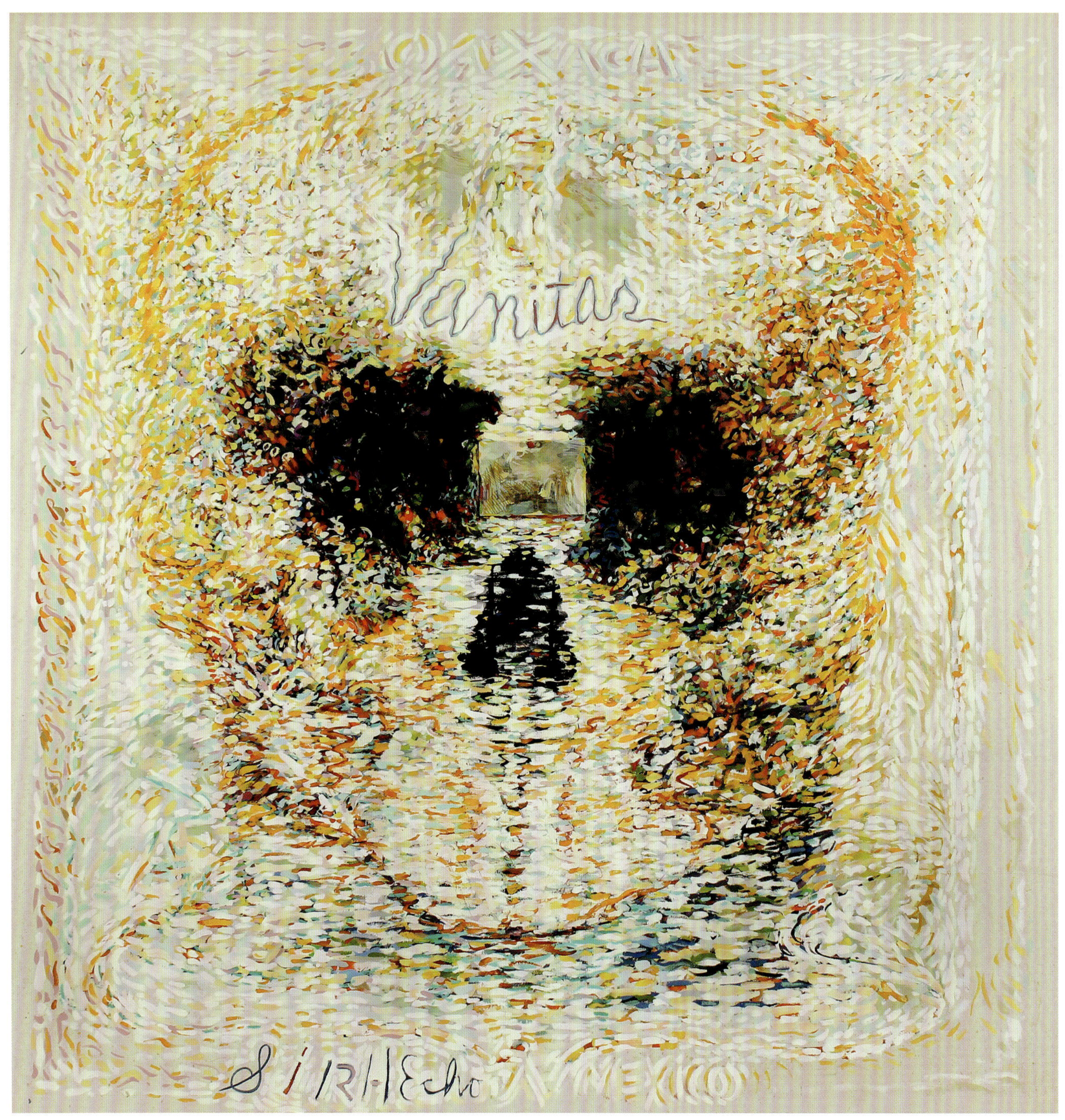

Camblin's large *Vanitas* painting dominated the exhibition, 1979. Oil on canvas. *Collection of Laura (Lollie) Dyke Reed Jackson Estate. Photograph by David P. Gray.*

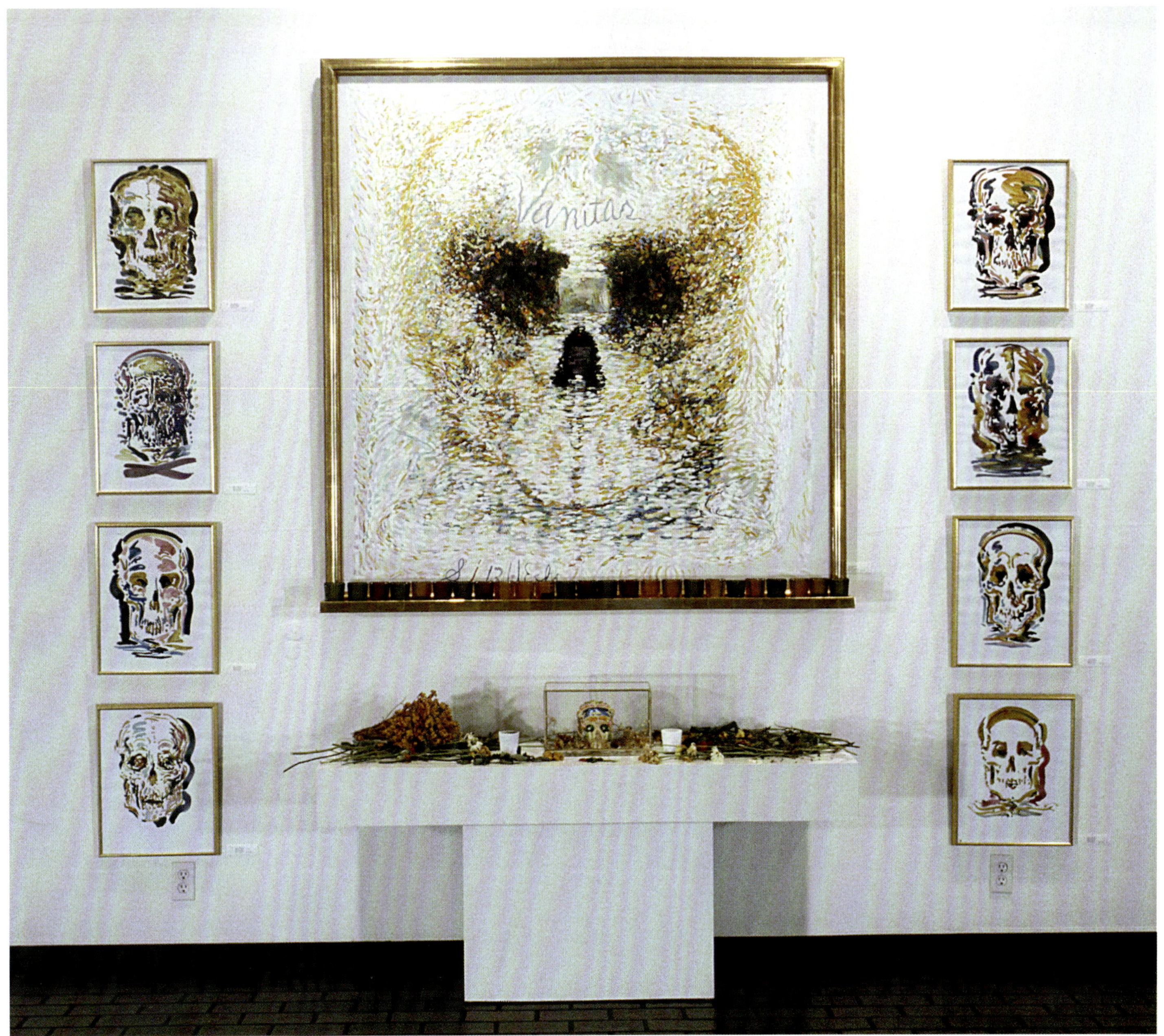

Installation photograph for Vanitas show. Camblin watercolored individual skulls to hang around large *Vanitas*.

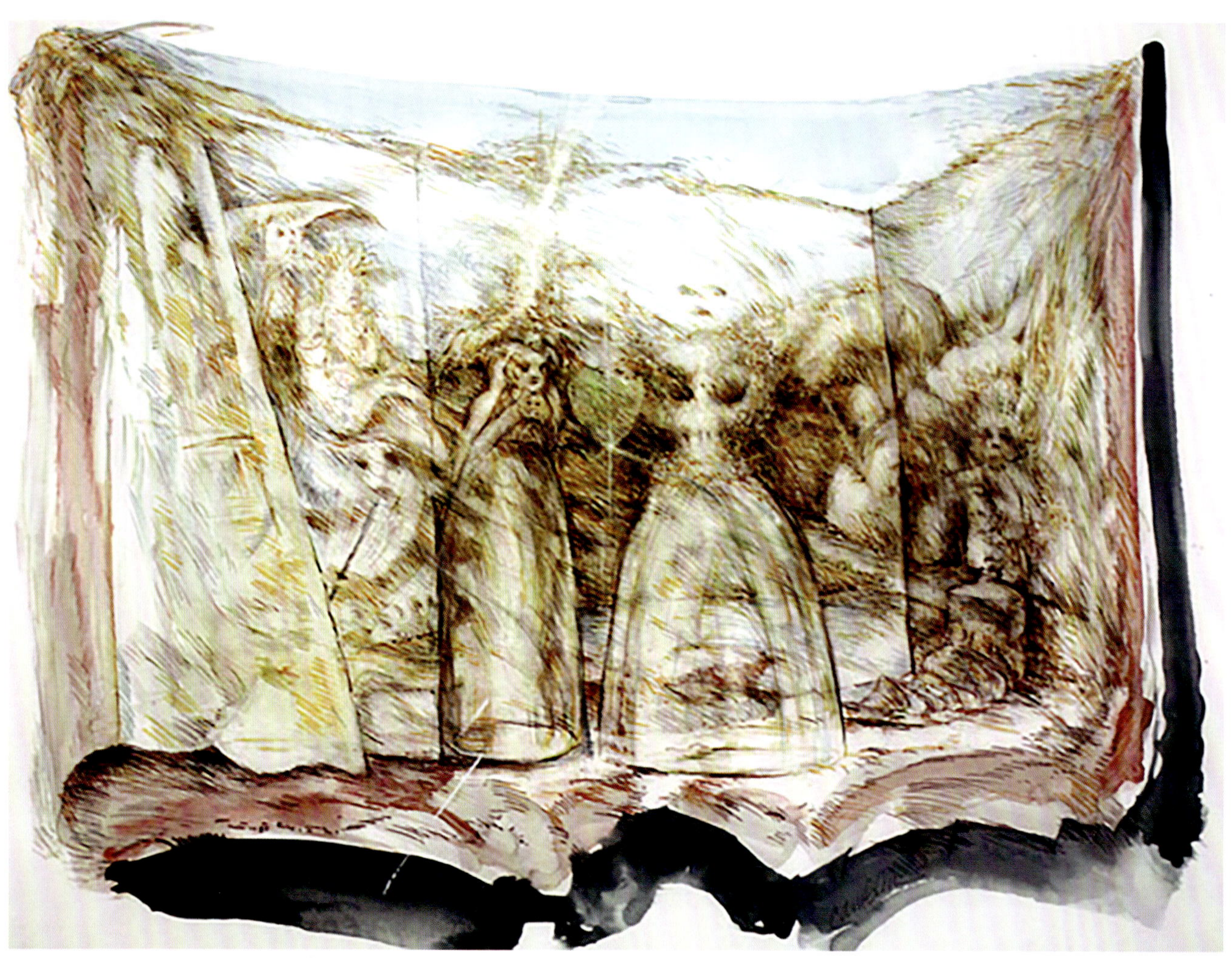

Las Meninas from *Las Meninas Series* in homage to Velasquez. Camblin created another mysterious work with transparent figures, some with skull torsos, who inhabit a pleated curtain environment in which the artist in sitting in the lower left. Velasquez painted his self-portrait in Las Meninas in the upper right corner.

The transience of life and relationships, and the inevitability of death filled Camblin's work for Moody Gallery's exhibition, *Vanitas: Works of Bob Bilyeu Camblin and Anonymous Box Co.* The show opened on April Fools' Day, 1979, and proved to be Camblin's last solo exhibit at the gallery. The focal painting of the show was a large-scale, frontal view of a skull[7] mounted above a protruding bottom shelf filled with votive candles. The skull includes references to both Venice and Oaxaca. Camblin attached two postcards from Venice to the skull: one in the nasal cavity and one between the eyes. He painted over both cards, using the impressionistic brush stroke he employed in his Venice series, but the stroke was much larger. The *Vanitas* skull hung over an altar, topped with a sugar skull in a glass box, bouquets of dead flowers, and candles. Eight smaller paintings of sugar skulls flanked the sides of the work, four on each side. The scale of the *Vanitas* painting and the skull's frontal presentation challenged the viewers to face the reality of death and to consider their own vanities.

The exhibit included the three wooden reliquaries that contained Camblin's LEE skull print as well as watercolors from his *Las Meninas Series*. Judith Dunham, art critic and writer, wrote about his Velasquez inspired series in *Art Week*:

In the *Las Meninas Series*, which nods to Velasquez, formally attired women are posed in a quasi-landscape space also inhabited by sinister-looking figures, hazily discernible forms or, in one work, the figure of an artist. Here and in other pieces Camblin interweaves drawing and watercolor into rich, illusionistically deep surfaces that hint at presences beyond definite perception. On some works he has printed, in William Wiley fashion, one word over another to create a new configuration with its own meaning. One of the strongest conjunctions of surface treatment, subject choice and illusion occurs in the drawing of a skull that is almost camouflaged within the face of a cliff, offering ominous entry to a cave that is the initial focus of interest. Camblin's combinations and treatment of subject sometimes belie his sensitive draftsmanship. His skill can be confirmed, if need be, by looking at a self-portrait which stares out from a matrix of other images in a drawing hanging in Betty Moody's office.[8]

Besides the *Vanitas* exhibition, two Houston group shows commanded Camblin's attention: *Fire! An Exhibition of 100 Texas Artists* at the Contemporary Arts Museum and *Doors: Houston Artists*, done in conjunction with the Houston Festival and shown at the Alley Theatre. Camblin created pieces for both. The same year he included paintings in three exhibits outside Houston: *Five Artists from Texas* at George Belcher Gallery in San Francisco and *Twenty-First Annual Invitational Operation Update—1979* at the Longview Museum in Texas and *Works on Paper*, an exhibition curated by Dianne David for the Nave Museum in Victoria, Texas.

CHAPTER NINETEEN

The Last Years in Texas

Six months after his *Vanitas* exhibition, Camblin moved to a motel in Santa Cruz, California. He hoped he would be inundated with Houston guests who would lure him back to the city, but that was not to be. Feeling ignored, he reluctantly returned to Houston. The 1980s seemed full of difficulties: Camblin worried about things financial, political, and personal. The Iran-Iraq war began. The rise of a new right and Reaganomics replaced the hippie culture of the 1970s, a culture more suited to Camblin. Mount St. Helens erupted. An obsessed fan gunned down and killed John Lennon. Rather than concentrate on real problems, American citizens watched television: millions of fans waited to find out who shot JR Ewing in the soap opera *Dallas*. Camblin seemed to focus on the world's vicissitudes in an effort to avoid facing his changing and challenging personal issues.

Camblin's interest in art waned. His friend and collaborator, Allan Otho Smith, tried to cheer him up by silkscreening a photograph of Camblin's face on a brown paper grocery bag using only black ink. Cerling remembers, "Bob had some of his friends put the paper bags over their heads and the whole group, including Camblin, all with bags over heads, entered Moody Gallery so the gallerist wouldn't know who was the real Camblin."[1] The bag mask parade was a success and demonstrated Camblin's ability, and perhaps desire, to hide behind his own countenance.

Friends tried to help ease Camblin's gloomy state of mind, but once alone, he would be overtaken by his melancholy. He tried to socialize and attend art events, including a Kite Flying contest. He recorded his feelings in sketchbooks that he would deposit on my doorstep in hopes of long thank-you calls.

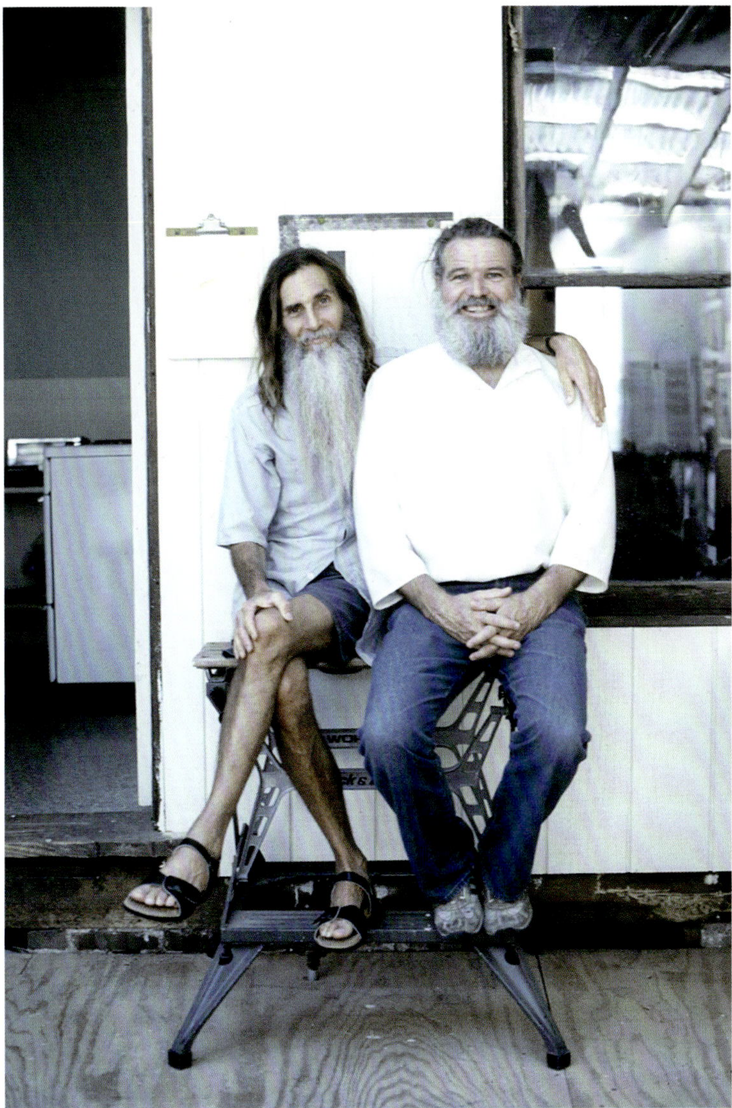

Camblin with Forrest Prince, another Houston artist and Camblin's good friend.

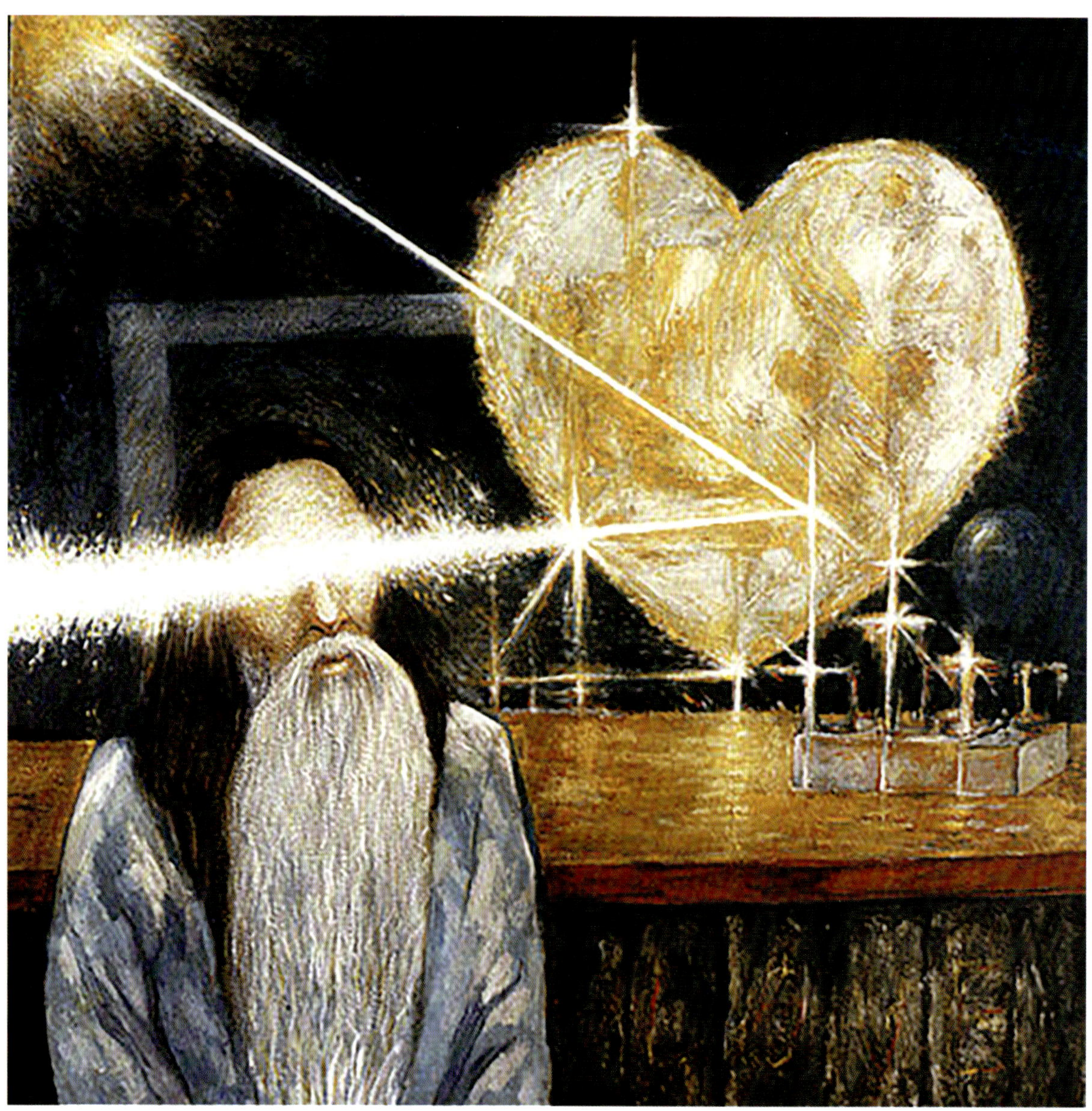

Painting of Forrest Prince and Heart. Camblin knew Forrest to be a man of God, thus the rays of enlightenment.

On a page torn from a sketchbook, Camblin wrote, "full moon April 11, 1979, Sandra, AT last—first night in the NEW PLACE. (Thanks to Dave and all those that bought my pictures). It seems so strange that we have these different planes. So difficult to balance so many different lives that have to be lived . . . I continue

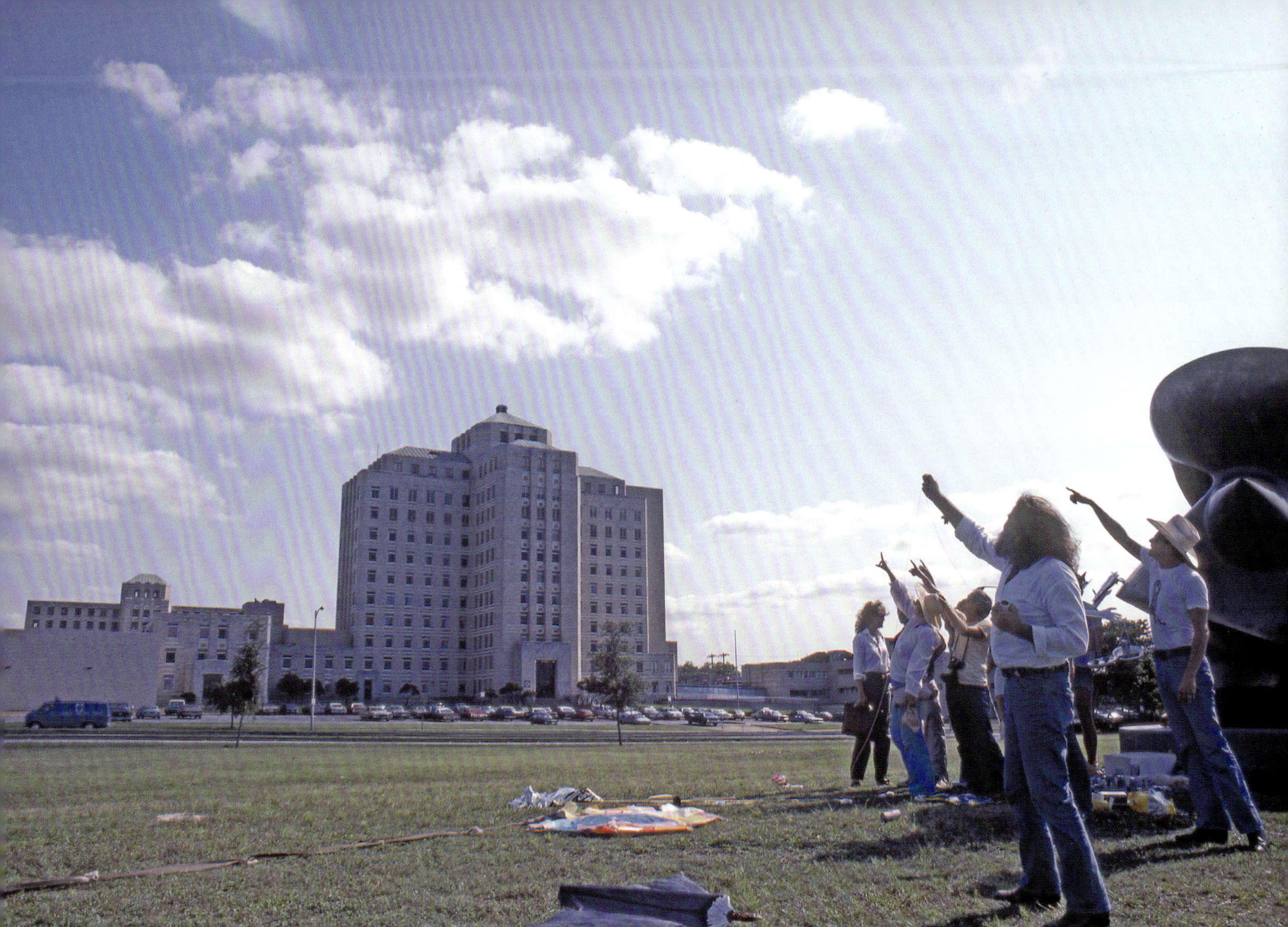

Camblin participating in a kite flying contest, organized by Allan O. Smith, on Allen Parkway. *George O. Jackson photograph.*

to believe that 'Time' can't change what is. Most people believe in some incredible THINGS/IDEAS?! and I too—keep a few to myself. C U Later L bob"

While he worried about his personal life, the evolution of the art world also troubled him. His sense of his place in the world was eroding. His life seemed to be turning into a trope, and he loathed being the individualistic and solitary artist betrayed by love. He felt he was no longer a part of the larger art world

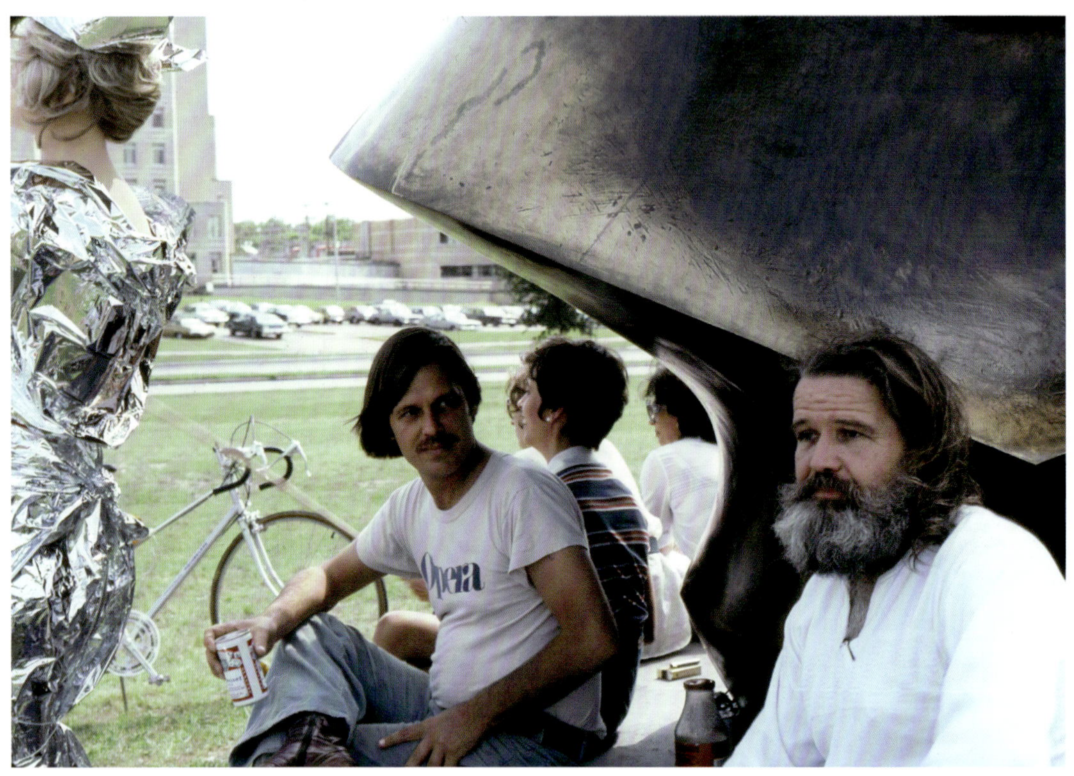

Lucas Johnson and Camblin sitting on a Henry Moore sculpture on Allen Parkway, Houston.

because his version of it no longer existed. With the rise of international art fairs, he believed art was becoming a commodity and that artists were tailoring their work to feed the fairs and the monied collectors, something he could not do. He understood that the selling of art on any level was commerce, but he liked the personal touch of a gallery dealer, even though his representation with any particular gallery did not usually last long. Camblin wanted viewers who took the time to really see his art. He didn't want to paint big works just to satisfy a trend that seemed to price art by the inch for the rich and powerful. If the first question a viewer, museum goer, or art enthusiast asked was, "How much is it worth?" he knew the looker would not engage with his art. For him, money was not the magic; he resented having to think about money at all. The art world and his life took opposing paths. To him it seemed as if he and I were doing the same, and that stopping the divergent directions was beyond his abilities. He wrote, "Nearly sunset on the waning MOON July 11, 1979, and I know that if you are reading this at sunset one day, you will remember that its all 'ONE LONG DAY ONE LONG NIGHT'—anon Lover Forever"

Exhibitions helped to distract him from his angst and kept him occupied. He had work in *Contemporary Drawings and Watercolors*, at the Memorial Art Gallery at the University of Rochester in New York and in group exhibits at Moody Gallery in both 1980 and 1981. His friend, Dallas artist David McManaway, had a show at the Meadows School of the Arts at Southern Methodist University in Dallas that included collaborative pieces done with Camblin. In 1980 Camblin's art was showcased in *Inside Texas Borders, Recent Works by Artists of the Southwest*, and the *Beehive Postcard Show* in Salt Lake City.

Back to Ireland and Return to Houston

Camblin decided to return to Ireland, the land of his genetic coding. He hoped that something in his makeup would respond positively and profoundly to restore him to his former self. He arrived in the fall of 1980. Before departing for Ireland, Camblin had begun a series of paintings titled *Touching Palms* with Nancy Giordano Echegoyen, a highly trained artist. From this point on, she would become the most influential female in Camblin's life. The duo signed their collaborative work "Anonymous Artists." Lollie Jackson[2] and Giordano[3] traveled to the Emerald Isle for a long visit with the artist during the spring of the following year. During their visit, Camblin painted collaboratively with Giordano. In the company of two devoted women, his mood improved.

Thrust back into solitude after the departure of his friends, Camblin decided to return again to Houston. Once in Texas, he felt ghosts lurking around every corner. Every person and place bought back memories. Texas wasn't proving to be productive, however, so he went to San Jose, California, in August of 1981, and stayed with Joe Tate for two months. He spent his time painting large canvases of Tate's Bascom Street studio. When he left San Jose, Camblin took a road trip to Page, Arizona; Carlsbad, New Mexico; and St. George, Utah, where he paid an

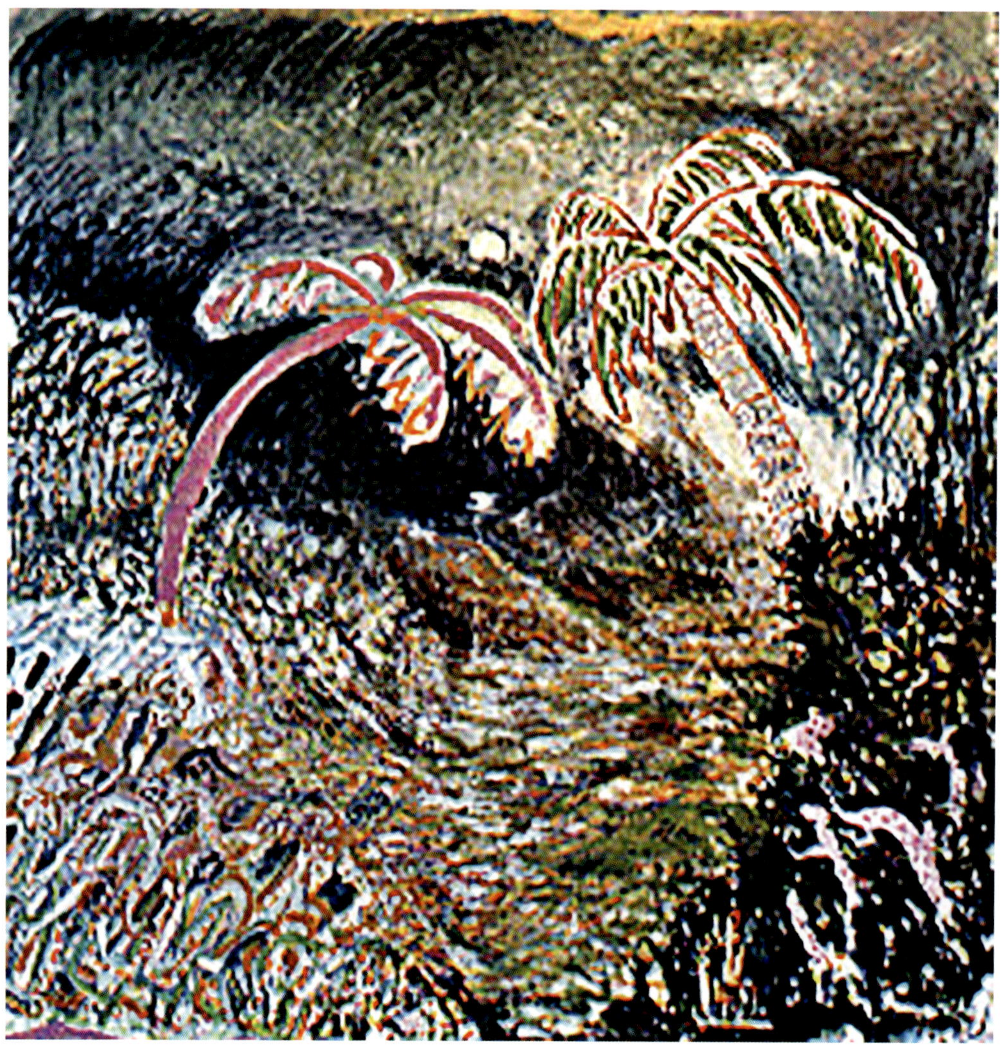

Camblin painted *Rock and Roll Palms* with Nancy Giordano.

unannounced and difficult visit to my parents. Returning to Houston, he no longer felt as if he were coming home.

He worked. In 1981, Camblin's art appeared in the Assistance League of Houston's *Collection '81—The Road Show* at 2 Houston Center and in the University of Houston's Lawndale Annex: *The Image of the House in Contemporary Art*. The next year Moody sent an exhibition of her gallery artists' work to Linda Durham Gallery in Santa Fe, New Mexico; the show included art by Camblin. Roberto Molina Gallery in Houston hung *Little Egypt—Waterworkshop* that exhibited Camblin's collaborative works. The *1981 Houston Arts Calendar* published a photograph of Bob, biographical information, and a colored reproduction of a ten-year-old watercolor *St. Bambola* from 1971. Whether Camblin purposely chose the decade-old watercolor of the masked, cast-off saint or if someone other than Camblin submitted the work is unknown. Either way, the selection for the calendar exposed his indifference to the project.

In January of 1982, I married. Camblin wrote me a congratulatory letter. Then he left town. Having visited Galveston regularly for years, he knew that being near water seemed to calm him, so he moved to Galveston, Texas, in February and remained there through November. He needed some distance between himself and his history in Houston. Galveston provided the first step of his extraction from Texas. While there, he entertained friends, painted, and walked the beach regularly; but he discovered that the island was not a long-term solution for his angst. Before his November departure, he assembled personal objects and placed them in a treasure chest. With the assistance of his longtime friend, Mike DeGeurin, whom he bound to secrecy, Camblin buried a treasure on Galveston beach. Having contemplated a permanent move from Houston for some time before his Galveston venture, he had been leaving signs, clues, and ciphers in his art for the recovery of buried treasure. Curiously, art critic Eleanor Freed wrote an article for the September 1982 issue of *Houston Arts Magazine* titled, "Treasures for the Finding." Even though the reference was not to Camblin's buried

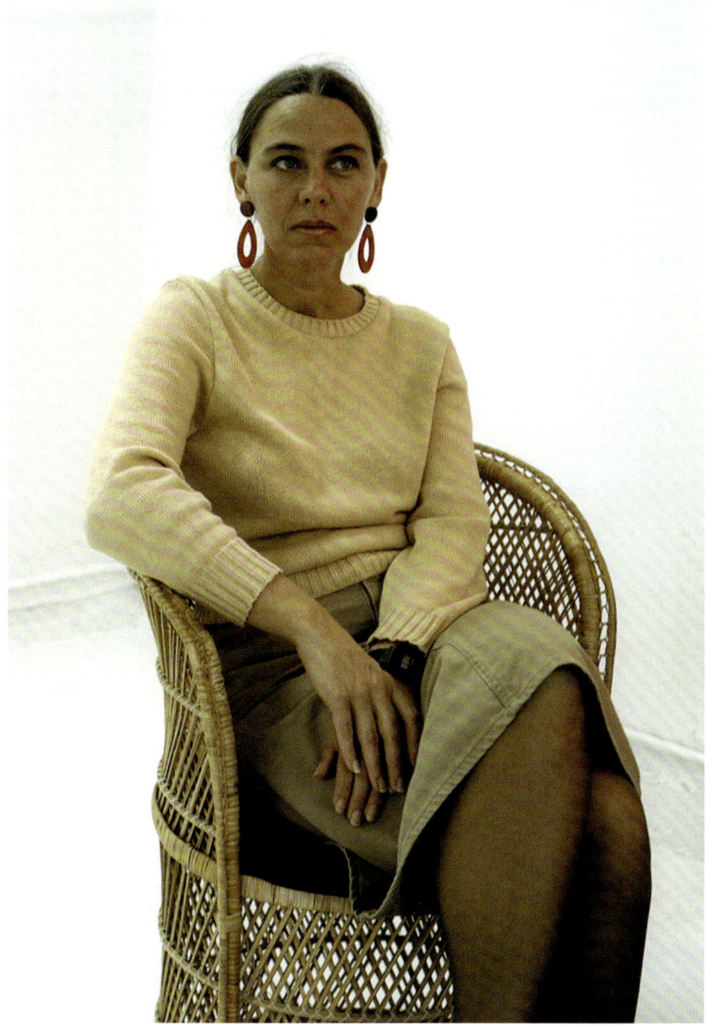

Nancy Giordano began collaborating with Camblin as Anonymous Artists in 1980.

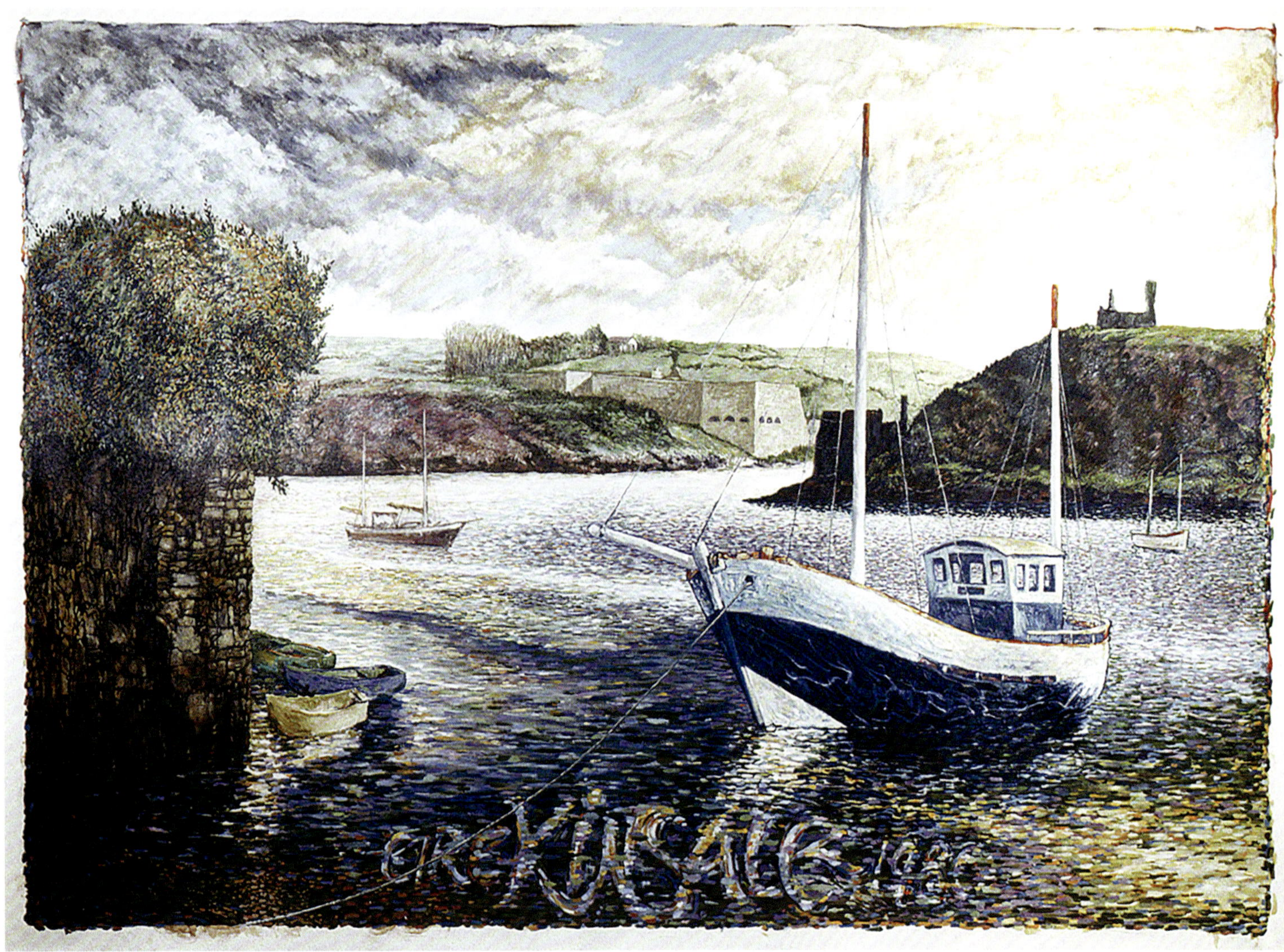

Kinsale, Ireland, 1980s, another collaboration with Nancy Giordano. The brushstrokes are tighter than those in *Rock and Roll Palms*.

treasure, Freed included a photo of Camblin along with a page from a sketchbook, exemplifying the treasures to be found in the Archives of American Art, including documentation on Camblin's art and life.

The year 1982 also involved an exotic art venue when *Art From Houston in Norway* exhibited Camblin's work in Stavanger Kunstforening, Norway. The

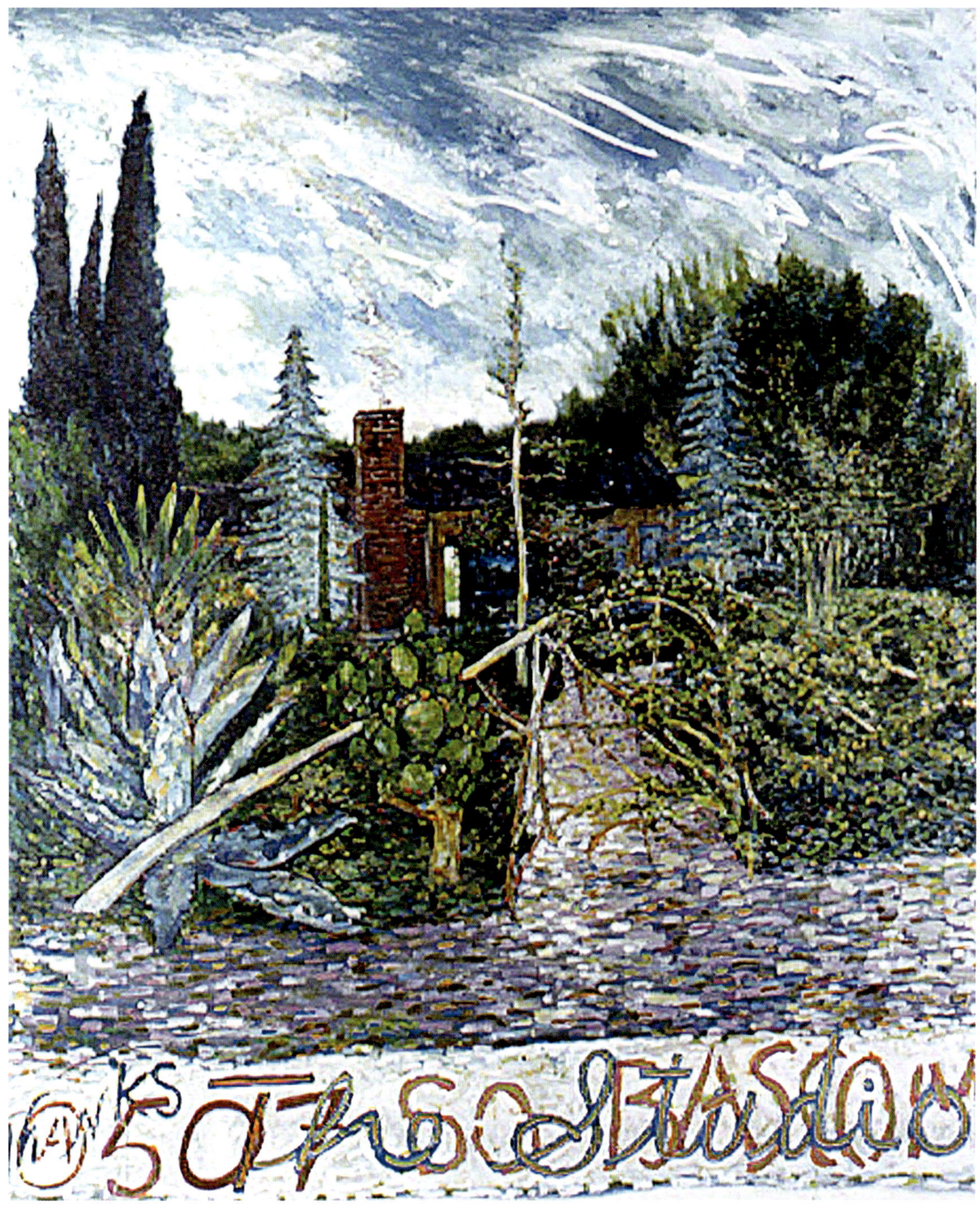

While visiting Joe Tate in California, Camblin painted Tate's studio, *507 So. Bascom*.

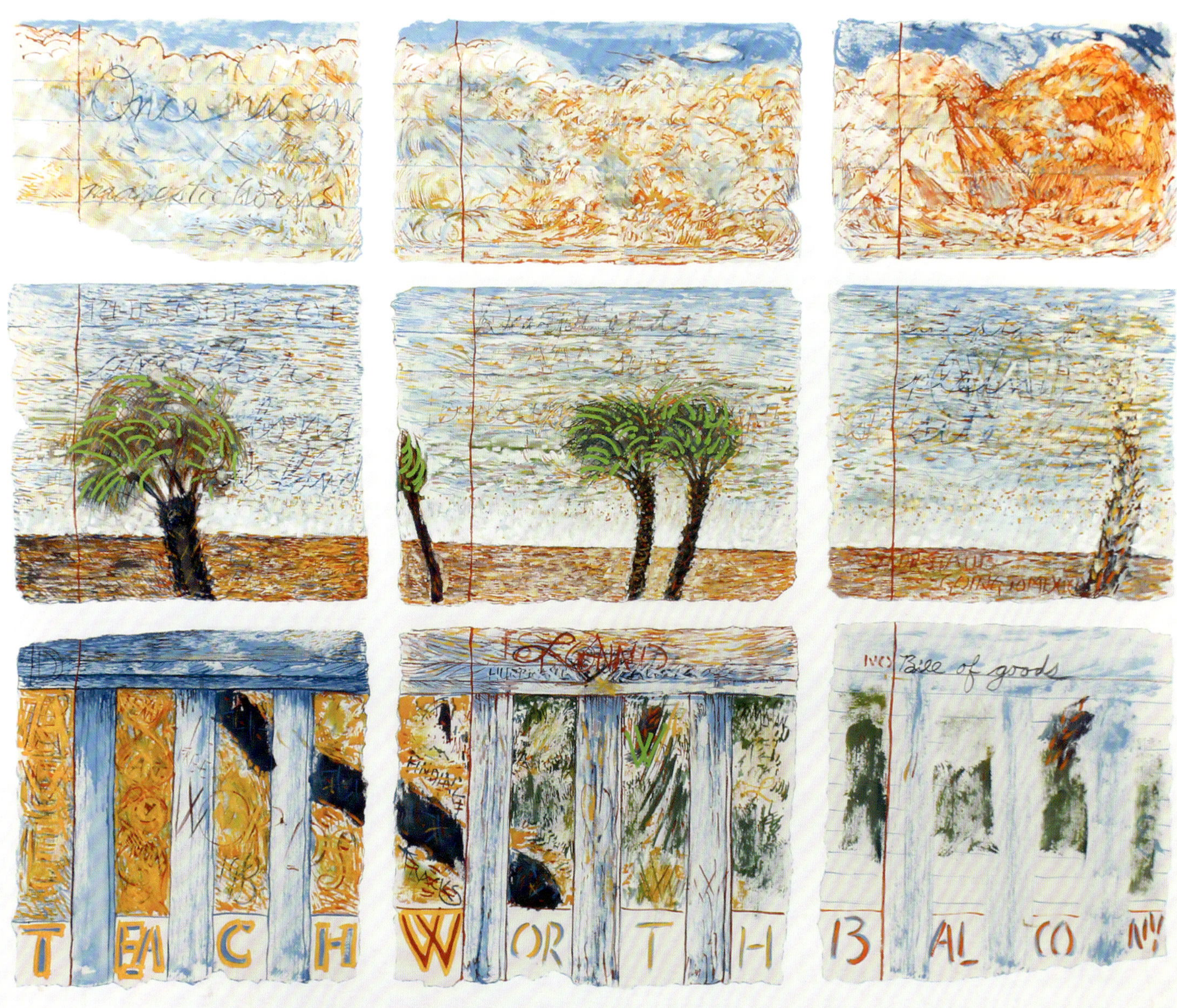

In *Teachworth Balcony*, 1981, Camblin returned to the cell format of his existential comics although this time a single landscape continues from one frame to the other. Oil on canvas, 5' X 6'. *Annie DeGuerin Collection. David P. Gray photograph.*

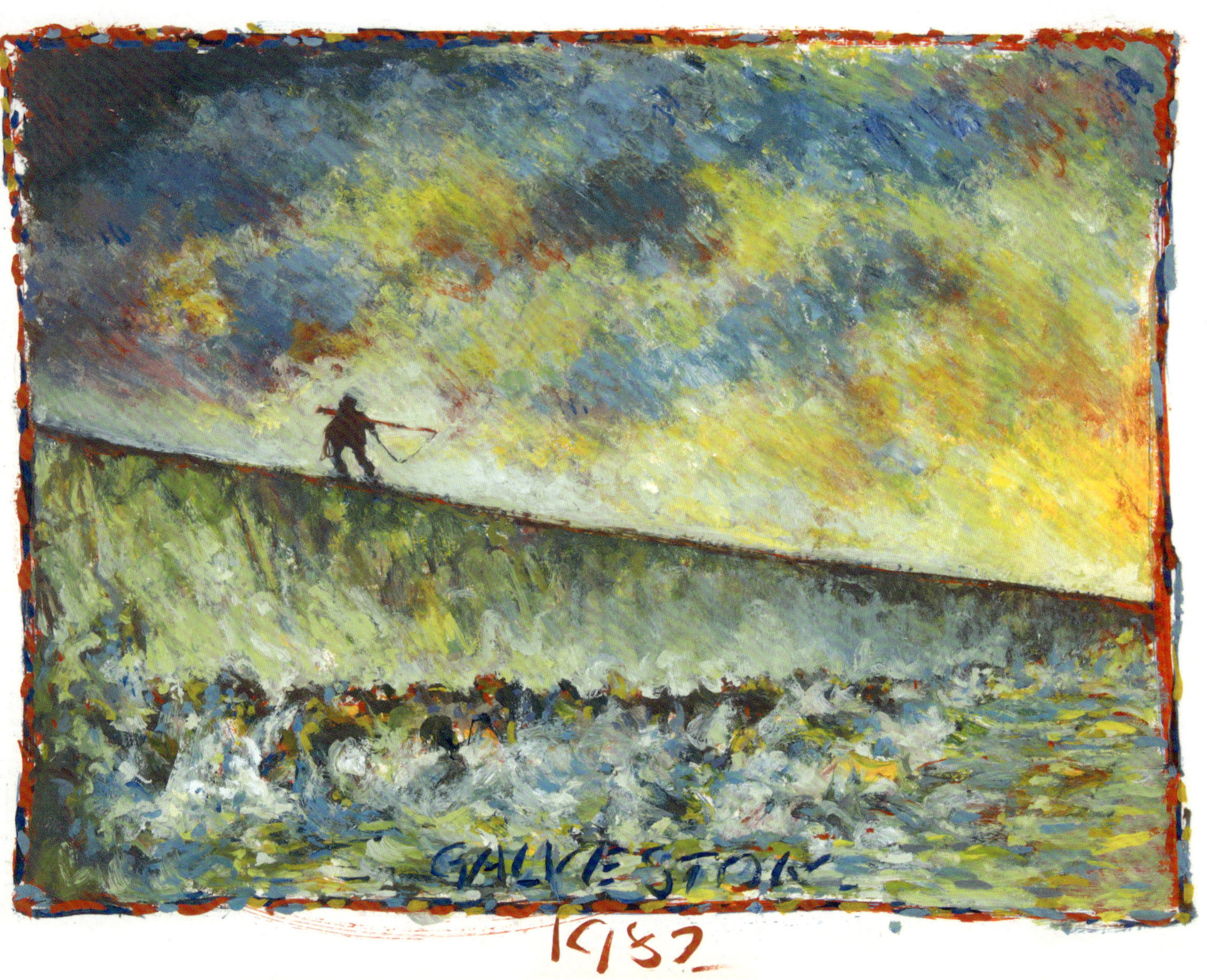

Camblin moved to Galveston in 1982 and painted on the beach or from Teachworth balcony. In *Galveston* he painted his fisherman character walking down the seawall using broader, more impressionistic brushstrokes.

following year, the University of Texas in Austin hung *Texas Images & Visions* in the Archer M. Huntington Gallery. The show was organized by William Goetzmann and Becky Duval Reese, who also wrote the accompanying catalog. Reese notes the Earl Staley–Bob Camblin connection: "Camblin's paintings, like Staley's, are often concerned with the Texas and Mexico landscapes. Camblin purposefully paints in a style resembling that of the impressionists. His painting *Big Bend* (*Homage to Earl Staley*) *1980* goes beyond a stylistic restatement, however. The painting combines highly colored impressionistic brushstrokes with collage, which Camblin has included in his work since 1974."

I received a note from Galveston: "Dear Friend, September 1982, Loveritas," a word combination of love and veritas. Love and truth or true love?

Sponsored by Houston Women's Caucus for Art, 2 Houston Center presented *1984 Show: An Exhibition of Contemporary Houston Art.* Camblin did not manage to get his art to the exhibit although his name appears in the *Artist & Catalogue Listings* and is followed by a series of periods. He may have been too busy to get involved with the 2 Houston Center exhibition due to his upcoming solo show at Houston's Midtown Art Center: *Bob Camblin: A Houston Retrospective, 1968–1984.* Patricia Johnson, art critic for the *Houston Chronicle* wrote on March 23, 1984: "The 100-plus works in a variety of media at the Midtown Art Center are . . . an homage to and a long overdue presentation of one of Houston's 'old' masters. His influence on the city's art community is sensed like an undercurrent whose power may catch you by surprise."

As a leftie, the figure, whom we presume to be Camblin, holds his pen in his left hand, and it appears that a strange figure with rays emanating from his back is guiding Camblin's hand. Camblin's double v=W followed by "Electricage" (electric age or electri cage?) is written from his shoulder to his wrist. A one-winged "Liberty" with torch raised in her right hand, places her index finger over her mouth. Camblin's hat is pulled down and covers the top part of his glasses which hide his eyes. His right index finger is raised under his hat. A skeletal figure in the background to Camblin's right is holding a pencil with its tip pointed down. Looking at the painting, the upper right corner reveals the word "Write" followed by text too dark to be read. The lower right corner includes the date April 1, 1985,

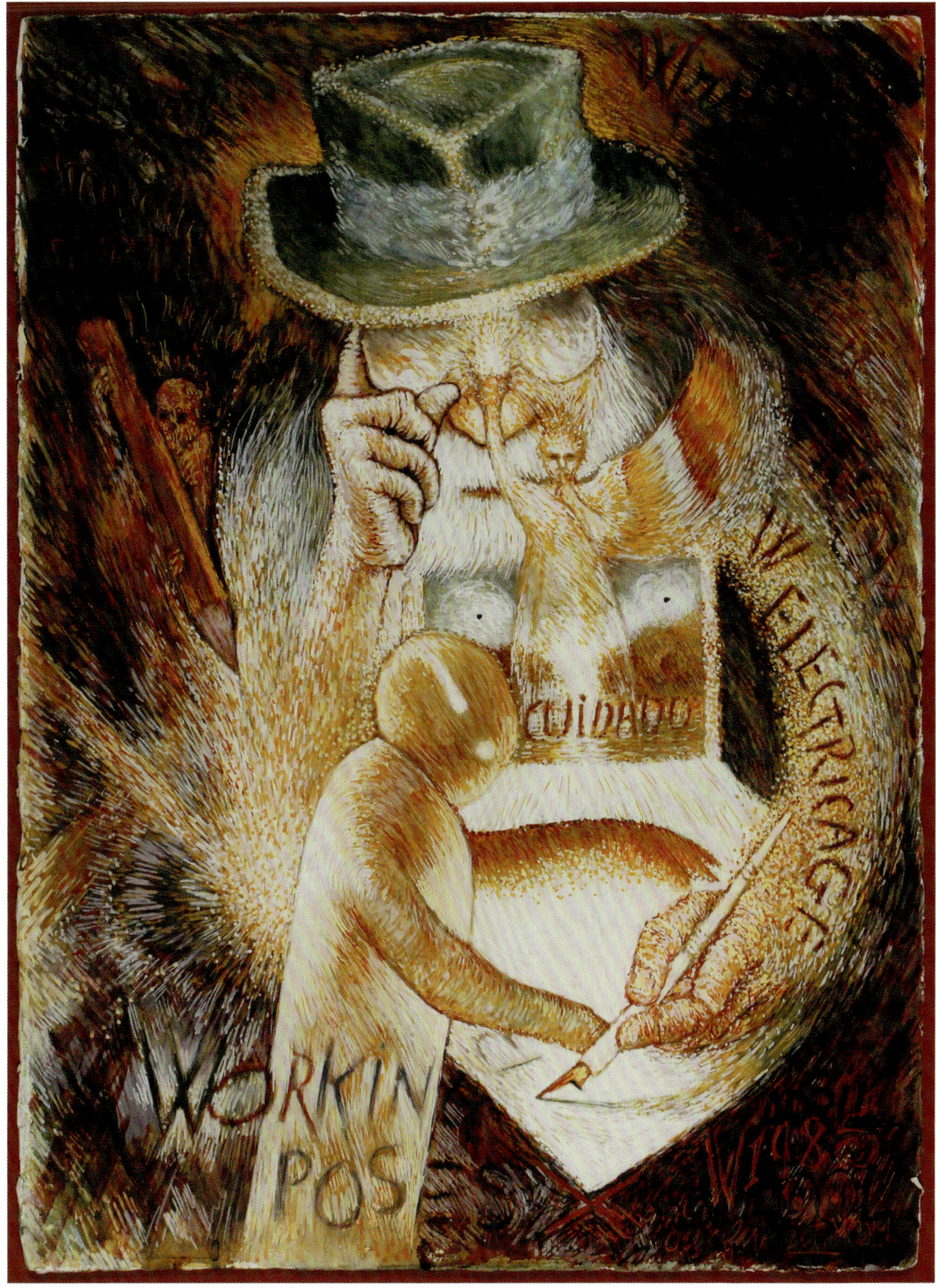

Cuidado, Working Poses April 1, 1985. In this painting, Camblin gives the viewer a warning. Be Careful. Keep it Under Your Hat. Don't tell.

under which "FOOL" can be discerned as can the word "MODEL." The painting has few hard edges and is less exuberantly expressionistic than other works from the period. The electrical energy emissions from the torch which is placed between Camblin's eyes, from the angel's one wing, and from the back of the pen-guiding creature seem to imbue the whole with energy from the electric age. Then there is the warning: Be careful. Keep it under your hat. Don't tell. April Fool

Camblin continued corresponding with me. Some of his letters reflected a lift in his mood. Referencing our earlier travels through the clever inclusion of the names of some of his favorite authors, in 1984 he wrote:

Going/Coming All the Time Leaving/Arriving—Time Traveling along Vonnegut Lines, Via Sagan Conduit, By Heinlein Express, in the Castenada Creeper, with Emerson Light Ship, on Shakespeare Unlimited, and the famous Oriental Express. HG Well, well, well, Clickety Clarke 2002,1984, Brave New Huxley, et al . . .

Where it is going—Red Stick, the pirate; where it has been—Robert Camblin, the professor/cartographer; What's happening Now—Robin Goodfellow, the practical joker & the prisoners—Anonymous Bosh, Kay Sage, Cindy Klaus et al.

RED BLUE YELLOW As far as I can see . . ."

CHAPTER TWENTY

Big Al Looms Large

In the mid-1980s, Camblin began a series of Albert Einstein portraits. His drawings, paintings, and prints of the scientist, affectionately dubbed *Big Al*, give evidence to his admiration and awe of the man. In Camblin's drawritings, he wrote "LOOK" across Einstein's face, placing the Os over the scientist's eyes. LOOK becomes a half-mask that invites the viewer to gaze into the eyes of Einstein to gain insight into the genius.

As if participating in Camblin's theater, the Hebrew University in Jerusalem and the Einstein Foundation filed a legal infringement for Camblin's recreation of Einstein's image. In response Camblin sent the foundation "The Unwritten and Untold Story of Big Al,"[1] (I received copies of all the correspondence) featuring a comic book version of Einstein that

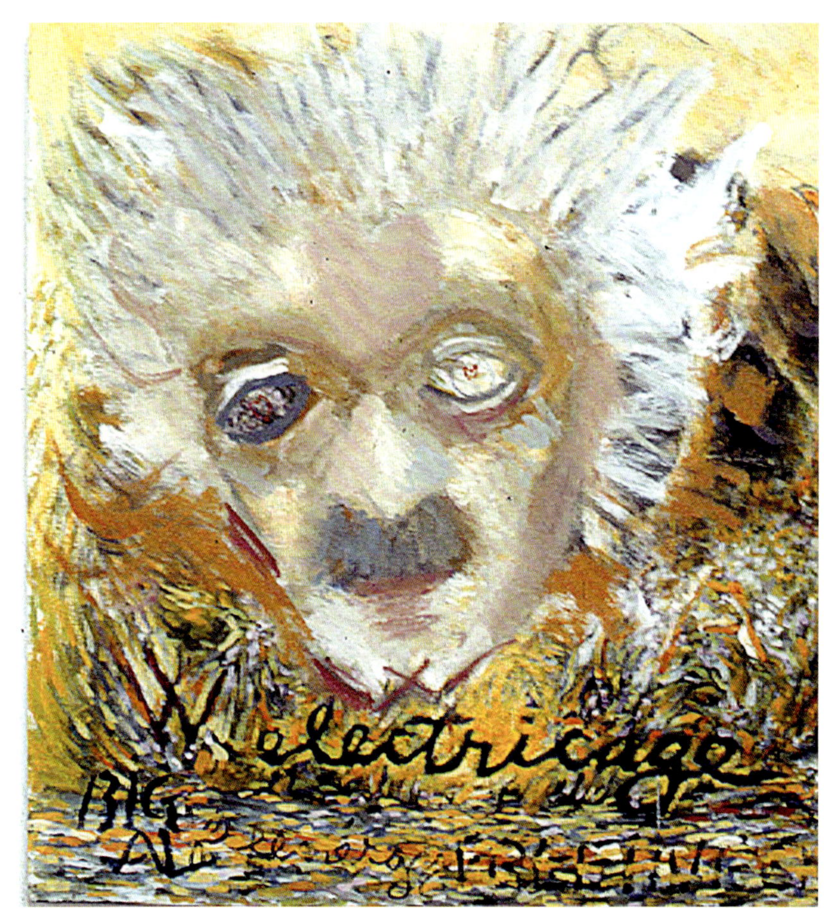

Big Al Electricage, 1985. Acrylic, 44" X 33". Big Al looks electrified and he certainly did electrify the world. *Collection of Mike DeGeurin. Photo Credit: David P. Gray.*

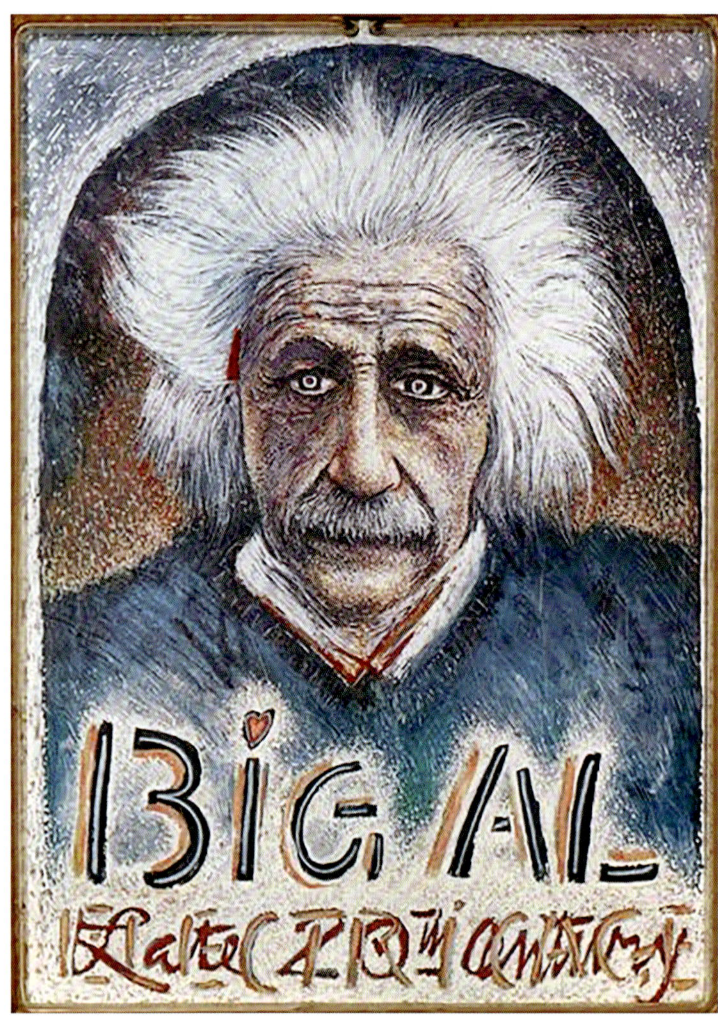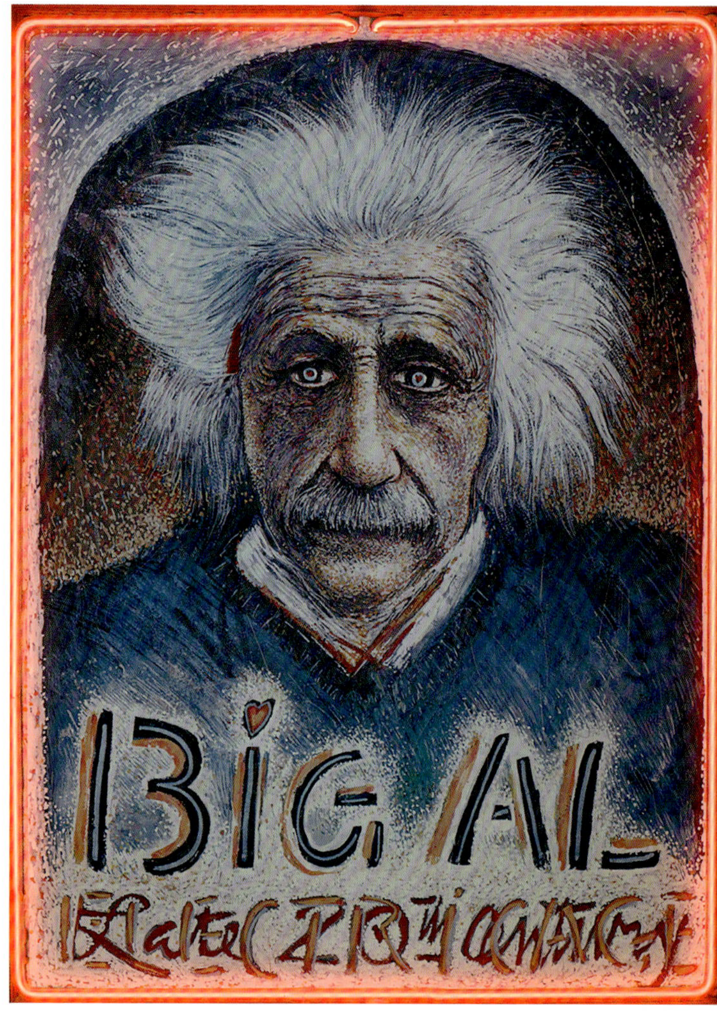

Big Al, Late 20th Century. Mixed media including neon, 32" X 24" X 4" deep. Camblin did electrify *Big Al* with a ring of red neon. *Collection of Dr. Carolyn Farb. Thomas DuBrock photograph. On the right:* with neon on. *One the left:* with neon off.

explained Camblin's continued use of the cartoon character. On one page Camblin noted, "The Write to re.member BIG AL no matter what he LOOKS like." He was amused and flattered by the fact the foundation even knew of his existence. Of course, Camblin continued using Einstein's image in his work. He even surrounded one portrait of *Big Al* with red neon.

Curator and writer Annette Carlozzi included one of Camblin's *Einstein* etchings in her 1986 book and exhibition *50 Texas Artists: A Critical Selection of Painters and Sculptors Working in Texas*. Next to the reproduction of the etching Camblin wrote, "Picasso sed. Paintings are not to decorate the Walls of a room or apartment, but are instruments of WAR AGAINST BRUTALITY and DARKNESS. . . . Sincerely anonymous."[2]

The Houston photographer Gay Block took the perfect accompanying photo of Camblin whose eyes are masked in sunglasses. His eyes obscured, he seems to be looking directly at the camera.

By 1985 Camblin seemed his old self. The shows from that year included *Self Images* at the Houston Women's Caucus for Art; two shows at Midtown Art Gallery in Houston: *Propaganda, Too!* and *The New Nude;* and a *Houston Drawing* show in the Museum of Fine Arts' Glassell School of Art. But the exhibition that caused the most stir for all artists in Houston was *Fresh Paint: The Houston School*, organized by Barbara Rose and Susie Kalil for the Houston Museum of Fine Arts. True to form, Camblin was the only artist who did not include an artist's statement in the catalog. Instead he added a drawriting, signed "Sincerely, anonymous." He exhibited two large paintings he had created while staying with Joe Tate in San Jose, California in 1981: *Joe's Backyard* and *The Bascom Street Studio*.

I received a drawriting. Over a blank piece of paper Camblin had traced his right hand on which he wrote, "Write HAND 1985." The hand covered the letter so only some of the words could be read. "Dear SAND_A, June Moon 1985. Nice _o __e __u again. Best wish__ in your future _______ We are happy _________ that everything has_________out so well, well and remember me _________your _________ "

His notes and letters arrived fairly regularly throughout the 1980s.

In 1985, the Cultural Arts Council of Houston presented Camblin with a grant for the work of Anonymous Artists. He was honored, but the award was not enough to keep him from entertaining thoughts of leaving Texas. Joe Tate was gone. He and Earl Staley had been distant for over a decade. Camblin no longer felt integral to the art community of the city. His strongest Houston art connection remained Dave Folkman, who kept Camblin busy making lithographs. Supportive of the Camblin-Folkman lithographic endeavors, Lollie Jackson, always the consummate patron, asked to purchase an example of every work the duo produced.

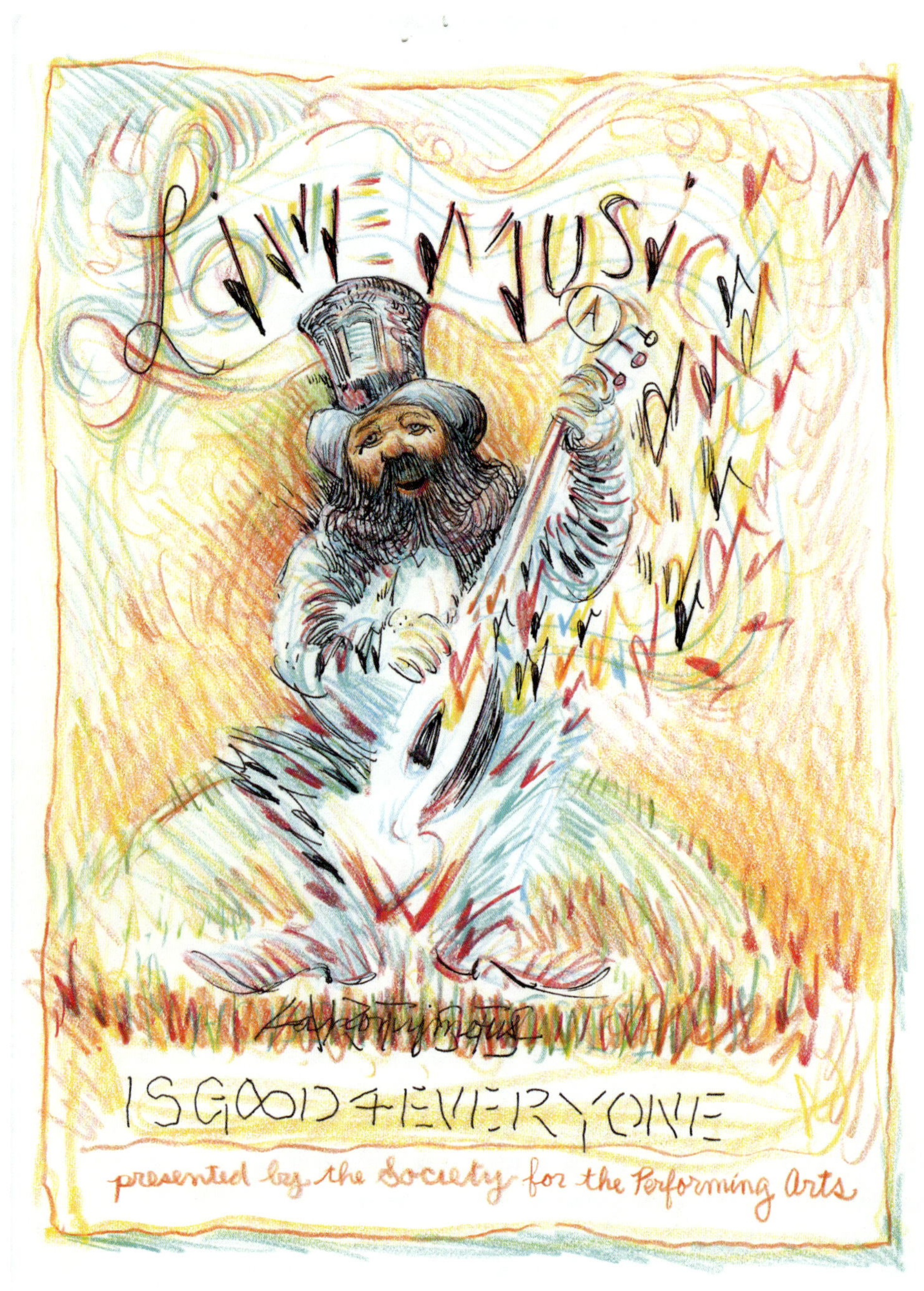

Love Music, the Society for the Performing Arts, 1985. Camblin was given a grant by the Houston Arts Council. He was grateful to be appreciated, but he was ready to leave the state.

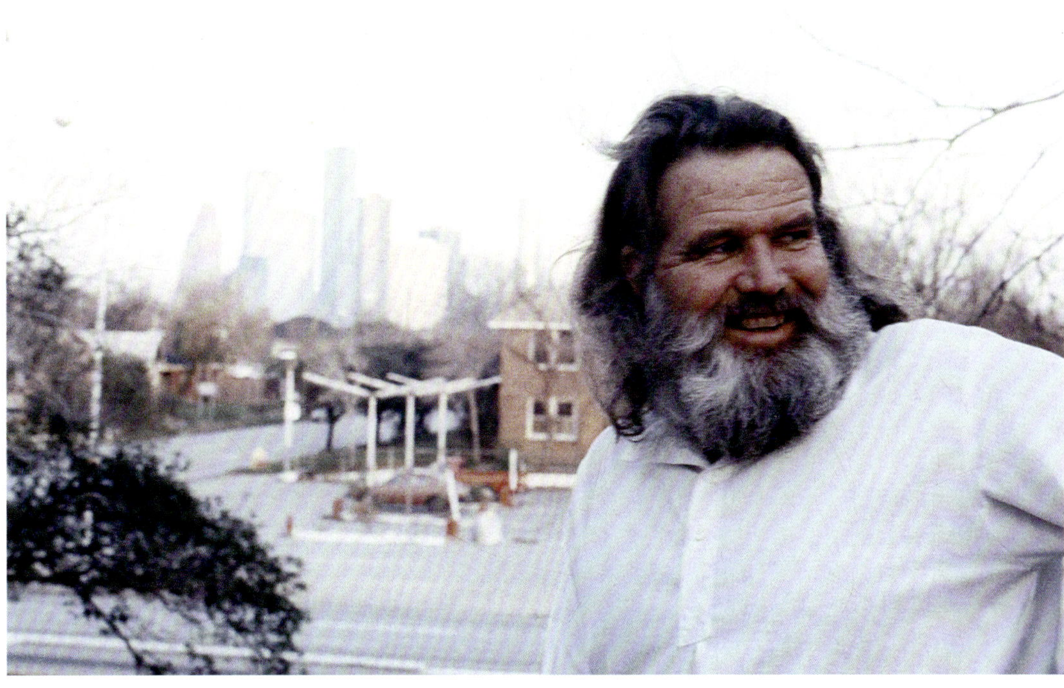

Photo of Camblin on balcony of W. Gray Studio 1986.

To house the lithographs, Folkman built a large wooden chest over which Jackson hung Camblin's large *Vanitas* painting[3] that she had purchased during Camblin's 1979 exhibition. Because of her devotion, Camblin asked that Jackson store and care for an archive of his work including his lithographs, some large paintings, sketchbooks, journals, newspaper articles, and memorabilia.

In February of 1985, "Mrs. Sandra Levy" received a note from Anonymous Artists, "Mort, sum c'est." Camblin was either feeling very mortal or alerting me to the death of our involvement. Another letter followed: The "Dead, some say." Camblin no longer wanted sympathy; he was "Still Dancing in my Head."

When David Folkman changed the production location of his studio,[4] Camblin moved into Little Egypt's old building. Once there, he and Giordano, who were living together, worked on their collaborative paintings as "anonymous artists." They also created their individual works and together painted directly on the walls of the space. Feeling the need to talk to his brother, Dennis, Camblin ventured back to Honolulu, Hawaii, where he spent several weeks walking the beach, floating in the ocean and talking with Dennis. When he returned to Houston, he was more relaxed. He began seeing things in a positive light.

The year 1986 began with *Texas Visions*, a traveling exhibition that visited eight Texas cities. The show was organized by the Art League of Houston. From May 17 to September 7, 1986, the Houston Museum of Fine Arts celebrated the Texas sesquicentennial with an exhibition and catalog, *The Texas Landscape, 1900–1986*, curated and written by Susie Kalil. Camblin had three works in the show. In the accompanying catalog Kalil notes: "In Bob Camblin's atmospheric impressionist views of Houston's Buffalo Bayou, we are placed in the artist's world; he pushes us to the edge of the bank, directing our eyes to examine its swamps and thickly massed foliage and to contemplate the skyline beyond."

The exhibition *Cinq x Cinq: Houston Texas* took Camblin and his work to Paris in late 1986. In the show's catalog essay on the artist, Gerard-Georges LeMaire wrote, "What fascinates Bob Camblin is clearly the complex and very delicate relationship between image and language." The artist created a large painting of the Paris rooftops. He also painted his Irish heaven.

While in Paris, France, Camblin and Ray Balinskas posed in front of the poster announcing the *Cinq X Cinq* show that included Camblin's work, 1986.

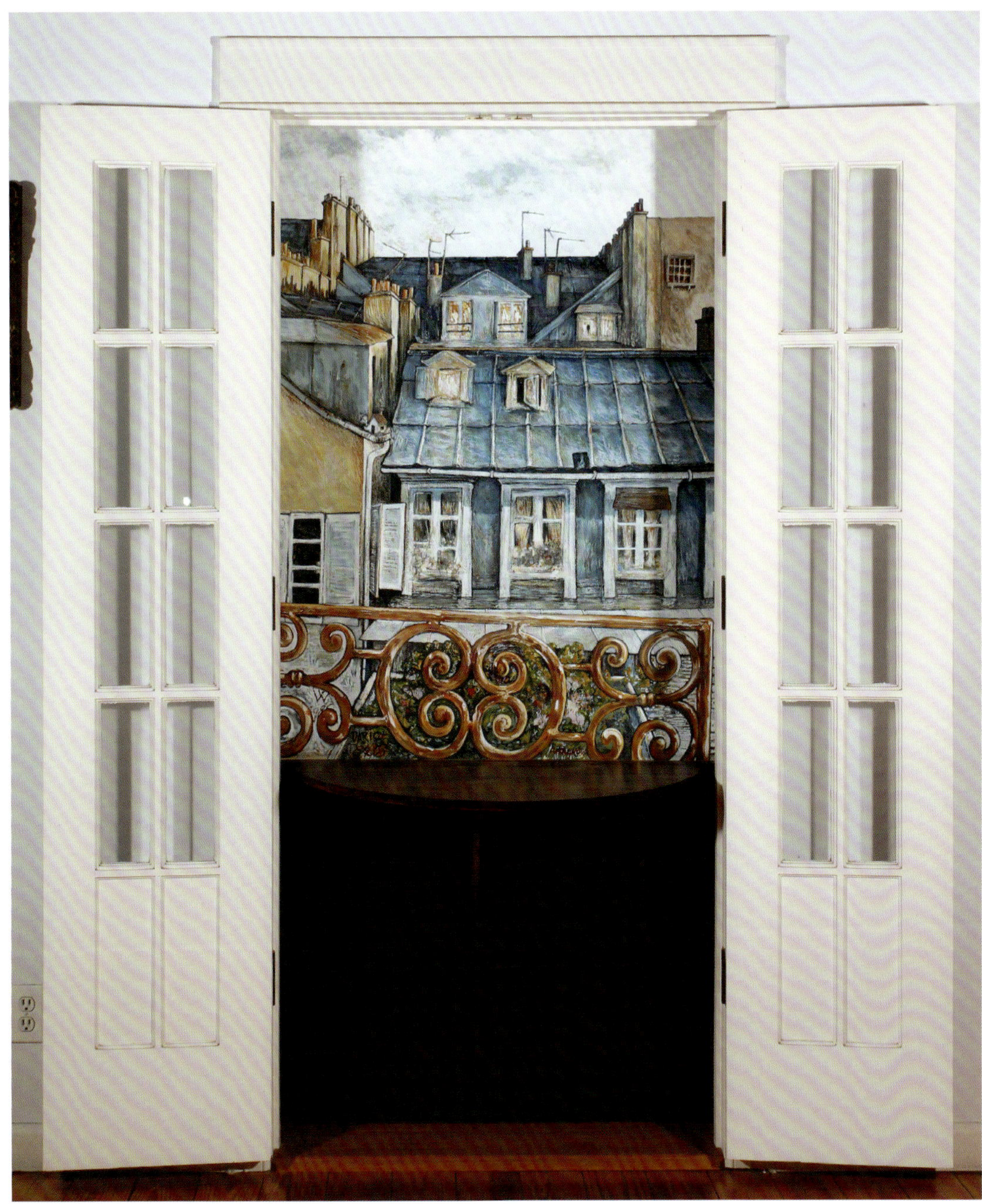

The DeGeurin installation of *Paris*, 1986, 54" X 40", between French doors in their home. *Collection of Gayle and Mike DeGeurin. Photograph by David P. Gray.*

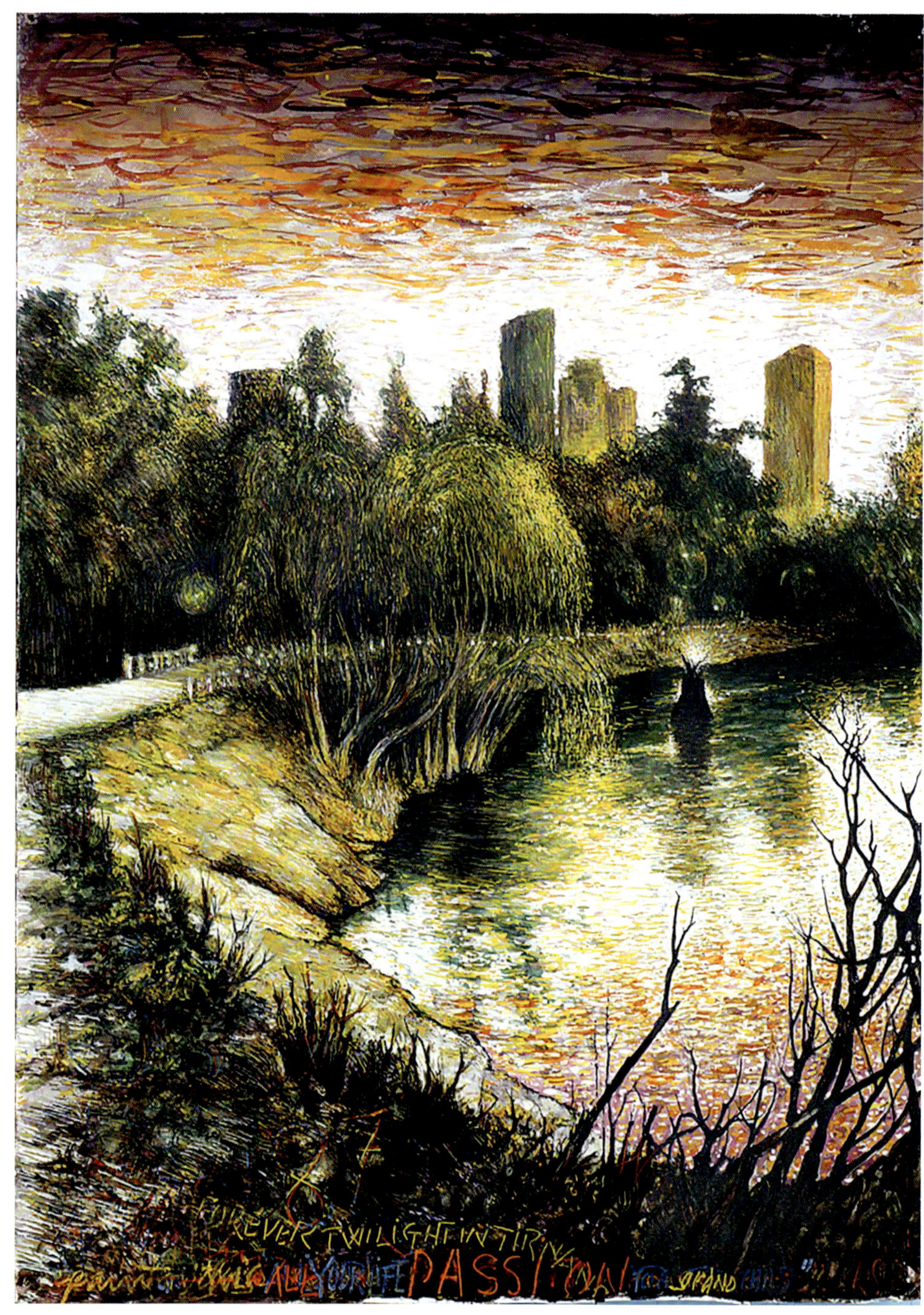

The Irish heaven is called Tirnanog, and Camblin tried capturing heaven in paint with *Forever Twilight in Tirnanog*, 1987. Houston appears in heaven's background.

The colored reproduction in the catalog for *Cinq x Cinq* is *Venus*, done in 1973. At the other end of the thematic spectrum, Camblin included a skull titled *Cuidado* (be careful) from 1982 and *Just Leave (Yes)* completed in 1979. *Venus, Cuidado, Just Leave (Yes)?*—The selection of artworks for the exhibition seems to present a curious, and perhaps subconscious, narrative.

The year ended with Janet Landay's *Collaborators: Artists Working Together in Houston 1969–1986* at the Glassell School of Art of the Museum of Fine Arts. Camblin and the Holding Firm reunited and provided help and art for the show. Camblin recalled that he was happiest in Houston during the 1970s when he was part of the dynamics of the Holding Firm. Now in 1986, with the help of Giordano and the work demanded by exhibitions, his sense of humor returned.

Camblin participated in Diverse Works' 1987 *Found* exhibit and in two 1988 shows: *Handmade Paper* at Little Egypt and *Robert Morris/Paintings & Bob Camblin/ Paintings, Drawings* at the Nave Museum in Victoria, Texas. The same year, shortly before Camblin's permanent departure from the Lone Star State, he decided to have a final Houston exhibition, partly promoted by the sale of the West Gray home and studio. He and Giordano organized *Artists Anonymous LAST DAZE Silent Auction*, the last show at their West Gray studio. They sold as many of their works as possible; then the artists took their leave, from Houston, from Texas, and from old friends.

After his departure, I received a note, "Thanks Borges. The false Aleph is the BEST WE can SI. anonymous"

Camblin had been a fan of Jorge Luis Borges most of his adult life. The Argentine's use of magic realism corresponded to his own understanding of "reality." Having long questioned "reality," Camblin was drawn to the layering and mystery found in the many realities offered by Borges in "The Aleph," a favorite story. (The author uses his own name for the central character.) It begins with the narrator, Borges, remembering the death of his love, Beatriz. He vows not to allow life to change him and dedicates himself to honoring the memory of his beloved. Borges regularly visits Beatriz's father, Daneri, who confesses to having seen the Aleph in his cellar. Finally Daneri invites Borges to the cellar to see the Aleph for himself. "I saw the coupling of love and the modification of death; I saw

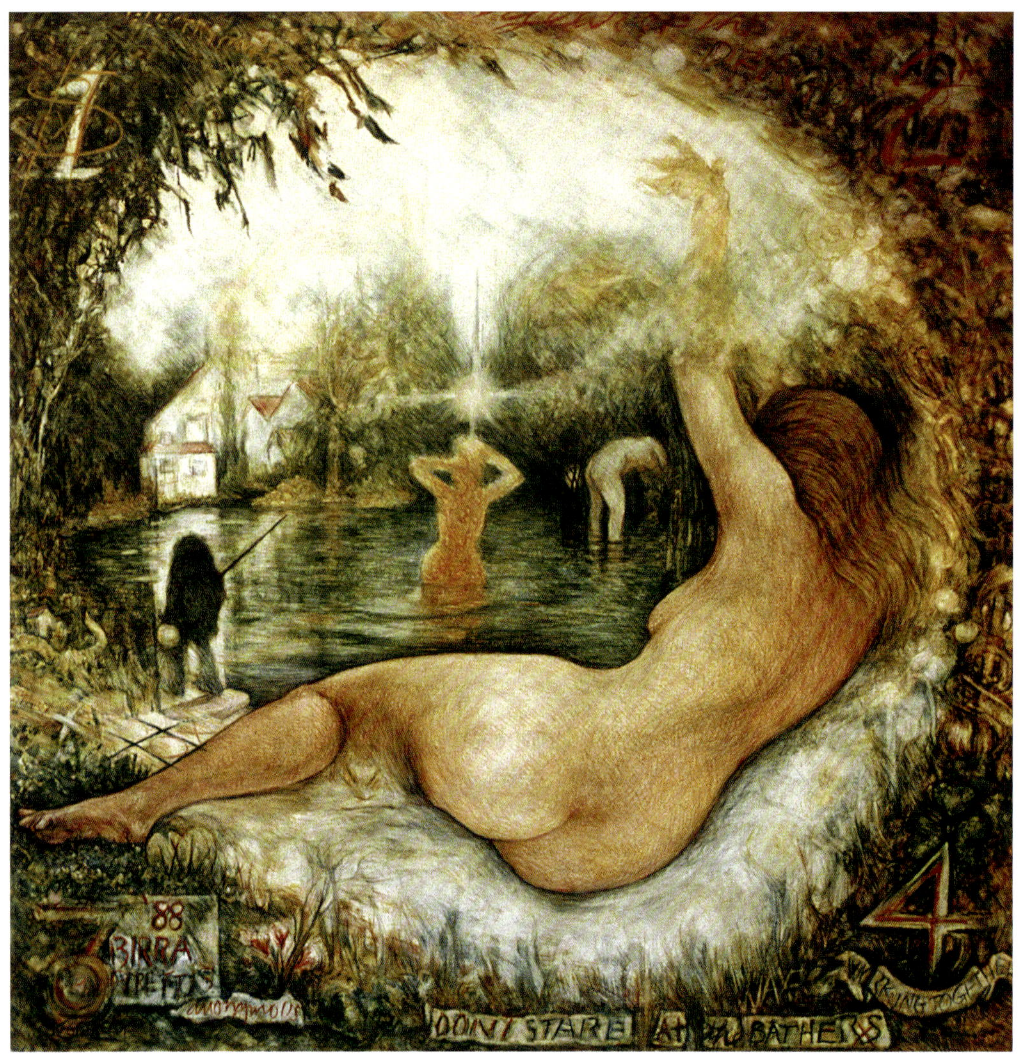

The Bathers, 1988. A mysterious dollar sign on the upper left, an 8 on the upper right, 4 working together on the lower right, and Birraporetti's on the bottom left, Camblin filled his bathing beauties with lots of clues. Undoubtedly he is the little creature who is fishing.

the Aleph from every point and angle, and in the Aleph I saw the earth and in the earth the Aleph and in the Aleph the earth." However, he later decides he saw only the false Aleph. Camblin may have seen the magnificence of the false Aleph, as described by Borges, as something so powerful that it defied human logic. Perhaps both Camblin and Borges considered that even a glimpse of the authentic Aleph would have been beyond human capabilities. The character, Borges, continued to question what he experienced because "under the wearing away of the years, his porous mind and his forgetfulness" were losing the face of Beatriz.

When Camblin delivered his drawriting to me, I felt like the "false" aleph. His choice of author, story, and words, and his timing were perfect. On the one hand, the words stung. On the other, they reminded me that we had truly experienced something unique, something I had chosen to discard, thereby proving I was not ready for its significance.

For years Camblin had been intrigued with the Alpha and Omega of the Greek alphabet and its attendant interpretation as beginning and end, or Christ and God, but the more complex symbolism of the Hebrew alphabet truly captivated him. He had long been fascinated and perplexed by the Aleph. All the letters of the Hebrew alphabet have names and numeric values. Each is a basic unit for the plan of creation and is connected to universal creative forces. Being the first letter of the Hebrew alphabet, the Aleph is believed to combine the "divine, spiritual and physical worlds." Scholars[5] of the Torah tell us that if the alphabet ceased to be, even for even a nanosecond, "all of creation would become absolute nothingness." Camblin's bottom line may have been that our relationship had been reduced to nothingness, or perhaps he was just forgetting my face.

CHAPTER TWENTY-ONE

Sojourner: Having No Destination, I am Never Lost[1]

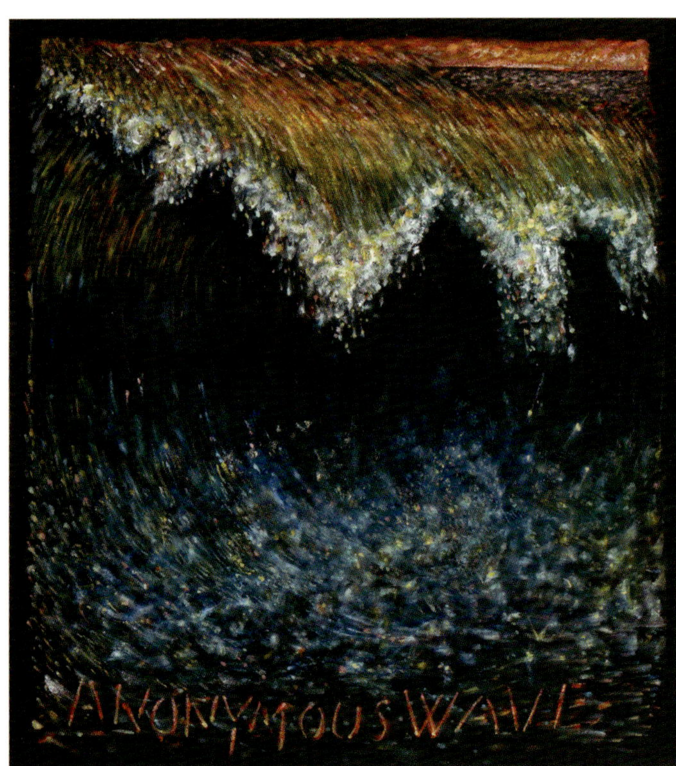

Anonymous Wave, 1988, 19" X 18", allowed Camblin to have the sensuous experience of working with loaded paint brushes on black velvet. The result is a rich, exuberant good-bye wave to Houston. *Collection of Lourdes and Ray Balinskas. Photograph by David P. Gray.*

Camblin's personal and professional worlds had long been complicated. His expectations from a dealer and his demands on a gallery did not result in longtime professional representation. After he left Moody Gallery, he chose only to be represented by an occasional show at Graham Gallery in Houston. He and the gallery owner Bill Graham developed a fond, working relationship. Still, he was experiencing his chronic financial problems. Camblin realized that large art often sold more readily than intimate works. He and his work were expanding; consequently, in the 1980s and '90s, he did a series of large-scale sky-scapes and seascapes painted with expressionistic, exuberant color, applied in a slashing impressionistic *mouche volantzes*-style that he had begun with his Kuwaiti commission.[2] His emotional response to the paint, the pigments, and the process bespoke his state of mind. His mojo was back.

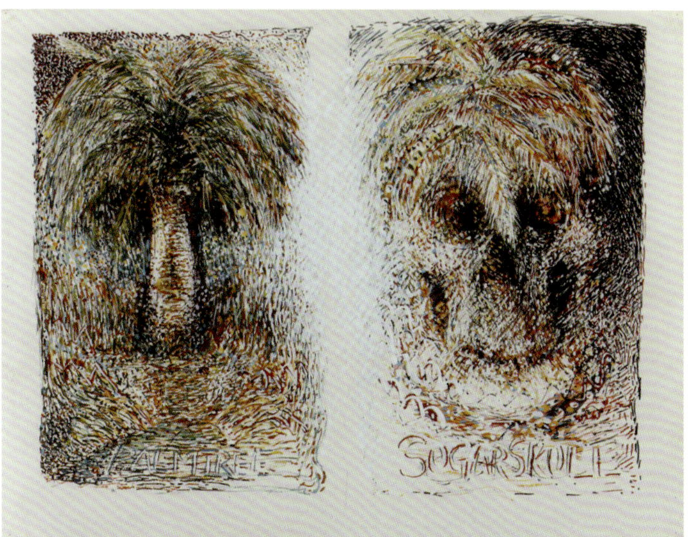

Even though his magic was back, Camblin was still drawn to skulls. Not being morbid he painted a visually playful pair titled *Palm Tree and Sugar Skull*. Watercolor, 22" X 30". He used his large impressionistic brushstroke and combined it with pointillism. The juxtaposition of these two images, a palm tree in which the composition, shading, and surrounds coalesce into a hidden skull, and a non-menacing skull with palm-tree hair, emphasizes the fact that both are illusions. The result is a tour-de force. *Collection of Lourdes and Ray Balinskas. Photo Credit: David P. Gray.*

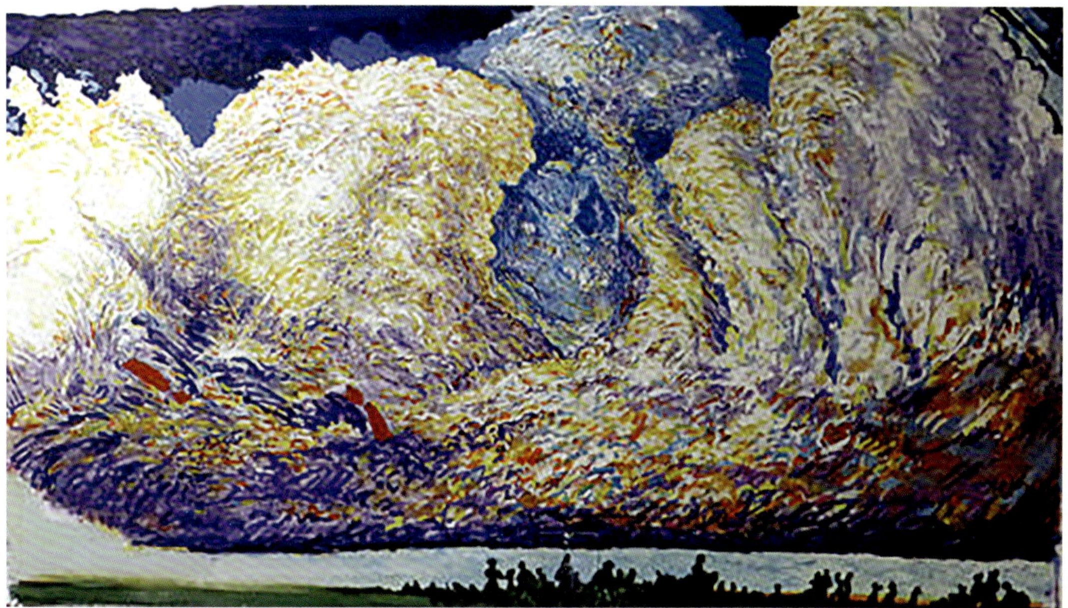

Deciding to let the paint take him where it would, he painted several large canvases before he departed. *Wild Clouds* fill the sky, and a creature stares out before it transforms into something else. Again the soft, dense brushstrokes and the brilliant colors convey exciting drama.

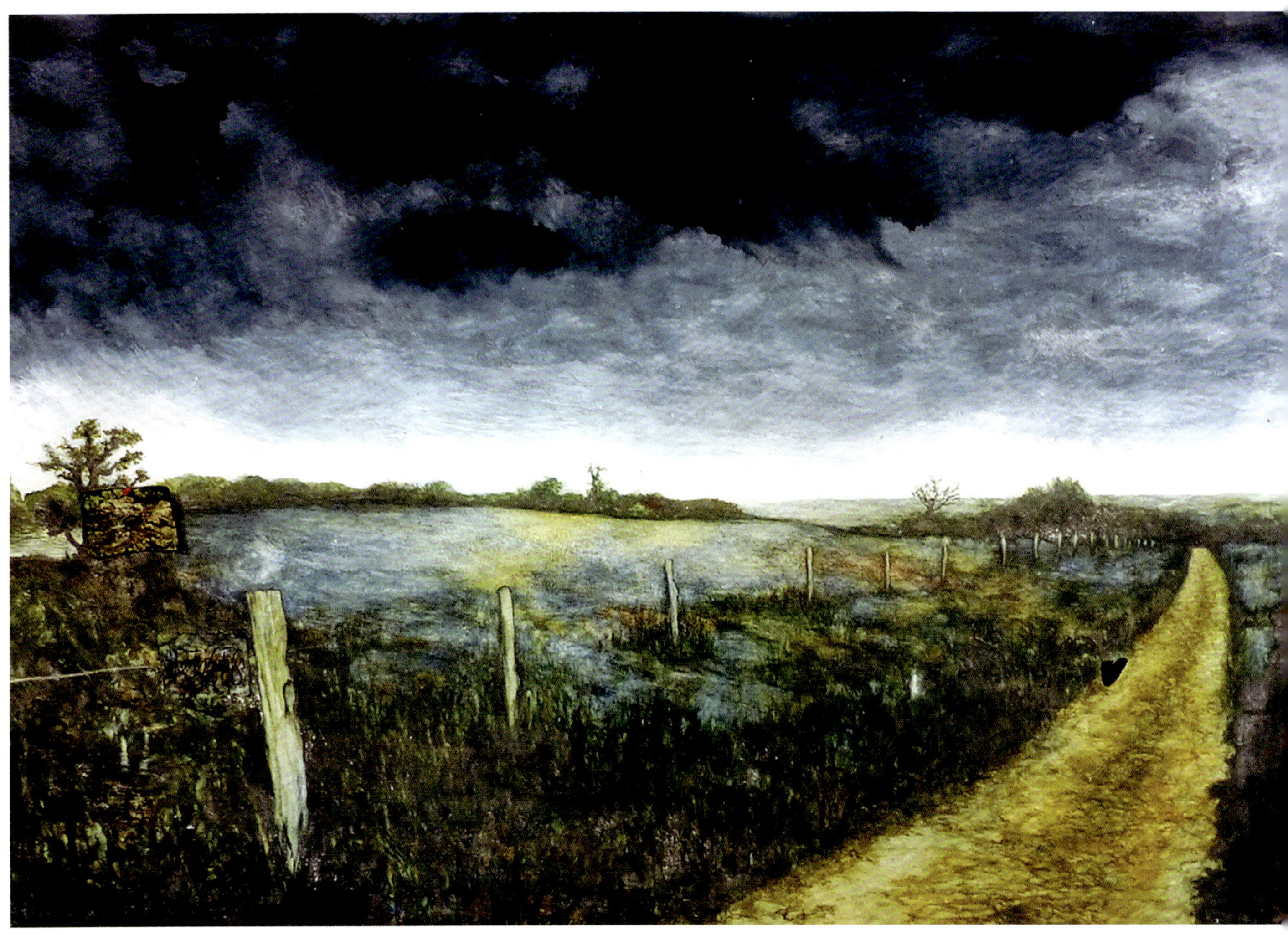

Dramatic Sky. Again the sky allows us to anthropomorphize its clouds. The light earthen, curving road takes the eye toward clear skies. *Photograph by David P. Gray.*

Loyal supporters purchased enough of his large acrylic canvases to keep him going. He spent time at the country house of his friends and collectors, Gayle and Mike DeGeurin, who had begun representing his work. Gayle wrote, "Joe, Bob, Nancy and Lollie made several trips to our place in Burton, Texas, to watch spring roll in." Celebrating spring and friendship, Camblin painted two exuberant and large canvases of *Texas Springtime.* The two large paintings were very similar except that he painted one with a yellow horizontal beam of light traversing its center.

Sometime in the mid-1980s, Camblin abandoned his cast of characters except for Santa Claus and Mort. To his friends he appeared less interested in art. He created a new "running man" logo, and abandoned his "It's All Art." His state of mind indicated that his personal identity was in flux. The elimination of his old personae may have helped solidify his changing sense of self. No longer feeling emotionally connected to Houston, Camblin, along with his new running man logo, left the city for good. He flew to San Francisco to join Giordano. They drove up the coast to Washington State and visited Orcas Island in the San Juan Islands before continuing on to Victoria, Canada. On their return, the couple stopped in Yachats, Oregon, and found a house that needed a sitter. They agreed to occupy the house.

Camblin's physical removal from Houston may have been prompted by his need to resolve his final works and to remove himself from his Texas identity. After residing in Texas for twenty-one years, Camblin left the state and rarely returned. As his old friend Earl Staley said in an interview in 2016, "When Camblin visited Texas, he seemed anxious, as if he couldn't wait to leave."[3]

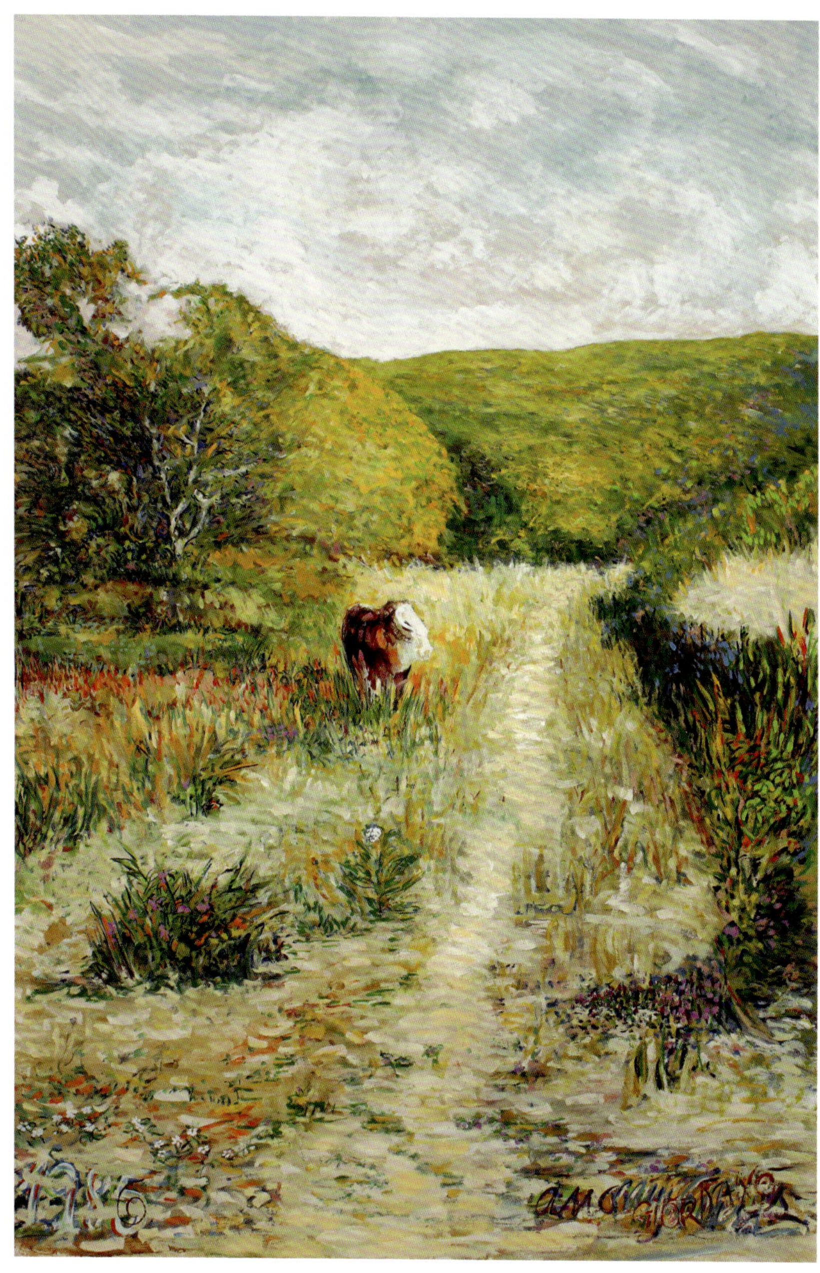

Park Avenue Cow, 1986. Oil and Acrylic, 6' X 4'. *Collection of Susu and Robert P. Ross, Jr.* Camblin softened his dramatic palette for this piece, making it more bucolic. *Photo Credit: David P. Gray.*

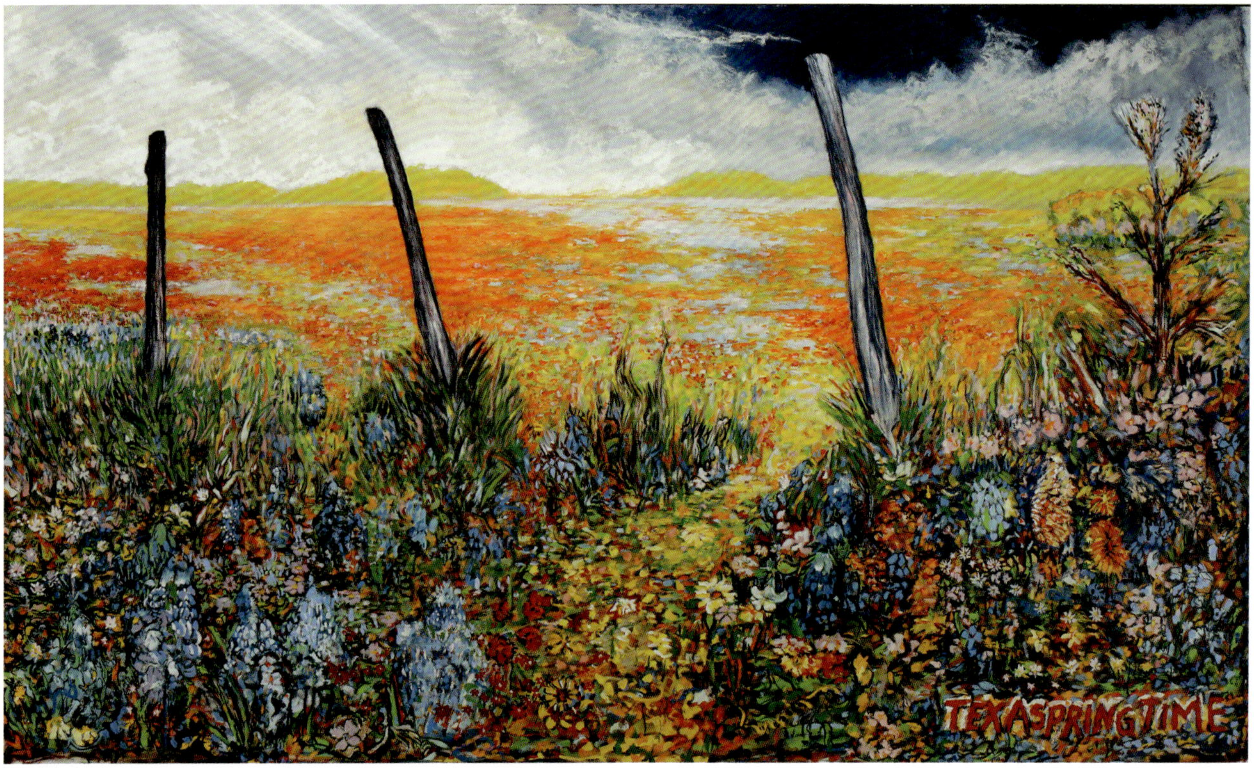

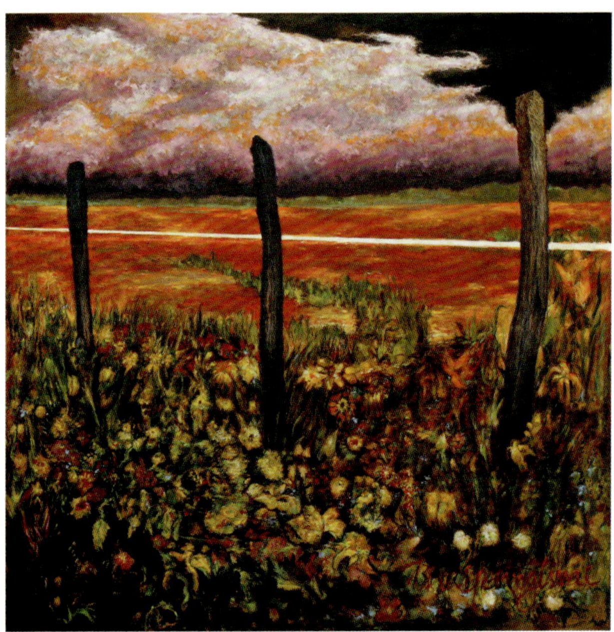

Above: Gayle DeGeurin pointed out that Lollie, Joe, Nancy and Camblin often made several springtime trips to her and Mike's country home in Burton, Texas, where the wildflowers bloomed in abundance. *Texas Springtime*, 1988, Acrylic, 48" X 80", may have been Camblin's version of springtime in the country. *Collection of Mike and Gayle DeGeurin. David P. Gray photograph.*

Left: The lushness of *Borderline*, Oil/Acrylic, 5' X 5', combined with what looks to be a sharp white laser beam that races horizontally across the red earth, charge the painting with tremendous energy. The black sky promises change. The colors, the brushstrokes, the compositions, and the subject matter are testaments to Camblin's positive outlook. *Collection of Susu and Robert P. Ross, Jr. David P. Gray photograph.*

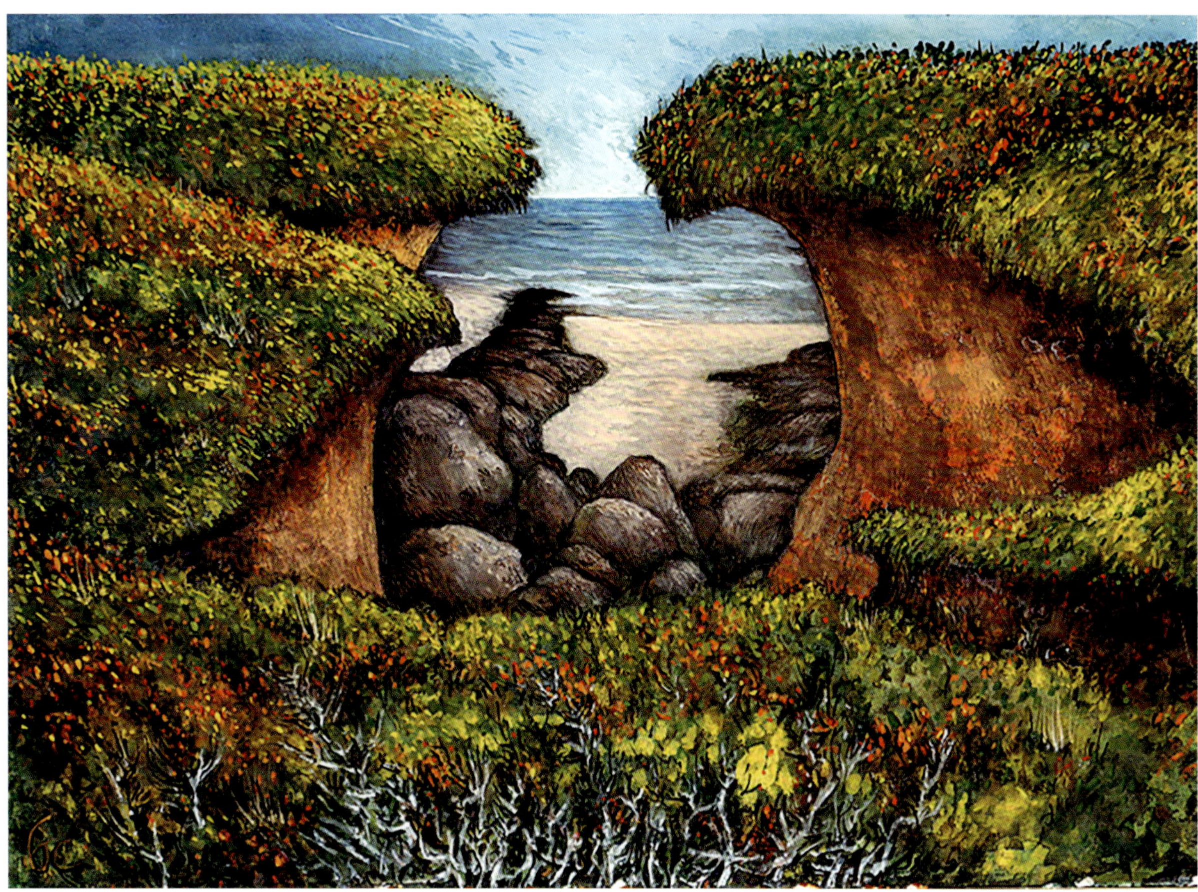

After settling in Yachats, Oregon, Camblin painted *Yachats View*. He carried with him the enthusiasm he had before leaving Houston.

After leaving Yachats, Camblin and Giordano traveled to Waldport, Oregon, where they found a house on the Pacific coast with eight miles of unimpeded beach. While there, Camblin occasionally exhibited work at a local gallery. Partly because an itinerant lifestyle made hauling canvases and art supplies difficult, painting stopped being a driving force; but Camblin continued his drawritings. He settled into a more contented life after his sixties, and at the age of seventy-six, he and Giordano married.

The first year of the last decade of the twentieth century, Ramsey Reimers, a businessman on Mujuro, Marshall Islands, invited Camblin and Giordano to spend time on the island as his guests. As Dennis Camblin wrote:

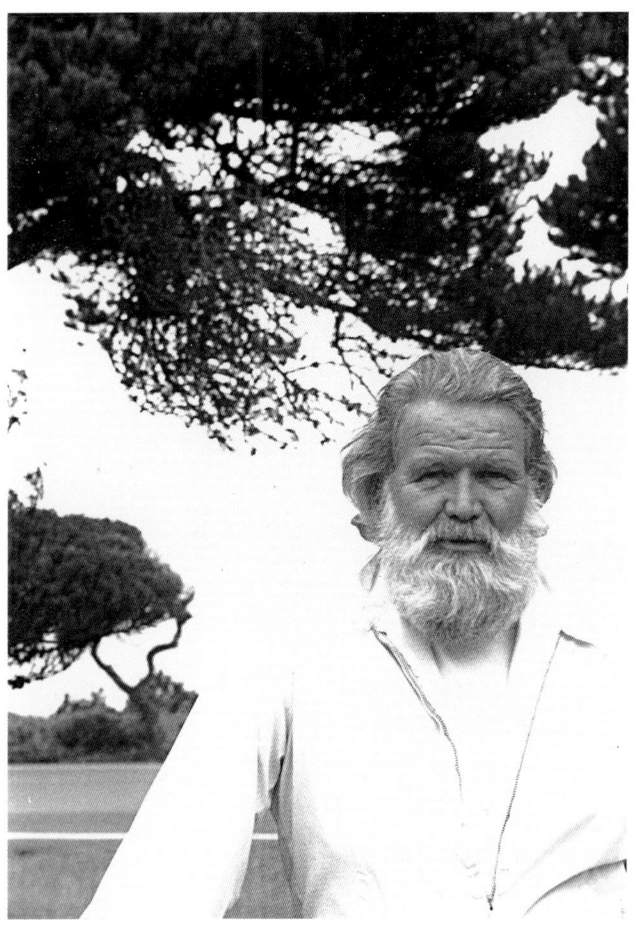
Bob Camblin in Oregon in the late 1980s.

Ramsey was scion of the largest business enterprise in the Marshall Islands. He built the largest and most elegant house in the islands. I talked him into bringing Bob out on commission to make a large painting as centerpiece to the central room. He paid Bob (and Nancy's) travel, provided a studio apartment and gave him free hand on subject matter. He stayed in Majuro (central island) for, as I recall, 3 months. At the end, he presented Ramsey with a large, acrylic on canvas—lagoon scene with outrigger canoe on beach. He also painted and drew much more, then put on an opening (so to speak) in his studio with everything for sale. Most were sold for varying amounts. Ironically, the best piece of work did not sell because it was pen/ink/pencil/wash in grey tones, no color), so I bought it from him. I also kept several, small watercolor studies of this and that. The paintings he sold remain there in prominent locations—no one will part with them.[4]

Following their time on Majuro, Camblin and Giordano moved back to the West Coast and spent time in Waldport, Oregon. Giordano worked and sold her paintings at the Whittler's Workshop. Camblin drew, read, walked the beach, and painted.

When a teaching position with the Orleans Parish Arts Connection at Abramson High School in New Orleans became available in 1994, Giordano took the job. She and Camblin moved to Olivier Street in New Orleans. The masked *mardi gras* culture of the city[5] inspired Camblin to return to his masked portraits. The individual watercolors from the series are numbered, and each is titled *New Orleans Mask*. The masks in Camblin's series would still be ideal for Mardi Gras revelers.

Giordano changed teaching positions and commuted to LaPlace (on the east bank of the Mississippi River in the New Orleans metropolitan area) from Algiers

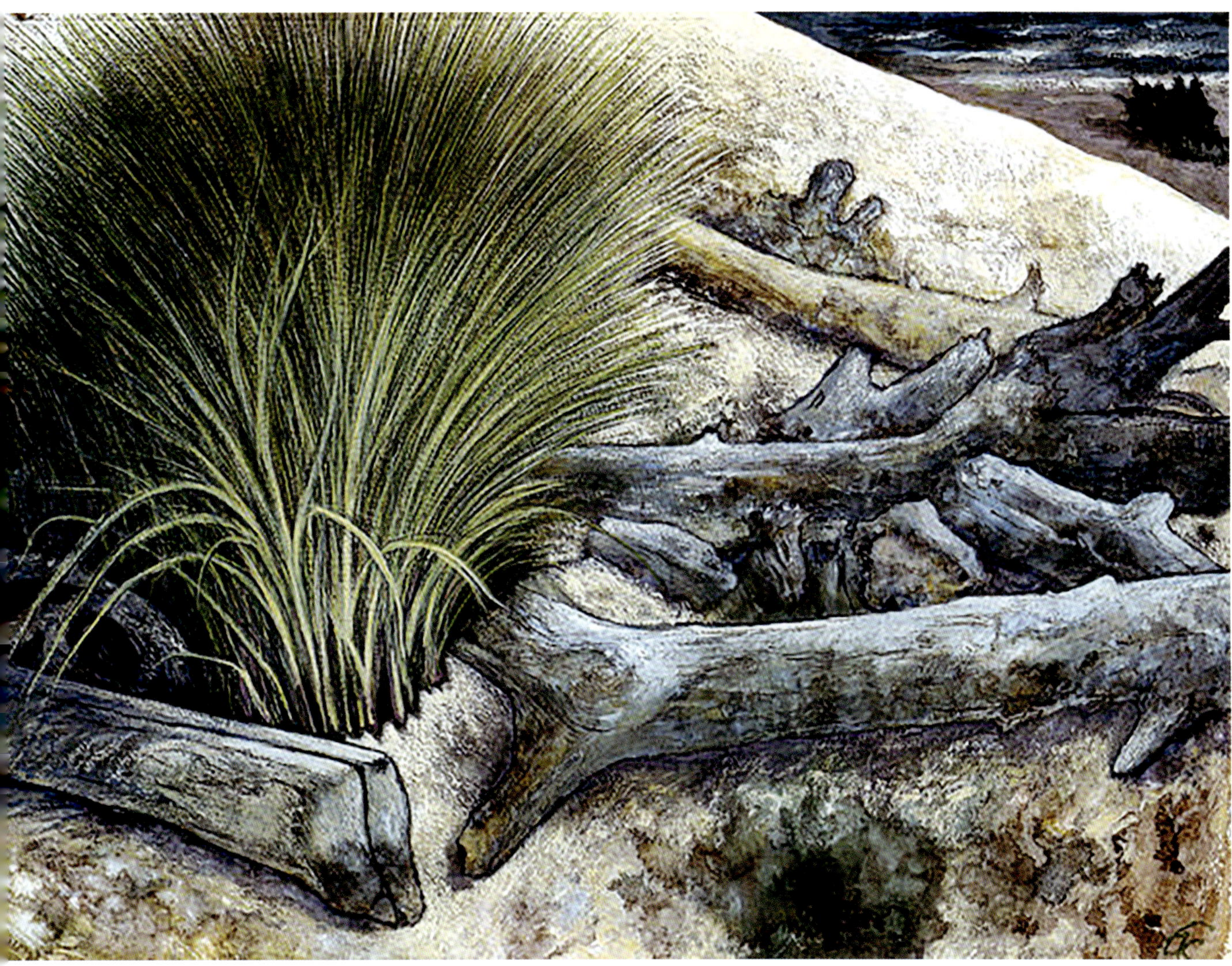

Beach Detail

Point (across the Mississippi from Market Square in New Orleans) where she and Camblin occupied a Mississippi River houseboat. In 2001, Giordano purchased a home in LaPlace where the couple lived happily until a stroke forced Camblin to a care center. Sixteen years after his move to Louisiana, Bob Camblin, along with his final character, Mort, shuffled off this mortal coil. He departed into the mysterious silence with the belief that life and death are ever intertwined.

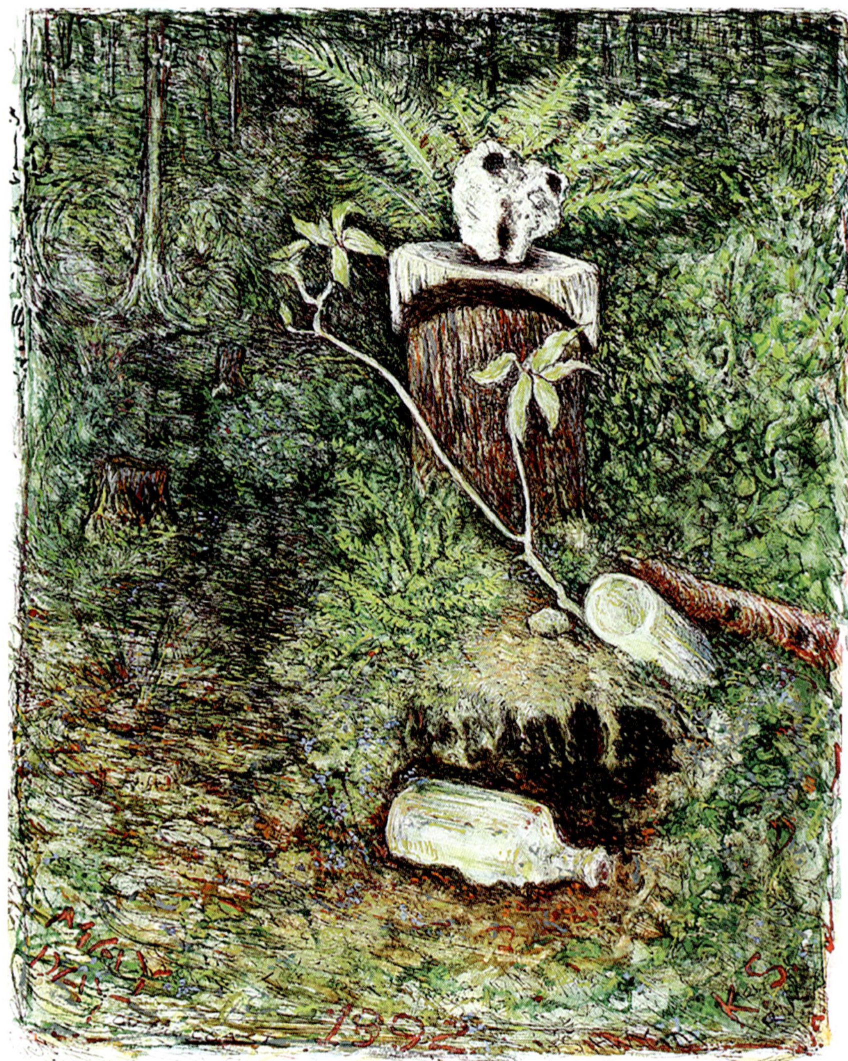

Message in a Bottle, 1992. Camblin had put messages into bottles since he was a child. The central bottle under the root cave contains rolled paper, ostensibly, a message. He also used what looks to be an animal skull rock. May Day is written on the lower left while K S [Kay Sage] appears on the lower right. Lots of clues to accompany the message in the bottle.

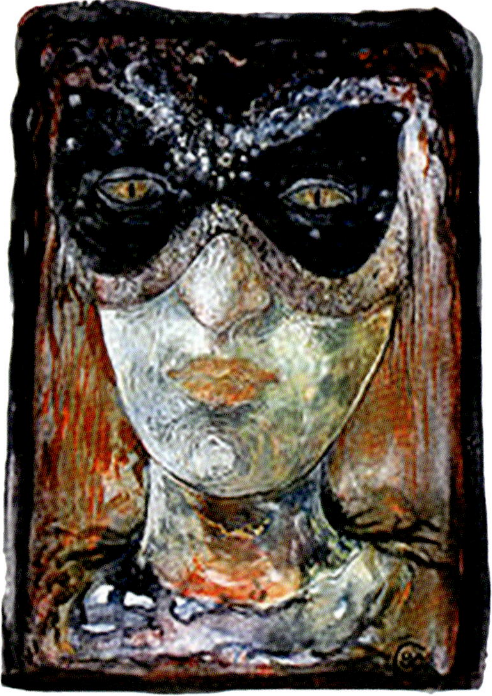

New Orleans Mask: Camblin's personae did not wear masks except for sun glasses even though the artist was taken by masking practices. With the tradition of Mardi Gras, his move to New Orleans seemed appropriate.

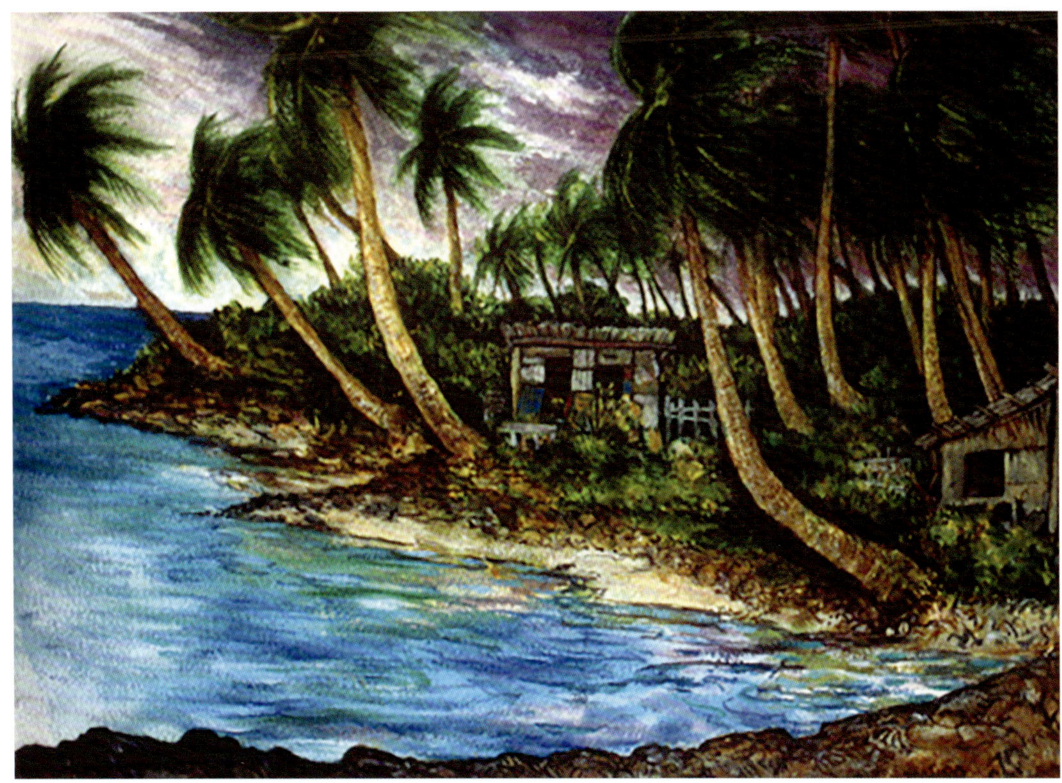

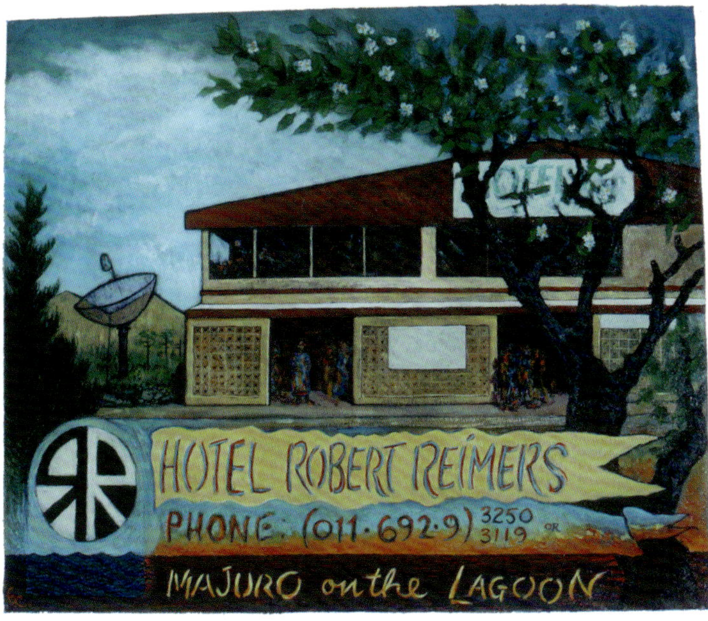

Above: Majuro Beach with Bending Palms, Marshall Islands, 1999. Glowing water, foreground beach details, dramatic skies, and bending palms, all favorite subjects for Camblin.

Left: *Hotel Robert Reimers*, Marshall Islands, 1999.

Photos from Nancy Giordano's personal scrapbooks.

Exhibitions after Exiting Texas

Graham Gallery represented Camblin's work and had shows of his art until 1992 when Bill Graham died. In 1989 Transco Gallery at the Transco Energy Company in Houston exhibited *Toy Show*, curated by Dianne David and for which Camblin not only made a toy but also drew the invitation flyer. In 1990 the Modern Art Museum of Fort Worth held the exhibition *Printmaking in Texas: The 1980s.* James L. Fisher curated the show and wrote a book that served as the catalog. For the book and exhibit Camblin created *Ox Herding*, printed by Cerling Etching Studio. Three years after Camblin left Houston, *Texas Selections from the Menil Collection; A Tribute to the University of Texas Medical Branch Centennial Celebration* included a Camblin watercolor drawing, *Trotline Memorial*, in the Galveston Art Center exhibition. After his stroke, Camblin's friend, Sarah Balinskas, organized and hung his work at her business, Fine Framing, Houston: *Bob Camblin: Unframed Drawings and Paintings on Paper* in 2010. By December of that year Camblin was dead. Even so, his work continues to be discussed and to be included in exhibitions.

Richard Stout narrated a You Tube series on Texas artists: *Modernism in Houston Art: 1950–1970*, Part 7. The series was done for *Houston Modern Market Week* Exhibition at the William Reaves Fine Art Gallery, Houston, Texas, April 28, 2012.

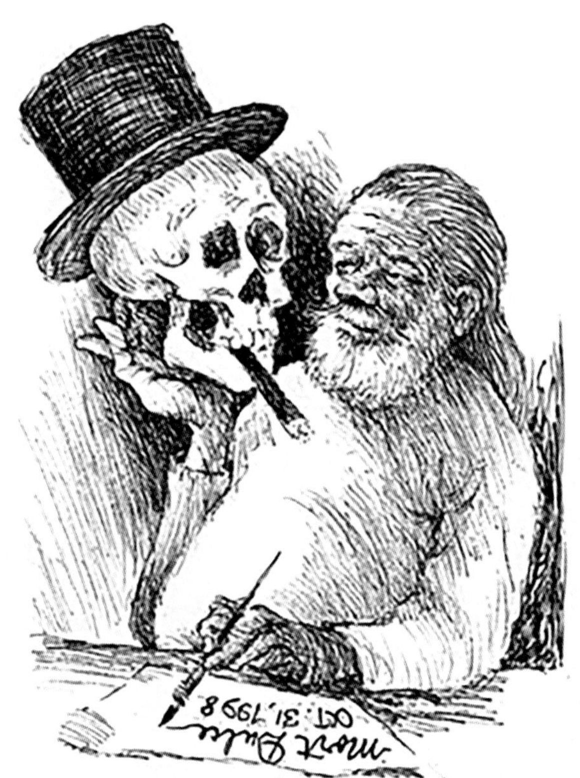

Mort Dulce [*Sweet Death*]. Camblin gave his sketch the date Oct. 31, 1998. Maybe dying on Halloween would make death sweeter.

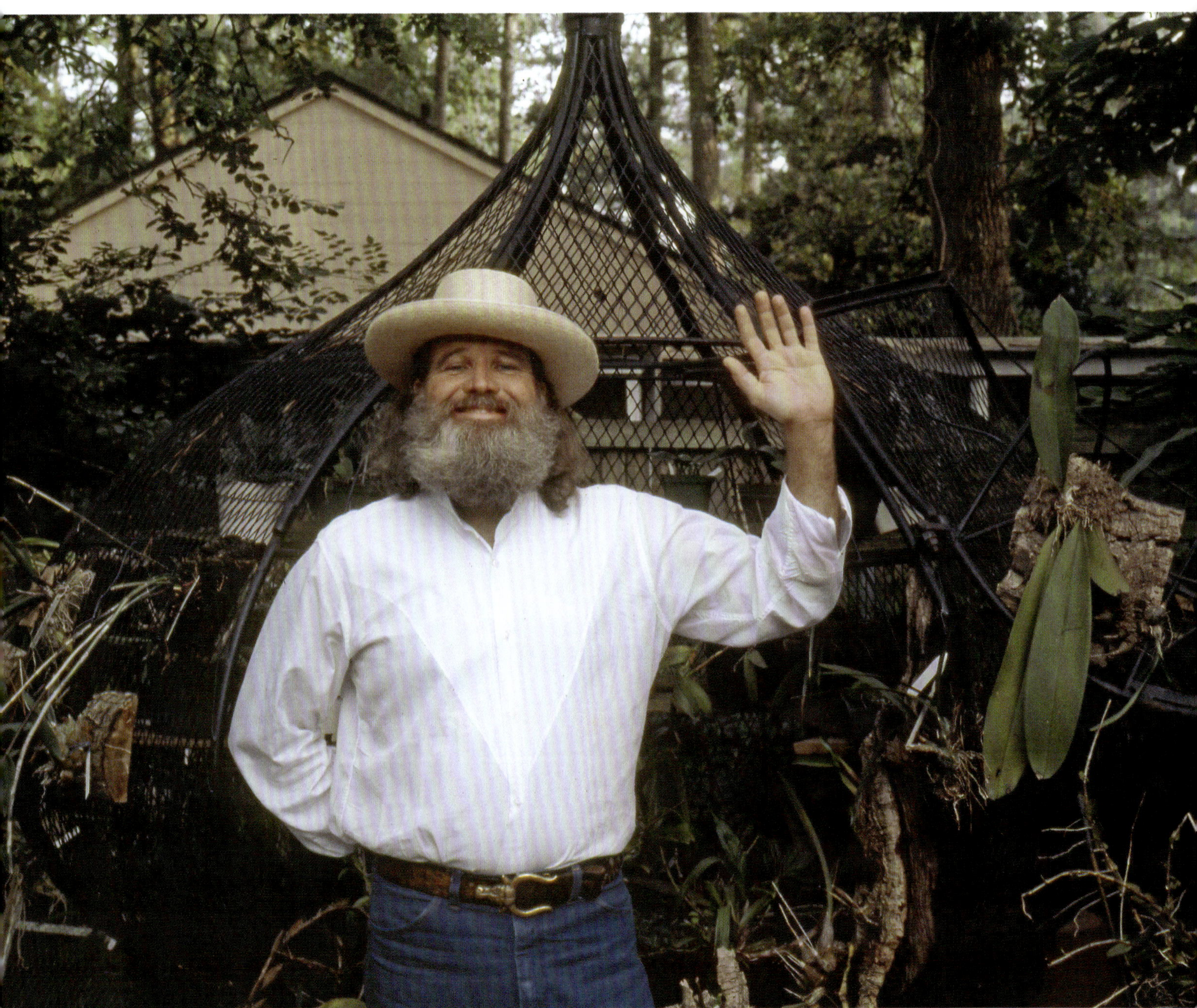

Camblin waving

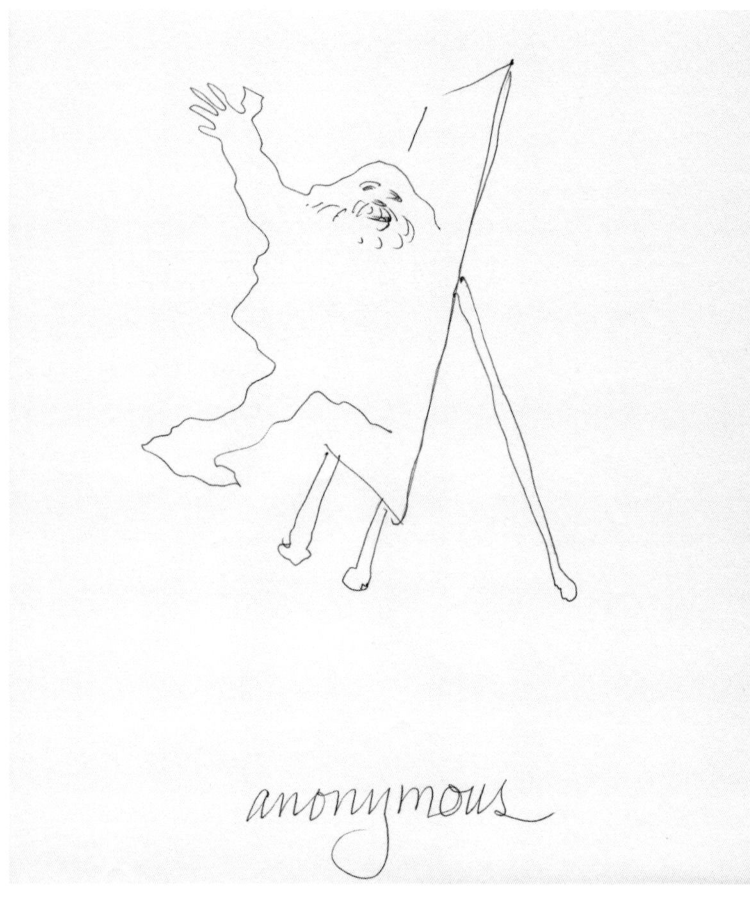

Anonymous. Camblin waves as he disappears into an artwork on an easel.

Flatbed Contemporary Print Fair, Flatbed Press, Austin, Texas, organized a fair in Austin, to which print publisher Penny Cerling donated a print by Bob Camblin, titled: *Gone Fishin'*. The fair ran February 14–15, 2014.

Focus on the 70s and 80s: Houston Foundations Part II, Deborah M. Colton Gallery, Houston, Texas, was a group exhibition of multimedia works by artists who contributed to the Houston art scene in the '70s and '80's. The show included works by Bob Camblin and ran from August 26 to November 4, 2017.

Presentation: *Pete Gershon presents "Collision" at Deborah Colton Gallery.* Gershon's presentation was in conjunction with Colton Gallery's show on the artists of Houston from the '70s and '80s. Gershon spoke about his then-forthcoming book *Collision*, on September 30, 2017.

Pete Gershon included Camblin and the Holding Firm in his book *Collision: The Contemporary Art Scene in Houston, 1972–1985*, published by Texas A & M University Press, College Station, TX, 2018.

An exhibition, *Prints and Ceramics from LIttle Egypt Enterprises and Related Studios* was shown at Glassell School of Art in the Leslie and Brad Bucher Gallery in September–November of 2019.

Fearless in his philosophy of art and confident in his talent, Camblin freed himself from trends and expectations. In doing so he was open to create work that pleased him. His ability to see and to transform his vision into art allowed him to examine the numinous in everything. He believed in, and created, magic. He lived in the intangible, ineffable realm of creativity. Devoted to the artistic manifestation of his personal metaphysical journeys, Camblin wanted to share his visions with those willing to take the time to see that "It's all art." He exhibited work in over one hundred exhibitions during his time in Texas and even managed to get his art to all but two of the shows.

Bob Bilyeu Camblin, the artist, professor, masked impersonator, and art activist, impacted the state's artists and their work just as Texas and other artists impacted his art. A great storyteller and a larger-than-life character with a love of the dramatic, he and Texas were the perfect fit. His exit from the state changed the dynamic and direction of the art and art history that followed.

He spent his last years on coastlines and never tired of looking at the sea. The love and companionship of his wife Nancy, his connection to his children, Brian and Robyn, and their children, and the challenges of a new piece of paper or an empty canvas gave him purpose. In his merger of Catholicism and existentialism, he remained true to himself and to his work. Camblin and his art were authentic.

Following Socrates's dictum,[1] he lived a well-examined life. His obituary ran in *The Times-Picayune*, December 12, 2010:

Robert (Bob) Bilyeu Camblin, age 82, passed away on December 4, 2010 at 12:35 PM in the Southeast Louisiana War Veterans Home in Reserve, LA. Born in Ponca City, OK, on August 1, 1928 to Viva Bilyeu Camblin and Donald Barr Camblin, he was the eldest of three brothers. He grew up in Ponca City, OK, and after serving in the U.S. Army and Air Force during the Korean War, received a BFA and MFA at the Kansas City Art Institute. After receiving a Fulbright Fellowship in 1956 to work in Rome, Italy, for a year, Bob began his career as both as an art professor at several major universities including the University of Detroit and Rice University, and a highly esteemed artist whose prolific works have appeared in prominent collections such as the Chicago Art Institute, NYC Whitney Museum of Art, Dallas Museum of Art and Houston Museum of Fine Arts. Bob is survived by his wife Nancy Giordano-Echegoyen of La Place, LA; brother Michael and sister-in-law Marilee Camblin of Portland, OR, and brother Dennis and sister-in-law Sneh Camblin of Hawaii; son Brian and daughter-in-law Kris Camblin of Tyler, TX, daughter Robyn and son-in-law Jim Rodriguez of Royal Oak, MI; and stepdaughter Maria Giordano-Echegoyen of Nashville, TN. Bob's grandchildren are Ian and Annie Camblin, Ryan and Allyson Rodriguez and grand stepdaughters Sophia and Isabel Giordano-Scott. A Memorial Service in honor of beloved Bob will be held in Ponca City, OK at St. Mary's Church on January 15, 2011.

Bill Davenport wrote an online Camblin obituary for *Glasstire*: *Texas Visual Art*:

Legendary Houston artist Bob Camblin died Saturday in La Place, LA from complications following a stroke he suffered last year. Born in Oklahoma in 1928, Camblin studied painting at the Kansas City Art Institute, earning an M.F.A. in 1955. He taught at Rice University from 1967–73 [actually 1974] with Joe Tate and Earl Staley, with whom he shared studio space. His influence was a constant undercurrent in the city's art scene until he left in the early 80's. Volatile and gregarious, Camblin saw himself as a vehicle for artistic inspiration, not always fully responsible for his highly personal, narrative polemic works. Wary of interpretation, he assumed multiple artistic personas, signing himself Anonymous Bosch, Red Stick the Pirate, and Mr. Peanut and is the only artist without a written statement featured in the seminal 1985 *Fresh Paint: The Houston School* catalog.

When Duchamp noted that it takes fifty to one hundred years for an artist to find a true audience, he did not say when to begin counting the years: birth, mid-career, death? Camblin still waits to find his true audience, but his time is quickly approaching.

Earl Staley: Memories of Bob Camblin:

I learned everything about the craft of art from Bob. I met Bob in the Fall of 1967 when he became a faculty member at Rice U. He rented the house I vacated on Wroxton when I bought a house. We became friends. He often came by at night to smoke and exchange ideas. This was part of his weekly evening visitations [at] my house or Dianne David's Gallery/home. We had an intense exchange of ideas. He was 10 years older and full of so many ideas and life experiences.

We rented a studio together. I cannot remember where it was. Then we rented a studio off Montrose on Jack Street. We each had a working space. That year we started talking about collaborations. I was also informed my contract would not be renewed by Rice after the next year. Our first collaborative event was in November of 68; we got our classes to spend the weekend on Galveston's West Beach for a Creation/Destruction event.

Thanks to Dianne David we did several shows at her gallery: The Tattoo Show and The Document Show and Bob's Barter Show. These were under Bob and Earl Productions. It was a fertile period. Bob already had a working style while I was still searching for mine. In Fall 1969, I began the new Art Department at U of St Thomas with Jack Boynton and Pat Colville. Joe Tate took my place at Rice. He and Bob quickly became close. We did another Creation/Destruction event on West beach using our combined schools. Joe became a member of the studio and using the I Ching we named ourselves The Holding Firm. I cannot remember how we began to do collaborative drawings. We would meet at one of our homes and draw from an animal outline (drawn by Bob) and fill it in using pen and ink. Every 30 minutes we would turn the paper around so we all worked on each other's work. It was clear that Bob was the draftsman and could clean up the messes that Joe and I made. It was during these sessions that I began to learn how to draw, I watched Bob. Those drawings were made into lithographs by David Folkman many years later. Joe built his back Yard Show in the studio then we moved it to the Art Gallery at St Thomas. There we did the large Joe's Backyard collaborate painting. Again, Bob cleaned up and I learned by watching. We did another collaborative show like the Camp Out show in the gallery at St Thomas. Then we were forced to move out of our studio.

We found a two-story house on Sul Ross and cleaned it up. Bob and Joe were real tight. Joe had a strong effect on Bob. They were having a hard time with the new Rice Department. The Sul Ross studio became their fixation . . . An open space for collaboration, So, walls needed to be torn down, an enormous deck and staircase to be built, a third story lookout and finally a fence. It totally consumed us that summer. Another person from Rice Architecture school, Mark? [Batista] was there along with Al Smith from Rice. The next school year Bob and Joe were released from Rice. I hired Joe to teach Sculpture at St Thomas. His and my philosophies were totally different. Their philosophy of collaboration was losing my attention. I became estranged from their constant conversations fueled by coffee and smoke. I wanted to paint in my studio, and they had other ideas.

Joe did not work out and I fired him the same year. I found another studio and one night I went and moved all my stuff and never looked back. I did not see them for many years and when I did we were all different.

What did I learn? Nothing from Joe. From Bob everything: he taught me composition, watercolor and drawing. Things he learned at Kansas City Art Institute. I was given the art-as-sand box approach common in Art Departments beginning in the fifties and still common today. Collaboration was fun, it was part of the late 60s and early 70s, when all things were possible. Just before I left the Holding Firm I did one of my first large paintings relating to my life experiences. This too came from discussions with Bob. He was 10 years older and had had many.

The ending was Bad. I was not welcome. Bob told me that they were working as a jazz ensemble, but I wanted to play solo. That was true. I began a new stage of my life with a new confidence after learning all I needed from Bob and that the incestuous spirit of collaboration was not good for my creative life. Looking back the Holding Firm was a second graduate school from which I actually learned. I left when I got all I needed from what was being offered.

Earl Staley

Note: The Camblin quotes in the book are from personal material on him found in the Smithsonian Institution's Archives of American Art. His sketchbooks, newspaper and magazine articles, exhibition catalogs, recordings, notes from his friends Earl Staley and Penny Cerling, personal letters, and Staley's Super 8 film footage, were mined for pertinent information. The research for the book includes Camblin articles, exhibitions, catalogues, and memorabilia, all of which are listed in the Bibliography and the Exhibition Schedule.

Beginnings, 1928–1967

1928

August: Viva Faustina Bilyeu and Donald Barr Camblin gave birth to Bob Bilyeu Camblin on August 1, 1928, in Ponca City, Oklahoma. Donald was educated through the eleventh grade after which he worked at a gas station in Tulsa, Oklahoma. Once married, Donald and Viva moved to Ponca City, Oklahoma. He worked for Conoco, starting in the refinery's tool crib. During thirty-five years at Conoco, he moved up to personnel manager. Domestically, he made drawings and took his family camping and fishing.

Viva painted and Donald sketched for most of their lives. Bob had no formal training during his high school years, but his parents encouraged him in art. His mother's watercolors of birds and still lifes are linear and skillful. Her son included those qualities in his work. Camblin would add her name "Viva," in Spanish, Italian, and Portuguese as *"long live,"* on some of his later work. His father Donald "mostly pencil sketched."[1] Both parents had a determining influence on Camblin's preference for drawing.

1929

October: The stock market crashed on Black Tuesday, October 29, 1929, the onset of the Great Depression. It began ten months after Camblin's birth and continued until he was eleven. The Camblin family was able to survive the Depression because Ponca City, founded by and supported by a major oil company, had an economy built around petroleum and provided steady employment.

1934

Milton Caniff's *Terry and the Pirates* comic strip began newspaper publication in 1934. The strip, with its teenage hero Terry, ran until 1973. Matching wits with pirates and other villians, Terry proved his mettle for nearly forty years. 31 million newspaper subscribers read the comic between 1934 and 1946. A connection between the wily pirates and Camblin's Red Stick the Pirate is possible.

1939

September 1: Germany invaded Poland, starting a war in Europe that evolved into World War II.

1941

December: On December 7 fighter aircraft from the Imperial Japanese Navy bombed Pearl Harbor, Hawaii. The US declared war against Japan the following day, entering into World War II. Camblin was thirteen. He was seventeen when the war ended.

1942

Fall: Camblin entered Ponca City High School. During four years there, he played football and wrestled, played clarinet in the school band, wrote articles for the school paper, and was art editor for the yearbook.

During Camblin's youth, the *Krazy Kat* comic strip, created by George Herriman, ran in newspapers across the country. The cartoon characters had a distinctive language, a wacky surrealism, and a playfulness. Even though Herriman died in 1944, his series was popular for more than 80 years.[2]

Boxed cereals were popular in the 1940s. Wheaties became the "Breakfast of Champions" three years before Camblin was born and the brand's recognition continued to grow. Cereal boxes were printed with puzzles, traps, cartoons, sports heroes, mazes, and games such as "Hook the Fish": all advertising designed to influence children.

1945

May: On May 8 Germany surrendered unconditionally to the Allied powers of the United States, Great Britain, and the Soviet Union.

August: On August 6 the United States dropped a five-ton atom bomb on the Japanese city of Hiroshima. On August 14 the Japanese surrendered unconditionally to US General Douglas MacArthur.

1946

May: Camblin graduated from Ponca City High School and went to work for Conoco.

1947

March: On March 11 Camblin enlisted in the Army. The Army sent him to basic training in Fort Ord, California, then transferred him to Fort Sill, Oklahoma, where he worked as a mechanic for the Artillery.

1948

August: Camblin received his honorable discharge from the Army on August 2.

He enrolled in Kansas City Art Institute (KCAI) and moved to Kansas City, Missouri, the same year Robert Rauschenberg enrolled in the interior design department of KCAI.

1950

February: On February 4, 1950, Camblin enlisted in the Air Force Reserve.

June: On June 25 North Korean forces, supported by the Soviet Union and China, invaded South Korea. Two days later the United States, with twenty other United Nations countries, joined together to defend the South. Because of the onset of the Korean War, the Air Force extended Camblin's one-year term of enlistment an additional year and five months. He was stationed at Selfridge Air Force Base, Detroit, Michigan, for five months before being transferred to Hamilton Air Force Base, California, for the remainder of his service.

1952

July: Camblin received his honorable discharge from the Air Force, July 17.

August: Camblin resumed his studies at Kansas City Art Institute.

1953

September: Camblin met 22-year-old Kansas City, Missouri, native, Bonnie Bertram. They married on September 5, 1953, Kansas City, Jackson County, Missouri. (Marriage License No. B 49437)

1954

May: Camblin received his Bachelor of Fine Arts degree from Kansas City Art Institute.

Camblin had his first formal exhibition: *8th National Missouri Valley Exhibition*. He won a Purchase Prize.

1955

May: Camblin received his Master of Fine Arts degree from Kansas City Art Institute. With his degree Camblin received the Margaret Allen Barnett Memorial Award as the outstanding student of the 1955 class.

The article, "Gives Meaning to Life," in *The Kansas City Times*, Friday, May 27, 1955, recounts the commencement address and the awards given at the graduation ceremony for the Kansas City Art Institute and notes Camblin's receipt of the Outstanding Student of the Year.

November: The war in Vietnam began November 1. The United States entered the war with the aim of containing the spread of communism. The televised bloodshed and compulsory military draft instigated an anti-Vietnam war movement that introduced widespread use of drugs and an anti-establishiment counterculture.

During 1955 Camblin had two exhibitions of his work: *Bob Camblin*, Kansas City Art Institute, Kansas City, Missouri; and *4th Midwestern Biennial*, Prize.

1956

May: On May 19, 1956, Camblin learned he had won a Fulbright award. It was announced in "Robert Camblin, 27, of 4950 Oak Street, has won a Fulbright award to Study Art in Rome,

Beginning in September," and "One Year of Study in Rome. A Fulbright Award Is Given to Robert Camblin, a Painter," *The Kansas City Times*, Kansas City, Missouri, Saturday, May 19, 1956, p. 8.

Senator J. William Fulbright began the Fulbright Scholar Program in 1946. Harry S. Truman signed it into law on August 1, 1946, Camblin's eighteenth birthday. "[Fulbright's] vision for mutual understanding shaped the extraordinary exchange program bearing his name . . . and continues to increase mutual understanding between the people of the United States and the people of other countries." See Fulbright Scholar Program, A program of the United Sates Department of State, Bureau of Educational and Cultural Affairs.

When Camblin received his Fulbright, the program provided transportation to and from the host country, money for room and board, accident and sickness benefits, and dependent benefits.

September: Camblin and his wife Bonnie moved to Italy for a year. They spent time in Rome and Venice. The couple frequented museums, galleries, and historic sites in both cities. They also traveled to Florence and visited the Galleria degli Uffizi numerous times. Camblin was especially interested in the Flemish painter Hugo Van der Goes's *Portinari Altarpiece* in the Uffizi.

Camblin had three exhibitions during the year:

May 10–June 10: *Sixth Mid-America Annual*, Nelson Gallery of Art, Atkins Museum, Kansas City, Missouri. Camblin exhibited *Still Life with Pomegranates*, Duco, and won a Purchase Prize. Note: Duco is a DuPont trade name for an automobile lacquer. Jackson Pollock, as well as Camblin, sometimes used the medium. Catalogue: *Sixth Mid-America Annual Exhibition*, Nelson Gallery, Atkins Museum. *Still Life with Pomegranates* was illustrated in the catalogue.

Undated: Joslyn Memorial Art Museum, Omaha, Nebraska (renamed Joslyn Art Museum in 1987) Camblin won a Purchase Prize.

Undated: *Bob Camblin*: Cottey College, Cottey Gallery, The Philanthropic Educational Organization Foundation Art Gallery (Cottey Gallery), Nevada, Missouri.

1957

While in Italy, Camblin was included in a group exhibition.

January 17–March 3: 62nd *American Exhibition: Painting and Sculpture*, Art Institute of Chicago, Chicago, Illinois. Camblin exhibited *Still Life with Pomegranates*, Duco. The painting was loaned by the Nelson-Atkins Museum, Kansas City, MO. Catalogue: 62nd *American Exhibition: Painting and Sculpture*. Art Institute of Chicago, Chicago, Illinois. Catalogue foreword by Frederick A. Sweet, curator of American Painting and Sculpture.

A voracious reader, besides fiction Camblin read William S. Burroughs's *Naked Lunch* and *Junkie*, Albert Camus's *The Stranger* (*L'Etranger*), Jean Paul Sartre's *Being and Nothingness* and *No Exit*, Franz Kafka's *The Metamorphosis*, among others. Belief in an indifferent universe and existential helplessness contributed to images of death and destruction. Camblin contrasted the hopelessness of death with the possibllity of metamorphosis in some works.

September: Camblin returned to USA at the end of the Fulbright Award year in Italy. He accepted a job as a cartographer with Trans World Airlines in Kansas City, Missouri.

October: The Soviet Union launched the first artificial Earth satellite Sputnik on October 4. The launch caught the USA off-guard and began the space age. America and and the USSR entered the competitive but unofficial space race.

During the year Camblin had four more exhibitions, two involving Italy.

Undated: *Fulbright Artists Exhibition*, Schneider Gallery, Rome, Italy.

Undated: *Exhibition of Self Portraits*, Milan, Italy.

Undated: *American Federation of Arts International Traveling Show of Students' Work*, Fulbright Scholar Program.

Undated: *Bob Camblin—Drawings and Paintings*, Kansas City Art Institute, Kansas City, Missouri.

1958

Still working at TWA Camblin was included in two group exhibitions in January.

January 30–February 23: *153rd Annual Exhibition of the Pennsylvania Academy of the Fine Arts*, Philadelphia, Pennsylvania. The exhibition traveled to the Detroit Institute of Arts, Detroit, Michigan, March 13–April 13. Camblin's participation was noted in the *Fulbright Painters* catalogue, p. 17.

January: *American Art of Our Time*, Provincetown Art Association, Provincetown Arts Festival, Provincetown, Massachusetts.

Catalogue: *American Art of Our Time*, Provincetown, Massachusetts.

Brochure: "Program 1958," Provincetown Art Association, Provincetown Arts Festival, Provincetown, Massachusetts. The list of participating artists included Bob Camblin.

Article: "Artists Do Well at Art Exhibit," *The Daily Intelligencer*, Doylestown, Pennsylvania, January 30, 1958, p. 27.

Summer: Camblin accepted a teaching position at the School of Art, John and Mabel Ringling Museum of Art, Sarasota, Florida, and moved to Sarasota. He had five more exhibitions during the year.

September 17–October 5: *10th Fulbright Painters Exhibition*, Whitney Museum of Art, New York, New York.

Article: An article on the show included the Camblin quote from *Fulbright Painters* catalogue plus added: "Ponca City-born Robert Camblin reported his painter's dream come true, a year abroad with nothing to do but soak up the scenery, visit the museums and paint his head off. The results of his year in Italy—along with paintings by 59 other equally lucky artists—are on view this week at Manhattan's Whitney Museum of American Art. They were picked by the museum's new director, Lloyd Goodrich, from among the 194 U.S. artists who have worked abroad on U.S. Government (Fulbright) scholarships, paid in local currencies from the sale of U.S. surplus property abroad. The painters used their year abroad to feast their eyes, rather than to pick up the mannerisms of a foreign school. They soaked in "the golden glow of Rome." *Time Magazine*, "A Year Abroad," October 6, 1958, p. 69.

Undated: *Fulbright Painters*: The exhibition was circulated by the Smithsonian Institution in cooperation with the Institute of International Education, 1958–1959, New York, New York. The show traveled to 20 US locations.

Catalogue: J. William Fulbright, *Fulbright Painters*. Institute of International Education, Circulated by the Smithsonian Institution, 1958. For the catalogue Camblin wrote: "Now take a boy from the Midwest, from Ponca City, Oklahoma, for instance, teach him to speak Italian, then put him in an apartment that is twenty years older than his own country's government; put his apartment in the center of Rome about a block from where Julius Caesar was killed; where from his studio window he can see the church in which the first act of 'Tosca' takes place; where each morning he can feed the cats in the *scavi* in front of his apartment and where a short walk will take him to the *Colosseo* and *Foro Romano*. Let him become acquainted with the many of the people in this area and close friends with several Italian families. Let him visit the major museums and cities of Europe and live the last three months in Venice. Then bring him back and put him again in the Midwest . . . the results are these paintings." Camblin exhibited *Reliquaries No. 2*, 1958 and *Citta Del Mare*, 1958.

Undated: *Collectors Market Exhibit*, Nelson-Atkins Museum of Art, Kansas City, Kansas.

Article: "Collectors Market" exhibition, *The Kansas City Times*, Kansas City, Missouri, March 3, 1958, p. 4.

Undated: *Childe Hassam Purchase Fund Show*, American Academy of Arts and Letters, New York City.

Undated: *ART: USA 58*, Madison Square Garden, New York, New York, an exhibition organized by Lee Nordness in 1958. The exhibition was confirmed in the *New York Times*, "Obituaries: Lee Nordness," May 23, 1995. No artists or dates for the exhibition were specified.

1959

Camblin continued teaching at the John and Mable Ringling Museum of Art, Sarasota, Florida. He also taught art classes at the Longboat Key Art Center, Longboat Key, Florida. He had four exhibitions.

January 3–January 15: *Two Fulbright Artists: Bob Camblin and Eric Von Schmidt*, Sarasota Art Association, Sarasota, Florida.

Article: "Bob Camblin of Kansas City, Mo., is presently teaching at the Ringling School of Art . . . Among the exhibitions in which he has been represented are The 1957 American Painting-Sculpture Show in Chicago, the Fulbright Artist Show in Rome, the 153rd Annual Exhibition of Old Painting and Sculpture in Philadelphia and the 10th Fulbright Exhibition at the Whitney Gallery in New York City. Camblin is exhibiting drawings only in the current exhibition of the Art Association." "Show Opens Here Today," *Sarasota Herald-Tribune*, January 4, 1959, p. 7.

Article: "Only 16 Sarasota artists succeeded in entering the Sarasota Art Association Nation Show. . . . Those admitted to the show from the southeastern region are: . . . Bob Camblin . . ." "48 out of 280 Entries Accepted, Only 16 Local Artists In National Art Show," *The Sarasota Herald-Tribune*, February 21, 1959, p. 7.

March: *The Sarasota Art Association National Show*, Sarasota, Florida.

December: *21st Annual Exhibition of Contemporary American Painting*, The Society of the Four Arts, Palm Beach, Florida.

Article: Three others in the oil section received equal awards. Bob Camblin, Longboat Key, Florida, won for "Icarus Descending," which Washburn described as an example of his admonition that "we try not to penetrate the mystery of life but instead embrace it with love." "Contemporary Painting Show Opens At Four Arts Society," *The Palm Beach Post*, December 5, 1959, p. 13.

Article: "The show itself . . . has some good points. Abstract-expressionism isn't all bad and some of our Sarasota artists, like . . . Bob Camblin, come out very well indeed, although some of these are not out-and-out abstractionists and have agility enough to leap from one style to another when occasion requires." "Palm Beach Shows Hold Warning for Sarasota," *Sarasota Herald-Tribune*, December 11, 1959, p. 53.

Article: "Bob Camblin, Teacher at the Longboat Key Art Center, Won a $50 Four Arts Award for His oil 'Icarus Descending.' Camblin won honors in one of the most modern and highly-rated art competitions in the country." "Art Roundup," *St. Petersburg Independent*, Sunday, December 20, 1959, p. 5D.

Undated: *Five Artists*, St. Armands Gallery, St. Armands Key, Florida.

Article: "Collins to Officiate at All Florida Show," *Sarasota Herald Tribune*, December 18, 1959.

1960

Camblin began a series of paintings paying homage to Hugo Van der Goes's *Portinari Altarpiece* that he had seen at the Uffizi Gallery in Florence while on his Fulbright. He used the painting's structure rather than its subject matter, creating abstract works.

Article: "In his paintings, Camblin has been preoccupied with the 'Adoration of the Shepherds' by Hugo van der Goes, which he saw in Uffizi, Italy. This is Camblin's explanation for the series, 'Homage to Hugo:' The paintings are a transformation of the figures in 'Adoration' into abstract color relations, with an attempt to retain the poetic suggestions." Jan Dickerson, "New Aim Turns Toward the Classical," Art and Artists, *The Kansas City Star*, Sunday, December 25, 1960.

Camblin exhibited in five shows during the year.

January: *Governor's All-Florida Show*, John and Mable Ringling Museum of Art, Sarasota, Florida.

Article: "Governor LeRoy Collins officiated at the opening of the All-Florida show held at the Ringling Museum of Art. He said the exhibit was 'to stimulate public interest in art, especially Florida art and to encourage Florida artists by developing a market for their work and fostering deserved praise and commendation.'" "Show Opens Here Today," *Sarasota Herald-St. Tribune*, Music and Art Section, January 4, 1960.

Article: "150 Objects Picked Here for Governor's Show," *Sarasota Herald-Tribune*, January 8, 1960. "Collins to Officiate at All Florida Show," *Sarasota Herald Tribune*, January 8, 1960.

Article: Lawrence Dame, "Hundreds of sightseers . . . have remarked on the preponderance of abstract-expressionism and its imitations at the First Annual Governor's 'All-Florida' Art Show. . . . The first work most visitors see upon entering the newly refurbished large gallery is a pen, ink and collage paper of a chimerical beast by Bob Camblin, distinguished for its intricate and delicate line." Lawrence Dame, "Abstract-Impressionism Preponderant at Show," *Sarasota Herald-Tribune*, January 12, 1960, p. 8.

Article: "'Go fly a kite' was the last phase of an assignment given to students in two color and design classes at the Ringling School of Art. Instructors Bob Camblin and Gerald Purdy had 70 students working on what seemed—at first—a simple project." "Go Fly a Kite," *Sarasota Herald-Tribune*, February 7, 1960, p. 29.

Article: "Bud Wall of the Ringling School, apparently a follower of Bob Camblin, achieves a feeling of glowing space in 'Pencils for Sale' and took second prize." "Teachers' Imprints Discernible, Little Revolt Against Traditional Standards at Art Students Show," *Sarasota Herald-Tribune*, March 24, 1960, p. 16.

Article: "An announcement of award winners on Saturday night at the Ringling Museum will open the National Show of the Sarasota Art Assn., featuring some 200 paintings and sculptures. . . . Among acceptances from Sarasota are . . . Bob Camblin." "National Art Show Set Here," *Sarasota Journal*, March 30, 1960, p. 13.

April: *National Show of the Sarasota Art Association*, Ringling Museum, Sarasota, Florida, 1960.

Article: "One of the strongest and most pleasing oils is that of Bob Camblin, who has blown up clinging shellfish, like barnacles, into a bold pattern, where the pleasures of both form and color, along with ingenious, original treatment, are apparent." Lawrence Dame, "In National Exhibition West Coast Artists' Works Are Analyzed," *Sarasota Herald-Tribune*, April 15, 1960, p. 18.

Summer: Camblin left John and Mable Ringling Museum of Art, School of Art.

He accepted a position as an Instructor at the University of Illinois, Urbana, for the school year 1960–61.

November: *Bob Camblin—Recent Drawings and Paintings*, Kansas City Art Institute, Kansas City, Missouri.

Article: "Bob Camblin is an artist who believes that paintings are a 50–50 proposition—they should bring something to the viewer and the viewer should bring something to them. That is why, for himself, he likes neither abstract art (which demands too much) nor social realism (which screams too loud). He has tried both, and found the results a little forced. Now he is working somewhere between in a manner that might be called allegorical. 'I have found a direction, and it's nice to be going somewhere,' Camblin said genially last week when he visited the Kansas City Art Institute. Camblin, a member of the faculty of the art department of the University of Illinois, Urbana, Ill., has studied and taught at the art institute here. A collection of his recent drawings and paintings is now featured as a major exhibition at the school." Jan Dickerson, "New Aim Turns Toward the Classical," *The Kansas City Star*, Art and Artists, Sunday, December 25, 1960.

Undated: *Bob Camblin*: St. Armands Gallery, St. Armands Key, Florida.

Camblin began to focus on drawings of Greek myths, especially those involving themes of enigmatic change through metamorphosis, transmutation and transformation. His personal studies centered around Marcel DuChamp.

1961

Summer: Camblin resigned from the University of Illinois at Urbana. He accepted a position at the University of Detroit Mercy. Bruno Leon, AIA, chair of the Department of Architecture at the University of Detroit Mercy, had made the Department of Architecture autonomous from the department of Architectural Engineering with a six-year degree program. One of the first faculty positions he filled was Robert Camblin to teach first-year design and drawing. Camblin stayed until 1965. Leon became dean of the School of Architecture in 1964. In 1971 the chair went to Buckminster Fuller.

Bruno Leon offered the Camblin family one of the homes he had designed in Grosse Ile Township. The Camblins accepted his offer.

Bonnie gave birth to a son, Brian.

Camblin had three exhibitions during the year:

Undated: *Bob Camblin*, Oklahoma State University, Stillwater, Oklahoma.

Undated: *9th National Sarasota Art Association Exhibition*, Civic Center, Sarasota, Florida. Prize.

Fall: *Young Artists Exhibit*, Southwestern College, Winfield, Kansas.

Comment: "The aesthetic approach of three young modern artists was revealed last fall in the Fire Place Room exhibit. The study of such paintings as . . . Camblin's 'Fennigan Transfigured,' resulted in varied expressions." 1961 Yearbook, *Moundbuilders*, Volume 50, Winfield, Kansas, p. 90.

1962

According to his daughter Robyn, during part of the year (dates unrecorded), Bruno Leon and Bob Camblin traveled to Italy together. He began a series of drawings based on the Greek myths.

Robert Smithson made a series of drawings that incoporated words.

Camblin had a one-man exhibition:

November: *Bob Camblin: Drawings & Collage*, Art Education Gallery, University of Wisconsin, Madison, Wisconsin. November 13–November 30.

Press Release: "Prof. Don Anderson, chairman of the department of art and art education, termed the show a powerful collection with many religious themes. The artist has exhibited nationally in one-man and group shows. He has taken prizes at a number of shows including the eighth National Missouri Valley, the fourth Midwestern Biennial, the sixth Mid-America Annual, the Ninth National Sarasota Art Associate, and the 21st annual Contemporary American Painting at Palm Beach where four awards were taken by Camblin. He holds bachelor of fine arts and master of fine arts degrees from the Kansas City Art Institute and gained further training in Italy on a 1956–57 Fulbright grant. Prior to his present position at Detroit, Camblin taught at Ringling Art Institute, Sarasota, Fla., and at the University of Chicago." Press Release, *Madison News*, Nov. 13, 1962.

1963

Bonnie gave birth to a daughter, Robyn. Camblin exhibited in two shows:

April 14–May 12: *An Exhibition of Art Objects Collected by the Faculty of the University of Illinois, Urbana*, Krannert Art Museum, Urbana, Illinois. Camblin exhibited *The Fate of Miss Daphne Peneius*, pencil and color wash. Lent by Marvin Martin.

Catalogue: *An Exhibition of Art Objects Collected by the Faculty of the University of Illinois*: Number 56, Krannert Art Museum, Urbana, Illinois.

Undated: *Bob Camblin*, St. Armands Gallery, St. Armands Key, Florida.

November 22: President John F. Kennedy was assassinated during a motorcade in Dallas.

1964

Camblin was part of a group gallery show:

July–August: *Gallery Artists*, St. Armands Gallery, St. Armands Key, Florida.

Article: "The St. Armands Gallery has a group show of their regular artists, most of whom are either currently working in Florida or who have spent considerable time here. They include Bob Camblin . . ." Clyde Burnett, "From My Point of View, Summer or Not, Art Events Are Plentiful Here," *The Sarasota Herald-Tribune*, Sarasota, Florida, July 5, 1964, p. 11C.

Article: "The group show at St Armands Gallery contains some very interesting work by several artists whom the gallery regularly represents . . . One of the artists whose work interests me very much is Bob Camblin, who once taught at the Ringling School and now is teaching at the University of Illinois. Camblin's work is very representational in nature, but he has an eye for the unusual. His tight, immaculate draftsmanship, combined with an eye for the visually unique, puts his work into the realm of the surreal. For instance, 'Victim No 1' shows a crab on a beach, a clump of beach grass and a brilliant moon against a deep black sky. In another drawing he uses a complex pre-Columbian Indian motif. 'Sea Memory' is a form vague in its specific identification, but sharp in execution. In my opinion, Camblin combines great imaginativeness with a highly developed skill." Clyde Burnett, "From My Viewpoint," *The Sarasota Herald-Tribune*, Sarasota, Florida, July 12, 1964.

A group of Chicago imagists began working under a group name: The Hairy Who. Uninvolved in the New York art scene, their art involved grotesqueries, the outlining of shapes with dark lines, filled-in color, and sexual imagery emerging from surreal places. It is unknown if Camblin ever saw the group's work. His art incorporated similar components after his move to Houston.

1965

Summer: Camblin left the University of Detroit Mercy School of Architecture. He accepted a position as Assistant Professor at the University of Utah in Salt Lake City, Utah.

Camblin participated in four exhibitions during the year:

August: *Windows*, Plumtree Gallery, Salt Lake City, Utah. Camblin exhibited works of ink, casein, wash, and collage, 1965.

Article: "Bob Camblin, newest staff member of the University of Utah's Art Department has an exhibition of drawing at the Plumtree Gallery. These are brilliant and perceptive studies in the medium of ink, casein, wash and collage. The Windows series, achieved in sensitive statements of sheer virtuosity are graphite. Fragile lines, supple washes and luminous cross hatches are the means through which the artist develops his facile images. A series of skulls emerge in fascinating devices in a panel of small drawings entitled 'The Wheel.' 'The Birth of Venus,' 'Carousel of Four' and 'Dream of Crete' are particularly exciting." George Dibble, "U. Exhibit Features Modern Artists," *Salt Lake City Tribune*, Sunday, August 22, 1965, p. 43.

October: *Art Department Faculty Show*, Department Gallery, Building 441, University of Utah, Salt Lake City, Utah.

Article: "Works of 11 members of the Art Department faculty are on exhibit. The 28 works include some by two new faculty members, Philip G. Morton and Bob Camblin." "Faculty Show Hangs in Gallery at U," *The Salt Lake Tribune*, Sunday, October 3, 1965, p. 14.

November 17–December 31: *Exhibition of Works by Members of the University of Utah Art Faculty*, The Movie Gallery, Salt Lake City, Utah.

Calendar: "The exhibitors included Alvin Gittins, V. Douglas Snow, Ed Maryon, Earl Jones, Bob Camblin and Gerald Purdy." "Calendar of Salt Lake Civic Events," The Movie Gallery, *The Salt Lake Tribune*, Sunday, November 14, 1965; November 28, 1965, and December 31, 1965.

Undated: *Bob Camblin*, The Art Gallery of Windsor, University of Windsor, Ontario, Canada.

During the year, Camblin read Michel Foucault's *Madness and Civilization: A History of Insanity in the Age of Reason.*

1966

Camblin showed work in five exhibitions during the year. He began a series of paintings based on the theme of "St. Bambola," a fictitious saint that was a doll.

March 20–April 2: *Paintings, Prints and Drawings by Bob Camblin*, Plumtree Gallery, Salt Lake City, Utah.

April 7–June 5: *Drawings—U.S.A. '66*, Third Biennial Exhibition, St. Paul Art Center (named changed to Minnesota Museum of American Art in 1969), St. Paul, Minnesota. A national exhibition in which Camblin received a Purchase Prize for his ink drawing *Cicada Song.*

Catalogue: *Saint Paul Art Center, Third Biennial Exhibition, Drawing U.S.A. '66*, St. Paul, Minnesota, 1966.

November 20–December 11: *Drawings by Bob Camblin: Chrysalis Series*, Plumtree Gallery, Salt Lake City, Utah.

Article: "Creativity is a current concern of Mr. Camblin, as evidenced by his 'Chrysalis Series.'" Under a photograph included with the article: "An art innovation, painted plaster forms enclosed in plastic bubbles, feature exhibit by Bob Camblin." Also in Halliday's article, Camblin said he considered anyone an artist "who can live in an open-ended society, can adapt to constant change.

The prevailing philosophy in our society is now existential. Politicians don't agree; religions don't agree; parents don't agree—so each person has to construct his own values. Art foundation: A sound knowledge of drawing serves as a check point for the artist, regardless of which direction he takes. With this as a solid point of departure, the artist can tell when he is rationalizing. Drawing is the basic discipline. Yet, in the individual struggle, being clumsy represents a more human statement in art than facility with drawing. There are two sides to people. There's the intuitive and the rational. And they're both important. We use rationality for the next giant step into intuition. Art is a success if the student can get back to being a child again. It's all a process—becoming something. And it's important for the artist to recognize the process. Artists are always a threat to the status quo, to the existing values and attitudes of society. They are iconoclasts, establishing the next steps that society will take. Not that all creativity is necessarily good, in the sense of being beneficial to society, but change is inevitable and it is the natural role of the artist to point out new ways." Bob Halliday, "U. Instructor to Exhibit New Work, Cites Artists Role to Effect Change," *The Salt Lake Tribune*, November 20, 1966, p. 18.

Article: "Bob Camblin, a member of the University of Utah art department faculty, is featured in a one-man showing of drawings and sculpture which opened Sunday at the Plumtree Gallery." "One-Man Showing," *The Deseret News*, November 22, 1966, p. 10B.

Article: "Drawings by Bob Camblin at the Plumtree Gallery extend the two dimensional aspects of drawing through sculptural accessories. The provocative effect of projected planes rising in subtle values from severe white, are involved with overlaid plastic bubbles or shields which develop additional dimensions in the design. In the 'White Gull,' sensitively inscribed elements are imposed on the surface of the bubble. The effect of an even more fragile shadow, cast in the canvas sculpture and drawing beneath, include strange illusory conjunctions that draw on the disciplines of both. Thematic involvement with metamorphosis and development of the life cycle is explored in the exhibit of new works by the University of Utah art staff member." George Dibble, "Drawing, Sculpture Wed in Exhibit," *The Salt Lake Tribune*, Sunday, November 27, 1966, p. 19W.

December: *Open House*, Plumtree Gallery, Salt Lake City, Utah.

Article: "Max and Joan Smith, gallery owners, are inviting the public to view this cross-section of contemporary Utah art, including works by such prominent Utahns as Dorothy Bearnson, Bob Camblin . . ." "Plumtree Holds Open House at Gallery Today," *Salt Lake Tribune*, Sunday December 11, 1966 p. 18W.

December 16, 1966: Camblin began his scarecrow series.

Undated: *Bob Camblin*, Baker University, Baldwin City, Kansas.

The Houston Years, 1967–1988

1967

Camblin had eight exhibitions during the year:

February 4–28: *Bob Camblin: Recent Drawings*, Fred Jones Jr. Museum of Art, University of Oklahoma, Norman, Oklahoma.

Article: "One of the major responsibilities of a museum is the encouragement and recognition of talented artists from the geographical area. It is a pleasure to present this exhibition of superb drawing by a native Oklahoman. Mr. Camblin has had nine one-man shows in this country and abroad since completing his formal studies in art. He has received numerous awards and honors in national competitive and invitational exhibitions—the most recent, a Purchase Prize in the 1966 *Drawings: USA*, a national show at the St. Paul Art Center. The stamp of quality is immediately discernible in the sensitive certainty of line which clarifies his intensely personal vision." From the museum's online "Gallery Guide," written by S.O. Camblin exhibited 27 drawings in the exhibition: *Bambola Morte #4*, pastel; *From the Sea*, ink; *The Wheel*, ink; *Sea Chalice #2*, ink; *Death of Odysseus*, ink; *Doll Face #2*, pastel; *Doll Box*, pastel; *Scarecrow #2*, pencil; *The Seven-Souled Man #3*, pencil; *Canto III Metamorphosis*, ink; *Heart of St. Bambola*, ink and collage; *Altar of St. Bambola #2*, ink; *Dream of Crete*, ink; *Canto II Metamorphosis*, ink; *Window 7*, ink and pencil; *Window 3*, pencil; *Window 4*, pencil; *Window 5*, pencil; *Martyrdom of St. Bambola*, ink and embossment; *One-Eyed Doll*, ink; *Scarecrow #3*, ink and wash; *The Seven-Souled Man #5*, ink; *Sea Chalice #3*, ink and wash; *The White Gull*, pencil; *Seven-Souled Man #6,7*, ink; *Mark of the Beast*, ink; *Altar of St. Bambola*, ink and wash. A photograph of *Metamorphosis* was reproduced for the article. "Above is a recent drawing by Bob Camblin of Ponca City. Camblin's drawings are on exhibition through Feb. 28 at the OU Museum of Art. Camblin received his M.F.A. in 1955 from the Kansas City Art Institute, was awarded a Fulbright grant for studying in Italy and was awarded a 1966 Purchase Award in the *DRAWINGS; U.S.A.* exhibition. Camblin is presently on the faculty of the University of Utah." "Metamorphosis," *The Oklahoma Daily*, University of Oklahoma, Norman, Oklahoma, February 10, 1967, p. 14.

March 5–April 12: *The Intermountain Biennial*, The Salt Lake Art Center, Salt Lake City, Utah. Camblin exhibited a sculpture titled *Head* and a mixed media work, *Doll Box #2*.

Article: "Sculpture seems to come on stronger than in previous shows. Bob Camblin's 'Head' . . . attests to the versatility of . . . sculptural interest." Dibble, George, "Art Center Chooses 5 Works," *The Salt Lake Tribune*, Salt Lake City, Utah. Sunday, March 5, 1967, p. 14.

May 1–26: *4th Annual Small Sculpture and Drawing Exhibition*, Western Art Gallery, Western Washington State College, Bellingham, Washington.

July: *Drawings: Group Show*, St. Armands Gallery, St. Armands Key, Florida.

Article: "Gallery Director Murray Lebwohl has recently re-opened St. Armands Gallery, 302 John Ringling Blvd, St. Armands Key, after a month's absence . . . He has installed a group show of drawings by . . . Bob Camlbin . . . Bob Camblin's drawings are very carefully executed—he is a draughtsman in the classic sense, but who also must deal in a very serious allegorical exploration of the meaning of life and death." "New Exhibits at St. Armands Gallery," *The Sarasota Herald-Tribune*, Sunday, July 16, 1967, p. 7F.

Summer: Camblin accepted a position of Assistant Professor at Rice University in Houston, Texas. He and his family moved from Salt Lake City, Utah, to Houston, Texas, a move he hoped would catapult him from conservative environments. Camblin described his idea of Houston at the time of his move: "In 1968 Houston was a place with no past history, lots of money, and open doors." "Bob Camblin," *Art, Seven One Three*, 1988, p. 39.

Other artists teaching in the Art Department at Rice University were Earl Staley, John O'Neil, and David Parsons. A few months after the beginning of classes, Camblin and Staley moved into studios on the third floor of a new Rice building, Allen Center. Recounting the history of Allen Center, Sandy Havens, a faculty member, remembered: "The Fine Arts studios were a source of some dismay for some of the more traditional administrators who had to make peace with sharing space with very non-traditional artists like Earl Staley and Bob Camblin whose paintings and life drawing classes were very much a presence on the third floor. It was usually a somewhat mixed crowd on the elevators. Many stories there." Sandy Havens, "Comment," *The Rice History Corner: Gleanings from the Rice University Archives.* Allen Center Open House, November 1967.

Rice University Art Department had only been functioning for two years when Camblin arrived. Artist John O'Neil's organizational experience at the University of Oklahoma guided him as he developed the new department. Susie Kalil wrote, "In 1965 Rice University had brought John O'Neil from his post as director of a large department at the University of Oklahoma to establish an art department at Rice. O'Neil, in turn, had asked Bob Camblin, Earl Staley, and Joe Tate to join the faculty."[3]

Earl Staley said, "John O'Neill had the great ability to hire people that he immediately didn't like. He didn't like me right away, and he didn't like Camblin and after that, Joe Tate. John—he was quite a character. He hired Joe Tate to replace me, and of course, Tate was worse than me. Bob Camblin and I were sharing a studio together off of Montrose near Richmond. We had a studio together, then Joe Tate showed up and he had a part of the studio. Then we rented a big place down the street from St. Thomas on Sul Ross, and we took it over as a collaborative studio. We were hanging out there and conversing and talking constantly. We taught ourselves. Camblin actually taught me how to paint. He taught me the rules by watching him, and he and Joe and I worked together on projects and ideas and shows at St. Thomas, and whatever happened there."[4]

Artist and friend, Roy Fridge, worked as a guest lecturer for Rice University Art Department. Every Friday for two semesters Camblin had Fridge work with the students of one of his drawing classes. Fridge taught the students animation while he made his own Camblin-influenced film, *Reflections of St. Bambola.* Fridge received a Cash Award for the film in the 1971 Seattle Film Fest.[5]

November 8–December 10: *Seventeenth Exhibition of Southwestern Prints and Drawings*, Dallas Museum of Art, Dallas, Texas.

Undated: *Beaumont Annual*, Beaumont, Texas.

Undated: *Dickinson State College Exhibition*, Dickinson, North Dakota.

Undated: Norfolk Museum of Arts and Sciences (became the Chrysler Museum of Art in 1971), Norfolk, Virginia.

1968

Camblin led one "Happening" and had three exhibitions during the year.

Allan Kaprow coined the term "happening" and presented *18 Happenings in 6 Parts* at the Reuben Gallery in New York in 1959. "He chose the word happening to suggest 'something spontaneous, something that just happens to happen.'" Kaprow was interested in the process of creation. Hans

Namuth's 1951 film of Jackson Pollock painting a large canvas made Kaprow realize that the action of painting was an event, a performance. Kaprow began staging events that involved audience participation, "blurring the boundary of art and life."[6]

The Contemporary Arts Museum, Houston, Texas, exhibited *Allan Kaprow and Wolf Vostell: Two Happening Concepts*, January 9–February 11, 1968. There is a good possibility that Camblin went to the exhibition.

Rice University invited Kaprow to Houston where he created the happening, *Baggage*.[7]

January 13–February 16: *American Drawings 1968*, Moore College of Art and Design, Philadelphia, Pennsylvania.

Catalogue: *American Drawings 1968*, Moore College of Art and Design, Philadelphia.

Article: "The gallery, located at 819 Richmond Avenue, features many works by Rice students, graduates, faculty, and their wives. A new addition is a salad bar featuring hand made sandals by Bonnie Camblin, wife of Rice art professor and underground film magnate Bob Camblin." "Forum Exhibiting Student Creations," *The Rice Thresher* 55, no. 18, ed. 1 (Thursday, February 22, 1968): 6.

Spring: The assassination of Martin Luther King, Jr., on April 4, the attempted murder of Andy Warhol on June 3 and the assassination of Robert Kennedy on June 5 shocked the world. Camblin reacted by pulling further away from organized religion.

June 16–September 8: *1968 Invitational Drawing Exhibition*, Sales and Rental Gallery, Nelson-Atkins Museum of Art, Kansas City, Missouri.

Catalogue: *Invitational Drawing Exhibition*, Nelson-Atkins Museum of Art Calendar, June –August, 1968, Sales and Rental Gallery.

Advertisement: "Bob Camblin, David Gallery," *Art in America*, September–October 1968.

October: Happening, *Side Show*: Camblin and Staley as B& E Productions took Rice students to the West Beach, Galveston, for movie making with Roy Fridge editing. *Side Show* was the first of three Camblin-led Construction/Destruction "happenings."[8]

Article: "Sunday, Oct. 27, a group of students and faculty met on Galveston Beach. . . . The event, organized by Bob Camblin and Earl Staley, . . . has been called by one or the other of them: 'An Experience in Extra Curricular Intermedia Discipline: A Construction-Destruction Event to Be Filmed on the Beach (Another B & E Production: A Real Swell Time)' " Russ Lyman Georgia Lyman, *The Rice Thresher*, "Communal beach happening yields sideshow film footage," Houston, Texas, Thursday, December 12, 1968, p. 4.

Article: "Bob Camblin and Earl Staley, Rice Fine Arts profs, will present the world premiere of "Side Show," starring Rice students, in the Brown Commons." *The Rice Thresher*, "Notes and Notices," Houston, Texas, Thursday, December 5, 1968, p. 7.

Article: "Faculty help on the second edition includes Larry McMurtry, Earl Staley and Bob Camblin." "Janus presents photographic issue to go on sale next Monday, Dec. 16," *The Rice Thresher*, Thursday, December 12, 1968, p. 4.

December 24, Apollo 8, NASA's first manned mission to the moon entered the lunar orbit, circled the moon ten times and returned to earth on December 27.

Undated: *Bob Camblin*, Allen Center Art Gallery, Rice University, Houston, Texas.

John de Menil and his wife Dominique Schlumberger moved the entire art history department, known as the Institute for the Arts, from St. Thomas University to the Art Department of Rice University in 1968–69. With this major move, Rice University gained a significant art history department. St. Thomas professors Mino Badner, William Camfield, Walter Widrig, Philip Oliver-Smith and Thomas McEvilley joined Rice art historians, Katherine Brown and James Chillman, Jr. The Rice art department studio professors consisted of Bob Camblin, David Parsons, Earl Staley and John O'Neil.[9]

Camblin and Staley moved to a studio on Oakley Street and formed B & E Productions. "When Bob Camblin and Earl Staley set up studios next door to each other they set in motion a pattern of working together that yielded rich results over the next four years."[10] *Collaborators: Artists Working Together In Houston 1969—1986*, The Glassell School of Art, The Museum of Fine Arts, Houston, Texas. September 18–October 19.

1969

David Gallery, owned by Dianne David, began representing Camblin. "Dianne's star shone brightly. Her pioneering David Gallery in the late '60s was the most influential of its time and enlivened the Houston art scene with creative exhibitions that introduced the works of her brother Dorman David, Bob Camblin, Lucas Johnson, Earl Staley, Foy Fridge, Jim Love, David McManaway, Charles Pebworth, Donald Roller Wilson, William T. Wiley, Larry Rivers, Seymour Leichmann, Guy Johnson, amongst others and in doing so influenced the direction of contemporary art in Houston."[11]

During the year, Camblin gave a public lecture at Rice University, participated in an art auction, judged a photography contest, led a happening, and exhibited in five shows.

The Society of Rice University Women presented a seminar series titled "Contemporary American Culture." Camblin gave a lecture on "Art in the '50s and '60s."[12]

Article: Roy Fridge said: "I began to be interested in mirrors, in dolls and that is why Bob Camblin's drawing [St. Bambola] appeals to me. He also does stages sets with his boxes and time machines." Article: "Mixed Media Man," Art, *The Houston Post*, February 23, 1969.

At Rice University the Menils constructed two metal buildings: one to house an exhibition space, nicknamed the Art Barn, and the other to house a media center. The buildings opened in March 1969. After the Art Barn's opening, "the building became an exhibition space associated with Rice's Institute for the Arts, a project the de Menils, and a studio home for the school's art faculty, including John O'Neil, David Parsons, Bob Camblin and Joe Tate."[13]

Article: "The panel of judges for the contest . . . includes Alton Parks, Bob Camblin, John O'Neil and Mrs Kathryn Brown of the Rice Fine Arts Department." "Annual Wiess Photographic Contest Features 'Life' as Principal Theme," *The Rice Thresher*, Thursday, March 20, 1969, p. 6.

March 20–April: *Bob Camblin: Recent Paintings and Drawings*, David Gallery, Houston, Texas.

August: Woodstock, White Lake, New York, a music festival held at a dairy farm in the Catskills changed the popular culture. Beginning with the music and art fair, "the Age of Aquarius" defined the counterculture generation and Camblin immediately felt that he belonged. He grew long hair and beard.

August 7–September 3: *Stable Work by Stable Artists*, David Gallery, Houston, Texas.

Benefit: Pacifica Art Auction, September 28, 1969, St. Thomas University, Houston, Texas.

Article: "Artwork contributed by many of Houston's finest artists, will be auctioned off Sunday, September 28, at the first annual Pacifica Art Auction. Works include those of Bob Fowler, Bob Camblin . . ." "Pacifica Art Auction Slated at St. Thomas," *The Bellaire Texan*, Wednesday, September 24, 1969, p. 10.

October 29–November 30: *Eighteenth Exhibition of Southwestern Prints & Drawings*, Dallas Museum of Art, Dallas, Texas. Camblin exhibited: *The Folded Scarecrow*, pen, ink and wash; *Time Machine #8*, ink.

Catalogue: *Eighteenth Exhibition of Southwestern Prints and Drawings*, Dallas Museum of Art, Dallas, Texas, 1969. Press Release: "The 18th Annual Southwestern Print and Drawing Exhibition will open at the Dallas Museum of Fine Arts on Wednesday, October 29 highlighting sixty-nine works by sixty-one of the finest regional artists. The print and drawing show is the only competitive exhibition of its kind held in the area and as in the past, drew excellent response from artists in seven states. There were over 400 entries submitted by 220 artists from New Mexico, Arkansas, Colorado, Arizona, Oklahoma, Louisiana and Texas. The drawings were juried by Henry Hopkins, Director of the Fort Worth Art Center Museum, and will tour a circuit of ten museums and universities through December of 1970." Press Release: October 23, 1969.

October: Happening: *Construction/Destruction Event II*, Galveston, Texas. In his *Holding Firm Movies* printout, Earl Staley noted that a second *Construction/Destruction* event followed the year after *Side Show* of 1968. Staley also said that Joe Tate participated in the event (actually Tate came to Rice University the following year) as did students from both Rice and St. Thomas Universities. Camblin's 1975 resume listed 1972 "Construction-Deconstruction Events 1 & 2, Galveston Texas, B & E Productions."

Undated: *Bob Camblin*, University of Wisconsin, Madison, Wisconsin.

Undated: *Bob Camblin*, Allen Center Art Gallery, Rice University, Houston, Texas.

Camblin began highly detailed drawings and watercolors that incorporated bizarre imagery in surreal landscapes. He created a series of paintings with fish, followed by a series of Figure 4 Traps.[14]

Rice University did not renew Earl Staley's contract. He moved to the University of St. Thomas to help start an art department.

1970

Camblin participated in eight exhibitions and created a theater set design.

January 4–25: *St. Paul Art Center Permanent Collection, Drawing U.S.A.*, Laguna Gloria Museum (later named Austin Museum of Art), Austin, Texas.

Article: "Neil Havens is director of the show and is assisted by Bob Camblin, Houston artist and member of the Fine Arts Faculty at Rice, in set design." "The Rice Players will present 'The Devils,'" *The Rice Thresher*, Thursday, January 29, 1970, p. 6.

Article: "The Rice Players will present "The Devils" by John Whiting, on Monday, Feb. 9, through Saturday, Feb. 14. Bob Camblin, Houston artist and member of the Fine Arts faculty at Rice, is designing the production in conjunction with Neil Havens . . . Camblin got his BFA and MFA at the Kansas City Art Institute. Thereafter he went to Rome, Italy, on a Fulbright scholarship. He has taught art at a variety of universities in Kansas, Florida, Illinois and Utah, as well as at Rice. Camblin's paintings are currently on view at David Gallery in Houston." "The Devils to Open At Rice," *The Bellaire & Southwestern Texan*, Bellaire, Texas, February 9, 1970, p. 2.

April: A protest occurred at Rice University over the cancellation of Abbie Hoffman, radical leader of the Chicago 7, a group of activists who were accused of inciting riots at the Democratic National Convention. In Houston, non-students and students from other Houston universities instigated the protest against Hoffman's cancellation. Rice students resisted it. Fire gutted the dean of student's office. Several days later Hoffmann spoke at the university for about 5 minutes and only fifty Rice students attended. Camblin found the conservative stand of the Rice president and faculty as well as the student body very worrisome and began encouraging his students to examine their own beliefs regarding civil and social liberties.

May: After President Nixon declared the de-escalation of the Vietnam War in 1969, he increased the attacks in Cambodia. As a result, antiwar demonstrations broke out in the US. One of the protests resulted in the Ohio National Guard shooting fourteen Kent State university demonstrators, killing four. The incident underscored political and social divisions in the US. Conservatives backed the police shootings of unarmed students while liberals were horrified that those charged with protecting US citizens had opened fire upon its civilians. A decade of conflicting political positions on the Vietnam War, civil rights riots, the assassinations of Martin Luther King, Jr., and President John F. Kennedy, battles over voting rights, and general unrest divided the country.

Article: Ann Holmes, "Where It's At (If You Can Find It)," *The Art Gallery*, May 20, 1970, p. 37.

Summer: Joe Tate accepted a position in the Art Department of Rice University to replace Earl Staley. Tate aligned himself politically, socially, and artistically with Camblin and Staley.

September 10–October 1: *Boxscapes: Bob Camblin, Drawings—Watercolors*, David Gallery.

Article: "Childhood memories are those little film strips of incredulous horror and innocent amazement that reflicker their private scenes against the back walls of our adult heads. What a scene Robert Camblin's make. His flickerings have escaped from his cranial projection room and can now be seen playing, each like a little walk-up drive-in showing selected short subjects from Camblin's youth, on the walls of the David Gallery. 'Boxscapes' 42-year-old Camblin calls this surrealistic marble fudge of catfish heads, rubber gloves and mountain ranges entwined in miles of visceral tubing. The title is an allusion to the shipping crate motif into which Camblin watercolors his moderate size youthful recollections. Camblin's youth, not yours. Chances are good the show will not pluck any sympathetic strings of youthful melancholy in the eyes of the viewer. It's not that Camblin's experiences were probably that esoteric. It's just that their resurrection is so arresting, with their caricature and unscary visions of things scary. What could be more scary than "Spavinaw Ancestor Masks," for instance. Nearly every one of the 30 watercolors in the show has at least one. Anybody else would recall them as catfish heads. The title of the single construction in the show is "Time Machine"—somewhat self-explanatory. Essentially, it's the key to the show. Positioned at the entrance to the gallery, the viewer in passing it may visually equip himself from its compartments of Camblin memorabilia, with the symbols which echo throughout the show. Technically, Cambllin's subtle blend of muted colors worked in clean detail, enhanced by the symmetrical lines of the box format alluding to Albertian perspective studies, becomes a secondary evocation of faded early Rennaissance frescos. It's enough to cajole a wide empathetic grin for Camblin's adventure of remembering." "Distant Flickerings Color Camblin Show," *Houston Chronicle*, September 20, 1970.

October–November: *Opening Group Exhibition*, Cranfill Gallery, Dallas, Texas.

Article: Jan Butterfield, "Dallas Galleries Feature Art of Talented Young Artists," *Fort Worth Star Telegram*, November 12, 1970, p. 6G.

Undated: *Drawings in America*, Museum of Fine Arts, Houston, Texas.

Catalogue: *Drawings in America*, Museum of Fine Arts, Houston, Texas, 1970.

Undated: *Tattoo Show*, B & E Productions, David Gallery, Houston, Texas. Camblin, Staley, and David gallery owner Dianne decided to have a tattoo exhibition in the David Gallery. Staley filmed some highlights from the show in Super 8.

Undated: *St. Paul Annual Drawing Show*, Minnesota Museum of American Art, St. Paul, Minnesota.

Undated: *The Highway Show*, Rice University, Houston, Texas.

Catalogue: *The Highway Show*, Rice Gallery, Rice University, Houston, Texas, 1970.

Undated: *Drawings from Nine States: A Regional Exhibition*, Museum of Fine Arts, Houston, Texas.

1971

Camblin participated in eleven exhibitions and one happening.

Camblin and Staley added Joe Tate to B & E Productions and renamed themselves, B. E. & J. Productions.[15] Camblin began drawing specimen bottles with disconcerting contents. He started stenciling titles in large letters above the compositions.

January: *Construction/Deconstruction Beach Event III*, B & E Productions Galveston, Texas. Camblin and Staley, joined by Joe Tate, organized and led a collaborative "earthwork" for a Galveston "happening" on the beach. Nearly 200 students, as well as other interested men and women, participated. At dawn the group gathered objects and detritus they found on the Galveston seaside and they built a construction. According to the *Houston Chronicle*, when completed, their creation rose more than forty feet. After working through the day, the group ritualistically circled their construction at dusk, and then walked into and out of the sea before setting fire to "The Thing."

Article: Dreyer wrote that the students revelled in the creative process. In the same article, Camblin said, "Nicest thing about it, they're all enjoying it." Martin Dreyer, "The Night They Burned The Thing," *The Houston Chronicle*, Texas Magazine, Sunday, January 10, 1971, cover and pp. 14, 16, 17, 20.

Article: "Students of Bob Camblin's and Joe Tate's drawing and painting classes will have an exhibition of their work at the Rice Memorial Center Jan. 18–31. The works to be exhibited were selected by the students themselves and will be judged for special awards by Earl Staley and Jack Boynton of the University of St. Thomas." "Elsewhere on campus," *The Rice Thresher* 58, no. 14 (Thursday, January 14, 1971).

February 18–unknown: *Document Show*, David Gallery, Houston, Texas. As B & E Productions Bob Camblin and Earl Staley produced the exhibition. B & E Productions wrote: "'Original Statement of Purpose,' Art becomes definition. Definition becomes perception. Document is concrete perception. Definitions change as perception increases. Knowledge demands documentation. Art is documented knowledge. Man is document in form of art. Life is series of art documents. Knowledge of life becomes art. Meaning of art equals document. Documents are definitions of art. History documents change. Art has presented documents of change. Change is visible non-visible. Mental participation demands participation. Participation becomes perception. Art is mental participation made concrete. Man asks precident: Dada, 1916, Duchamp, Surrealism, Happening, Environment, Conceptuals, Participation. This exhibition is art. Individual pieces are art. Openings are art. Attendance is art through participation. Without participation there is no art."[16] Camblin and Staley contributed their own documents, both real and fabricated.

Article: "Questionnaires were to be corralled at the door on opening night with pertinent and impertinent data demanded. Much of it could enrich the sexual researchers, Masters and Johnson, for new statistics at the love life of the artist." Eleanor Freed, "Documenta," *Houston Post*, Art Section, February 21, 1971, p. 28.

Dorman David, brother of Dianne, influenced the exhibition. Dorman sold documents, some of which were forged, including the Texas Declaration of Independence.[17]

March 1–31: *3rd Biennial National Exhibition of Prints and Drawings*, Dickinson State College, Dickinson, North Dakota.

March 8–April 15: *The Other Coast*, University of California, Long Beach, California. The show included work by ten Texas artists (as noted on cover with photograph of the artists): Bess, Tracy, Larson, Love, Rapho, Hood, Turner, Wray, Stout and Camblin. Camblin exhibited: *Time Machine*, *Two Funky Hands*, *Spavinaw Crystal*, and *Bone Jawr*.

Catalogue: *The Other Coast (10 Texas Artists)*, University of California, Long Beach, California, 1971. In the catalogue, an unnamed interviewer asked the participating artists about their "Reflections." Camblin said: "[It]Took him forty-two years to begin to understand his work and doesn't see why it should be made any easier for the viewer."

Article: "On Sunday's calendar will be a preview from 5–8 at Cranfill Gallery, which will also present the work of two Texas artists—Bob Camblin and Lee Baxter Davis. Camblin and Davis were both included in the gallery's opening last fall and work in drawing, watercolor and printmaking. Camblin teaches at Rice University, while Davis teaches printmaking at East Texas State University." "Seven New Shows to Preview," *Times Herald*, Dallas Texas, March 19, 1971.

Article: "Bob Camblin's funky drawings are surrealistic, inventive, witty and intricate." Virginia Laddey, "'Other Coast' Shows New Approach to Art," *Independent Press-Telegram*, Long Beach, California, Sunday, March 21, 1971, p. W6.

March: *Two Texas Artists, Bob Camblin and Lee Baxter Davis*, Cranfill Gallery, Dallas, Texas.

April 4–September 3: *Bob Camblin: Painting and Drawing*, David Gallery, Houston, Texas.

Article: Janet Kutner, "Variety Exhibited by Camblin at David Gallery," *Dallas Morning News*, April 13, 1971, p. 10E.

June 22–July 18: *34th Tarrant County Annual*, Fort Worth Art Center, Fort Worth, Texas. Camblin exhibited: *Fish Target #2* and *Red Tide*.

Brochure: *34th Tarrant County Annual*, 1971.

Article: "Texas," Arts, *Summer (Ete)*, 1971, pp. 49–50.

July 14–September 6: *Texas Painting and Sculpture 71*, Dallas Museum of Fine Arts, Dallas, Texas. The show included a work by Camblin, *Joe Tate's Jelly Bean Machine*, watercolor on paper.

Catalogue: *Texas Painting and Sculpture 71*, Dallas Museum of Fine Arts, Fair Park, Dallas, Texas.

October 26–November 25: *Project South/Southwest*, Fort Worth Art Center, Fort Worth, Texas.

Article: Ann Holmes, "Fantastic Artists," *Southwest Art Gallery Magazine*, October 1971, p. 34.

Article: In an article on the Abilene artist, Minter mentioned Camblin: "Other artists included in the exhibition include 6 painters and 3 sculptors . . . Bob Camblin, Houston." "Minter Included in Art Exhibit," *Abilene Reporter-News*, Sunday, October 24, 1971, p. 23.

Article: "Second Installment—'South X Southwest'," *Dallas Morning News*, November 7, 1971, p. 4C.

Article: "Percentage wise, Rice has a good record of bringing new blood into the department. For the past several years, the art department has had a visiting associate professor in studio who came from out-of-state for a year or two. Bob Camblin and Check Boterf were brought on that program." Charlotte Moser, "Before the Glamor of Art," *The Houston Chronicle*, undated ca. 1971.

December 7–unknown: *Rice Faculty Exhibition*, Sewell Art Gallery, Rice University, Houston, Texas.

December: Prompted by Joe Tate's dismissal a year after his arrival, Camblin sent a three-page "OPEN LETTER CONCERNING METHOD OF CHANGING STUDIO POLICY" to Norman Hackerman, Rice University President, Virgil Topazio, Dean of Students, and the Rice faculty of the Fine Arts Department. He wanted "to clarify why I feel abused and outraged." After outlining his issues, Camblin ended the letter: "On closing I would like to state that if the University, Faculty and Students permit themselves to be used in this manner knowingly then as an artist I would have to find this environment unsuitable for my approach to art and teaching which always will be to create 'humanity.' Since art is not only pencils and pigments, but is seeing one's life as an In-Process art form, then I must live it as honestly as I paint."[18] By sending the letter, Camblin insured that the renewal of his contract, as well as possible tenure, would not be considered.

Undated: *Drawings USA*, Minnesota Museum of American Art, St. Paul, Minnesota.

Undated: *Two-Man Exhibition*, Cranfill Gallery, Dallas, Texas.

1972

Camblin exhibited in six shows and one happening.

Brooke Alexander Gallery, Inc., New York, began representing Camblin.

Camblin, Staley, and Tate decided that BE & J Productions was too lengthy a name, so they threw the *I Ching* or *The Book of Changes19* and came up with the hexagram "8. Pi / Holding Together." The subject of the hexagram is "Holding Together means uniting. Holding Together brings good fortune." The trio agreed that they had found their new name and adopted it after deciding to replace 'Together' with 'Firm.' As the Holding Firm they first built out their shared studio, added a tower, and installed a pay phone. Their space attracted gatherings of other artists.

As words became more important to his work, Camblin began to make titles part of his compositions.

April: In a "Personal" letter from the Office of the President of Rice University dated April 5, 1972, President Hackerman told Camblin his upcoming contract would not be renewed. On the back of the termination letter envelope, Camblin wrote: "Dear Pres. Hackerman, I am in receipt of your letter of April 6th notifying me of the termination of my contract next June 30, 1973. I wanted to thank you for the offer of assistance in finding a suitable position elsewhere, but in a discussion with Prof. Camfield I find that since the department feels that I am valuable to them, I will be offered the post of Artist-in-Residence. Thank you again for your concern."

The Rice University Art Department asked Camblin to stay on for an additional year as Visiting Artist and he accepted.

Article: Judy Lunn, "Prowling Artists—Right in Your Backyard," *Houston Post*, July 21, 1972, p. 1B.

October 22–unknown: *Recent Works by Gallery Artists*, Smither Gallery, Dallas, Texas.

October 8–September 2, 1973: Main Street Ii, Fort Worth, Dallas, Houston Invitational: 11 Artists, Houston's Chamber Of Commerce's Cultural Affairs Committee, Traveling Exhibition:

First City National Bank, Houston, Texas: October 8, 1972.

Contemporary Arts Museum, Houston, Texas: October 18–November 12, 1972.

Marion Koogler McNay Art Institute, San Antonio, Texas, April 23–July 12, 1973.

Art Museum of South Texas, Corpus Christi, Texas, July 30–September 2, 1973.

Article: "There is no one around these parts who can handle oil wash and watercolor with the combination of subtlety and precision that Bob Camblin manifests. The imagery is perplexing and often uncomfortable and bizarre as in these examples of his recurrent fish saga. For good measure he has here juxtaposed a sculptured fish trap." Eleanor Freed, "Texans, Titled and Subtitled," *Houston Post*, October 29, 1972, p. 1B.

October: One-week visit to the Architecture Department of the University of Manitoba, Winnipeg, Canada. Camblin conducted Design Labs, Freehand Drawing classes and a seminar in the Theory of Environmental Design.

November 3–4: *The Former David Gallery Presents The Next to The Last Garage Sale*, David Gallery, Houston, Texas.

Camblin brought some art for Dianne David to sell. He assisted in the event, dramatizing and making up stories for every item being sold. "Cards announcing The Last Garage Sale were sent out by Dianne David, who announced recently that she was closing her David Gallery. That's where the sale was, adjacent to The Bookman where Larry McMurtry was once manager."

Article: "The Last Garage Sale May Not Be," *Houston Chronicle*, Section 4, September 26, 1972, p. 4.

Article: "New Faces," *The Houston Post*, 1972.

December 14–16: *Bob Camblin: Money Is No Object, Barter Show* (B E & J Holding Firm Bartering), David Gallery, Houston, Texas.

On the invitation: "Money Is No Object." Camblin said he would barter with those in attendance who wanted to trade their objects for his work. Dianne David added to the invitation: "we'll trade his strange and unusual art for your stranger and unusual objects." Staley and Tate helped with the transactions but Camblin had final say on all bartering. Staley filmed the exhibition.

Article: "Dianne made the initial trade—a bowl of Oklahoma acorns for a Camblin drawing." Eleanor Freed, "Oklahoma Acorns a Fair Trade," *Houston Chronicle*, Section 7, December 13, 1972, p. 3.

Article: [Camblin] People were very fair. I liked their version of what they thought I'd like. Without leaving my studio I amassed all of this . . . What was gained in person to person rapport was worth the whole experience." In the same article, Freed said of Camblin, "His superbly detailed drawings and watercolors contain bizarre and unlovely objects frozen into perpetuity in specimen jars. These are often linked with tubing to the outside world." Eleanor Freed, "Montrose Bateau Lavoir," *Houston Post*, "Spotlight," January 7, 1973, p. 34.

Article: Contemporary Art Museum Houston, curator Jay Belloli: "'There are more artists here than you'd ever believe,' he says, his eyes dancing. 'All these amazing, marvelous, wonderful peole like Joe Tate, Bob Camblin, Earl Staley. They're really nifty people to know.'" Elizabeth Bennett, "New Faces," *The Houston Post*, 1972.

Undated: Southern Illinois University Art Museum, Carbondale, Illinois.

Undated: *Construction-Deconstruction Camp-Out*, The Holding Firm, Texas.

Undated: *Camp-Out Show*, St. Thomas University, Houston, Texas.

1973

Earl Staley wrote about Camblin: "His place was a treasure tableau of the curious and outrageous that he had collected or traded . . . it was as entering a wizard's den."[20]

Article: "On the mantel piece in Camblin's studio stands an array of strange, strange objects . . . a stuffed armadillo, a head from a wax museum, a penitente rattle, an ivory elephant train, a polished bone, rattlesnake rattle and entire skin, a rather askew set of antlers, bells, fur, feathers, trade beads, an apache wife beater, a walrus tusk, dinosaur fragment, books with escutcheons and other insignia . . . a leather medical school training doll from the 19th century with foetus and placenta . . . a trunk full of childhood tricks. Much of Camblin's work contains the aura of magic. 'We all have our magic snake skins. We slough them off. That is what I have done.'" Eleanor Freed, "Montrose Bateau Lavoir," *The Houston Post*, Sunday, January 7, 1973, p. 34.

In 1973 H. C. Westermann carved his *Untitled (First Peanut)* a wooden two-foot-long peanut sculpture. On an unfisinished lithograph Camblin listed Westermann as one of five influential artists.

Camblin started signing notes and letters with two different personas, both based on an image of Santa Claus: Cindy Claws (Santa's image upside down, beard becomes hair) and Santa, the bearer of good tidings and gifts.

Camblin exhited in fifteen shows, three in New York City. B E & J collaborated on a poster for KPFT.

January–February: *Made in Houston*, Louisiana Gallery, Houston, Texas. The artists in the show were: Pat Colville, Earl Staley, Bob Camblin, Ben Woittena, Latane Temple, James Boynton, and John Fairey.

January 15–February 15: *20th Century Drawings*, Museum Consortium Tour, Texas Commissions on Arts and Humanities, Amarillo Art Center, Amarillo Texas.

Catalogue: *20th Century Drawings*, Modern Art Museum of Fort Worth, Fort Worth, Texas.

Article: "Staley, Tate and Camblin, however, did not choose Houston, it chose them by bringing them to the city for teaching jobs. They all like the environment of Houston, but, if they have to go to another city for another 'livable' money-making job, they will. 'We're the way we are because of what we are,' said Camblin. 'We'd be different someplace else.'" Sussan L. Butler, "So You Want to Be an Artist," *Houston Chronicle*, January 28, 1973.

February 26: The last day Camblin and Staley spent in the Oakley Street studio.

Article: "This month the Clear Creek Art League presented a triple header, the B. E. and J. Holding Firm of, by any other name, Bob Camblin, Earl Staley, and Joe Tate. These three artists combined talents and brought us their collective theories and thoughts on art today; as they see it. Originally brought to Houston to be part of the Rice University faculty in Fine Arts, Staley heads the Art Dept. of the University of St. Thomas, while Camblin and Tate are currently still at Rice. This summer the trio will hold seminars, in their shared studio on Montrose Blvd. in the old David Gallery, where students will be exposed to real art as a total life experience." "CC Art League Hears Trio," *The Deer Park Progress*, March 22, 1973, p. 18.

Article: Henry Hopkins, "Contemporary Art in Texas: On the Road to Maturity," *Art News*, May 1973, p. 43.

May 25–July 22: *American Drawings 1963–1973*, Whitney Museum of American Art, New York. Camblin exhibited: *Trotline Memorial*, 1972, Ink & watercolor, 22 X 30 and *Backyard Spiral*, 1972, Ink and watercolor, 22 X 30. Brooke Alexander, Inc., New York, made the loan of Camblin's works for the exhibition.

Catalogue: Elke M. Solomon, *American Drawings 1963–1973*, Whitney Museum of American Art, New York. Illustration of *Trotline Memorial*, p. 57.

Benefit: KPFT's Radio Guide poster. In August the Holding Firm drew a Venus from Botticelli's *Birth of Venus* and filled the image with drawings and doodles. The goddess wore glasses in the shape of the infinity symbol. The trio stamped "B E & J Holding Firm" on to the poster.

Another flyer, "Artists for Pacifica" listed the contributor of the door prize as The Holding Firm, and the individual names of the artists as donors to the auction. Dianne David was chair of the fundraiser.

August 8–October 11: *20th Century Drawings*, Museum Consortium Tour, Texas Commissions on Arts and Humanities, Tyler Museum of Art, Tyler, Texas. The Modern Art Museum of Fort Worth loaned Camblin's *Galveston Finger Snare*, 1971, watercolor and pencil. 30 X 22 inches.

Catalogue: *20th Century Drawings*, Modern Art Museum of Fort Worth, Fort Worth, Texas, 1973.

August 26–September 20: *Contemporary Paintings, Graphics and Sculpture*, Smither Gallery, Dallas, Texas.

"Exhibition included Juergen Strunck, Robert Wade, George Green, Vernon Fisher, Jack Mims and Bob Camblin." *Texas Monthly*, "Around the State," "*Contemporary Paintings*," Dallas: Smither Gallery, August 1973, p. 20 and September 1973, p. 21.

August: *Bob Camblin*, Contemporary Arts Museum, Houston, Lower Gallery.

Texas Monthly, "Around the State," Houston: The Contemporary Arts Museum, Houston, Quaytman in the Main Gallery and Bob Camblin in the Lower Gallery. August 1973, p. 26.

August 7–September 4: *Private Works: Works on Paper*, Contemporary Arts Museum, Houston. BE & J Holding Firm exhibited a mixed media collaborative drawing. Camblin exhibited: *Glass Bead Gamer #1—Change the Distance*, 22 X 30, pencil, watercolor on board; *The Ideal*, 22 X 30, pencil, watercolor on board; *Message in a Bottle*, 22 X 30, pencil, watercolor on board. A detail from *Message in a Bottle* was illustrated in the catalogue.

Pamphlet: *Private Works: Works on Paper*, Contemporary Arts Museum, Houston, Texas.

Article: "[F]rom what I can tell from the documentation and drawing, constructed on site, gathered data at it (thus, in a sense, making it anthropological), made a map of it and then reconstructed it in another place using the drawing as a guide. It's a story, within a story, within another one, a takeoff on historical discoveries and a complicated joke which is probably more fun to the Holding Firm than an outsider." Susan L. Butler, "Private Works," *Houston Chronicle*, Art Circles, September 1973.

September–October 18: *Group Show: Wade, Fisher, Strunck, Winter, Camblin, Davis*, Smither Gallery, Dallas, Texas.

Texas Monthly, "Around the State," Dallas, Smither Gallery: Group show: Wade, Fisher, Strunck, Winter Camblin, Davis, thru Oct. 18. October 1973, p. 23.

October 16–December 2: *Extraordinary Realities*, Whitney Museum of American Art, New York. The exhibition traveled to Everson Museum of Art, Syracuse, NY, January 15–February 18, 1974, and to the Contemporary Arts Center, Cincinnati, Ohio, March 8–April 27, 1974. Camblin exhibited: *Drawn Dry*, Pencil and watercolor, 20 X 28, p. 62.

Catalogue: Robert Doty, *EXTRAORDINARY REALITIES* (New York: Whitney Museum of American Art, 1973), 62 (illustration of work) and 64.

November: *Hand Colored Prints*, Brooke Alexander Gallery, Inc., New York, New York. The exhibition of prints opened at Brooke Alexander Inc. in New York and then traveled. Camblin exhibited: *Round-Up: See King the Longhorn*, Etching with watercolor, 1973. 22½ X 26½ inches, 26 examples numbered A.P. # 1 through A.P. #26 on Millbourn paper.

Catalogue: Carter Ratcliff, *Hand Colored Prints*, Brooke Alexander Gallery, Inc., New York, November 1973. Noted in the catalogue for Camblin's prints: "Printer: R Camblin at B & J Holding Co., Houston, Texas." Works by 26 artists from around the country were included in the show.

December 5–January 5, 1974: *20th Century Drawings*, El Paso Museum of Art.

December 11–January 11, 1974: *Drawings*, Cusack Gallery, Houston, Texas.

December 15–January 11, 1974: *Texas Drawings*, Smither Gallery, Dallas, Texas.

Calendar Listing: "Around the State," Dallas: *Texas Drawings*, Smither Gallery, December 15, 1973–January 11, 1974. December issue, p. 33.

Undated: *Joe Tate's Back Yard*, St. Thomas Art Gallery, University of St. Thomas, Houston. Earl Staley, chairman of the art department of St. Thomas University, asked Joe Tate to create an installation for the university's art gallery.

Undated: *Faculty Exhibition*, Rice University Gallery, Sewall Hall, Rice University, Houston, Texas.

Undated: *Drawings from the Permanent Collection, Fort Worth Art Museum Drawings: An Exhibition of the Collection of the FWAM*, Fort Worth Art Museum, Fort Worth, Texas, 1973.

Brochure: *Drawings from the Permanent Collection*, Fort Worth Art Museum, Fort Worth, Texas, 1973.

Camblin became Visiting Artist at Rice University. 1973–74 was his last teaching year at Rice. Believing it was time to make his living with his art, Camblin did not apply for other teaching positions. The subject of his artwork became less fantastic than previously. He began painting landscapes almost exclusively.

The Holding Firm completed a collaborative portrait of Fannie Goldfine Benton whose daughter commissioned the artwork after Fannie's death in February 1973.

Camblin moved out of his family home to his studio at 519 Sul Ross in Houston. Together with Staley, Tate, Allan Otho Smith, Mark Batista, and other workers, Camblin began building a three-story tower in the backyard of the studio building. Staley made a Super 8 movie of the undertaking.

After the completion of their backyard tower, B E & J Holding Firm and Assoc. posted a "News Release" in local galleries and art supply stores: "THREE HOUSTON ARTISTS are opening their private studio at 519 Sul Ross for the study of Fine Art."[21] An unknown number of local art students signed up for classes. The venture closed after a year.

1974

In the early '70s, Camblin began quoting French philosopher Michel de Montaigne who was known for his common sense and for making the essay form into a literary genre. Camblin's favorite Montaigne quote was "*Qeu scais-je?*" an Old French phrase that translates to "What do I know?" The question became Camblin's motto. Camblin created his own alter-ego, Kay Sage, a name with a close pronunciation to contemporary French "*Que sais-je?*."

Camblin reread Sartre and Camus.

For balance, he read the *Essays* of Ralph Waldo Emerson whom he considered America's equivalent to Montaigne. From the *Essays* he hand-scripted, "Self Reliance," and printed and hand-colored a series of lithographs with the essay.

Camblin participated in eleven exhibitions:

January 15–February 15: *20th Century Drawings*, Amarillo Art Center, Amarillo, Texas.

February 1–March 1: *Sixteenth Annual Invitational Painting & Sculpture Exhibition*, Longview Museum, Junior Service League of Longview, Longview, Texas. Camblin exhibited: *Two Versions of the Galveston Deadfall*. Longview Museum purchased the work for their permanent collection.

February 2–March 1: *1974 Houston Area Exhibition*, Sarah Campbell Blaffer Gallery, University of Houston.

February 9–unknown: *Hand Colored Prints*, Smither Gallery, Dallas, Texas. The exhibition was circulated by Comprehensive Exhibition Services in Los Angeles to 12 museums throughout the US and Canada.

Article: "In a number of the prints in this show color is surprisingly contained by, even subservient to, line. This is particularly true of certain of the etchings (Neil Oliver, Richard Hass, Bob Camblin and Susan Hall)." Diane Kelder, "Prints: Artists' Alterations," *Art in America*, March–April, 1974, p. 97.

February 25–March 27: *20th Century Drawings*, Abilene Fine Arts Museum, Abilene, Texas.

April 7–May 7: *20th Century Drawings*, Museum of the Southwest, Midland, Texas.

May 17–June 17: *20th Century Drawings*, Wichita Falls Museum and Art Center, Wichita Falls, Texas.

May: *Drawings*, Nancy Hoffman Gallery, New York City, New York.

Catalogue: Nancy Hoffman, *Drawings* (New York: Nancy Hoffman Gallery, May 1974). Hoffman wrote for the catalogue: "Recently the artist's attitude toward drawing and the public's understanding and acceptance of drawing combined to elevate this form of expression to major work. During the 60's barriers between art forms were breaking down . . . This new commitment to drawing by artists and the receptivity to the splendors of drawing—new and old—by the public led to an explosion of activity in this area. The main focus of this exhibition is to explore drawings as a prime form of expression of the artist." Twenty-four artists were included in the exhibit. Camblin exhibited: *As Far As I Can See Fence*, watercolor and pencil on paper, 22" X 30", 1974.

July 6–31: *20th Century Drawings*, Longview Museum and Art Center, Longview, Texas.

Undated: *Gallery Artists*, Cusack Gallery, Houston, Texas.

Undated: *Nineteenth National Print Exhibition*, The Brooklyn Museum, New York, New York.

Camblin completed the *Elements* series, the first lithographs done by Little Egypt Enterprises after the print shop relocated in Houston.

Staley left the Holding Firm and moved to his own studio,[22] basically ending the Holding Firm.

1975

Delahunty Gallery in Dallas, Texas, began representing Camblin's work.

Camblin had nine shows and one commission from the Houston Grand Opera.

"On April 1, 1975, at 12:01 A.M., C.S.T., I passed through the chronological matrix of one billion four hundred fifty five million three hundred seventy six thousand seconds of Real Time . . . This stated, let me begin: For whatever it means and to the 'best of my knowledge' and with proper documentation, I, Bob Camblin, was born on August 1, 1928, to Viva Faustena Camblin nee Bilyeu and Donald Barr Camblin in Ponca City, Oklahoma, U.S.A., World, Galaxy, et.al. The rest is perfectly average." Camblin included his education experience, his working experience, and his family experience. He added: "1973–75: Working full time as an object maker, specifically in graphite and watercolor pigments as applied to 100% rag paper, although I have continued: 1. Small three dimensional objects; lectures, teaching: A. design at the Museum of Fine Arts School, Houston B. guest lecturer, University of Winnipeg, Canada 3. Mosaic murals A. Sacred Heart Byzantine Rite Church, Detroit, Michigan 4. Prints: A. collaboration with Dave Folkman of Little Egypt Enterprises in a suite of 4 prints. My work is handled by: Myself, Houston; Brooke Alexander Inc. New York, New York; Delahunty Gallery, Dallas, Texas. I am located at: 1426 West Bell, Apt. #5 Houston, Texas, 77006 U.S.A. North America; Latitude 30 degrees Longitude 95 degrees; World; Third Planet-Solar System; Galaxy, et. al. More information available on request. Love." Camblin's 1975 Resume[23]

January: The Houston Grand Opera chose Camblin to create a program cover and poster for its 1975 opera series. He was assigned *Der Rosenkavalier*. The Opera had 250 posters printed of each participating artist's cover and sold them for $25.00 each. Barbara Duff, the editor, added a photograph and brief biography of "BOB CAMBLIN, Cover Artist," and included a quote by the artist, who noted his only goal was "to make an object that, if found in the attic, wouldn't get thrown out." The inside back cover of the program had a color reproduction of Camblin's *Gully Washer* watercolor. The production was performed and the program distributed in January 1975. Program: Houston Grand Opera, *Der Rosenkavalier* 4, no. 3.

January: *Made in Houston*, Louisiana Gallery, Houston, Texas. A poster for the show listed the artists as: Huband, O'Neil, Harris, Hickman, Stevens, Shaw, Camblin, Burton, Beauboeuf, Broussard, Luna, Hedrick, FRB Rapho.

Article: Madeleine McDermott Hamm, "Fine Art Posters: A Good Look, a Reasonable Price," *The Houston Chronicle*, January 1975.

March: Camblin traveled to Honolulu, Hawaii.

April: Saigon fell to the communists, ending the Vietnam War.

Article: "His [Folkman's] first project was a 10-color (and one 11-color) plate edition of four images by artist Bob Camblin published by Bob Lowe, a Houston art publisher. It took them a year to complete 50 copies of the suite and it cost Lowe $16,500 for everything from ink to printer's time." Charlotte Moser, "Master Printmaking in Houston," *Houston Chronicle*, May 31, 1975, Section 2, p. 1.

June 1–July 20: *1975 Houston Area Exhibition*, Sarah Campbell Blaffer Gallery, University of Houston. Camblin exhibited *Air* lithograph from the *Elements* suite.

Article: "Wedged somewhere in between Houston's burgeoning new art galleries and the city's fast-spreading reputation as 'a place to watch' in the art world are some 200–300 people who spend their days stretching canvas, spilling paint on old jeans or welding strips of Corten steel into sculptures. Bob Camblin has worked with a private art dealer in New York, Brook Alexander, one of the Big Apple's most respected print publishers." Charlotte Moser, "The Art Boom," *Houston Chronicle*, July 20, 1975, p. 9.

Newsletter: "Bob Camblin: *Elements* (1974) a suite of four lithographs in color signed and numbered by the artist in an edition of 50. Each print is 22 ½ x 30 in. and was printed on Twinrocker handmade paper by David E. Folkman at Little Egypt Enterprises in Houston. The four elements—*Air, Earth, Fire, Water*—are rendered with the sensitivity of a Camblin watercolor. The suite derives from 40 plates, the first four, explains the artist, usually drawn in a sumi-ye manner, the next four in a tighter delineation of form but still in tusche, and the last two in tight lines. Each print is based on a structure of triangulation that grids the work area into quarters. The 40 plates could be used in different combinations, and artist and printer are presently compiling *Four Books*, with text, proofs, photos, and acetate overlays to clarify their experiments and show alternative directions the prints could have taken. For example, *Water*, the most beautiful *Element*, was conceived first as a night scene but with a geometric line plate buried to give more structure to an amorphous image. Through trial, the line plate emerged as an ambiguous overlay suggesting marking, perspective, even navigation. Such ambiguity pervades the suite, rife with graffiti and open to simultaneous interpretations. Color is too delicate for black and white reproduction, but *Elements* is an ambitious project clearly realized. Price: suite of four $800. Published by Robert S. Lowe, Houston." "Prints & Portfolios Published," *The Print Collector's Newsletter* 6, no. 3 (July–August 1975): 72.

September 1–30: *Works on Paper*, Brooke Alexander Inc., New York.

September 10–October 31: *The Classic Revival*, Illinois Bell, Chicago, Illinois. The exhibition traveled to Lakeview Center for the Arts, Peoria, Illinois; Quincy Art Center, Quincy, Illinois; Illinois State Museum, Springfield, Illinois; Kirkland Gallery, Millikin University, Decatur, Illinois; Mitchell Museum, Mt. Vernon, Illinois; Ella Sharp Museum, Jackson, Michigan; University Gallery, University of Minnesota, Minneapolis. Organized by Illinois Bell Telephone.

Catalogue: Robert H. Glauber, *The Classic Revival*, Illinois Bell Telephone, Lobby Gallery, Chicago, Illinois. For the Introduction, Glauber wrote about Camblin: "Surrealism has left its indelible marks on Bob Camblin."

September: *Exhibition of Former Instructors*, Ringling School of Art.

Article: "Ringling School of Art Continues to Move Toward Accreditation," *Sarasota Herald-Tribune*, September 14, 1975, p. 8E.

September 25–unknown: *Inauguration: Drawings—Dibujos*, Covo de Iong Gallery, Houston, Texas. Camblin was one of 10 artists in the gallery's opening show.

Interview: "I started showing the artists I thought were really good: Jim Love, Roy Fridge, Bob Camblin, Don Shaw, Lucas Johnson. When I closed the gallery, I think in 1970, Bob Camblin, who was one of my artists, told me that he thought that art had died and that the galleries were going to stay open—I think that was the main reason I closed the gallery—he said that the galleries that were going to stay open were going to be like tombs and that if I would watch, that the art was going to start becoming more minimal, more nonperceptive—no realism. He was really right, because the galleries that are staying open are showing very, very minimal art that I could do myself, lines, showing art by people who cannot draw. Like Salvador Dali said, he thinks we ought to get back to realism so we can find out who's got some skill." Dianne David interview by Louis J Marchiafava, Archive # 0H036, The Houston Metropolitan Research Center, Oral History Project Interviews, October 2, 1975.

Article: "She [Deborah Marie Saccomanno] also studied drawing under Lowell Collins and Houston artists Bob Camblin and Earl Staley." "Artist from Houston Sets Display Here," *The Baytown Sun*, Baytown, Texas, October 30, 1975, p. 4.

Article: ". . . Jack Boynton recalled: 'Three people got into a collaborative thing in 1973. Bob Camblin, Earl Staley and Joe Tate got involved in a joint effort, doing collaborative drawings where they worked on them either independently or simultaneously. Also Joe did a backyard show. It was a lot of dirt. It was an earthwork in a sort of sense. He did a backyard in a gallery. There were plants, clothes lines. He did a lot of wood things. The clothes pole worked on that and then there was a big painting all three worked on, a painting of the backyard. They started with a literal backyard. The were trying to get to different levels of reality. I worked on a collaborative piece with Camblin that I showed in January at the DuBose Gallery. We were doing 'find the image' type of things. Like Max Ernst. The general category I think would be surreal—looking for different levels of reality. If it's 'find the image,' everybody finds what their imagination sees so they come out different. We did a collaborative piece where I did two identical watercolors on a page and he [Camblin] did two identical watercolors on the page. Both of us did the painting first, then the drawing. Inasmuch as we sort of work similarly, we decided to do the same thing to see what the difference was. Any information exchange goes on during the process where each one says what they see or puts down what they see. It's a a springboard in a sense—not only do you always have all your own options but you see all their options, too. You understand what they're seeing in the thing so it gives you another facet. It enlarges your perceptions so you grow. It broadens your vision by whatever is exchanged. With these people there was a certain amount of competition involved. We had established ground rules and proceeded from them. Anyone could draw over anyone's work, erase it or whatever. Everyone worked on a corner at a time. Then every thirty minutes, we'd turn the drawing around by 90 degrees. You had to make something really nice to be sure it stayed because the next time it came around, it might be gone or entirely different. If you don't have any preconceptions about what this thing is supposed to be and you take your ego out, it works. In this case, it stayed competitive and it turned out to be a somewhat interesting drawing visually but a very interesting experience . . . Then the school [St. Thomas University] did a camp-out project with a lot of students and faculty." Mary Fuller, "Marcel Duchamp Lives: One View of the Texas Art World," *Currant*, October–November 1975, p. 20.

Fall: Camblin accepted an offer to teach a semester at Louisiana State University as Visiting Artist. He temporarily moved to Baton Rouge. He began engaging his students with personas he developed: Red Stick the Pirate (obviously the literal translation of Baton Rouge), Robin Goodfellow, the Professor. He knew of personas created by Marcel Duchamp.

December 2–30: *Objects from the Life of Bob Camblin*, Union Art Gallery, Louisiana State University, Baton Rouge. Dressed in cowboy boots, a black hat, and sunglasses, Camblin attended the opening as Red Stick the Pirate. The invitation to the exhibit had a red flying W in the shape of a skull with two triangular eye sockets. A cross was drawn underneath the red skull, Red Stick's flag. The address side of the postcard invitation had printed: "The Flag and Play were designed by Kay Sage. It was performed in Baton Rouge, Louisiana in the Fall of 1975. Red Stick, the Professor, and Robin Goodfellow were all played by the vagabond Teacher, Bob Camblin of Houston, Texas." Camblin also wrote the exhibition information.

Article: "Visiting Artist—On display in the Union art gallery are the paintings of visiting artist Bob Camblin. Amazingly enough, Camblin has extremely weak eyesight and sports a white cane and shades to prove it." Under the printed photograph, Camblin circled his name and added "printer's error. This is Robin Goodfellow." "Visiting Artist," *LSU Daily Reveille*, December 2, 1975.

December: *Holiday Show*, Covo de Iongh Gallery, Houston, Texas.

Advertisement: *Texas Monthly*, List of artists exhibiting at Covo de Iongh Gallery, Houston, beginning in January 1976, December issue 1975, p. 108.

Undated: *Gallery Artists*, Delahunty Gallery, Dallas, Texas.

By the end of the year, Camblin decided it was time for him to go back to Venice, Italy, marking twenty years since his Fulbright. Hoping to find fresh inspiration in Italy, he began making plans to make his Venice venture happen.

1976

Camblin exhibited in twelve shows.

January 3–31: *Made in Houston*, Louisiana Gallery, Houston, Texas. Nine Houston artists, including Bob Camblin, John O'Neil, Pat Colville, Earl Staley, James Boynton, Hannah Stewart, Ben Woitena, Joel McGlasson, and Latane Temple.

Article: "Take for instance Bob Camblin's drawings, as bizarre as ever! In soft tones he combines real and not-so-real to create demanding and somewhat esoteric works." Susan L. Butler, "Art Circles," *Houston Chronicle*, January 1976.

January: *Gallery Artists*, Covo de Iongh, Houston, Texas.

Article: "Johnson gathers such names as Jose Luis Cuevas, Rufino Tomayo, Pedro Friedeberg, along with Houston's Bob Camblin and Lucas Johnson," "The January Gallery Scene," *Subject: Fine Art*, January 1976, p. 115.

March 7–18: *Bob Camblin: Watercolors and Prints*, Baker University, Baldwin City, Kansas.

Article: "Sunday, March 7, featured in the library art exhibits will be the works of Texas artist Bob Camblin and local artist Evonne English . . . Camblin, a former Kansas City area artist, and former student of Tom Russell, Baker professor, will be showing water color works and prints . . . Monday March 8 and Tuesday March 9, Camblin will hold workshops for interested persons." "For Two Weeks Baker Hosts Artists," *The Baker Orange*, March 5, 1976.

March 14–April 25: *Contemporary Images in Watercolor*, Akron Art Institute, Akron, Ohio. Watercolor lent by Brooke Alexander Inc. Exhibited *Trot Line Forgery*.

March 29–August 8: *Contemporary Images in Watercolor*, Indianapolis Institute of Art, Indianapolis, Indiana.

April 12: Bonnie and Camblin signed divorce documents.

April: *Origin of the Birds: Bob Camblin and Bill Steffy*, Covo de Iongh Gallery, Houston, Texas.

Article: "Camblin is an exquisite watercolorist, and his infinite skill at drawing takes him to the look of Victorian aquatint etchings. The brown colors, light tiney lines and images of boats, flowers, clouds, birds and possibly people keep disappearing into rocks and leaves, as fine as the skeleton of a dried leaf. His current work is reminiscent of Beatrix Potter drawings, and touches of Arthur Rackham. Though the "Origin of the Birds" is the loose theme of this two-man show, you have to look hard for the bird or the origin in Camblin's leafy world." Mimi Crossley, "Art: Gallery Roundup, Bob Camblin and Bill Steffy at Covo de Iongh," *The Houston Post*, April 15, 1976, p. 6B.

Article: Charlotte Moser, "Between Fantasy and Surrealism," *Art News*, April 1976, p. 66.

Article: "Houston artist Bob Camblin has installed his recent ink and watercolor drawings at Covo de Iongh Gallery . . . All the drawings are small in scale and are filled with tiny intricately-drawn details. Words are also used either in the drawing or as involved poetic titles explaining the drawings. As complicated as the ideas of the drawings are, there is also an open innocence about their ideas . . . Camblin is involved with natural phenomena as the source of a kind of earthy, mystical wisdom . . . The artwork deals almost exclusively with landscape . . . Recognized over the years got his delicately detailed phantasmagoric drawings, Camblin has taken a moodier, more medieval approach in his new drawings. Drawn while looking through a large magnifying glass, they are filled with surprising details and convoluted forms that change with each glance like figures formed by a puffy white cloud on a windy day. The most obvious change in Camblin's new drawings is his color, now deep browns, blacks and greens instead of the watery pastels of the past. These dramatic colors make the drawings more powerful, more defined and aggressive, and more menacing than the early works. Based on an idea about the origin of birds, the drawings are highlighted by a starkly un-Camblinesque 'Origin of the Birds' of a black, ink pond in a whimsical landscape: a glowing earthly still life of a fish, frog, rat and bird; and a drawing called 'They Only Mate This Way Once': framed in a drawn proscenium-like curtain. There is an unmistakable sense of presence in these drawings that approaches a viscious psychology more than the fragile, almost contrived drawings of the past." Charlotte Moser, "Folk Tales and Totems: Mythology Is Theme of 3 Art Shows," *The Houston Chronicle*, April 17, 1976, p. 6.

June 6–October 31: *Permanent Collection: A 75th Anniversary Retrospective*, Modern Art Museum of Fort Worth, Texas.

June: Camblin asked Brooke Alexander Inc. to return all his unsold work. He said he believed he and the New York dealer were "not on the same page." Alexander responded graciously and returned Camblin's art.[24]

July: Camblin was engrossed in the United States Bicentennial ceremonies. He drew the ships in his sketchbooks while he watched TV coverage.

July 7: *The Box Show*, Covo de Iongh Gallery, Houston, Texas.

Article: A photograph of Camblin's watercolor, placed inside a box by Dave Folkman, illustrated the article on artists and boxes. Charlotte Moser, "Box Is Both Form, Content of Developing Art," *Houston Chronicle*, July 7, 1976.

Article: "In Houston Bob Camblin and Jack Boynton are involved with very refined Surrealist-type drawing: Camblin, in the Wileyesque tradition of landscapes teeming with dots, dashes, words and animals." Roberta Smith, "Twelve Days of Texas," *Art in America*, July/August 1976, p. 46.

To fund his journey to Venice, Camblin offered "subscriptions" for future art created in Italy. He sold twenty subscriptions with help from Betty Moody, owner of Moody Gallery. He began using more personas: Mr. Peanut, Santa Claus/Cindy Claus, Anonymous Box Company, Anonymous Bosh (after Bosch) Company. He noted that the "c" in Bosch was intentionally omitted because his Camblin presence represented the missing "c."

Fall: Bonnie married Bruno Leon.

August: Camblin journeyed to Venice for five months. He recorded in a sketchbook: "Every 10 years the celebration of the *Feste del Oseo del Vero* takes place. Glass birds of various designs are launched from the flat top of the campanile in Campo Santa Margarita. The success of this 'miracle' vouchsafes another 10 years of prosperity for the inhabitants of *Sestiere Dorso Duro*. It is carried out usually during the first week of November at night during the time of the Full Moon. The small lights shining in the crystal birds like so many floating Xmas ornaments are a sight to behold. Although at the request of the residents and since it is only once every 10 years, little official attention is paid to this centuries old custom." Writing about Venice in a sketchbook he observed, "Sort of a spatial Venturi effect. The buildings funnel the action although the buildings have very busy textures, decoration, etc. For me they are the props for the intense drama above—below and through. Most of the viewers forget they are part of this theater. The paintings are expressionistic in subject, but impressionistic in color and composition. The camera has fixed things in our perception. Venice is *scene* instead of acted . . . and yet we all participate in it even if the individual brain is acting out other dramas. For me to paint it now, it must have some of all I 'experience' and this living theater is it—not a building, a scene, a portrait but the controlled chaos of nature flowing through the past and present of Venice water, earthquakes, sinking, industry, etc. and yet reflecting beauty even in old age." Camblin goes on to note, "In Venice nothing goes to one vanishing point. This is not Renaissance Italy. It wanders, it breaks, it changes a straight line; an unbroken line is unseen and unheard of here."

October 14, 1976: Camblin: "Picasso opened a door and Duchamp stood in it—The rest of us have to crawl through the window and wait."

October 1–November 14: *Contemporary Images in Watercolor*, Memorial Art Gallery, University of Rochester, New York.

October: While living in Venice, Camblin visited London for a week.

November 10: *Seven American Artists*, Gulf Street, Kuwait City, Kuwait. An exhibition of Houston artists. Military officers closed the show without explanation.

December: Camblin returned to Houston.

Undated: *Bob Camblin*, Louisiana State University, Baton Rouge, Louisiana.

Undated: *Bob Camblin*, Louisiana Gallery, Houston, Texas.

During the year, he signed his letters and artwork with: "bob," "anonymous bosh," "Robin Goodfellow," "Kay Sage," "Anonymous Box Co."

1977

Moody Gallery began representing Camblin. Betty Moody, the gallerist, and Camblin began plans for an end of year solo exhibition.

During the year, Camblin exhibited in seven shows.

May: Camblin received a Kuwaiti commission for a large oil painting.

June 26–unknown: *Little Egypt Enterprises: 13 Artists*, Moody Gallery, Houston, Texas.

Article: "While Bob Camblin was working out four prints—with 10 plates used for each—Folkman moved his press over to Camblin's studio; through various phases, the Camblin prints took over a year to produce." Mimi Crossley, "Little Egypt Rolls On," *Houston Post*, June 26, 1977.

August 9–30: *Joe Atteberry, Bob Camblin, and Bill Steffy*, Moody Gallery, Houston.

Article: Charlotte Moser, "Camblin's New Work Sparks Moody Show," *Houston Chronicle*, August 19, 1977.

Texas Monthly, "Around the State," Houston: Moody Gallery: Bob Camblin and other artists, thru Aug., p. 48.

September: Camblin's resume lists him teaching a class at the University of Houston, Texas. The university's art department is unable to confirm.

Camblin traveled to San Jose, California, and visited Joe Tate.

Article: ". . . 30 artists from this area will have one-man shows in Houston's top 10 galleries. Among those to look for will be Bob Camblin (Moody Gallery in November)." Charlotte Moser, "Gallery Prospects Better," *Houston Chronicle*, September 11, 1977, p. 23.

September: *Houston Area Exhibition*, Sarah Campbell Blaffer Gallery, University of Houston, Houston.

September: *Important American and European Printmakers*, Editions Gallery, Inc., Houston.

October: Camblin entered into a Trade Agreement with McFaddin & Kendrick, Inc. He traded a watercolor *Venice*, 1977, for $1000.00 worth of meals at McFaddin & Kendrick's private club, Ciao.[25]

November 12–December 3: *'N Compleat Workes: Bob Bilyeu Camblin in Collaboration with the Anonymous Box Company*, Moody Gallery, Houston, Texas. Camblin designed three different invitations, each with a unique postcard of his creation. All three versions were printed as announcements for the show along with a separate, larger fold-down color invitation. The exhibition included recent watercolors and drawings. Camblin attended the opening as Mr. Peanut, and he stayed in character the entire evening, his Mr. Peanut costume by his side.

Article: Patricia Johnson, "Camblin Paintings Merge Magic and Metaphysics," *Houston Chronicle*, November 18, 1977, p. 24.

Article: "For several years, Bob Camblin has worked over his lush, incredibly rich watercolors and drawings, done with the aid of a magnifying glass—so small and detailed were the puzzle pieces he created with multiple images everywhere. After travels in Italy and California, Camblin returned to Houston and decided to paint very large works on canvas. From the intricately wrought, layered images with ghost writing he is known for, Camblin turned Turner and maybe Cezanne and a little Monet, too. Recapitulating the Impressionists, Camblin splashes bright color and light on big canvas. The result looks experimental, always interesting, but transitional with more promise for what is to come out of all this. Still present are the wonderful Camblin stories hinted at: half hidden animals, secret places, strange vegetation, travels to magical lands (as in 'Going to California'), clues left behind in the form of postcards tacked to the picture plane, and everyday references to painting in Earl Staley's backyard. The Impressionists loved gardens. Above all, Camblin has painted a magic garden scene for many years. Though he manages to transfer and keep his own stroke on the big works, the canvases suffer from a lack of sureness about what happens on a large scale: the potentials for more illusion, flatness and how white space can just get away from you and take over. If Camblin has taken this route to loosen up, he must be happy, for they are big, loose, vibrant works. Lord knows what's next but it's going to be fun to find out." Mimi Crossley, "Gallery Roundup—Bob Camblin: Paintings and Watercolors," *Houston Post*, November 25, 1977, p. 17AA.

Texas Monthly, "Around the State," Houston: Moody Gallery, recent watercolors and paintings by Bob Camblin, Nov. 12 to Dec. 3, p. 78.

Undated: *Moody Gallery Artists*, Waco Art Center, Waco, Texas.

Undated: *The Collection of the Junior Service League of Longview*, The Longview Museum and Art Center, Longview, Texas. Camblin exhibited *Two Versions of the Galveston Deadfall.* watercolor on illustration board, 25 X 16 in., 1974. Purchase 1974.

Catalogue: *The Collection of the Junior Service League of Longview* (Longview, TX: The Longview Museum and Art Center, 1977), pp. 32 & 36. Camblin is the only artist with no biographical information in the catalogue.

Undated Benefit: Channel 8 TV Auction Round-Up, 1977. Bob Camblin donated an offset lithograph.

Camblin changed the signature of Red Stick from a skull and cross bones to two circles (eye sockets), under which are four short vertical lines (teeth).

During the year, Camblin signed his work: "anonymous box," "K S," "Robin Goodfellow," "Old Paint," or used the flag of Red Stick, a red skull with either a red cross beneath it or with four vertical lines for teeth.

Camblin continued to work with Little Egypt Enterprises. He completed *Glass Bird Cage*, a lithograph and silkscreen combination and *Summer*, a lithograph and silkscreen.

The Holding Firm (Camblin, Staley, and Tate) collaborated on a series of six lithographs of six phantasmagorical animal prints, titled *Bestiary*, at Little Egypt Enterprises. The prints included a vulture, an alligator, a walrus, an anteater, a bat, and a fanged dog-like creature with a scorpion tail. Nearly all available space within the outlines of each creature is filled in by the artists' intricate graphics, the style similar to that of the earlier "Birth of Venus" flyer.

1978

Camblin participated in four exhibitions and two benefit auctions.

January: Camblin began work on the Kuwait commission. He was aware of the historical depiction of skulls in art. Besides representing death and mortality, he knew the apotropaic properties of skulls. Like Picasso, Camblin kept a skull in his studio. He wrote in a 1978 sketchbook for the Kuwaiti commission that he chose a memento-mori skull composition, a composition employed by Velasquez and Picasso.

For the commission, he began use of a dot and dash painting technique.

In a sketchbook for the Kuwait commission Camblin wrote: (Each "\" marks a new page in his journal.)"

"Al-Naqeeb Family Portrait, 1978 ABC . . . Variation on Las Meninas as/ A painting for the Royal family Al-Naqeeb of A Kuwait B London C Salt Lake City\ (a drawing with a skull as the main element of the composition) Memento Mori after Velazquez and Picasso et al\ The Skull behind all things (even our children have one) and yet beyond the mirrors of every imaginable KIND the man stands in the DOOR\ with his BACK to the Light and Reflects on it . . . Flickering brush eye and MIND and in Time\ We stand in this/that ROOM and the Difference disappears and we SEE Velazquez, Picasso and ME2\ watching the YEARS ROLL BY and WE are in [a] ROOM using the SW wall to stretch Las Meninas again\ and let that room blend into those 3 things Never forgetting that this will include the 4thing That this is to be for the Royal family\ Al-Naqeeb with photos, history, Arabic . . . This homage to ART/FAMILY/HISTORY will be abstracted and distilled and along with the BOOK will be buried in KUWAIT the xcess will be my homage A Velazquez/Picasso and [the patron can] add continually to the piece that\ is a collaboration with [the patron]. My paintings will even be lighter in value than either Velazquez or Picasso\ A Reversal of all the Values creating a LIGHT painting with a light man standing in front of a BLACK HOLE and the mirrors\ are always the same COLORless showing a little less (each time) ('Where does that little bit go?') anon—than expected\ This painting—out of the Desert Rose came this idea—MOR les and the people I know and the ones I've only heard about\ Photos of the house, Arabian Nights and the stories she tells\ and weaving these KUWAITing Dreams I can paint as if I was already hanging in the living room seeing this DREAM of coming TRUE, Best

Wishes, senza dubbio\ and I the painter living that dream through [the patron's] eyes/voice stand in the Mediterranean sun and laugh with Earl N Picasso Velazquez N Silverman aMore serious PAIR\ and on and on the COURT PAINTER immortalizes the FAMILY and HIMSELF This painting is 4ALL\ Patrons N Artists sharing SOME TIME together even if they\ NEVER MEET in This/ That TIME SPACE called NOW."[26]

May: Camblin traveled to Claremont, California, to see artist friend Gerald Purdy.

May: *The Art of Texas*, The Renaissance Society, University of Chicago, Chicago, Illinois, 1978. Fifteen artists from Texas exhibited work in the show.

Article: "There are realists, surrealist, abstract expressionists, conscious primitives and unconscious geniuses among the artists. The occasional appearance of a mountain, sagebrush, rodeo rider, or piney wood recall the region, but this Texan art is art first and Texan thereafter." Abbe Martin, "Review," *The Chicago Reader*, May 1978.

July: Feeling discontented in Houston, Camblin traveled to Kalamazoo, Michigan. Sojourns brought Camblin some respite from his depression.

July 15–August 5: *Prints & Posters by Bob Camblin & Other Artists, with Little Egypt Enterprises*, Moody Gallery, Houston, Texas.

Texas Monthly, "Around the State," Houston: Moody Gallery, Prints & Posters, in conjunction with Little Egypt Enterprises. Thru Aug. 5, p. 51.

August: Camblin moved to Mexico and spent two months at the Casa Marcum in Oaxaca. In a letter to M.J. he wrote, "I feel that my plans are to return to Houston sometime in November—a longer stay here without a car is difficult. This voluntary X-isle has worked admirably. I have found it possible to 'go on living' with no one around, but it is not my true nature." Camblin expected visitors to come to Mexico to lure him back to Houston. No visitors materialized. He experienced Mexico's Day of the Dead and was fascinated with the sugar skulls that were used during the celebration. He purchased a boxful to take with him when he returned to Houston. Camblin began drawings and watercolors of skulls. During the year he signed work: "Mr. Peanut," "K S," "anonymous box co.," "anonymous," "anon," "Robin Goodfellow," "Red Stick," "camblin."

Benefit auction: "Fiesta de las Flores," Benefiting The Art Center, Waco Texas, September 9, 1978. Camblin donated the lithograph *Earth* from the *Elements* series.

September 12–October 29: *Watercolors and Lithographs by Bob Camblin*, Projects Gallery, Art Museum of South Texas, Corpus Christi. Exhibited *Elements* suite of 4, *Glass Bird Cage, Four Seasons* suite of 4, *Texas Dandelion, Rainbow Pie, Waterhole, Untitled, It's All Natural Red Stick, Everyone Is in The Lone Star State, Post Card* series.

Texas Monthly, "Around the State," Corpus Christi, Art Museum of South Texas, Projects Gallery: Watercolors and Lithographs by Bob Camblin thru Oct., p. 24.

September 17–October 20: *Spirit of Texas*, John Michael Kohler Arts Center, Sheboygan, Wisconsin. Exhibited *Baton Rouge Log* or *The Red Stick Log*.

Moody Gallery gave The Brooklyn Museum Camblin's suite of four, *Elements*.

Benefit Auction: *Houston Symphony Marathon II Art Sale*, Saks Fifth Avenues Center of Fashion, Houston, Texas: Over 300 works from 20 galleries, November 8–9, 1978.

Article: Betty Ewing, "Sold and on Hold: A $20,000 Concert," *Houston Chronicle*, November 1978.

Texas Monthly, "Around the State," Houston Symphony Marathon, November 1978, p. 99.

In Houston Camblin continued working with Little Egypt Enterprises. He completed: *Winter*, a lithograph and silkscreen combination, and *Dandylion State 1*, a colored etching.

1979

Camblin was included in seven exhibitions.

January: Camblin worked on his Kuwaiti commission and prepared for a solo show, *Vanitas*, at Moody Gallery. Besides a large oil painting and several watercolors, he built three skull altars: One had attached black blinds hanging behind and below the wooden box frame; one employed a draped background and drawers filled with relics, milagros, and personal items; the other was a free-standing sculpture. He used the same skull print as a focus in all three works.

February 16–April 15: *Fire! An Exhibition of 100 Texas Artists*, Contemporary Arts Museum, Houston, Texas.

Catalogue: *Fire! An Exhibition of 100 Texas Artists*. Contemporary Arts Museum, Houston, Texas, p. 24. For the artist's statement in the catalogue, Camblin writes: "To: James Surls, From: Bob Camblin, from the center of the anonyousboxco [draws symbol for 'It's All Art'] as far as I can si! ITSPEAKS4ITSELF _____but we say, Thanks Amigos and let me know if you need any help . . ."

March 10–29: *Twenty-First Annual Invitational Operation Update—1979*, Longview Museum and Arts Center, Longview, Texas. Exhibited *Post Card Series*.

March: *Doors: Houston Artists*, *The Houston Festival*, The Alley Theatre, Houston, Texas. No specific dates given.

Catalogue: Trudy Sween, *Doors: Houston Artists, The Houston Festival*, The Alley Theatre, Houston, Texas, 1979, pp. 13–14.

Article: "Doors Open Aesthetic Vistas at the Alley." "One of the best pure artworks in the show, Bob Camblin's punctured and hooked door is braced by ropes and huge stones." *Houston Chronicle*, March 18, 1979, p. 17.

April 1–21: *Vanitas: Works of Bob Bilyeu Camblin and anonymous box co.*, Moody Gallery, Houston, Texas.

Article: "All appears to be vanity in Bob Camblin's latest spring show of watercolors and assemblages. But don't be fooled, even though Camblin would love to have it so. Through series of veil-like drawings and washes, Camblin paints illusionary scenes of the human comedy, with skulls ominously winking out of the picture. They are intricate, lacy works with great skill and message. In typical Camblin style, each picture is filled with dozens of emerging and disappearing shapes and letters in a mysterious soup of color and form. They are puzzle pictures, with a not-so-hidden meaning." Mimi Crossley, Review, "Bob Camblin: *Vanitas*, Moody Gallery," *The Houston Post*, April 6, 1979.

Article: "Mexican folk art with its heavy flavor of ethnic anthropology is inspiring a growing number of Houston artists. Bob Camblin, whose new paintings and sculptures revolve around the folk festival, The Day of the Dead in Oaxaca, Mexico, is the latest. With this new work now showing at Moody Gallery, Camblin has reached another pinnacle in his progression from the eccentric Durer-like fantasy drawings for which he was first known in Houston. His show a year ago reflected his recent travels in Venice, Italy and these new Mexican-inspired pieces represent an amalgam of cultural experiences, despite their specific subject matter. The central image in these works is the skull, the primary symbol in Day of the Dead ceremonies. A day of celebrating the excesses of life in anticipation of death, the festival features a candy skull made from hard sugar and festooned with bright colored icing. In keeping with the idea, Camblin has executed his mysterious, impressionistic skull paintings with pastel frills and exorbitant detail. The largest skull painting in the show is called *Vanitas*, suggesting personal excesses and most of the works are decorated with ornate Spanish-inspired frames. The link between Camblin's original European inspiration and his current Mexican one is the 17th-century Spanish painting by Diego Velasquez called *Las Meninas*. Washed in mysterious sepia veils, sections of this famous painting—which once served as inspiration for Picasso—incorporate the bell-shaped skirts of the painting's female subjects with the spectre of a Mexican skull. Occassionally, Camblin's shimmering painting technique suggests the sparkling romantic waterways of Venice. Camlin has brought all these themes together with remarkable authenticity. In three reliquary sculptures, Camblin has re-created folk environments but, in general, he has adaptd his folk images to a personal style that has enriched with time. Drawn curtains painted onto the canvases convey theatrical dreaminess, sepia tones suggest antiquity and a magical watercolor technique reflects matchless skill. Camblin's orchestration of myth and visuals has a unique poignancy." Charlotte Moser, "Art Celebrated Mexican 'Day of the Dead' Festival," *Houston Chronicle*, April 7, 1979, Sec. 3, p. 9.

Texas Monthly, "Around the State," Houston, Moody Gallery, Vanitas, paintings, drawings and mixed media by Bob Camblin thru April 21, April 1979, p. 58.

Article: "Texas, like other places, has its own perspective and reference ponts. The east coast looks to Euroope, the west coast to the orient, and Texasm affectionately called the third coast, to Mexico. Bob Camblin, like fellow Houstonite Earl Staley, was drawn to Mexico. He returned after a two-month stay near Oaxaca to create a new group of works, on view through April at the Moody Gallery, which integrate his experiences there with his previous pictorial interests. Skulls and other images evocative of the Mexican Day of the Dead celebration appear in various contexts throughout the show, most prominently in the large *Vanitas* painting and repeated in lithographs placed within collaborative assemblage-altars. The scultures, created with David Folkman and a group called the Anonymous Box Co., are wall mounted or freestanding. Made with old wood units like drawers, frames and sills, they contain, in addition to space for Camblin's skull lithograph, shelves and niches for characteristic Mexican artifacts, bones, faded, drying flowers and votive candles. In the drawer of one assemblage Folkman has filled two tiers of compartments with neat assortments of pottery shards, old type, bullets, small skulls, beads, *milagros* and other objects. The arrangement could stand alone as a fascinating work. One of Camblin's watercolors of the Mexican landscape on display in the middle room of the gallery shows a view of the Oaxaca environs, bordered on one side by a window and on the other by a convenient vertical tree trunk. This irregular frame within a frame, illusion within illusion, is the format of many—and the best—of his drawings and watercolors on display. Instead of windows, the overall images are softly draping curtains bearing scenes that resemble stage sets. In the *Las Meninas Series*, which nods to Velasquez, formally attired women are posed in a quasi-landscape space also inhabited by sinister-looking figures, hazily discernible forms or, in one work, the figure of an artist. Here and in other pieces Camblin interweaves drawing and watercolor into rich, illusionistically deep surfaces that hint at presences beyond definite perception. On some works he has printed, in William Wiley fashion, one word over another to create a new configuration with its own meaning. One of the strongest conjunctions of surface treatment, subject choice and illusion occurs in the drawing of a skull that is almost camouflaged within the face of a cliff, offering ominous entry to a cave that is the initial focus of interest. Camblin's combinations and treatment of subject sometimes belie his sensitive draftsmanship. His skill can be confirmed, if need be, by looking at a self-portrait which stares out from a matrix of other images in a drawing hanging in Betty Moody's office." Judith Dunham, "Texas Overview," *Artweek* 10, no. 16 (April 21, 1979): 4.

November 18–January 6, 1980: *David McManaway Works—Twenty Years*, University Gallery, Meadows School of the Arts, Southern Methodist University Dallas. The exhibition included collaborative works of McManaway and Camblin.

Catalogue: Anne Livet, *David McManaway Works—Twenty Years*, University Gallery, Meadows School of the Arts, Southern Methodist University Dallas, 1979.

Undated: *Five Artists from Texas*, George Belcher Gallery, San Francisco, California.

Undated: *Works on Paper*, Nave Museum, Victoria Regional Museum Association, Victoria, Texas.

Camblin collaborated again with Little Egypt Enterprises. They created: *Midsummer Night's Dream*, first making the paper and then creating the lithograph. Working with memento mori he created *Skull*, a colored lithograph, three of which he used to make reliquaries.

Camblin was one of twelve artists who created etchings with Undermain Studio.

The Smithsonian Institution, Archives of American Art, collected 440 Slides of Bob Camblin and his work, New York, New York.

1980

Camblin participated in five shows. He and Nancy Giordano-Echegoyen began collaborating on a series, *Touching Palms*. One painting would be exhibited in the *Collaborators: Artists Working Together in Houston* exhibition in 1986.

Article: Sandra Curtis, "Texas Project," *Archives of American Art Journal*, Smithsonian Institution, January 20, 1980, p. 31. The report outlines the contents of the documents found in the Bob Camblin donation.

January–February: *Moody Gallery Artists*, Moody Gallery, Houston, Texas.

Texas Monthly, "Around the State," Moody Gallery, Moody Gallery Artists, Houston, Texas. Thru Feb. 1980.

September 12–October 19: *The Grand Beehive Exhibition*, Salt Lake Art Center, Salt Lake City, Utah. Camblin participated in an assemblage of original postcards in the form of a beehive.

October: Camblin traveled to Kinsdale, Ireland. He returned to Texas over four months later. Painted *Adieu Vat Boat* and Carmelite Monastery (in collaboration with Nancy Giordano-Echegoyen).

Article: Charlotte Moser, "Playing Cowboys and Artists in Houston," *Art News*, December 1980, pp. 124–128.

Undated: *Contemporary Drawings and Watercolors*, Memorial Art Gallery, University of Rochester, Rochester, New York; Akron Art Institute, Akron, Ohio; and Indianapolis Institute of Art, Indianapolis, Indiana.

Undated: *Inside Texas Borders*, Corpus Christi State University, Corpus Christi, Texas.

Undated: *Recent Works by Artists of the Southwest*, Gensler and Associates/Architects, Houston, Texas, 1980. The exhibition was organized by Gensler architects and included art by Bob Camblin. The show hung in the Transco Tower lobby, main floor.

Working with Penny Cerling at Little Egypt Enterprises, Camblin completed 12 drypoint "postcards" for the six-page interior of *Scrapbook*, black paper 10.5" X 15". The cover page, over which is a clear acetate cover, is a lithograph with "Scrapbook" handwritten.

Publication: Robert S. Olpin, *Dictionary of Utah Art* (Salt Lake Art Center, 1980), 30. The publication entry: "Camblin, Robert, was a faculty member of the Department of Art, University of Utah, from 1965 to 1967. By the mid-60s, a flood of non-traditional work in prints and painting beginning in Utah, at the University of Utah the works of Bob Camblin (B.F.A., M.F.A., 1954, '55, Kansas City Art Institute) and others registered a recent and fascinating set of local thrusts in various stylistic and technical directions."

1981

Camblin exhibited in four shows.

January: Camblin returned to Houston from Ireland.

March 5–April 3: *Collection '81—The Road Show*, 2 Houston Center, Assistance League of Houston, Houston, Texas.

Catalogue: *Collection '81—The Road Show*, 2 Houston Center, Assistance League of Houston, Houston, Texas.

May: Camblin visited Kinsale, Ireland, for the month. He started signing "anonymous artists" or "artists anonymous" to his art.

August: Camblin traveled to San Jose, California, to spend time with Joe Tate at The Studio, 507 South Bascom, San Jose, California. Camblin painted a large oil canvas of the Bascom studio.

August 28–September 30: *Moody Gallery, Houston, Visits Sant Fe*, Linda Durham Gallery, Santa Fe, New Mexico.

Article: "Moody [brought] the work of 12 Moody Gallery artists to Santa Fe: . . . Bob Camblin, whose oils and drawings of the Irish landscape are rich in hidden imagery . . ." David L. Bell, "Houston Show Visits Santa Fe Gallery," *Albuquerque Journal*, August 30, 1981, p. 46.

October: Camblin made sojourns to New Mexico, Arizona, and Utah.

November: *The Image of the House in Contemporary Art*, Lawndale Annex of the University of Houston, Texas.

Article: Patricia C. Johnson, "The Image of the House Through Artists' Eyes," *Houston Chronicle*, November 15, 1981, pp. 18–27; 47–49.

Undated: *Little Egypt Waterworkshop*, Roberto Molina Gallery, Houston, Texas, 1981.

Publication: *1981 Houston Arts Calendar* (Houston: Wordworks, Inc, 1981), 7–8. Camblin's art was *St. Bambola*, watercolor, 30" X 22". The 1971 work (the published title includes a copyright mark dated 1980) was printed on the page opposite the third calendar page of January (January 12–18). In the artist's biographical information, Camblin noted his university teaching positions, including the University of Houston. He concluded with, "His art is included in the collections of the Fort Worth Art Museum, the Fogg Museum of Harvard University, the Yale Museum, and the Brooklyn Museum."

1982

Camblin moved to Galveston from February to November. He exhibited in five shows.

April: *Hearts and Flowers*, The Waco Art Center, Waco, Texas. The exhibition celebrated the Tenth Anniversary of the Art Center. The artwork chosen was created by nearly 100 artists who had shown work at the Art Center during the previous decade, including Bob Camblin, Marc Chagall, David Hockney, and Andy Warhol.

Article: "The Art Center Tenth Anniversary Celebration," *The Waco Citizen*, Waco, Texas, Friday, April 16, 1982, p. 6.

June 3–28: *Art From Houston in Norway: 1982*, Stavanger Kunstforening, Stavanger, Norway. The exhibition featured Houston artists for the Houston-Stavanger Sister City Society's Festival celebration in Norway. Bob Bilyeu Camblin exhibited: *Kings X*, 1975. Watercolor on Paper, 23" X 29", Courtesy: Moody Gallery, Houston.

Catalogue: *Art From Houston in Norway: 1982*, Stavanger Kunstforening, Stavanger, Norway., pp. 20–21. In his Introduction, David Brauer wrote: "Our responsibility was to produce the best, most representative selection of contemporary art in Houston. This, to the best of our abilities, we have done, and we are honoured to be instrumental in the presentation, for the first time in Europe, of the art of our city to our sister city of Stavanger."

September 3–October 17: *Contemporary Landscapes*, Art Museum of South Texas, Corpus Christi. Camblin exhibited *507 Bascom—The Studio*, 1981, oil on canvas, 73 X 65 inches; *Joe's Backyard*, 1981, oil on canvas, 65 X 73; *Houston, Texas*, 1982, oil on canvas, 48 X 73.

"If the concept for this exhibition includes a devil's advocate then that artist would be Bob Camblin. Most recently living and working in Galveston, Texas, Camblin's career includes paintings and watercolors executed in tight versus loose, and narrative versus non-narrative styles. I doubt that he would consider himself a landscape painter in the traditional sense. Of the three paintings included in this exhibition, two were done in San Jose, California, at the home of his friend, the painter

Joe Tate. In both 'Joe's Backyard' and '507 Bascom—The Studio' Camblin depicts the home's front and backyard with lush color and paint application. The yard has a domesticated wildness about it, seemingly not so much for lack of care as for a preference for the untamed. A narrative quality creeps in as titles are written across the base of the paintings. At nearly dead center of '507 Bascom—The Studio' Camblin has collaged a post card onto the surface of the panting only to paint over it. Energy and a robust nature breathe through these works. They are in a true sense collaborative in that Camblin asked Joe Tate to also contribute to them. Without knowing Bob Camblin we can still imagine him handing a loaded brush to his friend and saying something like 'Here, Joe, you do something to it.'" Catalogue: Jim Edwards, *Contemporary Landscapes* (Corpus Christi, TX: Art Museum of South Texas, 1982), 4, 10, 11.

Article: Photograph of Camblin and sketchbook page illustrated in "Treasures of the Finding," by Eleanor Freed. "The Archives of American Art Preserves Fragile Testimony to the Lifework and Spirit of American Artists," *Houston Arts Magazine*, Society for the Performing Arts, September 1982, p. 24.

October: *Print Show*, referenced in *The Houston Chronicle*, October 14, 1982, p. 24.

Article: Patricia Johnson, "Print Show Lights Up Some of City's Masters in Field," *Houston Chronicle*, October 14, 1982, p. 24.

Article: "Contemporary Landscapes, an exhibition of recent works by 10 American artists, opens Tuesday at the Nave Museum . . . Artists represented are . . . Bob Camblin . . ." "Art Exhibit Planned at Nave," *The Victoria Advocate*, November 2, 1982, p. 2.

November: *Contemporary Landscapes: Ten American Artists*, The Nave Museum, Victoria, Texas.

Publication: "Recent acquisitions [of the Amarillo Art Center] also include works by Bob Camblin," "Museums and Public Exhibition Spaces," Amarillo Art Center, Amarillo, Texas, 1982.

Publication: "Moody Gallery: Bob Camblin usually works in a series related to places he has traveled to (Ireland, for example), and always using a highly personal vocabulary of elements—drawings, watercolors, and oil on canvas paintings." Les Krantz, *The Texas Art Review* (Houston: Gulf Publishing in conjunction with The Krantz Company Publishers, Inc., 1982), 8, 175.

1983

Camblin had work in an exhibition that traveled to three museums.

February 25–October 3: *Texas Images and Visions*, Archer M. Huntington Gallery, University of Texas at Austin, Texas. The exhibition traveled to the Art Museum of South Texas, Corpus Christi and to Amarillo Art Center. Camblin exhibited: *Big Bend (Homage to Earl Staley)*, 1980 an oil and postcard collage on canvas, 48" X 60".

Catalogue: William H. Goetzmann, and Becky Duval Reese, *Texas Images and Visions* (Austin: Archer M. Huntington Gallery, University of Texas at Austin, 1983), 44, 128.

Camblin completed four lithographs with Little Egypt Enterprises: *Untitled*, *Wave with Rock*, *Wave & Seawall*, and *Stake in Wave*.

1984

Camblin was listed in the catalogue of the Houston Women's Caucus for Art exhibition to which he did not deliver work. A large retrospective of his work opened at Houston's Midtown Art Center three days after the opening of the Houston Women's Caucus show.

March 6–24: *1984 Show: An Exhibition of Contemporary Houston Art*, 2 Houston Center, Houston Women's Caucus for Art.

Catalogue:*1984 Show: An Exhibition of Contemporary Houston Art* (Houston: Houston Women's Caucus for Art, 1984). Bob Camblin was listed in the catalogue, but he did not get work or biographical information to the show or catalog.

March 9–April 14: *Bob Camblin: A Houston Retrospective, 1968–1984*, Midtown Art Center, Houston.

Article: "His influence on the city's art community is sensed like an undercurrent whose power may catch you by surprise . . . Camblin holds two beliefs that offer clues to 'reading' his art. First is that art is a gift and that he is an artist, a circumstance over which he has no real control. Second is that everything is true. Given both these premises, it follows that he is but an instrument and as such may not be necessarily responsible for what he creates. In turn, that allows him to paint, draw and sculpt in any number of styles or fashion. He does, generally superbly. Tight line figure or architectural drawings, tongue-in-cheek caricatures of Mr. Peanut (Planter's logo), exquisite and pale watercolors done with a feathery touch and anxiety-ridden canvases bursting with gesture and strident colors—all are Camblin . . ." Patricia Johnson, "Camblin's Personal Artwork Explored," *Houston Chronicle*, March 23, 1984. Sec. 5, p. 10.

Began a series on Albert Einstein.

1985

In 1985 Camblin participated in seven shows, one of which traveled to seven locations. He received the Cultural Arts Council of Houston Grant for Anonymous Artists.

January 5–unknown: *The New Nude*, Midtown Art Center, Houston. Camblin exhibited *Long After Courbet.*

Catologue: Michael Berryhill, *The New Nude* (Houston: Midtown Art Center, 1984), 10.

January–April: *Fresh Paint: The Houston School*, Museum of Fine Arts, Houston, Texas. The show traveled to P.S. 1, Long Island City, New York, and to the Oklahoma Art Center, Oklahoma City, Oklahoma. Camblin exhibited: *The Studio*, Oil on canvas, 1981, 73" X 65", pp. 31, 33, 37, 41, 68, 69, 72, 79, 112, 113, 197, 198, 199, 248.

Catalogue: Barbara Rose and Susie Kalil, *Fresh Paint: The Houston School* (Houston: Museum of Fine Arts, Houston, Texas Monthly Press, 1985). Camblin was the only artist in the catalogue without an artist's statement. Instead, Camblin wrote: "WOW OF silenz 4 1984," signed "Sincerely anonymous."

Article: "'Pioneer' artists such as Bob Camblin and Jack Boynton focus on landscape imagery which continues to be a major theme in Houston painting." "'Fresh Paint' Art Exhibit Recognized Houston Regional School," *The Baytown Sun*, Baytown, Texas, Friday, January 11, 1985, p. 15.

Article: Kay Larsen reviewed *Fresh Paint: The Houston School* while the show was exhibited at PS1, New York. "[T]he range is enormous, from Bob Camblin's wily, Wiley-like realism to Melissa Millers unnervingly sweet Disneyland-diorama- style animal pictures." Kay Larsen, "Art," *New York Magazine*, June 17, 1985, p. 64.

July: Camblin traveled to Hawaii for a month.

September: Camblin received letter from Einstein Foundation attorneys telling him that they filed a legal infringement for his use of Einstein's image. The letter amused but did not deter Camblin.

Becky Reese used Camblin's *Bascom Street Studio*, oil on canvas, 73 X 65, 1981, for an illustration in an article. Becky Reese, "Is Regionalism Dead?" *Texas Trends in Art Education* 3, no. 1 (Fall, 1985): 16.

December 6–January 28, 1986: *Texas Visions*, Transco Energy Company & Museum of Art of the American West, Art League of Houston. Exhibited *Texas Springtime*, oil on canvas, 48 X 72 inches. Camblin signed the work: "Anonymous Artists." The show traveled to: The Museum of Western Art, Kerrville; Live Oak Art Club, Columbus; Abilene Fine Arts Center, Abilene; Lufkin Historical and Creative Art Center, Lufkin; Rockport Art Center, Rockport; McAllen International Museum, McAllen; Fort Bend County Museum, Richmond, Texas.

Catalogue: *Texas Visions: A Celebration of Texas Artists* (Houston: Transco Energy Company and Museum of Art of the American West, Art League of Houston, 1985.

Undated: *Self Images*, Midtown Art Center, Houston, Texas.

Undated: *Bob Camblin*, Graham Gallery, Houston, Texas.

Undated: *Propaganda, Too!*, Midtown Art Center, Houston, Texas.

Undated: *Houston Drawing*, Alfred C. Glassell, Jr. School of Art, Museum of Fine Arts, Houston, Texas.

With Cerling Etching Studio, Camblin did a series of prints on Albert Einstein, *Big Al and the Electricage*. Camblin had one of the *Big Al* etchings surrounded by red neon. He also created *Oxherding Picture I* between 1988 and 1990.

Award: Bob Bilyeu Camblin received the Cultural Arts Council of Houston Grant for Anonymous Artists.

1986

Camblin had four shows during the year, one of which was in Paris, France. He was included in a book about Texas artists.

May 17–September 7: *The Texas Landscape, 1900–1986*, The Museum of Fine Arts, Houston. Camblin exhibited: *Year of the Buffalo*, 1985, Casein on paper, 30 X 32; *First Sighting*, 1985, Casein on paper, 30 X 32; *USA 1985*: Sincerely, Anonymous, 1985 Casein on paper, 30 X 32.

Book: Susie Kalil, *The Texas Landscape, 1900–1986* (Houston: The Museum of Fine Arts, Houston, 1986), 47 and 91.

Article: "A number of pieces directly reflected artists' interpretations of the land: . . . Bob Camblin's tangled views of water and lush vegetation around the Gulf are examples." Mel McCombie, "Houston, The Texas Landscape 1900–1986," *The Nation*, October 1986, p. 25.

July: *Bob Camblin: Slides of the North Wall 1985–86, anonymous Artists*, Camblin's Studio at 1401 W. Gray, Houston, Texas. Camblin, together with son Brian, daughter-in-law Kris, and various friends celebrated Camblin's one-year anniversary at 1401 West Gray, former home of Little Egypt Enterprises. The invitation noted that the event was "in our appreciation to the CULTURAL ARTS COUNCIL OF HOUSTON."

September 18–October 19: *Collaborators: Artists Working Together in Houston 1969–1986*, The Glassell School of Art, The Museum of Fine Arts, Houston. Camblin exhibited: As The Holding Firm: *Bestiary*, original drawings, c. 1971–72: Lithographs, c. 1975, Suite of 6, Each 22" X 30"; *Rhinoceros*, c. 1971–72, Ink on board, 28 X 36, Loan by Rachel W. Davis Gallery; *Joe Tate's Backyard*, 1973. Oil on canvas 6' X 12'; *The Meltzer's Backyard*, 1973, Watercolor on paper 22" X 30"; *Emerson's Self-Reliance*, c. 1973. Hand-colored etching, 27½" X 22½"; by The Holding Firm and Friends, *Flatonia*, c. 1972–73, Mixed media 24" X 32" X 8½"; by Bob Camblin and Earl Staley, *History Test*, c. 1971. Pencil on paper 22" X 30"; By David McManaway and Bob Camblin: *Jomo Collaboration*, 1971. Mixed media, 18" X 16"; by Bob Camblin and Joe Tate: *Portable Beach Vacations*, c 1972. Mixed media, 2¾" X 7¼" X 5"; by Bob Camblin and Robert Heintges: *Figure Four Traps*, c. 1972–73. Mixed media, 24" X 32" X 8½"; by Bob Camblin and David Folkman: *Untitled*, c. 1974–75. Mixed Media (wood, magnifying glass, watercolor) 15" X 17" X 2¾"; by Jack Boynton and Bob Camblin: *Through the Looking Glass Lightly*, 1975. Watercolor and pencil on paper, 23" X 29"; by Jack Boynton and Bob Camblin: *Cosmic Co. Mix*, 1975. Watercolor and Pencil on paper, 23" X 29"; by Jack Boynton, William Wiley, Richard Cabral and Robert Hudson with Sharon Boynton, Earl Staley, Bob Camblin and Allan O. Smith, *Untitled*, 1977. Collage and mixed media, 60" X 60"; by Bob Camblin, Allan O. Smith, Ron Arena, *Reliquary*, 1978. Mixed media, 67" X 30" X 11¼"; with base 16" X 25½" X 12¾"; by Bob Camblin, Nancy Giordano, Don Redman, Earl Staley, *Oil Tankers*, c. 1978–79. Acrylic on canvas, 60" X 60"; Bob Camblin, Joe Tate, Gary and Don, *Joe Tate's Backyard in California*, 1981, Oil on canvas, 60" X 72"; by Anonymous Artists (Bob Camblin and Nancy Giordano): *Touching Palms*, 1980. Oil on canvas, 48" X 48"; Anonymous Artists, *Homage to Earl Staley*, 1980. Oil on canvas, 48" X 60"; by Jack Boynton, Richard Cabral, Earl Staley, Pat Colville, Robert Heintges, Bob Camblin, Joe Tate, Jim Martin, Jack Freeman, Jeff McManus, Chris White, Burney Wilson, Susie Rosmarin, Mary McCrain, Gerald Furstenerg, McCullough, *Camp Out*, 1972. Watercolor, ink and pencil on paper, 23" X 29", and Videotapes of the Holding Firm collaborations. The exhibition included six artworks and one videotape created by The Holding Firm. Twelve collaborative works executed by Camblin with other artists or friends, dating from 1971 to 1981, were also exhibited. Another two pieces made by Anonymous Artists (the name being Camblin's own creation) completed the Camblin contributions to the show.

Referring to Camblin as "Houston's art collaborator par excellence," Landay wrote in the catalogue: "He suggests that artists, like band members, sometimes take turns soloing, other times they play harmony. Furthermore, when artists, like musicians, agree on a preliminary subject or theme, their improvisation is more likely to yield successful results. Camblin should know. Since 1969, he has been at the heart of numerous collaborative affairs. There was B&E (Bob Camblin and Earl Staley), transformed to BE&J when Joe Tate joined up and which eventually became the Holding Firm, then disbanded when Tate left Houston for California and Camblin and Staley went their separate ways."

Catalogue: Janet Landay, *Collaborators: Artists Working Together in Houston 1969–1986* (Houston: The Glassell School of Art, The Museum of Fine Arts, Houston, September, 1986), Introduction plus Plates 3, 4, 5.

Article: "Here we see young Earl Staley, Bob Camblin, and Joe Tate going on camping trips to Flatonia in the early '70s to discuss and build art projects, and coming away with objects such as fur-covered suitcase containing a bizarre rabbit-trap built of sticks. . . . Perhaps the best known are Staley, Camblin, and Tate, who between 1969 and 1974 called themselves 'The Holding Firm,' organized art excursions, and drew and painted on each other's pictures, changing positions or turning the works collaboratively, signing the work 'Anonymous Artists.'" Susan Chadwick, "Glassell Exhibit Calls to Mind 'the Good Old Days' of Art," *The Houston Post*, Sunday, September 28, 1986, p. 3F.

Article: "Paraphrasing Bob Camblin, who is Houston's art collaborator par excellence, Landay writes: 'He suggests that artists, like band members, sometimes take turns soloing, other times they play harmony. Furthermore, when artists, like musicians, agree on a preliminary subject or theme, their improvisation is more likely to yield successful results.' Camblin should know. Since 1969, he has been at the heart of numerous collaborative affairs. There was B&E (Bob Camblin and Earl Staley), trnansformed to BE&J when Joe Tate joined up and which eventually became the Holding Firm, then disbanded when Tate left Houston for California and Camblin and Staley went their separate ways. But currently active and active since around the late 1970s, is Anonymous Artists, which is the collaborative partnership of Camblin and Nancy Echegoyen. In between there have been more ventures in which Camblin has participated with numerous other artists and his name appears on the bulk of this exhibition. The exhibition bears out Camblin's description of successful collaborations, too, as evident in 'Jomo Collaboration,' a 1971 mixed media by Camblin and David McManaway (from Dallas), that combines the two artists' fortes—Camblin's exquisite draftsmanship and McManaway's equally exquisite eye for assemblage—in a work where the two-dimensional and three-dimensional qualities echo each other in delicate counterpoint . . . as in the Surrealist game of 'Exquisite Corpse' where each artist added his or her marks to a folded piece of paper that hid what had been done before, collaboration can also be a free-flow of information that may or may not ultimately 'make sense.' The untitled collage from 1977 where the principals were Jack Boynton, William Wiley, Richard Cabral and Robert Hudson aided by Sharon Boynton, Staley, Camblin and Allan Smith, is an example of how the elements are separate and unified." Patricia Johnson, "Collaborators Leave Their Marks on Art Works," *Houston Chronicle*, Houston, Texas, October 4, 1986.

November: Camblin traveled to France for opening of the *Cinq X Cinq* exhibition.

November 27–February 7, 1987: *Cinq X Cinq Houston Texas*, Galerie Dario Boccara, Paris, France. The exhibition included works by five American painters: Lucas Johnson, Bob Camblin, Gael Stack,

Bert Long, and Ron Hoover. Camblin exhibited: *Cuidado*, 1982, gouache and ink on paper, 88 X 73 cm, *Just Leave (Yes)*, 1979, gouache and ink on paper, 87 X 68 cm; *Venus*, 1973, gouache and ink on paper, 67 X 88 cm.

Catalogue: *Cinq X Cinq Houston Texas*, Stedman/Hubbard, essay by Gerard-Georges Lemaire, Galerie Dario Boccara, Paris, France, 1986, p. 12–13.

Camblin was inspired by Paris and created *French Window*.

Article: "Cinq Pour Cinq," *Houston Chronicle*, November 21, 1986, p. 9. The newspaper ran a photograph with the exhibition's artists and exhibition dates.

Book: Annette Carlozzi, *50 Texas Artists. A Critical Selection of Painters and Sculptors Working in Texas.* Camblin's *Big Al—April Proof*, etching 1985, 12" X 8" was illustrated in the book, p. 28 & 29. For his artist's statement, Camblin hand printed: "some say Picasso sed. 'Paintings are not to decorate the walls of a room or apartment, but are instruments of war against brutality and darkness . . .' Stop, Look, Listen, Sincerely, anonymous."

1987

Camblin exhibited in two shows and designed the invitation for a DiverseWorks fundraiser.

Graham Gallery began representing Camblin's work.

Article: "Attending the festivities in Paris were artists Lucas Johnson and wife Patricia; Bob Camblin and collaborator Nancy Echegoyen Giordano; and Bert Long and wife Connie." Betty Ewing, "These Americans in Paris Hit the Town with Art from Texas," *Houston Chronicle*, January 11, 1987, p. 8.

May 2: *Escape to the Wild Side*, DiverseWorks Artspace fundraiser, Camblin designed the invitation and map.

May 30–July 11: *Found*, DiverseWorks, Houston, Texas.

Article: "*FOUND*, an exhibit on view at DiverseWorks, lives up to its name with some 100 objects ranging from the whimsical to the frightening . . . Bob Camblin and Jack Boynton also have a lengthy history of working with assemblages of found materials occasionally. Camblin especially reminds one of the delicacy of Cornell's boxes with its poetic allusions residing exclusively in the kinds of object chosen—a clear glass sphere, for example—and situation within a context." Patricia C. Johnson, "'Found' Objects: Junk or 'Junque?'" *Houston Chronicle*, June 28, 1987.

December: *The Toy Show*, The Nave Museum, Victoria, Texas. Camblin created a toy for the exhibition.

Article: "'The Toy Show,' organized by Dianne David, is as much fun as it is beautiful. There are pieces by 43 people, most of them artists . . . Bob Camblin." "Artists Exhibit Their Playful Side in Victoria's Fanciful 'Toy Show,'" *Houston Chronicle*, December 18, 1987.

Undated: *Bob Camblin*, Graham Gallery, Houston, Texas.

Camblin traveled to Detroit to be with his daughter during a bone marrow transplant.

Late Work, 1988–2010

1988

Camblin had work in five exhibitions plus held a silent auction of the work by artists anonymous.

May 8–June 12: *Robert Morris—Bob Camblin—Paintings Drawings*, Nave Museum, Victoria Regional Museum Association, Victoria, Texas. Camblin exhibited: *Electricage Working Pose, Cuidado, Round Up No. 1, Taming the Bull, Rainbow Pie, Backyard Bash, Luna Moth, Table of Contents, Log Jam, Self Portrait, Time Machine.*

Article: "Houston artist Bob Camblin's work is a lot like life itself. It has elements of comedy and tragedy, reverence and irreverence, heaven and hell. Some like Camblin's work, some don't. Most of the young people in Victoria who have seen his work at Nave Museum have been fascinated with it even if they don't understand it, according to Clara Kilgore, executive director of Victoria Regional Museum Association. It is Camblin's artistic magic that has them awed, she said. Camblin is sharing the limelight at the museum through June 12 with Robert Morris . . . Camblin's work can be savage, erotic, satirical and at all times mystical. His 'Backyard' watercolors, for example on close inspection take on a threatening appearance, although even there he can express humor. In 'Camping in the Backyard' Camblin presents a torturous hell of body-shaped tree limbs and sexual symbols. Unlike the hell of Hieronymus Bosch, Camblin doesn't preach any sermons. His hell is what the viewer makes of it. And, in the midst of it he puts a comical pumpkin face with a tongue sticking out, as if to say it's all in fun. Like Morris, Camblin's technical skills as an artist are superior, and this alone makes his work fascinating." "Camblin, Morris Art Continues at the Nave," *The Victoria Advocate*, June 5, 1988, p. 12A.

July 22–September 2: *Handmade Paper*, Little Egypt Enterprises, Houston, Texas.

Calendar Notice: "Works by Eric Avery, Jack Boynton, Bob Camblin . . . at Little Egypt Enterprises." "Art Involving Handmade Paper," *The Texan Newspaper*, Events, Houston, Texas. A notice of the exhibition ran in the newspaper on July 22 and 27, August 3, 10, 17, and 24, and September 2.

November 11–January 5, 1989: *Toy Show*, Transco Gallery, Transco Energy Company, Houston, Texas. Dianne David recreated the original 1987 show. Camblin drew the invitation and made another toy for the exhibition.

November 22–29: *Bob Camblin: Artists anonymous LAST DAZE silent auction*, Camblin's studio at 1401 W. Gray. Camblin and friends used the artist's studio as an exhibition space for selling Camblin's art.

Camblin departed Houston. He flew to San Francisco with Nancy Giordano. They drove up the coast to Washington State and the Orcas Islands, Victoria, Canada. On their return, they stopped in Yachats, Oregon, and found a house that needed a sitter. They agreed to occupy the house.

Article: Camblin talked of his Houston years in the article: "In 1988, 20 years after he came to Houston, Camblin is vanishing, moving away." (did not include the writer's name or date) "Bob Camblin," *Art, Seven One Three*, Houston, Texas, 1988.

Undated: *Bob Camblin: Watercolors*, Rice University, Sewall Hall Gallery, Houston, Texas.

Undated: *Bob Camblin at Graham Gallery*, Houston, Texas.

Camblin continued working on *Oxherding Picture I* at Cerling Etching Studio.

1989

During their stay in Yachats, Camblin's mother Viva came for a visit. His son Brian with wife Kris came for a stay during which they found a house in Breakers, Oregon, they wanted to buy. Camblin and Giordano paid the mortgage as rent for a room and moved to Breakers with Brian and Kris. Giordano later purchased the lot next door. The couple had numerous visitors: Mary Lentz, Nancy's daughter Maria, Nancy's brother-in-law Josefa Vaughan. Penny Cerling of Little Egypt Enterprises together with Lollie Jackson, Annie DeGuerin and Gayle DeGeurin made the trip.

Giordano worked at Whittler's Workshop.

Camblin and Giordano left Yachats and traveled to Waldport, Oregon. Camblin and Giordano found a home with 8 miles of unimpeded beach on Highway 101. They moved in and stayed. Camblin occasionally exhibited work at Art-on-the-Rocks Gallery. Camblin painted: *To the Sea*, *Missummer Eve and Do You Have Fall*.

September 8–October 7: *Little Egypt Silent Auction*, 1511 Welch, Houston, Texas.

Article: Johnson reported on a print auction, an effort by Little Egypt Enterprises to raise money to buy the building LEE occupied. Johnson noted that Bob Camblin was the first artist LEE printed after Little Egypt's move to Houston. Patricia Johnson, "Master Printmaker Counting on Silent Auction," *Houston Chronicle*, September 7, 1989.

November 13–December 30: *The Artist's Eye: Fourteen Collections*, DiverseWorks, Houston, Texas.

Article: "'The Artist's Eye: Fourteen Collections', curated by Patricia Johnson." Holmes wrote that the studio of Jim Love had several portraits of Love, one by Bob Camblin. Ann Holmes, "What Artists Collect," *Houston Chronicle*, November 14, 1989.

December: *Messages from the South*, Sewall Art Gallery, Rice University, Houston, Texas. Camblin exhibited two watercolor landscapes.

Article: "Two watercolors by Bob Camblin, now a resident of the Oregon shores, offer masterful clarity of technique and, more importantly, the sense of connectedness to the [exhibition's] subject landscapes, not as abstract form but as living meaningful reality." Patricia C. Johnson, "Ignore Theme to Enjoy Exhibit," *Houston Chronicle*, December 5, 1989, p. 4.

December: Installation: *Outsider Art*: Texas version of a Mexican Nacimiento (Nativity Scene), Mixed media. Art Car Museum. Camblin was one of dozens of artists who collaborated to build the nacimiento in December 1989. Boyd posted photographs and text on his blog about the event: "When Ray Balinskas and Tito Ramos decided to build their own version of a Mexican nacimiento, they invited many of the artists of Houston to help . . . If any single piece in the show represents a collapsing of artistic categories, *Texas Nacimiento* is it." Bob Camblin was one of the artists invited to help build the mixed-media assemblage.

Blog: Robert Boyd, "What Is Outsider Art," *The Great God Pan Is Dead* online, Sunday, September 14, 2014.

Publication: Peter Hastings Falk, ed., *Annual Exhibition Record, 1914–68*, 3 vols. (Madison, CT: Pennsylvania Academy of the Fine Arts, Sound View Press, 1989). Includes Bob Camblin.

Little Egypt Enterprises closed. In its place, Penny Cerling, who began working at Little Egypt nine years earlier, opened the Cerling Etching Studio.

1990

Camblin exhibited in a traveling printmaking exhibition. He was included in a book on printmaking.

December: *Printmaking in Texas: The 1980s*, Modern Art Museum of Fort Worth, Texas. Camblin exhibited *Gone Fishing.*

Book: James L. Fisher, *Forty Texas Printmakers* (Modern Art Museum of Fort Worth, 1990), 6, 30, 31, 105, 106. A Camblin etching, purchased by the Modern Art Museum in Fort Worth, was illustrated.

Article: "Houston artists Derek Boshier, Bob Camblin, Earl Staley and Dick Wray are primarily painters." Janet Kutner, "Impressions from the Edge," *The Dallas Morning News*, December 13, 1990.

August: Camblin and Giordano traveled to Majuro, Marshall Islands, to paint for one month at the invitation of Ramsey Reimers, a businessman on the islands. "Ramsey was scion of the largest business enterprise in the Marshall Islands. He built the largest and most elegant house in the islands. I talked him into bringing Bob out on commission to make a large painting as centerpiece to the central room. He paid Bob (and Nancy's) travel, provided a studio apartment and gave him free hand on subject matter. He stayed in Majuro (central island) for, as I recall, 3 months. At the end, he presented Ramsey with a large, acrylic on canvas—lagoon scene with outrigger canoe on beach. He also painted and drew much more, then put on an opening (so to speak) in his studio with everything for sale. Most was sold for varying amounts. Ironically, the best piece of work did not sell because it was pen/ink/pencil/wash in grey tones, no color, so I bought it from him. I also kept several, small watercolor studies of this and that. The paintings he sold remain there in prominent locations—no one will part with them." Personal communication from Dennis Camblin, November 2015.

Camblin and Giordano returned to Waldport, Oregon.

Penny Cerling and Jeff Skarda donated 131 Bob Camblin prints, created by the artist with Little Egypt Enterprises and with Cerling Etching Studios, to the Museum of Fine Arts, Houston.

1991

Camblin had work in two exhibitions and participated in one benefit.

March 9–April 21: *Texas Selections from the Menil Collection; A Tribute to the University of Texas Medical Branch Centennial Celebration*, Galveston Art Center, Galveston, Texas. From the Menil archives: "An exhibition of 50 drawings, sculptures, and paintings by artists living and working in Texas from The Menil Collection shown at the Galveston Art Center, Galveston, TX." Camblin was one of 26 participating artists. He exhibited: *Trotline Memorial*, 1971, pencil and watercolor.

Benefit: Camblin donated work to KLRU-TV, Austin, Texas, public television station. "This year's list of artist who have donated works to the auction is impressive, as always. It includes Jack Boynton, Bob Camblin . . ."

June: *The House*, Laguna Gloria Museum, Austin, Texas.

Article: J. R. Oleson, "Two Laguna Gloria Shows Strike Balance," *Austin American-Statesman*, June 8, 1991, p.13.

1992

Camblin enlarged his Old Santa character from the 1970s and had him living in Tirnanog. Camblin continued to live in Waldport, Oregon. His son Brian moved to Santa Fe where Bruno and Bonnie Leon had built a home.

He had work in two exhibitions.

June 6–August 2: *Printmaking in Texas: The 1980s*, Austin Museum of Art, Austin Texas.

August 26, 1992–July 12, 1993: *Island Inspired*, Stephen F. Austin Gallery, Stephen F. Austin State University, Nacogdoches, Texas, August 26–September 20; Williams Tower, Houston, Texas, November 15–December 31; and the Galveston Arts Center, May 23, 1993–July 12, 1993. Camblin exhibited: *Teachworth Balcony*, 1981, oil on canvas. The exhibition was organized by the Galveston Arts Center and curated by Clint Willour and Jim Edwards.

Catalogue: Jim Edwards and Clint Willour, *Island Inspired* (Galveston, TX: Galveston Arts Center, 1992). Camblin's *Teachworth Balcony* was used as the cover for the catalogue.

Near the year's end, Camblin moved to Algiers Point, Louisiana, with Giordano.

1993

April: Camblin had an angiogram on April 21 that revealed badly blocked arteries. He underwent a carotid endarterectomy at East Jefferson General Hospital in Metairie, Louisiana. When he recovered from the procedure, he seemed unlike himself. While the doctors did not diagnose a minor stroke, Camblin's family believes he must have experienced one during the surgery.

November: *A Matter of Time*, DiverseWorks, Houston, Texas.

Article: "The selection at DiverseWorks is not the best of Little Egypt, but it is a slice of Houston's art history. 'Old-timers' of the scene include Bob Camblin, a former professor at Rice University and one of Houston's most underestimated, under-represented and influential artists (now living in Oregon)." Patricia C. Johnson, "Folkman: Artist and Technician. His Own Creations Shine alongside Little Egypt Editions," *Houston Chronicle*, November 15, 1993.

Publication: *1983–1993, DiverseWorks Artspace, The First Ten Years*, "Found," (Houston: Diverse Works Artspace, Inc., 1993). The exhibition "Found" was held in 1987.

1994

Camblin and Giordano moved to New Orleans. Camblin's son purchased the lot next to his Breaker's house from Giordano. Giordano purchased a duplex, shotgun house from her daughter with the funds from the Breakers' sale.

Besides visits from family and friends including Bonnie and Bruno Leon, Jack and Sharon Boynton, and Patricia and Lucas Johnson, Camblin and Giordano traveled to see family in Baton Rouge and Camblin's son and wife in Santa Fe.

1997

Giordano begins teaching at St. John the Baptist Parish Schools in La Place.

1999

Artist quotes: "So in 1968 I was a visiting artist, working with Bob Camblin and some others [at Rice University]." "Roy Fridge, interviewed by Michelle W. Locke," p. 19.

"You work on the same project with someone and try to do it as straight as you can. And you see other things happening. Other ways to draw. Like when I would draw with Staley, Bob Camblin and Joe Tate and we were all sitting around a table like this . . . and we'd rotate the paper around the table, and they learned something from the way that you did it and you learned something from the way that they did it." "Jack Boynton, interviewed by Marco Villegas," p. 27.

"Earl Staley and Bob Camblin came [to Houston] in the sixties—wonderful additions to the scene. They did some really brilliant work." "Richard Stout, interviewed by Toni Beauchamp," p. 31.

"It's funny, when I started showing at the David Gallery, there was no doubt that it was the best gallery in Texas. At least to my mind, I showed with Roy Fridge, Jim Love, Bob Camblin and Jack Boynton." "Lucas Johnson, interviewed by Jim Edwards," p. 54. *Art Lies* 24 (Fall 1999).

Publication: Peter Hastings Falk, ed., *Who Was Who in American Art, 1564–1975*, 3 vols. Listings include Bob Camblin.

2000

Article: "Her [Betty Moody of Moody Gallery, Houston] first real break came when Rice University faculty members Bob Camblin, Don Shaw and Jack Boynton joined the stable." Janet Kutner, "Gallery Owner Revels in Her Work," *The Dallas Morning News*, August 27, 2000, p. 1C.

2001

Interview: "Moving back to ancient times, in 1970 Betty Wright and I opened a gallery to show young artists from Texas and Mexico. Some of the artists were . . . Bob Camblin." Interview: "Murray Smither Interviewed Bruce and Julie Webb of the Webb Gallery, located in Waxahachie," *Art Lies* 30 (Spring 2001): 6.

2003

Undated: *Collins House Exhibit of the University Collection*, Baker University, Baldwin City, Kansas—the first university in Kansas—loosely associated with the Methodist Church, held an exhibition that included a pen and ink drawing by Camblin titled *Metamorphosis #2*. The drawing was a University Purchase from Elsie Allen Funds.

Brochure: *Collins House Exhibit of the University Collection*, Baker University, Baldwin City, Kansas.

2005

Article: "Folkman used his technical expertise and his artistic sensibility to help those such as Jack Boynton, Lamar Briggs, Bob Camblin and Earl Staley realize their vision in print form." Mark L. Smith, "Way Out Here, Printmaking in Texas," *Art Lies* 46 (Spring 2005): 45.

Publication: Lonnie Pierson Dunbier, ed., *The Artists Bluebook 34,000 North American Artists to March 2005*. Camblin is listed.

2008

Gift: The *Annual Report 2007–2008, Museum of Fine Arts Houston*, listed Penny Cerling as a donor to the Museum's print collection: Bob Camblin, *April Proof*, 1991, etching and drypoint, 20 X 15⅜ sheet, 11¾ X 7¾ plate.

2009

Camblin began treatment for Parkinson's Disease. He also continued taking medication for high blood pressure.

September: Camblin suffered a stroke that left him unable to walk. He was sent to River Parishes Hospital in La Place. After treatment, he was transferred to a nursing home, SE Louisiana War Veterans' Home, in Reserve, Lousiaina.

2010

January 16–17: *Bob Camblin: Unframed Drawings and Paintings on Paper*, Sarah Balinskas Fine Framing, Houston, Texas. The exhibition was held before Camblin's death in an effort to help defray expenses from the hospitalization after his stroke.

While in the War Veterans' Home, Camblin experienced difficulty swallowing. During a feeding session, fluid got into his lungs. He quickly developed pneumonia that led to congestive heart failure.

December: On December 4, Bob Bilyeu Camblin died in the Veterans' Home in Reserve, Louisiana. His obituary read: "Camblin Robert (Bob) Bilyeu Camblin, age 82, passed away on December 4, 2010 at 12:35 PM in the Southeast Louisiana War Veterans Home in Reserve, LA. Born in Ponca City, OK, on August 1, 1928 to Vava Bilyeu Camblin and Donald Barr Camblin, he was the eldest of three brothers. He grew up in Ponca City, OK, and after serving in the U.S. Army and Air Force during the Korean War, received a BFA and MFA at the Kansas City Art Institute. After receiving a Fulbright Fellowship in 1956 to work in Rome, Italy, for a year, Bob began his career as both an art professor at several major universities including the University of Detroit and Rice University, and a highly esteemed artist whose prolific works have appeared in prominent collections such as the Chicago Art Institute, NYC Whitney Museum of Art, Dallas Museum of Art and Houston Museum of Fine Arts. Bob is survived by his wife Nancy Uter Giordno-Echegoyen of La Place, LA; brother Michael and sister-in-law Marilee Camblin of Portland, OR, and brother Dennis and sister-in-law Sneh Camblin of Hawaii; son Brian and daughter-in-law Kris Camblin of Tyler, TX, daughter Robyn and son-in-law Jim Rodriguez of Royal Oak, MI; and stepdaughter Maria Giordano-Echegoyen of Nashville, TN. Bob's grandchildren are Ian and Annie Camblin, Ryan and Allyson Rodriguez and stepgrandaughters Sophia and Isabel Giordano-Scott. A Memorial Service in honor of beloved Bob will be held in Ponca City, OK at St. Mary's Church on January 15, 2011." *The Times-Picayune*, December 12, 2010.

"Legendary Houston artist Bob Camblin died Saturday in LaPlace, LA from complications following a stroke he suffered last year. Born in Oklahoma in 1928, Camblin studied painting at the Kansas

City Art Institute, earning an M.F.A. in 1955. He taught at Rice University from 1967–73 with Joe Tate and Earl Staley, with whom he shared studio space. His influence was a constant undercurrent in the city's art scene until h left in the early 80's. Volatile and gregarious, Camblin saw himself as a vehicle for artistic inspiration, not always fully responsible for his highly personal, narrative polemic works. Wary of interpretation, he assume multiple artistic personas, signing himself as Anonymous Bosch, Red Stick the Pirate, and Mr. Peanut and is the only artist without a written statement feature in the seminal 1985 "Fresh Paint: The Houston School" catalog. Camblin is survived by his wife, Nancy Giordano." Bill Davenport wrote Camblin's obituary for *Glasstire*: Texas Visual Art online.

An obituary also ran in the *Ponca City News*, December 19, 2010, Page 3A.

After Camblin's death, his daughter Robyn mixed her father's ashes with Paynes Grey oil paint and created three portraits of him with the paint for family members.

Posthumous Exhibitions and Publications:

2012

April: YouTube: Richard Stout, *Modernism in Houston Art: 1950–1970*, Part 7, YouTube series done for Houston Modern Market Week Exhibition at the William Reaves Fine Art Gallery, Houston, Texas, April 28, 2012. Stout mentioned Bob Camblin's influence on Houston art.

May 12: *Collection of Ursula Brinkerhoff*, Canal Street Gallery, Houston, Texas. Camblin's work was featured in the sale of Brinkerhoff's estate after her death.

2013

Article: Molly Glentzer, "Penny Cerling: A Life of Needles and Pins," *Houston Chronicle*, June 26, 2013. In the article about Cerling's involvement with printing in Houston, Glentzer wrote: "The art collection that fills her home's upstairs walls suggests the dynamic of that period, with prints by dozens of artists who helped build Houston into the hotbed of visual art it is today: Karin Broker, Bob Camblin . . ."

Newsletter: The article records the history of Rice University's Womens Organization and notes: "The seminar series, 'Contemporary American Cuilture,' began in January 1969. Bob Camblin was asked to speak on 'Art in the 50s and 60s.'" *The Cornerstone*, Society of Rice University Women, Rice Historical Society, vol. 19, no. 2 (Summer 2013): 10.

2014

February 14–15: *Flatbed Contemporary Print Fair*, Flatbed Press, Austin, Texas. Flatbed Press organized a print fair in Austin, and Penny Cerling donated a print by Bob Camblin, titled: *Gone Fishin'*, Medium: Intaglio, 18 inches x 15 1/2 inches.

2017

August 26 –November 4: *Focus on the 70s and 80s: Houston Foundations II*, Deborah Colton Gallery, Houston, Texas. Opening postponed until September 9 due to Hurricane Harvey.

NOTES

Preface

1. Henri-Robert-Marcel Duchamp, *Marcel Duchamp: Meditations on the Identities of an Artist* (Smithsonian Institution Scholarly Press, December 2014).

Introduction

1. William Shakespeare, *As You Like It*, Act II Scene VII. "All the world's a stage, And all the men and women merely players." Spoken by Jaques.

Chapter One

1. Sixteen years before Camblin's birth, far-sighted Poncans, who wanted to lure developers to their city, had voted to create a municipal electric utility (PCUA). Two years later PCUA began electrical service, an important piece of the city's infrastructure and a necessity for development.

2. At the time the thirty-four-year-old E. W. Marland and his wife Virginia arrived in Oklahoma, Ponca City's population was 2,500. Having made a fortune in West Virginia's oil fields, only to lose his money in the panic of 1907, Marland came to Ponca City broke. But he still had an eye for surface geology that promised oil. He observed ideal landforms south of the city, so he and his wife set up their home in the Arcade Hotel, using extended credit from the hotel manager. A talented self-promoter, he borrowed enough money to search for black gold.

3. Ten years after his first oil strike, Marland controlled 10 percent of the world's oil supply.

4. E. W. Marland was Oklahoma's governor from 1934–1939. He paved the way for building projects carried out by President Franklin D. Roosevelt's New Deal: The Civilian Conservation Corps (CCC) and the Works Progress Administration (WPA). The WPA Federal Art Project provided jobs for twenty-eight Oklahoma artists who painted murals for public buildings.

Post offices were not the only public building receiving funds from FDR's Federal Art Project. In total, the U. S. Treasury employed 10,000 artists who created 100,000 paintings, 8,000 sculptures, and 4,000 murals for public buildings all over America. The artists received $23.86 a week, a stipend that kept them alive and working during the Depression. Even though Ponca City's first post office was established in January 1894, there is no record of a mural in the original or subsequent Ponca City post office buildings.

5. The residents of Ponca City kept close tabs on the Marlands, who seemed to grow more prosperous by the day. But they were childless. To rectify the absence of children, Marland and his wife adopted a niece Lydie, sixteen, and a nephew George Roberts, nineteen, who were children of Virginia's sister Margaret. The family of four lived together for ten years until Virginia's death in 1926. Marland waited two years after his wife's death before having Lydie's adoption annulled—then he married her. Under Marland's guidance, Lydie transitioned from niece to adopted daughter to wife, which made her brother George also her "stepson." The marriage of an oil baron to his daughter caused a national scandal and introduced Ponca City to millions of gossip column readers. The *New York Times* covered the event on page one, and the tabloids had a heyday.

The fracas did not seem to upset Marland, but Lydie was mortified. To ease her concerns, Marland gave his bride a wedding present: his newly completed mansion. Shortly after moving into the estate, the wildcatter lost Marland Oil in a hostile takeover by JP Morgan, Jr. Once again his money was gone. Six years later, a resilient Marland became the tenth Governor of Oklahoma in 1934, making Lydie the First Lady of the state. Two years after leaving office, Marland died and was buried in Ponca City. LydiE became a recluse for a decade and then vanished for twenty-two years. When her brother George filed a missing person's report in 1955, newspapers again exploited Lydie's story. She became an elusive legend, with unconfirmed sightings of her occurring all over America. She returned to Ponca City in 1975 and died in the Chauffeur's Cottage on the Marland mansion grounds twelve years later.

6. Bryant Baker created the sculpture. Baker studied at the Academie Julian in Paris. Camblin kept several postcards of the *Pioneer Woman*, one pinned to his studio wall, another on which he wrote, "Wow, Mom. I did my homework." He added a heart with an exclamation point running down the middle. The note is only visible when the card is viewed at an angle.

7. Camblin drew the *Pioneer Woman* in his art, using the figure to honor his mother, Viva. He employed *Viva* as a title, intending *Viva's* meaning, "long live!" (in Spanish and Italian), to be part of his homage to his mother. He often shortened Viva to two overlapping Vs, forming a W that extended its symbolism to include "You get What you deserve."

8. The Arcade Hotel was razed in 1973.

9. Wentz also founded and supported the Oklahoma Crippled Children Society. He created foundations to underwrite Project Awards at four Oklahoma universities and funded higher education at several colleges.

10. The ceilings of atmospheric theaters were usually smooth domes filled with low-wattage lights to simulate stars. Fantasy outdoor settings often decorated the walls.

11. The nickname for Oklahoma is "The Sooner State." The name derives from the people who raced into the unassigned lands of the Oklahoma District to claim land before the official time for the 1889 Land Run. Those people arrived sooner.

12. Oklahoma Historical Society, *World War II*, Oklahoma History Research Center.

13. The high school building sits on land donated by Marland.

14. U.S. President Franklin D. Roosevelt signed into law the Servicemen's Readjustment Act of 1944, also know as the G.I. Bill of Rights.

Chapter Two

1. Robert Rauschenberg also registered in KCAI's interior design department in 1948.

2. *Life Magazine*, "Life Presents R. Buckminster Fuller's Dymaxion World," a fifteen-page pullout section of Fuller's Dymaxion World, with cutout and assembly directions, published March 1, 1943.

3. Buckminster Fuller Institute.

4. In 1952, art critic Harold Rosenberg coined "Action Painting," a term that dominated the Abstract Expressionism movement.

5. Camblin was also in the *4th Midwestern Biennial* and won a purchase prize. Because all his known exhibitions are noted in the Time Line, the text will not discuss each individual show.

Chapter Three

1. Italian food hadn't yet become a Midwestern American staple in 1956.

2. William J. Fulbright, *Fulbright Painters*, "Artist Statement" (The Smithsonian Institution and The Institute of International Education, 1958).

3. Three years before Camblin's arrival in Rome, Robert Rauschenberg had an exhibition at the Galleria dell'Obelisco in March 3–10, 1953. The gallery followed his show with an exhibition of work by Kay Sage, March 16–31, 1953.

4. The Rorschach Inkblot Test is used to investigate psychological personality traits.

5. Franz Kafka (1883–1924), *Racconti* (Stories), illustrated by Renzo Vespignani, Feltrinelli Editore, Milano, Italia, 1957. The text is in Italian, suggesting Camblin purchased and kept the book for its illustrations, not for its text.

6. Samsa represents the absurdity and hopelessness of the human condition. Kafka's 1915 novella foresaw The Theatre of the Absurd.

7. From the official website: *http://www.palermocatacombs.com*.

8. An essay from 1944: Sartre's first attempt to defend existentialism. Jean-Paul Sartre, *Selected Prose The Writings of Jean-Paul Sartre*, vol. 2. "A More Precise Characterization of Existentialism" (Evanston, IL: Northwestern University Press, 1974), 155.

9. French: *Mauvaise foi.*

10. Jean-Paul Sartre, *Being and Nothingness: An Essay in Phenomenological Ontology* (New York: Citadel Press, 1965).

11. The Greeks and Romans both understood linear perspective, but during the Middle Ages the concept was lost.

12. From 1476–79, Tommaso Portinari, a Medici banking agent living in Bruges, commissioned Hugo van der Goes to create an altarpiece for his family chapel in the church of the Florentine Hospital of Santa Maria Nuova. Moved from the Portinari chapel in 1900, the altarpiece now hangs in the Uffizi Gallery. *Galleria degli Uffizi, Florence.*

13. Jan Dickerson, "New Aim Turns Toward the Classical," *The Kansas City Star*, Sunday, December 25, 1960.

Chapter Four

1. While in Sarasota, Camblin also taught classes at the Longboat Key Art Center. He had several solo exhibitions and was included in a group show at St. Armand's Gallery, whose owner promoted his work. Sarasota Art Association and the Ringling Museum of Arts Governor's All-Florida Show included his art in exhibitions.

2. Jan Dickerson, "New Aim Turns Toward the Classical," *The Kansas City Star*, Sunday, December 25, 1960.

3. Dickerson, "New Aim."

4. Jan Dickerson. "New Aim."

5. Detroit Mercy's architectural department went on to hire Buckminster Fuller five years after Camblin left the university.

6. The format and the fantasy have much in common with Henry Darger (1892–1973), an American writer and artist who became famous posthumously with the discovery of his illustrated manuscript *The Story of the Vivian Girls, in What is Known as the Realms of the Unreal, of the Glandeco-Angelinian War Storm, Caused by the Child Slave Rebellion*. Camblin, however, created his series in the early 1960s and Darger's work was not discovered until his death in 1973.

7. Bob Halliday, "U. Instructor to Exhibit New Work, Cites Artists Role to Effect Change," *The Salt Lake Tribune*, Nov. 20, 1966, 18.

8. Camblin used the German word, *hintergedanken*, to represent ulterior motives. Allan Watts (1915–1973) defined *hintergedanken* as "a thought way, way, way in the back of your mind. Something that you know deep down but can't admit." *The Tao of Life: A Life without Definition.*

9. Jesmira Bonoan, "The Influence of Existentialism on the Theatre of the Absurd," prezi.com, posted May 6, 2011. A phrase coined by critic Martin Esslin (a Hungarian-born English producer, dramatist, journalist, critic, scholar and professor), the "Theatre of the Absurd" tries to instill the lost sense of cosmic wonder and primeval anguish and hopes to achieve this by shocking man out of an existence that has become trite, mechanical, and complacent.

10. Bob Camblin, Sketchbook *Venezia* (referring to Albert Camus's *The Myth of Sisyphus*), October 1976. Camus wrote a philosophical essay about "pushing a rock" titled *The Myth of Sisyphus* (1942, translated into English in 1955). In the Greek myth, Sisyphus is condemned for eternity to push a rock up a hill, only to have it roll to the bottom again. He despairs at the meaninglessness of his task. He eventually reaffirms his life through a free-willed rebellion against his fate, thereby experiencing value and meaning for his efforts.

11. Albert Camus, *The Myth of Sisyphus: And Other Essays* (New York: Vintage Books, 1955). Camus's essay on the absurdity of Sisyphus's task influenced dramatists of the 1950s and '60s, including playwrights Harold Pinter, Samuel Beckett, and Eugene Ionesco, whose existential plays resulted in the Theatre of the Absurd. Note: The Theatre of the Absurd was only a literary concept. No formal organization existed.

Chapter Five

1. The official name for Mormonism is The Church of Jesus Christ of Latter Day Saints.

2. The Italian definition of Bambola: A reproduction of a human (adult or child), of a humanoid form, of an animal or of an imaginary personage, generally realized in plastic, ceramic or biscuit ware. Camblin increased his production of St. Bambola images while in Salt Lake.

3. Putto (singular) Putti (plural): A representation of a cherubic infant, often shown winged. In the art of the Renaissance, the figure of an infant boy—often the Christ child. In Italian, putto means boy. *Merriam-Webster Dictionary.*

4. Spirit guide: A term used by the Western tradition of Spiritualist Churches, mediums, and psychics to describe an entity that remains a disincarnate spirit in order to act as a guide or protector to a living incarnated human being. *The Free Dictionary* by Farlex.

5. Anima: In Jungian psychology: The feminine inner personality, as present in the unconscious of the male. It is in contrast to the animus, which represents masculine characteristics. *The Free Dictionary* by Farlex.

6. Jane Munro, *Silent Partners: Artist and Mannequin from Function to Fetish* (New Haven, CT: Yale University Press, 2014).

7. Putti are found as messenger spirits in art from the Greek Eros to the Roman cupid, but their use fell out of favor during the Middle Ages. Donatello is credited with reviving putti, and infusing them with Christian meanings in the 1420s. Renaissance art was largely religious and portrayed the Christ child as a cherubic, often naked baby. Creating nude putti to sing to or to attend the Christ child was an easy evolution of the form, for which artists used dolls as models.

8. Bob Camblin, *Libro de Ricordare*, September 20, 1976, to October 14, 1976.

9. Bob Camblin wrote the text on the back of his sketch of a scarecrow.

10. Suzuki's popular books and essays on Buddhism introduced Zen Buddhism to the West. Camblin kept books by Suzuki in his studios.

11. D.T. Suzuki, *An Introduction to Zen Buddhism*, Foreword by Carl Jung (New York: Grove Press, 1964), 39–40. Camblin owned a copy.

12. Sendai Gibon, "The Universe," a treatise on this subject called *Tengan Yaku* (Medicine for the Eye), written in a dialogue form, Zen Painting, early nineteenth century.

13. Suzuki, *An Introduction to Zen Buddhism*.

14. "Insights: Art of Awakening." mymeditativemoments.com.

15. Camblin's remaining haigas have a prescience, which stems from his combination of poetry and image.

16. Bob Camblin, *Untitled Sketchbook*, vol. 2, February- March 1975.

17. John G. Rudy, *Wordsworth and the Zen Mind: The Poetry of Self-Emptying* (Albany, NY: State University of New York Press, 1966), 118. *Wu-Shih*: A term for non-ideological ordinariness and the accompanying piety it supports.

18. Bob Camblin, A handwritten assignment for his University of Utah students. The Smithsonian Institution's Archives of American Art, 1966.

19. Camblin, Undated sketchbook.

Chapter Six

1. Camblin created "drawritings," sketches with accompanying text (his version of Japanese haiga). Drawritings became his preferred method of self-expression and communication from the 1970s until his death.

2. Drawings in France's Chauvet Cave are more than 30,000 years old, but the cave was only discovered in 1994.

3. Robert Fowler email to author, June 6, 2016.

4. Bob Halliday, "U. Instructor to Exhibit New Work, Cites Artists' Role to Effect Change," *The Salt Lake Tribune*, November 20, 1966, 18.

5. The Horsemen are described in the New Testament of the Bible in the Book of Revelation of Jesus Christ to John the Apostle, 6:1–8.

Chapter Seven

1. Bob Camblin, Undated sketchbook.

2. The Ringling Brothers and Barnum and Bailey Circus celebrated their first African-American ringmaster when Johnson Lee Iverson won the position in 1999.

3. Camblin departed Houston in 1988.

4. Howard Beeth and Cary D. Wintz, eds., *Black Dixie: Afro-Texan History and Culture in Houston, 13 Essays About the History of African-Americans in Houston, Texas* (Bryan: Texas A&M University Press, 1992).

5. Mies van der Rohe designed Brown Pavilion in 1974. The expansion held to van der Rohe's earlier design.

6. The Menils, who later built their own museum, the Menil Collection, and MacAgy have become cultural legends in Houston because of vision, discriminating "eyes," patronage, art collections, and art installations. The Menils also built the Rothko Chapel.

7. Unnamed reporter, "Bob Camblin," *Art, Seven One Three*, Houston, Texas, 1988, 39.

8. Marilyn McAdams Sibley, *The Port of Houston: A History*, "A Port Fifty Miles from Sea" (Austin: University of Texas Press, 1968).

9. Funk was an antiestablishment art movement that began in the San Francisco Bay area and included many artists from the Bay Area Figurative Movement. It was not a cohesive style but shared biting humor, vulgar references, and sly wit as commentaries on social justice.

Chapter Eight

1. Allan Kaprow, "Happenings in the New York Scene (1961)," *Essays on the Blurring of Art and Life* (Berkeley: University of California Press, 1993), 15–26

2. Achim Hochdorfer, ed., Benjamin Buchloh, Joseph Branden, Claes Oldenburg, *The Sixties* (Munich, Germany: Schirmer/Mosel Verlag GMBH & Co KG, 2012).

3. Kaprow, "Happenings," 16.

4. Kaprow, "Happenings," 16.

5. Kaprow, "Happenings," 16.

6. The Contemporary Arts Museum, Houston, Texas, exhibited *Allan Kaprow and Wolf Vostell: Two Happening Concepts*, January 9–February 11, 1968. Camblin's attendance is highly likely.

7. The first beach event happened when one of Camblin's classes spontaneously decided to make a collective trip to Galveston. The subsequent pair of happenings involved more students, and therefore required planning for transportation to and from the beach, which was forty-seven miles south of Houston.

8. Earl Staley filmed the 1968 collaborative event on Galveston's West Beach. Camblin and Staley held a "world premiere" of the film at Rice University Commons.

9. Martin Dreyer, "The Night They Burned The Thing," *The Houston Chronicle*, Texas Magazine, Sunday, January 10, 1971, cover and p. 16.

10. Earl Staley wrote about his memories of Camblin. Staley's text appears on the final text pages of this book.

11. The year after Camblin's third Galveston happening, Allan Kaprow was invited to Rice University to lead a happening he called *Baggage*. Kaprow wanted the participants to examine the "baggage" that influenced their lives, to realize how heavy it was and to find a way to dispose of it. The happening involved taking baggage to Galveston, filling the suitcases with sand, driving to the airport, placing the bags on a passenger shuttle that returned the bags to the owners who then drove the baggage back to Galveston and dumped the sand onto the beach.

12. Dianne David Interview by Louis J. Marchiafava, Archive # 0H036, *The Houston Metropolitan Research Center*, Oral History Project Interviews, October 2, 1975.

13. *Wunderkammer*: A place where a collection of curiosities and rarities is exhibited. Oxford English Dictionary.

14. Ann Holmes, "Fantastic Artists," *Southwest Art Gallery Magazine*, October 1971, p. 34.

15. "Reflections," *The Other Coast: 10 Texas Artists*, University of California, Long Beach, California, 1971.

16. Camblin in a 1970 sketchbook.

17. Eleanor Freed, "Stark realism, dramatization of a hitchhiker; Documenta," *The Houston Post*, February 21, 1971, 28.

18. Bob Camblin, Earl Staley, Joe Tate. B, E & J Productions letter to potential exhibitors for the Document Show, 1970.

19. In 1972, Camblin, Staley, and Tate decided to change their name from B, E & J Productions. They "threw" the *I Ching* (*The Book of Changes*) and came up with the hexagram "#8 Pi / Holding Together" that they modified to The Holding Firm. *I Ching*, Wilhelm translation, Bollingen Series 19 (New York: Princeton University Press, 1950), 35–39.

Chapter Nine

1. Allan Otho Smith was a graduate student when he moved into the Holding Firm's Sul Ross and Jack Street studio. He helped build the tower and assisted with exhibitions and events. He created his own silkscreened art and was represented by Harris Gallery in Houston. He attended Red Stick's exhibition in Baton Rouge and participated in Camblin's "Glass Bead Game" as J. R. Cane.

2. McManaway may have discovered the term "Jomo" in the 1942 film *Juke Girl*. Jomo was a character who sold fetishes.

3. The Archives of American Art Microfilm Reel 3462 includes a copy of the letter.

4. Camblin's handwritten letter on back of the envelope containing Camblin's termination notice sent from Norman Hackerman, Rice University President, April 1972.

Chapter Ten

1. Eleanor Freed, "Montrose Bateau Lavoir," *The Houston Post*, Sunday, January 7, 1973, 34.

2. Staley Blogspot.

3. Freed, "Montrose Bateau Lavoir."

Chapter Eleven

1. Camblin owned Alfred Frankenstein, *The Reality of Appearance: The Trompe L'Oeil Tradition in American Painting* (Berkeley University of California Press, 1970). Peto's *The Cup We All Race 4*, however, is not mentioned or illustrated in the book.

2. Jasper Johns's *Figure 4*, 1959, and Robert Indiana's serigraph *4 FOUR*, from his numbers series, 1968, used numbers for the subject and structure of the works as did numerous conceptualists. Note: May 16, 2007, Christie's sold John's Figure 4 for $17,400,000.00.

3. Some examples of the boxed fish series were displayed in David Gallery's *Boxscapes* exhibition, 1970.

4. Bob Camblin, Sketchbook, November 1976, Venezia.

5. Richard Brautigan, *Trout Fishing in America* (New York: Dell Publishing, 1967).

6. Brautigan, *Trout Fishing*, 8.

Chapter Twelve

1. The highest peak in the Chisos is Emory Peak at 7,825 feet above sea level.

2. Camblin read Freud and knew that valleys and gullies are common Freudian female dream symbols.

3. Jim Edwards, *Contemporary Landscapes* (Corpus Christi: Art Museum of South Texas, 1982), 10.

Chapter Thirteen

1. Sometimes called the *Ten Ox-herding Pictures of Zen*, the series of ten pictures and commentaries illustrates the stages of Buddhist practice that lead to enlightenment. Camblin owned *Zen Flesh, Zen Bones: A Collection of Zen and Pre-Zen Writings* including ten Ox-herding pictures, 1957, and D.T. Suzuki's *Manual of Zen Buddhism* with eight Ox-herding pictures.

2. Alexander exhibited twenty-six of Camblin's hand-colored etchings in his traveling exhibition.

3. Semiotics: a general philosophical theory of signs and symbols that deals especially with their function in both artificially constructed and natural languages and comprises syntactics, semantics, and pragmatics. Merriam-Webster Dictionary.

4. Ferdinand de Saussure, *Course in General Linguistics*, edited by Charles Bally and Albert Sechehaye with Albert Riedlinger, Translated by Roy Harris (Geneva, 1915), 68–73.

5. Michel Foucault, *History of Madness*. Translated by Jonathan Murphy and Jean Khalfa (in English), 1964. Quote from the Preface to the 1961 edition. p. xxvii–xxxix. In 1965, Vintage Books of Random House, New York, published an abridged edition of Foucault's *The History of Madness*, translated by Richard Howard, with some changes and an additional chapter, as *Madness and Civilization: A History of Insanity in the Age of Reason*.

6. Michel Foucault, *Les mots et les choses (The Order of Things: An Archaeology of the Human Sciences)* (New York: Pantheon Books, 1970), 1–15.

7. Elizabeth Gross, *Derrida and the Limits of Philosophy* (Thousand Oaks, CA: Sage Publications,1986), 27.

8. Jacques Derrida, *Writing and Difference* (Chicago, IL: University of Chicago Press, 1978).

9. From a 1966 Camblin sketchbook.

Chapter Fourteen

1. Bob Camblin, Sketchbook, May 1974.

2. Cerling continued to operate Cerling Etching Studio from 1990 until she opened Tembo-Cerling Collaborative Studio with Holly Lewis in 1998.

3. From a letter Camblin wrote from Baton Rouge dated Aug. 30, 1975.

Chapter Fifteen

1. Camblin continued to counsel "caution" in his art, especially in the 1970s. He drew from the Spanish influence found in Houston as well as from his numerous travels to Mexico when he wrote *Cuidado* in his work: Spanish for "watch out" or "beware."

2. *Prima facie*: Accepted as correct until proved otherwise.

3. The Face of Jesus appearing on the veil of Veronica derives from the story of a woman who wiped Christ's face with her veil as he carried the cross. His "Holy Face" was miraculously imprinted upon her cloth.

4. Zurbaran signed two works of the *Holy Face*, 1631 and 1658. His workshop produced more than twelve paintings using the theme.

5. The French translation of "red stick" is *baton rouge;* however, red was the color of magic in ancient folktales and a stick is the hand instrument into which a compositor places the letters to be set up for printing, turning red stick into a magic stick for words.

6. As a boy, Camblin may have identified with the character Terry from *Terry and the Pirates*, created by Milton Caniff. Thirty-one million newspaper subscribers read the comic strip between 1934 and 1946.

7. *Raconteur*: A person who tells anecdotes in a skillful and amusing way.

8. In the English fairy-court, Robin Goodfellow was sometimes called Puck and was the son of King Oberon, a domestic spirit. He was full of tricks and fond of practical jokes. Shakespeare used the character in *A Midsummer Night's Dream*. Camblin created Robin Goodfellow on October 31.

9. "Visiting Artist," *LSU Daily Reveille*, Louisiana State University, December 2, 1975.

10. Marcel Duchamp created *Rrose Selavy* in 1920. When pronounced, the French double *r* sounds similar to 'ehr' and together with rose becomes "Eros." Selavy is *C'est la vie*, "It's life." Rrose Selavy thus becomes "Eros is life."

11. Camblin's evolution of *Que sais-je* into Kay Sage occurred before he realized a real Kay Sage (1898–1963) had existed. A wealthy American painter and poet, Sage was married to an Italian prince, Prince Ranieri di San Fastino for ten years and later married Yves Tanguy. Eight years after Tanguy's death, Sage shot herself through her heart.

12. Michel de Montaigne (1533–1592) was a French philosopher who championed the essay form. "His work is noted for its merging of casual anecdotes and autobiography with serious intellectual

insight; his massive volume *Essais* (translated literally as "Attempts" or "Trials") contains some of the most influential essays ever written." *wikipedia.org The Complete Essays of Montaigne*, translated by Donald M. Frame (Stanford: Stanford University Press, 1957) (originally published in France, 1580). Camblin owned and read the *Essays*.

13. *Que scay-je?* (sometimes written *Que scais-je)* is Middle French. The question "What do I know?" is now written *Que sais-je?*

14. Besides Mr. Peanut, Camblin incorporated an Italian Mr. Peanut, *Signor Arachide*, and a Spanish one, *Señor Cacahuate*.

15. A photograph of a smaller person in the Mr. Peanut outfit exists.

16. Westermann, like Camblin, represented an eccentric artist who followed his own path regardless of artistic movements. In him Camblin found many similarities: the work of both men provided social commentary; both refused to interpret their art when asked; both used Surrealistic elements in their images; both were influenced by the existential theme of human helplessness; both were witty and both created their art with meticulous detail.

17. Kevin Griffin, "From: Vincent Trasov: The Interview," *Vancouver Sun*, May 22, 2012.

18. *File Magazine* photographed Trasov in his Mr. Peanut costume for the magazine's cover for April 1972. *Esquire Magazine*, August 1974, p. 52 had a photograph and description of Mr. Peanut.

19. C. G. Jung, *Two Essays on Analytical Psychology* (London: Routledge Publishing, 1953), 190.

20. "Founded in 1969 by Michael Morris and Vincent Trasov the Image Bank helped facilitate the exchange of ideas, images and information between artists through the use of the postal system." Morris / Trasov Archive.

21. Rudolph Otto, a prominent German Lutheran theologian in the first half of the twentieth century, originated the word "numinous" to describe a mysterious, non-rational religious experience. The word *numen* is Latin for divine power.

Chapter Sixteen

1. Born August 1, Camblin was born under the Zodiac sign of Leo.

2. Wikipedia.org

Chapter Seventeen

1. Camblin Sketchbook, November 1976, Venezia.

2. Wiley and Camblin were friendly acquaintances. They corresponded and collaborated. Critics often compared Camblin to Wiley, perhaps because the two artists both liked words and play-on-words.The two shared a similar sense of humor. Both drew complicated landscapes and referenced geometric symbols. Both produced linear works with outlined color and form. Even so, the two artists' works cannot be misread as the other's art.

3. Camblin Sketchbook, November 1976, Venezia.

4. Anamorphosis: A distorted projection or drawing which appears normal when viewed from a particular point or with a suitable mirror or lens. *Oxford Dictionary.*

5. Personal Letter, Private Collection, 1978.

6. 1978 Sketchbook, Private Collection. Note: The composition is based on underlying eye sockets and nasal cavities of a skull.

7. Ibid.

Chapter Eighteen

1. "Aztec Skull Trophy Rack Discovered at Mexico City's Templo Mayor Ruin Site," *The Guardian*, Archaeology, Associated Press in Mexico City, August 20, 2015.

2. In the early 1500s, the Spanish brought a celebration of ancestors, All Saints Day, to Mexico. The Mexicans added skeletons, home altars, and graveyard celebrations to the Catholic rituals.

3. Frances Ann Day, *Latina and Latino Voices in Literature* (Westport, CT: Greenwood Publishing Group, 2003), 72.

4. The lithographs were printed by David Folkman and Susan Latinovich of LEE. The smiling skull implies that death always has the last laugh.

5. *Milagro:* The word *Milagro* means "miracle." Milagros are small metal religious talismans found in many areas of Latin America, especially Mexico. They depict arms, legs, hearts, praying people, farm animals and a wide range of other subjects for which the user needs a miracle. The charms are nailed or pinned to crosses or wooden statues of saints, sacred objects, or hung with little red ribbons or threads from altars and shrines.

6. Forrest Prince, a Houston artist and visionary, has the wooden construct from the largest Camblin reliquary in his home and uses it as a shelf. He learned of the piece's origin only recently. Prince placed a globe, a duck, and various other items on the shelves.

7. Camblin had long included skulls in his work, but he increased his use of the skull as subject after his time in Oaxaca, influenced by his increasing age as well as the Day of the Dead.

8. Judith Dunham, *Artweek*, April 21, 1979, 4.

Chapter Nineteen

1. Penny Cerling, email of August 6, 2017.

2. Lollie Jackson became Camblin's most devoted collector.

3. Nancy Giordano Echegoyen is referred to as Giordano from this point forward.

Chapter Twenty

1. Camblin's response to the Hebrew University and to the Einstein Foundation can be viewed on camblin.com.

2. Undated Camblin Sketchbook.

3. Note: The Jackson estate did not allow photographs of the chest's contents. As a consequence, an unknown number of Camblin's last lithographs are buried in Jackson's art collection, awaiting discovery.

4. Little Egypt Enterprises closed in 1989.

5. Amir Aczel, Dov Ber, Paul Coelho, along with numerous others, have spent their lives studying the significance and the complexity of the Hebrew alphabet.

Chapter Twenty-One

1. A quotation from Ikkyu, Japanese Zen Buddhist priest, poet and calligrapher (1394–1481).

2. Camblin exaggerated the impressionistic brushstrokes he had used for his Kuwaiti commission and labeled the technique *Mouches Volantes*, French for "flying flies." (He sometimes wrote "Moosh Volantz" in his sketchbook drawings.) The system limited Camblin's as well as collaborating artists' brushstrokes to dots and dashes, which downplayed individual styles in joint efforts.

3. Author interview of Staley at his Houston studio, May 7, 2016.

4. Personal communication to Robyn Camblin from Camblin's brother, Dennis Camblin, November 2015.

5. New Orleans Metropolitan Convention and Visitors Bureau: "The Europeans brought their carnival customs [to New Orleans], and Creole society was soon masking and dancing at private balls while revelers in disguise roamed the streets. The year 1837 marked the first documented procession of masked revelers in New Orleans. Masked Mardi Gras still continues."

Epilogue

1. During his trial for corrupting the youth of Greece, Socrates explained, "The unexamined life is not worth living." Reported in Plato's *Apology*.

Timeline Endnotes

1. Robyn Camblin, Email dated December 29, 2015.

2. Elizabeth Crocker, "Some Say It With a Brick: George Herriman's *Krazy Kat*," uncredited essay, February 28, 2008.

3. Barbara Rose and Susie Kalil, *Fresh Paint: The Houston School*, Kalil "Introduction" (Houston: The Museum of Fine Arts, Houston, 1985).

4. cnx.org Earl Staley

5. *Roy Fridge*, Brochure. Self published, edition of 100, 1972.

6. Kirstie Beaven, The Tate, Blog, "Performance Art 101: The Happening, Allan Kaprow," May 30, 2012.

7. Sandy Havens, "Allan Kaprow's Happening," *The Cornerstone* 16, no. 2 (Spring 2011): 1–3.

8. Discrepancies in the dates for the Construction/Deconstruction events: Earl Staley used the year '1968' as the first event in his narrative of a *Super 8 movie* with images of the event. Landay used the year 1969 as the beginning of the events. Roy Fridge's biography in *Roy Fridge*, An Exhibition Organized y the Art Museum of South Texas, Corpus Christi, April 12 – June 9, 1985, used 1968 as the year Fridge participated in the Side Show.

9. Stephen Fox, *The Campus Guide, Rice University* (New York: Princeton Architectural Press, 2001), page 172.

10. Janet Landay, *Collaborators: Artists Working Together in Houston 1969–1986* (The Glassell School of Art).

11. Obituary of Dianne David, November 9, 1938 – March 2, 2012. Moody Funeral Services, March 2012.

12. "The Cornerstone," *Rice University Historical Society* 19, no. 2 (Summer 2013).

13. Radio Show, Mark Lamster, Architecture Critic, "Rice University to Demolish Houston Landmark," *The Dallas Morning News*, 11:53 am on March 1, 2014.

14. A favorite Camblin quote: "The fish trap exists because of the fish; once you've gotten the fish, you can forget the trap. The rabbit snare exists because of the rabbit; once you've gotten the rabbit, you can forget the snare. Words exist because of meaning; once you've gotten the meaning, you can forget the words. Where can I find a man who has forgotten words so I can have a word with him?" Chuang Tzu, 4th Century BC Chinese philsopher (translated by Burton Watson).

15. There is some confusion as to the actual date of the birth of B E & J. In a *Houston Post*, September 28, 1986, review of the Glassell School *Collaborators* exhibition, Susan Chadwick wrote: "Staley, Camblin and Tate, between 1969 and 1974 called themselves The Holding Firm . . ." In the catalogue for the 1986 *Collaborators* show, Janet Landay wrote: "When Joe Tate moved from California to join the Rice faculty in 1970 . . . B E & J Prodluctions was born . . . [they] came up with 'Holding Firm' (1972) . . . [that lasted] over a three year period."

16. Microfilm Reel 3461from the Smithsonian's Archives of American Art, Museum of Fine Arts Houston, Hirsch Library.

17. Influences of Dorman David on Document Show: Gregory Curtis, "Forgery Texas Style," *Texas Monthly*, March 1989. Calvin Trillin, "Knowing Johnny Jenkins," American Chronicles, *The New Yorker*, October 30, 1989, pp. 79–95. Lisa Belkin, "Lone Star Fakes," *New York Times Magazine*, December 10, 1989.

18. Microfilm Reel 3461, Smithsonian Institution, Archives of American Art, Museum of Fine Arts Houston, Hirsch Library.

19. *I Ching* or *The Book of Changes*, Wilhelm translation, Baynes English translation, Bollingen Series XIX (New York: Princeton University Press, 1950). Note: The I Ching is an ancient divination text and the oldest of the Chinese classics. Its roots can be traced back to the 8th Century BC. The book impacted the counterculture of the 1960s and continues to be consulted to this day. Camblin turned frequently to the book's wisdom, calling it "consulting the Chinaman." Hexagrams and quotations from the I Ching are found in his work.

20. Staley Blogspot.

21. Microfilm Reel 3462, Smithsonian Institution, Archives of American Art, Museum of Fine Arts Houston, Hirsch Library.

22. Earl Staley's notes have him leaving the group in 1973. Landay *Collaborators* catalogue has him leaving the Holding Firm in 1974.

23. Private Collection.

24. Microfilm Reel 3462.

25. Microfillm Reel 3462.

26. 1978 Sketch Book, Private Collection.

REFERENCES

Archives

Yale University's Library archives, American Painting Section of the Mounted Photograph Collection, in Box 24, Description C, Miscellaneous Artists: one photograph of Bob Camblin is acknowledged.

The Brooklyn Museum Library & Archives, Artist file: with miscellaneous uncataloged material.

The Museum of Modern Art, Queens, New York, Artist file: Bob Bilyeu Camblin, 1928.

Guggenheim,org. Archives Collections/Artist Files, A008, 643493, Bob Bilyeu Camblin.

Philbrook Museum of Art, Tulsa, Oklahoma, Artist file, Bob Bilyeu Camblin.

John and Mable Ringling Museum of Art Library, Archives, Bob Camblin.

The Archives of American Art, Bob Bilyeu Camblin papers, 1951–1985.

The Archives of American Art, Summary of the David Gallery records. 1963–1982.

The Archives of American Art, Summary of the Sandra Curtis Levy photographs and slides, 1935–1984.

The Archives of American Art, Summary of the Little Egypt Enterprises records, 1965–1979.

The Archives of American Art, Summary of the Covo de Iongh Gallery scrapbook, 1975–1978.

Note: All Archives of American Art collections listed above can be found in the AAA New York, or in the Museum of Fine Arts, Houston, Hirsh Library, Texas.

Rice University Information Files UA 36, 1910–2015, Identification: UA 361, 49.5 Linear Feet, Repository: Woodson Research Center, Rice Univesity, Houston Texas.

Chronological List of Published Works

1942

Ponca High School Yearbook, *Cat Tales '46*, the Ponca City News, Ponca City, Oklahoma, 1942, pp. 27, 29, 56, 62.

1955

"Gives Meaning to Life: Institute Graduates Hear of the Value of Art." *The Kansas City Times*, Friday, May 27, 1955, p. 5.

1956

"One Year of Study in Rome. A Fulbright Award Is Given to Robert Camblin, a Painter." *The Kansas City Times*, Saturday, May 19, 1956, p. 8.

"Fulbright Painters: Press Release," Smithsonian Institution, Traveling Exhibition Service, Washington, D.C., 1956.

1957

62nd American Exhibition: Painting and Sculpture. Chicago: Art Institute of Chicago. Catalogue foreword by Frederick A. Sweet,

1958

"A Year Abroad." *Time Magazine*, October 6, 1958, p. 69.

Lewis, Jo Ann Sukel, and J. William Fulbright. *Fulbright Painters*. New York: Institute for International Education, 1958.

1959

"Contemporary Painting Show Open at Four Arts Society." *The Palm Beach Post*, West Palm Beach, Florida, Saturday, December 5, 1959, p. 13.

"Art Exhibit Set in Little Theater." *Fort Myers News Press*, Sunday, November 29, 1959, p. 20.

1960

"150 Objects Picked Here for Governor's Show." *Sarasota Herald-Tribune*, January 8, 1960.

"Show Opens Here Today." *Sarasota Herald-St. Tribune*, Music and Art Section, January 4, 1960.

Dame, Lawrence. "Abstract-Impressionism Preponderant at Show." *Sarasota Herald-Tribune*, January 12, 1960, P. 8.

"Go Fly a Kite." *Sarasota Herald-Tribune*, February 7, 1960, p. 29.

"Teachers' Imprints Discernible, Little Revolt Against Traditional Standards at Art Students Show." *Sarasota Herald-Tribune*, March 24, 1960, page 16.

"National Art Show Set Here." *Sarasota Journal*, March 30, 1960, p. 13."

Dame, Lawrence. "In National Exhibition West Coast Artists' Works Are Analyzed," *Sarasota Herald-Tribune*, April 15, 1960, p. 18.

Dickerson, Jan. "New Aim Turns Toward the Classical," *The Kansas City Star*, Sunday, December 25, 1960.

1961

"Young Artists' Exhibit." *Southwestern College Yearbook*, Winfield, Kansas, 1961, p. 90.

1962

Press Release. *Madison News*, Nov. 13, 1962.

1964

Burnett, Clyde. "From My Point of View, Summer or Not, Art Events Are Plentiful Here." *Sarasota Herald-Tribune*, Sarasota, Florida, July 5, 1964, p. 11C.

Burnett, Clyde, "From My Viewpoint." *Sarasota Herald-Tribune*, Sarasota, Florida, July 12, 1964.

1965

Dibble, George. "U of U Staff Member, Bob Camblin." *Salt Lake Tribune*, Sunday, August 22, 1965.

"Faculty Show Hangs in Gallery at U." [University of Utah], *Salt Lake Tribune*, Sunday, October 3, 1965 p. 36.

"Exhibit of Works by 11 Members of University of Utah Art Faculty" *Salt Lake Tribune*, Sunday November 14, 1965, p. 17.

"Calendar of Salt Lake Civic Events." *Salt Lake Tribune*, Sunday, November 28, 1965.

1966

Halliday, Bob. "U. Instructor to Exhibit New Work, Cites Artists Role to Effect Change." *Salt Lake Tribune*, November 20, 1966, p. 18W.

Bob Camblin. A handwritten assignment for his University of Utah students. The Smithsonian Institution's Archives of American Art, 1966.

"Plumtree Holds Open House at Gallery Today." *The Salt Lake Tribune*, Sunday, Deember 11, 1966, p. 18 W.

1967

"Metamorphosis." *The Oklahoma Daily*, University of Oklahoma, February 10, 1967, p. 14.

Dibble, George. "Intermountain Biennial: Art Center Chooses 5 Works." *Salt Lake Tribune*, Sunday, March 5, 1967, p. 14 W.

Havens, Sandy. "Allen Center Open House, November 1967," Posted by Melissa Kean, June 24, 2013, and Havens's comment added same day. *The Rice History Corner*, Gleanings from the Rice University Archives, November 1967.

1968

"Bob Camblin: David Gallery," *Art in America*, September–October, 1968.

"Communal Beach Happening Yields Sideshow Film Footage." *The Rice Thresher*, Houston, Texas, December 12, 1968, p. 4.

1969

Freed, Eleanor. "Mixed Media Man." *Houston Post*, February, 23, 1969.

1970

Butterfield, Jan. "Dallas Galleries Feature Art of Talented Young Artists." *Fort Worth Star Telegram*, November 12, 1970, p. 6G.

Holmes, Ann. "Where It's At (If You Can Find It)." *The Art Gallery*, May 20, 1970, p. 37.

"Distant Flickerings Color Camblin Show," *Houston Chronicle*, September 20, 1970.

1971

Dreyer, Martin. "The Night They Burned The Thing." *Houston Chronicle*, Texas Magazine, Sunday, January 10, 1971, cover plus pp. 14, 16, 17, 20.

"Elsewhere on Campus." *The Rice Thresher* 58, no. 14, 1st ed. (January 14, 1971).

Laddey, Virginia. "'Other Coast' Shows New Approach to Art." *Independent Press-Telegram*, Long Beach, California, Sunday, March 21, 1971, p. W 6.

"Seven New Shows to Preview; Bob Camblin and Lee Baxter Davis." *Times Herald*, Dallas, Texas, March 19, 1971.

Holmes, Ann. "Fantastic Artists." *Southwest Art Gallery Magazine*, October 1971, p. 34.

Freed, Eleanor. "Stark Realism, Dramatization of a Hitchhiker; Documenta." *Houston Post*, Art Section, February 21, 1971, p. 28.

Moser, Charlotte. "Before the Glamor of Art." *The Houston Chronicle*, ca. 1971.

Kutner, Janet. "Variety Exhibited by Camblin at David Gallery." *Dallas Morning News*, April 13, 1971, p. 10E.

"Texas," Arts, *Summer (Ete)*, 1971, pp. 49–50.

1972

Lunn, Judy. "Prowling Artists—Right in Your Backyard." *Houston Post*, July 21, 1972, p. 1B.

Bennett, Elizabeth. "New Faces." *The Houston Post*, 1972

"The Last Garage Sale May Not Be." *Houston Chronicle*, Section 4, September 26, 1972, p. 4.

Freed, Eleanor. "Texans, Titled and Subtitled." *Houston Post*, October 29, 1972, p. 1B.

"Oklahoma Acorns a Fair Trade." *Houston Chronicle*, Section 7, December 13, 1972, p. 3.

1973

Freed, Eleanor. "Montrose Bateau Lavoir." *Houston Post*, "Spotlight," January 7, 1973, p. 34.

Butler, Susan L. "So You Want to Be an Artist," *Houston Chronicle*, January 28, 1973.

Doty, Robert. *Extraordinary Realities*. New York: Whitney Museum of American Art, 1973, p. 62.

Hopkins, Henry. "Contemporary Art in Texas: On the Road to Maturity." *Art News*, May 1973, p. 43.

Butler, Susan L. "Private Works." *Houston Chronicle*, Art Circles, September 1973.

Solomon, Elke M. *American Drawings 1963–1973*. New York: Whitney Museum of American Art, 1973.

Ratcliff, Carter. *Hand Colored Prints*. New York: Brooke Alexander Gallery, 1973, p. 9.

1974

"CC Art League Hears Trio," *The Deer Park Progress*, Deer Park, Texas, Thursday, March 22, 1974, p. 18.

Kelder, Diane. "Artists' Alterations." *The Art Journal*, March–April, 1974

1975

Amen, Kelly Gale, and Madeleine Hamm. "KGA Talks Interior Design with the *Houston Chronicle*," Houston: *KGA Blog*, 1975.

Duff, Barbara. "Artist Information," *Der Rosenkavalier*. Poster, Program Cover, Back inside cover. Houston Grand Opera, January 1975, pp. 40, 43.

Moser, Charlotte. "Master Printmaking in Houston." *Houston Chronicle*, May 31, 1975, Section 2.

Moser, Charlotte. "The Art Boom." *Houston Chronicle*, July 20, 1975, p. 9.

"Bob Camblin: Elements (1974)." *The Print Collector's Newsletter* 6, no. 3 (July-August 1975).

Glauber, Robert H. *The Classic Revival*. Catalogue for exhibit in Illinois Bell Telephone, Lobby Gallery, Chicago, Illinois, 1975.

Dianne David interview by Louis J. Marchiafava, Archive # 0H036, The Houston Metropolitan Research Center, Oral History Project Interviews, October 2, 1975.

Fuller, Mary. "Marcel Duchamp Lives: One View of the Texas Art World." *Currant*, October–November 1975, p. 18.

"Visiting Artist." *LSU Daily Reveille*. Louisiana State University, December 2, 1975.

1976

Butler, Susan L. "Art Circles," *Houston Chronicle*, January 1976.

"The January Gallery Scene." *Subject: Fine Art*, Houston, January 1976.

Smith, Dan. "Baker Hosts Artists for Two Weeks." *The Baker Orange*, Baker University, Baldwin City, Kansas, March 5, 1976.

"Review: Art Gallery Roundup." *The Houston Post*, Thursday, April 15, 1976.

Moser, Charlotte. "Between Fantasy and Surrealism." *Art News*, April 1976, p. 66.

Moser, Charlotte. "Box Is Both Form, Content of Developing Art." *Houston Chronicle*, July 7, 1976.

Smith, Roberta. "Twelve Days of Texas." *Art in America*, July/August 1976, p. 46.

The Collection of the Junior Service League of Longview. Longview, TX: The Longview Museum and Art Center, 1977.

1977

Crossley, Mimi. "Little Egypt Rolls On." *Houston Post*, June 26, 1977.

Crossley, Mimi. "Gallery Roundup—Bob Camblin: Paintings and Watercolors." *Houston Post*, November 25, 1977.

Moser, Charlotte. "Camblin's New Work Sparks Moody Show." *Houston Chronicle*, August 19, 1977.

Moser, Charlotte. "Gallery Prospects Better." *Houston Chronicle*, September 11, 1977, p. 23.

"Camblin Paintings Merge Magic and Metaphysics." *Houston Chronicle*, November 18, 1977, p. 24.

Crossley, Mimi. "Review: Gallery Roundup: Bob Camblin: Paintings and Watercolors." *The Houston Post*, Friday, November 25, 1977.

1978

Martin, Abbe. "The Art of Texas." The Renaissance Society, *Chicago Reader*, May 26, 1978.

1979

Moser, Charlotte. "'Doors' Open Esthetic Vistas at the Alley." *Houston Chronicle*, March 18, 1979.

Crossley, Mimi. "Review: Bob Camblin: Vanitas." *The Houston Post*, April 6, 1979.

Holmes, Ann. "Where It's At (If You Can Find It)." *The Art Gallery*, May 20, 1979, p. 37.

Sween, Trudy. "Doors: Houston Artists." *The Houston Festival*, The Alley Theatre, Houston, Texas, 1979, pp. 13–14.

Moser, Charlotte. "Art Celebrates Mexican 'Day of the Dead' Festival." *Houston Chronicle*, April 7, 1979, Sec. 3, p. 9.

Dunham, Judith. "Texas Overview." *Artweek*, April 21, 1979, p. 4.

1980

Curtis, Sandra. "Texas Project." *Archives of American Art Journal*, Smithsonian Institution, January 20, 1980, p. 31.

Olpin, Robert S. *Dictionary of Utah Art*. Salt Lake City: Salt Lake Art Center, 1980, p. 30.

Moser, Charlotte. "Playing Cowboys and Artists in Houston." *Art News*, December 1980, pp. 124–128.

1981

"1981 Houston Arts Calendar." Wordworks, Inc, Houston, Texas, 1981, pp. 7–8.

Bell, David L. "Houston Show Visits Santa Fe Gallery." *Albuquerque Journal*, Sunday, August 30, 1981, p. 46.

Johnson, Patricia. "The Image of the House Through Artists' Eyes." *Houston Chronicle*, November 15, 1981, pp. 18–27; 47–49.

1982

"The Art Center Tenth Anniversary Celebration." *The Waco Citizen*, Waco, Texas, Friday, Aril 16, 1982, p. 6.

Freed, Eleanor. "Treasures of the Finding." *Houston Arts Magazine*, Society for the Performing Arts, September 1982, pp. 16–24.

Krantz, Les. *The Texas Art Review*. Houston: Gulf Publishing with The Krantz Company Pub., 1982, p. 8.

Johnson, Patricia. "Print Show Lights Up Some of City's Masters in Field." *Houston Chronicle*, October 14, 1982, p. 24.

1983

Goetzmann, William H., and Becky Duval Reese. *Texas Images and Visions*. Austin: Archer M. Huntington Gallery, University of Texas at Austin, 1983, pp. 44, 128.

1984

Johnson, Patricia. "Camblin's Personal Artwork Explored." *Houston Chronicle*, March 23, 1984. Sec. 5, p. 9.

1985

Rose, Barbara, and Susie Kalil. *Fresh Paint: The Houston School*. Houston: Texas Monthly Press, 1985.

"'Fresh Paint' Art Exhibit Recognizes Houston Regional School." *The Baytown Sun*, Baytown, Texas, Friday, January 11, 1985, p. 5.

Larsen, Kay. "Art." Review of *Fresh Paint*, *New York Magazine*, June 17, 1985, p. 64.

Reese, Becky Duval. "Is Regionalism Dead?" *Texas Trends in Art Education* 3, no.1 (Fall 1985): 16.

1986

Landay, Janet. *Collaborators: Artists Working Together In Houston 1969–1986* Houston: The Glassell School of Art, The Museum of Fine Arts, Houston, 1986.

Kalil, Susie. *The Texas Landscape, 1900–1986*. Houston: The Museum of Fine Arts, Houston, 1986.

McCombie, Mel. "Houston: The Texas Landscape, 1900–1986." Art News, *The Nation*, October 1986, pp. 15–16.

Johnson, Patricia C. "Collaborators Leave Their Marks on Art Works." *Houston Chronicle*, October 4, 1986.

"Cinq Pour Cinq." *The Houston Chronicle*, November 21, 1986, p. 9.

Carlozzi, Annette. *50 Texas Artists. A Critical Selection of Painters and Sculptors Working in Texas*. San Francisco: Chronicle Books, 1986, pp. 28–29.

1987

Ewing, Betty. "These Americans in Paris Hit the Town with Art from Texas," *The Houston Chronicle*, January 11, 1987, p. 8.

Johnson, Patricia C. "Found Objects: Junk or 'Junque?'." *Houston Chronicle*, June 28, 1987.

1988

"Bob Camblin." Art. *Seven One Three*, Houston, Texas, 1988.

1989

Falk, Peter H., ed. *Annual Exhibition Record of the Pennsylvania Academy of the Fine Arts 1913–1968*. Madison, CT: Sound View Press, 1989.

Johnson, Patricia C. "Master Printmaker Counting on Silent Auction." *Houston Chronicle*, September 7, 1989.

Chadwick, Susan. "Glassell Exhibit Calls to Mind 'the Good Old Days' of Art." *The Houston Post*, Sunday, September 28, 1989, p. 3F.

Holmes, Ann. "What Artists Collect: New Location, Revealing Show at DiverseWorks." *Houston Chronicle*, November 14, 1989.

1990

Fisher, James L. *Forty Texas Printmakers*. Fort Worth: Modern Art Museum of Fort Worth, 1990, p. 6, 30, 31, 105, 106.

Kutner, Janet. "Impressions from the Edge." *The Dallas Morning News*, Art Section, December 13, 1990.

1993

Johnson, Patricia C. "Folkman: Artist and Technician. His Own Creations Shine alongside Little Egypt Editions." *Houston Chronicle*, November 15, 1993.

1999

Falk, Peter Hastings, ed. *Annual Exhibition Record, 1914–1968*. Pennsylvania Academy of the Fine Arts, 1999.

2001

Transcript of the Murray Smither interview with Bruce and Julie Webb of the Webb Gallery in Waxahachie, Texas, *Art Lies* 30 (Spring 2001): 6.

2005

Dunbier, Lonnie Pierson, ed. "The Artists' Bluebook." *AskArt.com*, 2005.

Smith, Mark L. "Way Out Here Printmaking in Texas." *Art Lies* 46 (Spring 2005): 45.

2010

B. Davenport, Bill. "Memorial Tribute to Bob Camblin." *http://glasstire.com/2010/12/06/bob-camblin-1928–2010*.

Staley, Earl. earlvstaley.blogspot.com, 2010.

Quaintance, Don. "Comment," *http://glasstire.com/2010/12/06/bob-camblin-1928–2010*.

2012

Stout, Richard. "Modernism in Houston Art: 1950–1970," Part 7, YouTube series done for Houston Modern Market Week Exhibition at the William Reaves Fine Art Gallery, Houston, Texas, April 28, 2012.

2013

Glentzer, Molly. "Penny Cerling: A Life of Needles and Pins." *Houston Chronicle*, June 26, 2013.

2014

Rice University. "Allen Center Open House, Nov. 1967." *Rice History Corner* from the Rice Archives (Sandy Havens's letter), June 24, 2013.

"Rice University to Demolish Houston Landmark." *Dallas Morning News*, March 1, 2014.

2017

Whitehead, Eliot. *Family Portrait: The Lost Sketchbooks of Bob Camblin 1956–1974* Running Man Press, April 1, 2017.

2018

Gershon, Pete. *Collision: The Contemporary Art Scene in Houston, 1972–1985.* College Station: Texas A & M University Press, 2018.

Misc:

1968:

Earl Staley filmed the 1968 Rice University collaborative event on Galveston's West Beach.

Bob Camblin sketchbooks:

Senza Dubbio, 1974.
Volume I & III, 1975.
Volume II, February – March 1975.
Finding the Source, 1976.
Libro di Ricordare, Sept 20th, 1976 to October 14th, 1976.
October, Venezia, 1976.
November, Venezia, 1976.
ABC, Venezia, November 1976.
A Fable, 1977.
Family Portrait, 1978.
Plus sketchbooks in Archives of American Art (microfilm in the MFAH)

2011:

Donation made, in Camblin's memory, to High School for the Performing and Visual Arts, Houston, Texas

2014:

George O. Jackson de Llano's Webpage dedicates photograph "En Homenaje a Bob Bilyeu Camblin

Webpage of Lewis A. Flacks, a student of Camblin's, lists the artist as his inspiration

Note: Besides archives from various galleries, material on Camblin can be found in the Houston Museum of Fine Arts Archives, which houses the work done by the Texas Project for the Smithsonian's Archives of American Art (AAA) as well as records from the Graham Gallery/William A. Graham Archives. The Archives of American Art, Smithsonian Institution, Washington D.C. has original material from 1963–1982 including photographs of the artist.

Getty Research Institute, Selected Dealer Archives & Locations:

David Gallery, Houston

Established by Dianne David. Artists include: William C. Agee, Jack Boynton, Bob Camblin, Roy Fridge, James Kearns, Seymour Leichman, Jim Love, David McManaway, Robert Morris, Futzie Nutzle, Peter Paone, Mike Selig, and Don Shaw.

Venice, Italy
 in 1957 (Fulbright year),
  24–25, 33
 in 1976, 180, 181–96, *185,
  196*
 letter with watercolor image
  from, *182*
 works in sketchbooks from,
  183, 195
 works inspired by, *199,* 201
Venus (Camblin), 237
Vespignani, Renzo, 22–23, 58,
 69
*View from my studio window,
 The* (Camblin), *21*
Volto Santo (Zurbaran), 166